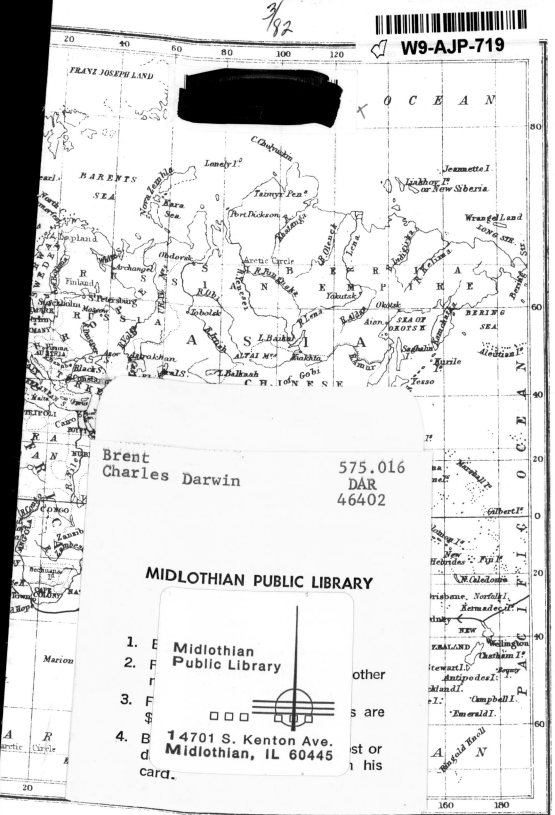

CHARLES
DARWIN

By the same author

GODMEN OF INDIA
ANTARCTIC TRAGEDY – a Biography of Captain Scott
THE VIKING SAGA
THE MONGOLS
BLACK NILE – a Biography of Mungo Park
FAR ARABIA
T. E. LAWRENCE – a Biography

Peter Brent

CHARLES
DARWIN

"A Man of Enlarged Curiosity"

. . . et pourquoi l'histoire naturelle n'aurait-elle pas
aussi un jour son Newton?
Cuvier, *Recherches sur les ossemens fossiles*

He who understand baboon would do more toward
metaphysics than Locke.
Darwin, '*M*' *Notebook*

1817

HARPER & ROW, PUBLISHERS, New York
Cambridge, Philadelphia, San Francisco
London, Mexico City, São Paulo, Sydney

ISBN: 0-06-014880-2

LIBRARY OF CONGRESS CATALOG NUMBER: 80-7889

81 82 83 84 85 10 9 8 7 6 5 4 3 2

Contents

List of Plates

Acknowledgements

—◁◁◁—

I would like to thank the many Darwin and other scholars upon whose expert advice I have leaned. I owe a particular debt to Nancy Mautner, herself completing a dissertation on the early days of Darwin, who has been both unstinting with suggestions, all of great practicality, and totally unselfish with the finds she has made in the course of her own researches. I also want to thank the Syndics of Cambridge University Library for permission to use the great store of original Darwin material they hold, and Peter Gautrey, directly responsible for the Library's Manuscript Reading Room, without whose friendliness, generosity and encyclopedic knowledge no book on Darwin would ever be successfully completed. My thanks, too, to the London Library, for the indispensable fact of its existence and the helpfulness of its staff.

I would also like to express my appreciation of a certain British publisher who, presented with an outline for this book emphasizing Darwin's crucial role in the intellectual history of the West, reeled back with the remark, "But what I want to know is, did he pay his tailor's bills!" In the three years it has taken me to complete this biography, his words have gleamed like a beacon marking the shallows to be avoided. Nevertheless, he will be able to find the solution to this important problem on page 355.

Introduction

Charles Darwin died a century ago, in the plain, secluded house sixteen miles from London where he had lived for forty years. The pale green early growth of trees stretched across the mottled skies of an English Spring. Beyond the grounds they guarded, the world waited for the news, its tributes ready. On 26 April, 1882, an awestruck nation placed his body among those of its greatest heroes, in Westminster Abbey. The learned, the aristocratic and the powerful gathered to mourn him. Clergymen muttered prayers, each one of which might be thought a reconciliation between their certainties and his. It was a reconciliation to which he would have been indifferent; the eulogies, on the other hand, would have pleased as well as embarassed him. Beneath his true, yet slyly conscious modesty, there would probably have been the feeling that they were his due.

In his seven decades he had altered the way human beings thought about the world they inhabited, the creatures they shared it with and, above all, themselves. He had proposed and seen accepted a history of living things quite different from that which had prevailed when he was young. He had outlined the processes of change through which life expressed its unrestrainable restlessness. As a result, an earth which had been thought essentially immutable, at rest within the eternal concern of its creator, could be seen as an interplay of forces sufficient, in its context of aeons, to bring into being a myriad of life forms.

His central idea he had termed natural selection. It suggested that scarcities of sustenance or the abrasions of adverse conditions were constantly at work upon the plants and creatures of the earth. The weakest or worst-adapted did not survive these environmental assaults. The strongest or best-adapted overcame them and in time bred offspring. To these they passed on their strengths or adaptations. When members of a species were isolated from their fellows, this process ensured that over the generations they would change more and more from what had been the norm. Eventually, these changes became so marked that they defined an entirely new species. The vast transformations and enormous time-span of geology provided the conditions which made these fundamental alterations possible.

The foundation for ideas such as these was laid during the five years in which Darwin was naturalist and captain's companion on board *HMS Beagle*. This was the period in which Darwin grew up as a scientist, making the transition from eager amateur to methodical professional. What he saw – in South America, the Galapagos, the South Seas – meshed with what he read, notably Lyell's *Principles of Geology*, to create for him a new view-point and perhaps even a new way of seeing. When he returned home, he had the material he needed for the years of intense speculation into which he was about to enter.

Darwin worked over his theories for more than twenty years. Other naturalists had toyed with evolutionary ideas; none had proposed a method by which such an evolution might be brought about, and then compiled the evidence to support his proposition. When in 1859 Darwin published his beliefs in *On the Origin of Species*, he included a massive array of relevant observations, as well as the persuasive logic of his theory. It was this rigour in his intellectual attitudes, this strictness of scientific principle, that disting-uished him from all the other writers who had at one time or another suggested a mutational scheme. What he thought true, the reasons why he thought it and the facts that bore upon those reasons made in his work a single unity. Nothing was forced, though the inadequacies of what he could know meant that his theory had gaps – gaps of which he himself was well aware.

When his book had been published, there began controversies which have never entirely died down. The most important saw the advocates of evolu-tion face and then beat off the outraged champions of divine creation. The victory of the scientists had the unexpected effect of elevating them in the public eye to the position from which the theologians had been forced. What religion had been unable to deliver, science, a knowledge true because directly verifiable, would in time be able to provide. By disproving the scientific claims of theology, science had, paradoxically, become not more of a science, but more of a religion. At the centre of this process – indifferent, nervous, even taciturn, and there certainly against his wishes – stood the benign, bearded figure of Charles Darwin.

From the other side there rose the equally acerbic, if less clamorous, voices of his scientific critics. For many of these, his theory seemed little more than a tautology, saying only, "Whatever survives, survives; whatever has changed, has changed". For others it appeared to explain many things; if it were true, however, it had to explain everything. During the last twenty years of his life Darwin basked in the world's respect, but had at intervals to rush off and plug another newly discovered hole in the great dyke he had constructed.

Arguments on the subject have varied in virulence, but they have never ceased. A century after his death, both the validity of evolution within science and the confrontation between science and other, less objective forms of knowledge remain live issues. Indeed, new ways of understanding reality and new agreements about its nature and extent may cause us to reassess the part science plays in our perception of the world, and in creating the ideas we have of it. Yet Darwin retains his stature as one of the great forerunners of modernity, a member of that small handful – Marx, Kierkegaard, Freud, Cézanne, Einstein must be others – who have among them created our contemporary sensibility. So central to our situation are his conclusions, so directly do the debates they cause bear upon it, that he seems of our time more than that of Victoria. Biology, geology and palaeontology owe him a profound debt; the questions he posed helped to bring into being such entire fields of knowledge as psychology, ethology, genetics and ecological studies.

As a result, most of the many books that have been written about Darwin have concentrated on his scientific work. They have seen his private life through his published letters and his *Autobiography*. The first, selected by his son, used the correspondence mainly to explain the genesis of his ideas. The second, written by Darwin in his old age, ostensibly at least for his family, is orthodox in its sentiments and reticent about his inner life. Indeed, Darwin never revealed very much of what he truly felt; it may even be that the emotional vagaries to which other men are subject were burnt away by the intensity of his intellectual effort.

This absence of available evidence, reinforced by his almost morbid modesty, has allowed various myths about Darwin to grow up. One suggests that his father disliked him, that he himself felt a reciprocal detestation, that his expressed love for his father later in life was therefore a neurotic overcompensation for his true sentiments, and that his overturning of theological certainties was a metaphorical enactment of the patricide which was his deepest and darkest desire. Freudians like Ernest Jones and Phyllis Greenacre half a century ago had a psychoanalytical field day with such assumptions.

Another myth is that of his early laziness and scholastic incompetence, from which he emerged, like butterfly from grub, as the complete naturalist, flashing his wings in the great sunlight of scientific truth. A legend which also delights laymen is that Darwin, while in the Galapagos Islands, was struck by the transporting clarity of vision on which his entire theory was to be based, a sort of Archimedean "Eureka" which showed him the path that he would follow.

While misconceptions and half-truths of this kind accumulated, there was slowly becoming available an enormous body of notebooks, diaries, journals, annotated texts and, above all, letters. Some of these were published, notably under the scholarly supervision of Nora Barlow, Darwin's grand-daughter, but many others lay in the archives, almost entirely unremarked. Not bearing directly upon the work, they seemed to the scientifically orientated scholars who entered the field of Darwin studies to be little more than gossip. What was written continued, to the extent that it was biographical, to rest upon the published material.

As the centenary of Darwin's death approached, it seemed time to gather together some of this evidence, whether still unpublished or, if in print, hitherto read only by the obsessed eye of the specialist. So reticent was Darwin about his inner life, so wide were the ramifications of his scientific interests, so complex were the philosophical, theological and social consequences they led to, so undramatic – though frequently charming – were the events of his personal life, that every clue making possible a deeper and more comprehensive understanding of these matters becomes of the greatest importance.

When all the new evidence has been added to the old, there emerges a portrait of Darwin much more detailed than any before – especially of the younger Darwin as he was during the years of his development and early maturity. Wealth cocooned him: the Darwins turn out to have been unexpectedly rich. Riding and shooting fascinated him – but so did the pursuits of the naturalist and the experimenter. Long visits to friends and relations varied the rhythm of his life. Those to his cousins, the Wedgwoods of Maer, are well known; less so are his trips to Woodhouse, near Oswestry, where lived the enchanting, self-willed Fanny Owen, almost certainly the first and possibly the most passionate love of his life.

His years as a pupil at exclusive Shrewsbury School were succeeded by his period as a medical student at Edinburgh, and this by his time at Cambridge. There his long-time fascination with entomology brought about his fateful friendship with Professor Henslow – it was through Henslow that the invitation arrived that led eventually to his five wandering years aboard the survey ship, *HMS Beagle*. The attitude taken to this voyage by Darwin's father, long believed to have been one of total opposition, shows him in fact to have been rather different from the stern domestic tyrant of legend.

Not long after his return, already marked for fame, Darwin began to fret about his still unmarried condition; it is not necessary to accept at face value the apparent singleness of mood with which he selected his cousin, Emma Wedgwood, to be his bride. He may have had others in mind before Emma, and may have approached her with emotions in which affection was, for a while, diluted by calculation.

During the years that followed his return from South America and the

Pacific, he was compiling his *Transmutation Notebooks*, those marvellous collections of scribbled insights, observations, quotations and perceptions through which he struggled towards his evolutionary thesis. The toughness of mind and muscularity of purpose with which he constructed his theory have an abiding excitement for us who know what they led to: for a true understanding of how Darwin's ideas developed, however, it is essential to restore to their central place these seminal *Notebooks*. During all the rest of his intellectual life he was to draw on them. But because he used himself as a subject for the psychological observations with which he filled them, they may also offer clues to the inward self which otherwise he kept so carefully hidden.

On the whole, Darwin led a life of blameless serenity. Illness and convention circumscribed it. A horror of direct confrontation as well as the unremitting sweetness of his temperament kept him far from the feuds and factionalism of more worldly scientists. Removed from metropolitan distractions, protected by the centripetal energies of an affectionate family life, he nevertheless worked courageously at the intellectual time bomb that might have blown away this happy calm. Instead, family tranquility resisted all the outrage and fury that his theories aroused. Safely within it, championed on the battlefields of philosophic controversy by souls more robust than he, Darwin survived intact and unembittered. As execration died down, adulation took its place. This too, though he enjoyed it and perhaps thought it his due, he kept at a safe distance.

Love sustained him: that of his father and sisters, later that of his wife and clever, successful children, and always that of a series of loyal and profoundly talented friends. Thus supported he worked at ideas the complex significance of which has not even yet been wholly understood. The debate they have engendered can still not be put to its concluding vote. That this was likely to be so, he must have realized as the clamour he had caused continued into his old age. When he died a century ago, he died fulfilled.

PART ONE

Housemaid and Postillion

1

Dr Postillion, I *entreat* your acceptance of a *leetle* Purse which I hope you will *condescend* to use in remembrance of the *Housemaid* of the *Black Forest*.

Fanny Owen

The boy is sturdy, high-complexioned, with fine, chestnut-coloured hair now in some disarray. Where he stands, the ground slopes gently, the dappled green of meadowland flowing away towards the gleam, half hidden by elm and willow, of the nearby river. He is quite still, all attention; the butt of the fowling-piece he holds rests on the moist grass. A few yards from him sits a dog, tongue loose between soft jaws, eyes bright with the anticipation of commands and movement. The boy gives no commands. He lifts his face; light catches the brown of his strangely deep-set eyes, flicks at the tip of his blunt, no-nonsense nose.

Between him and the river, a heavy shape beats its way into the air. Dark-grey wings hammer out its ponderous progress. "Look at the heron", says the boy, but the dog does not shift its gaze from his face. The boy smiles, taps his thigh and, as the dog responds, walks on. He makes his way diagonally towards the river; ahead of him, standing four-square on a bluff that overlooks the water, is the house where he lives. Beyond it, in the distance, he can see, above trees and the glimpsed roofs of the town, the fine spire of a church.

A yellow chaise turns towards the house from the Holyhead road. Briefly, in delighted alarm, pigeons flick to and fro against the bulbous clouds. The boy begins to run, his gun at the trail. The bag he carries, made substantial by the weight of two shot snipe, slaps against his side. The dog lollops happily at his heels. The boy lengthens his stride. His father has finished his rounds, has diagnosed the last patient of his day and has come home to supper. He himself should have been back half an hour before.

As he nears the house, he can hear a woman's voice. Its Shropshire accents, high and clear, call out his name.

2

———— ◁◁◁◁▷▷▷▷ ————

When Charles Darwin was just over eight years old, his mother died. It is hard from his own account to decide whether her death was the most significant event of his childhood – but hard from what one knows of childhood not to conclude that this was the case. He had been born on 12 February, 1809, the second son, the fifth of six children, in the household of a prosperous provincial doctor with a flourishing practice in Shrewsbury and the surrounding Shropshire countryside. Considering the effects of his mother's early death, Charles himself tells us in his *Autobiography* that he thought it "odd that I can remember hardly anything about her except her death-bed, her black velvet gown, and her curiously constructed work-table". This forgetfulness, he felt, was "partly due to my sisters, owing to their great grief, never being able to speak about her or mention her name; and partly to her previous invalid state". In another fragment of his recollections he recorded the vivid memory of his father's crying on the day of her death, but almost every other remembrance of his mother had vanished. He was astonished at how much detail his younger sister, Catherine, seemed able to recall.

Thus Susannah Wedgwood, who married tall, corpulent Dr. Robert Darwin, lies twice-buried in the memory of the dead. Her son, whose books and letters, notebooks, reminiscences and papers we have in engulfing profusion, could leave us no more than two sentences of description to dress the bare fact of her name. Those who remembered her better left no record of what they kept alive in their imaginations. In Charles, the silence has, perhaps, its own meaning. Those who have been equally bereaved in childhood can usually offer some small stock of images, fragments of a life, highly lit moments in the short passage of a person towards the unexpected grave. When grief erases these, the resultant silence acts like a scar over a wound. We know the wound was there because the scar remains; the pain cannot be reached because it is wrapped around by the silence.

For the young Darwin, however, the importance of his mother's death lay not only in the fact that it occurred. It also created the conditions in which he grew up. He was a young boy in a household largely run by older sisters; only Catherine, a year younger than he, at first made cause with him – years later he would speak with his own sons about the chestnut tree in which they had

had their favourite place, a green retreat of slowly swaying branches. In time, naturally enough, Catherine learned to stand with the other girls; though always his friend, she too took up the attitudes of an affectionate protectiveness. The older sisters, Susan and Caroline (the oldest, Marianne, was married in 1824), were too young to be as distanced from him as a mother, yet too distanced to be the allies they might have been had they not had to take up quasi-maternal responsibilities. Had there been a mother, all the children could have been children together; as it was, the girls were forced by that absence to play the vacant adult role. As for Charles's brother, Erasmus, the four years between their ages placed him in an entirely different childhood generation; a boy of twelve and thirteen has little in common with an eight-year-old.

The father seems rarely to have played more than a father's role. An early death was commoner then and people made less accommodation for bereavement than we – perhaps the expectation of good health and long life has softened us. Widowers were not rare, and Dr. Robert felt no apparent need to act the mother while he had daughters – and servants – able to take that part. He was busy, intelligent, loquacious, respected and well off, a man of girth and presence, a doctor widely consulted by people of all kinds drawn to him by his reputation as the best medical practitioner in Shropshire. He had already been established in Shrewsbury for twenty-three years by the time that Charles was born, and with his friendships, connections, mortgages and loans, as well as the ramifications of his practice, had become an integral and eminently visible part of the local community.

He looms darkly across the stories, often retold, of Charles's first twenty-five years: in them, his shape is that of a domestic bully and his effect on his son a continuing disaster of neurosis and disability. Dr. Rankine Good's theories about the roots of Charles's genius, arrived at in the 1950s, stem from his view of Dr. Robert as "tyrannical". A decade later Dr. Phyllis Goodacre's conviction that repressed hostility – a "massive aggression" of which he never allowed himself to become conscious – lay beneath both Charles's scientific theories and his ill-health, implied a reaction to a similarly severe and oppressive parent. Sir Julian Huxley and H.B.D. Kettlewell, in their *Charles Darwin and his World*, write of "the inflexible will of his father". In a recent biography, John Chancellor described Dr. Robert as "this crassly unimaginative colossus".

It is hard to see how such an extreme portrait has been arrived at, except to answer the needs of classical Freudian analysis. It seems blithely to disregard the centuries, and the shifts in behaviour their passing causes. Once accepted as truth, however, it is difficult to refute, since every affirmation Charles makes of his affection and respect for his father is taken to prove its opposite.

Certainly Dr. Robert's character was imposing and, in a period when age and authority were synonymous, when the paternal dictate was monarchical in its expectation of obedience, it will have tended to subdue the young. Over half a century later, Emma, Charles's wife, by then his widow, who had been a Wedgwood and had known the Darwins all her life, remembered how the "household had to run in the master's grooves, so that the inmates had not the sense of being free to do just what they liked". But nobody has ever suggested that Dr. Robert was easy-going. He was a widower, a hardworking doctor and if "the noise and untidiness of a boy were unpleasant to him", that was not to be wondered at. Elsewhere, Emma recalled a certain "want of liberty at Shrewsbury whenever Dr. Darwin was in the room; but then he was genial and sympathetic, only nobody must go on about their own talk". Charles, in his own old age, described his father in terms that bear this out. "His spirits were generally high, and he was a great talker. He was of an extremely sensitive nature, so that whatever annoyed or pained him, did so to an extreme degree. He was somewhat easily roused to anger." If Emma, in the 1880s, thought that Dr. Robert had not liked Charles, that he did not "understand or sympathize with him as a boy", Caroline, Charles's older sister, felt the opposite was true and that the Doctor had liked his son far more than Charles ever realized. The final picture that emerges is of an autocratic, rather overbearing man, the firm master of his house, but neither violent nor unreasonable. He fits, perhaps a little too easily, into the expectations of his times, accepting his privileges with an unconcern we might consider unattractive. Yet his children lived, on the whole, the lives they wished; neither son pursued a career that Dr. Robert chose, neither was ever threatened with economic reprisals for the decisions he took, both – and Charles in particular – remained on good terms with their father.

One looks in vain, too, in Charles's *Autobiography* for the kind of self-lacerating hatred that, for example, both created and disfigured Samuel Butler's account of his father. Nor is Dr. Robert magnanimously pardoned by a son come late to understanding, or dismissed in a few lines by a writer who, unwilling to suspend a proper filial respect, is yet unable to muster an undiminished filial affection. On the contrary, Charles goes out of his way to draw a sympathetic portrait of his father, and the picture that emerges is of a sympathetic man. It cannot be doubted that Dr. Robert had periods of dissatisfaction with his son; looking back, Charles had similar reservations about his own youthful achievements. But where is the record of constant disapproval, of harsh treatment and unjust decisions, of indifference, contempt and violence that one would expect from the parental bully postulated by the biographical theorists? A few words of early criticism are followed by decades of increasing satisfaction. Whenever work and health permitted during the years that followed the *Beagle* voyage, Charles would visit Shrewsbury. Never for a moment did he hint, in letter or journal, that seeing his father was either a bore or a duty, nor is there the slightest sign of that obsessive concern suggestive of an inner guilt. His affection for his father seems to have flowed truly and easily; it was not the poisoned, counterfeit spring that wells up from those murky strata where unresolved Oedipal tensions keep their patricidal secrets.

Dr. Robert's father had been the famous Erasmus Darwin; one may believe that the memory of the family's great man was kept trim and in good order by the Shrewsbury household. He had been a man of multiple attainment, the sort of polymath who flourished in the days when the various areas of human knowledge still had discernible connections and a common vocabulary. A student of classics and mathematics at Cambridge, and a published poet, he studied medicine in Edinburgh before returning to Cambridge to take his doctorate. He too had been taller than average and somewhat overweight, with strong, heavy limbs and the ruddy complexion that Robert and Charles would in turn inherit. In middle age he became grossly corpulent; a hole had to be cut in his dining table to accommodate his bulk. The scars of smallpox marred his face and a bad stammer dammed his speech, but swiftness of intellect and a savage unconcern for the wounds he caused made him effective in argument and, especially to those he had not forced to limp from the field of battle, a sought-after companion.

He was a teetotaller, but is said to have imposed no such restrictions on his sexual activies. His appearance hardly suggests the lover, but perhaps his vigour of body, force of character and sharpness of wit were able to overcome both his own disabilities and the resistance of the women he desired. He settled first in Lichfield and later in Derby, became a successful doctor and soon saw that success expressed in an income of over £1,000 a year – in the second half of the eighteenth century, a sum well on the pleasant side of comfortable. The personal price he paid was his long silence as a poet, a pause of thirty years during which he wrote nothing as frivolous as verse for fear that it would damage his medical reputation. He remained human enough to care for the poor, however, treating them without pay and at need even providing them with food. So well-known did he become that George III suggested that he might come to London as a royal physician – an unofficial invitation which, to the delight of Derby, he turned down.

Around 1760 he first met Josiah Wedgwood, then still rising to his position of fame as the country's greatest potter. It may be that at first Erasmus was Wedgwood's doctor, but soon the two men, each representative in his own way of England's new professional class, had become firm friends. Erasmus's more abstract philosophical and scientific interests were served by the Lunar Society, a group well known in the history of ideas, who met at the time of the full moon (ostensibly for no more mystic a reason than that members might ride home in that midnight brilliance). They were, on the whole, serious, anti-clerical pragmatists, radical in politics, supporters of the American colonists in their struggle against the British crown, admirers of the French Revolution, opponents of slavery, advocates for democracy, and propagandists of an enlightened humanism.

With his medical reputation secure, Erasmus began to re-establish himself as a poet and intellectual. Briefly, he corresponded with Rousseau and, at slightly greater length, with the geologist Hutton, whose ideas, disseminated by Playfair and filtered by Lyell, were to have a profound influence on the as yet unborn Charles. He began the publication of his long poem, *The Botanic Garden*, bringing together his early fascination with poetry and his newer interest in botany. In 1794, he brought out *Zoönomia*, subtitled *The Laws of Organic Life* and intended principally as a medical textbook. In it, however, Erasmus propounded a developmental theory, though he argued it in speculative rather than factual terms. It would almost certainly have become one of the minor curiosities of scientific history, had his grandson not formulated a much more comprehensive theory of a similar kind and supported it by evidence which, in essence at least, still continues to convince.

It was Erasmus himself who had brought Robert Darwin to Shrewsbury. He had half-forced his son to follow him into medicine, sending him to study at Leyden in Holland, and his own old medical school of Edinburgh. Now, it is said, he gave young Robert, still only twenty, a pound for every year of his life and returned to his own Derby practice; later, an uncle sent the novitiate practitioner another £20. Forty pounds, even in 1786, was no great sum with which to finance one's entire life; other authorities, however, put the amount involved at over £1,000. In any case, as Charles related in the *Autobiography*, "his fees during the first year paid for the keep of two horses and a servant". Soon Dr. Robert could afford both marriage and a house in which to keep it secure. He bought a plot of land overlooking the River Severn, to the north-west of the town, conveniently near the Holyhead road. There he built The Mount, his practical, well-proportioned, red brick house with its wide-awake windows and its grandiose entrance (since extended by a pillared porch); and to it he brought his wife, already in her early thirties, Susannah Wedgwood, Josiah's favourite daughter.

Josiah had died in 1795, a year before the wedding, leaving a flourishing business and, after earlier bequests, a quarter of a million pounds. His daughters, Susannah among them, received £25,000 each; the bulk of what remained went to his destined successor, also named Josiah. Soon the family house, Etruria Hall, was up for sale: young Josiah was moving south, to

Dorset, hoping that distance and the deployment of money would establish him as a true member of the gentry. He was, however, over-ambitious. As the wiseacre comment on social mobility had it. "The third generation makes the gentleman". Somewhat more authoritatively, F.M.L. Thompson points out in his *English Landed Gentry in the Nineteenth Century*, "It usually took two generations . . . or the passage of about half a century, for a new family to withdraw from the scene of its commercial success and settle entirely in the life of country gentlemen". Charles's Uncle Jos, therefore, failed in his endeavour; and not only failed, but also stretched his resources almost beyond bearing. Luckily, he was intelligent and – even better in the circumstances – sensible. He beat a retreat, back to Staffordshire and the supervision of his father's business, which had in the meantime been left under the care of a manager. Seven miles from the Etruria Works stood Maer Hall; it was a plain stone house, built about two centuries earlier, and overlooked a little lake (or "mere" – hence its name). That first, great landscape gardener, "Capability" Brown, had shaped the water and the grounds; the house was surrounded by meandering paths, stands of trees, small coppices, gentle slopes and flashing gardens. This was the seat which the younger Josiah Wedgwood now bought – and to do so, borrowed from his brother-in-law, Dr. Robert. With Maer only twenty miles from Shrewsbury and such a community of finances, it is not surprising that a close connection developed between the Darwins and the Wedgwoods.

It is customary for biographers to make much of the contrast between the civilized gaiety of Maer and what they take to be the sullen gloom of The Mount. There is no doubt that for Charles there was a freedom about the life he experienced there which contrasted with the constraint he felt at Shrewsbury. Indeed, he says so in his *Autobiography*: "Life there was perfectly free . . . and in the evening there was much agreeable conversation, not so personal as it generally is in large family parties, together with music". His daughter, Henrietta, wrote years later, "I can remember his description of these enchanted evenings, and his happy look and sigh of reminiscence, as he recalled the past . . ." But if he and his sisters, and his brother when not at university, delighted to visit the Wedgwoods of Maer, it must not be forgotten that The Mount, too, received its quota of visitors. Families like the Wedgwoods and the Darwins lived in the style of country gentry and, like them, followed a year-round course of leisurely visits, mostly to the houses of friends or relations in the vicinity, a few further afield, to London, Brighton, Edinburgh or the West Country.

This ordered existence, reminiscent of that portrayed in Jane Austen's novels, raises – as did Uncle Jos's social failure in Dorset – the complex question of class. Where exactly did the Darwins and their cousins the

Wedgwoods stand in the intricate webbing of relationship, courtesies and snubs within which each such family had to find its place? Both families came from yeoman stock, honest rather than clever. Clever marriages and hard-headed management over several generations had brought the Darwins and their Lincolnshire estate of Marston prosperously into the seventeenth century. In the Civil War, William Darwin fought for the King and with the royal defeat almost lost the family holding. At the Restoration of the Stuarts in 1660, however, he was compensated by a law office. Thus, with his own estate and solidly established as the Recorder of Lincoln, he was able to send his son to Cambridge.

This son married the only daughter of a local landowner, a young lady called Anne Waring who thus, in 1680, brought into the family the name that would be carried a century later by her great-great-grandson, Dr. Robert Waring Darwin. More importantly, she also brought the Waring family estate, Elston Hall, near Newark, in Nottinghamshire, and there the Darwins now established themselves. By the eighteenth century, therefore, the Darwins had, as lawyers, become members of a new professional middle class, but had at the same time acquired a respectable roof of their own. The great Erasmus had been the grandson of the first Darwin of Elston Hall, by his work adding to the name a certain intellectual and artistic grandeur.

In the century and a half in which Darwins had been so solidly established in the provincial middle class, they had often found the leisure to pursue various interests of their own. The great Erasmus's father, Robert, had been noted for proficiency in natural history; his elder son – yet another Robert – wrote an introduction to the work of Linnaeus, entitled *Principia Botanica,* during the time that his younger brother was spreading his fame from the security of Lichfield and Derby. Erasmus, in due course, became a Fellow of the Royal Society, as did his son, Dr. Robert (a tradition that, uniquely, was to run through three more generations). Dr. Robert's elder son, Erasmus, showed an early predilection for science, though it was to be submerged in due course by ill health, indolence and the gentle dissipations of a metropolitan dilettante. Again, it would be the younger son who attracted the world's attention.

In the world of rank, however, the Darwins' standing was made plain by their lack of connection with families of title. Their only real link with the echelons of the aristocracy was through Bessy, Charles's aunt by marriage – his Uncle Jos's wife, Elizabeth Allen. The Allens of Cresselly were somewhat tortuously connected to those late Tudor grandees, the Cecils. However, when it came to lifestyle and, more especially, income, the distinctions between the Darwins and the surrounding gentry became much less clear. The fact is that Dr. Robert was, by the standards of the gentry if not those of the landed families of the great aristocracy, a more than tolerably wealthy man.

There survives his last comprehensive account book, a ledger bound in a now-faded red cloth, with impressive marbled endpapers, in which are recorded his investments, loans and land purchases, his debts, allowances and gifts. The Doctor opened it in 1831, so it reveals his financial activities only over the last sixteen years of his life. When one tots up the income that its pages detail, one finds that it rarely dropped below £7,000 a year and was frequently over five hundred pounds more than that. To this, of course, must be added the money he made from his highly successful practice, which can hardly ever have been less than £1,500 a year. Since the fruitful outlay of his capital was already well established by the time the ledger begins – his income totalled £7,574 6s. 9d. in 1832, the first full year recorded – one may assume that he had had sums of this kind to dispose of for many years previously.

"For most of the nineteenth century," F.M.L. Thompson has calculated, "it would be reasonable to adopt a landed income of £1,000 a year as the lower limit for the gentry, and . . . £10,000 a year formed the upper limit . . . Such a range of wealth obviously embraced a variety of types, and these included . . . the man whose landownership was quite subsidiary to his main profession." The Darwin money did indeed come partly from land owner-ship – there was a farm in Lincolnshire that brought in £200 a year, and Sutterton Fen, rented by a Mr. Carrington for £42 annually. It is clear from the most superficial glance at the accounts, however, that land was a totally unimportant source of income for the Darwins, its absence making one essential difference between them and the gentry.

Some of the Doctor's money came from solidly safe investments – he had put well over £20,000 into 3% and 4% Consols; there were canal shares in significant numbers, sums lent to Shrewsbury's roadbuilding funds that paid a steady 5% – but by far the greatest proportion of his capital (or the capital that he controlled, since some already belonged to his children) had been lent out, often in mortgages, to some of the landed, aristocratic families in the neighbourhood. The Earls of Powis, for example, at one time owed Dr. Robert over £50,000; the Noel-Hill family, otherwise the Barons Berwick of Attingham, were paying interest on some £25,000; and Sir John Hanmer, in the 1830s the Liberal member of Parliament for Shrewsbury, was yet another with a five figure debt. Dr. Robert, with the help of his solicitor, Thomas Salt, seems to have been as financially agile as he was physically ponderous.

The ledger, often with entries in his own hand, offers us sudden, brief glimpses of him, the man directly seen and not filtered through the nervous perceptions of his relations. One sees the meticulous care with which he made provision for his children. Marriage settlements, transfers of mortgages, loans and the interest payments on them mark his economic shepherding of Charles and the others. The sisters were given small sums every year, the interest on Wedgwood legacies which their father had "borrowed" from them; the eldest, Marianne, long married to Dr. Parker, was by the 1840s receiving over £200 a year. Dr. Robert seems to have taken care of his other dependants, too; complicated transactions with "Edward Evans my servant" ensured an income for the latter from the interest on loans to the Doctor that may have been no more than notional, while other advances, sedulously repaid, enabled him to "purchase the stable &c of Jos Phipps in the Durnall garden". In 1846 there is the simple entry, "Nov 10 E. Evans died this day, a faithful friend & servant". "Mrs Sara Price Housekeeper" was paid the annual five per cent on a £100 loan, which was repaid in 1835, and one assumes that this too was some form of disguised pension. Edward Evans's old mother had similarly "lent" Dr. Robert £42, and every half year received a guinea as her five per cent interest payment, a sum which was made up to £1 6s. "to make it a shilling a week", as the entry explains. With rents at sixpence a week, this was no negligible sum.

If he was, within the limits of good sense, a benevolent master to his servants, Dr. Robert was also a reasonably magnanimous landlord. In 1831 there is an entry for the property at Sutterton – "Nov 22 a years rent due Lady Day 1831 – forgive the half year due 29 of September 1831 for W. Carrington"; the £50 the straitened Mr. Carrington was able to pay seems to have been acceptable. Since the rent was £42 a year, his payment, covering eighteen months, was £13 short. A year later, "on account of rent due at Lady Day 1832," he could manage only £22, with another £12 the following May. In September, 1833, however, his affairs began to look up: he paid £38 that month, and in November another £60. His landlord's faith had been rewarded – he had caught up the arrears. The sum, of course, was of no great consequence to a man whose income ran in thousands, yet it may be taken as indicative of a basic largeness of spirit that such adjustments and postponements were allowed.

The ledger also offers us an insight into Dr. Robert's curious filing system. Documents were, he wrote, "in tin box under Back stairs" or "In drawer in Bureau". A mortgage securing a large loan to Viscount Clive, Lord Powis's son, could be confirmed by following a pencil note, "Title deeds under my bed 30 June 1832". Haphazard though all this seems, Dr. Robert's system was meticulously indicated and easy to follow. What is less clear is where all the capital it refers to had actually come from. Erasmus Darwin, after all, had had after his second marriage another family to provide for.

Whatever the sources of this prosperity, the fact remains that Charles passed his boyhood in a household which, though always frugally run, was one of the wealthier ones in the neighbourhood. The result of this was that he, his brother and the girls could follow a way of life hardly different from that of the landed gentry round about. Young Charles, for example, became passionately interested in shooting, a sport that, during the early nineteenth century, was becoming more and more the prerogative of the upper classes. The fact that the landowners spent money to preserve game which at times attacked the tenant farmers' crops meant that who shot what, and why, gave some indication of the hunter's social standing; as Thompson points out, "it would be a mistake to suppose that the normal tenant farmer was allowed any shooting by his landlord". This was, after all, the period when game laws almost as severe as those of the Middle Ages hemmed in further a peasantry whose ancient freedoms the enclosure of the great estates had already noticeably diminished.

The Darwin daughters, meanwhile, lived a life no less leisured than that of the young ladies of the landed gentry, punctuating it in the same way with a genteel concern for the household, involvement in a variety of philanthropic enterprises and such charitable works as visits to the sickbeds of the poor. Caroline, Susan and Catherine, born respectively in 1800, 1803, and 1810, really do seem at times like peripheral, though precisely delineated, characters in a Jane Austen novel. Their preoccupations, as one reads their surviving letters, are instantly familiar. Good works, gossip, and an undisturbing appreciation of the arts suggest a typical conformity.

When one looks more closely, however, one notices a vigour and intelligence which Miss Austen usually permitted only to her heroines – and an interest in politics that she allowed to no one.

> I am afraid Parliamentary Reform will occupy them almost all this Session, but I do fully expect when that is carried into effect, the Slavery Question will be done at once. I never hoped for anything so capital as Mr. Brougham being Lord Chancellor . . . Every body in Shropshire that I see are so horrified at Mr. Brougham's elevation, that they really are dumbfounded and cannot express their sentiments about it.* I think they are all young Lord Eldons† in this County.

Thus Catherine, at the end of 1830, writing to her cousin Fanny Wedgwood; nothing quite so independent or radical ever sullied mind or pen in the lives Miss Austen depicted.

---

* Henry Peter Brougham (1778–1868), soon to become the first Baron Brougham and Vaux, was a leading Whig politician, a strong advocate of parliamentary reform.

† John Scott, first Earl of Eldon (1751–1838), the son of a coal dealer who became Lord Chancellor. He was an arch-conservative and considered the leader of the "ultra-Tories".

It is not surprising, therefore, that the Darwin daughters, Caroline and Susan in particular, with their father in active and supportive partnership, should have established an infant school not far from The Mount; nor that they should have turned to educational reformers like the French writer and politician Guizot (whose two-volume work on educational theory stood on their library shelves) to give them guidance. They took enthusiastically to the methods of the Swiss Johann Pestalozzi, still alive when they first opened their doors, and so in their small way helped to pioneer developments in education which still have their effect today. (Money for the school came in part from Dr. Robert's periodic repayments of a sum notionally "borrowed" from Caroline.)

Nevertheless, in their fascination with the marriages of their friends and neighbours, their delight in the dances and gaieties of a provincial town, their frequent visits to the commodious houses of acquaintances or relations and the secure financial foundations of their lives, the Darwin sisters seem representative of the young women familiar to us from the literature of the age. Their voices float down to us across the decades in tones we almost know, the frivolities they deal with part of our expectations of them. One sees them, in sweep of gown and chestnut ringlets, smiling to themselves as their busy quills rush across the paper and the superficial details of their lives tumble out for the delectation of their brother, locked into his education in Edinburgh or Cambridge, and later in his naturalist's exile in South America and on the South Seas. In such moods, one could imagine that they never had a real thought in their heads.

The reality of their lives, however, was broader than lightheartedness allowed; they read, they stood up for the liberal causes traditional both among the Darwins and the Wedgwoods, they attended to their natural duties at home and those to which they had appointed themselves in the town, they tried to keep an eye on the upbringing of their young brother. They took early to that maternal tone of affectionate anxiety by which boys in a household of women are often in danger of being swaddled: "I must say dear Charles," writes Caroline, "how glad I am that you have been studying the bible . . ."; Susan, a little earlier, is equally happy. "I am very glad to hear you are such a good boy with your French . . ."; and even the young Catherine chips in: "I must just mention that Edinburgh is spelt with an *h* at the end; and *altogether* has only *one 1*. . . ."

They could, however, make fun of each other; Caroline at the end of 1825 was reading a novel apparently entitled *Moses Sherridon* and Susan, too, had been enjoying it, "but unfortunately any particular part that is mentioned in conversation she can not quite call to mind, his marriage for instance: 'Dear me! Married, was he! Well, I suppose I missed that chapter' and many other incidents – 'Dear me! Well, I suppose I missed that page' – Do you read your magnificent work on Zoology in that manner? . . ." They did not always read novels, either, as the stereotype would let one expect; Caroline mentions Coleridge's *Aids to Reflection,* Catherine has been deep in Southey's account of the Peninsular War, while Susan is delighted to hear that Charles has taken to "studying 'The Morning Chronicle' instead of *odious* John Bull; what is the use or pleasure of reading a paper which everybody abuses & allows to be so unfair?"

So one returns to the sisters' politics, for *John Bull* was an anti-reform and pro-slavery publication of an unpleasantness only matched by its liveliness. It was not calculated to please Susan, who, as Catherine put it, in April, 1826, "is hotter than ever about Slavery. – John Bull pretending that the Slaves lead a life of *Comfort* and *Happiness* really seems as if he was quizzing* the subject . . ." Through their school and their visits to the sick they were able to express the humanism from which their liberal opinions sprang. "We all get up early & are good & industrious," wrote Susan in March the same year, and that seems to have been the case. They did not hesitate to draw even the languid Erasmus into their activities: they had, she wrote, been making him very useful, "taking him to Doctor all our sick poor people" – he was at the time still a medical student. "He goes pretty often to visit poor Mrs. O. Jones who has been quite confined to her bed for some time. The other day when he was there, she gave him an old Guinea wrapped up, saying 'she wished very much to give him his first fee & hoped he would keep it as a love token from her' – This little mark of friendship & kind manner of doing it please Eras very much."

In this atmosphere of occasional high spirits, happy flirtation, social concern and applied, if not very profound, intelligence, the young Charles Darwin grew up. It is a far cry from the gloomy house which has so often been described, the ice-bound home from which, it is assumed, he must always have been happy to escape. If he was glad to get away – and like most young men, he enjoyed adventuring under other people's roofs – it was to avoid, not indifference or tyranny, but rather the oppression of too active an affection. The lives of his sisters were reasonably full, given the standards of the day – but hardly full enough for energetic, clever young women barred from all ordinary careers. It is not unreasonable that they should have turned some of their energy on him, surrounding him with advice and admonition no less tedious for springing from their love and concern.

---

* Quizzing – making fun of.

3

In March, 1826, when Charles was already a medical student in Edinburgh, Caroline wrote him a little homily about reading the Bible,

> not only because you think it wrong not to read it, but with the wish of learning there what is necessary to feel & do to go to heaven after you die. I am sure I gain more by praying over a few verses than by reading simply many chapters – I suppose you do not feel prepared yet to take the sacrament – it made me feel quite melancholy the other day looking at your old garden, & the flowers just coming up which you used to be so happy watching. I think when you & Catherine were little children & I was always with you or thinking about you was the happiest part of my life & I dare say always will be.

When Charles was small, Caroline was his teacher. He and Catherine were given their educational rudiments at home, their older sister acting as a sort of governess. Ten years later, recalling those days – "the happiest part of my life" – Caroline sets down this glimpse of the infant Charles, happy when watching the new flowers thrusting towards spring and so already noticeably enthralled by the workings of nature. Her tone suggests her approach to teaching; it is clear that she had not inherited the rational, even atheistical, attitudes to religion that were almost traditional with the Darwin men. One may assume that Charles, therefore, like most children of that time, approached life, literature and the mysteries of the alphabet by way of Bible stories and uplifting little parables. In his *Autobiography,* Charles remembered that:

> I was much slower in learning than my younger sister Catherine, and I believe I was in many ways a naughty boy. Caroline was extremely kind, clever and zealous; but she was too zealous in trying to improve me; for I clearly remember . . . saying to myself when about to enter a room where she was – "What will she blame me for now?" and I made myself dogged so as not to care what she might say.

By this time, he had begun to collect "all sorts of things, shells, seals, franks, coins and minerals", a taste which in the family only his brother shared. He was also, he tells us, "much given to deliberate falsehoods", though that seems a phrase dignifying with the full panoply of wickedness what was little more than schoolboy joking. One example he gives us shows him picking and hiding a pile of valuable fruit, then running "to spread the news that I had discovered a hoard of stolen fruit". This sounds like the attempt of a boy, in general unsure of approval, to gain praise and approbation from his family. He did, however, take forbidden plums, peaches and apples, some to eat himself, some to offer to the lads who lived in the nearby cottages (gifts one can see as part of another attempt to secure approval). With Darwinian ingenuity, he used a flowerpot on the end of a long stake to pluck fruit from which a high wall and a gate were supposed to keep such rascally intruders.

Nearly sixty years after the event, Caroline contradicted Darwin's modest account of his childhood:

> Instead of being "a naughty boy" he was particularly affectionate, tractable & sweet tempered, & my father had the highest opinion of his understanding & intelligence. My father was very fond of him & even when he was a little boy of 6 or 7, however bustled & overtired, often had Charles with him when he was dressing, to teach him some little thing such as the almanack – and Charles used to be so eager to be down in time. Charles does not seem to have known half how much my father loved him.

Was this the past seen in the glow cast by half a century, the reaction of praise that follows bereavement? When she wrote that, Darwin had already been three years dead. Or was there an element of truth in it, marking the difference between the way we see ourselves and that in which others see us? And if the young Charles thought himself wicked and doubted his father's affection, if he felt his older sisters' interest oppressive, yet found it necessary through invented stories to gain his family's approval and that of the boys in the neighbourhood, does that not point to a central and, in time, perhaps a fruitful insecurity?

It is a strain that is to run through all his dealings in and with the world – a constant self-denigration, a repetitive conviction of unworthiness and inadequacy. The world, for its part, will respond, and seems to have responded then, with an unfailing affection and a stream of praise. Having decided, however, that the world was constantly on the point of criticizing him, Darwin throughout his life seems to have pursued his nursery policy – he made himself dogged and did not care what it might say. Thus there developed in him that solitary stubborness, that determination to walk his own path towards his chosen direction, which made his work so original in its ideas, yet so meticulous in its detail. Outer diffidence, a public pliability, the constant appearance of agreeableness; inner certainty, undeviating will, the pursuit of his own objectives – Darwin, like most people, seems to have established the main outlines of his character long before the age of six.

In Shrewsbury a Unitarian minister named George Case ran a primary school and, early in 1817, Charles became a pupil there. He himself had been baptised into the Anglican Church, but his mother sometimes worshipped at the chapel to which the school was attached, and he too had on occasion been taken to services there, either by her or his elder sisters. It must have seemed natural to place him with Mr. Case. W.A. Leighton, one of those clerical naturalists who in such large numbers combined reverence with research in the nineteenth century, later one of Darwin's many scientific correspondents, was a schoolfellow there and remembered the young Charles across nearly seven decades:

> In figure he was bulky and heavy-looking, and did not then manifest any particular powers of mind. He was reserved in manner, & we thought him proud inasmuch as he did not join in any play with the other boys, but went directly home from school.

Leighton may not have known Charles very well at the time, since he was some five years older – old enough, indeed, to be called on at times to hear the younger boys' lessons. "I can therefore say that [Charles's] lessons were always carefully prepared & correctly said. No doubt his Mother attended to all this . . . Though reserved in manner he was of a kind disposition and seemed pleased to do any little acts to gratify his fellows – one instance of which was his bringing plants from his father's garden for our little gardens." Bringing one such plant for Leighton, Charles "told that his Mother had been teaching him how by looking into the interior of a blossom he could ascertain the name of the plant. This greatly aroused my attention & curiosity and I enquire of him repeatedly how this could be done. His reply was that he could not remember . . ." Leighton, thinking back, felt that Charles's mother might have been trying to introduce him to the Linnean system of classification; in any case, the entire incident helped to turn Leighton towards an interest in botany and this in time would lead him to write such works as *Lichen Flora of Great Britain* and *The Flora of Shropshire*. If the effect was so profound at second-hand, one feels the firsthand experience, Darwin's own early experience of his mother's fascination with plants, must have had a similar importance. Susannah Wedgwood herself had throughout her youth been especially close to her father, who had been sufficiently interested in science to collect the "books, prints, pictures, cabinets of Experiments and Fossils and of Natural History" which eventually figured in his will. The shelves at Maer held many books on botanical subjects and the accounts of eighteenth-century voyagers, full of biological observations. Most of these must have come from Etruria Hall and must therefore have been available to Susannah before her marriage to Dr. Robert. There was also, of course, the Darwins' own scientific tradition to inspire the young Charles.

After just over a year with the Rev. Case, Charles was sent to the long-established and reputable public school which for many years was probably as well known as the town from which it took its name. Shrewsbury School, with its battlemented tower, its Tudor windows, its Gothic chapel, decorated sundial and imposing porch, looked the very type of famous English school. It had, however, passed through a long period when its reputation for quality had almost evaporated; over the previous two decades, under the redoubtable Dr. Butler, it had been energetically thrust back into its traditional position among the seven great schools in the country.

Considering the role of the early nineteenth century public school, F. Musgrove, in an article in *Economic History Review*, has pointed out that it "was the appropriate educational institution not for children who had their way to make in the world, but for those who would have no need to earn their own livelihood, having fortunes or estates to inherit, and unpaid or inadequately paid careers in Parliament, the Army, the Church, voluntary public services or the Bar to pursue". It was also, then as now, the route along which ambitious parents pushed their young, hoping in this way to heave them a rung or two up the social ladder. Then as now, such attempts frequently built in the next generation aspirations they could not fulfil and, by corollary, skills that proved valueless in the situations in which they actually found themselves.

For a while Dr. Robert hoped, naturally enough, that both his sons would follow him into the medical profession, though in Charles's case the decision that he should study for it may not have been taken until he was sixteen. That he sent both boys to Shrewsbury School may have been for no better reason than geographical convenience – it was the nearest good school. To the extent that his choice was related to social attitudes, it probably reflected a position achieved, rather than one only hoped for. An annual investment income of £7,000 represented, at the interest rates then common, capital of around £175,000 – more than enough to secure the future of the Darwin children. Dr. Robert, therefore, will not have doubted the suitability of his sons to be pupils in Dr. Butler's establishment. Charles, in particular, with his passion for the outdoors and his special pleasure in shooting, fitted very well with the young sons of the county's gentry. The Darwins were not landed, perhaps, but they were certainly gentlemen.

If the suitability of Charles for Shrewsbury School was beyond question, the same could hardly be said of the school's suitability for him. The curriculum for the fifth form, which reflected the standards set for the entire school, began on Mondays with Greek, Roman or English history, continued with Greek grammar, went on through readings of Thucydides, Plato, Aristotle and the rest, returned to Greek grammar, took a glance at Cicero's

Orations and ended with Virgil. The rest of the week called for the same concentration on the ancients: the Greek and Roman dramatists, poets, philosophers, rhetoricians and historians came jostling past day after day upon that pedagogic conveyor belt. Modern pupils expect weekends of freedom; not so the public school boy in the nineteenth century. Juvenal or Horace would be reopened on Saturday mornings, classroom sessions later enlivened by lectures on the geometry of Euclid. (A special tutor also taught Charles the mysteries of Euclid privately and not without effect: Darwin remembered many years later "the intense satisfaction which the clear geometrical proofs gave me"). Saturdays ended with "Open lesson, generally English translation into Greek or Latin prose, or lesson in Greek play . . ." Even Sundays had their share of labour, though in deference to the day no "pagan authors" were set: "Upper boys examined in Watts's *Scripture History* or Tomline's *Theology*. Lower boys examined in Catechism." In the sixth form, a similar list was extended by the addition of occasional lessons in geography, philology and religion, as well as the history, Euclidean geometry and algebra offered to the fifth.

The respectability of this curriculum is proved by the fact that Dr. Butler included it in a letter he sent to Mr. Brougham, urging him to categorize Shrewsbury as a school of high status in new measures being contemplated for the regulation of the country's education. Writing in his *Autobiography*, Darwin stated quite categorically, "Nothing could have been worse for the development of my mind than Dr. Butler's school, as it was strictly classical . . . The school as a means of education to me was simply a blank." The formalized constructions of the dead languages, the discipline of writing Latin verses, the endless learning by heart of great swathes of ancient epics, all bored and frequently defeated him: "I had many friends, and got together a grand collection of old verses, which by patching together, sometimes aided by other boys, I could work into any subject." With the help of this ingenious library of poetic oddments, he managed to scrape by, and he became adept at "learning forty or fifty lines of Virgil or Homer, whilst I was in morning chapel", forgetting them as soon as their usefulness had come to an end. With a conscientiousness that he was often to display, he worked hard, "not using cribs", finding after a while that for some of the poetry, especially the odes of Horace, he was developing a genuine liking.

Although the school was close to his home, Charles was sent there, in the gentlemanly way, as a boarder, and as a result was integrated into so close a community much more completely than if he had remained that object of boyish suspicion and scorn, the day-boy in a boarding school. However, "as the distance was hardly more than a mile to my home, I very often ran there in the longer intervals between the callings over and before locking up at night", a practice that enabled him to maintain a certain measure of intellectual independence of the school. His scientific interests, for instance, diffuse and rudimentary though they were, could not easily have been kept up in a place where a boy was hardly ever alone, working in great classrooms and sleeping in dormitories with twenty or more companions.

Such evening runs may occasionally have been spiced with a certain danger, since the boys of the school and those of the town were at times in a state of war. In May, 1819, Dr. Butler felt it necessary to write to the overseer of the local factory, "I have received information of an intention of some of the boys belonging to your factory to attack my pupils on their way to the water", a piece of proposed rowdyism that seems to have been an overspill from the antagonisms aroused by an election*. Dr. Butler proposed that a couple of "trusty workmen" should keep an eye on their younger colleagues – he would "give them a reasonable compensation when the election was over . . ."

Violence among the Shrewsbury boys was expected and not uncommon; quarrels should be settled, wrote the Headmaster, "between themselves by a trial of mastery . . . But no master can either say or encourage it." When it actually came to a fight, he and the other teachers usually kept out of sight. But discipline was strict, with corporal punishment as its most important sanction; when Butler first took over at Shrewsbury, he asked his own old headmaster, Dr. James of Rugby, for advice. Whipping seems to have been the teacher's first resort, though punishments included "imposition of translations . . . the more troublesome repetitions, or solitary confinement when the weather admits". Dr. James's attitude seems to have had political overtones, not surprising in one who lived through the final decades of the eighteenth century: indiscipline and departures from the norm might not be immediately significant, he wrote to Butler, "but everything new afterwards will in this age stir up revolutionary principles; for some such spirits must exist, and there is no garden without weeds".

Quite apart from the discipline, life at Shrewsbury cannot always have been pleasant or easy. All his life, Darwin was vividly to remember the "atrocious smell" of the dormitories in the morning. Yet it was not true to say that the boys' welfare was not considered, or that they had no redress when conditions fell below an acceptable standard. In 1819, Erasmus – perhaps on his younger brother's behalf – complained that the beds were damp. Instantly asked for an explanation by Dr. Robert, Butler defended himself vigorously. He was, he wrote, anxious "always to attend to real complaints, but not to justify boys in foolish whims or prejudices". The bed

---

* 1819 was a year of much political disturbance, especially in the Midlands and the North, culminating in Manchester's "Peterloo Massacre".

had, in fact, "been certainly for two and I think for three days constantly before a large kitchen fire". Closer questioning of Erasmus would doubtless elicit the truth – "if you think it desirable that an addition should be made to the boys' blankets after what you hear from him, you cannot do me so great a kindness as by recommending that measure, and they will immediately be put on every bed in my two houses . . . as what is done for one must certainly be done for all". The incident not only illuminates the Headmaster's concern, it also offers another demonstration, in the vigour with which Dr. Robert took up the cudgels for his sons, of how far he was from being the domestic tyrant of legend.

Charles was, perhaps, fortunate in having an older brother who could sometimes smooth the path for him a little, and especially one who was always widely popular. Believed to be taking medicine to "strengthen his skeleton", Erasmus, tall, thin and delicate, was early given the nickname "Bones". The Welsh scholar, naturalist and teacher, John Price, a school-friend of his, remembered that he had been "universally beloved as a gentle, kind hearted creature with talent far beyond his physical powers". Charles, on the other hand, had then been merely one of the "Little-fellows" in a society where Price himself – and Erasmus – had been "Big-fellows". These were castes between which there could be only limited contact, and Price's memories of Charles were in later years imprecise and hazy. When himself a senior boy, Charles seems to have been a little more flexible; a younger contemporary of his remembered that, "as a new boy all forlorn in 1823 he at once took notice of me", partly because he was connected with family friends of the Darwins. "He showed me great kindness . . . I do not think it was in his nature to be unkind to anyone – never was a boy less cut out for a bully or School Tyrant." He appeared old for his age, both "in manner & in mind", but neither showed any distinction in his work nor developed into "a hero of the cricket field or river". Another schoolfellow, J. H. C. Cameron, who went into the Church and died as Rector of Shoreham, reinforced the view of Charles as gentle, friendly and popular. Cameron shared a dormitory with him for several years and the boys "often beguiled the night with pleasant conversation." Young Charles "was always cheerful & good tempered & much beloved."

It is obvious, however, that during the years Darwin spent at school, all his most important activities occurred outside it. Field sports and natural history were his twin interests, and it was these he pursued with the zeal Dr. Butler would have preferred to see directed towards the classical poets – a preference Dr. Robert will have endorsed. Thus from the beginning Charles set the pattern that was to hold good throughout his education. The subjects presented to him formally, as the necessary part of his student destiny, he worked at only as hard as he was driven to by a sense of duty, unenlivened by the slightest enthusiasm. His best efforts he kept for what really interested him, which was natural history in various simple versions, and an indiscriminate itch to collect the forms, products and organisms with which the natural sciences dealt. As a result, the belief gained ground that he was essentially indolent – a belief which he himself came to share.

As time went on, however, there grew up a quite different set of ideas on the subject of his intellectual energy, and how one assessed his character depended upon which set of criteria one chose. Those who put the curriculum first – Dr. Butler, naturally, probably the Darwin sisters, certainly Dr. Robert – saw Charles's student years as marred by consistent failure; those, on the other hand, who knew him primarily as an enthusiast of the natural sciences considered his school and university days as essential only in the leisure they allowed him to prepare for his scientific career. The first group were surprised and gratified by his later success; the second, while no less gratified, felt rather that Charles had simply fulfilled their long-held expectations.

His love of shooting, of course, came into a different category. It was a part of his general delight in nature and the open air, but it was also one element in the sporting heritage of a gentleman. Later, he would take more pleasure in riding; now, in his early and middle teens, it was the gun that fascinated him. There are still in existence notes that he wrote for himself on a hunter's arts and skills, perhaps basing himself on a manual of "instruction to young Sportsmen" which he noted on the back, perhaps distilling everything that he had learned. There is detail about the preferred size of shot, and on the filling of cartridges – 280 pellets of No. 7 shot to an ounce of powder seems to have been the recipe – and some basic instructions about the act of shooting itself: "Never take down your gun when once up" and "One or two feet before the bird at 60 yards". Charles listed for himself some of the salient points of the game laws: "Penalty for killing game out of season 20 l or not less than 10", he wrote; and "An unqualified person can only be convicted once in a day"; and "A person with neither qual: nor lic: may carry a gun so that he does not take game". It sounds almost as though he were preparing for a poacher's career. Then there are "Instructions for [here 'Shooting' has been crossed out] Young Sportsmen By an old Sportsman", and these tell us, "There are two ways, Snap & taking steady aim. Snap must be done immediately, the other steadily." These basic observations are briefly elaborated: at the bottom there is a sort of claim to authorship, "C. Darwin fecit", and then the agitated postscript, "In Hares & Rabbits, for Gods sake, shoot above them," which sounds like a direct quotation from some knowledgeable companion – or perhaps a cry of anguish after a disastrous miss. The whole, for all its youthful ring, fore-shadows later methodical approaches to more serious matters.

His chief mentor in the art of shooting was William Owen of Woodhouse, near Oswestry, whose fondness for Charles was almost boundless: Charles, in response, seems for a while to have regarded Woodhouse as, like Maer, a second home. Nicknamed "The Forest", it became for his sisters, too, one of those agreeable ports of call where one could find relief from the monotony of one's own hearth. The house stood no more than a dozen or so miles from The Mount, at West Felton, on that endlessly convenient Holyhead road.

It was with William Owen to show him how, therefore, that Charles, as he says in his *Autobiography*, became in the latter part of his schooldays "passionately fond of shooting . . . How well I remember killing my first snipe, and my excitement was so great that I had much difficulty in reloading my gun from the trembling of my hands. This taste long continued and I became a very good shot." But, more even than shooting, natural history and especially the collecting and classification of beetles became the focus for his energies. In his *Autobiography* he recalled "collecting minerals with much zeal, but quite unscientifically", he took greater care over insects for "when ten years old (1819) I went for three weeks to Plas Edwards on the sea-coast in Wales, I was very much interested and surprised at seeing a large black and scarlet Hemipterous insect, many moths (Zygaena) and a Cicindela, which are not found in Shropshire . . . From reading White's *Selborne* I took much pleasure in watching the habits of birds . . . In my simplicity I remember wondering why every gentleman did not become an ornithologist". John Price could remember the very spot in Shrewsbury School "where he brought me a shell of *Purpura lapillus* and said, 'Price, what's this?' I believe I translated the Welsh name *Gwichiad y cwn* into Dog periwinkle, which satisfied the little man for the time . . ." It was a piece of information which for several years thereafter turned Price, in Charles's view, into an oracle on natural history. Cameron, too, associated the young Charles with natural history – he had not been particularly successful at his formal lessons, Cameron recalled, "but was always busy collecting beetles, butterflies, etc."

There was, however, another, inward element in the young Charles Darwin, a strange, locked-away somnambulistic strand to his character, chambers of the self to which others then, and he later, could find no access. As a very young boy, he tells us he had "a strong taste for long solitary walks; but what I thought about I know not". Once he became so absorbed that he fell seven or eight feet to the ground, off the truncated walls that long before had fortified the town. It was the time in a child's life when the imagination constructs a reality more compelling than anything the merely physical world can offer; later, while a schoolboy, he developed a taste for poetry, reading Shakespeare, Byron, Scott and that less durable work, Thomson's *Seasons*. When he grew older he "wholly lost, to my great regret, all pleasure from poetry of any kind . . ."

Where did that pleasure go, and why? What happened to the capacity to respond, to the childhood intensity of the imagination? Darwin himself believed they simply vanished, but such qualities cannot easily be lost. They may be buried, disregarded, to surface in the distortions of dream and neurosis; or they may be redirected. Surely in Darwin's case the latter was true, the profound energy that had made vivid his imaginings, that had made real the kings and lovers of Shakespeare or the journeyings of Byron's Childe Harold, being refocussed upon the workings and variegated artefacts of nature? The lonely intensity of his childhood fantasizing was to be matched twenty-five years later by the lonely intensity of his scientific speculations. The poets' probing of the secrets of the heart was to be matched by his own probing of the secrets of life itself.

It was science, meanwhile, that forged the strongest overt bond between Charles and his brother Erasmus. The older boy, as the *Autobiography* testifies, "at school encouraged me to read, lending me books", but Charles was nevertheless compelled to add, "Our minds and tastes were . . . so different that I do not think I owe much to him intellectually . . ." Science, however, was a shared passion: Erasmus and Charles cooperated in turning a tool shed in the garden into a laboratory, and performing there a number of simple experiments. When in 1822 Erasmus went up to Cambridge, his letters back to Charles (or "Bobby", as from time to time he called him) make plain how seriously the two boys took their venture.

> I am very glad to hear that all the glass & earthenware apparatus has arrived safe . . . I should recommend ye first two or three shillings there are to spare in ye Lab, to have a shelf put up either in ye place over ye retort shelf or else under it; or both. The 10£ which poor Miss Congreve has left . . . will come in very nicely for an Air Pump or some such thing. As far as I can make out you are not carrying on any experiments in ye Lab. I will recommend you a few which will employ you some time, & will not be expensive.

The suggestions Erasmus made included obtaining "pure alumina from alum" and "ye silver in a sixpence free from ye Copper"; he also described a lecture by Professor Henslow which included "ye test of Arsenic by burning it with a blow pipe", but found himself too far away to smell "ye garlic odour which they describe". Erasmus found the Henslow lectures "very entertaining, & this is his first course so that he will have improved by ye time you come up". His next letter suggested more shelves that might be put up in their laboratory, and promised that he would "obtain some specimens of rocks for you, for Professor Sedgwick said that at the Gog Magog hills (about 4 miles distant) there were a vast number of specimens, which I shall certainly some day go & explore". As early as this, therefore, Charles was made aware of two academics who were to be closely bound up in his later career and one of whom, Henslow, was to become an intimate friend.

At the end of 1822, Erasmus was writing about the need for "as many of the large green stoppered bottles as possible . . . & then I shall not be obliged to *persuade* you quite so often to run down to Blunt for some water". Blunt was a chemist, which leads to the deduction that Erasmus meant distilled water for their experiments; the underlined persuasion suggests that relations between the brothers had their robust side. Erasmus also hoped that Charles would "practice making gases" and this he seems to have done; his son, George Darwin, remembered his father's describing the far-off days when, as a pupil at Shrewsbury School, he had been dragged by Dr. Butler before the assembled boys and, holding him firmly by the ear, the Head-master had said, "This stupid fellow will attend to his gases and his rubbish, but will not work at anything really useful". Charles Darwin himself tells us that his schoolboy nickname was "Gas". Yet he regarded the work he had done in that garden laboratory, assisting his brother with his experiments until late in the evening, "the best part of my education at school"; it is of course typical of Darwin's scholastic career that it had nothing whatsoever to do with his prescribed lessons.

Erasmus relied on Charles to send him the books he needed at Cam-bridge, rather in the way that, a decade later, Charles was to rely on him to send out packets of books to the *Beagle*. Many of the books that Erasmus needed were, naturally enough, medical texts, but early in 1825 he also called for *"Linnaei Systema Naturae* wh. is among ye books in ye Morning Room & unbound". The only personal part of that letter was brief and practical: "The next time you go home please to let them know I am alive & well . . . I shall at all events be giving ye Dr a practical proof shortly that I am alive: by sending for some money." If Dr. Robert was a tight-fisted domestic martinet, he was one arousing singularly little awe in his elder son.

By this time, there was talk of curtailing Charles's schooldays – it was obvious to everyone that he would never do well at Shrewsbury. Erasmus had his misgivings about these intentions. "Let me hear more about your school plans," he wrote in a postscript, "I should vote for your staying on until at least 18 years." His postscripts were often of interest; in another letter that February he added one to his father. He had lent someone £13 "in your name & wh. I believe he wrote about, & is I hope all right"; he signed his message with an insouciant mock formality, "I remain your lendpenny & spendpenny son, E. D. –" If there was an apology implicit in the designation, it was a fairly lighthearted one.

That summer, Erasmus, who had gone through his three stipulated Cambridge years, was due to go to Edinburgh, to follow in his father's and grandfather's footsteps at the University medical school there. Charles, when Shrewsbury School broke up for the holidays, began busily helping his father on his medical rounds. "At one time I had at least a dozen patients, and I felt a keen interest in the work. My father, who was by far the best judge of character whom I ever knew, declared that I should make a successful physician – meaning by this, one who got many patients." Perhaps it was this precocious zeal, perhaps it was Charles's general interest in science, but, whatever the reason, that summer decisions were made about his future which at the time must have seemed crucial. "As I was doing no good at school", he admitted in the *Autobiography*, "my father wisely took me away at a rather earlier age than usual, and sent me (October, 1825) to Edinburgh University with my brother . . . My brother was completing his medical studies, though I do not believe he ever really intended to practice, and I was sent there to commence them."

At more or less the same time, however, if his own account is to be believed, a new realization struck him. He became aware of the actual wealth of his father. It was not something to which he had probably given much thought before. All his friends, after all, were members of families that ranged from the comfortably off to the noticeably wealthy. Money was the underlying fact of their lives – they were the owners, the payers of wages, the consumers of good food and fine linen, the people upon whom the economy of the entire region depended for capital or, as in his father's case, professional services. (In fact, Dr. Robert provided both, as we have seen.) Now, at sixteen, Charles began to be aware of what wealth might mean. In Edinburgh he was able for the first time to speak man-to-man on the subject to an older brother almost certainly more aware of the facts than he. He had begun to understand, as he put it in the *Autobiography,* "that my father would leave me property enough to subsist on with some comfort, though I never imagined that I should be so rich a man as I am; but my belief was sufficient to check any strenuous effort to learn medicine". In other words, in Edinburgh, as at Shrewsbury, he felt justified in directing the main thrust of his education towards areas outside those nominated as his own. He felt free to follow his own inclinations – a course of action that, entered into haphazardly, acquires in retrospect the clamorous power of destiny itself.

4

"I don't know whether to be sorry or glad about your Edinborough plans," wrote Erasmus to Charles on 24 February, 1825.

> I think it is a thousand pities that you do not come to Cambridge . . . & I shall venture to add that it is a pity you leave school so soon, but to this latter doctrine you will hardly give credit. It will be very pleasant our being together, we shall be as cozy as possible, & I almost think that when you have arrived at the dignity of a "Varsity" man, that I shall leave off licking you. We shall have some good amusement in scheming out our plans next summer . . . there will be no earthly use staying at Shrewsbury, for it is out of the question reading there, the Lab on one hand & no room on the other, whereas if we get domiciled at E– we can both read like horses that is to say if we like it . . ."

Erasmus went on to describe "a little case-hardening in anatomy" using a dead body – "I was not the least annoyed while an old Physician also present kept leaving the room perpetually". He added, prophetically, "I don't fancy it will have suited your stomack especially before breakfast . . ."

Darwin was not yet seventeen when he attained "the dignity of a 'Varsity' man", charged with the task of attempting to redeem what he remained convinced all his life was the low opinion others held of him. "When I left school . . . I believe that I was considered by all my masters and by my Father as a very ordinary boy, rather below the common standard in intellect. To my deep mortification my father once said to me, 'You care for nothing but shooting, dogs and rat-catching, and you will be a disgrace to yourself and all your family'." Quoting this in his *Autobiography*, Darwin adds that his father, "who was the kindest man I ever knew, and whose memory I love with all my heart, must have been angry and somewhat unjust when he used such words". These were nevertheless the words that Charles remembered all his life, and not those of kindness or even justice; it seems unlikely from all the other evidence that this was because Dr. Robert was neither kind nor just to him. The feeling that he was doubted by those closest to him must have been even stronger in those days, yet the stoicism that Charles had shown when facing Caroline's strictures sustained him still. Any determination he may have had to excel in his Edinburgh studies did not survive long after his move to Scotland's capital.

Yet the alteration in his circumstances was spectacular. He had, after all, never lived anywhere but at home; even his period as a boarder was at a school in the town of his birth. To travel nearly three hundred miles and establish himself in lodgings, albeit under his brother's care, was a fundamental change. Perhaps even more important, however, was the change in the intellectual atmosphere by which he was now surrounded. Shrewsbury had been a backwater, dominated by the sporting ambitions of the gentry, the seasonal anxieties of the farmers, the orthodoxies of church and chapel and the classical priorities of Dr. Butler. Edinburgh was a capital, and one that throughout much of the previous century had been amongst the most powerful intellectual and academic centres in Europe.

Although the principal of its great university had always been, as was customary, a clergyman, the man who held that post during the last decades of the eighteenth century, William Robertson, had encouraged the development of scientific studies and so brought in as heads of department some of the most influential scholars in Britain. In natural history and medicine, the reputation of Edinburgh University stood as high as any in the world. By the 1820s, almost all of this generation of great teachers had stepped aside and the magnetism that they had exerted had as its most obvious consequence the overcrowding of the classrooms and lecture halls; whereas in the 1790s the number of students had rarely exceeded one thousand, by the 1820s that figure had doubled. Nevertheless, the excitement that the older generation had helped to create, the sense of attending and becoming a part of one of the world's foci of intellectual endeavour, had not diminished; and, if their successors had not always their distinction, professors still taught in Edinburgh whose words were heard with respect in Paris, Heidelberg, Leyden and Boston. For a receptive sixteen-year-old, the effect of becoming a part of such a community must have been exhilarating.

Charles responded by finding and going his own way with singleminded zeal. The very fact that he so much enjoyed his self-selected studies and their unofficial status concealed even from him the fact that they were central to his education. Even had his life taken on a shape completely different from the one that made him famous, the way he passed his time in Edinburgh, though having little enough to do with learning about medicine, could never have characterized him as a wastrel. When he arrived in 1825, however, medicine was what he intended to study and there survives among his papers one headed "The Classes for the different branches of Education will be opened, the ensuing Session, as follows", in which the lectures that applied to him stood fourth, after Literature and Philosophy, Theology and Law. There were Anatomy and Pathology to be studied under Dr. Munro and "Principles and Practice of Surgery", Mr. Russel was due to give "Clinical Lectures on Surgery" and Dr. Home "Clinical Lectures on Medicine". A few of Charles's notes survive from lectures he attended on the Materia Medica, by Dr. Duncan, and on Chemistry, Dr. Hope.

Although Darwin does not mention it, Professor Hope's performances with his banks of equipment and his self-satisfied – but admirably clear – expositions of what he was doing with it were among the most popular not only in the University, but in the city at large. Audiences of up to five hundred gathered to hear him, making his course of twenty-two lectures one of the focal points in the social life of a middle class which took the maintenance of Edinburgh's intellectual reputation as partly their own responsibility. "The fashionable place here now is the College", wrote Henry Cockburn in the 1820s; "where Dr. Thomas Charles Hope lectures to ladies on Chemistry. He receives 300 of them by a back window, which he has converted into a door. Each of them brings a beau, and the ladies declare that there never was anything so delightful as these chemical flirtations. The Doctor is in absolute extacy with his audience of veils and feathers . . ." And one of the students, a Polish prince who was at the university between 1820 and 1823, thought Hope's teaching methods superior to those of most of the other professors "in the neatness of his demonstrations, in his skill in carrying out his experiments, and in his mode of expression which is elegant to the point of affectation". As J.B. Morrell points out, in the article upon which these descriptions are based*, the main drawback to Hope's lectures was that he jealously kept the manipulation of his substances in his own hands; students were not encouraged to do their own practical work. In 1823, he did permit his assistant to inaugurate a class where students were able to work with the equipment; there is no record of Charles Darwin's having attended it.

Hope's lectures were nevertheless, as far as Charles was concerned, the only ones that were bearable – the rest rivalled each other only in tedium. In January, 1826, he was hailing a letter from Caroline as "a great relief after hearing a long stupid lecture from Duncan . . . Dr. Duncan is so very learned that his wisdom has left no room for his sense." Even twenty years later, Charles was to remember vividly Dr. Duncan and his purgatorial lectures on the Materia Medica: "A whole, cold, breakfastless hour on the properties of rhubarb." As for Munro on anatomy, "I dislike him & his lectures so much I cannot speak with decency about them. He is so dirty in person & actions." That these views were not unique to Charles seems proved by a letter from Erasmus, written in 1826, after he had moved south to continue his studies in London.

---

* "Science and Scottish University Reform: Edinburgh in 1826", published in *The British Journal for the History of Science*. Vol. 6. No. 21. 1972.

There certainly must be some radical difference in the London & Edinburgh lectures, for I can attend four hours in the day without the least weariness: the students are no comparison better behaved than on the other side of the Tweed . . . I have not heard a single scrape & excepting at the close of ye opening lecture no applause . . .

Charles's notes are neat and serious; the text is stilted, the attendant little drawings are all diagrams of apparatus and never doodles. There are useful underlinings and appropriate lists. Among them are entries that he may have brought with him from Shrewsbury, observations gleaned from his father's practice and experience. When he set down his father's views, he often gave them scholarly attribution – 'Dr. Darwin' – and they covered a variety of ailments. There were three kinds of palsy – in the one that "comes on by degrees recovery has hardly ever been known. – These notes hold good chiefly for old women"; epileptics who had an attack after a long interval "without confusion afterwards there may be expected in the next 48 hours 23 more fits . . . In Apoplexy, if the patient appears better, but respiration difficult, it generally terminates fatally . . . In Mania Emetics seldom act, but if a dose of Laudanum be given 12 hours previous it acts freely, & so in other cases . . . My Father never gives [*sic*] Digitalis in Mania, except in that which follows childbirth."

Clearly, respect for Dr. Robert's views had developed early and sunk deep roots – certainly as far as medicine was concerned. It looks, too, as though for a time Charles was committed to his proposed medical career, sufficiently at least to make these notes, presumably voluntarily composed and not stemming from his obligatory lectures. Perhaps he was whisked into temporary enthusiasm by his father's determination and his own brief summer holiday experience of the Shrewsbury practice. If it ever existed, however, this enthusiasm did not survive for any lengthy period.

It may have been his experiences in the operating theatres which finally destroyed what medical ambitions he had left. He watched "two very bad operations, one on a child, but rushed away before they were completed". He never returned – the agony of patients before the days of chloroform was more than he could bear: "The two cases fairly haunted me for many a long year." In this delicacy of reaction, however, he was only following family tradition, since in the *Autobiography* he wrote of his father, "To the end of his life, the thought of an operation almost sickened him, and he could scarcely endure to see a person bled . . ." But Charles hardly needed a reason to turn away from medicine. The fact is that it simply did not interest him. Perhaps it already involved an openness to the world, a willingness to be approached by all and sundry, a vulnerability to interruption, that was unendurable to him, even in prospect. Thus, when he had to attend hospital wards as a part of his course, he found to his own suprise that the interest he had had in his Shrewsbury patients had not survived to focus his attention on these Scottish ones.

Not that he disliked being in Scotland – as early as October, 1825, Catherine was now writing how glad she was "that you are so much pleased with Edinburgh"; adding, somewhat mysteriously, "I assure you, I miss you very much, both to walk with me, and also for *you know what*; . . ." But, across the miles, the strong grasp of the sisters still managed to reach out. In December, Susan was busily passing on advice: "Papa says Erasmus may wear Flannel next his skin in cold weather by all means, and that he may *sleep* in it also, tho he does not think that very advisable – but in warm weather he very much objects to it." For a long time, indeed, the bonds of a natural nostalgia were to remain strong – Elizabeth Wedgwood, writing a couple of years later to her sister Fanny, remarked that Charles and Erasmus "are quite troublesome in being so fond of letters from home . . ." It is clear, nevertheless, that, established at Mrs. Mackay's, at 11 Lothian Street, Charles at first settled happily enough into his Edinburgh life. He and his brother shared "two very nice and *light* bedrooms and a sitting-room", strolled about the town, and went to the theatre and the opera. Soon after his arrival he had written home that "we are going to Der F– (I do not know how to spell the rest of the word)", suggesting that the Darwin brothers were among those who made Weber's *Der Freischütz* such a success after its Edinburgh opening in 1824. (It is a measure of Edinburgh's standing at the time that the opera opened there only three years after its first night in Berlin; London and Philadelphia saw it the same year, New York not until the following season.)

It was not long, however, before the lectures began to assume their unbearably burdensome aspect. In March, 1826, his misery increased, for his brother left Edinburgh and returned to Shrewsbury, before moving on to continue his studies in London. "I hope you are a little reconciled to Erasmus' absence by this time", wrote Caroline towards the end of the month. That same March, Susan wrote, hoping that "you are getting in better humour with Edinburgh now that Spring is come". In a very few lines, however, she was berating him for his lack of interest in his medical studies.

> My reason for writing so soon is, that I have a message from Papa to give you, which I am afraid you won't like; he desires me to say that he thinks your plan of picking & chusing what lectures you like to attend not at all a good one; and as you cannot have enough information to know what may be of use for you, it is quite necessary for you to bear with a good deal of stupid & dry work: but if you do not discontinue your present indulgent way, your course of study will be utterly useless. – Papa was sorry to hear that you thought of coming home before the course of Lectures were finished, but hopes you will not do so.

It is hard to be sure whether this relayed parental disappointment actually stemmed from Dr. Robert, or whether "Papa" had been turned into Susan's stalking horse; in either event, it made plain the fact that Shrewsbury would not take kindly to Charles's giving up his Edinburgh studies before due time. Family gossip, a smattering of politics and news of pets made up the rest of the letter: "I am so sleepy I must wish you Good night," wrote Susan at last, before spattering the back flap with maternal little injunctions. "Remember to write *slow* and then you will form each letter distinctly . . . Don't waste your time by going to the Play as it must prevent your getting up early, or attending to your studies. – For this next month devote yrself to wisdom & you will be much happier." As the good advice comes tumbling out, well meant, deserved, and mixed with benevolence and even high spirits though it was, it becomes increasingly clear why her family nickname should have been "Granny".

Charles's way of devoting himself to wisdom, however, was not that of his sisters. What sustained him as the weeks passed by, and linked him to the intellectual life around him, providing at the same time the basis for almost all his friendships, was his more and more serious involvement in natural science. His formal studies included a certain amount of basic biology, and among his notes one can find a list based on Lamarck's classification of non-vertebrate animals, the first record of Darwin's recognizing the existence of that great naturalist. He borrowed from the University Library an eclectic collection of biological works: works on entomology, zoology, on shells and shellfish were taken out and, presumably, read with patient avidity. His reading, of course, took in a wider compass than this – both he and Erasmus borrowed more books than the average Edinburgh student. The bias, however, was strongly towards natural history; it was as if he had made a quite independent decision, owing nothing either to the wishes of the family or the intentions of the university, about the kind of course he had really come to Edinburgh to follow. The fact that this was a decision almost certainly not consciously arrived at, did not make it any the less firm.

Because his notebooks survive, if only partially, one can trace the development of his scientific approach from a schoolboyish listing to something approaching the analyses of the mature naturalist. In 1826, he kept in a desultory manner a diary of his doings and sightings. The book in which he made his entries remains impressive; entitled *The Edinburgh Ladies & Gentlemens Pocket Souvenir for 1826*, it opened with an obsequious dedication, in black, romantic gothic type: "To the Nobility and Gentry of Edinburgh, This little Work is respectfully inscribed, by their most obedient, and most faithful Servant, The Publisher." Then follow pages and pages of useful information: the Post Office box closed at 7 a.m. for letters to the Cape of

Good Hope and China, as well as Berwick, Falkirk, "and the Penny-Post Villages in the neighbourhood of Edinburgh". It closed at "$\frac{1}{2}$ past 4 p.m.", however, for letters to the West Indies, North America – and Carlisle. (The postage to China, incidentally, was 1s 11d – somewhat less than first class internal mail in Britain today.)

There were eleven daily mail- or stagecoaches to Glasgow: the Royal Mail "left every alternate evening at half-past 8", and did the journey in forty-eight hours, with "only two nights out on the road". There was a table giving rates of porterage: "Every cart of coals not exceeding 12cwt. to a house or cellar . . . or to first storey up or down a stair, 3d. Every succeeding storey after the first, additional 1d." There were listed the Kings of Scotland, the Kings and Queens of England, the Sovereigns of Europe – and those other sovereigns in the realms of gold, the bankers of London. So one flicks past the table "by which the interest of any sum at any rate, and for any time, may be readily found" and another "to calculate wages", to arrive finally at the first, characteristic entry by Charles himself. On 18 January he wrote, "Saw a Hedge Sparrow late in the Evening creep into a hole in a tree; where do most birds roost in winter?"

A precise observation, followed by a simple, comprehensive and totally relevant question – Darwin thus established early the outlines of his approach to nature. All his life, he was to have this gift of looking at the actual object, organism or event before him, rather than at some other thing which textbooks had suggested was there, and then asking questions about it – questions which often had the paradoxical quality of being naive in themselves, but demanding replies of an extreme sophisitication. This time there is no sign that his query was ever answered.

On 9 February, he wrote, "Caught a sea mouse, *Aphrodita Aculeata*, of Linnaeus . . . when its mouth was touched it tryed to coil it self in a ball, but was very inert; Turton states it was only two feelers, does not Linnaeus say 4? I thought I perceived them . . ." The entries make it clear that he was often on the shore during that Spring; others have a curiously innocent straightforwardness: ". . . Heard a lark singing at 20' past 7 o'clock & two bats at $\frac{1}{2}$ 8 o'clock. Saw a humblebee." On 1 May, back in Shrewsbury, he could announce to himself, "Susan heard a Cuckoo" and add the next day, "I believe I saw a swift late in the Evening but am not sure." As these early arrivals became commonplace, he noted other birds in profusion throughout that summer – corncrakes, "Kitty Wrens", flycatchers, sand martins (though these were "very few", whitethroats, stone-chats, green linnets, a nuthatch; but ominously, week by week, one can hear beyond his watchfulness the intermittent clangour of his gun. On 22 May, "Killed a Red-backed Shrike"; on 12 June, "Shot a bird with bright red breast & crown of head. Sonnet or

Redpole?"; on 26 June, "Shot a cormorant . . ."

That summer, the diary was unopened, partly because Charles was touring Snowdonia on foot, walking up to thirty miles a day and on one occasion clambering to the top of Snowdon itself; some of the rest of his vacation was also occupied by a riding tour of North Wales that he took with Caroline, "a servant with saddle-bags carrying our clothes". Autumn brought a different occupation: he began to keep a record of the game birds he shot – $7\frac{1}{2}$ brace of partridge and a hare on 1 September; next day, $6\frac{1}{2}$ brace; $2\frac{1}{2}$ two days later; four brace and a hare on the 5th, and so on. In the field, he kept his score by tying knots in a strap hung from his button-hole, meticulously safeguarding his achievements.

Marked by sightings of a Larger Titmouse, a Grey Wagtail, a Water Ouzel, the year drew on, sparsely annotated. He made his last entry on 25 December – "Monday and Holiday", the diary tells us – writing, "A remarquably foggy day, so much so that the trees condensed the vapour & caused it to fall like drops of rain. Saw a hooded crow feeding with some rooks by the seashore near Leith." He had returned again to the North Sea shores near Edinburgh. Even in its individual orthography, the entry was typical.

By the end of 1826, however, Charles had become a member of the Plinian Society, one of those groupings of the educated and the curious to which the spread of knowledge in the eighteenth and nineteenth centuries owed so much. This one, devoted to the study and discussion of the sciences, was intended largely for the students of Edinburgh University and so provided the young Darwin with a combined forum and lecture theatre far more congenial than anything the professors could offer. He had become a friend of Robert Grant, already an active zoologist who was soon to be appointed Professor of Comparative Anatomy and Zoology at London University, a chair he would hold for nearly half a century. With him Charles would often wander along the rocky foreshore, "to collect animals in the tidal pools, which I dissected as well as I could". This attitude to his own skills was not one of conventional modesty, as he had already made clear in his *Autobiography*: "It has proved one of the greatest evils of my life that I was not urged to practice dissection . . . the practice would have been invaluable for all my future work". Not until, in the 1840s, he struggled for eight years to classify all the species and varieties of the Cirripedes was he able to make good part of this deficiency by dedicated perseverance.

The notes he made in 1827, therefore, influenced by the professionalism of his new friends, were much more systematic and detailed than anything to be found in his diary of the year before.

> Procured from the black rocks Leith a large *Cyclopterus Lumpus* (common lump fish). Length from snout to tail $23\frac{1}{2}$ inches, girth $19\frac{1}{2}$ inches. It had

evidently come to the rocks to spawn and was there left stranded by the tide; its ovaria contained a great mass of spawn of a rose colour. Dissected it with Dr. Grant . . .

Two of the notes became the germs of the first scientific papers he ever composed, the first faint pipings of an expertise he was to develop over the next fifty-five years. "Having procured some specimens of the *Flustra Carborea* (Sam:) from the dredge boats in Newhaven I soon perceived without the aid of a microscope small yellow bodies studded in different directions on it . . ." Then came, "One frequently finds sticking to oyster and other old shells small black globular bodies, which the Fishermen call great Peppercorns. These have hitherto always been mistaken for the young *Focus loreus* to which it bears a great resemblance . . ." In his *Autobiography*, Darwin gives "about the beginning of the year 1826" as the date when he read his papers to the Plinian Society, but he did not become a member until November of that year. The papers pointed out "that the so-called ova of Flustra had the power of independent movement . . . and were in fact larvae", and "that little globular bodies which had been supposed to be the young state of *Fucus loreus* were the egg-cases of the wormlike *Pontobdella muricata.*"

These papers demonstrated that Charles was developing what is perhaps the basic requirement of a scientist – the capacity to ask simple questions that others have overlooked, questions which refuse to take anything on trust, and then by observation to discover the right answers to them. The small black globes that bobbed about in unison with the seaweed *Fucus loreus* had simply been assumed to be the seeds of the plant; everyone thought so, Dr. Grant said it was so, it was not a matter open to discussion. Only the young Darwin, apparently, seventeen years old, had enough basic scepticism to open up these enigmatic vesicles, and so discover that they had no organic connection with seaweed at all, but held the young of a green, vermiform leech. It is hard not to believe that this experience helped to reinforce in Darwin that intellectual stubbornness, that undeviating readiness to go his own way, which was to mark the major triumphs of his career.

The lesson he may have derived from his investigations into the so-called eggs of the *Flustra* was rather different. This little invertebrate was a special study of Dr. Grant's, who was somewhat put out to see his protégé thus rampaging across scientific territory to which he had staked the prior claim. It was perhaps by arrangement between them that Darwin did not speak of his discovery at the Plinian until Grant had, three days earlier, read a paper at the more important Wernerian Society "regarding the anatomy and mode of generation of Flustrae", and that Darwin never published his findings at all. In Grant's monograph on the subject, however, Darwin is given credit for his discovery. Thus very early, Charles was brought face-to-face with the problem of priority in science and given a demonstration of how jealously precedence was guarded; thirty-two years later, this would create for him one of the great crises of his life.

As Professor Howard Gruber* has pointed out, there was another, rather more sinister, lesson that Darwin might have learned from his experience of Plinian Society meetings. On occasion, papers of some ideological daring were read. For example, in February, 1827, a certain Mr. Grey had submitted his theory "that the lower animals possess every faculty and propensity of the human mind", a conviction foreshadowing Darwin's own later conclusions. Towards the end of March, a member named W.A. Browne proposed that mind and thus consciousness had an entirely material basis. So offensive was this idea to orthodox opinion, and so lively – and thus, to some ears, blasphemous – the discussion that followed the talk, it was decided to remove all trace of both from the records: even Browne's advance announcement of his paper at the previous meeting of the society was expunged. That Darwin attended the meeting is certain, since it was then that he read his own less controversial papers. Perhaps, overwhelmed by the personal importance of that evening, he hardly took in the controversy aroused by Browne, but as a member he cannot have been unaware of the scandal that followed. To strike a whole debate from the records was not, after all, a very common occurence. What did he make of it? He mentions nothing in his *Autobiography*, yet it was his first taste of the strong controversy that scientific theories can arouse. Later, he was to be horrified by the squabbling of the London savants and, later again, to realize that his own ideas were bound to make him the target of orthodoxy's most virulent defenders. Did he then remember Browne and the fate that had befallen his paper? It seems likely that, even if it no longer retained any importance among his conscious memories, so complete an act of censorship will have contributed to the formation of his own attitudes and the buttressing of his already established caution.

Other notebook entries demonstrate his scientific activities. "Procured on 15th April from deep water in Firth of Forth a good many specimens of *Pennatula mirabilis*", he wrote; his *Autobiography* tells us how he procured them. "I also became friends with some of the Newhaven fishermen, and sometimes accompanied them when they trawled for oysters, and thus got many specimens". Another entry reads, "Observed with Mr. Coldstream at the black rocks at Leith an *Asterias rubens* doubled up as it were . . ."

---

* In that invaluable book, *Darwin on Man*, an examination of the psychology of creative thought which is essential reading for anyone interested in Darwin. It includes fully annotated transcriptions of the "M" and "N" Notebooks by Professor P.H. Barrett.

Coldstream, a medical man, was an amateur zoologist who was later to have some published work to his credit; he was among those whose advice Darwin sought while preparing himself for his *Beagle* adventure. But Darwin had other companions, and on one occasion described for his fellow-Plinians a "Zoological Walk to Portobello" which he had taken "with Mr. McKay on Saturday morning".

The weather had proved wretched, "as it usually does in such cases . . . even near objects being rendered totally invisible by the dense and impenetrable mist". As a result, "disappointment succeeded disappointment, in short, to use a familiar term, it was a complete failure". On the shore itself, "an impenetrable cloud of obscurity" rendered everything invisible, but allowed the brash young Charles the opportunity to air an over-familiar joke. "But there yet remained one view, that view, which both English & Scotch unanimously agree in giving their just tribute of praise, that view, which once beheld renders all others totally insipid & devoid of interest, in the words of our illustrious countryman, Dr. Johnson, it is *'the highroad to England'*." The shoreline, however, "appeared perfectly destitute & void of every thing that could interest the Zoologist"; even when they had made their way towards some rocks said to be promising, they had found them covered by the tide. "But if we failed in adding to our stock of Zoological knowledge, we had on our return, the satisfaction of discussing in a most scientific manner, an excellent dinner, not of Haggis or Scotch Collops, but of substantial Beef steaks."

It is pleasant to realize that the preternatural gravity of the student days described in the *Autobiography* were shot through with such broad schoolboy humour. Young Englishmen at Edinburgh University today probably still make the same simple jokes. Nevertheless, Darwin's central interests remained serious and absorbing. Grant, sixteen years older than he, took him to meetings of the Wernerian Society, a more senior grouping than the Plinian and more exclusively devoted to natural science; and there he heard, among others, lectures by the famous American ornithologist, Audubon, whose illustrations of birds, always famous for their accuracy, have become a collector's delight because of their beauty.

Still uninterested in training to become a doctor – he attended meetings of the Royal Medical Society, but was bored with most of what was said there – Darwin seemed almost consciously to be arming himself for a career as a naturalist. It is usually assumed that his interest in science was at this stage more or less haphazard, something of a hobby, and yet it is hard to see how he could have taken it more seriously. He walked, he went out with the fishing fleet, he attended meetings, he collected specimens and struggled to make sense of them with his inefficient dissection techniques and his "wretched microscope"; when he saw anything of interest he prepared a paper and read it to his peers.

Indeed, his preparations went further, since he found that Dr. Duncan's black servant, now retired, had once travelled with the naturalist Waterton and, in his service, had learned to stuff birds. Darwin employed him, at a guinea an hour, to teach him the rudiments of taxidermy. Charles Waterton had published a book entitled *Wanderings in South America* and one can assume that Darwin asked his teacher, as they worked together over the mounting of the skins, about his experiences in that distant continent. The effects on Darwin of reading about Humboldt's travels are well known; those of hearing the stories of this unnamed man remain no more than possibilities: attractive guesswork.

Perhaps in order to extend his scientific experience still further, Darwin in that same year of 1827 enrolled in the geological classes of Professor Jameson. An "old Mr. Cotton in Shropshire" had a few years earlier spoken to the schoolboy Charles about local formations, pointing out in particular a boulder, the "bell rock", transported to Shrewsbury from the north, perhaps even from Scotland – "he solemnly assured me that the world would come to an end before anyone would be able to explain how this stone came to where it now lay". The "deep impression" that this produced on Darwin may have induced him to enter, ten years later, the continuing controversy about how erratic boulders had actually been moved. Now it helped to lure him to Jameson's lectures, but to his despair he found them "incredibly dull", to the point of repelling him from the entire subject.

Darwin's view of Jameson, frequently repeated, is perhaps a little unfair to the professor. Certainly he was no charismatic performer in the lecture theatre, but, as Morrell points out, "the gown and the town, the young and the old, attended him; regular students, surveyors, civil engineers, army engineers, silversmiths, jewellers and farmers all crowded into his class-room". Appointed in 1804, he taught for half a century and had, over the years, inspired a number of students who were later to become distinguished; in a class not compulsory for graduation, he had also increased the attendance at his lectures from some fifty people to four times that number. It is difficult not to conclude that Darwin's lack of patience was as much to blame for his not staying the course as Jameson's lack of dramatic virtuosity. If, as Darwin remembered vividly enough to repeat contemptuously to his son, George, Jameson's opening words actually were, "Gentlemen, the apex of a mountain is the top and the base of a mountain is the bottom", one has to make some allowance for a man lecturing to an audience of mixed backgrounds and abilities. There is actually no harm in a teacher's beginning a course of lectures by making sure that everyone present agrees on the meaning of the words he is going to use.

The fact is that Darwin was never a man who took kindly to being lectured. He liked reading, so taking in information at his own speed, or eliciting what he wanted to know through question-and-answer sessions, thus controlling the flow of information. Otherwise, he preferred activity, collecting, classifying and examining with his own hands and eyes the organisms or formations that interested him. He was not a person who took easily to sitting passively in an audience. Nevertheless, through Jameson he did become directly aware of one of the great scientific controversies of that epoch. He refers to it in the *Autobiography*, where he describes Jameson among manifestly volcanic formations insisting that the blocked fissure before him had been "filled with sediment from above, adding with a sneer that there were men who maintained that it had been injected from beneath in a molten condition."

5

With Jameson's tendentious aside we are abruptly flung into the wider world of science, that world which Darwin is nearly on the point of entering. He himself does not yet know his life's direction, being unaware that he has already made choices influencing everything he is to do and become. We, watching him precisely because we do know his future, conversely know very little yet of this world of science that awaits him. Seeing him, spotlit at the centre of his stage, placed in a handful of sketchy settings – Shrewsbury, Maer, Edinburgh – we have had no chance to examine that other setting, the setting of scientific knowledge and belief, in which he is to play so major a role. The fact is that there is a direct connection between the convictions of Professor Jameson, the arguments upon which they bear and the evolutionary theories on which Darwin's fame rests – theories which, after all, constitute the only reason why his Edinburgh apprenticeship to natural science should be of the slightest interest to us 150 years later.

It is Time that forges this connection. The first essential for an evolutionary theory is to establish that enough time has passed since the earth began for its infinitely slow processes to do their work. It was the geologists who first, as it were, made available such periods of time for the biologists to contemplate. That they should have done so was sufficiently provocative of controversy; but it was followed by more detailed argument.

For what events had punctuated the vast aeons geology was now proposing? What tremendous originating moment had preceded them? What was the actual length of time that had to be considered? And, in that connection as well as in considering the origins of life itself, what was the precise significance of the fossil record? On questions like these discussion was denunciatory and apocalyptic as often as it was reasoned and scientific, and it had led to very little agreement. The scientists were divided into camps which the necessities of history have demarcated much more sharply than actuality ever did. There were gradations of opinion from the sternly theological to the harshly materialistic, while many of those who took their stand on the Bible accepted much of the scientific evidence, and many of those who put science in the forefront did so against a background of Mosaic certainty.

Well over a hundred years before, men like the Danish anatomist, Nils

Steensen and John Ray, the English preacher, had struggled with the problem of geological time, forced to face it by the clear antiquity of fossils, and the fact that they appeared to prove the earlier existence of creatures since drastically altered or totally vanished. In an age when the Bible was among the primary sources of knowledge, absolute in a way that the evidence of one's senses could not be, the conflict this set up caused them, and other, similar savants, considerable anguish. Steensen solved his personal dilemma by conversion to a fundamentalist Catholicism that stopped all questions; Ray, on the other hand, busied himself over many years in attempting to reconcile what he saw to be a fact with what he knew to be the truth.

It took a polymath natural scientist of the French Enlightenment, an eighteenth-century intellectual adventurer of the right boldness of mind, to smash down the cramping barriers of Biblical certitude. This was Georges Louis de Buffon, not the first man to find himself tamed by the achievement of ambition. Becoming the Director of the Jardin du Roi by methods more political than scientific, Buffon settled to his duties, which were nothing less than to act as curator for the central botanical garden and natural history museum in France. It was to catalogue the collections, which had sprawled across a number of scientific boundaries since the first herb garden had been founded in 1635, that Buffon began the enormous *Histoire naturelle* by which he has since been remembered.

He started, as was only proper, with some account of the history of the earth. His view discounted totally that of Church or theologian: no six millennia, as divined by Bishop Ussher, would limit his account of terrestrial development. It was he who defined the fundamental categories into which geologists have ever since divided rocks: igneous, sedimentary, and metamorphic. He considered the earth as very old indeed, and he divided its span into seven periods, in only the last of which human beings appeared. He accepted the logic of fossil discoveries, and thought it likely that once there had been whole species which had since died out. When the Faculty of Theology at the Sorbonne decided to censure him, their grounds make curiously modern reading. They accused him of saying that seas had produced the mountains, that the planets were once part of the sun and that the sun would one day burn out, that there were several varieties of truth and that everything, apart from mathematics and physics, was no more than appearance and probability. The importance of Buffon is that he declared what had previously been unthinkable, that he forced those who read him to take a stand on matters about which dogma had hitherto allowed them to be evasive. After him, time was never to be completely imprisoned again.

The world-scheme of Buffon seemed to permit flexibility; that of the later Cuvier, not yet twenty when Buffon died in 1788, attempted to reimpose rigidity. A Protestant, of Swiss parentage and German education, Georges Cuvier was by the end of the eighteenth century established at the Jardin des Plantes in Paris – where his colleagues included Lamarck and Geoffroy Saint-Hilaire. All three men had their parts to play in the arguments and elucidations which would culminate in a tenable theory of evolution. As an anatomist, Cuvier became convinced that the structure of each creature, and of each grouping of creatures, was particular, intended for the purposes of that creature or grouping and for no others. Nature, he wrote, 'has realized all those combinations which are not inconsistent and it is these inconsistencies, these incompatibilities, this impossibility of one modification existing with another which establish between the divers groups of organisms those separations, those gaps, which mark their necessary limits and create the natural branches (*embranchements*), classes, orders and families." Thus the natural world was frozen in its present shape, every property of each specimen compatible only with its own life situation, and no conceivable development could alter those properties in a way which would permit one species to develop into another.

Yet, paradoxically, Cuvier was the founder of and earliest expert in the science of palaeontology. So cunning was he in the art of reconstructing the skeletons of long-vanished creatures that he claimed he could do so if he had only a single bone as evidence. Thus he was every day faced in his studies with the contradiction between his view that nature was essentially immutable and the clarity with which the fossil record pointed out that in the distant past there had been species which had since entirely vanished. If no alteration was possible in God's Creation, where had they gone, and why? For Cuvier, the answer was based, at least partly, on his acceptance of the Mosaic outline of world history. Genesis had given us the story of the Flood, a fact which pointed out how suceptible the earth was to the effects of natural catastrophe. If one postulated a repeated rising and falling of the oceans, a succession of vast floods throughout the course of history, these would explain the disappearance, during the various epochs, of once-flourishing species. This theory had the advantage of, as it were, halting all development between catastrophes. During those times, nothing changed, everything remained as Nature had ordered. Only when the natural disaster of a gigantic flood intervened would whole families of creatures be swept away, to be replaced by others already existing elsewhere and ready to spread into the now unoccupied regions.

Cuvier based his rejection of any kind of transmutation on two pieces of evidence and one assumption. First, the fact that no intermediate, interspecies forms had been discovered among the fossils so earnestly unearthed by the age's scientists; and, second, the identity, absolute in every detail, of

mummified specimens brought from Egypt with the living animals of which
they were the ancestors. His assumption was based on the classificatory
work upon which much of his fame rested, and still rests today. It was he who
divided living creatures into four great groups, and named them *Vertebrata,
Mollusca, Articulata* and *Radiata*. Having done so, he concluded that these
were absolute definitions. Nothing that belonged to the animal kingdom
could fail to find its place in one of these great divisions. Mutability from one
to the other, therefore, demanding intermediate forms, however temporary,
was by its nature an impossibility.

His first point retains some merit; argument persists about the precise
placing in the mosaic of nature of this or that fossil. The vagueness, the
problems of definition, that surround the earth's creatures, however, provide their own counter to the absolutism of the *Diktat* through which he
attempted to impose a universal order. As for the identity of the animals the
Egyptians knew with those that surround us today, the fact that he took this
to be significant suggests his inability to accept the vastness of the time-scale
upon which rested the very science he had founded. What he had to accept,
nevertheless, was that in the course of geological time there had, apparently,
been some increase in the complexity of the organisms that inhabited the
globe. He was thus forced to concede that, by way of the catastrophes he
postulated, some sort of natural development had taken place. This seemed
to him evidence that there existed in the world an overriding progressive
principle, ensuring that the results of those destructive floods should in the
end prove beneficial. However, once the world had settled down after each
such catastrophe, no alteration in the fixed varieties of creatures would take
place until the next arrived. Time alternated between long periods of immobility and abrupt bursts of energy during which the hands of the cosmic clock
leapt forward.

Cuvier had always been at pains to separate his religious and his scientific
views, a separation made possible precisely because he was convinced that
the two could legitimately exist side by side. While the acceptance of a
Creation was always implicit in his theories, he certainly diverged from the
orthodoxies of Genesis, believing that there had been at least three previous
ages during which creatures of various kinds had roamed the earth, leaving
their scattered bones for a Cuvier to decipher. Only in the present period,
which he believed of no great antiquity, had the human species and the
domestic animals that supported and sustained it made their appearance.
This conviction made it possible after all to link his vision with that of the
orthodox: one might believe that it was at the beginning of the present age
that Adam, the great progenitor, had been set upon the earth.

Cuvier himself, however, rarely ventured an overtly theological statement in any of his geological, palaeontological or zoological works. This, in a man known to be a pious Lutheran, a vice-president of the Bible Society, is an exemplary demonstration of intellectual restraint. Others, with whose works Darwin may have been more familiar, bent Cuvier's conclusions to more directly Christian uses. The evangelical Thomas Chalmers, discussing Cuvier's *Theory of the Earth*, wrote:

> Moses may be supposed to give us not a history of the first formation of things, but of the formation of the present system . . . giving us the full history of the last great interposition, and . . . describing the successive steps by which the mischiefs of the last catastrophe were repaired.

John Bird Sumner, who rose to be Archbishop of Canterbury, saw no reason to suppose that ours was the first earth, or the Flood the first catastrophe; what now existed might well, he felt, have been created out of the debris of what had previously been destroyed.

Not everyone was quite so deft in linking the Mosaic model with geological theory. Yet, for most geologists, the Bible remained the background against which they drew their conclusions, its statements as solidly evidence as any rock. At the very least, it had to be included among the prime elements to be considered when they constructed their versions of what had happened in the past. Among the more liberal was the influential William Buckland, Reader in Mineralogy at Oxford from 1813, who became in one way or another the teacher of almost all the important British geologists active in the middle decades of the century. He followed Cuvier in believing that the earth had passed through several discrete periods, punctuated by catastrophes, but had no hesitation in linking the last of these disasters with the Flood of Genesis. Becoming Oxford's first Professor of Geology in 1820, he said in his inaugural lecture that he took "the word 'beginning' as applied by Moses in the first verse of the book of Genesis, to express an undefined period of time, which was antecedent to the last great change that affected the surface of the earth, and to the creation of its present animal and vegetable inhabitants; during which period a long series of operations and revolutions may have been going on; which, as they are wholly unconnected with the history of the human race, are passed over in silence by the sacred historian . . ."

The consequence of such convictions was that Buckland, despite doing much precise work of lasting value, could regard everything he saw as evidence for what he already believed and was thus on many matters kept at bay by the truth. He testified to his Bible-based catastrophism by inventing the term "diluvial detritus", a phrase which, implying the proven factuality of the Flood, was to help misdirect geologists for many years.

These were not the only views, however, that prevailed in geology. There was another, even longer-running controversy which had a quite different basis. Its theorists did not necessarily subscribe to catastrophist or diluvial ideas – though they were certainly doctrinally free to do so. At the end of the eighteenth century, Abraham Gottlob Werner, a professor at the Freiburg School of Mines, had proposed that the earth had once been covered by a planet-wide ocean. The rock strata had been laid down by the slow deposit of material carried in suspension by the water; all were sedimentary. The salts found amongst them had once been in solution in these primeval seas. The action of wave, current and tide had shaped the features and formations which now varied the surface of the earth. Most geologists in the early nineteenth century accepted this theory. They were therefore known as Neptunists.

Those who took a different view – and were consequently known as Vulcanists or Plutonists – believed that many rocks were volcanic in origin, and that the central heat retained by the globe had been the prime force determining the shape and nature of its surface. What both these versions of the earth's history had in common was that they described it as a single process, continuing constantly, uninterrupted by a series of vast, disruptive accidents. Those who accepted them were thus able, if they wished, to avoid entirely that circularity of argument which took the Bible as the evidence for its own truth, and to free themselves from the trammels of Biblical time.

The originator of the Vulcanist theory, and a man who has often been considered the founder of modern geology, was Dr. James Hutton, of Edinburgh. He had died at the end of the eighteenth century, not very long after the publication, in 1795, of his *Theory of the Earth*. As a man who had also developed a theory of strictly empirical knowledge, he took his stand on what could be known by direct observation. From a scientist's point of view, all that could be known was the condition of things as they were in the present. Some entirely unique event in the past, such as the Flood, was debarred from his picture of geological reality since by its nature it was beyond present experience or definition. He was therefore what came to be known as a "uniformitarian" – that is, a natural scientist who accepted that the processes he could observe in the present had always been in operation and that, as a result, the earth had throughout its history been subjected to the same forces working by the same laws and producing the same consequences as those he could actually study. (This did not necessarily mean that everything had always been the same, since often the cumulative effect of such processes would be radical changes.)

Hutton's views, propagated by John Playfair, professor of mathematics at Edinburgh University until 1805, at first persuaded only a minority of geologists. From about 1810, however, more and more of them began to adopt his opinions. Perhaps it was this that gave such an edge of bitterness to Jameson's comments on the day that Darwin noted. For it was Jameson who was the leader of Wernerian opinion in Britain, it was he who most rigorously upheld the Neptunist position. Just before being appointed to his chair, he had spent four years in Freiburg as Werner's student and clearly idolized him. He went so far as to call Werner's investigation into the formation of the earth "the most perfect of its kind ever presented to the world" and it was to honour his master and disseminate his views that he founded that Wernerian Natural History Society to which Grant had introduced Darwin.

Yet Jameson was fighting a losing battle, and by the time he was lecturing to the impatient young Charles, he knew it. The third Volume of his *System of Mineralogy*, published in 1808, had outlined and eulogized the theories of Werner. The second edition, eight years later, made no mention of the Freiburg sage. Thus Darwin was faced by an already defeated man, whose growls were the retreating thunder of a rearguard action. Wernerism animated the Wernerian Society only in name; everywhere the volcanic theory was gaining the day. Darwin was, in a sense, flogging the deadest of horses when he pointed out in his *Autobiography* how striking it was "that I, though now only sixty-seven years old, heard Professor Jameson, in a field lecture at Salisbury Crags, discoursing on a trap-dyke . . . with volcanic rocks all around us, and say that it was a fissure filled with sediment from above . . ."

But Jameson was to defend catastrophe as the originator and index of terrestial change, even into the years when, himself as broodingly silent as a burnt-out volcano, he had to hear his lectures read by a deputy. For it must always be remembered that these geological theories did not have in practice the rigidity they have on paper. There were no fault lines criss-crossing the science, marking out irrevocable divisions. There were, of course, fierce controversies, first between Wernerians and Huttonians, later between catastrophists and uniformitarians. But the antagonisms of the second argument could cut across those of the first – it was, after all, quite logical to be a Wernerian uniformitarian or even a Huttonian catastrophist – and individual scientists were constantly altering their own positions. Thus distinctions were frequently blurred by a general volatility of opinion, a state of affairs made even more imprecise by the spectrum of religious views on display.

This was the complexity that awaited Darwin's intervention, its debates as confusing as they were vociferous, on the day that he entered Jameson's lecture hall. And this was the scientific area from which he was beaten back by Jameson's dullness. He wrote of the professor's lectures, "The sole effect they produced on me was the determination never as long as I lived to read a book on Geology or in any way to study the science." Yet as a young man fascinated by natural science, and interested enough to attempt Jameson's course, he must have been well aware of the underlying controversies – indeed, it may have been his purpose in studying geology to understand the arguments better. However faintly the doctrine of Neptunism still animated the Wernerian Society, it remained the base upon which it had been founded. At the end of 1826, the Plinian voted down a proposal to elect Cuvier as an honorary member, demonstrating that it kept an eye on international developments. And Darwin's grave mentor, Robert Grant, once startled him by revealing an adherence to the evolutionary views of Lamarck, an admission which at the time passed right over young Charles's orthodox head (though it made sufficient impression to remain for fifty years in his memory). The swirl of new ideas, the marches, battlefields and casualties of academic strife, the frowning ramparts of the righteously con- servative, the bombardments of the divines, all surrounded science – and especially natural science – with a hubbub that, however faintly, must have reached the ears even of the neophyte Darwin, offering him subliminal hints of a myriad questions as yet unresolved.

6

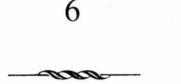

Darwin's period in Edinburgh was nearly over. He had for the first time demonstrated what he would prove again in Cambridge and London – that, despite the modesty of his own account, there was some quality about him, perhaps his gentle doggedness, perhaps his sweetness of temperament, perhaps the naive yet fruitful directness of his queries, which made him acceptable company for men older and much more established than he. There was the taciturn Grant, who had studied in Paris and was about to become a professor; there was the geologist Leonard Horner, twenty-four years older than Charles, one of the pioneers of factory reform, who took him to a meeting of the Royal Society of Edinburgh presided over by Sir Walter Scott ("I looked at him and at the whole scene with some awe and reverence", commented Darwin, remembering his younger self of half a century before). Through attending those lectures by Jameson, who in 1804 had founded the city's Natural History Museum and still held the title of Regius Keeper, he became friendly with William Macgillivray, the Curator, thirteen years older than he, later to write *A History of British Birds* and, in the last year of his life, to become a professor at Aberdeen University. Darwin recalled that he "had much interesting natural-history talk with him, and he was very kind to me".

If Darwin had really been the hearty outdoor dullard of legend, if his assiduous collecting of stones and shells and insects had been little more than an extension of his sportsman's interest in partridges and hares, it is inconceivable that he could long have held the interest of men like these. It is even more unlikely that they would have been of the slightest interest to him. Every university has – and had in even greater abundance then – its quota of yelling rowdies and complacent musclemen, the heroic enthusiasts of the physical; had Darwin been no more than one of these, it is from their ranks that he would have chosen his friends. Perhaps he did so and does not mention it, in notes, letters, diary or *Autobiography*; what is certain is that he did not do so exclusively and that men of consequence thought it profitable, to him or to themselves, to allow him to cultivate and maintain their companionship.

What also remained true, however, was his disenchantment with medicine, though it was more than he could manage to face his father with this reluctance. In the *Autobiography* he tells us, therefore, that Dr. Robert "perceived or he heard from my sisters, that I did not like the thought of being a physician . . . He was very properly vehement against my turning an idle sportsman, which then seemed my probable destination". There was already no chance of Darwin's spending his life in idleness, though sport took up a great deal of his leisure. Nevertheless, the activities he was shying away from were those of which his father approved; those that had captured his interest were simply peripheral, in his father's view, to the life of a properly occupied gentleman. Darwin was a little in the position of an artist, determined to take seriously what all his family and friends thought of as a pleasant hobby; the difference was that the definition "scientist" had hardly any of the independent existence which had for centuries attached to the description "artist". Even in the few universities the sciences were still establishing themselves; elsewhere, those who pursued them either worked in museums and botanical gardens or combined their interest with their profession. Thus it was that lawyers, politicians, medical men, soldiers, sailors, clergymen and the wealthy dilettanti thrown up by the abrupt expansion of the economy were among the most important lay contributors to the swift development of natural science. Charles, whether conscious or not of his destiny as a naturalist, had reason to consider it, like his father, just one variety of idleness.

It was not of his future that he was thinking, however, as he rattled home in that summer of 1827, for it would be months before the decision whether to return to Edinburgh would have to be taken. At eighteen, months might as well be years – and, in the meantime, he had another journey in mind. On 14 May, Dr. Robert wrote to Jos Wedgwood, "Charles goes to London in place of a servant to attend his sister, and see some of the sights, as he never has been in town. He has a lark in plan, which is, if you allow him, to join you & cross the sea, that he may have been in France, then return back again." Once again the Doctor belies his tyrannical legend.

It was in scheduled attendance on Caroline, therefore, that Charles a few weeks later dined at the London house of Dr. Holland. A second cousin of both the Wedgwoods and the Darwins, the doctor was later to become physician to Queen Victoria and a knight; on this occasion, however, he shocked the budding naturalist by proclaiming that whales were cold-blooded. Two days later, Jos Wedgwood was writing to his daughters, Fanny and Emma – who were themselves staying with their aunt in Geneva – about the journey to Paris. "I am very glad that I induced Car. D. to come with me. I need not tell you how agreeable a companion she is, and she has so much taste for beauty that it is a pleasure to travel with her." They had arrived in Dieppe at eleven in the morning, after an overnight crossing: "Caroline was ill, but took not the least harm, and Charles, though not quite well, made a very hearty dinner on roast beef." Caroline herself wrote to the girls on the same day: "It was very good-natured of Uncle Jos to think of me, but there never was a kinder person and the pleasantest travelling companion. I am quite losing all my former fear, and Charles, who came with us as far as Paris, joins me in a chorus of admiration whenever he leaves the room . . ." So Charles had his "lark", it seems; of his stay in Paris, if indeed he stayed any time, and of his return journey, we know nothing. The chorus of praise and mutual admiration moves on into Europe, while Charles, one must presume, his ambition to cross the Channel fulfilled, turned on his heel and hurried back to Shrewsbury, and summer; and Fanny Owen.

So the name emerges, casually, demurely, cobwebbed by the decades, almost overlooked by biographers, mentioned not at all by Darwin when, a staid and revered old man, he set down all that was important about his life for his family to read. But Henrietta Litchfield, his daughter Etty, remembered the mature Darwin remembering Fanny and his own youth; he had, she tells us, "evidently been greatly attracted by Fanny Owen. He told me once how charming she looked when she insisted on firing off one of their guns, and showed no sign of pain though the kick made her shoulder black and blue. I was then only a child, but I can still remember the expression of his face . . ." There were two Owen girls among the young people at Woodhouse who were the particular friends of the Darwins, but although Charles maintained an intermittent acquaintance with the older, Sarah, his feelings for Fanny seem, at least for a while, to have been much stronger than friendship.

One clue to his sentiments comes from the occasional remarks he makes about Fanny Owen in his letters to William Darwin Fox. Of all the farflung Darwins, Fox, a distant cousin, was perhaps closer to Charles than anyone except Erasmus. A little older than Charles, it was Fox who first ushered him into the serious mysteries of natural history, and especially of entomology. Strangely, after the years when they were students together at Cambridge, the two men hardly met. Both were to live in seclusion, Fox working out his destiny as a country clergyman, Darwin his very different one as the founder of a new kind of natural history. Yet, year after year, their correspondence continued, the letters passing steadily to and fro for a full half century. For us, conversation has been curtailed into monologue – we have only Darwin's letters. The questions, reminiscences, gossip and opinions they contain, however, illuminate not only Darwin, but also the gentle, encouraging man to whom they were addressed.

Now, in the 1820s, the two were young, active, ambitious and clearly had few secrets from each other. Thus, from time to time, Charles could allow himself what by the standards of the day were clear indiscretions. Towards the end of 1828, for example, he wrote to his cousin about a snuffbox (he had been fashionably tapping and pinching and sniffing for a year or two by then) that he had accidentally exchanged for Fox's: "doubtless yours is the most valuable; but mine was the gift of Mr. Owen, & he is the Father of Fanny, & Fanny, as all the world knows, is the prettiest, plumpest, [most] charming personage that Shropshire possesses, ay & Birmingham too . . ." Nor was this only his opinion – Catherine, writing to him in Edinburgh in April, 1826, had stated categorically, "Fanny Owen has quite the preference to Sarah among the gentlemen, as she must have everywhere; there is something so very engaging and delightful about her".

As a result, Woodhouse, always attractive to Charles, took on a glamour which drew from him unwonted epistolatory extravagances. Again writing to Fox, this time in October, 1828, he describes his feelings.

> Home is doubtless very sweet, but like all good things one is apt to cloy on it; accordingly, I have resolved to go to Woodhouse for a week. This is to me a paradise, about which, like any good Mussulman I am always thinking; the black-eyed Houris however do not merely exist in Mahomets noddle, but are real substantial flesh & blood.

A year later he was, if more prosaic, still passionate: "The Owens of Woodhouse, the idols of my adoration . . . But if I begin to talk about Woodhouse & la belle Fanny I never shall conclude this letter . . ."

Catherine Darwin, writing to her cousin Emma – who a decade later became the one who actually married Charles – described one Woodhouse gathering*. She had been to a ball where a group from Woodhouse had been prominent, and the next morning the Owens' pony carriage had come for her. "There was an immense party there . . . It is hardly possible for common mortals in my opinion to wind up their spirits to the Woodhouse pitch; more than half the gentlemen indeed were a little too much stimulated." The next day, a Friday, new guests had been invited to dinner,

> . . . under the belief that the former party in the house would be gone by that time . . . It was a grand puzzle how in the world to dine 29; it was at last settled to have two side-tables, each of 6; 2 gentlemen, a President and Vice-President, and 4 ladies. We drew lots for our places, and each had a ticket; the rival side-tables betted who could make most noise. Of course each party stand

---

* Henrietta Litchfield, who printed the letter in her *Emma Darwin: A Century of Family Letters*, placed it in 1830. However, it mentions what was clearly Charles's first visit to the Darwin Fox household: "I am so glad to find that he likes the Foxes as much as I did". That visit took place in 1828, for that October Charles wrote what was obviously his letter of thanks after his return: "Formerly, I used to have two places, Maer & Woodhouse, about which, like a wheel on a pivot, I used to revolve. Now I am luckier in having a third . . ."

up for themselves; we certainly had famous fun this evening. There were quantities of waltzing, dancing, games, &c till about 1 . . . Fanny Owen was the belle. I do not wonder, for I never saw such a charming girl altogether as she is. Susan was in her glory and in violent spirits. She would call this a most unfair account of things if she was to see it, and would send you a far more flaming description.

In a postscript, however, Catherine gives an authorized quotation from Susan, for "she has just said 'what a delightful visit I have had. I never enjoyed anything like it – so gay – we never talked a word of common sense all day.' Guaranteed by me. Susan gives leave for this anecdote."

With the scene thus set and the characters disposed about the stage, it is possible to turn to the beginning of the sketchy scenario that time has left us. No scrap of a letter from Charles to Fanny appears to have survived; perhaps she destroyed those she received, either at the time or later, meticulously avoiding the slightest chance of damage to her reputation. What we care to believe about their relationship must be inferred from the tone of Fanny's correspondence, itself incomplete and perhaps, even in her high-spirited case, somewhat vitiated by the conventional caution of the day. One has the feeling, nevertheless, that what was always rather frivolous for Fanny was always rather serious for Charles – serious enough, in any case, for him to have preserved her letters over fifty years. If they were playing a game, it was one that rarely seemed likely to become more in her case, while for Charles one can imagine that it often threatened to do so. But her lightness of tone may have been no more than a personal style reinforced by a socially protective manner, while what one assumes to have been his slightly more purposeful, perhaps even plodding approach, remains no more than an assumption, a possibility, a guess.

At the beginning, it is clear, all was adolescent lightheartedness. For what fantasy, what childhood make-believe, what images, culled from romantic fiction, or aristocrats forced by poverty, ignorance or guile to adopt the role of servants, lay behind the lowly titles Charles and Fanny gave themselves? In a note, undated but possibly written to mark Charles's departure for Edinburgh, Fanny scrawled, "Dr Postillion, I *entreat* your acceptance of a *leetle* Purse which I hope you will *condescend* to use in remembrance of the *Housemaid* of the *Black Forest* – I remain Dr C yrs truly Fanny O". There was a postscript perhaps calculated to disturb the adolescent Darwin: "Pray remember me most kindly to *my friend* Mr Charles Mogg –" So by, say, 1825 or perhaps before, there they were, twelve miles apart, established in the roles that Fanny at least was to maintain for years – Housemaid and Postillion. It was a vision to which she remained faithful until her marriage, by which time Darwin was already far away, bucketing painfully about the

South Atlantic in the tiny, fateful *Beagle*. Did he sign himself "Postillion" when he wrote to her? It seems probable – she was unlikely to have kept up so intimate a fiction for so long without encouragement.

They had in common gossip about their neighbours and relations and a love of the countryside, of riding in particular. "Owen is at this moment scouring the country on my Golfinder", she wrote on a 4 October that was probably in 1824, but may have been six years later (1830 is the only other appropriate year that matches the day, "Monday morning", with the date), ". . . if he should come home lame – I shall be *bereft* indeed". It is quite clear that she meant the horse and not the man. However, very swiftly she turned to discussing Woodhouse visitors, of whom a Miss Anson had laid siege to "The Hill"* in a manner that "astonished all our weak minds. I *could imagine* a good deal but the *forces* were brought on so well the *cannonade* so quick, and the barricades so *dexterously* managed, I'm sure no *General* of the age could come near her in *skill* & *science* . . . How long the Ansons will stay I can't guess, but Owen says till *May*. Milady† is going over to consult Dr. Darwin & I really think the best advice he can give her is *change of air*! give him a *hint* if you can – I must finish this scrawl as I am wanted to *mount guard* the Duty comes *very heavy* now." Clearly the leisurely visits of the gentry in those easy-paced horse-drawn days had their tedious side.

"My dear Postillion", she wrote, on a date unknown, but which may from the neatness of the writing be even earlier. "Of course you are well initiated in all the *black mysteries* which I am sure are going on at the Forest, I think *you know* that if I *have* a *punchon* it is for a *thorough good mystery*, so I implore you to write me a full account of all that has been going on *lately* between the noble houses of the *Forest, Bliss Castle*** & *Darwin Hall*, I am dying by inches to know *all*, & your *well known* and *laudable thirst* for useful *knowledge* has I am sure made you acquainted with *every particular* before

---

* Shropshire was full of Hills, many very distinguished. Among them were the Noel-Hills who became the Lords Berwick (one of whom became Fanny's uncle by marriage and all of whom were among Dr. Robert's debtors), Rowland Hill, who became Wellington's successor as Commander in Chief of the Army and, somewhat later, his namesake who introduced the penny post. There was also an ancient line of this famous Shropshire clan who were known charmingly as the Hills of Court of Hill.

† Almost certainly Anne Margaret, the Dowager Lady Anson, a daughter of the Earl of Leicester. The Ansons were a Staffordshire family who owed their prominence to the exploits of that famous circumnavigator, Admiral Anson.

** On the cover of a letter Sarah wrote to Charles in 1828 she added the note, "Owen returned today from the *bliss* at Chillington". This suggests that "Bliss Castle" was Chillington Hall, in Staffordshire, bought by the Giffard family in 1178 for twenty marks and a charger of metal. At this time, the 24th Giffard in succession to inherit the house lived there; he had three daughters who may have been the cause of the pervading bliss.

this so pray sit down and relieve me from my dreadful *state* of *haggitation*
. . ." She was away, on a long, almost indefinite visit to a family named Dean
and having "heard of your honoring the Forest with your presence" regretted that she had not been there to beat him at écarté "or to make a *beast of
myself* in the *strawberry beds*".

They were evocative, those strawberry beds, redolent of summer and
self-indulgence; we come on them again in a letter Susan wrote to Charles in
the July of 1833. She had been spending four days at Woodhouse: "It was
high Strawberry season & Caroline Owen said *that* always put her in mind, of
when you & Fanny used to *lie full length* upon the Strawberry beds grazing
by the hour". One sees them at their languid orgy, half children, half adults,
the green and purple tendrils of the plants curling about them, their bodies
almost buried in that knee-high jungle, faces bending to the dark-red fruit,
the juice delicately tinting their pouting lips, their cheeks and chins, their
reaching fingers: now and then they laugh, now and then their eyes meet, the
heat haze shakes and shimmers across distant fields, they are happy in that
moment, and in more ways perhaps than they will ever understand. His older
sister, her younger, stand aside, in shadow it may be – one imagines Susan
with a parasol – watching a spectacle that stirs them, too, in complicated
ways; it becomes a picture in their personal histories, an event experienced
and witnessed, a moment to which they can all return from time to time and
take their bearings.

But Fanny had present dramas to play out. She conjured up "Mrs.
Burton", who seems to have been a vigorously watchful local dragon; for a
moment we glimpse standards of propriety very different from our own, and
so extensive that they provided many opportunities for an innocent delin-
quency. "I am sure", Fanny wrote, "if *Ma'm* Burton could hear of my
corresponding with Mr. Charles Darwin, she would say *dear me*, ma'm *what
a sense of propriety* Miss Fanny Owen must have, indeed I think it is quite
incorrect, but *it is to be hoped* it may not *reach her ears*." Her pen had split,
which put her "in a horrid passion", and so she made an end: "I remain dr.
Postillion yr. dutiful Housemaid, Fanny Owen". She could not resist a
postscript – "I must post this in an envelope *well sealed, sisters* I know *peep
so*, and *pray make* a mystery of it, tell them there is something *very* particular." Fanny adored the apparently indecorous, the trappings of drama, the
paraphernalia that accompanied romance: nothing proves more conclu-
sively that prosaic Charles Darwin had in youth his quota of poetry in the
soul than the fact that Fanny thought it worth her while to play Housemaid
to his Postillion.

Toward the end of 1827, Fanny and her sister Sarah travelled to Brighton,
and spent a season of several weeks there. Some of the sprightly brilliance of

the Regency, the special magnetism of a town patronised by princes, still enveloped – as, faintly, they do to this day – the stones and streets of this elegant resort. It had for fifty years been the place where fashionable London maintained its good manners but relaxed its inhibitions, where courtesans might be treated like ladies – it was in Brighton that brilliant, notorious Harriet Wilson began her career – and ladies at times behaved like courtesans. There was a garrison, and the pavements, like the parties, dinners and balls, were brilliant with the pomp of uniforms. Rake-hells wilder even than the notorious Lord Cardigan rode or sauntered past its neat, bow-fronted houses, regarding with sophisticated eye girls who both did and did not understand so mesmerizing a regard. It was a place for enjoyment, most of it innocently high-spirited, but some of it ranging across the spectrum of sensuality – though tending towards an immoral Roman coarseness rather than an amoral Greek delicacy when it came to the actual choice of pleasures.

For the Owen girls, Brighton meant excitement, flirtation, admiration, and the possibility, faint perhaps, but always there, of a good marriage into the Army or one of the professions. So both Sarah and Fanny were much taken with the abundance of what they called "shootables", a word which meant anything that was fair game, but in particular eligible men. Sarah wrote to Charles at the end of the year, to tell him that she had "been very gay since I came here. I like Brighton *very* much, we are out almost every night, which *I* think very wonderful, considering we knew so few people when we first came. Last week we were at *three* Balls, besides Parties, & are engaged to four or five more. You make such particular enquiries after *Red coats & shootables* that I cannot resist telling you that they are most of them 'remarkably frightful' & the *scarlet shootables* & Scorpions are also remarkably useless as very few of them go out & dance." She had "had the supreme bliss of *chauncing* to meet my very favourite shootable yesterday, viz Mr. Charles Jones", but added nevertheless, "Brighton is so *horribly* windy that there is very little pleasure in walking here, & besides we are in sad want of a *walking* chaperon, & I often wish you were here to take pity on two *desolate Females* . . ."

They did not sound in the least desolate. Rather, it was Charles who seems to have voiced despair at Fanny's silence. In mock consternation – one can almost see her pretty eyes opening wide – she replied:

> My dear Charles, I never was so horror struck as to receive your little note the other day. My conscience upraided me so much as really to prevent my eating any *breakfast* altho' a plate of *hot* toast was smoaking before me. I reproach myself bitterly with ingratitude for your entertaining budgets in having delayed so long sending you an effusion. Pray forgive the *penitent* Housemaid. She is truly sorry for her crime.

And then she commented briefly on what must have seemed a major alteration in Charles's planned destiny. "I was very much surpris'd to hear from Sarah that you have decided to become a DD instead of an MD, you never let me into the secret". For in staid, faraway Shrewsbury, Dr. Darwin had come to a new decision about his son. It was now apparent even to him that Charles had neither liking nor ambition for a medical career. With the intention, therefore, of having him qualify to become a clergyman, Dr. Robert had decided to send his son to Cambridge. This decision, of great moment to Charles, made only the slightest dent in Fanny's self-absorption. Having allowed herself her moment of astonishment, she returned swiftly to the seaside delights that surrounded her. "We are", she reported gravely, "very dissipated here, at a Ball or Party almost every night, which you may suppose I find not bad sport in its way. But all must come to an end and I fear we shall be dragg'd away to the shades of the Forest and leave Brighton at the hights of its gaiety . . . Pray tell me some Shrewsbury scandal, you well know if the Housemaid has *a faiblesse* it is for a *mystery* . . . I hope you will not be gone from Home when I return, I shall expect *cart loads* of *black mysteries* after so long an absence, pray collect all you can . . . I am too stupid & sleepy tonight to do anything but sleep in the armchair. I am sure you will say what a *stupid, prosy* creature the Housemaid is become, but remember it is *1828* & she is a year *older* – indeed my dr Postillion believe me ever yrs truly Fanny O." Then, true as always to the over-excited spirit of romance, she added a note: "Burn this".

However, the Housemaid had perhaps let her Postillion languish letterless for too long, while she allowed herself to be drawn away into those flaring, dancing, music-rich Brighton evenings. Compared with the provincial calm of Shropshire, after all, she now had an almost metropolitan stage on which to deploy her beauty, wit and coquetry. Charles, insecure, probably jealous, preparing to set off for the strangeness of Cambridge and an entirely new life, seeems to have felt the pinch of despair. It made him predictably irresolute. He must have written, protesting – and then written again, terrified by visions of the fury Fanny would fall into when she read his strictures on her silence. One can reconstruct something of his note from the mingled contrition and excuses of her reply.

> My dear Postillion, [she wrote] You must have thought the Housemaid most *awfully* changed by the Brighton air to suppose for a moment that she had dashed with *indignation* your agreeable letter into the flames and determined to treat its author with *merited disdain* – The real reason why I did not long ago send you a leetle effusion was that you told me you were going to Cambridge the end of the month, now that word *Cambridge* sounded most formidable to my ears; I had visions of Mrs. Burton *constantly* starting up before me, which seemed to say, "Dear me, ma'am, would you believe it, Miss *Fanny Owen*

corresponds with a young man, ma'am, *at the University"*; this horrid phantom appear'd to me so often and worked upon my heated fancy to such a degree that after *mature deliberation* I thought it best to *remain silent* and if the Postillion should be in a *fury* at *my ingratitude* I [shall] explain it all away when we shall meet once more at the Forest. Thus you see Mrs Burton has been the cause of all this, I hope you will forgive the poor Housemaid . . .

Questions about Shrewsbury doings and gossip about those at Brighton followed. "I was at a very gay Ball on Wednesday night plenty of *red Coats – moustachios* which *you say must* be pleasant. I like *Blue & silver* better." We do not know why at this moment she preferred the Navy to the Army, if this is in fact what she meant: neither preference was calculated to calm her sporting naturalist waiting at The Mount. "Excuse this scrawl," Fanny wrote at the end, "but I have *such a Pen*! and besides never could write like any thing but what *I am* a *Housemaid* and so, dr. Postillion ever yrs F. Owen." This time the note on the cover was more vehement: "Burn this as soon as read – or tremble at my fury and revenge".

Soon after the two Owen girls had returned to Shropshire, Sarah wrote to Charles, now settling into Christ's College. It was mid-February, 1828, and probably the young Owen sisters were having their own problems in adapting once more to the staid rhythm of a winter countryside, where the weekly meet of the local Hunt and an evening game of picquet were the normal limits of social outrageousness. They had, she said, stayed a week longer in Brighton than they had intended, having already extended a proposed three-week visit into one of three months,

on account of a very gay Fancy ball given by *five & twenty* Batchelors, indeed it would have been too provoking to have missed it, for it was an admirable Brigadoon, everybody in fancy dresses or uniforms. Fanny & I went as *She Turks* that is in the dress of Fatima if you ever chaunced to see it, this Festivity took place on the first of February and lasted till 7 o clock A.M. on the 2nd of Feby. We had 3 balls, three successive nights before & even *my constitution* began to fail, whatever Mrs Burton may say or think to the contrary.

The girls' return to Woodhouse brought boredom and tedium in its wake. "The tranquillity here is indeed truly awful . . .", wrote Sarah, before moving on to the subject of Charles himself: "Pray tell me if *your sentiments* continue the same – I heard of your paying visits to the Forest during our absence, I am glad *some people were missed*, as that circumstance may perhaps induce you to stay longer *when some people* are to be found in Paradise." Only she and her sister had been absent – and she had, after all, signalled her interest in young Mr. Jones by doubling her exclamation marks. That left the unnamed Fanny as the "some people" of these innocent hints. Sarah ended her letter less dramatically than Fanny, but to the same effect. "I really must conclude this scrawl, you have wasted too much time already in reading it, pray put it on the Fire which is now blazing in your room . . . I need not remind you of your promise not to shew my stupid effusions to *any body* on any account whatsoever . . . I remain *always* Yours most truly, S.H. Owen." The tone is friendly, but it lacks the intimacy of the "Housemaid" when she addresses the "Postillion". However, Shropshire's proposed marriages prompted Sarah to a late addition; one was to be between Miss F. Forrester and Mr. Biddulph – a ceremony which, as we shall see, never took place.

When Fanny wrote again, her voice carries to us, eavesdropping across Time with a deceptive clarity. We hear her, but find it hard to make out the exact meaning of her words, the precise feelings which impel her. That both words and feelings are sprightly rather than profound, however, cannot be gainsaid. Addressing him this time as "Dear Charles", she had again to cover her preceding silence. The date of the letter must have been late in that same February of 1828, for she wrote, "I tremble at having the boldness to begin a letter to you after having allowed your last effusion to remain such a time unanswered, but as I believe I have told you before I *cannot* & *will not* play *second fiddle* & as Sarah wrote to you very soon after we came home I thought I had better delay doing so *till now* . . ." One wonders on what occasion she had told Charles that before, and whether then too it had been Sarah to whom she was playing second fiddle. Now, her only news, she wrote, was of two days of "quite *brilliant festivities*", where Lloyd Kenyon* had been "the Hero of the fête, it being a sort of *farewell Brigadoon* before that *interesting* youth join'd his regiment which he did a few days ago to our *unspeakable dispair* – for Oh! how he used to come and *sit* and *eat* and *sit* till we thought he must have *grown to his chair*." A Wedgwood visit had prevented Charles's sisters from calling at Woodhouse, but, when they finally arrived as promised, "I wish you were to be of the party but '*brighter hours will come*' and I look forward to yr paying us a long visit in yr next vacation – I am shocked to inform you that I have not yet learnt to play at *Billiards*, I hear you exclaim what a lazy creature, but it is not *my fault* I assure you for I can get no one to give me some lessons, Owen votes it a *fat bore*, so I suppose I must *trust to fate* for a *master* or wait till *you come*." But epistolary inspiration was beginning to run down and soon she was making her familiar excuses for bringing her letter to an end: "I must conclude for I find myself getting *awfully dull* and *prosy*, but what can you expect from an *unfortunate exile* of the Forest *pity* and *forgive* is all I ask – & believe me my

---

* Later the third Baron Kenyon; a nephew of that political Sir John Hanmer who figured on the list of Dr. Robert's debtors.

dr Postillion ever yr faithfull Housemaid Fanny O". As always, she could not resist the excited postscript: "For *Heavens* sake burn this, or if it fall into the hands of any of the *young men*, what would they think of a *Housemaid* writing to Mr. Charles Darwin – Ma'm Burton *would die of it I think*."

The last of this group of letters, addressed to "Charles Darwin Esqr, Christ's College, Cambridge", and posted in Shrewsbury in April, 1828, was from Sarah again. In it she recollected "the memorable old Hunt Bazaar which *impoverished* so *many misguided shootables* Mr Charles", and told of how she had to "mount the strictest guard" on the visiting Congreve* family, "for Fanny was ill & did not leave Paradise Row till they left the lower Regions – hers has certainly been a *well timed* sickness . . ." Paradise Row – was it so named because it stood above, while the rooms on the ground floor were designated "the lower regions"? Was there a hint of something less innocent, some thought of loveliness unveiled, of angels at their orisons, of unattainable delights? Probably there was not – the rigidities of middle-class property, the innocence of protected lives mingling with the ignorance of immaturity, and the unsophisticated self-acceptance of a pre-Freudian age all combined to keep in check what has become the easy prurience of our own day.

"I suppose you have been officially informed", wrote Sarah, "of the marriage which is shortly to take place in *your* Family!! so I need hardly mention names . . . I have suspected it *long ago* !!!" But the oldest Darwin daughter, Marianne, was already four years safely married to her Dr. Parker, and it would be over ten years before there was another marriage in the family: one wishes that she *had* mentioned names. She was sorry not to see him come to Shrewsbury in the vacation, "though perhaps if you had, you would not think it worth while to visit the Forest, *out of the shooting Season*, now that all the *Muslin* is collected there." They used the word "muslin" as a collective noun for young ladies, and Charles had himself referred to it when writing of his university life.

"By the bye, Charles", asked Sarah, "what can you mean by saying you have not *set your eyes on* Muslin since you left Shropshire. Have the Doctors, Proctors, Deans &c &c &c neither Wives nor Daughters!! or are the Cambridge shootables thought too *dangereux* to be seen by them?"

Now a long summer silence descends on the correspondence. It is in the autumn of this year that Charles writes so enthusiastically of Fanny to William Darwin Fox. She too, when she writes again that October, takes a tone that seems livelier and more intimate than before, not in what she has to say, but in the relaxed style: a certain strain seems missing from the playful-

---

* The Congreves belonged to the Staffordshire gentry, having settled in the county shortly after the Norman Conquest.

ness, the archness has diminished, the voice one hears seems more truly her own. The substance is as superficial as ever. She has been to the theatre in Oswestry, "but the wonder ceased when we found that the *gay, darling, handsome, dissipated, General Despard** was the only *shootable in the Play House*". The Woodhouse party travelled back in a van, packed so tightly that "I really thought some valuable lives would have been lost for the *Black Hole* at *Calcutta* must have been a *fool* to it". Charles had sent her some books, and made her a present of a butterfly, a Swallow Tail "which has absolutely *astounded* my weak mind, there is *something* about it so *werry pecoolier* . . ." Once again, visitors are expected, the Williams family (perhaps including the Edward Hosier-Williams who became Sarah's first husband), "so I think we shall be Williams'd . . ." and in the meantime she has again been unable to find anyone with whom to play billiards, "& am afraid for *want* of *practice* I shall forget all my *fine shotses*." An injunction to burn the letter, a warning that he need not expect another too soon, and then the note ends: "Believe me in haste yrs truly an 'Unbelieving Jew' ", with underneath the line, "Paradise Row ½ past 12 – Saturday night". The words are scrawled, the letters loosely formed and over-large, her pen has not been sharpened; one seems to see her, candlelit, drooping over the paper, the quill with its faint scraping racing her fatigue, her bed already opened, perhaps at the end of October a fire lit in the grate and, outside, autumnal breezes rattling the fading leaves.

Winter settled in. The year turned; a second winter pinned the country. In July of 1829, Miss Owen had been Charles's "la belle Fanny"; at the end of the year he had sent a message to her by his sister Catherine, certainly to ask her to write. In January, 1830, she sent him a letter.

I received your little message from Catherine when I was staying at the *Darwin Hotel* for the Hunt week. I have delay'd so long complying with your modest but I can't help thinking *unaccountable* request that I fear you are thinking me an *illtempered creature, sulky, idle*, &c, &c, but I have been so busy lately or so cold & frost bitten that I have never had time to scribble you a few lines. [Her news is as always: there have been Balls] . . . and a little sort of *fandango* or as Owen calls it a "Blow-out" at the Leightons, which was pleasant for Clare with her usual good nature sang to the *admiring & awe struck* multitude almost all night. What more could we wish for? She pitched her voice in its *shrillest* key and oh, ye powers!! Heavens & Earth, I wish you could have heard her. But why did you not come home this Xmas? I fully expected to have seen you, but

---

* John Despard came of an Irish military family. His elder brother, embittered by the treatment he had received after long and distinguished colonial service, attempted to seize the Tower, the Bank of England and the King with an army of some forty unfortunates; not unexpectedly this attempt was unsuccessful and he was executed for his pains. John Despard fought in the American War of Independence, being captured twice, and rose to become a full general. He retired to Oswestry and, despite so exciting Fanny's praise in 1828, died there in 1829.

I suppose some *dear little Beetle* in Cambridge or London kept you away. I know when a *Beetle is* in the case every other *paltry* object gives way – if I could have sent to tell you that I had found a *Scrofulum morturiorum* perhaps you might have been induced to come down! How does the *mania* go on, are you as constant as ever? don't think me impertinent but tell me – *pity* and *forgive* my ignorance.

In the meantime, there were still Williamses, playing out "that eternal never to be ended Williams affair . . . I never was so sick of anything, and see no chance of it coming to an end – anything wd be better than this uncertainty, and always hearing the same thing – the *name* now quite puts me in a fury – *Human patience* can bear it no longer & my *little stock* has been long exhausted on *that subject*". A year later, however, Sarah would be Mrs. Williams – and a dozen years on, would find herself a widow. Not, fortunately, for the rest of her life.

As the letter meandered on, Fanny's mood became increasingly angry and bitter. Perhaps she was beginning to discover that there was a profound discrepancy between her aspirations and her means: only having been born a great heiress would really have satisfied Fanny. In any case, she burst out, "Hard times these! upon my word Charles – Xmas may be a joyful time but I'm sure it does not *seem so* to *me* – my finances are in a most pitiable state & the *mortgage* on my Estate *incalculable* – the *duns* begin to *ride* – and the *King's Bench* stares me in the face." No wonder that, telling Charles of a painting she is reluctantly finishing for her father, she had written in an earlier letter that "I'll have my *revenge* for I'll be *paid well for it*. I won't pass the best part of my life in a *dirty cheese room* for nothing. No! No." Now she commented, "What a situation! but I can't say my spirits as *yet* suffer *much*. I drive *dull care* away wonderfully – and hope that Providence will carry me through my difficulties – it *often has*, so I must trust to it – I dare say you are in the same situation so can have a fellow feeling for me – What a HORRID DISGUSTING THING MONEY is." The underlinings doubled and tripled here. "I hate the name of it – don't you – it is fit for vulgar souls – *not* BEETLE HUNTERS – and *Paint Brush Drivers*!!!" The words sprawl, enormous, over the page, blurred by the pressure of her hand on the pen: there is no doubt that she was in earnest. After her signature she scribbled, "Burn this I *do* desire *Sir*", and reinforced the command with a series of pen-strokes as peremptory as the cracking of a whip.

Although this bitterness was real enough, it is hard to know what to think about Fanny Owen. Even in the one-sided correspondence that survives, one seems to see signs that the feelings flowing between her and Charles were equally one-sided. Her vanity, self-centredness and shallowness, like her beauty and her quick, if childish, wit, meant that unworldly Charles could never have been, in any sense of the word, a match for her. One cannot imagine that she ever spoke of him in the terms he used of her when writing to Fox. He read Shakespeare – or Newton's *Optics*. She read *The Mysteries of Udolpho*. "Do bring me a JUICY book of some kind", she pleaded, in the last of this group of Owen letters; "anything you can purloin, for I sadly want one – I don't care what it is – a *book* is a BOOK – truism!" It was the Spring of 1831 by the time she wrote that, and the bitterness still seems to be there. The brightness had faded; the world had turned prosaic. To read was to leave it for a while. Much later, Darwin too would read for relaxation, or have read to him, light romances with pretty heroines at their core. But Fanny, locked in the tedium of a largish house near a smallish village not very far from a sleepy little town, taking to books as to a drug, must have felt already that their life was, as it were, collapsing into itself, turning to dust, and to the same dust she could discern as the substance of the lives around her. She had been the belle of ball after ball, but what had it gained her? Her stage was so narrow, the cast upon it so undistinguished, the audience full of faces known too long and too well – or not well enough. Had she lived elsewhere, been rich, spent these years in the true glitter of the metropolis and not this faint provincial reflection, how differently everything would have turned out! It is inconceivable that with her temperament such thoughts did not from time to time torment her. As it happened, she was to have one chance and, when it appeared, she took it; but as 1830 turned into 1831, she did not yet know this.

And Charles? He was young and, if not volatile, he had his own imaginative powers – and then, there was always Maer. In September, 1830, he was writing to Fox that he found it "just as delightful as ever & Charlotte just as agreeable as ever: id est, as agreeable as possible." Charlotte Wedgwood, however, was twelve years older than he – though that did not prevent his coupling her name even with the once-sacred one of Fanny, early in February, 1831: "I could not write a long letter", he told Fox, "even to Charlotte Wedgwood or Fanny Owen . . ." The goddess of his earlier monotheism had become just one in a pantheon – even if for the moment it was a pantheon of only two deities.

Was his passion for Fanny therefore no more than a summer moment of adolescent self-delusion? Perhaps the shimmering weeks of the long vacation in 1828 saw the peak of his feelings for her – of their feelings for each other – but they were close for several years, longer than would have been possible had it all been just a passing infatuation. And then, we have Henrietta's testimony, her report of Darwin's expression when, years later, he would speak of Fanny. Above all, we have the letters. If Fanny, whom he mentions not at all in his *Autobiography*, had been of such small significance, if she had been no more than just another friend in a Shropshire full of friends – why is it that her letters and those of her sister have survived, maintained with the same care as was lavished on those written by the Darwin girls themselves? There are so many letters from the Owens, so few from anyone else outside Charles's family, which have remained in being from those early years. Why was it Fanny's letters above all that were kept over the five decades of his life that followed the *Beagle* voyage – decades during which, even if he always remembered her, he hardly ever saw her again?

7

The friends Charles had in common with the young Owens were, perhaps, with their titles and their lineages, surprising companions for a provincial doctor's son. Eligibility may have remained the true social criterion – when it finally came to marriage, it was to the Wedgwoods that Charles was linked – but it is also obvious that the Darwins moved easily and as of right among the Shropshire gentry. In the same way, the education of both Erasmus and Charles had been modelled upon what was considered suitable for the sons of the long-established families, with a great public school – albeit a local one – followed by one of the great universities. It was by no means generally established that the offspring of a professional man such as Dr. Darwin would necessarily be sent to a school like Shrewsbury, and even less that they would move on afterwards to Oxford or Cambridge.

The great Erasmus Darwin, Charles's grandfather, whose own father had been called to the Bar after studying at Lincoln's Inn, had taken his degree at Cambridge, where two of his brothers had also been educated. The only one of his sons, however, to go to either ancient university had been the oldest, Charles, who had studied at Oxford; he had died, wastefully, at the age of only nineteen. Dr. Robert himself, as we know, had been sent to Leyden, in Holland, as well as Edinburgh, but he had sent his oldest son, Erasmus, to Cambridge and, in selecting the same university for Charles, reinforced a family tradition which was to see Darwins linked to Cambridge – the city as well as the colleges – over several generations.

The decision to send Charles to the University was obviously accompanied by considerable parental anger, a furious analysis of Charles's shortcomings and dark forebodings about the lacklustre future that awaited him. Dr. Robert's solution, which he was not the first unhappy father to seize on, was to install his son in some undemanding vicarage or rectory. Through the ramifications of his familial, financial or professional connections, there seems no doubt that respected Dr. Darwin could quite easily have found his younger son some quiet country living, a retreat demanding no very vigorous cure of souls nor necessitating much in the way of evangelical fervour. All over the English countryside, the Church spread somnolently in its unpretentious patchwork of parishes, maintained by scattered regiments of vicars, rectors, parsons and curates. These, making up in stamina for what they lacked in energy, fitted into their little districts as snugly as the churchyard yew-trees, smiling at babies and droning from pulpits for decade after comfortable decade. They were the props and adjuncts – and, frequently, the offspring – of the gentry and the aristocracy, by whom they had in many cases been appointed. In their gentlemanly, apathetic hands Christianity sagged, faded and shredded like the ancient banners that adorned their churches. The fact that the clerical profession was often chosen as the last resort of the family dullard did nothing to lead to a revival.

Is that how his father regarded Charles? It seems probable. The law, for example, seems never to have been considered as a profession, although there was a certain legal tradition in the family. No one pondered that other standby, the Army, soon to be the destiny of two of the Owen boys and not an unthinkable choice for the kind of sporting young man Charles appeared to be – even if that was also the kind of young man deplored by his father. There may have been, of course, another and much more positive considera- tion. Most of the foremost naturalists of the day were clergymen. There was a long, honourable and serious history of men following these intertwined careers. If God was expressed in his creation, how could one better serve him than by elucidating its marvellous mysteries? Since Darwin was already so competent a naturalist, the argument might have gone, he was already part of the way to becoming a clergyman. At the very least, a career in the Church promised to permit him enough free time to pursue these distracting inter- ests of his.

For Darwin himself, there was, even if only briefly, a slight problem of conscience. He found it difficult to declare his allegiance to the Thirty-Nine Articles, that curious doctrinal base, promulgated in the reign of Elizabeth I, upon which the Church of England rested. "I asked for some time to consider . . . though otherwise I liked the thought of being a country clergy- man." He read a little theology, added it to his belief in the absolute validity of the Bible, and so "soon persuaded myself that our Creed must be fully accepted. It never struck me how illogical it was to say that I believed in what I could not understand and what is in fact unintelligible." He needed, now, a degree from an English university; family tradition was in this case applied and Cambridge selected. It must have seemed at first that to graduate would pose very few problems – had he not been crammed throughout his school- days with the necessary classics, five days a week and half-days on Satur- days? When it came to it, however, his detestation for what he had learned trapped him, for "as I had never opened a classical book since leaving school, I found to my dismay that . . . I had actually forgotten . . . almost everything which I had learnt even to some few of the Greek letters". The autumn and early winter of 1827, therefore, Charles spent at home, bent doggedly over those hated languages out of his and the world's dead past, while twelve miles away the Owen sisters prepared themselves, packed and fled away to the whirligig gaieties of Brighton. By Christmas, he had 'recovered my school standard of knowledge" – simple Greek no longer held either secrets or terrors. After the Christmas vacation, therefore, he rattled away eastwards to Cambridge.

The years that followed were to change Darwin's life, fundamentally and absolutely, yet in an entirely unexpected fashion. But that was not principally why he was always to remember them with pleasure and affection. It was for the companionship he discovered at Cambridge, especially that centering on the pursuit of natural history, that Darwin felt a lifelong nostalgia. In 1855 he wrote to T.C. Eyton*, "Ah the good old times of Entomology, I have never enjoyed anything in Natural History so much since." Twenty years later, he could still write of "never-failing pleasant rememberances of old days". When in 1860 he asked Albert Way – once his student companion, by then a Fellow of the Society of Antiquaries and a co-founder of the Archeological Institute – some questions about the history of the dray-horse, he could not resist adding, "Eheu Eheu, the old Crux Major days are long past". Again the reference is to entomology rather than to professors, lectures and examinations: Darwin never forgot his capture of *Panagaeus crux major*, nor the fenland walks he took in order to hunt it and other beetles. The mere mention of some old companion's name was enough to set the ghost of that long-pinned insect scuttling across the reed beds and water meadows of his inner landscape, the landscape that framed so many of his most important memories.

Although it was Cambridge that later stimulated some of his most vivid moments of nostalgia, Darwin always considered his years there a period of academic failure. His time, he wrote, "was sadly wasted there and worse than wasted"; it was, indeed, "wasted, as far as the academical studies were concerned, as completely as at Edinburgh and at school". One might assume from this self-castigation that Charles was eventually "ploughed" or "plucked", as the slang of the day might have put it, and given no degree at all; or at best a very bad one. But he had worked hard to revive his knowledge of the classical languages driven into him during his years at Shrewsbury, had retained his pleasure in Euclidean geometry, the clarity of which always delighted him, and had meanwhile discovered a similar delight in the logic of Archdeacon Paley's *Evidences of Christianity*, a work which, with its com-

---

* Thomas Campbell Eyton, from a well-known Shropshire family that had lived in Shrewsbury since the twelfth century, a school and university contemporary of Darwin's, later became a noted amateur ornithologist and one of Darwin's many scientific correspondents, though he was to oppose Darwin's theories on the mutability of species.

panion volume, *The Principles of Moral and Political Philosophy*, was required reading for B.A. candidates, just as Euclid and the classics were. Darwin thus went into the examination hall well prepared in these essential areas. Recalling those days many years later, when he was writing his *Autobiography*, he felt that he could still "have written out the whole of the *Evidences* with perfect correctness . . ." – though not, he added, side-stepping arrogance, "in the clear language of Paley".

In the *Evidences* Paley tried, by logic and the evidence of Scripture, to prove the divinity of Jesus, but it was another of his books that would, in the long run, prove of greater importance to Darwin. This was Paley's *Natural Theology*, a work which, though not compulsory, was also much studied and one which Darwin greatly admired during his student days. Later, by inverting its logic, he was to make it a powerful element in his reassessment of the natural world.

In *Natural Theology* Paley argued that, observing so complex a construction as the material universe, we are bound to hypothesize its constructor. It is obviously just as much an artefact as a watch we might find on the ground – and, "when we come to inspect the watch, we perceive . . . that its several parts are framed and put together for a purpose . . . This mechanism being observed . . . the inference, we think, is inevitable, that the watch must have had a maker: that there must have existed, at some time, and at some place or other, an artificer or artificers who formed it for the purpose which we find it actually to answer: who comprehended its construction, and designed its use." The book then examines in great detail the vast mechanism of the earth and its creatures, in all the complexity of their adaptations, drawing from their effective use of natural resources, and their successful defence against natural forces, the same inference of a maker, a designer. It was when Darwin ceased to find this inference inevitable that he realized he was beginning to look in a quite different direction for his answers.

In the meantime, however, his admiration for these books, and the arguments they set forth, was unequivocal, and he studied them with pleasure. When the time came, therefore, to sit his examinations, by "answering well the . . . questions in Paley, by doing Euclid well, and by not failing miserably in Classics", he achieved tenth place in the list of those who gained ordinary, as opposed to honours, degrees. This may not have been scintillating achievement, but it was not failure either, nor deserving of a self-accusation so impressive and long-lasting that in a textbook of the 1970s he could still be characterized, simply, as a "three-time academic dropout".

Darwin, assessing his student career, did so – as in so many other instances – from the viewpoint of some censorious overseer. "With respect to Classics I did nothing except attend a few compulsory lectures . . . In my second year

I had to work for a month or two to pass Little Go, which I did easily. Again in my last year I worked with some earnestness for my final degree . . ." This sounds like the normal university process undergone by an intelligent student with more important things on his mind than the aridities of the curriculum. Darwin might have written, "I spent as little time on my purely academic work as seemed consistent with obtaining a good ordinary degree of B.A."; and if he had done so his reputation as a poor student would never have been created. Instead, he wrote of wasted time and academic failure, discounting his university successes because they were unofficial and impossible to quantify. In other words, he took up the position his father might have done, or Dr. Butler, and regarded himself with the eye of authority. He has nothing to say in his own defence, except apologetically, and describes his extracurricular activities self-critically, where they seem to have been frivolous, and, where they were not, as though they did not really excuse his central shortcomings.

Whatever his unexpressed expectations of posterity's interest, Darwin, of course, was ostensibly writing his *Autobiography* for his family, especially its youngest members, and perhaps even for future generations of Darwins. His approach may therefore have had its hortatory element, but this cannot obscure the readiness to display and find fault with his inadequacies that so frequently appeared throughout his life in his letters and journals. One might regard his attitude as that of a small boy so often criticized, yet in such a high-minded and loving manner, that he has finally been seduced into identifying with his critics. In this sense it might be said that he has ended by learning to side against himself. Darwin always had what might be termed a public, visible part of his personality which tended to be the first to point the finger of blame at his supposed delinquencies. Yet at the same time this swiftness to accept and even to initiate blame hides a paradox – with all his apparently sincere contrition, he never made any discernible efforts to reform. Instead, this public self-accusation may have had the effect of giving an inner, private and much more genuine aspect of himself its freedom. By so readily agreeing that he was blameworthy, he was always able to purge his "sins". This put him at liberty to commit them – again and again. It was a device, in other words, that left him in the last resort free to do exactly as he wanted.

Since what he wanted to do – these "delinquencies" of his – consisted of nothing but the wholehearted pursuit of his scientific and sporting interests, it was not really easy to call up any high moral imperatives either to support the criticisms of others or to justify his own clamorous self-indictments. Not even Darwin can finally have believed that his compelling though innocent pleasures, whether with the gun or the butterfly net, were truly wicked, or could even be dubbed, with any honesty, "idleness". The fact is that much of Darwin's behaviour can best be understood as partly or wholly self-protective, whether it was his attractively equable temperament, his later absorption with his constant ill health or, as here, his frequent and vociferous self-denigration. Thus guarded, the true Charles Darwin could stalk his ideas, and his ambitions, down the long, undisturbed years that they demanded.

It would be untrue to say, however, that Darwin's diversions were not often self-indulgent – he was, for example, a tireless sportsman. "From my passion for shooting and for hunting and when this failed, for riding across country I got into a sporting set, including some dissipated low-minded young men. We used often to dine together in the evening, though these dinners often included men of a higher stamp, and we sometimes drank too much, with jolly singing and playing at cards afterwards." All this sounds convivially innocent enough, but Darwin cannot help judging, condemning, excusing and asserting himself in what seems like a single, moralizing breath: "I know that I ought to feel ashamed of days and evenings thus spent, but as some of my friends were very pleasant and we were all in the highest spirits, I cannot help looking back to these times with much pleasure". Albert Way, however, confirmed Darwin's Cambridge reputation as a smoking and drinking man by devising for him a mock coat-of-arms, its shield supported on one side by an American Indian, with feathers and bow, on the other by a bearded student in smoking-cap and jacket, the two sharing a waterpipe that stands above; on the quartered shield itself short pipes, heads sporting cigars, groups of church-warden pipes, and ashtrays vie with mugs, spigots, and barrels to convey their message of conviviality. Below, the motto "Yallo baccoque repleti" seems to translate as "Filled with Beer and Baccy". (It must have taken all Albert Way's budding skills as an antiquary to dig out the late-medieval Latin word *yalos,* meaning "glass".)

Darwin retained his pleasure in sport. "In the autumn, my whole time was devoted to shooting, chiefly at Woodhouse and Maer, and sometimes with young Eyton of Eyton". Herbert* remembered years later Darwin's making a resolution not to shoot again because once, while out with William Owen, "he picked up a bird not quite dead, but lingering from a shot it had received on the previous day; and that it had made and left such a painful impression on his mind, that he could not reconcile it to his conscience to continue to derive pleasure from a sport which inflicted such cruel suffering". It was a resolution Darwin did not keep; he was at Maer for the shooting when in

---

* John Maurice Herbert, at St. John's, Cambridge, while Darwin was at Christ's, later a highly respected County Court judge. Darwin called him "Old Cherbury" because of his family's possible connection with the Lords Herbert of Cherbury.

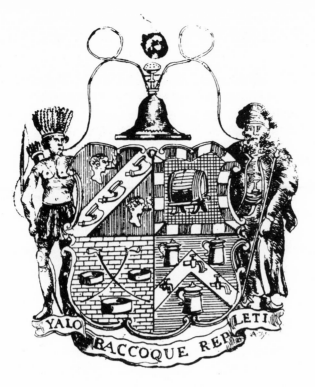

YALO ... LETI

BACCOQUE REP...

Car. Darwin

amico opt. amicus fumosior.

Albertus Way. e C. S. Trin.

D . D . D .

5. Ap. 1828.

Albert Way's notion of Darwin's coat of arms.

1831 his Uncle Jos intervened in the discussion that followed his invitation
to join the *Beagle* expedition; during those years of exploration, too, he
often went ashore in South America with the ship's officers in order to bring
down some of the local game-birds.

The *Autobiography* gives the impression that his shooting was carried on
in his family's despite and against a background of paternal disapproval.
This may well have been true at times, but "The Case of the Distressed
Sportsman", which he wrote out and presented in October, 1828, suggests

that they had more sympathy with these country pursuits than in memory he permitted them.

> Charles Darwin gent. humbly petitions all benevolently disposed persons to pay attention to his case. Whereas he the aforesaid formerly gained a comfortable livelihood by destroying hares, pheasants, partridges & Woodcocks with the aid of a double barrelled gun & the said gun becoming dangerous & liable to destroy the aforesaid Charles Darwin hys arms, body & brains & consequently unfit for use, he is reduced to lay his deplorable case before the charitable & humane, being utterly unable to raise the sum requisite for the purchase of a new Double barrelled Gun, Value of £20.

Underneath stand the signatures of his father and his three sisters; each has set £5 beside the name as their pledge to support this benevolent enterprise.

Among those who remembered Darwin at Cambridge when they themselves looked back to a youth by then fifty years distant was the same John Price who had been at school with Charles and his brother Erasmus. It was the latter whom Price remembered better, at Cambridge as at Shrewsbury. Erasmus had wanted to be a doctor and he had, in Price's opinion, "every mental qualification"; however, "his Father told me he must not attempt, with his delicate frame, a career like his own, involving, if successful, a severe strain upon body and mind. For all that, he pursued the study of human anatomy *con amore* . . ." (His professor of anatomy, incidentally, was nicknamed "Bone" Clark, pleasantly distinguishing him from the Cambridge mineralogist, "Stone" Clark, and the well known Doctor of Music, "Tone" Clark.) Later, after Erasmus had set himself up in London, Price would sometimes stay with him at his Spring Gardens apartment. On one occasion the two of them visited a menagerie where "a huge Man-drill called Peter 'indulged in a pipe & a glass of grog daily' ". Price, his memory perhaps kept green by Charles's later fame, recalled that at the time "our descent from Monkeys became a popular topic (I suppose thro' Lamarck's romancing)".

It is from another fellow student, Frederic Watkins, later Archdeacon of York, that we learn of the "Gourmet Club" of which Charles was a member. The purpose of the club was to provide feasts of "birds & beasts which were before unknown to human palate". Having tried hawk, bittern and other unlikely dishes, the club "came to an untimely end by endeavouring to eat an old brown owl, which was indescribable!" Running through these indigestible proceedings there was of course a satirical element, a cocking of snooks at the exclusive and largely aristocratic dining clubs which were and remain a feature of the two senior universities. Darwin's membership of this disrespectful assembly illuminates both his social position and his social attitudes.

Presumably such unfortunate creatures as were eaten by the (perhaps equally unfortunate) members of this investigative group, were shot for the purpose. Darwin kept hand and eye sharp by aiming his gun at the candles in his room, pulling the trigger and letting the hammer fall on caps. The constant sharp snapping sounds that this produced amazed his tutor: "Mr. Darwin, why are you always cracking whips in your room?" he asked. The question was not entirely without point – Darwin had been developing his skills as a rider. On one occasion, he insisted on taking a friend's place in the saddle of a horse which had over and over again refused a jump. With Darwin up, it leaped the uninviting hurdle at the first attempt – and threw him in the process. Typically, he used to recall the tale not as a demonstration of his skill or heroism, but because of the opportunity it had given his friends to laugh at him. (On the other hand, it was an opportunity to laugh which also demonstrated his skill or heroism – there was on occasion a touch of slyness about Darwin's modesty.)

On another occasion there was a fire at Linton, some eleven miles from Cambridge; Darwin and a few companions, "seeing the reflection so plainly in the sky . . . thought we would ride & see it, we set out at $\frac{1}{2}$ after 9 & rode like incarnate devils there & did not return till 2 in the morning, altogether it was a most aweful sight . . ." At this age Darwin was obviously robust and energetic, good-naturedly ready to take part in any "larks", to use Dr. Robert's word, and happy to take life easy in the vigorous manner of the healthy young. "I have been in such a perfect & absolute state of idleness," he wrote to his cousin, William Darwin Fox, in April, 1829, "that it is enough to paralyse all one's faculties: riding & walking in the morning, gambling . . . to a most disgusting extent in the evenings, compose the elegant & instructive routine of my life." It may be jokingly, but even to his closest friends (and Fox remained his friend for over forty years) Darwin could not resist using the self-distancing vocabulary of authority. He went on, however, "The only thing that is talked about in Cambridge is Little Go which has been unusually strict . . .", a circumstance which apparently did not stir him to any great academic activity, in preparation for his own trial, then scheduled for the following year.

Yet to portray Darwin exclusively as a red-cheeked riding, shooting, fishing sort of fellow ("For you must know I am become a 'Brother of the Angle'," he had written to Fox in the summer of 1828), boisterous, unrestrained and boring, would be to deny the far more complex reality. J.H. Cameron, who like so many of Darwin's Cambridge contemporaries went into the Church and was Rector of Shoreham when he died, remembered how "I used to read Shakespeare to him in his own room & he took great pleasure in these readings. He was also very fond of music, though not a performer . . ." Darwin's youthful love of music was slightly paradoxical, since he could neither hold nor easily recognize a tune. It was his friend

Herbert who, himself an amateur musician, as mathematicians often are, introduced him to these unexpected delights. Darwin records how as a result he "acquired a strong taste for music, and used very often to time my walks so as to hear on weekdays the anthem in King's College Chapel. This gave me intense pleasure, so that my backbone would sometimes shiver." Because he often went alone to the chapel, he was even in retrospect convinced that "there was no affectation or mere imitation in this taste", yet it puzzled him: "I am so utterly destitute of an ear, that I cannot perceive a discord, or keep time and hum a tune correctly; and it is a mystery how I could possibly have derived pleasure from music."

His friends shared his bemusement. Writing to him in 1836, Herbert defended himself against "the charge of having defamed yr. musical taste, tho' I have often spoken of yr. want of musical memory, the coexistence of which with yr musical taste & sayings has been often the subject of my most curious speculations . . . Faith, I think I see & hear you now, on my having tried you with 'God Save the King' or 'Cherry Ripe' – 'By G— old fellow, I don't know but isn't it the Halleluyah I heard in King's last Sunday?' At times I imagine yr. fondness for music must have been the result of reasoning, tho' the intensity of yr. feeling it, as evinced by yr. *backbone* criticisms on Handel's Choruses wd. lead one to infer a very large development of the organ of Tune." Much later, writing his Cambridge recollections for Darwin's son, Herbert described Darwin's greatest musical delight as coming from "some grand symphony or overture of Mozart's or Beethoven's, with their full harmonies". Sometimes, too, Darwin would spend hours regarding the prints and pictures collected in the Fitzwillian Museum, a solitary and introspective pursuit at odds with the image of the young sporting man only happy in some moiling group.

The fact is that Charles Darwin was in aimost all respects a fairly standard example of the nineteenth century student, well off, active in field sports, working hard enough to avoid academic failure, but a long way from academic success, with a circle of like-minded friends among whom he could relax, at times quite boisterously; yet at the same time, as happens with the intelligent young, responsive to ideas and to the arts, affected by music and poetry, liberal in his opinions, agreeable in company but able to sustain and even on occasion happy to seek solitude. Where he differed from the others was, not so much in his pursuit of, as in his passion for natural history, and entomology in particular. Albert Way's surviving caricatures of Darwin riding on the backs of enormous, quasi-equine beetles show how specific to him his passion was thought to be.

In the *Autobiography* he tells us that nothing "was followed with nearly so much eagerness or gave me so much pleasure as collecting beetles." Looking back, he realized that he had been no more than a collector, neither dissecting nor examining his specimens in any really disciplined way, but of the singlemindedness with which he pursued them there could be no question. He tells here the story, much repeated since, of how, with an insect already in each hand, he saw on a tree trunk a rarity he could not bear to leave. Without thinking, he stuffed the beetle in his right hand into his mouth, and reached for the prize. "Alas it ejected some intensely acrid fluid, which burnt my tongue so that I was forced to spit the beetle out . . ." It was lost and, by the time he had recovered, the coveted third insect had also vanished. Few collectors would admit to the kind of acquisitive intensity that makes nothing of carrying a live beetle in one's mouth.

Darwin employed a labourer to scrape and collect the moss off ancient tree-trunks, and gather the lively rubbish that fell to the bottom of the barges bringing reeds in from the fens. One can imagine the eagerness with which Darwin would watch his helper empty the bags he had brought, and the greedy care with which he would sift the soft piles before him. It was Fox who first introduced him to entomology, and Darwin's letters to his second cousin are full of the gossip, reminiscences and plans of dedicated beetle hunter. "I am dying by inches", wrote Darwin from Shrewsbury in the summer vacation of 1826, "from not having anyone to talk to about insects . . . I was not fully aware of your extreme value before I left Cambridge. I am constantly saying 'I do wish Fox was here' ". At once he launched into descriptions and discussions of the specimens he had caught – "my sister has made rough drawings of them" – but then apologized "for sending such a very selfish, stupid* letter, but remember I am your pupil, so you must forgive me. – I hope you will write to me soon . . . write me a good long letter about yourself & all other insects." On the back, neat amidst the surrounding scrawl, stand the sisterly illustrations.

In the summer of 1828, Darwin went for the first time to Barmouth, on the coast of Wales, where the soft waters of Cardigan Bay moved to the endless Atlantic echoes; he was attempting to gain some hold on the complexities of mathematics. He struggled under his tutor, Betterton, but found himself, then and later, utterly unable to penetrate the mysteries of algebra, "chiefly from my not being able to see any meaning in the early steps . . . This impatience was very foolish, and in after years I have deeply regretted that I did not proceed far enough at least to understand something of the great leading principles of mathematics . . ." All this, however, was far from Darwin's mind as he scampered across the Barmouth hills in search of the craters, crevices and shadows where his six-legged prey lay waiting for him.

---

* Darwin, here and elsewhere, uses "stupid" to mean "dull" or "boring".

That he had from the beginning had beetles on his mind as seriously as algebra is clear from the letter he had written to Fox about *"the science"* – entomology – as he was about to make his holiday move to Barmouth. "On Wednesday I set out on my Entomo-Mathematical expedition . . . by the blessings of Providence I hope *the science* will not drive out of my poor noddle the Mathematics. – Talking of *the science*, I must tell you that since beginning this letter, I think, sir, upon my soul, sir, I will take my oath, sir (as Way would say), that I have discovered that I possess a valuable insect, viz *Melasis Habellicornis* . . ." The revelation seems to confirm what he wrote in the *Autobiography* about his haphazard methods of identifying his specimens. At the end of August, Darwin wrote again, now from Barmouth, chiding Fox for not having replied.

> I hope it arises from your being 10 fathoms deep in the *Mathematics* & if you are God help you, for so am I, only with this difference I stick fast in the mud at the bottom & there I shall remain in static quo . . . I go on very badly with Mathematics; neither have I succeeded as well as I expected in entomology . . .

With Darwin at Barmouth were Herbert and Thomas Butler, the son of Shrewsbury School's Dr. Butler, later to have his own paternal inadequacies immortalized in his son's writings, but for the moment as fresh-faced a student as the other two. The three, all under Betterton's boring tutelage, became, in Herbert's words, a "somewhat exclusive triumvirate, separate from the rest of the Cambridge party". Darwin, himself collecting constantly, gave Herbert a bottle of alcohol in which to drop anything interesting that he saw during their long walks together, "but alas! my powers of discrimination seldom enabled me to secure a prize. Usually – 'Well, old Cherbury, none of them will do'."

Butler remembered Darwin on "long mountain rambles in which he inoculated me with a taste for botany which has stuck by me all my life. His own speciality at that time however was in the capture of beetles & moths . . ." Darwin did not share the other students' interest in trying to reach, as Butler said, "mountain tops & spots of remarkable scenery & he was not very often of our party"; instead, as Herbert remembered him, he "entomologized most industriously, picking up creatures as he walked along, and bagging everything which seemed worthy of being pursued or of further examination". They walked, sailed, or went fishing – Darwin, with a typically soft-hearted humanity, finding himself unable to set live bait on his hook – or hiked across country, sometimes as far as Dolgelly, ten miles away. There, Herbert recalled, Darwin would sit "in a natural 'chair' on the edge of the cliff, where he shot any bird on the wing below him, which he wished to secure, & the guide who was at the foot of the Cliff had to pick it up & carry it home for preserving".

In September, 1828, while Darwin was making his first visit to Osmaston, Fox's home, he wrote to Herbert about the results of his energetic pursuit of the insects of western Wales. "In the first place, I must inform you that I have taken some of the rarest of the British Insects, and their being found near Barmouth, is quite unknown to the Entomological world: I think I shall write and inform some of the crack entomologists." Herbert cannot have been quite as hopeless a collector as he later professed, since Darwin in this letter asked him to "oblige me by procuring some more specimens of some insects which I dare say I can describe."

In October Darwin sent Fox "glorious news" – not surprisingly, it was entomological news. "I have been introduced, & if I may presume to say so, struck up a friendship with Mr. Hope." Twelve years older than Darwin, an Oxford graduate and a clergymen, Hope was one of the country's leading authorities on beetles and thus could hardly help but be one of Darwin's heroes. Ten years later he was to enshrine his knowledge in a three-volume work, the *Coleopterist's Manual*, and some ten years on again, would present a large part of his enormous collection to his old university. Darwin relayed Hope's conversation and his compliments – "for 4 or 5 years back, he had not seen such a rich case", he wrote; then, mindful of Fox's seniority in "the science", added hastily, above the line, ". . . yours must be still richer". Hope thought that some of Darwin's specimens had not been captured in Britain before: "My head is quite full of Entomology. I *long* to empty some information out of it into yours."

Early in January, 1829, he wrote to Fox to congratulate him on his degree, and wished he were with him in Cambridge "to join in all the glory & happiness, which dangers gone by can give." Typically, he calls this "a very selfish wish . . . as I was not with you in all your troubles & misery". Now, however, "How we would talk, walk & entomologise! Sappho should be the best of bitches, & Dash*, of dogs: then should be 'peace on earth, good will to men,' – which, by the way, I always think the most perfect description of happiness that words can give." Fox had sent the Darwins a swan for Christmas, but "We have not yet eat it," wrote Charles, "& it is probable it will keep some time longer."

During this winter Darwin was plagued by one of the illnesses, their genesis so difficult to define, which were to distress him throughout most of his life. This was an eczema of the lips and in this letter of 2 January, 1829,

---

* Darwin's dog seems to have accompanied him to and from Cambridge: "I & Mr. Dash arrived quite safe here on Saturday morning," he wrote to Fox just before Christmas, 1828. "He rises in my opinion hourly & I would not sell him for a £5 note."

one sees it mentioned for the first time. "My life is very quiet & uniform & what makes it more so: my lips have lately taken to be bad . . ." Herbert could recall this disability: "He had at one time an eruption about the mouth for which he took small doses of arsenic. He told me that he had mentd. this treatment to his Father – & that his Father had warned him that the cure might be attended with worse consequences . . ." Such possible consequences included, Herbert thought, partial paralysis. That he remembered it at all suggests that the eczema lingered for some time, or occured more than once; there is indeed a letter written to Fox that summer from Barmouth, to which Darwin had returned as Hope's entomologizing companion. For a few days, everything had been as absorbing and successful as he had expected, "but for the rest of the week my lips became suddenly so bad & I myself not very well that I was unable to leave the room & on the Monday I retreated with grief & sorrow back again to Shrewsbury . . . I am determined I will go over the same ground that he does before Autumn comes & if working hard will procure insects I will bring home a glorious stock."

Clues as to the causes of these eruptions are scanty, perhaps non-existent; one reads the letters and seizes upon possibilities. In January 1829 there were two. One was Darwin's anxiety about the Little Go, the examination that had to be passed to allow one to continue at Cambridge: "About the Little Go", he wrote, "I am in doubt & tribulation". The second possible source of stress was a shooting accident that had occurred at Woodhouse a few days before, when "first shot one of the young Owens cut his eye so badly with a Copper Cap that he has been in bed for a week. – I think I never in my life time was half so much frightened . . ." Being present at (or as later hints suggest, having caused) the possible mutilation of Fanny's brother, perhaps having to explain what happened, at least to her, may have been enough to bring out his own disfiguring rash. As for the summer eczema, it may have needed no more than seaside sunshine to induce it; on the other hand, a year later, in 1830, once more with Hope in Barmouth, Darwin was writing to Fox, "I am quite disgusted with Hope's egotism & stupidity: how I wish you were here; the very thought of a day's entomologising with you is quite refreshing." It seems unlikely that Hope should have developed these disagreeable qualities quite suddenly, in the space of a year, or that Darwin, thrown together with a man whom he had greatly admired, should not, consciously or unconsciously, have become aware of them in 1829. The resultant tensions may have been enough to stimulate his tendency to skin eruptions round the mouth. What is undeniable is that, from the beginning, Darwin's medical history creates its characteristic enigmas.

Meanwhile, early in 1829, Darwin, as a precocious entomologist, had visited London and there seen not only Hope – "he has given me about 160

new specimens & actually often wanted to give me the rarest insects ..." –
but also S.J. Stephens, a civil servant who had been seconded from the
Admiralty to help arrange the British Museum's insect collection, had just
brought out *Illustrations of British Entomology* and was in the process of
preparing his *Systematic Catalogue of British Insects*. Darwin described him
as "a very good humoured pleasant little man" whose cabinet of specimens
"is more magnificent than the most zealous entomologist could dream of."
While in London, Darwin had made his scientific pilgrimage, going "to the
Royal Institution, Linnean Society, Zoological Gardens & many other
places where naturalists are gregarious. – If you had but been with me." He
always had a sensitivity to what others might make of his words, was always
anxious to forestall resentment, criticism or dismay. So now he saw how
easily Fox might become envious of the way his erstwhile follower was
beginning to outstrip him. At intervals throughout their long association he
would carefully revive his early gratitude for Fox's tutelage, though the
occasion for it had by then long passed.

"I think London", stated the young Darwin, doubtless euphoric at his
easy acceptance by the great, "would be a very delightful place; as things
were it was much pleasanter than I could have supposed such a dreary
wilderness of houses to be ..." It was a view he was to modify within a
decade. In any case, the University still chained him. Under advice, he
decided not after all to take Little Go in 1829; on the other hand, he was
interested to learn what books Fox was reading for his divinity studies. By
April, he was missing Fox's companionship more than ever. "I find Cambridge rather stupid & as I know scarcely anyone that walks & this, joined
with my lips not being quite so well, has reduced me to a sort of Hybernation
..." Meanwhile a dealer named Harbour, with whom Darwin obviously had
an arrangement to get the pick of any new consignments of beetles, had
actually allowed a fellow student called Babington* to take first choice –
and, "accordingly, we have made our final adieus, my part in the affecting
scene consisted in telling him he was a d—d rascal & signifying I should kick
him down the stairs if ever he appeared in my rooms again; it seemed
altogether mightily to surprise the young gentleman ..."

Did Darwin feel free to express anger and outrage because of the difference in class between himself and "Mr. Harbour"? If true, this was perhaps
ignoble; yet Darwin always had the practical attitudes of his time about
servants and social inferiors. Nevertheless, he had as we have seen some flaw
of self-confidence, some absence of certainty, that made him emphasize his

---

* Almost certainly Charles Cardale Babington, also a Shropshire man, from Ludlow, who
graduated the year before Darwin. Nicknamed "Beetles", he became one of the founders of
the Entomological Society and in 1861 was appointed to the chair of botany at Cambridge.

shortcomings when dealing with those in authority. It seems plausible that, when he himself held the authority, he should become confident, assured and even assertive in his dealings.

At this time Darwin clearly held a simple, unquestioning Christian belief, similar to and probably influenced by that of his sister, Caroline. Thus, when in April, 1829, Fox's sister died, Darwin wrote to him, "I feel most sincerely and deeply for you and all your family; but at the same time, as far as any one can, by his own good principles and religion, be supported under such a misfortune, you, I am assured, will know where to look for support. And after so pure and holy a comfort as the Bible affords, I am equally assured how useless the sympathy of all friends must appear, although it be as heartfelt and sincere, as I hope you believe me capable of feeling." Darwin, empathetic always, may simply have been offering Fox, a man destined by character and belief to be a clergyman, the most suitably helpful words he could muster. Yet the passage carries conviction; we know from the *Auto-biography*, too, that when reading Paley, Darwin "did not at that time trouble myself about (his) premises", but rather took them on trust.

If these were his convictions, however, what are we to make of Herbert's testimony, written admittedly sixty years later? According to this, "we had an earnest conversation about going into Holy Orders; I remember his asking me with reference to the questions put by the Bishop in the Ordination Service, 'Do you trust that you are inwardly moved by the Holy Spirit, etc.' whether I would answer in the affirmative; and on my saying 'I could not' he said, 'neither can I, & therefore I cannot take Orders'." It seems obvious that in Darwin's mind his clerical destiny remained very much in question. His doubts imply that religion was potentially open to scrutiny – and what eventually comes under the scrutiny of a Darwin is liable to reveal unsuspected fragilities. It is likely, too, that the beliefs he expressed to his family were different from those he allowed himself when amongst his Cambridge cronies, and that a scepticism acceptable at the University might have been somewhat out of place in Shrewsbury.

By mid-July, 1829, Darwin had sufficiently recovered from his eczema to plan an entomological expedition to Maer. Meanwhile, however, he had stepped for the first time on the public stage, a fact he announced to Fox in a very matter-of-fact style: "You will see my name in Stephens' last number. I am glad of it if it is merely to spite Mr. Jennyngs*." The *Autobiography* gives a more honest account of his exultation: "No poet ever felt more delight at

---

* Darwin's inaccurate spelling of "Jenyns". Rev. Leonard Jenyns was a naturalist, up at Cambridge during the previous decade, a member of the Linnean, the Entomological and Zoological Societies. He was to prove a lifelong friend to Darwin, and also became Henslow's brother-in-law.

seeing in Stephen's *Illustration of British Insects* the magic words 'captured by C. Darwin, Esq.' " To Fox, however, he played his pleasure down, hastening instead to recall earlier days. "I shall not soon forget my first entomological walks with you & poor little Way . . ."

For the rest of that vacation he planned "to lead a perfectly idle & wandering life, always taking care to have as little of home & as much of Woodhouse as possible". Beyond, potential Nemesis lurked – Little Go, which was again beginning to make him distinctly nervous, partly because he had learned that it was to be stricter than before: "they were determined they would make it a very different thing from any previous examination". As a result, "I am sure it will be the very devil to pay amongst all idle men & entomologists" – Darwin continued to equate the energetic pursuit of beetles, whether recognized in print or no, with the generality of student idleness.

In September, Darwin was again a visitor at Fox's home, Osmaston. Shortly afterwards, he attended a music meeting at nearby Birmingham which was, he informed Fox, "the most glorious thing I have ever experienced; and as for Malibran*, words cannot praise her enough, she is quite the most charming person I ever saw." Happiness, however, has its limits; towards the end of the letter he uses a phrase which, to us who know his future, has an ominous ring: "It knocked me up most dreadfully, & I will never attempt again to do two things the same day." During his sickness-ridden middle years, exertion was constantly to "knock him up"; the phrase sounds like a drumbeat throughout his correspondence. For the moment, however, it is heard this once, then vanishes; he still had a decade of physical activity ahead of him.

Around Christmas, Darwin spent three weeks in London, sleeping on an air-cushion mattress at his brother's apartment. He wrote to Fox, "I never was there for so long a time before & enjoyed it much more than I expected". But the year turned; 1830 began its progress. Little Go, avoided once, was now imminent, looming threateningly across Darwin's university path. "I shall if possible withstand temptation & not ride this term", he wrote to Fox in rather tentative resolve. Resolution was rewarded: "I am through my Little Go!!!" he scribbled in jubilation in March, 1830, each exclamation mark a witness to his earlier anxiety. "I am too much exalted to humble myself by apologizing for not having written before. But I assure you before I went in, and when my nerves were in a shattered & weak condition,

---

* María Felicia Garcia, who sang under her first married name of Malibran. She studied under her father, a famous tenor who became a composer and a teacher active on both sides of the Atlantic. One of the greatest contraltos of her day, she died in 1836, still in her twenties. Her brother, also a renowned singing teacher, outlived her by seventy years, dying in 1906, aged 101.

your injured person often rose before my eyes & taunted me with idleness. But I am through, through, through. I could write the whole sheet full with this delightful word." He expected Fox to arrive in Cambridge: "What fun we will have together; what beetles we will catch; it will do my heart good to go once more together to some of our old haunts . . . Heaven protect the beetles and Mr. Jenyns, for we won't leave him a pair in the whole country . . . And now for the time – I think I shall go for a few days to town to hear an opera & see Mr Hope; not to mention my brother also, whom I should have no objection to see."

By the end of August, Fox had made his first visit to Maer and had written about it to Darwin, who was summering with Hope in Barmouth (it was during this stay that he remarked on the entomologist's "egotism & stupidity"). Darwin replied, "I am delighted that we agree so well about the Wedgwoods . . . I trust that Charlotte has driven out of the field your musical enchantress at Ashby. Cannot you imagine how very pleasant I must find Maer. Not one drawback." In September, he was at Maer himself and finding it "just as delightful as ever". He had been energetically occupied with entomology, "& to day have worked so hard that I can hardly see to write . . . But beetles, partridges & every thing else are as nothing to me now that I have got a horse. I am positively in love with him, stands 11 hands & one inch and I think will make a very good hunter."

By November, university matters had become serious again – the degree itself was looming ahead. "I have not stuck an insect this term", wrote Darwin sadly, "and scarcely opened a case . . . really I have not spirits or time to do anything. Reading makes me quite desperate; the plague of getting up all my subjects is next thing to intolerable." In the end, therefore, Cambridge had been reduced for Darwin to the same desperate scramble that it was for the rest. Like them, he imagined he had arrived at the critical moment of his stay there. Not for many years was he to understand that his degree and almost all the work he did for it had been totally irrelevant; even when he understood this, he could not, as we have seen, condone his comparative neglect of the decreed curriculum. Yet this was not to have the slightest impact on his life. What changed him and altered his future was his association with and friendship for Professor Henslow.

One has to realize that, by this second year, Darwin had established a small reputation among Cambridge scientists. As the readily given companionship of men like Hope and Stephens proves – continuing in this the story of his Edinburgh days – he had an intense dedication and a level of success which placed him in a different category from the average up-hill-and-down-dale undergraduate beetle hunter. Insects, like rocks and shells, were items that both young gentlemen and young ladies thought it fashionable to collect. The lecture audiences in London and Edinburgh showed how unscholarly and general was the interest in natural science. It is common to set Darwin against this background and define him as no more than another untutored enthusiast pursuing a spare-time hobby. He was by no means a fully fledged naturalist, but equally he was no frivolous dilettante whiling away a few outdoor hours. He spent time, money and endless effort over his search for specimens and, as a result, had begun to put together one of the better collections in England. He ranged himself, albeit modestly, with men like Jenyns and Hope and Stephens, and they in their turn took him with a seriousness that expressed their respect.

Darwin's friends were under no illusion over the importance to him of entomology, nor over his proficiency in it. This led to one of the pleasantest episodes of his stay at the university – the arrival one day of an unexpected gift, carefully packed and accompanied by a note. "If Mr Darwin will accept the accompanying Coddington's Microscope, it will give peculiar gratification to one who has long doubted whether Mr. Darwin's talents or his sincerity be the more worthy of admiration, and who hopes that the instrument may in some measure facilitate those researches which he has hitherto so fondly and so successfully prosecuted." No signature identified the donor. Darwin, delighted, wrote to Fox. "Some goodhearted Cambridge man has made me a most magnificent anonymous present of a microscope: did you ever hear of such a delightful piece of luck? One would like to know who it was, just to feel obliged to him." This was written in 1831; not for many years did Darwin learn that it was Herbert who had made the gift, but he never forgot it. "I never see that old Microscope", he told Herbert in a letter nearly forty years later, " which to my amazement I received anonymously without thinking with pleasure of our old friendship."

Herbert, almost from the beginning, expected Darwin to become a successful, even an eminent, natural scientist, and he was in a position to know, for, like Fox, he belonged to Henslow's circle. Darwin learned to think of Henslow with a kind of veneration: "His moral qualities were in every way admirable", he wrote in the *Autobiography*. "He was free from every tinge of vanity or other petty feeling; and I never saw a man who thought so little about himself or his own concerns. His temper was imperturbably good, with the most winning and courteous manners; yet, as I have seen, he could be roused by any bad action to the warmest indignation and prompt action." He cited as an example Henslow's attempt to rescue from an enraged crowd two body-snatchers, products of the prevailing law limiting the supply of cadavers for medical dissection, who had been attacked while on their way to prison.

Darwin wrote a very similar assessment of Henslow's character just after the latter's death in 1862. It was published in the *Memoir* edited by Leonard Jenyns – who had recently changed his named to Blomefield – in which the various contributors described their feelings for the lovable Henslow. Darwin recalled his "remarkable power of making the young feel completely at ease with him; though we were all awe-struck with the amount of his knowledge." This ease was due to "the transparent sincerity of his character", "his kindness of heart", "a highly remarkable absence in him of all self-consciousness" and the fact that "his manner to old and distinguished persons and to the youngest student was exactly the same". Like Darwin, Jenyns – or Blomefield – commented on Henslow's equable temper, his absence of vanity or any kind of ill nature, "though very far from blind to the foibles of others". Despite this unruffled benevolence of temperament, "there was no insipidity of character . . . When principle came into play, no power on earth could have turned him one hair's breadth."

Henslow in his time had helped to construct whole areas of Cambridge intellectual life. Joining the older Sedgwick, he had organized the Cambridge Philosophical Society, with its objectives of "promoting Scientific Enquiries and of facilitating the communication of facts connected with the advancement of Philosophy and Natural History"; among the facts that would be communicated were those Darwin included in his letters to Henslow during the voyage of the *Beagle*. Later, Henslow was the main driving force behind the establishment of the Zoological Museum, the nucleus around which the other scientific museums of the university were created. In due course, Henslow became professor of mineralogy and, perhaps more importantly, botany. "His lectures on Botany", wrote Darwin, "were universally popular and as clear as daylight".

More valuable than the formal teaching of this modest and approachable man were the weekly gatherings he organized for students interested in natural history. These enthused and encouraged young men just beginning to get a grasp of the biological sciences, brought them in contact with each other, and provided both a forum for the discussion of what interested them and an informal seminar presided over by one of the university's most distinguished minds: "all who cared for natural history attended these parties". At times, too, those who formed part of his classes in botany would follow him on excursions into the countryside. "He was, on such occasions, in as good spirits as a boy, and laughed as heartily as a boy at the misadventures of those who chased the splendid swallow-tail butterflies across the broken and treacherous fens. After our day's issue we used to dine at some inn or house, and most jovial we then were . . ." So Darwin in his cool fifties, remembering warmer, younger days.

From the very beginning, Darwin found Henslow exceptionally sym-

J.S. Henslow, Darwin's mentor in natural history.

pathetic. It was Fox who had introduced him to the weekly meetings, and so
it was Fox whom he could tell, early in April, 1830, "I have been seeing a
good deal lately of Prof: Henslow; I took a long walk with him the other day:
I like him most exceedingly, he is very goodnatured & agreeable". In May he
again reported frequent meetings with Henslow – "& the more I see of him
the more I like him. I have some thoughts of reading divinity with him the
summer after next." In the event, the *Beagle* adventure intervened; thoughts
of a clerical career slowly faded in the glare of tropical suns, and the shadow
of South American mountains.

In November, 1830, Darwin seems to have missed Fox quite keenly:
"Many many times do I think of our cozy breakfasts & even wish for you to
give me a good scolding for swearing or being out of temper or any of my
hundred faults". It was some compensation that his promenade with Henslow now took place almost every day, "so that I was called by some of the
dons 'the man who walks with Henslow'; and in the evening I was very often
asked to join his family at dinner." It is not surprising to find that, in a letter
to Darwin some ten years later, Henslow – addressing him as "My dear
Brother Benedict" – should have stated, "I know no one beyond the circle of
my own family in whom I feel a more hearty interest . . ."

Darwin, in assessing Henslow, felt that he lacked "original genius", but
had one intellectual quality that may well have influenced Darwin's own
development, so clearly was he to display it: "His strongest taste was to draw
conclusions from long-continued minute observations." If Darwin took any
direct legacy from Henslow, it was perhaps the ability to harness his own
talent for devising straightforwardly pertinent questions to his disciplined
observational powers. In this way by-passing received opinion, Darwin was
eventually to reach conclusions very different from Henslow's own and with
which Henslow at the end of his life would find himself unable to agree, but
his method must have owed much to the lessons he absorbed at Henslow's
fireside, on the professor's botanical field trips and during their frequent
friendly walks together.

By the end of January, 1831, Darwin knew that he had obtained his
degree. His letter to Fox on the subject is curiously subdued.

> I do not know why the degree should make one so miserable, both before &
> afterwards. I recollect you were sufficiently wretched before, & I can assure
> [you] I am now, & what makes it the more ridiculous, I know not what about. I
> believe it is a beautiful provision of nature to make one regret the less leaving
> so pleasant a place as Cambridge; & amongst all its pleasures – I say it once &
> for all – none so great as my friendship for you . . . My plans are not at all
> settled. I think I shall keep this term, & then go & economise at Shrewsbury,
> return & take my degree.

The kind of future that now awaited him was outlined in a letter from a fellow student, George Simpson, who congratulated him somewhat ironically "on your *very very good degree*, tho' I must say I should have been disappointed had you not been a leading man, knowing your predilection for Mathematicks." He himself, although he had been out hunting, was beginning "to think of studying divinity which is more profitable to the soul than field sports . . . I suppose you will shortly look out for a partner for your future Vicarage, as well as a pretty pattern for Nightcaps . . ."

In fact, because Darwin was not formally to receive his degree until the early summer, he remained up at Cambridge for the time being; as he wrote to Fox, "I have so many friends here (Henslow amongst the foremost) that it would make any place pleasant." A few weeks later, he added to this: "I expect to spend a pleasant Spring term, walking & botanizing with Henslow . . ." It is clear that at this time Darwin hung on and valued every word of the older man. During one lecture Henslow praised the beauty of a passage by the late Roman, Egyptian-born Claudian, a poet much given to writing florid panegyrics. Darwin immediately hunted it out; a description of the countryside, it prompted him to simple-minded comment: "There were botanists then before Linnaeus!" He made the remark just before one of Henslow's scientific soirées; he often arrived early for these in order to help arrange the room, setting out the specimens that were to be discussed by the assembled naturalists.

These glimpses of Darwin as a fervent disciple are given us by J.M. Rodwell, a fellow student who became Prebendary of St. Paul's and a noted oriental scholar (he translated the Koran). It is from him, too, that we have the story of Darwin, out with Henslow, seeing on the far side of a ditch a plant he wanted to gather. In fenman fashion, he tried to vault over with the aid of a strong staff. The thick mud held the pole fast; Darwin lost all momentum, hung for a moment clinging to the stick, then slid ignominiously into the ditch. Being Darwin, he stretched out an arm as he descended and plucked the plant, then pulled himself from the mud and, bespattered but triumphant, brought his prize to Henslow. Watkins, who also often walked with Darwin, remembered him "in the meadows between Cambridge & Grantchester, & many is the wretched animal that he unearthed from a rotten willow tree or some other obscure hiding place . . ." With such clues, one can imagine the two men, Henslow and Darwin, walking slowly beside the winding river, behind them the grey, spired and crenallated silhouette of Cambridge, ahead of them the churchtower and village roofs of Grantchester. Henslow will be smiling, his wide, well-shaped mouth benign, a small wind stirring his hair and his greying mutton-chop whiskers. From time to time Darwin, cheeks blazing with health and deepset eyes bright, will break off and frisk busily away, heavyset yet boyish, ranging after plant or insect like a terrier, returning after a while with some new specimen for Henslow, and to continue once more their eager, endless conversation.

Henslow was an infinitely patient, infinitely diplomatic teacher. When Darwin in ignorance one day discovered some fact already long established in botany, it was to Henslow that he rushed in his excitement. When he looked back, Darwin realised that no "other Professor of Botany could have helped laughing . . . But he agreed how interesting the phenomenon was, and explained its meaning, but made me clearly understand how well it was known; so I left him not in the least mortified, but well pleased at having discovered for myself so remarkable a fact, but determined not to be in such a hurry again to communicate my discoveries." All his life, Darwin was to leap unrestrainedly to conclusions; it was perhaps from Henslow that he learned, not only how to verify, support or falsify these by endless close observation, but also to be cautiously slow in making them public. When the time came to state his most controversial assumptions, it would take him twenty years to gather his evidence and formulate his theories. Yet even as a student the fundamental characteristic of a scientist was well established in him, and Henslow was not slow to recognize it: "What a fellow that Darwin is for asking questions!" he would remark; one can almost hear the sigh that must have modified the admiration in his voice. Darwin's untiring propensity to ask questions may have wearied Henslow, but as a teacher born, dedicated and boundlessly talented, he cannot have helped but respond to it.

Partly through Henslow, Darwin met another man who, at rather greater distance, would attend his progress from undergraduate to world figure, one of the heavyweights of scientific polemics who was, in 1831, already the president of the Geological Society: Adam Sedgwick. In 1818 he had been appointed Professor of Geology at Cambridge; he was to hold the chair until he died fifty-five years later. Knowing him brought Darwin in direct contact with the controversies by which geology had been racked since before the turn of the century. In those debates, Sedgwick had been among the foremost figures, though – to his credit – by no means unwavering in his views.

Sedgwick had begun in the conviction that the truth of divine revelation could never be falsified by scientific truth – the latter existed to clarify rather than contradict the former. This led him to adopt the extreme catastrophist position of accepting the Biblical Flood as an event accurately described in Genesis and true in geological fact. From this he went on to adopt, like Jameson and many others, the full Wernerian hypothesis; the world's rocks were sedimentary, laid down through the wide silting of the floors of ancient oceans. In time, however, although he never entirely gave up the catastrophist position, he did alter his allegiance from Werner to Hutton.

A. Sedgwick, geology professor who became Darwin's implacable opponent.

This transfer from Neptune to Vulcan perhaps needs a Virgil to record it; we must make do with Charles Lyell, who described Sedgwick on 7 June, 1829, as having "decided on four *or more* deluges", though with the proviso that one should "doubt, not dogmatise" when considering the nature of such floods. Three days later, in an account of a meeting on the subject at the Geological Society, Lyell was reporting, "Sedgwick, now president, closed the debate with a terribly anti-diluvialist declaration. For he has come round . . ." By the end of October he could write of Sedgwick, "Throws overboard all the diluvian hypothesis; is vexed he ever lost time about such a complete humbug; . . . says he lost two years by having also started a Wernerian". Sedgwick himself did not so easily admit conversion; however, in 1831 he wrote:

> It was indeed a most unwarranted conclusion, when we assumed the contemporaneity of all the superficial gravel on the earth. We saw the clearest traces of diluvial action, and we had, in our sacred histories, the record of a general deluge. On this double testimony it was, that we gave unity to a vast succession of phaenomena, not one of which we perfectly comprehended, and under the name of *diluvium*, classed them all together.

As he admitted when in his presidential address of 1831 he stood up "thus publicly to read my recantation" to the assembled geologists, the fact those formations which had been thought evidence of the Flood contained no human remains was enough to undermine that claim.

Thus the terms of natural science's most fundamental discussion, rumours of which will have reached him in Edinburgh, however briefly he attended Jameson's lectures, will once more have presented themselves for Darwin's attention. In the *Autobiography* Darwin tells us that he was "so sickened with lectures in Edinburgh that I did not even attend Sedgwick's eloquent and interesting lectures. Had I done so I should probably have become a geologist sooner than I did." Rodwell, however, had two memories of Darwin's reacting to Sedgwick's lecture hall assertions: in one of these, typically, he tested Sedgwick's claim that a certain spring contained carbonate of lime which it deposited as a white coat on nearby twigs and branches. Darwin, finding that this was indeed the case, left a bush in the water and, when it was completely coated, presented it to Sedgwick, who afterwards used it in his lectures.

> On another occasion we were talking over one of Sedgwick's lectures in which he had spoken of the enlarged views both of Time & Space that Geology could give, he said to me – It strikes *me* that all our knowledge about the structure of our Earth is very much like what an old hen wd know of the hundred-acre field in a corner of which she is scratching! – & afterwards, "What a capital hand is Sedgwick for drawing large Cheques upon the Bank of Time!" – which of

course was a reference to some speculation of Sedgwick's as to the probable antiquity of the world.

If Rodwell's memory, in 1882, was accurate – verbatim accounts of sentences spoken must always be suspect, even when half a century has not intervened – Darwin may have attended at least a handful of Sedgwick's lectures; if the second story is true, he will certainly have considered the arguments that bore upon the age of the earth, even if he dismissed the more radical speculations. His tone filtered through Rodwell's recollections certainly sounds sceptical even about Sedgwick's reluctant and limited unorthodoxies.

Another witness, J.W. Heaviside, a mathematical cleric who achieved some distinction in both his careers (he became tutor to a royal prince, as well as Canon of Norwich), has memories different both in detail and in mood. "About the time of our intimacy Geology was coming to the front as a science – [Darwin] certainly at that time avidently [*sic*] took up the subject – and I can remember how genially he bore with the chatt of those, who like myself . . . knew nothing about the subject, as to Moses being a better authority òn mundane cosmogony than he & the geologists." From this testimony one may assume that such questions occupied at least some part of Darwin's mind long before they were more acutely brought to his attention by all that he experienced during the voyage of the *Beagle*. One may perhaps assume even more: the fact that Heaviside places Moses on one side, championed by the ignorant, while on the other "he & the geologists" held to an alternative view, suggests that Darwin may have stepped out of the Biblical straitjacket rather earlier than most people have imagined. In any event, he may have moved from a fundamentalist acceptance of Genesis at least as far as Sedgwick had.

Teachers, however, need not be present in the flesh: sometimes their books are sufficient. During this time at Cambridge Darwin read two books that influenced him profoundly. One was by the astronomer John Herschel, and had the slightly forbidding title, *Preliminary Discourse on the Study of Natural Philosophy*. It presented as virtues with a wide general application the disciplines demanded by scientific methods. The "taste for scientific inquiry" provided "an inexhaustible source of pure and exciting contemplations"; the scientist, "his faculties in constant exercise, and his thoughts perpetually on the wing" was necessarily diverted from all "frivolous, unworthy and destructive pursuits". Herschel considered all the various branches of science, pondered the limits of usefulness of mathematics and suggested that certain spheres of study – he included, optimistically, chemistry – needed no highly developed mathematical skills. That among these were the natural sciences must have uplifted Darwin's spirits considerably.

Herschel was a propagandist for science, exhilarated by the challenge implied in human ignorance, and Darwin's high regard for his book may have played its part in the decisions he was to make about the course of his own life.

Another such was *Personal Narrative of Travels to the Equinoctial Regions of the New Continent*, by Friedrich Heinrich Alexander, Baron von Humboldt. Forty years older than Darwin, he was one of the creators of modern geography, as well as an endlessly resilient and resourceful traveller. The information he brought back was often based both on knowledge and observation; his speculations about how the living organisms of the world fitted in with their environment and each other were therefore informed and valuable. In 1796 he made a long and scientifically fruitful journey to South and Central America, studying the whole range of natural phenomena from volcanoes to insects and the whole range of natural processes from earthquakes to ocean currents. At the same time he did not flinch from presenting these observations in a prose that was always literate, sometimes mellifluous and occasionally overblown. His descriptions of Tenerife in the Canaries Darwin copied out and read aloud to Henslow and his other companions.

Watkins, in his memories of Darwin, recalled "the long & very interesting conversation that we had about Brazilian scenery & tropical vegetation of all sorts. Nor do I forget the way & the vehemence with which he rubbed his chin when he got excited on such subjects & discoursed eloquently on lianas & orchids & other treasures of the almost impenetrable Forest." It seems plausible that this fascination was a consequence of his devotion to Humboldt's book. If from Herschel Darwin gathered a view of science as an all-embracing discipline, from Humboldt he derived a sense of the unity of nature. It was Humboldt's ambition to present the natural world as a single interlocking entity, a process to which all its parts contributed, each affected by all the others. This vision enabled him among other things to take the first steps towards establishing meteorology as a science. And it was this vision that Darwin kept constantly before him when considering the exotic phenomena that surrounded him on his excursions from the *Beagle,* and later when he was struggling with the ecological concepts, as yet undefined by science, that underlay his evolutionary theories. No wonder that when, in 1845, he wrote to his friend Hooker about Humboldt's sad decline into senility (he was ninety when he died in 1859), he said, "If you see him again . . . say that I never forget that my whole course of life is due to having read and re-read as a youth his *Personal Narrative*".

With his degree examinations over, Darwin in 1831 settled to an idyllic Spring and early Summer. Only a certain shortage of money caused him any dissatisfaction. Fox invited him to Osmaston again, but he was forced to refuse. "The Governor has given me a £200 note to pay my debts, & I must be economical. On the per contra side of the question, Henslow's lectures come into play & I should have been sorry to have missed even one of them." He added that he saw a great deal of Henslow, "whom I do not know if I love or respect most." Money, or its absence, dragged him back to Shrewsbury instead; in July he wrote complainingly to Fox, "I arrived at this stupid place about three weeks ago . . . I am staying here on exactly the same principle that a person chooses to remain in the King's Bench." In his mind's eye, The Mount had turned, monstrously, into a debtors' prison.

This exaggeration of his own poverty – not dissimilar to Fanny Owen's exclamations of despair – does not mean that Darwin was unaware of genuine suffering. The affair of a fellow student named H. Mathew shows Darwin as a young man who, though compassionate, was fully aware of complicated kinds of suffering and degradation. Heaviside was at Sidney Sussex with Mathew and recalled:

> [Darwin] was much at Sidney & I think his principal inducement in coming into our set, was that he was rather fascinated by a man there, named Mathew, a man of considerable ability, a fair scholar & tolerably read in general literature & with manners that attracted towards him many . . . Mathew unfortunately was a very intemperate man & I think [Darwin] took great pains to try & break him of his ill habits but not then with much success. It was strange that Makepeace Thackerey* was equally attracted by Mathew & was equally concerned to put him straight.

It is from Mathew himself that we learn more about his situation, since he wrote to Darwin early in February, 1831, from Cecil Street, just off the Strand. He complained bitterly of being in London "without a human being to exchange a word with . . . I can not describe the horrors and depression of spirits to which it subjects me." For fifteen shillings a week, he wrote, "I am furnished with a Study, Sitting Room, Bed room, Kitchen and Dressing Room. Is not this a splendid establishment for a single person? There is one circumstance which *does* however slightly diminish the grandeur of the thing and that is the painful fact that this long enumeration of apartments is only one room with many names." His circumstances, however, were "a mighty secret" and Darwin was to let no one know he was in London, "much less in such a degraded condition".

He scribbled down desperate plans – he would write prose, he would write

---

* This was of course the novelist, author of *Vanity Fair.* He was not strictly a contemporary of Darwin, but Heaviside commented, "I remember saying to Thackeray not long before his death how strange it was, that so many of his early acquaintance who had taken high University honors had subsided comparatively into oblivion, whilst he & Charles Darwin both of whom were little appreciated among their fellows for their specialities, had made European reputations for themselves . . ."

verse, he would pawn his coat, he would pawn his books. But poverty and solitude were not his only troubles, nor were his troubles only his own. "As if I had not curses enough to bear in my own proper person I am harassed with moaning supplications, letters from my wife and another whom you know, full of entreaties to be allowed to join me and vehement assertions of their being willing to go through anything with me even to living on potatoes and salt. All this is very fine, but I have not even potatoes and salt to give them." It is hard to know whether he is here referring to two women, or to a woman and child.

A little further on he made this Dickensian situation even clearer. "I forgot to add to my history of blessings that I am going tomorrow before a magistrate about my bastard, with one sovereign in my pocket to meet law expences, arrears, and advance for a quarter – I suppose you guess by this time where I shall lodge tomorrow night – I do not date my letter because I do not mean to let you know where I am . . ." The nobility of this self-restraint is rendered somewhat suspect by that fact that the address has in fact been included; the letter is an indirect plea for help, to be understood in the context of a society to which there was, so to speak, no bottom. Today, we are used to the organized compassion of the state. It creates a net which catches the deprived and the unfortunate, and prevents their falling into the last desperation of poverty. Not so the Britain in which Mathew (and the mother of his child; and the child) suffered and which Dickens portrayed. In that society, once individuals fell through the layers of which it was composed, nothing and no one had the slightest obligation to offer assistance, at least until the doors of the Poorhouse had finally clanged shut behind them. A haphazard private charity helped some, but by its nature could not provide security for all. (It would, indeed, have considered such provision dangerous, even immoral, undermining the useful urge to work long hours for low pay.)

Mathew appears to have been among the fortunate; Darwin responded to his unspoken request. "I answer your kind letter", wrote Mathew twelve days after his first approach, "on the spirits engendered by a pint of porter, the days of gin are over. I answer for your generous remittance with a beggar's gratitude with thanks, though I am not yet practiced enough in the profession not to feel ashamed as I write. Do not think meanly of me. I assure you I had the hard choice of accepting your kindness or a jail, for I had already pawned my watch."

Once more he was making plans: he would keep himself by writing reviews; meanwhile he would spend two years working on poems and a book, or books. If he had had no success at the end of that time, he would have to reconsider. He felt lighthearted enough to tackle Darwin on a literary point: "And you dare to lift up your voice against the immortal Shelley, as if he was an insect . . . I wish I had you here in my garret where there is not room to run away. I would persecute you for hours." But, relenting, he paid Darwin a grateful compliment: "Most humanized of insect killers".

Somewhat later, Mathew sent Darwin a further bulletin. Beginning with protestations of lifelong affection – "Once for all I do love you and shall ever, come what may to either of us" – he went on to say that he was now . . .

> at home in the bosom of my family (as the novel writers have it) and I know of no bosom which I had not rather lie in. I came here like the prodigal son but was received more like the fatted calf. My father is fierce, my brother cold and my sisters in tears. Every post brings a Dun, and every Dun a scene. My father abuses me for wasting my talents, though he never discovered that I had such things until they were irrecoverably thrown away. But such is the trick of governors.

He had tried to have his poems published, "and received a civil note in reply beginning with compliments and concluding with 'Sorry that the poetical department was occupied', what a phrase, poetical department. Who ever heard of the department of Apollo." Finally, he had pawned almost all his clothes to pay for the coach and so had returned ignominiously home.

He spared a paragraph from his own affairs to ask Darwin about his. "Have you bottled any more beetles, or impaled any butterflies." He wondered, in a rather laboured fashion, about Darwin's political opinions – it was the year before the first Reform Act was passed. "Or are you still old quiet poco curante Darwin* caring for naught but your gin bottle and its constant accompaniment philosophy." He appears to have been a man given to swift and deep infatuations – "I have seen her who makes all others little worth seeing," he wrote. He had called the mother of his child his "wife"; this was clearly someone else: "Oh God what a woman; and then I feel myself tied to a fool. The chain drags heavily." Perhaps he was, after all, legally married; the "wife" was another woman, this paragon yet a third. In any case, in a moment he had moved on to praise Shelley once again. So Mathew passed out of Darwin's life; one feels that he was somehow outmatched by Cambridge and London, as well as the victim of his own excesses. He mistook ambition for ability; even if he possessed the ability, he had not the stamina to deploy it. It takes time to impress an uninterested world.

---

* Poco curante, an Italian term meaning one who cares for nothing, was one of the pedagogic insults with which Dr. Butler tried at Shrewsbury to startle Darwin out of "idleness". It made a deep impression on Darwin, for "as I did not understand what he meant it seemed to me a fearful reproach".

Did Darwin later ever think of him? His own situation was very different, secure both financially and emotionally. Yet he too searched for recognition, offering the world no more than his talents. That there were risks in such a course Mathew's experiences brought home to the observer. The reiterated lessons of his youth taught Darwin, if he cared to learn, that there were few advantages in recklessness. Perhaps Mathew's history reinforced Darwin's own tendency to caution. Not that in the end this beleaguered poet did so much worse than many of Darwin's other friends. Writing in 1882, Heaviside could relay that in due course he was "altogether weaned from his intemperate habits, married a person of good character but much beneath him in social life, obtained a small living & died about twenty years ago after being paralysed for some years before his death"*

This glimpse of a family far colder and much more bitter than his own, with a son unsupported by love or money, did not in that summer of 1831 lighten Darwin's disgruntled mood. Perhaps underlying this was an unease at having ended his three years at Cambridge, with the need looming to make new choices. For relief, he turned to a plan he had conceived of taking a party of fellow naturalists – he hoped that Henslow would be among them – on an expedition to the Canary Islands. Even before he had read the Humboldt passage to them, "I had talked about the glories of Teneriffe, and some of the party declared they would endeavour to go there; but I think that they were only half in earnest." Darwin, on the contrary, seized on the idea. It meant a chance to visit the tropics, Humboldt's tropics. It meant the possibility of gathering undreamed-of specimens for his entomological cabinet. It meant, too, that for another few months no firm decision would have to be taken about his future. Perhaps a whole winter might pass before that question reared up once more. To this point in his life, he had managed to keep at bay the necessary duties he had been asked to perform; he had side-stepped medicine, while at Cambridge he had done just enough to take his degree, on the slightly brighter side of mediocre. Meanwhile, he had pursued with a ferocity his unofficial status disguises from us, as it had from himself, his real and absorbing interest, natural history, expressed for the moment in his passion for entomology, but showing increasing signs of broadening out. With the end of his student days, he must have felt that these

---

* The central figure in this drama was almost certainly Henry Mathew or Matthew, who entered the university in 1827, spent a year at Trinity before transferring to Sidney Sussex, and took his degree in 1832. He was indeed popular, being elected President of the Union in 1830. Poverty, dissipation and a period spent away from Cambridge would explain the five years it took him to graduate. The final letter to Darwin is postmarked "Bridgewater", a town in Somerset – Matthew's father was rector of nearby Kilve. He himself eventually became rector of Eversholt, in Bedfordshire, and died in his fifties after what was described as "nearly 20 years of patient suffering". This bears out Heaviside's little biographical sketch.

activities, which he himself had at times equated with idleness, were under threat. Even if he managed to maintain his scientific interests, he would as a country parson be far from the Hopes or the Henslows, whose support and companionship had helped him so decisively in the past. Yet all such fears were, almost certainly, inarticulate and unsuspected. No alternative existed to the course that had provisionally been mapped out for him. He could, like his brother, abandon all thought of an official career, but the cost might well have been – or might have seemed to him – the contempt of his father. It is no wonder that for a few weeks the Canaries expedition appeared like a reprieve, however temporary, and that he seized on it with a vigour none of his friends could match.

In a letter to Shrewsbury, early that July, he said, "All the while I am writing now my head is running about the Tropics: in the mornings I go & gaze at Palm-trees in the hot-house & come home & read Humboldt: my enthusiasm is so great I can hardly sit still in my chair . . . I never will be easy till I see the peak of Teneriffe & the great Dragon tree; sandy, dazzling plains, & gloomy silent forest are alternately uppermost in my mind . . . I have written myself into a Tropical glow. Good bye." One imagines him sprawled in his chair, spreadeagled by the heat and burden of his dreams. To Fox he wrote, "The Canary scheme goes on very prosperously. I am working like a tiger for it, at present. Spanish & Geology; the former I find as intensely stupid as the latter most interesting . . . I have seen a good deal of (Jenyns) lately & the more I see him the more I like him. – I feel just the same towards another man whom I used formerly to dislike that is Ramsay* of Jesus, who is the most likely person . . . to be my companion to the Canaries." By then, Darwin had gone to the lengths of enquiring, through a London merchant, about suitable ships. Two days after writing to Fox, Darwin gave Henslow rather more detailed information. "Passage 20£: ships touch & return during the months of June to February. – But not seeing myself the Broker, the two most important questions remain unanswered. viz. whether it means June inclusive & how often they sail . . . I hope you continue to fan your Canary ardor: I read & reread Humboldt, do you do the same, & I am sure nothing will prevent us seeing the great Dragon Tree." But this enormous tree, its trunk nearly fifty feet around, which Humboldt had described, was after all not quite enough to fan Henslow's "Canary ardor". By the end of August, Darwin was writing to Fox, "The Canary

---

* Marmaduke Ramsay, son of a Scottish baronet, a Cambridge tutor some dozen years older than Darwin, who had graduated in 1818. He was one of the group that clustered about Henslow. He must have been in his last illness even as Darwin was writing; his early death that summer shocked them all. On 24 August Henslow, in a letter of the utmost importance to Darwin, began by suggesting that they "condole together upon the loss of our inestimable friend Ramsay . . ."

scheme does not take place till next June. I am sorry to hear that Henslow's chance of coming is very remote. I had hoped it was daily growing less so." Probably Henslow had never taken the expedition very seriously – Jenyns, his brother-in-law, claimed in later years never even to have heard of it. Had Henslow been as full of it as Darwin obviously was, it is unlikely that he would not have told his fellow clergyman and naturalist, a relative and a friend, something about it.

In the meantime, a more domestic expedition had been promised Darwin. He had been urged by Henslow and persuaded by his Canary Islands plan to develop his geological knowledge. As a result, he had bought a clinometer for twenty-five shillings and, leaning the tables in his room at various angles, had, as he reported to Henslow, "measured them as accurately as any Geologist going could do". He had not yet done any field-work, however, having "only indulged in hypotheses; but they are such powerful ones, that I suppose, if they were put into action but for one day, the world would come to an end." Darwin's youthful joke was, of course, to come to mature, if metaphoric, fruition; one wonders, all the same, what thoughts had been stirred in him by the first serious impact of geology. Perhaps underlying his remark there was, as Prof. Gruber has proposed, a pervasive and wholly orthodox catastrophism. In any case, he began at this time to make a simple map of the strata and deposits around Shrewsbury. To guide him further, Henslow had asked Adam Sedgwick, due to continue his examination of the rock formations of North Wales, to take him as companion. In his letter of 11 July, Darwin was a little anxious – "I have not heard from Prof: Sedgwick so I am afraid he will not pay the Severn formations a visit" – but by the beginning of August, Sedgwick had arrived.

He was to spend the night at The Mount; that evening, during a conversation Darwin had with him, he said something which the younger man was never to forget. A labourer had found a tropical shell in a gravel pit near Shrewsbury and Darwin had offered to buy it. The man's refusal seemed proof that he had not devised the story for profit, and Darwin asked Sedgwick what he thought about it. He replied that most probably someone had thrown the shell away and to Darwin, looking back much later in the *Autobiography,* this seemed the likeliest explanation. But then Sedgwick went further. He said that if the shell had really been embedded there, "it would be the greatest misfortune to geology, as it would overthrow all that we know about the superficial deposits of the midland counties". Darwin was nonplussed: why was Sedgwick not "delighted at so wonderful a fact as a tropical shell being found near the surface in the middle of England"? For the first time he began properly to understand what had previously been no more than words on a page to him – "that science consists in grouping facts so that general laws or conclusions may be drawn from them".

What follows from this is that a discovery of too radical a nature creates such conceptual turmoil that most people's sense of security will lead them to resist it. Whole areas of thought must otherwise undergo what may be violent changes in order that it can be accommodated. Facts, in other words, have consequences that are broad, far-reaching, fundamental. They do not stand alone, but relate to general conclusions. These are lessons that Darwin learned, perhaps beginning from this moment. Throughout the *Transmutation Notebooks,* in which ten years later he worked out the basis for his theories, he was quite overtly conscious of the way in which facts and hypotheses had constantly to be tested against each other – and that of the two, it was facts which were primary.

On 5 August, he entered North Wales at Sedgwick's side. They began their detailed survey to the sound of thunder crashing about Snowdonia's peaks and sodden by an irresistible downpour. Then and in the days that followed, Sedgwick would send Darwin off on a course parallel to his own, "telling me to bring back specimens of the rocks and to mark the stratification on a map". They worked their way westward across the Vale of Clwyd; in Cwm Idwal Darwin remembered how carefully they examined every detail of the rocks, "but neither of us saw a trace of the wonderful glacial phenomena all around us". Yet, as he remarked, if the valley "had still been filled by a glacier, the phenomena would have been less distinct than they now are". It was an example, which he only understood much later, of how easily one can overlook what has not yet been observed by anyone else.

At Capel Curig, Darwin left Sedgwick to continue on his own (in mid-September, the latter was still busily engaged, reporting with professorial self-satisfaction, "I have now been at real hard work, cracking the rocks of Caernarvonshire for rather more than three weeks . . ."). He himself set off across the wilds of Merioneth, travelling directly southwest "by compass and map", his objective the vacation centre at Barmouth, "to see some Cambridge friends who were reading there". Was this an attempt to have one last, small undergraduate fling? His Canaries expedition had been postponed for a full year; Henslow's lack of involvement in it must in any case have dampened his own enthusiasm. The study of divinity awaited him, with its enforced acceptance of doctrines about which he was far from certain. And then? The parsonage, a convenient marriage, lifelong stability: an ideal programme for the Darwin of the 1850s and 1860s. For a vigorous young man fascinated by the scientific romanticism of a Humboldt, aching to see the brilliant coasts and forests of the tropics, already accepted as a near equal by some of the country's most eminent entomologists, it lacked the attractions of activity and scope.

Certainly there were advantages to be found in the life of a country clergyman: there would be leisure enough, sport enough, even science enough, provided he practiced it locally; and with all that, an infinite security. His religious doubts, such as they were, concerned points of theology – his faith as a whole was secure. In short, a country vicarage would offer him a life devised by, designed for, and occupied by gentlemen. Nevertheless, it would remain a life chosen by him only for the want of one more congenial. If, with Henslow and Sedgwick among his examples, he looked forward in due course to a university post rather than a country living, he gave no sign of it.

Despite his severely limited choices, therefore, it is possible that Darwin, in the private turmoil of his thoughts, had still not finally made up his mind – or had not, at least, completely accepted what seemed the inevitable decision. If that was so, then his advance on Barmouth, arrow-straight across the hills and valleys of that almost unoccupied land, can be seen as an attempt to recapture for a few days more the careless certainties and well-defined doubts of the student days that were now over.

But then, after all, September was about to open, offering its autumn vistas of legalized marksmanship and bloodshed. Despite his earlier vow to Herbert that he would shoot no more, he was soon turning away from Barmouth, with its last taste of undergraduate glories, and hurrying back to Shrewsbury, intending to go on very soon to Maer – "for at that time I should have thought myself mad to give up the first days of partridge-shooting for geology or any other science". Waiting for him at The Mount was a letter in the now familiar handwriting of Henslow. It must have been with the slight smile of one anticipating the jovial messages of an old friend that he broke the seal.

The letter was dated 24 August, 1831. It began with the condolences over Ramsay's death. Had Darwin in fact had earlier news of that? If not, it must have been a distressing shock so abruptly to learn of what had happened to his intended travelling companion. The next sentence, however, may well have surprised him even more, sweeping away as it did his own puny plans and substituting for them the dramatic proposals of the real world.

> I will not now dwell upon this painful subject [wrote Henslow of their grief over their friend] as I shall hope to see you shortly, fully expecting that you will eagerly catch at the offer which is likely to be made you of a trip to Tierra del Fuego, and home by the East Indies. I have been asked by Peacock* . . . to recommend him a Naturalist as companion to Captain Fitz-Roy, employed by Government to survey the southern extremity of America. I have stated that I

---

* Yet another clergyman-scientist, a one-time Dean of Cambridge who was Lowndean Professor of Astronomy at Cambridge University.

consider you to be the best qualified person I know of who is likely to undertake such a situation. I state this not in the supposition of your being a *finished* naturalist, but as amply qualified for collecting, observing, and noting, anything worthy to be noted in Natural History. Peacock has the appointment at his disposal, and if he cannot find a man willing to take the office, the opportunity will probably be lost. Captain Fitz-Roy wants a man (I under-stand) more as a companion than a mere collector, and would not take anyone, however good a naturalist, who was not recommended to him likewise as a *gentleman*. Particulars of salary &c., I know nothing. The voyage is to last two years, and if you take plenty of books with you, anything you please may be done. You will have ample opportunities at command. In short, I suppose there never was a finer chance for a man of zeal and spirit; Captain Fitz-Roy is a young man. What I wish you to do is instantly to come and consult with Peacock (at No. 7 Suffolk Street, Pall Mall East, or else at the University Club), and learn further particulars. Don't put any modest doubts or fears about your disqualifications, for I assure you I think you are the very man they are in search of; so conceive yourself to be tapped on the shoulder by your bum-bailiff and affectionate friend.

Below the signature, "J.S. Henslow", there stood a postscript: "The expedi-tion is to sail on 25th September (at earliest), so there is no time to be lost".

It must have seemed to Darwin, as he put the letter down, as if the jaws of the future had at the last moment relented: poised to devour him, they had relaxed into a smile. The pretty parsonage with its dutiful wife, its necessary children and its ordered existence had, apparently, receded. It remained, a possibility that at times was delightful to contemplate; its reality, however, was suddenly something he did not yet have to take seriously. One sees him, rearing up, bright-eyed, tall, vigorous, the letter held high, his voice excited. "Susan!" he calls in this imagined scene. "Granny! Caroline!" The sister-hood comes running. A dog barks. Somewhere outside a horse clatters across stone. "Catherine!"

Did he, one wonders, call his father?

The main sources for Part One were:

The *Autobiography* of Charles Darwin, edited by Nora Barlow; volume one of *Emma Darwin: a Century of Family Letters,* edited by Henrietta Litchfield; the Wedgwood family papers at Keele University; and, above all, the Darwin papers at Cambridge University Library, of which the material from the Owen letters, much of the correspondence between Charles and his sisters and brother, and many of his Edinburgh and Cambridge notes and records have never been published before.

Other sources include the *Life and Letters* of Charles Darwin, edited by Francis Darwin; the *Life and Letters* of Dr. Butler, edited by S. Butler; and biographies of Darwin by De Beer, Ward and Woodall. The unpublished letters from Darwin to W.D. Fox can be found in the library of Christ's College, Cambridge.

Many books contributed scientific information, notably De Beer's *Charles Darwin: Evolution by Natural Selection,* Eiseley's *Darwin's Century,* Gillispie's *Genesis and Geology,* Hardy's *The Living Stream* and Himmelfarb's *Darwin and the Darwinian Revolution,* as well as the works of Buffon, Cuvier, Paley, Playfair and Lyell.

Burke's *Peerage* and *Landed Gentry,* and the *Dictionary of National Biography* have supplied most of the details about the people and families mentioned.

PART TWO

A Man of Enlarged Curiosity

1

> The undertaking would be useless as regards his profession, but looking upon him as a man of enlarged curiosity, it affords him such an opportunity of seeing men and things as happens to few.
>
> *Josiah Wedgwood.*

Now began a confused, and confusing, to and fro of messages and visitors, the result of which was that Darwin, himself strangely passive and indecisive, almost lost the *Beagle* appointment. If this was the crucial moment of Darwin's life, it also played a part in creating his father's reputation as one of the sterner tyrants of the age. For it was almost entirely Dr. Robert's doubts that persuaded the young Charles to begin by rejecting so astonishing an opportunity. We, primed with the hindsight of historians, can hardly believe that Henslow's invitation could have seemed anything other than fortunate and filled with promise. The Doctor's reluctance appears obtuse and his lack of support for his son monstrous. Yet if Charles had finally rejected the proffered place on the expedition, he would not have been the first to do so.

Leonard Jenyns remembered the sequence of events. "Captain Fitzroy was a great friend of Peacock, Fellow of Trinity and eminent mathematician, – and said to him – 'Can't you find me a man in our university to go out with me in my voyage as a Naturalist? I shd like to take one with me.' Whereupon Peacock came and applied to Henslow and myself . . . – and Henslow would have doubtless much liked to go & been very fit for the place. But being a married man with a family & holding University appointments he declined. – He & Peacock then pressed me to go; – and I was not at all inclined to it – though Henslow was very anxious I should consent. I took a day to consider of it; – at the end of which I was quite determined against going – thinking it not quite right to give up my parish & clerical work for such a purpose . . ." Jenyns, of course, was a university friend of Charles's and himself a naturalist as well as a clergyman, and prominent among the country's natural historians. It was by no means strange that he should have been thought a good choice, nor that he considered Darwin suitable for the post he had turned down. "Henslow and myself then both thought of Darwin, as a man in every way suited for the appointment . . ."

It is possible, too – though Jenyns stated he knew nothing of the story – that another clergyman-naturalist educated at Cambridge during the 1820s was approached before Darwin and turned the invitation down. This was

M.J. Berkeley, who later played a different part, applying his knowledge of fungi and algae to the vast collection of botanical specimens that Darwin eventually brought back. What all this makes clear, however, is that Dr. Robert's hesitant attitude was by no means unique to him. The trip was bound to be lengthy, hazardous and disruptive of normal life. The fact that, looking back, we see it as essential to Darwin's development does not mean that, looking forward, anyone would have been justified in coming to that conclusion.

Peacock's original letter to Henslow had pointed out that the expedition "will furnish . . . a rare opportunity for a naturalist & it would be a great misfortune that it should be lost . . ." Discovering that his letter was too late for the post, he had in his enthusiasm added a further note: "What a glorious opportunity this would be for forming collections for our museums: Do write to me immediately & take care that the opportunity is not lost . . ." It is not surprising, therefore, that he should have sent a covering letter of his own with Henslow's invitation to Darwin. In this he said that he had taken the opportunity "of seeing Captain Beaufort at the Admiralty (the Hydrographer) & of stating to him the offer which I have to make to you: he entirely approves of it & you may consider the situation as at your absolute disposal." Peacock also strongly recommended Captain Fitzroy, "a public spirited & zealous officer, of delightful manners & greatly beloved by all his brother officers: he went with Captain Beechey* & spent 1500L in bringing over & educating at his own charge 3 natives of Patagonia: he engages at his own expense an artist at 200 a year to go with him: you may be sure therefore of having a very pleasant companion, who will enter heartily into all your views." Pointing out that the *Beagle* was due to sail at the end of September, he added that Darwin "must lose no time in making known your acceptance to Captain Beaufort", but thought it necessary to include a short paragraph on money: "The Admiralty are not disposed to give a salary, though they will furnish you with an official appointment & every accommodation: if a salary should be required however I am inclined to think that it would be granted."

It must have been with the impact of a full broadside, the shock of an overwhelming cannonade, that this letter and Henslow's landed among the equable certainties and undramatic expectations of Shrewsbury. One can imagine the tensions in that restrained household, the debates among the sisters, the baffled comprehension of the servants, the sense of the great world having sent its envoys to startle the uneventful Shropshire harmony.

---

* An error by Peacock – it was Capt. P.P. King who commanded the first expedition on which the *Beagle* sailed, as companion ship to the *Adventure*.

The vast father, settled in authority, and the stripling son doubtful of his worth will have been closeted together, the conviction of the former, many times tried, long observed and trusted, set against the uncertain enthusiasm of the latter. It was an uneven confrontation; Charles, even at this crucial moment, allowed himself to be swept by habits of conformity and obedience into an agreement we assume, but do not know, was grudging, with Dr. Robert's negative.

Was it, however, in a suppressed turmoil of revolt or with some secret relief that Charles sat down on 30 August to write Henslow his letter of refusal? His geological excursion with Sedgwick was behind him; ahead beckoned the shooting months of autumn, partridges and pheasants crowding the coverts, ordained sacrifices to the pleasures of the gentry. His future had been charted out, directing him with increasing precision toward his destiny of a suitable marriage, a comfortable parsonage. All his life he had been passionately a naturalist, yet all his life that pursuit had been, at least nominally, peripheral, ancillary, no more than a hobby. He was now being asked to acknowledge that his interest in science was much more than that, was sufficiently central for him to give up several years to its practice, to make it for that period the main activity of his life, and to abide by whatever distortions this would create in his career, his prospects and his relationships. It seems clear that until this moment he had – at least when in Shrewsbury; and perhaps always in his heart of hearts – agreed with his family that natural history was a distraction from the real business of his life, was, indeed, an interest that had hampered him, held him back and undermined his chances of success. Suddenly he was being asked to reverse this opinion and, against all his training, make what he most loved not his recreation, but his work. It was a reversal so profound, a release from discipline so abrupt, he must in ordinary humanity have flinched from it.

The prospect of the journey itself, and the time that it would take, were daunting enough in themselves. He had been north to Scotland, west to Wales, east to Cambridge, but except for his single "lark" to Paris four years earlier, had never travelled beyond British coasts. Suddenly, he was being offered the world. It was true that he had been planning his excursion to the Canaries, but this was to have been a gentle prelude to, a short postponement of, the years of confining reality that awaited him. Meanwhile, he had his sisters, his friends at Woodhouse, his cousins at Maer, Henslow and his Cambridge circle, London and its scientific societies, among which he was beginning to create his own place; he had his new degree, his field sports, his home, the affectionate scepticism of his father still to win over – it would have been astonishing if there had not been something of relief in his acceptance of Dr. Darwin's view. "As far as my own mind is concerned", he wrote to Henslow, "I should, I think *certainly*, most gladly have accepted the opportunity which you so kindly have offered me." Is there not some hesitation there, some slightly dubious overemphasis? In any case, he has his excellent reason for rejecting the chance: "But my father, although he does not decidedly refuse me, gives such strong advice against going, that I should not be comfortable if I did not follow it." Then he describes his father's objections: "the unfitting me to settle down as a Clergyman, my little habit of seafaring, *the shortness of the time*, and the chance of my not suiting Captain Fitz-Roy. It is certainly a very serious objection, the very short time for all my preparations, as not only body but mind wants making up for such an undertaking. But if it had not been for my father I would have taken all risks . . . I am very much obliged for the trouble you have had about it; there certainly could not have been a better opportunity."

That final note of wistfulness at last lets out some of his inner regret; it is very probable that his feelings remained mixed and unsettled, veering between distress and relief in a very human manner. His mind in this turmoil, he made the short journey to the Wedgwoods' home; perhaps it is true that he intended little more than to tramp those familiar fields and copses and litter the countryside with the dead birds that mark the sportsman's exultation and define the labours of his dogs. In his pocket, however, lay a note from his father to his Uncle Jos. It began with medical matters – Dr. Robert had apparently prescribed half a dozen turpentine pills for Jos's use – but then continued, "Charles will tell you of the offer he has had made to him of going for a voyage of discovery for 2 years. – I strongly object to it on various grounds, but I will not detail my reasons that he may have your unbiased opinion on the subject, & if you think differently from me I shall . . . follow your advice." That was written on 30 August; the next day, Dr. Robert added a postscript: "Charles has quite given up the idea of the voyage".

The letter shows how open the subject still remained, how much less than definite Dr. Robert's attitude actually was. Far from issuing an imperious paternal fiat, he went out of his way to remain fair and to leave himself the opportunity of changing his mind. In the relaxed atmosphere of Maer, with all its friendliness, practicality and liberalism, Charles is likely to have found a sympathetic audience for his tale of disappointment. It may be, too, that, having safely refused the offer, he sharpened the outlines of that disappointment a little in order to engage the concern of his cousins (such, alas, are the wiles of uncertain youth).

It is not surprising to find that it was Hensleigh, Jos Wedgewood's youngest son, who was the most outspoken in urging Charles to reverse his decision and make the voyage. Five years older than Charles, he was to become a lifelong friend to both the Darwin sons, making of Erasmus over the years an almost constant companion. He too had been at Christ's College, graduating three years before Charles's arrival there (although among the best mathematicians of his year, he came last by such a margin in the classics examination that his friends, extending the expression "the wooden spoon", spoke of "the wooden wedge", a term that then remained in use at Cambridge for over sixty years). In later years he was to become fascinated by etymology, in the 1850s publishing an etymological dictionary that established his permanent reputation. He had an acute and unorthodox mind – later again, he was to take a close interest in spiritualism – and his determination to see Charles set off on a voyage of worldwide exploration was entirely in character.

It was perhaps less to be expected that Josiah would prove equally sympathetic. But he too very soon came to the conclusion which was to alter the outcome of the debate, turn rejection into acceptance and so change both Darwin's life and the intellectual history of the western world. For Darwin's father, in making his refusal conditional, had looked to Josiah Wedgwood to reinforce his own opinion. Earlier, he had said to Charles, "If you can find any man of common-sense who advises you to go, I will give my consent". Now, in Uncle Jos, the Darwins, father and son, discovered such a man. Human, forward-looking, as sharp in business as the Doctor himself, his common sense could hardly be denied even by those who differed from him in their conclusions. Now he came down, absolutely and energetically, on the side of acceptance.

There was an immediate despatching of letters to The Mount. Stiffened by Wedgwood support, Charles wrote to his father in a tone of obdurate diffidence, of respectful, even nervous, disagreement. "My dear Father", he began, "I am afraid I am going to make you again very uncomfortable. But, upon consideration, I think you will excuse me once again, stating my opinions on the offer of the voyage. My excuse and reason is the different way all the Wedgwoods view the subject from what you and my sisters do." He enclosed "what I fervently trust is an accurate and full list of your objections" and begged his father to give him in reply a firm yes or no. "If the latter, I should be most ungrateful if I did not implicitly yield to your better judgement, and to the kindest indulgence you have shown me all through my life; and you may rely upon it that I will never mention the subject again." He pointed out that neither the Wedgwoods nor he himself believe that any great danger was involved. "The expense can not be serious, and the time I do not think, anyhow, would be more thrown away than if I stayed at home. But pray do not consider that I am so bent on going that I would for one *single moment* hesitate if you thought that after a short period you should continue uncomfortable." He cannot think that the voyage "would unfit me hereafter for a steady life", and hopes fervently that the letter will give his father no uneasiness.

His list of the Doctor's objections as he has remembered them for Josiah to consider runs to eight items.

1.) Disreputable to my character as a Clergymen hereafter.
2.) A wild scheme.
3.) That they must have offered to many others before me the place of Naturalist.
4.) And from its not being accepted there must be some serious objection to the vessel or expedition.
5.) That I should never settle down to a steady life hereafter.
6.) That my accommodations would be most uncomfortable.
7.) That you should consider it as again changing my profession.
8.) That it would be a useless undertaking.

One must feel admiration for all three men involved in this debate. Had Dr. Robert been in fact the domestic tyrant later biographical legend made him, no debate would have been possible, above all not one in which he finally lost the motion. Nor would one be able to see in the tone of Charles's letters to his father much more than an unappetising servility. What one sees in fact is a determination to be asbolutely fair to his father's point of view and to the substance of his criticisms, and so to make it as easy as possible for the Doctor to be objective in his final decision. Now, from Josiah, there comes a letter, written on the spur of the moment, in great haste and perhaps with some emotion, which nevertheless deals clearly and intelligently with each of Dr. Darwin's reported uncertainties. He writes of the weight of responsibility he feels at discussing the matter,

> but as you have desired Charles to consult me, I cannot refuse to give the result of such considerations as I have been able to give it . . .
>
> 1. I should not think it would be in any degree disreputable to his character as a Clergyman. I should on the contrary think the offer honourable to him; and the pursuit of Natural History, though certainly not professional, is very suitable to a clergyman.
>
> 2. I hardly know how to meet this objection, but he would have definite objects upon which to employ himself, and might acquire and strengthen habits of application, and I should think would be as likely to do so as in any in which he is likely to pass the next two years at home.
>
> 3. The notion did not occur to me in reading the letters; and on reading them again with that object in mind I see no ground for it.
>
> 4. I cannot conceive that the Admiralty would send out a bad vessel on such a service. As to objections to the expedition, they will differ in each man's case, and nothing would, I think, be inferred in Charles's case, if it were known that others had objected.
>
> 5. You are a much better judge of Charles's character than I can be. If on

comparing this mode of spending the next two years with the way in which he will probably spend them, if he does not accept this offer, you think him more likely to be rendered unsteady and unable to settle, it is undoubtedly a weighty objection. Is it not the case that sailors are prone to settle in domestic and quiet habits?

6. I can form no opinion on this further than that if appointed by the Admiralty he will have a claim to be as well accommodated as the vessel will allow.

7. If I saw Charles now absorbed in professional studies I should probably think it would not be advisable to interrupt them; but this is not, and, I think, will not be the case with him. His present pursuit of knowledge is in the same track as he would have to follow in the expedition.

8. The undertaking would be useless as regards his profession, but looking upon him as a man of enlarged curiosity, it affords him such an opportunity of seeing men and things as happens to few.

It is likely that more persuasive than the cogency of the arguments was the fact that they were being presented at all. Originally the Doctor may well have spoken out of feeling more than consideration; if that was the case, and he had on reflection thought himself a little hasty, then Josiah's opinion gave him an excuse to change his mind. As for the Wedgwoods themselves, they proved too impatient to let mere paper do their work. Turning his back on sport, Josiah had horses harnessed and drove Charles to Shrewsbury, there to discuss the matter with the Doctor face to face.

Dr. Robert, however, seems not even to have waited for the arrival of the Wedgwood chaise. As that was still clattering through the Shropshire lanes, he was writing his reply to Uncle Jos. "Dear Wedgwood", he began, "Charles is very grateful for your taking so much trouble & interest in his plans. I made up my mind to give up all objections if you should not see it in the same view as I did. – Charles has stated my objections quite fairly & fully – if he still continues in the same mind after further enquiry, I will give him all the assistance in my power. Many thanks for your kindness." Thus, when Darwin and his uncle arrived, primed to assault the paternal citadel, they found its gates already opened and its flag run down. What has always been thought of as a debate, perhaps even an argument, ought more plausibly to be regarded as a celebration.

The one point not touched on in this correspondence is money. Some people have suggested that it was an issue: Charles had, after all, overspent his allowance at Cambridge – in the *Autobiography* he quotes an exchange between himself and his father. He had said, "I'd be deuced clever to spend more than my allowance whilst on board the *Beagle*", at which his father had smiled and remarked. "But they tell me you are very clever." Not only does that not sound as though this was a very serious point of contention between them, but the whole question of Charles's expenditure – of which he too was always very conscious – has to be put in its context. And that context is the family income, which in that year, from investments, rents and interest on loans, without considering the Doctor's professional fees, came to well over £7,500. Robert Darwin, as we have seen, was by no stretch of the imagination a struggling provincial medical man, living from one brace of unsolicited rabbits or bag of potatoes to the next. He was a substantial man of business, with a large amount of capital that he knew very well how to make work for him. The few hundreds that Charles's expedition might cost him would have become a significant factor in the discussion only if he had chosen to make it so. There is no serious evidence that he did. Certainly Peacock's suggestion that a salary might be forthcoming – spurious enticement though it undoubtedly was – elicited no response from the Darwins. (On the contrary, after accepting the post Charles became worried that even the £40 a year paid by the Admiralty for his food might jeopardize his ownership of any specimens he collected.)

In any case, Dr. Robert, beset by Wedgwood enthusiasm, had given way. Hastily, Charles scribbled a letter to Beaufort at the Admiralty, belatedly accepting the invitation. "Perhaps you may have received a letter from Mr. Peacock", he added, "stating my refusal; this was owing to my Father not at first approving of the plan, since which time he has reconsidered the subject: & has given his consent & therefore if the appointment is not already filled up I shall be very happy to have the honor of accepting it." But he felt the need to explain further: "There has been some delay owing to my being in Wales," he wrote; it is obvious that, the decision having been made, he was in terror that it had been made too late. "I set out for Cambridge tomorrow morning, to see Professor Henslow: & from thence will proceed immediately to London."

"Tomorrow morning" meant a benighted three o'clock. That was the hour when Charles clambered on board the swiftest of the express coaches – rightly named *Wonder* – and set off eastwards towards Cambridge and Henslow. Almost certainly still bewildered by the whirligig of yeas and nays, he rattled through the morning, over the still dusty roads of early autumn. Would his letter arrive in time to reverse the consequences of his earlier rejection? Would his arrival on Henslow's doorstep make the difference? As it turned out, it was as well that he travelled in person: his letter, though marked "For immediate delivery", still sat undispatched upon the post office shelf in Shrewsbury.

Despite all the activity, however, all the responses of an expected enthusiasm, he was not quite as committed as he seemed. In the Preface to the Journal of the voyage he was to write, of the days that followed his father's acquiescence, "I shall never forget what very anxious & uncomfortable days these two were, my heart appeared to sink within me, independently of the doubts raised by my Father's dislike to the scheme. I could scarcely make up my mind to leave England even for the time which I then thought the voyage would last."

Nevertheless, he sped across the breadth of England, leaving the coach at Brickhill and continuing from there in a series of post-chaises. By the evening of the same day he could sit in his room at the Red Lion in Cambridge and write to Henslow, "I am just arrived: you will guess the reason, my Father has changed his mind. – I trust the place is not given away. – I am very much fatigued & am going to bed. – I daresay you have not yet got my second letter. – How soon shall I come to you in the morning. Send a verbal answer. Good night." One may doubt that he himself had a good night; his exhaustion will not have been entirely physical and it may be that despite it he slept only fitfully in his Red Lion bed. "I trust the place is not given away" – it is likely that this thought in all its variants will have passed again and again through his anxious and uncertain mind.

When he saw Henslow the following morning, he discovered that he had been right to be fearful. His appointment still dangled in the limbo between acceptance and rejection. It was apparent that the one factor able to decide the question would be Fitzroy's own preference. The drama of selection would have to be brought to its crisis. On 5 September, Darwin travelled to London – and this despite having seen a letter written by Fitzroy to a friend which was, Darwin told Susan, "so much against my going that I immediately gave up the scheme". Clearly, Darwin's idea of giving up might not be everyone's.

Thus he came to the true turning point, the fulcrum from which his world was to be moved. He met Captain Fitzroy. It is from this moment, one senses, that his true commitment to the *Beagle* expedition began. The voyage, the ship, the opportunity, all were instantly transformed by being personalized in this single, magnetic young officer; "it is no use", Charles wrote to Susan, "attempting to praise him as much as I feel inclined to do, for you would not believe me". It is clear that from the moment they met, these two young men felt a personal affinity which the differences between them could not obscure or darken. If there were reservations, they were on Fitzroy's side. He had already written, in that discouraging letter Darwin had seen, of his doubts over Darwin, doubts that were apparently based on his Tory dislike of sharing his ship with a Whig – or, more responsibly, of his fears over the frictions this might cause. To these he now added the findings of physiognomy – in which, as in phrenology, he was fashionably a believer – discovering in the shape of Darwin's nose clear signs of a lack of energy and determination. These were not doubts that seem to have survived long. One can hear the helter-skelter enthusiasm that overwhelmed Darwin that evening, in the rushed sentences he wrote to Susan.

> He offers me to go share in everything in his cabin if I like to come, and every
> sort of accommodation that I can have, but they will not be numerous. He says
> nothing would be so miserable for him as having me uncomfortable . . . There
> is something most extremely attractive in his manners and way of coming
> straight to the point. If I live with him, he says I must live poorly – no wine, and
> the plainest dinners . . . I shall pay to mess the same as Captain does himself,
> £30 per annum; and Fitz-Roy says if I spend, including my outfitting, £500, it
> will be beyond the extreme . . . Fitz-Roy says the stormy sea is exaggerated;
> that if I do not choose to remain with them, I can at any time get home to
> England, so many vessels sail that way, and that during bad weather (probably
> two months), if I like, I shall be left in some healthy, safe and nice country; that
> I shall always have assistance, that he has many books, all instruments, guns, at
> my service; that the fewer and cheaper clothes I take the better . . . I like his
> manner of proceeding. He asked me at once, "Shall you bear being told that I
> want the cabin to myself? – when I want to be alone. If we treat each other this
> way, I hope we shall suit; if not, probably we should wish each other at the
> devil." . . . I hope I am judging reasonably, and not through prejudice, about
> Captain Fitz-Roy; if so, I am sure we shall suit. I dine with him today. I could
> write [a] great deal more if I thought you liked it, and I had present time. There
> is indeed a tide in the affairs of man, and I have experienced it, and I had
> *entirely* given it up till one today . . .

To Henslow, Charles wrote in similar mood. "*Gloria in exelcis* is the most moderate beginning I can think of. Things are more prosperous than I should have thought possible. Captain Fitz-Roy is everything that is delightful . . . What changes I have had. Till one today I was building castles in the air about hunting foxes in Shropshire, now llamas in South America . . ." By the next day, he is sending Susan a list of things to do and prepare – "a pair of lightish walking-shoes, my Spanish books, my new microscope . . . my geological compass . . . a little book, I have got it in my bedroom – 'Taxidermy' . . ." – and expressing his deep-rooted, if entirely new, optimism: "I write all this as if it was settled, but it is not more than it was, excepting that from Captain Fitz-Roy wishing me so much to go, and from his kindness, I feel a predestination I shall start . . . He must be more than twenty-three years old; he is of a slight figure . . . dark but handsome . . . and, according to my notions, pre-eminently good manners . . . This is the first really cheerful day I have spent since I received the letter, and it all is owing to a sort of involuntary confidence I place in my *beau ideal* of a Captain."

It is likely that Fitz-Roy, had he known of it, would have taken offence at having his manners scrutinized by the son of a Shrewsbury doctor. When he came to write his own *Narrative* of the voyage he described Darwin as "grandson of Dr. Darwin the poet . . . a young man of promising ability,

Plate 1

Dr. Erasmus Darwin, the
gargantuan grandfather
whose ideas, expressed in
poetry and prose,
stimulated Charles's own
theories.

Plate 2

Susannah Wedgwood,
Darwin's mother, whose
death when he was only
eight may have worked
profound changes in his
character.

Plate 3

Dr. Robert, Charles's
father: a man of power and
authority – but was he the
domestic tyrant many
have described?

Plate 4

Charles and Catherine,
the two youngest
Darwin children, in the
care of their older
sisters after their
mother died.

extremely fond of geology, and indeed all branches of natural history". The tone of lofty approval would have seemed right to him, despite the fact that he himself was only twenty-six. His name, Fitz-Roy, means "king's son"; his direct progenitor, the first Duke of Grafton, had been a bastard son of Charles II by Barbara Villiers.

He himself had been born in 1805 – the year of Trafalgar – and shortly before his thirteenth birthday, he had been entered at the Royal Naval College, Dartmouth. He passed out at the top of his class and, by the age of twenty-three, was serving as Flag Lieutenant to the commander of the South American station, Admiral Otway. The *Beagle*, accompanying HMS *Adventure*, was then on her first survey voyage; unable to face the loneliness, the difficulties of his task or some personal disaster, her captain, Commander Stokes, one day locked the door of the poop cabin and, thus secluded, shot himself. Otway appointed Fitzroy to the command: the *Beagle* and her most famous captain had been brought together.

This was the background of the man Darwin met, and upon whom he rested the full structure of his decision, and his hopes. He was, as Darwin had written, handsome, with long, rather sensitive features, the narrow, curving nose of autocracy (so different, therefore, to Charles's suspect snub) and dark eyes with long, slightly feminine lashes. It was a face expressing both a direct imperiousness and perhaps some disguised weakness; certainly it was a striking face that flew with great clarity the signals of a powerful personality. In his *Autobiography*, written four decades later, Darwin remembered him as, "devoted to his duty, generous to a fault, bold, determined and indomitably energetic, an ardent friend to all under his sway". His main drawback seems to have been the uncertainty of his temperament, leading at times to unreasonable furies and at others to the most self-destructive of depressions.

The high-spirited friendliness of the letters Fitzroy wrote to Darwin, however, shows clearly that there was another side to his character – a relaxed concern expressed through a quirky, idiosyncratic humour, very unexpected in the stony martinet or the melancholic fundamentalist so often depicted. It is not a side much in evidence in John Chancellor's "stern disciplinarian", nor in Gertrude Himmelfarb's Fitzroy, who "combined the normal authoritarian attitude of a naval captain with the abnormally authoritarian disposition of an intense, high-minded and puritanical aristocrat". Such views of Fitzroy are not incorrect, but they may be partial; they obscure the lightness of temperament revealed in the badinage he addressed to Darwin.

Yet, equally, it is true that the violence of that imperious temperament was always threatening to erupt. Fitzroy's scowling rancour, Darwin recalled in the *Autobiography,* "was usually worst in the early morning, and with his eagle eye he could generally detect something amiss about the ship, and was then unsparing in his blame. The junior officers when they relieved each other in the forenoon used to ask 'whether much hot coffee had been served out this morning?' which meant how was the captain's temper?" There were, too, even darker levels in the character of this complicated, difficult man: "He was also somewhat suspicious and occasionally in very low spirits, on one occasion bordering on insanity. He seemed to me often to fail in sound judgement and common sense". Yet, despite these complexities, the two men managed to live together for five years on that cramped ship, "on the intimate terms," as Darwin pointed out, "which necessarily followed from our messing by ourselves in the same cabin".

For Darwin, nevertheless, Fitzroy's outbursts must have been as novel as they were distressing – this fine-drawn aristocrat exposed him to something rather different from the equable, rational and liberal temperaments he had been accustomed to among his own family and Wedgwoods. It is an indication of Fitzroy's underlying magnanimity, however, that he was aware of the distress he sometimes caused and would often apologize for his excesses with an openess that must have been hard to resist. It was an effort of retribution which doubtless owed much to his religious beliefs. These were precise, profound, fervently held and, as time went on, more and more fundamentalist.

Among the ambitions and desires that led Fitzroy to invite a naturalist aboard the *Beagle* – his wish to give the expedition scientific respectability, for example, or his understandable need of a companion – must have been his belief that science would prove the truth of Genesis. In 1831, his ideas, though still forming, had already taken on their general fundamentalist shape. He was a man interested in the sciences, proud of his involvement with the savants of the age and anxious to take his place amongst them. He was still a very young man, engaged in the normal effort to hammer out a world view. But if his certainties about the Creation and the Flood became more solid as the years went by, setting at last into the concrete of bigotry, the lineaments of his creed were already firmly established.

Charles, on the other hand, seems not to have reached any profound conclusions on the question. His long-term objective remained a country parsonage, and there were certain forms and affirmations he would finally have to accept in order to achieve that. He believed that species were immutably fixed, and probably that they derived this fixity from the will of their Creator. But there was not, as there was with Fitzroy, any great passion behind these ideas – religion, like politics, sport and science, was simply a part of his social heritage.

It therefore seems probable that in part it was the fervour of the *Beagle*'s commander that itself honed to a new sharpness Darwin's curiosity about the fundamental questions. No young naturalist of the period can have been ignorant of, for example, the discussions that turned on the true age of the earth, nor of what these meant for the literal truth of Genesis. But that in the five years they spent together Fitzroy's religious preoccupations helped to shape Darwin's interests, that the captain's faith in the absolute veracity of the Creation story reinforced his own curiosity about the prehistory of natural forms, seems on the face of it more than likely.

If this is true, then the two men's reactions to each other's developing opinions was in the nature of a recoil. When Fitzroy wrote his account of the voyage, published in 1839, he added a chapter on his beliefs and certainties about the Flood: "A Few Remarks with Reference to the Deluge". In it he admitted early waverings – "I suffered much anxiety in former years from a disposition to doubt, if not disbelieve, the inspired History written by Moses" – but the rest of the chapter was a detailed testimony to his success in overcoming such spiritual hesitation. Yet elsewhere, at precisely the same time, Darwin was, as it were, travelling even more swiftly in the opposite direction.

At this moment of first meeting, however, no theological dissension dammed the swift, instinctive friendship that the two men felt for each other. Soon Darwin, in the hasty rhythms of his altered situation, was dashing from gunsmith to instrument-maker, part of the time as Fitzroy's companion as the captain rattled through the streets in his gig. On 14 September, he was writing to Susan from Devonport. He and Fitzroy had travelled from London to Plymouth together in one of the newfangled steamers, three days of Channel coasting during which the two men could deepen and strengthen their newly established knowledge of each other.

> I suppose breathing the same air as a Sea Captain is a sort of preventive . . . of course there were a few moments of giddiness, as for sickness I utterly scorned the very name of it . . . Perhaps you thought I admired my beau ideal of a Captain in my former letters: all that is quite a joke to what I now feel. – Everybody praises him (whether or no they know my connection with him), and indeed, judging from the little I have seen of him, he well deserves it. – Not that I suppose it is likely that such violent admiration as I feel for him, can possibly last; – no man is a hero to his valet, as the old saying goes; – and I shall certainly be in much the same predicament as one.

The analogy is almost too self-deprecating, perhaps answering the over-agreeable strain in Charles's character; yet the common-sense expectation that his infatuation would pass displays throughout this turmoil a continuing calm awareness of reality which is both admirable and endearing.

Meanwhile, Darwin had had his first opportunity actually to see the *Beagle*. His main impression was of her smallness. He wrote to Susan, "The want of room is very bad, but we must make the best of it." The ship was, in fact, not much over ninety feet in length; headroom on the lower deck was only just over five feet. When launched in 1820, the *Beagle* had had only two masts, but a mizen mast had been added and she was now, as was customary with these small survey vessels, barque-rigged (square-rigged on the fore- and main-masts, fore-and-aft sails between mainmast and mizen, with a fore-and-aft mizen sail). She had been given her new sail plan while being prepared for the first South American voyage, the one which Fitzroy had joined halfway through. During this rebuilding, she had also been given a fo'c'sle and a large poop cabin, increasing a little her internal roominess and giving her a little more protection from heavy seas. Apart from her size, the *Beagle*'s main disadvantage was that, like the rest of her class, when she shipped water her high bulwarks prevented its running off. The Navy had very early dubbed these little vessels "half-tide rocks", so vulnerable were they to high-rolling waves; more ominously, their other nickname was "coffin brigs". When enough water collected on the upper deck during a storm they simply rolled over, and several had over the years capsized and sunk. Alternatively, they became so heavy that they lost way, turned broad-side to the wind, and so lay at the mercy of the storm. Of the 107 vessels of the class that were built, twenty-six were lost from these or similar causes; the only other one to go down was the victim of a pirate ship. It is fair to say that the *Beagle* owed her record of safety more to Fitzroy's seamanship than to any inherent quality in her design.

As work was begun on her now, it became clear that most of her timbers were rotten, a fact Fitzroy used to make her safer by extensive restructuring. Nothing, of course, could be done to lengthen her, nor to increase her beam, which at its widest was only twenty-five feet. Into this cramped space, in degrees of discomfort varying directly with their degrees of authority and importance, seventy-three men and one woman would eventually be packed. There were the First and Second Lieutenants, John Wickham and James Sulivan; there was Lieut. Stokes, whose principal duty was to aid Fitzroy with the survey work; there were McCormick, the surgeon, never to be popular, and Bynoe, his assistant, destined in time to replace him; there were Rowlett, the purser, older than most; the master, Chaffers, and his asssistant, Usborne; there were Mellersh and King (the son of the previous expedition's commander), the midshipmen; a carpenter, a clerk, an instrument-maker; listed among the supernumeraries were Augustus Earle, the artist, whose title was Draughtsman – and Charles Darwin, Naturalist. There were all these and the rest of the crew, and Capt. Fitzroy's steward, and Mr. Darwin's servant – and three Fuegians, those "natives of Patagonia" mentioned by Peacock in his letter to Darwin.

In a sense, these aboriginals from Tierra del Fuego were as much the occasion of the *Beagle*'s voyage as was any need felt by the Admiralty to have accurate charts of South American waters. While commanding the *Beagle* on Capt. King's expedition, Fitzroy had taken and held three of the Fuegians, suspecting that their compatriots had stolen a whaleboat. To these three hostages, named by their British captors Fuegia Basket (the only woman), York Minster and Boat Memory, there had later been added a fourth, from a different group and speaking a different dialect. He had been called Jemmy Button. These bizarre names were not born of any pre-Surrealist fancy, nor to express contempt, but commemorated places or incidents connected with their capture. Once they were in his hands, Fitzroy, in the proselytizing spirit of the time, had decided to bring them back to England with him. It was his intention to help extend the world's one true civilization by educating and then returning them, as beneficial influences, to their own people. It was a venture he himself was largely to finance.

Housed in Plymouth, clothed in European style, at times delighted, at others bewildered, the four Fuegians waited while Fitzroy tried to arrange their future. As the Captain wrote his letters and bustled energetically about, Boat Memory died of smallpox. The other three, however, thrived; soon they were attending an infant school at Walthamstow, making this effort to span the millenia under the auspices of the National Society for Providing the Education of the Poor in the Principles of the Established Church. They were presented to the King and Queen. But Fitzroy was impatient to take them back to their bleak land, there to act as interpreters for him and infiltrators for Jesus and Great Britain among their countrymen. Had the Fuegians not existed, or had Fitzroy been a less determined (and well-connected) officer, the *Beagle* would not that September have been undergoing an extensive refit, preparatory to sailing through the dangerous storms that swoop and circle near Cape Horn.

Darwin travelled back to London by coach; at 17 Spring Gardens, the apartment of his metropolitan brother, letters from his friends were arriving as his news spread. One of the first came from Charles Whitley, a cousin of Herbert's and, like Herbert, an old Cambridge colleague and friend. Writing from Barmouth, Whitley said, "I congratulate you on the prospect of an employment after your own heart, & the opportunity it affords you of studying all the natural sciences at once, after your own taste." He mentioned Darwin's "cannibal shooting, fungus describing anticipations", suggesting that Charles's manner of telling his news had been somewhat light-hearted, and then asked whether Charles would be "at Salop again, and *when*? inasmuch as I desire greatly to see you again. You may be drowned, shot or fever-smitten, or I may die from pure vexation & disappointment before you return . . . there are few men I should miss more than yourself when the black day came to either of us."

But a bleaker note creeps into Whitley's letter now, a note of wistful envy which he was not the only one to sound, and which gives a darker definition to the congratulations Darwin was to receive from several of his naturalist friends. Most of them, of course, were young men facing almost hesitantly the long, repetitive years that awaited them now that their university days were over, and they saw in Darwin's opportunity the promise of a freedom which, it seemed, would always be denied to them. "Once more I congratulate you on your luck," Whitley writes, "(& I wish it were mine, for I have latterly had much vexation & am sick enough of England) as it will put it in your power to distinguish yourself in your favourite pursuits – & I flatter myself that you will not be slow to do so to your own satisfaction & the pleasure if not the envy of your friends . . ."

This was not the only demonstration of the fact that, far from being the amiable wastrel of repeated legend, Darwin by his early twenties had established among those who knew him solid expectations of success. His friends saw very well what the opportunity he had been given could mean, but they did so because they realized how perfectly equipped he was, by application as well as inclination, to take advantage of it. On 19 September, another Cambridge colleague, Frederic Watkins, wrote from Doncaster: "Never did I think so highly of our present Government, as when I heard they had selected Darwin for ye naturalist & that he was to be transported (with pleasure of course) for 3 years. Woe unto ye Beetles of South America . . ." He expected to see Darwin ranked with "Henslow, Linnaeus & Co – Whilst I, luckless wretch, am rusticating in a country Parsonage & shewing people a road I don't know to Heaven." It is hard not to believe that such views as these of Watkins helped to make more remote the chances of Darwin's accepting the life of a rural clergyman, so clear is the note of discontent. More to his taste will have been Watkins's nostalgia for Cambridge, memories of which seemed to warm Darwin throughout his life. Here, a tiny mystery creeps in, however, for someone has considered it necessary to excise almost the whole of two lines. "But at least, old fellow," Watkins writes, "ye worst fortune in the world cannot deprive us of many pleasant & sacred recollections . . . [*here the scoring out and actual excision occur*] . . . ye note of ye nightingale & ye voice of the cherubim, ye moonlight walk & ye social glass (query, bottle?) ye roll of the organ & ye clash of knives and forks, with small talk, arguments, billiard-balls & beetle-hunting enough to furnish ye most unfurnished head in Cambridge with ideas." One wonders what Watkins remembered, at this moment of parting, that necessitated so impenetrable a censorship.

From Maer, Charlotte Wedgwood wrote to him, displaying some signs of an active conscience. By this time, the two years originally planned for the expedition had extended to three, and this made her view the project with rather more doubt than before. "I wish you would not so completely set us down as your Lords of the Admiralty – when I think of your sisters my conscience is ill at ease & I shall feel guilty when I next see them – they will be very goodnatured if they do not bear us a grudge. I shall lay all the blame on my father & Hensleigh, & you can vouch for us that Hensleigh is the only one that gave a strong opinion." It is clear from her somewhat sanctimonious tone how widespread was the family impression that Charles was by nature an idler: "That it will oblige you to work is I know one of the advantages that you think this expedition will give you. I wish it may . . . I have an earnest desire that you should prove you have made a good choice, as well as that we have not done you an injury, for I cannot help remembering that but for that 1st September your family would have had you safe at home . . ."

Meanwhile, Darwin continued his preparations, gathering together the paraphernalia he needed and preparing to travel first to Cambridge, then on to Shrewsbury for his farewells. In the midst of all this, he evidently had time to attempt one alteration to the *Beagle's* complement. On 23 September, Fitzroy replied to this request, his sprawling writing and vigour of phrase reflecting both his energy and the easy relations he had by now established with his expedition's naturalist.

> I read the first sentence of your letter – "Before you judge my conduct" – and threw it away in a rage – saying "Damn these shoregoing fellows they never know their own minds," – "well let's see what crotchet makes him refuse to go" – when upon reading further I found that so desperate a beginning only ushered in a simple request about a Mid! – I made certain you were off your bargain, a *Lady* in the way, or something unforeseen! I am sorry it is out of my power to take young Owen – because the number of Mids allowed has been complete since the Vessel was commissioned. There is no *chance* of a Vacancy. You were surely quite right to *ask* – I could but refuse – yet I would not have refused had I been *able* to oblige you.

It is clear, therefore, that even at this critical moment in his life, Darwin would have liked to have with him some representative of "The Forest", an Owen to keep alive his connection with that alternative family of his and most particularly, perhaps, with Fanny.

Towards the end of September, Darwin returned as planned for his final farewells to Shrewsbury, once again taking that swift coach, the *Wonder*, to speed him home. Six days after his arrival, however, he was writing to

Henslow, "I heard from Cap Fitzroy yesterday he gives me a week more of respite, & therefore I do not leave this place till the end of this week, & London on the 16th of October. – I wish indeed that time was arrived, for I begin to be very anxious to start." The Doctor, however, was much happier about his departure, having now become used to the idea. The sisterhood, on the other hand, although taking their cue from their father, were probably free as always with their admonitions and advice, while at nearby Woodhouse, by contrast, a crucial absence will have made all bleak. Fanny was in Devon, visiting relations.

On 27 September, she sent him a letter. Caroline had told her, she wrote, "that you wish to have a *good bye* from me before you go. I had not the *least idea* you were to go so soon . . . I *hoped* and fully expected I should have been at home in time to see you – I *cannot tell* you how *disappointed* & *vexed* I am that that cannot be, little did I think the last time I saw you at the poor old Forest that it would be *so long* before we should meet again. This horrid Devonshire, fool that I was to come here . . ." The sentences fly under the press of emotion, the underlinings are double, treble, the tone trembles on the verge of tearfulness. "I would give any thing to see you once more before you go, for it does make me melancholy to think of the time you are to be away – & Heaven knows what may have become of all of us by this time two years, at all events we *must* be grown *old* & steady – the pleasant days and the fun we have had at the Forest can never come over again – how I wish I were there this week to have one *last chat* with you – I cannot bear to think you are really going *clean* away without my saying one *good bye*!! . . . They tell me you were at Plymouth about 10 days ago & so was I, how *very very* unlucky we never met, do you go there again?"

A moment later, however, her spirits and her wit perked up. She was about to go visiting – "awful flat work, dowagering about with the Aunts . . . I have expiated all my sins for a severe Penance I have had of it – I won't be *taken alive* again in that way when once I get home . . ." She returned to a subject that always had for her an equivocal fascination, but in a manner which shows how conversant she was with the details of Charles's life; she wondered, "did you throw yourself on the Governor's mercy, & confess your creditors, or what have you done? What a capital way of escaping *ungentlemanlike Tailors* &c – When you are *far from the Land* they may *whistle* for their cash for what you care! Well, don't be surprised if you hear I have *taken Ship* too and fled my duns." One wonders what debts she really had run up, extravagantly queening it among the beaux and belles of Shropshire and the West. Fanny, as always, was happily creating for herself a personality made of bits and pieces gleaned from her favourite romances; the punishing dues accumulated by the well born were a significant element in their complex plots.

She asked him to tell her all his plans and prospects – "and tell me too if I shall look out for a nice little wife for the *Parsonage* by the time you return, tell me what you require and I will look about and put one in *my eye* by the time you want her – a proper knowledge of the *Beetle* tribe of course you require . . ." Is this the teasing of old friends, a genuine offer humourously couched, or a sly nudging of Charles towards a proposal? What would he have asked had they been face to face, and how would she have responded? Or was the moment for that long over, leaving only the affection of lifelong neighbours behind it, a young man and a young woman who had been children together? "I most sincerely wish you every amusement & happiness possible – but only wish most heartily you were not going quite so soon that we might have one *more talk & laugh* first – but it is not to be . . ." She signed herself "Always yours most sincerely & affectionately, F.O." – and then could not resist a final, romantic flourish: "*Burn this before you sail* for pity's sake –"

This letter crossed with one from Charles, and one that seems from her immediate reply to have been written in a mood of some depression – "in a *Blue Devlish* humour", as she puts it, perhaps quoting him.

> You say what changes will happen before you come back – & you hope I shall not have quite forgotten you – I doubt not you will find me in *status quo* at the Forest, only grown *old & sedate* – but wherever I may be whatever changes may have happened *none* there will *ever* be in my opinion of *you* – so do not my dear Charles talk of *forgetting*!! – the many happy hours we have had together from the time we were *Housemaid & Postillion* together, are not to be forgotten – and would that there was not to be an end of them . . . Caroline tells me you were actually walking about Plymouth the *very day I was,* I never did know anything so unlucky we should not have crossed each other's path!! . . .

Such farewells were, in a sense, premature, for work on the *Beagle*, although thorough, was not swift. Even at the end of September Fitzroy had written, "The dockyard are making very slow progress – so that we shall not sail until the end of October." That her refit took longer than hoped for is not entirely surprising: Fitzroy wanted what was almost a new ship, the cost of the work to the Admiralty amounting in the end to only £220 less than the £7,803 they had spent originally to have her built. She was stripped to her oak skeleton and totally restructured; the upper deck was raised, in effect lowering the bulwarks and so letting any water she shipped run off more easily. The difference in height of eight inches to one foot had the added advantage of allowing even the tall Darwin to stand upright when below. New planks of two-inch fir sheathed the bottom, beneath outer layers of felt and copper; a new rudder was fixed, a patent windlass, a new galley-stove, as well as a set of recently invented lightning conductors. Six boats were specially built, unusually strong spars and the heaviest possible rigging were fitted, the best ropes, chains and sails that could be found were energetically procured. Special trysails, fore-and-aft rigged, between the masts provided an extra and extremely useful area of sail. Seven guns added a touch of belligerency which was perhaps a little out of place; the *Adventure* had carried none on her expedition and, though the *Beagle* had been designed to sport ten, the Admiralty could see little reason to supply her with armaments – especially as Fitzroy insisted that they were brass, in order to make sure that so much metal should not affect his compasses.

The autumn slipped by; Darwin became more and more restless and unhappy. He thought of his family and of everything that he was leaving, of the years of effort and discomfort that awaited him; the grey November days bowed him down with their snorting storms and their damp, brooding melancholy. His accommodation seemed unworkably small – he had just room to turn round, he told Henslow. He had been assigned a narrow space beyond the chart table, his hammock had been slung there, and for the rest of the voyage that was where he would have to do all his working, sleeping, dressing, reading, thinking and dreaming. For his clothes and effects he had a few drawers, and for specimens a tiny cabin no bigger than a cupboard. Although he had periods of enthusiasm when he felt that the space at his disposal was luxuriously large in the circumstances, he veered from this quite often into gloom. It is a fact, however, that once under way and at work, he hardly ever mentioned the cramped conditions again. Now, checked in his expectations, waiting interminably for the *Beagle* to be ready, he seems to have been increasingly depressed. The rash that had afflicted his hands in the past broke out once more, accompanied by pains and palpitations in his chest. He was afraid that he had been stricken by some disease of the heart – but even more afraid that some doctor might forbid his setting sail. At some level of his being he probably realized that these were symptoms of tension, rather than of genuine sickness; in any case, he took no medical advice. On 15 November, Fitzroy received his Admiralty instructions: "You are hereby required and directed to put to sea, in the vessel you command, so soon as she shall be in every respect ready . . ." Darwin, delighted, wrote to Fox, enthusiastic in his praise of the *Beagle*. "Everybody who can judge says it is one of the grandest voyages that has almost ever been sent out. Everything is on a grand scale. 24 Chronometers! The whole ship is fitted up with Mahogany, she is the admiration of the whole place . . ." But his thoughts took a more melancholy turn. "Why, I shall be an old man by the time I return, far too old to look out for a little wife. What number of changes will have happened. I suppose you will be married & have at least six small

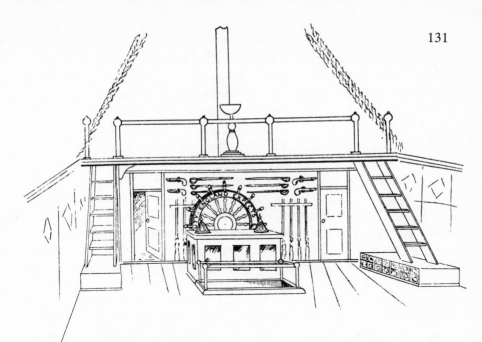

Note. The circle in centre of wheel was a drawing by Earle, the artist, of Neptune with his trident.

H.M.S. Beagles' Quarter-deck

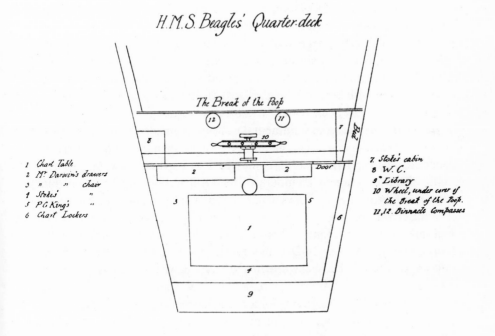

The Break of the Poop

1 Chart Table
2 Mr. Darwin's drawers
3 "   "   chair
4 Stokes'   "
5 P.G. King's   "
6 Chart Lockers

7 Stokes' cabin
8 W.C.
9 Library
10 Wheel, under cover of the Break of the Poop.
11,12. Binnacle Compasses

Poop Cabin

Plan of the *Beagle*, with space indicated for Darwin.

children. – I shall very much enjoy seeing you attempting to nurse all six at once . . . When I think of all that I am going to see and undergo. It really requires an effort of reasoning to persuade myself that all is true."

It must have, indeed, as November wound to its close with the *Beagle* still immobile. Darwin wrote to Henslow, "My chief employment is to go on board the *Beagle* & try to look as much like a sailor as ever I can. – I have no evidence of having taken in man, woman or child". It worried him that he was spending his father's money as he waited. It worried him, too, that there was so little space. "The absolute want of room is an evil that nothing can surmount," he told Henslow. "I think L. Jenyns did very wisely in not coming, that is judging from my own feelings, for I am sure if I had left College some few years, or been those years older, I *never* could have endured it." When, early in December, it seemed as if they were at last about to sail, he could write, "I look forward even to sea-sickness with something like satisfaction, anything must be better than this state of anxiety."

Meanwhile, back in a Shrewsbury that must already have begun to recede into the memory, the first significant change since his departure was taking place. Sarah Owen, Fanny's sister and his friend since childhood, was marrying. She was to live in London, in Belgrave Street, and had made him promise to visit her there as soon as he returned to England. "I hope & trust we may both meet with success in our respective new careers . . . God bless you, my dear Charles, believe that whenever I may change my *title*, I shall always remain your very sincere, affectionate Friend." In the letter, fixed to a piece of paper, there lies a small gold pin, designed in the shape of a thistle and decorated with semi-precious stones. The paper is folded over, has his name on it and has been sealed with black wax.

On the *Beagle*, far from sentiment, Darwin was gingerly practising how to climb into a hammock. "The hammock being suspended, I thus only succeeded in pushing [it] away without making any progress in inserting my own body." The presence in Plymouth of his brother, Erasmus, brought him some comfort during these days of impatience. On 5 December, a gale began howling down over their heads from the south; four days later, Charles and Erasmus were still taking walks on nearby Mount Edgecombe. On the following day, however, 10 December, Fitzroy attempted to set out. "Erasmus was on board," Darwin wrote in his diary, "& we had a pleasant sail, till we doubled the Breakwater; where he left us & where my misery began." The storm howled on, terrifying for a young landsman spending his first real day at sea – "such a whistling of the wind & roar of the sea, the hoarse screams of the officers & shouts of the men, made a concert that I shall not soon forget."

By the following noon, they were back in harbour again; eleven days later,

Fitzroy made a second attempt and once more was beaten back. Christmas intervened, with the whole crew far gone in revelry and its aftermath. The *Beagle* might have sailed on 26 December, Darwin noted, but "the opportunity has been lost owing to the drunkeness & absence of nearly the whole crew . . . Several have paid the penalty for insolence, by sitting for eight or nine hours in heavy chains . . . Dined in gun-room & had a pleasant evening." Abruptly, on 27 December, two months behind schedule, with the necessary east wind strong and steady, the crew presumably woolly-tongued but capable and the sea undemanding, the *Beagle* was on her way. Without a great deal of jubilation, Darwin noted that "with every sail filled by a light breeze, we scudded away at the rate of 7 or 8 knots an hour. I was not sick that evening but went to bed early". Thus anticlimactically he describes the moment towards which all his hopes and energies had been directed for four busy and bewildering months, the first day of the many hundreds which he was now to spend at sea, or among the unexpected creations of nature in endless unfamiliar lands.

2

—⁓⁓⁓—

Charles Darwin was still only twenty-two when the *Beagle* set course that December for the bleak winter reaches of the Atlantic. We peer down the decades in an attempt to see, in three-dimensional clarity, the figure of this young man at the outset of his crucial adventure, but try as we might, the image refuses to settle. We can achieve the two dimensions of a heroic portrait; the third dimension of reality escapes us. There was, then and during the remainder of his life, an enigmatic quality about Darwin's character. Not that he was ever intentionally mysterious. Rather the reverse – it is the very openess of his life that makes it, paradoxically, so impenetrable. We know so very little that was truly private. In none of his letters does he ever give way to resentment, fury, greed or any other of mankind's revealing vices. When, in his Diary, he came to express anger, it was almost always about public matters: slavery, the mistreatment of the South American Indians, the futile violence of South American politics. His tone to his sisters, as to his friends, was always one of disciplined affection, of a dutiful, though palpably genuine, love. It is as if he had no private persona, exuding instead a likeable simplicity in which everything was precisely what it seemed.

Yet one cannot help feeling that sailing on the *Beagle* was for him like an infinitely extended trip to the Owens and the Wedgwoods, offering him the possibility of a true freedom protected by the enormous ocean distances. One senses that the Darwin known to Henslow was not quite the same as the Darwin known by his Cambridge cronies; but that both had been rather different from the Shrewsbury Darwin his father and sisters recognized. The *Beagle* provided yet another stage upon which he could rehearse his truest role, that of Darwin among friends, Darwin convivial, Darwin easy in his mind because actively a scientist, a naturalist.

Certainly he had his doubts about the voyage: obvious ones concerned with the difficulties, discomforts and dangers of world travel at that time; and others somewhat less obvious, about what such a side turning in the progress of his life might lead to, about the loss of friends, of time, of opportunities for work and marriage. It may be, however, that many of these uncertainties were not really couched in his own terms at all. They were rather reflections of the self-doubt he had learned in his childhood. Its means of expression must have been the internalized voices of his father, of Caroline, of Susan, the loving "Granny" of his domestic government. Such voices could not be silenced, since the contempt he feared to hear in them was not theirs, but his own. The doubts he attributed to them were a part of himself and would never be entirely stilled, neither by distance nor by time.

Physically, Darwin in his early twenties was just under six feet tall, "rather thick-set in physical frame", as someone from Cambridge later recalled, ruddy in complexion, strong and energetic. He was also "of the most placid, unpretentious and amiable nature", and these agreeable characteristics were traits he must have had to call on, for although, as he had written to Henslow two months earlier, he found the officers "a fine set of fellows", they were also "rather rough & their conversation is oftentimes so full of slang & sea phrases that it is as unintelligible as Hebrew to me." Nor were the absence of truly compatible company and that lack of space over which he had been so anxious the only tribulations that he faced. Of far greater immediate concern was his constant sea-sickness, from which he suffered to greater or lesser extent throughout the whole voyage. Lieut. Sulivan (later, like Stokes and Fitzroy himself, an admiral) recalled that "whenever the ship was out of harbour he retired to his hammock in the chart room . . . his patience in persevering with his scientific work and not abandoning the voyage was most commendable". Charles tried to contain the sickness by a diet of biscuits and raisins; when he grew tired of that, "then the sovereign remedy is Sago, with wine & spice & made very hot. But the only sure thing is lying down & if in a hammock so much the better".

Nothing was ever to alleviate the illness. In February, 1832, he wrote to his father, "I was unspeakably miserable from sea-sickness"; in March a year later he told Caroline in a letter, "I suffered . . . much from sea-sickness"; two years later, in March, 1835, he was writing to Caroline again, "I continue to suffer so much from sea-sickness, that nothing, not even Geology itself, can make up for the misery & vexation of spirit", and in December of the same year, "There is no more Geology but plenty of sea-sickness." In June the next year he wrote to Catherine, "I positively suffer more from sea-sickness now than three years ago". It is against this background of misery and suffering that Darwin accumulated the vast store of specimens, observations, notes and comments that, brought back from the voyage, fuelled so much of his research work in the five decades that followed. What underlines his fortitude and application is that, unlike the officers and crew, he had the constant possibility open to him of giving up and going home. Late in the voyage, as homesickness drained the excitement from his travels, he was very conscious of this – and had he not been, his sister's pleas would have reminded him. Yet he persevered steadfastly at his immense and largely self-imposed tasks, meticulous through all viscissitudes of health, alterations of latitude and volatilities of mood.

Gales were swinging about that winter world as the *Beagle* bucked and swung down-Channel and across the Bay of Biscay. No really heavy weather actually struck them, but everywhere they felt the consequences of storms in other places and at other times. The seas were heavy, the winds strong, the skies lowering. Bad weather circled the North Atlantic – in the Channel, off the coasts of Africa, near their immediate destination, Madeira. In fact, when they finally reached that island, conditions were so poor and the wind so unfavourable that they simply passed it by. They had, however, had the wind with them for the crossing and, despite the bleak conditions, had made good time.

Their first time landfall was at fabled Tenerife – but, "Oh, misery, misery, we were just preparing to drop our anchor within half a mile of Santa Cruz, when a boat came alongside, bringing with it our death-warrant." The authorities had ordered them to spend twelve days in quarantine before landing. Instead, Fitzroy decided to leave at once; Darwin wrote that "we have left perhaps one of the most interesting places in the world, just at the moment when we were near enough for every object to create without satisfying our utmost curiosity". So the place he had dreamed of since first reading Humboldt's vivid descriptions of it, which for months he had planned to visit with Henslow, or with Ramsay, now fell unexplored astern.

However, anxious to begin his collecting and classifying, Darwin was soon setting a trawl and hauling aboard his first marine specimens. Eventually, when the *Beagle* finally dropped anchor off St. Iago, in the Cape Verde Islands, he was able to make his longed-for expedition on land. "It has been for me a glorious day", he wrote, "like giving a blind man eyes . . ." The volcanic terrain also occasioned a flurry of geological notes, and these make plain that at this point he still held largely orthodox views, very similar to those of Buckland and even Cuvier. Writing of Quail Island, near Cape Verde – described in his Diary as "a miserable spot, less than a mile in circumference" – he noted a scattering of ancient debris: "It looks to me like a part of the long disputed Diluvium". This use of Buckland's term suggests that in 1838 he too believed that there had been a flood in the past, worldwide and significant, whether this had been the Flood of Genesis or not. Four years later, on her return voyage, the *Beagle* halted once more at the Cape Verde Islands. Darwin amended his earlier record, with the comment, "I have drawn my pen through those parts which appear absurd". Among these was his reference to the "Diluvium".

Even if such fundamental questions did not occupy the forefront of his mind, he was nevertheless unable to spend so many years scrutinizing the alien profusion with which Nature sprawls across the southern hemisphere without being changed by the experience. Much of what he examined had been until then unknown; besides, he was young and, fortunately, sufficiently unschooled not always to know the conclusions at which he was supposed to arrive. The very fact that he was largely self-taught, made a naturalist above all by his disinterested enthusiasm and thus a scientist by vocation, untramelled by the exigencies of an academic career and unfearful of criticism brought by professors for whose conventions he felt no particular respect, meant that he was free to exercise both his natural curiosity and his equally natural ability to achieve, from the information he had collected, a new and interesting synthesis. A Henslow or a Jenyns, with the best will in the world, while they might have observed and collected precisely the same specimens as Darwin did, would have seen in them only what their training and established beliefs permitted them to see. In a real sense, the gathering of information would have been their only goal, and certainly their only achievement: it would still have taken a Darwin to fit that information into a general world scheme. Darwin, even if unwittingly, was gathering a stock of information which would provide much of the raw material he was to use during the rest of his intellectual life.

Twenty-three days after her arrival, on 8 February, 1832, the *Beagle* left the Cape Verde Islands and once more put to sea. "I find to my great surprise", wrote Darwin to his father, "that a ship is singularly comfortable for all sorts of work. Everything is so close at hand, and being cramped makes one so methodical, that in the end I have been the gainer." Returning to sea, he added, was like returning home – "if it was not for sea-sickness the whole world would be sailors". He now liked the officers better than he had, while for Fitzroy his praise remained as unstinting as ever. "He works incessantly, and when apparently not employed, he is thinking. If he does not kill himself, he will during this voyage do a wonderful quantity of work."

As the *Beagle* was preparing to leave the Cape Verde Islands, in faraway Cambridge, compact and calm beside its soggy fenland flats, Henslow was writing him the first of many letters. There was, as often between them, a touch of badinage: "Pray are you yet a Whig? for I heard from Wood that your Brother told you it was impossible to touch pitch & not be defiled." But towards the end of the letter, written both ways across the pages, it is clear that Henslow has been troubled by his conscience: "I sometimes blame myself for having hinted to you rather plainly little pieces of advice, lest you should have thought me troublesome – but I am sure your good heart will ascribe my suggestions to the right motive of my being anxious for your happiness ... I feel the more anxious for you as I have been so mainly instrumental in your adopting the plans you have – & should your time pass unhappily shall never cease to regret my having recommended you to take the step you have of devoting yourself to the cause of science." From this it is apparent that Henslow had no illusions that Darwin was simply taking a detour on his way to the intended parsonage: he was to be a scientist, not a clergyman, and this with Henslow's blessing. The phrase "devoting yourself to" is not the same as would have been, say, "spending such a long time in". It may well be that Charles, pliable as always, had been quite content to give one impression in Shrewsbury and Maer, but a very different one in Cambridge and London. Henslow addressed his letter to Darwin on the *Beagle*, "Rio de Janeiro (or elsewhere), South America"; for a moment we glimpse in the slight desperation of this how enormous were the distances, how impenetrable the silences, that lay between those who sailed on such demanding voyages, and those who waited at home for news of them. It is a situation which we, radio-linked and television-cossetted, can hardly imagine.

At almost the same time, Catherine Darwin was sending off from Shrewsbury news of the event that, perhaps more even than the invitation to join the *Beagle*, marks the end of Charles's boyhood. "Caroline spent two days at Woodhouse this week; she thought she should find them quite alone & quiet, and what was her surprise, on entering the room, to find Mr. Biddulph settled there. – You will be as much astonished as Caroline was, when Fanny took her out of the room, and told her that she was engaged to Mr. Biddulph; he had proposed a few days before and been accepted, in the course of a secret ride, Fanny meeting him at the Queen's Head." So Housemaid had turned her back finally on Postillion, the childhood games and the half-aware sweetnesses of adolescence were at an end; marriage, after all, was a serious and adult matter. Nor did Mr. Biddulph seem at first glance anything but a serious and adult proposition as a husband. The younger brother of a soldier who would become a general, Robert Myddleton Biddulph, himself only twenty-six, was a member of Parliament, a man of some means and of excellent family. He had, however, something of a reputation as a rake and a gambler. His home was at Chirk Castle and the marriage was a "good" one – though, to be sure, Fanny's aunt and namesake had married the still-future Lord Berwick thirty years before, as if to prove that the Owens were by no means out of their social depth in such waters.

So Fanny had contrived to be true to her romances to the end: Biddulph, the reformed rake, who had first made flirtatious advances to her sister, Sarah, had apparently fallen in love with her when seeing her misery after she had been jilted by an earlier suitor, John Hill; there had been Sarah's pique at being discarded; an unadvertised courtship had followed; Sarah's own marriage had smoothed the way; the affair had culminated in that secret ride, that private meeting; now, at the climax, a castle awaited her. How else, after all, was a Fanny Owen to find herself engaged? One senses that gentle, affectionate, science-obsessed Darwin, pliable, simple, knowing more of love than the manoeuvres of love, would never have been a husband Fanny could have chosen. Yet Catherine went on, "I hope it won't be a great grief to you, Charley, though I am afraid you little thought how true your prophecy of 'marrying and giving in marriage' would prove. – You may be perfectly sure that Fanny will always continue as friendly and affectionate to you as ever, and as rejoiced to see you again, though I fear that will be but poor comfort to you, my dear Charles."

Did Fanny's letter arrive by the same post, read under the bright South American skies, the news already months old, Darwin by now a hardened traveller, the *Beagle* at anchor in the harbour below Rio de Janeiro's mountains? Was hers the letter he picked out first, recognizing the Owen hand, happy to link himself to her across the thousands of miles of water that lay so bitterly between them? He makes no mention of it, his diary is silent, his autobiography gives us not a word. "Your sisters tell me", she wrote, "they informed you in their last letter of the awful and important event that is going to take place here – My fate is indeed decided, the die is cast – and my dear Charles I feel quite certain I have not a friend in the world more sincerely [interested] in my welfare than you are or one that will be more truly glad to hear I have every prospect of happiness before me in the lot I have chosen." She had, she wrote, known Mr. Biddulph a long time and always thought him "*most agreeable* and good hearted . . . I do think mine is a *happy end*, I have no misgivings about it – tho' it is indeed an awful and a melancholy thing to leave ones quiet happy Home . . . I would give a great deal to see you again & have one more merry chat, whilst I am still Fanny Owen, but alas that cannot be . . ." Once again she tells him that "when you do return to the little Parsonage and want *the little Wife*! pray give me a commission to look out for her." He will, she assures him, "always find me the same sincere friend I have been to you ever since we were *Housemaid & Postillion* together . . . Now adieu and Heaven bless you my very dear Charles . . ."

On the day that was written, 1 March, Darwin walked, in a daze of response to its beauty, through the countryside near Bahia (a town now named Salvador). He noted that he collected "a great number of brilliantly coloured flowers, enough to make a florist go wild. Brazilian scenery is nothing more nor less than a view in the Arabian Nights . . ." When, months later, he read Fanny's slightly chaotic farewells, was her voice already no more than a whisper out of his youth, a memory long put behind him? Did he notice its oddly passive tone – "My fate decided . . . the die cast" – and how that contrasted with the energetic manipulation of events of which Catherine had written? That Fanny wrote nothing of the secret meeting at the Queen's Head may have been no more than her fear of repeating what he already knew. On the other hand, she may also have drawn back from admitting how vigorously she had pursued such recently conceived ambitions.

Fanny, in her playfulness, her wit, her easy scorn, her make-believe, breaks down the fifteen decades that lie between her and us. She arises, more substantial and flirtatious than any ghost, from the cunning prattle of her letters. Experienced, in flesh and voice and sparkling eye, she may well have overwhelmed the young Charles Darwin. Emma Wedgwood, much solider, witty too, but in a more substantial, sardonic way, affectionate, sensible, made to be the steady wife of a preoccupied man – can she, loved and relied on though she was for nearly half a century, ever have hoped to obliterate all memory of that long-vanished glitter, that fey brightness, that determined, flashing romanticism, which had beguiled the student Charles?

He had thought Fanny "the prettiest, plumpest, most charming personage in Shropshire". Since then she had fallen in love with the slippery John Hill, and now had settled for Mr. Biddulph, M.P. She was, she wrote, "convinced he possesses every quality to make me happy, is most sincerely & Heaven knows disinterestedly attached to me" – it sounds as though a case were being made out. Would she have married Charles? If they had met before he sailed, would he have left betrothed? Would he have left at all? Or was it all no more than the summer flirtations of that era's long adolescence, a game for children: Housemaid and Postillion? She wrote, ". . . believe my dear Charles that no change of *name* or condition can ever alter or diminish the feelings of sincere regard and affection I have for you . . .", but of course everything had changed, both had already altered, the years were dragging them further and further apart, were demolishing childhood, their shared past, even the long friendship between them. For Fanny, motherhood waited, illness, a long struggle with a bitter mother-in-law: she would never be the Fanny of "The Forest" again. And for Darwin, deep affection, the joy of fatherhood, sickness, effort, fame – but never again the easy carelessness of the long afternoons at Woodhouse, nor the sprawling hours among the strawberry beds with this beguiling girl who had perhaps – who knows? – drawn from him the first unrepeatable energy of passionate love.

3

As these letters, gossipy or fateful, were beginning their slow journeys across the wide, pre-Victorian Atlantic, the *Beagle* set course for Bahia and Brazil, only pausing for a short while to land a party, Darwin among them, on the bleak rocks of St. Paul. The following day, they crossed into the southern hemisphere and all those who had never before reached the equator had to undergo the boisterous initiation that was traditional. These novices were nervously marshalled below decks; above, as the then Midshipman, King, was to record sixty years later, "Neptune was surrounded by a set of the most ultra-demonical looking beings that could be well imagined. Stripped to the waist, their naked arms and legs bedaubed with every conceivable color which the ship's stores could turn out, the orbits of their eyes exaggerated with broad circles of red and yellow pigments, those demons danced a sort of nautical war dance, exulting on the fate awaiting their victims below." No wonder that King felt that Darwin's "first impression was the Ship's crew from Captain downwards had gone off their heads".

The blindfolded Darwin was the first victim on deck, there to be lathered with pitch and paint, "shaved" with a piece of roughened iron and ducked in a large bath of water. King remembered that "Mr. Darwin readily entered into the fun", but the Diary records little enthusiasm: "I . . . found this watery ordeal sufficiently disagreeable". Despite these distractions, however, and the constant debilitating misery of his seasickness, Darwin had no intention of wasting those long days of South Atlantic sailing. His trawl was busy day by day, and as he swung to the waves' movement in his hammock or sat pale-faced in Fitzroy's cabin he was beginning to read some of the books he had brought with him. Humboldt remained his guide and support, Milton and the Bible offered him precept and sublimity, but it seems that Darwin spent most of his reading time absorbed in a book only recently published: the first volume of *The Principles of Geology*, by Charles Lyell.

Perhaps Fitzroy had been deceived by the book's unpretentious title. In any case, he had actually presented it to Darwin before the *Beagle*'s departure. Had he read it, it is unlikely that a man of his religious opinions would have found it acceptable. Henslow, too, both admired and feared it – gentle, scholastic cleric that he was, he advised Darwin to read it, but to believe it not at all. It sounds like one of the few moments when he may have sensed a threat to his lifelong reconciliation between the roles of scientist and clergy-man. For Lyell, directly or by implication, provided the counter-arguments for many of Henslow's, and Fitzroy's, certainties; far out on the South Atlantic, therefore, Darwin, passive between his Captain and his book, found himself caught willy-nilly in one of the central arguments of the age. It was, of course, the tumultuous dissension among geologists, with catas-trophist upholders of Genesis on one side, sternly objective uniformitarians on the other and all shades of compromise in between.

Two years earlier Lyell, touring in Sicily, had noticed how many craters there were on Etna, a record of intermittent cataclysm stretching far back into antiquity, and yet how much more recent they were than the limestone strata that passed beneath the volcano. The limestone itself, however, as its fossil content proved, was of no great geological age: in other words, the evidence pointed to slow and very powerful processes that needed almost limitless periods of time to create the landscapes and effect the changes for which they were responsible. Soon after his return he wrote to his geologist friend, Roderick Murchison – himself a catastrophist – that his book, by then "in part written, and all planned", would "establish the *principle of reason-ing* in the science". It would propose "neither more nor less than that *no causes whatever* have from the earliest time to which we can look back, to the present, ever acted, but those *now acting*; and that they never acted with different degrees of energy from that which they now exert". Endless time and an essentially unchanging earth – these were the ideas, expounded with the clarity of a trained advocate and the conviction of a scientist, with which Darwin now found himself faced. His response to them over the years that followed has, in a strange way, diminished Lyell, who is remembered more often as a forerunner to Darwin than as, in his own right, a scientific theorist of the highest quality. It remains true, however, that these and other ideas may well have struck home at the first reading, to sink deep into Charles's mind, working there as a forgotten bullet works into the flesh.

For example, one decision which Lyell proclaimed in his introductory chapter was to be echoed almost thirty years later by Darwin. Lyell stated with some emphasis that he was engaged in geology and not cosmogony – he was, in other words, concerned with how the surface of the earth had changed, not how it had come into being. Later, when his own time came to theorize, Darwin too – for all the promise of his title – would avoid discussion of the origins of life and restrict himself to its processes. Lyell said that in accepting this limitation he himself was following Hutton, and so proclaimed his general allegiance.

Lyell's arguments made it clear that he rejected any developmental view of the earth. The progressivism of Cuvier aroused his strong resistance: it was his conviction that no direction of any kind could be discerned in the processes to which the planetary mantle was subject. Things were not getting better nor life more complex – everything was in general terms exactly as it had always been. A few years ago our own cosmologists were postulating a "steady-state" universe, one which had in general, though not in detail, always and everywhere appeared the same; Lyell was proposing a "steady-state" earth. The events to which it was subject occured at random and without developmental effect, and the forces which caused them neither waxed nor waned throughout the millennia. It was a picture of moments of particular turmoil punctuating a constant, general serenity; of time marked by an infinite series of almost imperceptible changes, or of vast changes occuring too slowly to be perceived by their human observers.

Because these changes were so relatively small, however, and, though continual, spread over such incalculable ages, one could easily underestimate the energies involved. We, established on the surface of the globe, were in a poor position to calculate these: it was below ground and under the ocean beds that the vast mills of geology ground out their slow, irresistible results. These results were positive as well as negative – it was a false view that saw the geological past only in terms of catastrophe. Some effects had been restorative, renovative, constructing out of chaos landscapes of beauty, and of use. It was the balance of these processes, creative and destructive, that underlay the steady-state planet of Lyell's theory.

In the long term, it was probably the opening chapters of the second volume, not published until 1832, which most directly affected Darwin. These, dealing with the nature of the living species and discussing transmutation in terms of Lamarck's theories, raised questions and posed contradictions which, it has always been thought, eventually forced the increasingly restless mind of Darwin to search out solutions. For Lyell accepted that the organic world, like the inorganic structures of the earth, was in a condition of particular change but general constancy. Species appeared, adapted to their situations, but as the environment altered and ecological factors became increasingly difficult for them to combat, they vanished. Writing a book on geology, it was not necessary for him to speculate on the precise mechanism regulating these enormous comings and goings: it was sufficient to demonstrate that what happened at one level in nature was repeated at another and dependent level. Thus there were always species, settled in adaptation to their circumstances; over the huge periods that geological time represented, the particular species might change, one disappearing and another taking its place, but the overall picture would remain the same. Lyell never really faced up to the contradictions and omissions in this theory; the scientific community as a whole – in the continued absence of a Darwin – turned to the miraculous for a solution and postulated a repeated divine creativity to account for the appearance of new species. The deity their conclusion suggests seems more like Shiva, the Creator-Destroyer of Hinduism, than Christianity's loving God, but men like Buckland and William Whewell (later to be Darwin's bitter opponent) saw no contradiction between their opinions and their faith.

Yet during the early stages of the voyage even the first volume of Lyell's book offered Darwin, wanly seeking relief from his misery in its measured factuality, a new vision of the world and of its history. That the time span involved was almost incalculable natural scientists like himself knew very well. But Lyell had the ability to raise his reader's awareness of it, to make him face the full meaning of the aeons almost everyone now accepted so lightly. The epochs of prehistory were real, were, so to speak, there to be used, to be filled by the speculations of an informed and scientific imagination. It was with an awareness of the millennia involved that the geologist should look at the world. He should not be put off by the absence of obvious evidence, for what he observed altered so slowly that the most minute change became significant. And just as the periods of time were vast and the alterations almost imperceptible, so were the terrestrial forces involved gigantic, almost beyond imagining. The geologist was busy at a science the scale of which was almost out of reach of the human. He had to adjust his eyes and his thinking to that scale, he had to alter the very processes of his comprehension.

What Darwin, just out of university and aware of his inexperience, could gain from Lyell was not so much the information that the *Principles* contained as the principles themselves, and the act of the imagination which had gone into devising them. It was not facts that he was gathering, there among the moaning timbers and the endless slap of wind and wave, but a way of thinking, a way of seeing. If he had not learned then how slowly natural processes could afford to develop, how almost limitless was the time at their disposal, nothing he found later could have helped him towards discovery.

It was therefore with his mind in the first slow turmoil of the long intellectual revolution to come that Darwin confronted the biological exuberance of South America. The brilliant reality of tropical vegetation, tropical insects, tropical birds whirled him off his feet and away; he was like some adventurous swimmer spun exhilaratingly through endless dazzling rapids. He hardly knew where to look or turn; an object would engage his attention, but before he could properly focus upon it, he would be distracted by some alternative. "The delight one experiences . . . bewilders the mind; if the eye attempts to follow the flight of a gaudy butter-fly, it is arrested by some strange tree or fruit; if watching an insect one forgets it in the strange flower it is crawling over . . . The mind is a chaos of delight . . ." When he walked in the forest, its stillness awed him. When it rained, the power of the downpour demanded his respect. "To a person fond of Natural History such a day as this brings with it pleasure more acute than he ever may again experience."

After two days of this, he berated himself for laziness; he had been unable to translate his reaction into disciplined effort. But, after a day spent with Wickham and Sulivan at the local carnival – "being unmercifully pelted by wax balls full of water & being wet through by large tin squirts" – he took King with him "for a long naturalizing walk . . . It is a new & pleasant thing for me to be conscious that naturalizing is my duty, & that if I neglected that duty I should at same time neglect what has for some years given me so much pleasure." He learned as early as this, however, that the tropics were not only for his delight; he had cut his knee in some inconsequential way, and this now began to swell so severely that he could no longer walk. For eight days he suffered in his hammock while, near enough for him to hear the sussuration of its insects, the land awaited him.

Was it then, "early in the voyage at Bahia in Brazil", that Darwin had one of his most violent quarrels with Fitzroy? If it was, then Darwin's own frustrations may well have made him more combative than usual. Fitzroy had been to visit one of the area's great landlords, his estate naturally run by toiling regiments of slaves. Fitzroy had wondered if the slaves, who seemed well fed and contented, were actually happy in their conditions. Their owner had summoned several of them and asked them what they felt about the lives they led and whether they wished to be free. All of them, unsurprisingly, had replied that they had no wish for liberty. Darwin recalled in his *Autobiography* that he then asked Fitzroy, "perhaps with a sneer, whether he thought the answers of slaves in the presence of their master was worth anything." Fitzroy responded by an overwhelming fury, in which he not only forbade Darwin to share his cabin any longer, but also summoned Wickham later in order to abuse Darwin in his absence. The officers of the ship invited Darwin to mess with them, but Fitzroy's sense of outrage lasted only a few hours; then he "showed his usual magnanimity by sending an officer to me with an apology and a request that I would continue to live with him."

Whether this incident occured then or at a later visit to Bahia, it did not prevent Darwin's recovery. His wound healed with some days still to spare before the *Beagle* sailed, and he spent them in gently exploring the coastal lands. It was then that he began the geological observations that he was to condense into a single statement in his published *Journal*: noticing that for two thousand miles down the coast the only rock one found was igneous granite, he speculated as to its origins. Had it first appeared under the sea, or had it once been covered with sedimentary strata, since worn away? "Can we believe that any power, acting for a time short of infinity, could have denuded the granite over so many thousand square leagues?" It was, perhaps, Lyell that he was addressing.

On 18 March, the *Beagle* set sail for Rio de Janeiro. Filling his journals and notebooks, reading, writing letters – "I find living on board a most excellent time for all sorts of study", wrote Darwin. A water spout distracted him, the catching of a shark, the beginning of survey work and a landing on the tiny Abrolhos Islands. While he gathered specimens, "the rest began a more bloody [attack] on the birds". Using sticks, stones and guns, the sailors with a schoolboy ferocity killed more than the boats could hold. Then, at the end of the month, they exhibited a pleasanter – if still childlike – side to their natures, calling out the midnight watch for nothing, summoning carpenters to deal with nonexistent leaks, sending lads aloft to reef sails that needed no alteration: it was April Fool's Day. As for Charles himself, "Sullivan cried out: 'Darwin, did you ever see a Grampus: Bear a hand then.' I accordingly rushed out in a transport of Enthusiasm, & was received by a roar of laughter . . ." Pleasant that he should be caught, pleasanter that he could recount the fact so equably.

On 4 April, the *Beagle* entered harbour, to find the commander-in-chief, Sir Thomas Baker, preparing to land the marines. There had been a mutiny in the town, but as Fitzroy commented, in the offhand manner of a serving officer, "In these unsettled states . . . they recur so frequently, that even on the spot they cause little sensation . . ." By the next day, the skirmishing seems to have been over, for Darwin reports landing with the artist, Earle, and wandering admiringly through the "gay & crowded" streets. His impressions were rather different from those Fitzroy predicts in his *Narrative*: "Few strangers visit the metropolis of Brazil without being disappointed, if not disgusted. Numbers of almost naked Negroes, hastening along narrow streets – offensive sights and smells, an uncivil and ill-looking native population – indispose one to be pleased . . ." For Darwin, on the contrary, everything was of interest, and it was with delight that he and Earle took a house in Botofago, now a suburb well enwrapped by the city, but in those days just beyond its outskirts. In a short while King, too, took up his quarters there.

Earle had lived in the area before, a fact given its melancholy edge by the news that most of those he had known had died in the meantime. Darwin, however, was not to be cast down by the fate that overtook others – at nine in the morning of 8 April, he was setting off with five companions for his first journey into the interior. He was travelling with an old hand, Patrick Lennon, an Irishman who had spent twenty years in the country and who was now making his way inland to discover why he was receiving no income from a *fazenda* he had bought eight years earlier. They rode through a heat enlivened by the stuttering brilliance of enormous butterflies, then through forest shade, pressing on even through moonlit nights in which lurked the dark shapes of vampire bats. When, on the fourth day of the journey, Charles felt unwell, he cured himself with what seems the slightly unpromising mixture – delicious though it may have been – of cinnamon and port wine.

They had to cut their way through heavy jungle in order to reach the rigid lines of coffee trees that marked out the estate. Soon after their arrival, the party was embarrassed by a violent quarrel between Lennon and his agent, a man named Cowper. During it, to Charles's horror, Lennon threatened to sell Cowper's own illegitimate, half-caste child, the offspring of a slave mother, at the public auction – and, breaking up the established slave families, to do the same with every woman and child on the estate. In Darwin's reaction, detestation vies with fair-mindedness: "Can two more horrible & flagrant instances be imagined? & yet I will pledge myself that in humanity and good feeling Mr. Lennon is above the common run of men." Darwin's hatred of slavery, ingrained by family tradition and kept alive by his own constant generosity, was to be excited by many more instances than this. No distance or passage of time diminished his abhorrence; even here, at the very edge of cultivation, beside the Rio Macae, on the land of a man he had come to respect, his detestation remained firm, his understanding of what was involved quite clear. "Against such facts how weak are the arguments of those who maintain that slavery is a tolerable evil!"

The next day they rode to a nearby *fazenda* and here Darwin was able to spend two whole days ranging the forest, observing and collecting. The graceful trunks of the trees, soaring away to the canopy above, the elegance of the cabbage palms, the delicate ubiquitous mimosas – everything he saw lifted him to another peak of euphoria: "wonder, astonishment & sublime devotion, fill & elevate the mind". As for the *fazenda* itself, the food was so plentiful that "if the tables do not groan, the guests surely do". He recorded his admiration – with the usual caveat. "As long as the idea of slavery could be banished, there was something exceedingly fascinating in this simple & patriarchal style of living". Yet even in slavery there could be degrees of horror and Darwin conceded, "In such Fazendas as these I have no doubt the slaves pass contented & happy lives". Then came the return journey, over sands that made "a gentle chirping noise" as they crossed them, through lonely little towns with painted houses and dominating churches, past woods of acacias and across the local Rio Grande – where, having lost their passports, they were suspected of being horse-thieves – to arrive at last, on 24 April, at Rio harbour and the waiting ship.

Darwin now settled avidly to his life in the Botofago cottage. Writing to him at about this time (on 15 April), his old friend Herbert, among tales of Cambridge and the choral society, and nervous statistics about a developing cholera epidemic, proved again what expectations those who knew him as a naturalist held of him. His well-wishers, he thought, "ought to console themselves for your absence by the reflexion that you are now engaged in collecting materials for further fame; that you are about to couple your name, already intimately connected with Science, with those of a Cuvier and a Humboldt. Don't think me guilty of Flattery – I know you will do great things, as it is impossible that your assiduity and talents should not succeed." Darwin at this time was at the height of his vigour, stronger and healthier than he was ever to be again in the decades after the *Beagle*'s return. The picture that has come down to us, of the enfeebled, prematurely patriarchal figure, benignly reclusive in his house at Downe, is of little use when trying to imagine him in his Rio de Janeiro cottage. He had just come back from a two week journey, during which he had ridden some ten hours a day through a land made unfamiliar by language, vegetation, customs and climate, and had then suffered the losses and depredations of his move; yet very soon, in the enervating heat and the driving torrents of a tropical rainy season, had been outside collecting or inside collating (one hour's effort in the field produced specimens enough to keep him busy for the rest of the day). Meanwhile, he had breakfasted with the Admiral, dined with acquaintances, joined in the ceremonial of the flagship and, above all, kept up his notebooks, his Diary, his *Journal* and his letters home.

The *Beagle* set off on a return journey to Bahia on 10 May – Fitzroy had found a discrepancy of four miles of longitude between his measurements and those of a previous French expedition in the distance between Rio and Bahia. With predictable meticulousness, he was going back to calculate it again. Meanwhile, the personnel of the ship had slightly altered; it was here that the surgeon, McCormick, had been invalided out – "i.e., being disagreeable to the Captain and Wickham", as Darwin put it – his place being taken by the much more popular Bynoe, his erstwhile assistant.

More importantly, and a sign of the dangers that ringed about the naturalist's paradise of Darwin's descriptions, malaria had brought down with its chattering fevers several of the crew. They had been shooting in nearby marshlands and had been laid low; Darwin, though rejoicing in his Diary that he had been prevented from joining these wildfowlers, must nevertheless have realized once again what risks he himself would run in the course of his necessary expeditions.

He had in the meantime established a new routine, working in the field one day, arranging, collating and classifying what he had found the next. He walked long distances, observant always, constantly noting down what he observed. The southern winter was approaching: some days now it rained, on others it was unexpectedly cold; when the season brought in its low, sweeping clouds, he watched as they curled about the summit of Corcovado, some two thousand feet of quiescent volcano that overlooked the coastline. Towards the end of May, he climbed the mountain; the view from the peak, "which perhaps excepting those in Europe, is the most celebrated in the world", disappointed him. Beneath the smooth slopes of the Sugar Loaf, on another occasion, he collected insects – and, distracted by the familiarity of the task, found himself homesick for Barmouth.

At The Mount, meanwhile, the equable nature of the life had not in the slightest faltered. Erasmus fluttered the sensitivities of the sisterhood by paying, as Catherine wrote at the end of April, "a sentimental visit to his *friend*, Mrs Whitworth, one of the many female friends he made abroad. We were rather *scandalized* at this . . ." Everything turned out well, however; Erasmus reported that "she was the horridest brute that ever lived: and sang like a Barrel Organ", and besides, her husband was a Tory. Fanny's marriage still awaited celebration, but her sister was firmly Mrs. Williams. "You will not hardly know your old friend Sarah, under her new name", wrote Catherine, with the excited concern of the sentimental, "and I am afraid Mrs Myddleton Biddulph will be still more strange to you." Already, as early as this, she was suggesting that he return home soon, "before the Beagle's course is finished" – although in South America he would at least escape the cholera still spreading across England. "For Heaven's sake, take care of yourself, is all I entreat of you, and don't take any violent fatigues, and do your health great harm." By mid-May, when Susan wrote to him, the family had received his letters from Bahia and everyone, including the servants, was delighted with his health and evident contentment. Fascinated by the thought that one of their own had sailed away to such distant and exotic parts, the whole district expected to be kept informed of Charles's progress – and in a flurry of notes and copied extracts the sisters obliged.

Meanwhile, Fanny's wedding day, held up by financial matters – some question of the Biddulph estate, the arranging of an entail – had been postponed, but drew relentlessly nearer; Susan noted that Fanny had "much lost her former *housemaid spirits*". Charlotte Wedgwood, too, that cousin at whom Charles had in the past gazed with distinct admiration, was married to a gentle, somewhat melancholy clergyman; it was as Charlotte Langton that she became one of those to whom news of Darwin's adventures was instantly sent. (Fortunately her husband's gravity soon gave way to the enlivening delights of marriage, and he became "merry & joking, and chatty", as

Catherine was to write.) So the Owen girls had been snatched away and now, it seemed, one by one the Wedgwood girls were following suit. Darwin must have thought his chance of ever acquiring "that little Wife" was fast slipping away. "I have not yet ceased marvelling at all the marriages," he wrote to Catherine: "as for Maer and Woodhouse, they might as well be shut up." And then he made his only reference to Fanny Owen's news. "I received a very kind letter from Mr. Owen and Fanny." He said nothing more that survives on the matter, apparently wrote neither of heartache nor good wishes, sent no criticism and no congratulations. A few weeks later Fanny's sister, Sarah, unfamiliar now as Mrs. Williams of Belgrave Street, London, was writing to him, "I often think what a wonderful number of changes have taken place among *your* Friends, since you saw them. Fanny's marriage *must have surprised you* not a little, then the 'incomparable Charlotte's' and her Brother . . ." But Charles had either no will or no ability to express his feelings – quite possibly, he now had no feelings to express.

England had perhaps sunk too far below the immediate horizons of his mind, despite all the reminiscences of Barmouth that had confused him into a momentary nostalgia. Immediate and harsher tragedies, in any case, had obscured merely sentimental disappointments: three of those who had caught fever died. One was a cabin boy named Jones, snatched away on the eve of promotion, the second was Roberts, a seaman who had once, Darwin reports, "put a whole party of Portugese to flight", and the third was Charles Musters – "my poor little friend Charles Musters," as Fitzroy wrote, "who had been entrusted by his father to my care, and was a favourite with every one . . ."

Within a few weeks, news of these deaths was provoking Darwin's sisters into a small frenzy of advice and admonition. "I hope my dear Charley," wrote Susan, "this will be a warning to you to be *exceedingly* careful of not over tiring yrself lest you should bring on these fevers. Papa sends his most affectionate love to you & bids me again repeat what we have all said continually how much we hope we may depend upon your not allowing any false shame to prevent your returning whenever you feel inclined . . ." In April Charles had mentioned that he still had "a distant prospect of a very quiet parsonage, and I can see it even through a grove of Palms"; this delighted Susan, who wrote now that she could "fancy you settled there – and in spite of this marrying year I am sure you will find some nice little wife left for you". Caroline, writing that September, hoped that he would be "very prudent & consider the forlorn state you would be in a long bad illness with the miserable accommodation you would have in one of your scrambling expeditions, as indeed you had experience of from what your journal says." At Maer, Fanny Wedgwood, Charlotte's and Emma's sister, abruptly died. Emma had stayed with her during those last moments – it was her loss, wrote Caroline, that would be the greatest, "hardly ever having been separate, all her associations of her pleasures & youth so intimately connected with her". This was almost the first time any of the Darwins had mentioned Emma; they would doubtless have been astonished to see in her the "little Wife" of whom they had written so often and so hopefully to Charles.

Marriage remained in the forefront of matters discussed; even Erasmus, giving news of books bought and books unobtainable, writes of the new Mrs. Langton:

> Charlotte alas is very much deteriorated by her marriage . . . I fully expect that by the time you come home, she will have learned to talk quite fluently about Lords & their pedigrees: I am quite convinced that is their subject tête à tête. I long to have a good groan with you over the incomparable throwing herself away. I am sorry to see in your last letter that you still look forward to the horrid little parsonage in the desert. I was beginning to hope I should have you set up in London in lodgings somewhere near the British Museum or some other learned place. My only chance is the Established Church being abolished, & in some places they are beginning to demand pledges to that effect . . .

Clearly, if Charles was already half committed to a lifetime of science, he would not lack allies when the day arrived to go the rest of the way. Erasmus had established for himself a little laboratory, in which he worked with the intermittent assiduity of a dilettante, while, down in Shrewsbury, Dr. Robert, now partly retired from practice, had been inspired by tales of tropical wonders to establish a hothouse. According to Caroline, "it has quite revived his old interest about flowers, he is going to get a Banana tree principally from your advice . . ."

Darwin meanwhile maintained his routine in the natural hothouse he had dreamed of ever since first reading Humboldt. It delighted him, but he was nevertheless beginning to realize the task he had set himself. Writing to Fox from his Botofago base he asked to hear all his cousin's news of "such a stationary, slow sailing craft as a Parsonage" and added, "I suppose I shall remain through the whole voyage, but it is a sorrowful long fraction of one's life . . ." Was he already, or for the moment, a little weary, or was he, as he so often did, varying his responses to make them as palatable as possible to the person for whom they were meant? For in June Fox had written, "I often long so to be with you & join in your happiness, and think over the difference of our lots & the ridiculousness of my pursuits in Nat Hist: compared with yours." It was certainly in Darwin's nature to feign a fatigue which might please his faraway reader and lighten his dissatisfaction. So he added, "Do you think any diamond beetle will ever give me so much pleasure as our old friend *crux major*?" His rush of nostalgia was real enough and would be repeated many times throughout his life; nevertheless, it was the marvellous present that demanded his attention and all his energies were bent to the labour of probing and observing it.

He collected with indefatigable curiosity, making the constant observations and connections of a mind only recently liberated; he seemed prepared to range and study the whole of nature, to examine and find a place for every one of its artefacts. His published *Journal* is a little deceptive; he wrote it after his return and embellished it with the findings of hindsight. But his Diary and his notebooks testify to the swiftness of his comments, their immediacy and relevance, and, above all, the breadth of his vision. Nothing he saw passed unnoticed, and nothing he noticed was beyond the range of his speculation. At the same time, he kept alive his sensitivity to Nature as a whole; that tropical world never became to him simply an extension of his laboratory, a workplace in which classification took the place of awe.

Nor did he become a merely scientific automaton. He remained, for example, interested in the passage of that Whig measure, the first Reform Act, about which the sisters, and especially Susan, sent him regular information – although, as he wrote, the last keeness of his concern had not survived the "distance of time & space". He was always patriotic, in a simple, straightforward way: "Seeing, when amongst foreigners, the strength & power of one's own nation, gives a feeling of exultation which is not felt at home," he wrote on 1 July, a day on which he attended divine service on board HMS *Warspite*. The foreigners he found himself among had created in him a certain disillusion – he considered that the Brazilians "possess but a small share of those qualities that give dignity to mankind". He listed their shortcomings, then berated the clergy, upon whose faces, he wrote, one saw "plainly stamped persevering cunning, sensuality & pride". The old women were, if anything, worse – "Being surrounded by slaves, they become habituated to the harsh tones of command & the sneer of reproach . . . they are born women, but die more like fiends." In evidence, he cited the thumbscrews which they kept in their houses in order to discipline the slaves.

But, whenever he could, he worked, using his notebooks to collect his observations when he could not collect the actual specimens. In those pages, the characters he met went down, pinned in place like insects; the places in which he met them, the landscapes he crossed or saw from afar appeared with an even greater vividness. The response this demanded from him at length became impossible to sustain: "It is wearisome to be in a fresh rapture at every turn of the road. And . . . you must be that or nothing." When he came to sum up his stay in Botofago, he pronounced himself "tolerably contented" with what he had done, in a place where the geology proved less

Plate 5 Darwin's place of birth, Shrewsbury, on the River Severn, where even after his death controversy raged over his memory.

Plate 6 Shrewsbury School as it looked when Charles was a pupil there and Dr. Butler was vigorously recreating its reputation – though Butler's passion for the classics was never relevant to Darwin's interests.

Plate 7 Leith Harbour as it looked in the days when Darwin, a medical student at Edinburgh, would set out from it in the mussel boats, searching for zoological specimens.

Plate 5 Darwin's place of birth, Shrewsbury, on the River Severn, where even
after his death controversy raged over his memory.

Plate 6 Shrewsbury School as it looked when Charles was a pupil there and
Dr. Butler was vigorously recreating its reputation – though Butler's passion for the
classics was never relevant to Darwin's interests.

Plate 7 Leith Harbour as it looked in the days when Darwin, a medical student at Edinburgh, would set out from it in the mussel boats, searching for zoological specimens.

than interesting, the birds and plants were already known and much of the sea was unproductive: "The number of species of Spiders which I have taken is something enormous". For Darwin, insatiable in his search for fact and conscious of Henslow and the rest waiting for what he might send them, nature, even if tight-fisted in one direction, could always be persuaded to be generous in another.

On 5 July, 1832, the *Beagle* set off for the unknown coasts of Patagonia, hundreds of miles further south. The comforts of the tropics would now for a long time have to be abandoned. Darwin braced himself with the admonition that "the sooner such scenes are forgotten, the more tolerable will the present be". Whales, porpoises, flying fish, grampuses – as the days passed, the sea set up its energetic distractions. The weather turned cold and raw; at night, St. Elmo's fire played about the masts and spars – "the form of the vane might almost be traced as if it had been rubbed with phosphorus". Penguins and seals appeared, harbingers of antarctic waters. On the 26th the *Beagle* entered the bay at Montevideo, to find, as she had at Rio, that there was turmoil and insurrection in the city. The frigate *Druid* was in the course of sending ashore a party of marines to retrieve four hundred horses, comandeered by the new military government from their British owner. With the property of the British subject and the liberty of the British horse at stake, the *Beagle* prepared to give cover to the landing party. A promise that the horses would be given back, however, suspended the action. Observing local politics, Darwin noted, "The revolutions in these countries are quite laughable; some few years ago in Buenos Ayres, they had 14 revolutions in 12 months . . . both parties dislike the sight of blood; & so that the one which appears the strongest gains the day."

The next day he was on land again, taking a look at a small patch of soil and rock named Rat Island. At once he was collecting specimens – "one very curious; at first sight everyone would pronounce it to be a snake: but two small hind legs or rather fins marks the passage by which Nature joins the Lizards to the Snakes". A day later, he was on the summit of the little hill that gives Montevideo its name, looking around at a view that was "one of the most uninteresting I ever beheld . . . Whoever has seen Cambridgeshire, if in his mind he changes arable into pasture ground & roots out every tree, may say he has seen Montevideo."

Fitzroy, meanwhile, was writing a personal letter to Beaufort, expressing an almost unbounded satisfaction.

> All goes well – extremely well – on board. I can say, what seldom may be said, with truth, that I do not wish to change a single Officer or Man, and that I have not more sincere friends in the world than my own Officers . . . Mr. Darwin is a very superior young man, and the very best (as far as I can judge) that could

have been selected for the task. He has a mixture of necessary qualities which makes him feel at home, and happy, and makes every one his friend. By this Packet, the Emulous, he sends his first collection . . . I fancy that though of small things, it is numerous and valuable, and will convince the Cantabridgians that their envoy is no Idler.

In this happy frame of mind, Fitzroy now postponed Darwin's exploration of the uninviting landscape he had found, deciding instead to move on to Buenos Aires in search of certain old maps of Patagonia. The further shore of the River Plate, however, was destined to prove no more inviting, though for somewhat different reasons. "We certainly are a most unquiet ship", wrote Darwin; "peace flies before our steps".

A blank shot from the port's guardship, then a ball whirling through the rigging, a landing party stopped short of the shore and turned back – it was not the pleasantest welcome that Buenos Aires gave them. The city was, it seemed, afraid of cholera and would listen to no explanations – that the *Beagle* had been seven months on open water did not sway them. Fitzroy was furious; one can imagine those long features distorted, the brows contracted, the elevation of that imperious nose. He reported to Beaufort that he had told the Health Officer, "Say to your Government that I shall return to a more civilized country where Boats are sent more frequently than Balls". Darwin's account had Fitzroy sending a message to the local commander: "I am sorry I was not aware I was entering an uncivilized port, or I would have had my broadside ready for an answering shot". In any case, he turned the ship about, ordered the guns to be loaded and run out, then stood towards the impertinent guardship. His message this time was more direct: "If you dare fire another shot at a British Man of War you may expect to have your Hulk sunk; and if you fire at *this* Vessel, I will return a broadside for every shot." (That is his own account of what he said; Darwin's is even blunter. "Next time we enter port we shall be prepared as we are at present, and if you dare to fire a shot we'll send our whole broadside into your rotten hulk!" One may believe that in this unfamiliar situation the young naturalist had been somewhat carried away.) Fitzroy set sail for Montevideo again, and soon the busy *Druid* was off across the estuary to demand an apology. With schoolboy bloodthirstiness, Darwin wrote, "Oh I hope the Guard-ship will fire a gun at the Frigate; if she does, it will be her last day above water."

If he hoped for action, he was to come closer to it within a day or two. On shore, troops mutinied against their military government, occupied the citadel, and, in Darwin's words, "planted artillery to command some of the streets". Yawl, cutter, whaleboat and gig were launched – Fitzroy, with the approval of the Montevideo police chief, was landing men to protect civilian property. The *Beagle*'s neutrality was unforced since, as Darwin discovered, "the politicks of the place are quite unintelligible". Fifty-two men "heavily armed with Muskets, Cutlasses & Pistols" awaited the police chief, Dumas; then "we marched to a central fort, the seat of government . . . Whilst the different parties were trying to negotiate matters, we remained at our station & amused ourselves by cooking beefsteaks in the Courtyard. At sunset the boats were sent on board . . . As I had a bad headache, I also came & remained on board." Darwin, of course, as the expedition naturalist, had no need, and perhaps even no business, to involve himself in this little police action; it seems never to have occured to him, however, not to take part. With a brace of pistols in his belt, a cutlass at hand and the beard he had grown during his days at sea, he must have appeared as threatening a desperado as could be found along the River Plate. "It was", he wrote to Susan, "something new to me to walk with Pistols and Cutlass through the streets of a town." But the chance of battle receded; soon he was wide-eyed in a new landscape, recording his first sight of an ostrich.

The *Beagle* had her own business to attend to, and prepared to depart. Darwin sent letters ashore, and a box of specimens to be shipped to Henslow; then he was off again, with Fitzroy and his peripatetic base, to face the bruising, monotonous manoeuveres of a survey trip. At times the wind hammered at them, at others the cold brought its discomfort; there was dangerous work on lee shores and ominous bumps on unexpected shallows. There were periods of sunshine, fast runs down obliging winds, engulfing rainstorms: "This day last year", Charles wrote on 29 August, "I arrived home from N. Wales & first heard of this voyage. During the week it has often struck me how different was my situation & views then to what they are at present: it is amusing to imagine my surprise, if anybody on the mountains of Wales had whispered to me, This day next year you will be beating off the coast of Patagonia."

A few days later, however, he was writing, "I am thoroughly tired of this work, or rather no work; this rolling & pitching about with no end gained." On 6 September, they anchored in what Fitzroy calls "the extensive and excellent, though then little known harbour, called Port Belgrano", adding in a footnote "Often erroneously called Bahia Blanco"; Darwin, notwithstanding this expert precision by his captain, calls the place Baia Blanca. It had only been settled for six years and designed "as a frontier fort against the Indians".

The battle to dominate the native Americans was carried on at a level of cruelty that constantly outraged Darwin. As with the slaves, his sympathies were with the weak, although he never forgot or excused the murders and barbarities of which the Indians were guilty. Escorted by troops to a local fort – named Argentina – and there interrogated by a suspicious major,

Darwin learned more about this struggle between the indigenous people and the newcomers: "The Indians torture all their prisoners & the Spaniards shoot theirs".

Gradually, the Spanish garrison allowed their doubts to dissipate; the *Beagle* officers were soon busily at sport with gun and rifle. "I am spending September in Patagonia", wrote Darwin, "much in the same manner as I should in England, viz. in shooting . . ."

It was at this time, on 23 September, that he first visited Punta Alta, an area rich in fossils and famous in his own story. It was there that he discovered fossilized remains of a Megatherium, an enormous forerunner of the giant sloth, the unyielding bones of which would more than anything else first bring him to the attention of fashionably scientific London. On his first glimpse of this small plain, marked by the sea-shell evidence of its slow rise from the ocean bed, he found the fossilized "head of some large animal, imbedded in a soft rock. It took me nearly three hours to get it out. As far as I am able to judge, it is allied to the Rhinoceros." Now, and during a longer visit the following year, Darwin brought up, out of rock and time, a number of such ancient bones, between them creating the testimony from which skill and imagination might recreate a menagerie of prehistoric creatures.

Evolution explains the alteration and disappearance of species. Here was evidence enough that species had tramped their time upon the earth, then vanished. No wonder that again and again the discoveries at Punta Alta have been connected to Darwin's later theorizing, that what he found there has been considered an immediate quickening agent developing his ideas on species transmutation. His *Journal* has been taken to confirm this – but his *Journal* was written after his return, and amended during years when he had already begun his notebooks on transmutation. His notes on his fossil finds include precise decisions about the animals from which they came, decisions which were beyond his competence, and for which he later relied upon Sir Richard Owen, the most accomplished anatomist in Britain. Fossils had been dug up for many decades; even in South America, others before Darwin had found them. When on 8 September he "obtained a jawbone, which contained a tooth" and found from this that it must have belonged to the Megatherium, he pointed out that "the only specimens in Europe are in the King's collection at Madrid, where, for all purposes of science they are nearly as much hidden as if in their primaeval rock." There was no reason for him, aware as he was of the existence of such fossilized remains, to leap at once to a revolutionary conclusion. Indeed, his use of the adjective "anti-diluvial" to describe the Megatherium demonstrates the continued orthodoxy of his convictions. Even if the word was used only as a figure of speech, it was not one he would have chosen had he had the slightest doubt that the earth had included at least one universally catastrophic flood in its history.

Nevertheless, his finds at Punta Alta were ultimately of great importance. They led him into considerations of the ecology of the prehistoric world, and so faced him with the questions which Lyell had avoided. In his *Journal* he writes what amounts to a small essay about the amount of vegetation needed to feed animals so enormous, and came to the conclusion that there need be "no close relation between the *bulk* of the species, and the *quantity* of vegetation, in the countries which they inhabit". If that was so, however (though he seems not to have wondered how luxuriantly the plants might have flourished had there not been such bulky creatures to keep them in check), then that only increased the mystery of their disappearance. For if, as he declared, such creatures could have been sustained by the environment in which their fossils were found, then the problem of why they had not became both obvious and pressing. "I am far from supposing that the climate has not changed since the period when those animals lived", he conceded; but since it had not changed to such an extent as to make conditions impossible for them, it was a concession which did nothing to explain why they had vanished. This was particularly true of forms foreshadowing those still in existence, the most notable of which was an early version of the horse. "Certainly it is a marvellous fact in the history of the Mammalia", commented Darwin, "that in South America a native horse should have lived and disappeared, to be succeeded in after ages by the countless herds descended from the few introduced with the Spanish colonists!" The success of this later equine invasion must have stirred in his mind – a mind so active, so quick to seize on curiosities and anomalies – a number of key questions. He must have wondered, if only idly, about such things as the antiquity of species, their distribution over the earth, the nature and means of their survival. His thoughts about their need for vegetation must have emphasized for him what others, Lyell among them, had already pointed out: the necessary link between a species and its environment, the whole problem of adaptation.

In the *Journal*, he speculated about the differences to be found between the animals of North and South America, as against the similarities that used to obtain in quite recent geological times. Examining the fossil record and the evidence of such ancient animals as the mastodons trapped in Siberian ice, he developed a panoramic view of great terrestrial processes, appearing almost physically to see the subsidence of land and the creation of the modern continents, the spread of the great oceans and the subsequent separation of creatures which had previously meandered across a common range. But these were later ideas which he was prepared to display in the

Journal; they were not those of the *Beagle*'s young naturalist. And even in the *Journal* he did not allow himself to question why so late a separation had had such far-reaching effects upon the species, and by what mechanism the differences between the animals of the two American continents had come about. On matters such as these, his speculations would remain private for more than twenty years. Then, when he came to discuss the relationship between environment and extinction, the fossil horse of Punta Alta would leap from his researches to provide, for a passing moment, an example to embellish his argument.

Fitzroy, anxious to complete the survey of these shores as swiftly as possible, hired two small schooners which, by mid-October, were ready to set off on their independent tasks: "we gave them three hearty & true cheers for a farewell," wrote Darwin, but it was most of his closer friends who were departing, leaving him with the prospect of some weeks with little congenial companionship. The arrival of letters and newspapers from home as the month closed afforded some compensation for friendships postponed. Even more importantly, the same mail brought Darwin the second volume of Lyell's *Principles of Geology*, the book that was to have a more significant effect on his intellectual development than any other. In it, Lyell dealt with the zoological implications of his geological theories, made relevant by a recent revival of interest in Lamarck's ideas on the transmutation of species.

Lamarck remains a brilliant yet enigmatic figure, whose fate it has been to stalk like a spectre, now glimpsed, now vanished, the tortuous corridors and noisy debating chambers of the evolutionary establishment. A minor aristocrat, a hero of the Seven Years' War, at one time a starving medical student, he published in 1778 a book on the flora of France that established his reputation. Through the influence of Buffon he was engaged by the Jardin du Roi, there surviving the Revolution (and the politic change of name to Jardin des Plantes).

Over the years, Lamarck developed his evolutionary ideas into a system, first publishing his conclusions in his *Philosophie zoölogique*, which appeared in 1809. He had already brought out, seven years earlier, a work on geology in which he had exclaimed, "Oh, how very ancient the earth is!" and ridiculed those who still thought of its history in terms of six millennia. Having accepted the great age of the planet, Lamarck was able to take a long-term view of the life upon it and thus to arrive at a belief in the mutability of species. Creatures were always potentially liable to change over the generations, and that potential had been expressed in the great variety to which his own classifications – those classifications which Darwin had had to learn in Edinburgh – bore witness.

What has discredited Lamarck is the principle of change that he claimed as the underlying evolutionary process. It was what might be termed *change through use*. Any organ that was forced into use by the animal's need to fit in with or overcome its environment would begin to develop. Such a development would be passed on to its offspring which, faced with the same environmental factors, would through similar use promote its further development. Over a number of generations, therefore, such an organ would become more and more adapted to its function, until there had appeared the kind of specialization that could be seen throughout the natural world. In many specialized forms, however, there remained vestigial alternatives, rudimentary organs that, given a change in circumstances, began a new development which would, in the end, create a new specialization. The species were, therefore, in a constant actual or potential state of flux. So much was this the case, Lamarck believed, that he went even further and proposed that the demands of the environment and the organism's efforts to meet them could sometimes create entirely new organs, while the disuse of others led to their eventual disappearance.

Lyell seized on this, pointing out that "no positive fact is cited to exemplify the substitution of some *entirely new* sense, faculty or organ, in the room of some other supressed as useless ... It is evident that, if some well-authenticated facts could have been adduced to establish one complete step in the process of transformation ... time alone might then be supposed sufficient to bring about any amount of metamorphosis." The species, Lyell asserted, were real, true facts of nature, and the amount of variation which admittedly could be found between individuals, even between parents and offspring, did not amount to an "indefinite capacity of varying from the original type".

Lyell himself, as a convinced uniformitarian, suggested that new species appeared at a more or less constant rate throughout terrestrial time and space. The species that appeared later were not an improvement on those that had appeared earlier, they were simply responses to a creative principle in the universe which Lyell did not specify and about the mechanism of which he made no suggestion. Once present on the earth, adapted to the particular circumstances in which it had come into being, a species was free to spread in ways which the environment made possible or, at times, demanded; eventually, it would vanish altogether, for "amidst the vicissitudes of the earth's surface, species cannot be immortal ..."

In the rest of the volume, Lyell discussed the nature and reliability of the fossil record, pointing out how vulnerable it was to the accidents of both preservation and discovery. Thus, apparent variations in the distribution of different species were liable to be entirely misleading – a warning that stemmed as much from his rejection of directionality in terrestrial history as it did from observation. Only the non-appearance of human fossils, which in a species so widespread and active one might have expected to find, could be taken as clear proof of how recently mankind had appeared. There was also a brief examination, later to be of great relevance to Darwin, of the formation of coral reefs, the circular forms of which Lyell took as evidence that they stood upon the rims of craters submerged below the surface of the sea.

One may imagine Darwin seizing upon the book and, as the *Beagle* weighed anchor and set out a second time for Buenos Aires, spending the three days in which she struggled against headwinds devouring its ideas. During those cool, autumnal evenings, socially depleted by the absence of so many young officers, did he and Fitzroy discuss the matters Lyell had raised? It is impossible to believe that they did not, the fundamentalist officer veering between arrogance and humility, the young naturalist between politic conciliation and a dogged survey of the facts. Not that they were as yet in opposition: Fitzroy was still short of an absolutist position, Darwin far from an evolutionary one. Yet they must already have been moving apart, with Lyell's skirting of creation and rejection of the Flood less and less to Fitzroy's taste and more and more to Darwin's. If that was so, however, then the gaps in Lyell's presentation will have been increasingly disconcerting to Charles: a geologist could afford to ignore problems that a naturalist had to face. Somewhere, at some level of brain or consciousness, he must already have begun to grapple with them.

On 2 November, 1832 they once more passed the Buenos Aires guardship, "who this time treated us with greater respect", as Darwin remarked belligerently; soon he was examining the city, "large, & I should think one of the most regular in the world". It was one of the first to be laid out on a strict rectangular pattern, but the liveliness of the street events took from its straight lines and repeated angles all chance of monotony. There were the swaggering *gauchos*, with their heavy moustaches "and long black hair curling down their backs" and with "brightly-coloured garments, great spurs clanking about their heels, and knives stuck as daggers (and often used) at their waists . . . Their politeness is excessive; they never drink their spirits without expecting you to taste it; but whilst making their exceedingly graceful bow, they seem quite as ready, if occasion offered, to cut your throat." And there were the ladies, who wore in their hair "an *enormous* comb; from this a large silk shawl folds round the upper part of the body. Their walk is most graceful, & although often disappointed, one never saw one of their charming backs, without crying out, 'how beautiful she must be'." There was the great plaza, with its public buildings, the low houses built about their shady central courtyards; and, much less pleasantly, the place of public slaughter, where cattle were lassoed, dragged out of the herd, hamstrung and killed: "the ground is made of bones, & men, horses & mud are stained with blood".

Yet this exotic city on the River Plate had not excised older and gentler ambitions – or so it seems; he wrote to his cousin, William Fox, about his regret at having so soon to leave the tropics.

> My peep at these climates has quite spoiled me for any other; I must however except the English autumnal day, the clearness of the atmosphere of which will stand comparison with anything. – Poor dear old England. I hope my wanderings will not unfit me for a quiet life & that in some future day I may be fortunate enough to be qualified to become like you a country Clergyman. And then we will work together at Nat. History & I will tell such prodigious stories as no Baron Monchausen ever did before. – But the Captain says if I indulge in such visions as green fields & nice little wives &c. &c. I shall certainly make a bolt. – So that I must remain content with sandy plains & great megatheriums.

However, his discontent with South America and his hankering after English parsonages, or even English wives, was probably again being displayed more out of concern for Fox's feelings than out of any inner need. He mentions no parsonages in his Diary, nor demonstrates the slightest nostalgia for England. It was to be more than two years before homesickness began really to create its debilitating misery.

Fitzroy was impatient now to sail on towards the south and play out his Pygmalion contract with the Fuegians. On 26 November, two days after Darwin had basked in the easy music of Rossini's *La Cenerentola*, he was watching the seamen weigh anchor; three days later he was exulting like a true sailor, "Beautiful days, calm sea & a fine breeze; what can the heart of man desire more?" On 4 December, they made their rendezvous with the detached schooners, now beginning to show the first marks of their new duties; the meeting was short, the smaller ships were dispatched on another three months' survey trip, with the next appointment for the little fleet fixed for the following March in the Rio Negro, and the *Beagle* had set her stem to the south again.

On 16 December, 1832, Darwin could write, "We made the coast of Tierra del Fuego . . . Our ignorence whether any natives lived here, was soon cleared up by the usual signal of smoke; & shortly by the aid of glasses we could see a group & some scattered Indians evidently watching the ship with interest." Two days later, Darwin had the opportunity to see the local inhabitants at closer range. A large party of officers landed in order to establish some contact with the Fuegians, who, clustering on the shore – though without their women and children – made "without exception the most curious & interesting spectacle I ever beheld. I would not have believed how entire the difference between savage & civilized man is. It is greater than between a wild & domesticated animal, in as much as in man there is greater power of improvement."

The impression that the Fuegians made on him was profound. They became for the rest of his life the indicators of human degradation and at the same time the mark by which human advancement might be measured. To him, they seemed diabolic, "representations of Devils on the Stage . . . Reaching from ear to ear & including the upper lip, there was a broad red coloured band of paint; & parallel & above this, there was a white one . . . Their very attitudes were abject, & the expression distrustful, surprised & startled." He thought their language hardly human, though noting their talent for mimicry – "if you cough or yawn or make any odd motion they immediately imitate you."

Jemmy Button – whom the resident Fuegians instantly recognized as one of themselves – found that he could understand hardly anything they said, so different was their language from that of his own people, and so much of his own had he forgotten. Later, York Minster fared rather better, although the locals were disconcerted even by his sparse beard, telling him quite firmly to shave – "& yet he has not 20 hairs on his face, whilst we all wear our untrimmed beards". But the Fuegians were obviously aware of the signific-ant differences that existed between them and the Europeans, as they demonstrated when comparing skin colours; it is likely that they would have shrugged off no matter what bizarre behaviour from such unclassifiable strangers. One of their own, however, even if from some unknown group and accompanied by Europeans, was clearly expected to conform to their habits and customs. Such a conviction on their part had ominous implica-tions for the future of Fitzroy's project – the Fuegians were not, it seemed, disposed to accept novelty from anyone whom they accepted as one of themselves. Such individuals would, rather, have to conform to the conven-tions of the majority.

Darwin was struck by their apparent lack of property, even of huts – "Their present residence is under a few bushes by a ledge of rock," he wrote – and by the poverty of their diet. The *Beagle* contingent, meanwhile, amused themselves in making faces at the Fuegians and watching the "hid-eous grimaces" with which they were answered; with singing and dancing, to the delighted astonishment of people who must have been somewhat starved of entertainment in their bleak, nomadic lives; and with comparing the tallest Fuegian with their own tallest man. No wonder that Fitzroy records of his crew that "deeply indeed was I interested by witnessing the effect caused in their minds by this first meeting with man in such a totally savage state".

Soon Darwin was walking, scrambling or climbing the rocky uplands that overhung the sea, collecting specimens of the alpine flora and refreshing his sea-cramped spirit with a series of huge and dramatic panoramas. On 21 December, the *Beagle* sailed on, "doubtless to the grief of the Fuegians", and just before Christmas, in a yell and a clatter of gales, saw distant Cape Horn, "veiled in a mist & its dim outline surrounded by a storm of wind & water. Great black clouds were rolling across the sky & squalls of rain & hail swept by us with very great violence . . ." Christmas Day found the *Beagle* in sheltered anchorage, surrounded by the barren cliffs and mounds of America's southern tip, the officers wildfowling on shore, hallooing through their own echoing responses, causing their own tiny avalanches, Darwin himself tap-tapping his way about with his insistent geological hammer, and all observed by distant, half-hidden and doubtless astonished Fuegians.

Meanwhile, all through that Patagonian autumn, life in England had continued in its accustomed serenity; letters to Charles with news of it were beginning to pile up at Montevideo. Catherine mentioned that curious and burgeoning threesome of Hensleigh Wedgwood, his wife and cousin, Fanny, and his friend and cousin, Erasmus Darwin: "He and Mrs Hensleigh seem to be thicker than ever; she is quite as much married to him as to Hensleigh, and Papa continually prophecies a fine paragraph in the Paper about them." The Shrewsbury hothouse continued to prosper – a hole in the ground waited for the expected banana tree, which Dr. Robert intended naming "Don Carlos", in honour of his distant son. Fanny, who had been Owen and was now Biddulph, was struggling with her new family – "I should think there was a thorough hatred between them. – Fanny does not however at all beat under to them, but gives herself very proper airs." And finally Catherine offered again the sisters' hopes for Charles's future – "My dear Charles, how I long for you to be settled in your nice Parsonage. I hope you retain that vision before your eyes. – People here think you will find cruising in the South Seas such uninteresting work that it gives us some hopes you will perhaps return before the *Beagle*." How desperately they hoped to hold Darwin within their own comfortably narrow world, how afraid they were that he was bursting – had already burst – through its confining limits, how patiently they held to their cosy ambitions for him. But he was already gone, dazzled by the rocks and forests, the birds, beasts and human beings of a distant land, overcome by the wonder and variety of the natural world and drawn as if to the Holy Grail by the mysteries that lay behind its multifarious artefacts.

In November, Dr. Robert visited London and Sarah Williams, who had once been Owen, came to The Mount. Susan reported that she had said "she depended upon yr keeping yr promise of letting her be the first person you dine with upon your return as Belgrave St was very convenient for that purpose" and added, "I wish I cd foresee that before this time two years my dear Charley you wd fulfill that engagement." Palm trees had arrived for the hothouse, but were so large that they already touched the roof – "I don't see how they can ever flourish". And the tale of the *Beagle*'s landing men during the Montevideo insurrection had appeared in the papers; it made her impatient for letters from Charles himself.

His old Cambridge friend Herbert wrote at the beginning of December; as always, his letter was full of his admiration for Darwin. "You have I suppose become a good practical mathematician long ere this . . . I expect that the zeal, which you always had & which you once gave me credit for, will have carried you into the regions of the 'Mecaniques Celests' . . ." Alas, Darwin's mathematical skills were never to carry him anywhere very far, a deficiency he was in later years to deplore. Herbert had put his own mathematical studies to one side, retaining only as much, he wrote, as would enable him to understand the book that Darwin would inevitably write. "I have already begun to picture myself its appearance & the nature of its contents – one of Murray's 4tos in Davidson's type? 'Observations physical, political & moral made during a voyage rd the world in the years 1831–1835 by C. Darwin FRS &c &c'. You will of course stay its publication, till these hieroglyphic characters are affixed to your name – I shall indeed revel in its fresh-cut pages." Herbert, however light-heartedly, could see already the honours that were, to some of his friends, so clearly ahead of Darwin – just as he had a shrewder idea than many of how long it would be before the *Beagle* returned. Again, the zeal that Darwin "always had" testifies to an early energy which others have denied him.

By now the sisters had worked out a rota for sending Darwin one family letter a month; early in January, 1833, Caroline was forced by Catherine's dereliction to write one out of turn. "My Father is very well – which I know is the main thing so it will not matter how little else I have to tell . . . I do hope my very dear Charles the cold & rains whilst coasting Patagonia have not made you ill . . . and if you find all these changes of climate do not agree with your health come home & think of your snug Parsonage." Thus the cosy priorities of Shropshire continued to pursue Darwin across the Atlantic, as well as news of local deaths, illnesses and marriages and the health of animals: Pincher and Nina, his dogs, were both very well, Mrs. Biddulph was looking very handsome, "but I suspect she must find Mr. Biddulph a tiresome person to live with . . ." One imagines the triviality of this no more than gossip, but for Charles, locked into his unfamiliar world with all prospect of a swift return long vanished, it must have held the resonance of poetry, the latest stanzas in the saga of his own land and people.

Later that month, Fox wrote a letter that mixed information with envy. He had been ill, but was now beginning to improve, settled in some comfort on the Isle of Wight. "I have seen so many vessels on the point of setting out to South America from Portsmouth . . . that my erratic propensities have been often quite painfully excited and I have dreamt by the night that I was as busy as could be collecting with you, all around new, beautiful & strange." Alas, the nearest he had come to such a voyage was to examine a set of magnificent insects, brought from Rio and mounted in a cabinet. His destiny, he felt, was to be tied to the Continent at best, "not to say (as perhaps may be much nearer the truth,) the country I was born in, and of tropical regions I must be content to hear from *Humboldt & Darwin*." Herbert, too, felt similar stirrings; he had been ill and to the doctor: "A journey, or rather a voyage, to the Pampas would be the best way of carrying his prescription into effect, as he has ordered me to take an unlimited amount of exercise." It was as if Darwin carried on his shoulders, not only the scientific expectations of the English naturalists, but also the burden of representing every would-be adventurer and explorer in his circle of friends.

On 19 January, 1833, Fitzroy began the final preparations to settle his three Fuegians, as well as Matthews, the missionary who had come from England to bring the calming word of Jesus to these bleak regions. They set off in the four boats and ten days later reached what they called Woollya, Jemmy's country, where York Minster, too, had stated firmly that he and Fuegia Basket wanted to remain. As time passed, more and more of the local tribe arrived, among them Jemmy's mother, brothers and sisters. They met their prodigal without much in the way of emotional display; as Fitzroy remarked, "Animals when they meet show far more animation and anxiety . . ." Three strong wigwams were built, one each for Jemmy and the missionary, the third for York Minster and Fuegia Basket. A plot of land was dug and tilled and seeded, to provide them with a settled source of fresh vegetables.

At one time there were, Fitzroy estimated, more than three hundred Fuegians observing them with an overt, ceaseless and largely innocent curiosity, although for no discernible reason on 27 January almost all of them departed. Whether this had anything to with the seamen's demonstration of the power of firearms or not no one was able to establish; the behaviour of the Fuegians was on the whole so impenetrable to Fitzroy that he decided to leave Woollya and the new wigwams for a short trial period to see what might happen. Before he left, he counted up what had been stolen and found it to be remarkably little. He wondered how honest his own men might have been in similar circumstances: "Had they themselves been left among gold and diamonds, would they all have refrained from indulging their acquisitive inclinations?"

On the 28th, two of the boats began the return journey to the *Beagle* while Darwin and the others who were left, under Fitzroy's command, set off to examine some of the nearby islands and the deeply indented coast. They sailed away, through sunshine suddenly hot enough to burn their skins, down the Beagle Channel, a sound running straight and deep for over a hundred miles to the Pacific, and across waters pockmarked with the waterspouts of whales. The following day this enigmatic land revealed a little of its dangerous ferocity. Halted on a tiny beach at the head of a narrow bay, the party was admiring the gleaming blues and greens of a nearby glacier when, with a hollow, explosive booming, a great mass of ice broke free and fell thunderously into the water. Instantly the huge wave it had caused came curling up the inlet, gathering weight and speed as the cliff walls narrowed. Darwin tells us that "one of the seamen" saved their boats from being smashed on the rocks. But Fitzroy is clear that "had not Mr. Darwin, and two or three of the men, run to them instantly, they would have been swept away from us irrecoverably". Reward came the next day: Fitzroy, steering the leading boat out into a large, open area of water, named it Darwin Sound.

On 6 February, 1833, they arrived again at the tiny settlement in Woollya. To their surprise, everything had in their absence continued with only minor crises. Certainly there had been a quarrel or two and the garden had been destroyed – "My people very bad", Jemmy said; "great fool; know nothing at all; very great fool" – but at least everyone was healthy. Nevertheless, Matthews had decided that what signs he could read or predictions he could make were not good. It would be better, both he and Fitzroy thought, if he now left the settlement. So Fitzroy departed, saying farewell to his three half-taught Fuegians "with rather sanguine hopes of their effecting among their countrymen some change for the better . . . I hoped that through their means our motives in taking them to England would become understood . . . and that a future visit might find them so favourably disposed towards us, that Matthews might then undertake, with a far better prospect of success, that enterprise which circumstances had obliged him to defer, though not to abandon altogether."

It was 5 March, 1834, over a year later, when he was again at Woollya. There was no sign of York or Fuegia Basket, no sign of Jemmy Button. The wigwams were empty, and had been so for a long time. It seemed as though all his expectations had dwindled into this mystery. Then, from one of the islands, a canoe approached. In it, among the other paddlers, a man oddly familiar, certainly seen before, a Fuegian already known to them – and then, abruptly, known too well and, in that guise, welcomed with amazement: Jemmy Button. But a Jemmy totally altered, "thin, pale & without a remnant of clothes, excepting a bit of blanket round his waist: his hair hanging over his shoulders; and so ashamed of himself he turned his back on the ship as the canoe approached."

The story was one of treachery: York Minster had conspired with his brother and other members of his tribe to steal everything that Jemmy owned. Fitzroy, his plan totally awry, clutched at straws: "I cannot help still hoping that some benefit, however slight, may result from the intercourse of . . . Jemmy, York, and Fuegia, with other natives of Tierra del Fuego. Perhaps a ship-wrecked seaman may hereafter receive help and kind treatment from Jemmy Button's children . . ." Perhaps some idea of God would be retained; and certainly Jemmy was grateful, presenting cured otter skins to Fitzroy and to Bennett, one of the quartermasters; a bow and arrows to the school he had attended in Walthamstow; and two spearheads he had made to Darwin (though Darwin says that spearheads and arrows were "for the Captain"). Everything that might be spared and Jemmy would find useful was handed to him and his newly-acquired and somewhat suspicious wife, to his brothers and their mother, in an effort to establish him again. With York gone and his own people around him, it seemed possible that he would no longer be molested – though the price of that security was likely to be so stringent a conformity to the prevailing customs that what he had learned would bit by bit wear away.

Yet he had not learned much more of his own, original language; instead, to everyone's astonishment, it was his brothers and womenfolk who had picked up from him a rudimentary English, with which they supplemented their own vocabulary when speaking with him. Perhaps, for a while, it would indeed be possible for him to establish on that cloud-darkened, rock-dominated extremity of the Americas a little society marginally more complex, marginally better equipped, than anything that existed round about. But if he did, it hardly mattered; contacts with Europeans had begun and, here as in so many other places, would not cease until the last Fuegian had vanished. Fitzroy, his years of work undone and his hopes at an end, seems finally to shrug and turn away, setting down the bare facts: "As nothing more could be done, we took leave of our young friend and his family, every one of whom was loaded with presents, and sailed away from Woollya."

Thus Jemmy was left, to remember a distant land so different in wealth and style, in habit and religion, that even for him it must in time have melted into the brilliant vagueness of a myth; perhaps for the rest of his life, he would be in some corner of himself an exile, waiting for the resurrecting arrival that would allow him to sail away again with the powerful strangers who once, for so short a while, had utterly transformed his life. Darwin, looking back, tells us of the final contact: "He lighted a farewell signal fire as the ship stood out of Ponsonby Sound, on her course to East Falkland Island." It is not a detail Fitzroy bothered to record.

4

In March, 1834, Darwin wrote to Henslow, in terms which showed how insecure he still felt himself to be as a geologist.

> By the way I have not one clear idea about cleavage, stratification, lines of upheaval. – I have no books, which tell me much & what they do I cannot apply to what I see. In consequence I draw my own conclusions, & most gloriously ridiculous ones they are, I sometimes fancy I shall persuade myself there are no such things as mountains, which would be a very original discovery to make in Tierra del Fuego. – Can you throw any light into my mind, by telling me what relation cleavage & planes of deposition bear to each other?

His later reputation rises like a wall to hide from us this younger, tentative Darwin, still learning so many of the essentials of his multiple craft. It might be said that in many ways he was being forced to construct the sciences that interested him, before making himself a practitioner in them. In a later generation, such a task may have been beyond him, but during the first half of the nineteenth century more or less every ambitious scientist was in the same position: the natural sciences, certainly, were new, the divisions and definitions creating them recent, the knowledge they made available neither precise nor entirely reliable.

The advantage to Darwin lay in the scientific innocence this allowed. He could regard the world with an eye that saw only what was in front of it, unobscured by expectation. The only question was whether he had the courage to see with this childlike clarity. It was his lifelong gift and his intellectual salvation that he had. All the nobility of science, all the lonely stubbornness of the scientist, are implicit in Darwin's baffled reaction to his geological books: what they tell him he "cannot apply to what I see". Those who imagine that Darwin was merely fortunate, with no particular talent or distinction, and has therefore been grossly over-praised, are answered in that single phrase. In the innocence of his genius, he read the earth itself rather than his predecessors; thus he freed himself to arrive at knowledge from its testimony, instead of restraining its testimony within the bounds of what he thought was knowledge.

While Jemmy Button had suffered his year of treachery and deprivation, the *Beagle* had visited the Falkland Islands: "An undulating land," Darwin tells us in his *Journal*, "with a desolate and wretched aspect . . ." The drowning of Hellyer, the Captain's clerk, trapped by seaweed while swimming to retrieve a bird he had shot, did nothing to relieve the islands' inherent melancholy. Early in May, 1833, the *Beagle* was again in Montevideo, where the artist, Earle, had remained in a vain attempt to recover from sickness. A few days later, the ship was setting Darwin ashore at the town of Maldonado, a place he discovered to be dowdy, boring and unlovable. Nevertheless, he remained there for ten weeks, paying rent to his landlady, Donna Francisca, and grateful to be able to walk and ride again, even if only in the featureless countryside round about.

During his stay Darwin rode some seventy miles inland, to the banks of the Polanco; the ignorance and parochialism of the people he met struck him as surprising, though one might wonder how readily the inhabitants of Shropshire could supply information on the cities and artefacts of South America. Nevertheless, his pocket compass, his matches, even his washing in the mornings, seems to have excited wonder and comment wherever he went. "I am writing", he tells us in the *Journal*, "as if I had been among the inhabitants of central Africa". Aspects of the local manners, too, caused him some amused anguish: "a charming Signorita will perhaps present you with a choice piece from her own fork; this you must eat ... for it is a high compliment. Oh the difficulty of smiling sweet thanks, with the horrid & vast mouthful in view!"

All the while he was collecting specimens of the local animals and, especially, birds, both during his excursions and after his return. By mid-June, he could boast in his Diary that his collection was "becoming very perfect". Once more he settled into the old routine, gathering his specimens one day, preserving them the next. Doubtless he was helped in this by his servant, Covington, whom in July the previous year he had described merely as "fiddler & boy to Poop-cabin". Now, from Maldonado, he wrote to Caroline:

> The following business piece is to my Father: having a servant of my own would be a really great addition to my comfort, – for these two reasons; as at present, the Captain has appointed one of the men always to be with me, but I do not think it just thus to take a seaman out of the ship; – and 2nd when at sea, I am rather badly off for anyone to wait on me. The man is willing to be my servant, & ALL the expences would be under £60 per annum. I have taught him to shoot & skin birds, so that in my main object he is very useful.

Since he was spending no more than £200 a year, he felt that his father would allow him to spend this sum on Sims Covington, as indeed he did. Covington, a quiet and rather dour man, remained Darwin's servant until some time after his marriage to Emma Wedgwood.

Darwin's detestation of slavery burned as fiercely as ever. "What a proud thing for England", he wrote to Caroline, "if she is the first Europaean Nation which utterly abolishes it. I was told before leaving England, that after living in Slave countries, all my opinions would be altered; the only alteration I am aware of is forming a much higher estimate of the Negro character." Prophetically, he looked forward to the independence of Brazil – "it will be wonderful if at some future day it does not take place". And, in a postscript, he asked for more books to be sent out, including a treatise on Hutton's geological theories, a book on volcanoes, the most recent volume of Humboldt, and an awaited text by Sedgwick and his associate Conybeare on geology.

By the end of June, 1833, Darwin was back on board the *Beagle* and preparing to travel on: "My heart exults whenever I think of all my glorious prospects of the future", he wrote, hearing of Fitzroy's plans to make for the Pacific. He organized his collection: fly-catchers, mockingbirds, a local burrowing creature, the *tucutuco*, the whole spectrum of starlings – organisms of every sort, reptiles, mammals, over eighty kinds of birds – as the ship prepared to depart. At the beginning of August, the *Beagle* dropped anchor in the mouth of the Rio Negro.

The town of Patagones, past which the river flowed "about four times as wide as the Severn at Shrewsbury", became for a while Darwin's operational base. From here, he made or joined a number of small expeditions, one of which Sulivan recorded. What he seems to have remembered best is the comparative comfort of their excursions. "Tea is a great luxury in cruises of this kind. We always boiled a large boiler holding four gallons full every morning for breakfast, and the same for supper, and we never had any left . . ." Among a dozen men this provided relief enough. Food came in similarly generous portions, the same four-gallon pot, filled with "salt pork, fresh beef, venison, and biscuits", providing their dinner, with more meat at breakfast and supper. "Such hardships are hard to put up with," Sulivan commented ironically, "the idea of being among mud-banks in a boat with nothing but a waterproof awning to cover her with, and thick blankets to sleep in, with only two pounds of meat, two-thirds of a gallon of tea, one pound of bread, and a quarter of a pint of rum each man per day is dreadful!!!" They moored their boat to wait while Darwin and two men worked at the recovery of fossils – "he this morning found the teeth of animals six times as large as those of any animal now known in this country" – and watched thunderstorms march across the evening sky. Snug under their awning, keeping the insects at bay with the smoke of their pipes, they were far from distress. One can see them, on that low sandstone shore, the scattered islands fading from sight in the dusk, the black clouds standing high, flinging their lightning at intervals across the last glow of sunset, the wind flapping the canvas above the men's heads and the thunder stalking the passing minutes, the talk low, contented, broken at times by laughter or the sly insults of friends, the blue tobacco smoke floating uneasily below the awning: "I think I never in my life", Sulivan wrote in his journal, "saw people more happy than all our party were". One by one, the men roll themselves in their blankets and go to sleep; the thunder mutters like a lullaby. Darwin sits and ponders the stony bones he has collected, the creatures of whose skeletons they once formed a part, the long ages of the earth. He sighs, knocks out his pipe, lies down like the others to an easy sleep. These are the moments he will mine for memories, all the rest of his life.

On 11 August, he set out from Patagones to make an overland journey to Buenos Aires. Ahead of him, the wild, uninhabited country was criss-crossed by warring columns of Indians and soldiers, struggling through the bloody figures of their endless dance. Although he lost a day in order to answer an invitation from General Rosas, the Portugese commander, Darwin and his companions covered the 150 miles to Bahia Blanca in less than six days. During this time, Fitzroy wrote to him, a letter that in the lightness of its style evokes the curious friendship between these two extraordinary young men.

> My Dear Philos, [wrote Fitzroy in his enormous, sloping hand,] Trusting that you are not entirely expended – though half-starved, – occasionally frozen, and at times half drowned – I wish you joy of your campaign with Genl Rosas – and I do assure you that whenever the ship pitches (which is *very* often as you *well* know) I am extremely vexed to think how much *sea practice* you are losing; – and how unhappy you must feel upon the firm ground. Your home (upon the waters) will remain at anchor near the Montem Megatherii until you return to assist in the parturition of a Megalonyx measuring seventy two feet from the end of his snout to the tip of his tail – and an Ichthyosaurus somewhat larger than the Beagle . . . Take *your own time* – there is abundant occupation here for *all* the *Sounders*, – and so we shall not growl at you when you return."

Soon the *Beagle* had also arrived at Bahia Blanca, while in the rich soil of Punta Alta Darwin discovered yet more fossils – though these did not entirely conform to Fitzroy's exuberant description. One day, too, a column of soldiers arrived, in pursuit of a recalcitrant Indian tribe; their talk, and soon that of the townsfolk, was dark with tales of murder, battle, treachery and ambush. On both sides, prisoners had been hacked down or shot, the wounded killed, villages and settlements destroyed. The firepower, however, was with the government forces. Speaking to a local, Darwin learned all mature young Indian women were killed in cold blood. "I ventured to hint that this appeared rather inhuman. He answered me, 'Why, what can be done? they breed so!' Everyone here is fully convinced that this is the justest war, because it is against Barbarians. Who would believe in this age in a Christian civilized country that such atrocities were committed?" The desperate cry of a good man comes down to us across decades the blackness of which Darwin could hardly have imagined.

On 20 September, Darwin reached Buenos Aires, which seemed to him rather pretty, "with its Agave hedges, its groves of Olives, peaches & Willows; all just throwing out their fresh green leaves". It was only seven days, however, before he was riding out once more. By the end of the month, after a short bout of fever, he was in the town of Paraná, the guest of "an old Catalonian". Here he spent the best part of a week, studying the local geology and searching for fossils.

His remarks on what he found suggest that during those long rides and solitary forays of scientific prospecting, his mind was continuing to turn over the terms of that fundamental argument, that debate in which the antagonists could be taken to be Fitzroy and Lyell, and out of which as yet he had been able to create no glimmer of a synthesis. A recent profound drought had been followed by a season of exceptionally heavy rains. During the first, thousands of cattle had rushed into the Paraná and, too weak to crawl back up its muddy banks, had drowned there. When the downpour at length began, floods resulted during which the turbulent rivers had carried with them enormous quantities of mud and silt. These had been deposited upon the skeletons of the dead cattle. "What would be the opinion of a geologist", asks Darwin in his *Journal*, "viewing such an enormous collection of bones . . . thus embedded in one sticky earthy mass? Would he not attribute it to a flood having swept over the surface of the land, rather than to the common order of things?" To the extent that this represented Darwin's ideas at the time, it is clear that Lyell's uniformitarianism was beginning to win the day. The fossil evidence for catastrophe was suspect, making more plausible the theory that the natural laws obtaining in the present had always operated, and were sufficient to explain every apparent viscissitude in the geological record. Perhaps he was beginning to come to the conclusion that there had been time enough for many small changes to alter the earth, and that on the whole small changes were likelier than enormous natural convulsions. If this is so, however, it means only that he was keeping step with the more advanced scientific opinion of his day; he was not yet, for example, ahead of Lyell, nor on the way to accepting the mutability of species.

Back in Montevideo, Darwin met the artist, Martens, who had replaced the invalided Earle – a change about which Fitzroy had already written to him in his boisterous style: "Mr. Martens – Earle's successor – a *stone pounding artist* – who exclaims *in his sleep 'think of me* standing upon a pinnacle of the Andes – or sketching a Fuegian Glacier!!!' By my faith in Bumpology, I am sure you will like him, and like him *much* – he is – or I am wofully mistaken – a 'rara avis in navibus, – Carlo que simillima Darwin'! – Don't be jealous now for I only put in the last bit to make the line scan – you know very well your degree is 'rarissima' and that *your* tune runs thus – 'Est avis in navibus, Carlos rarissima Darwin'! – But you will think I am cracked so seriatim he is a gentlemanlike well informed man . . ." This high-spirited schoolboy classicism is typical of Fitzroy's eccentric, helter-skelter humour:

> *"Well, but the conjunctions – the conjunctions"* I hear you saying – *"you have got to the end of a sheet of paper without telling me one thing that I wanted to know"*. – This is the 4th October, – *"so the date of your letter tells me"* — well – hm – hum – but – we must consider – then – hum – tomorrow will be the sixth – *"Prodigious*!!!" Do you know what I mean – *"to be sure"* – so-and-so – so – & hm hmm hmm & off goes the head!! – I never will write another letter after tea – that green beverage makes one tipsy – besides it is such a luxury feeling that your epistle is not to go a chop the wide atlantick – and has only to cross the muddy Plata.

It must have been for Darwin like receiving a letter from Laurence Sterne. The feeling in it, however, makes plain how well Darwin was liked, as well as giving us a glimpse of how at times the conversation on the *Beagle* must have flung to and fro in a clatter of puns and tags which may well have reminded him of boisterous evenings at Cambridge.

This was a period when Darwin was almost distressingly active. His energy and ambition seems almost manic. On 14 November, 1833, he was setting out once more, again armed with passport, letters of introduction and the other appurtenances of a traveller in a land where credentials offer some security. Flood waters had enriched all the rivers and the men had to swim their horses across. "A naked man on a naked horse is a very fine spectacle . . . as the Peons were galloping about they reminded me of the Elgin marbles." Everything seemed to interest him, people, places, creatures, plants, climate, the structure of the rocks, the politics, the indigenous tribes; and nothing seemed for long to dim his sense of wonder or his awareness of what was beautiful: the River Uruguay at Punta Gorda is clearer than the Paraná, discernible when their waters mingle; though shut up tightly, a lime kiln may burst into flame again after many months; feats of lassoing catch his eye, and the speed of the *gauchos* in killing and skinning a mare; his host for the night demands, and gets, his praises for the beauty of the Buenos Aires women. And all these stand in his Diary under only a single date, 20 November. The next day is as full, and the next, and the one after that – for five years his passionate recording of the passing world did not flag.

Darwin returned to the *Beagle* with new specimens of fossils. For eighteen pence he had bought the head of a Toxodon; a tooth that was a perfect fit in one of its empty sockets was among those he had found 180 miles away, on the banks of the Tercero. The number of prehistoric bones that might be found in South America astounded him: "We may conclude", he wrote in the *Journal*, "that the whole area of the Pampas is one wide sepulchre of these extinct gigantic quadrupeds." During his journeys he had enormously increased his collections, and the knowledge he had of the past as well as the still extant fauna of the area; box after box, packed with care and dispatched with trepidation, crossed the Atlantic for the educated attention of Henslow. Although part of his year was now spent in the care of his new parish, Cholsey-cum-Moulsford, Henslow remained active as both teacher and scientist; at times his letters to Darwin read like those of the director of an expedition instructing his men in the field, while in England he arranged for some of Darwin's results and findings to become increasingly widely known. The fossil remains of the first Megatherium discovered by Darwin were, for example, exhibited at the third annual meeting of the British Association for the Advancement of Science, presided over by Sedgwick.

Henslow was not alone in following as closely as he could Darwin's progress. At Shrewsbury, the sisters were endeavouring to make good the deficiencies in their education: "I think Geology far the most interesting subject one can imagine," Susan wrote to her brother in March, 1833, "& now I have found a very easy way of learning a little smattering of it. The penny Magazines give a few pages (which the most foolish person can understand) in every Number . . . we all *swear* by it as it contains every kind of knowledge written so pleasantly with prints." From Susan above all among the young women one gets the feeling of a thwarted intelligence, a firm will frustrated by the even firmer conventions that locked in the daughters of the well-to-do; poor "Granny", she tried hard to stay in step with her brother, but in the circumstances of her time was doomed to be left farther and farther behind.

From Catherine, writing in May, Darwin received a slightly tongue-in-cheek account of the Erasmus scandal: "He seems to be more in love than ever with Fanny Hensleigh, and almost lives at Clapham. Papa has long been *alarmed* for the consequences, & expects to see an *action* in the Papers. I think the real danger is with Emma Wedgwood, who I suspect Mr Erasmus to be more in love with, than appears, or than perhaps he knows himself." Charles at this time was probably less interested in Emma and her possibilities than he was in news of that other Fanny who, long past the games of childhood, had produced a Biddulph daughter. "She looks deplorably ill & weak", Catherine reported, "and very lonely . . . Mr Biddulph seems fond & affectionate to her, but he is a gay dissipated man, and desperately selfish".

News of Darwin's travels and explorations always flustered his sisters and alarmed them into the kind of affectionate scolding he must constantly have had to suffer when at home. "Do take care of yourself my dear Charles you were so apt at home to over exert yourself that we are all afraid when ever we read of your enjoying yourself" – thus Catherine in September, before going on to give further news of Erasmus. "He is very constant to Mrs. Hensleigh Wedgwood & thinks her the nicest of women." She and her husband had been at The Mount with their baby "& Erasmus with all his horror of babies plays with the little thing and watches it for any length of time." In her next letter, however, she returned to her anxieties over Charles: "I cannot help being rather grieved when you speak so rapturously of the Tropics, as I am afraid it is a still stronger sign, how very long it will be, before we shall have you again, and I have great fears how far you will stand the quiet clerical life you used to say you would return to." Even for the sisters, it seems, that once-expected parsonage was, like an attractive dream, unable to resist the thrusts of an altered reality.

Fanny Biddulph was at Chirk Castle with "the detestable old Mrs & Miss Biddulph, whom poor Fanny perfectly hates . . ." Fanny herself – "delicate, pale, and thin; but so very charming" – had visited The Mount and "I wish you could have seen her pretty look, (when she was talking about you,) she turned to me, and said 'I suppose he never mentions me', with all her old sweet manner. – She talked a good deal about you very affectionately & warmly, & said how much she wished for your happiness." Erasmus, meanwhile, had been staying at Maer "with Fanny Hensleigh, her Baby, *Miss Snow,* as it is called (short for Snowdrop) and Emma Wedgwood; all his favourites around him."

In October, it was Susan who picked up the clerical theme: Charlotte Wedgwood's reverend husband, Mr. Langton, had become both busy and popular in his new parish; "I quite long for you to be settled in just the same kind of manner my dear Charley: I am sure I shall pitch my tent very near you in that case." Unmarried, yet forced to live through men in an age when few women had, so to speak, the use of their own lives, how she must have longed to have her young brother in a comprehensible occupation and an accessible home. Did these reiterations make Darwin in the slightest guilty? Did they place him under pressure? It is more likely that, used all his life to the admonitions of his sisters, he discounted much of what they said. It was Susan, however, who as much as anyone kept him aware of the political changes that were under way, and now she displayed her committed liberalism by rejoicing at the abolition of slavery, despite her resentment over the £20 million which the owners were to receive in compensation. Her independence of mind and underlying fierceness, implicit in the zest with which she attacked these political matters, perhaps owed something to her personal situation that October, for she was then in the process of rejecting the suit of a certain Mr. Panting.

That autumn, his family received the first installment of Darwin's *Journal* and read it with the avidity and enjoyment one might expect. It did not prevent Caroline from offering a little criticism. Charles had, she thought, been reading Humboldt a little too closely and had "occasionally made use of the kind of flowery French expressions which he uses, instead of your own simple straight forward & far more agreeable style". She sent him books by Harriet Martineau* "which are talked about by evry body at present" and mentioned Erasmus's admiration for the author. Like Susan, she praised the abolition of slavery; among the Darwins there seems never to have been the slightest dispute on public matters.

From Catherine, we have a picture of the family sitting in a group, hearing Charles's *Journal* read aloud, the great father, despite his weight, his age and his gout, listening intently to the adventures and opinions of his distant son. The manuscript, she wrote, "meets with great success, and is pronounced exceedingly entertaining" and Dr. Robert "desires me also to tell you how very much he is pleased with your Journal". Meanwhile, rumours of a shift in Darwin's opinions on terrestrial history seem to have percolated to Shrewsbury: "I hear that your Theory of the Earth is supposed to be the same as what is contained in Lyell's 3d Vol. Some of your Friends or Whitley's Friends meant to send out the 3d Vol to you; have you received it?" This was written on 27 November, 1833; had Darwin in fact moved all the way into the uniformitarian camp by then?

His geological observations on the coasts of Patagonia had convinced him that vast forces had been operating to elevate the land in comparatively recent times, and so might be taken to be still in operation. He knew this from finding, embedded in strata high above sea-level, the shells of still existing species of sea creatures. On the other hand, his various discoveries of the fossil remains of so many long-vanished creatures brought him to consider the causes of their destruction. "The mind at first is irresistibly hurried into the belief of some great catastrophe", he wrote in the *Journal*. Had such an event occurred, however, it would have shaken "the entire framework of the globe"; an examination of the local geology led, on the contrary, "to the belief that all the features of the land result from slow and gradual changes". Nevertheless, the central puzzle remained – "Certainly

---

* Harriet Martineau (1802–1876) was a well-known literary figure whose output ranged from fiction to books on Political Economy. She popularized the ideas of Ricardo and Malthus, and brought out a translation of Comte's *Philosophie Positive;* visited and wrote about America; and was involved in mesmerism, which was later to interest Darwin.

no fact in the long history of the world is so startling as the wide and repeated extermination of its inhabitants."

By the time even the first edition of the *Journal* was published, however, Darwin was almost at the end of those complex *Transmutation Notebooks* in which he laid the intellectual foundations for his later detailed theorizing. By 1845, when the second edition came out, he had written both the Sketch and the Essay which were the forerunners of his later published work. It is not surprising, therefore, to find in the *Journal* hints and echoes of familiar ideas; their display in those pages does not mean that they reflect the thoughts Darwin had as he swung in his hammock in the *Beagle*, travelling south towards Tierra del Fuego. His mind was not yet prepared to find a context for the rise and fall of whole groups of creatures, or to see the species as balanced within a system of constant growth and destruction. What he was now prepared to accept was the Earth of Lyell's vision, a place where constant changes added up to enormous – but incredibly slow – revolutions. Within these there might be at least a mobility of the species. How they arose and why they fell was as yet unclear; that they altered imperceptibly one into another must still have seemed as unacceptable to Darwin as it did to Lyell himself.

The third volume of Lyell's *Principles of Geology* had been published in April, 1833, and had soon after been sent to Darwin, who had asked for it. Perhaps he had read it while in Montevideo, perhaps he was reading it now, as the *Beagle* sailed southward into the cold and the storms of Cape Horn. Like the first two volumes, it was to have a profound effect on Darwin's view of the earth and its history. In the book, Lyell used in demonstration of his uniformitarian theories the third segment of the terrestrial past, the Tertiary Era. His approach was cautious – he took the trouble to point out, at some length, how misleading the geological record could be, laid down as it had been, in intermittent fashion, over millions and hundreds of millions of years. He suggested that the best guides to the relative ages of the strata were the fossils they contained. The greater the percentage of extant species represented in a stratum, the more recent it was. What is more, given the constancy of geological forces, over time and in space, it seemed to Lyell that an identity in this aspect of the fossil record could be translated into an identity of age. Thus, for example, thirty per cent of extant species found among the fossils in any stratum on earth would make it contemporaneous with every other stratum carrying the same percentage.

It was in this third volume, too, that Lyell made his persuasive analysis of the Etna region, demonstrating the great antiquity of even those rock deposits which were, in geological terms, comparatively recent. He re-examined some of the crucial evidence that had been offered by the catastrophists, and showed how, in the areas of Europe they had relied on, a uniformitarian explanation fitted the geological facts as well or better. He still, however, avoided any discussion of first and last things, asserting categorically that the beginning or end of the world could not, in the nature of things, ever be discovered. On the one hand you had "the finite power of man" and on the other "the attributes of an Infinite and Eternal Being". Since this was so, certain kinds of knowledge would always be beyond human capacity. What he gave his readers, therefore, was a world in which everything was process, a world which needed no direction because it had come from and was going nowhere. Its origins and its destiny were no one's concern – or, rather, were the concern of an intelligence so far beyond the human that its workings, and the information upon which it relied, could not even be discussed. It was a position that had overtones of deism, and as such not one that was likely to satisfy everyone for very long.

5

The *Beagle* sailed southwards, towards summer, the new year and the Straits of Magellan, accompanied now by a 170-ton schooner, nostalgically renamed *Adventure* (after Capt. King's original survey ship). She was a British-built yacht which had so appealed to Fitzroy that, as he wrote later, "my wish to purchase her was unconquerable". He had bought her at a personal cost of just under £1,300 and, also at his own expense, had had her refurbished. He hoped that the Admiralty would reimburse him at least for the costs of keeping her. "Perhaps it may shorten our cruize", wrote Darwin optimistically in his Diary.

Securely anchored in the mouth of the creek at Port Desire, on the Patagonian coast, the ships passed Christmas, 1833. Almost the whole crew competed for prizes offered by Fitzroy for those who could run fastest, jump farthest or wrestle their rivals to the ground. "These Olympic Games", Darwin called them, and they delighted him; he much preferred them to the usual festivities, which seemed to him notable only for "every seaman getting as drunk as he possibly can".

He too found sport of his own kind: the large guanaco which served as Christmas dinner was his contribution, brought down by his gun on the high plain that stretched away to the north. The general passion for hunting almost lost him one of his most valuable specimens. On the Rio Negro, as he wrote in his ornithological notes, "I repeatedly heard the Gauchos talk of a very rare bird which they called the Avestruz Petise . . . When at Port Desire . . . Mr. Martens shot an ostrich; I looked at it forgetting, at the moment, in the most unaccountable manner, the whole subject of the Petise, & thought it was a two-third grown one of the common sort. – The bird was cooked & eaten. – & my memory returned. Fortunately the Head neck legs, one wing & many of the larger feathers had been preserved." It is as well that he rescued its remains: it is classified today as the *Rhea darwinii*. Smaller than the more common flightless bird, the *Rhea americana*, it filled in its more southerly habitat the same ecological niche as the larger American ostrich did further north. The similarities between these species of Rhea, however, raised crucial questions in Darwin's mind. What made American fauna American? Why were these two South American birds so similar – and why were they so different from birds of broadly the same type in Africa and

The Rhea – one variety is named after Darwin.

The *Beagle* in the Magellan Straits.

Australia? His struggle with this problem was to lead him closer to the central mysteries of inheritance.

In mid-April, with the *Beagle* safely moored again, after having her bottom scraped and patched, Fitzroy decided to lead an expedition to explore the Santa Cruz river. Its headwaters lay in distant mountains that were a beckoning temptation to Darwin and as they made their way day after day upstream, it seemed that he would achieve his ambition of ascending their slopes. Thirty miles short of them, however, when they were 140 miles from the Atlantic coast and some sixty from the nearest arm of the Pacific, Fitzroy called a halt. They had run out of time and the peaks that Darwin had hoped to climb would remain for ever out of his reach. "We were obliged to imagine their nature & grandeur, instead of standing as we had hoped, on one of their pinnacles & looking down on the plain below." On 5 May, they began their return journey, allowing themselves to be whirled exhilaratingly along by the current. At noon on the 8th, they were back again on board.

Slowly the *Beagle*, with her attendant schooner, made her way under great cliffs, past lowering, snow-covered mountains and through a maze of rocky islands to the long, slow waves and great horizons of the Pacific Ocean. At the end of the month, they anchored off the island of Chiloe. They were burdened by an unwonted sadness – their purser, Rowlett, at thirty-eight the oldest officer on board, had died after a short illness. Nor was this Fitzroy's only loss. The Lords of the Admiralty had refused to help him maintain the *Adventure* and, furious, depressed, disdainful, hurt in pride as well as pocket, he was forced to sell the little schooner. In his *Narrative* he tells us that "the mortification it caused preyed deeply, and the regret is still vivid".

This setback, and the long strain of commanding a ship through unknown waters while meticulously charting a difficult coast, flung Fitzroy into the darkest of his abysses. Always liable to morose fits of silence or evil temper, to paranoia and a hair-trigger pride, he sank now into the most dire despair. His depression was so profound that he proposed to give up his command of the *Beagle*. From Valparaiso he wrote to Beaufort, on 26 September, 1834, "My Schooner is *sold*. Our painting man Mr. Martens is *gone*. The Charts &c are progressing slowly – They are not ready to send away yet – I am in the dumps." To his officers he was more outspoken, proposing that Wickham should take over the ship. He wrote to Beaufort again, on 28 September: "Troubles and difficulties harass and oppress me so much that I find it impossible either to say or do what I wish." His many problems seemed about to overwhelm him. "Letters from my friends – Having been obliged to sell my Schooner, and crowd everything again on board the Beagle – Disappointment with respect to Mr. Stokes – also the acting Surgeon – and the acting Boatswain – Continual hard work – and heavy expense – These and many other things have made me ill and very unhappy." He felt as though on the verge of insanity; for a while he kept to his cabin while Wickham acted as captain. But the *Beagle*'s officers knew that in this negative mood of abdication his weakness, paradoxically, would be his strength: they appealed to his sense of responsibility. If he gave up the command, it was the survey that would suffer. His skill and care for detail were essential for its success. Fitzroy allowed himself to be hauled back from the darkness; he took the command back from Wickham. Soon he was bustling about the ship in all his old, sharp-eyed belligerence.

Darwin, meanwhile, had settled himself in Valparaiso, in the house of an old school-fellow, Richard Corfield, who had providentially made his home in the town. With his habitual concern for domestic finances, Darwin noted that Corfield's annual household expenses, including "table, wine, 2 men, 3 or 4 horses", came to about £400, about half of what they would have been in England. Soon he was taking his long, observant rambles through the country round about, and examining beds of ancient sea-shells, "yet retaining their colours" which were to be found on land elevated to well over a thousand feet above the sea. When he put the reddish-black mould in which the shells were embedded under the microscope, he was amazed to discover from the organisms it contained that it had originally been marine mud. He noticed, too, that insects, birds and mammals were all surprisingly rare. His comment upon this in his Diary was pure Lyell: "It seems a not very improbable conjecture that the want of animals may be owing to none having been created since this country was raised from the sea." Significantly, perhaps, this speculative sentence made no appearance in the *Journal*.

During the second half of August, while making his first expedition into the Chilean mountains, Darwin's health began to let him down. "At night I was exceedingly exhausted ... Necessity made me push on ... It was wretched work; to be ill in bed, is almost a pleasure to compare to it." Thus run his diary entries. By 26 September he was forced to send for a carriage to transport him back to Corfield's house, and there he remained until the end of October. He described what had happened in a letter to his family. "I staid a few days at some Gold-mines, & whilst there drank some Chichi, a very weak, sour new-made wine. This half poisoned me . . . I consider myself very lucky in having reached this place . . . a man has a great deal more strength in him when he is unwell, than he is aware of."

Darwin sometimes felt that with this illness there began that undermining of his constitution which, before another decade had passed, would so severely circumscribe his life. Perhaps, however, his body was beginning to react to the apparent endlessness of the *Beagle's* voyage. In the same letter that describes his illness, Darwin also mentions the *Adventure*'s sale.

"Thank Heavens, however, the Captain positively asserts that this change shall not prolong the voyage" – a voyage which, he writes, "sounded much more delightful in the instructions than it really is". And he notes, "I find being sick at stomach inclines one to be homesick." The note of weariness is new; for the first time, there is the sense of a man jaded by the miles he has travelled. Perhaps, at some level below the conscious, being homesick inclined one to be sick at stomach.

His letters from England will, in any case, and whatever his mood, have helped him to pass the time. His entomologist friend, Hope, wrote about the founding of the Entomological Society, for which he had put forward Darwin's name, and asked him to work in particular on the association between volcanoes and certain insects. In a burst of chauvinism, he looked at entomology as a sort of scientific contest: "In our favourite pursuit we are likely to take the lead. Our Cabinets are very rich but unfortunately not everyone is so assiduous as a Darwin or a Stephens . . ." Once again someone who shares his interests praises Darwin's application. Nor is that the end of praise for Charles, because "from sending home the much desired bones of the Megatherium your name is likely to be immortalised. At the Cambridge Meeting of Naturalists your name was in every mouth & Buckland applauded you as you deserved."

From Catherine there came news that William Fox was to be married to "the daughter of a Sir Richard Fletcher who was killed at the siege of Zaragoza in the Peninsular War"; Darwin, as far as ever from finding his little wife, must have learned of this news with a mixture of feelings. It was as if the normality for which he and everyone he knew had always been intended was passing him by. Everyone else was behaving precisely as their age and station demanded; only he was pursuing this eccentric and now wearisome course along the barren coasts of South America.

On his birthday, 12 February, Susan had wished him many happy returns, "but not abroad", and reported that the Doctor, "who never forgets anniversarys remembered this day of course at Breakfast and sends you his best love & blessing . . ." She had, she wrote, enjoyed his *Journal*, but one part of it "as your Granny I shall take in hand namely several little errors in orthography of which I shall send you a list that you may profit by my lectures tho' the world is between us." And there the words are, set down with school-mistress precision: "loose" instead of "lose", "lannscape" instead of "landscape", "cannabal", "quarrell" and the rest, the errors underlined and the list with Susan's insistence that "as your Granny it is my duty to point them out".

Early in March Caroline reassured Charles about his concern over spending money. The previous November he had written, a little laboriously, about his need to spend an extra £50 in order to investigate certain geological formations in Uruguay. "I well know that considering my outfit, I have spent this year far more than I ought to do." Now Caroline wrote, "My Father . . . bids me say he did not growl or grumble at the last £50 you said you drew – & he says you must not fret about money, but be as good & prudent as you can." So much for Dr. Robert's supposed financial tyranny – the anxiety seems much more to have been on Charles's part, even if the Doctor also felt that he was being overcharged for the transport of Darwin's specimen boxes to Cambridge.

William Owen of Woodhouse wrote to Valparaiso in April, saying he was counting the days to Darwin's return "like a schoolboy before the Holidays". As for Sarah and Fanny, they were "now quite old steady wives", while two of the Owen boys were serving in India; perhaps during his travels Darwin would be able to meet them and the three of them could go out shooting. "What I would not give to be of such a party – but it is too late – I am getting very *hobbling* . . ." A message on the flap by Catherine did duty that month for a Darwin letter, but in May Susan was complaining of Erasmus, who had "behaved very shabbily this Spring & not paid his usual Easter visit: he half lives with the Hensleighs, & Mrs. H. has just had another child a boy . . .", a juxtaposition of information which, in view of Dr. Robert's doubts over the association, seems as unfortunate as it does innocent.

In September, Caroline once more expressed her sisterly anxiety over Charles's welfare: "My dear Charles do not let the having escaped so long make you careless & daring for the time to come". Fanny Biddulph and her husband had been on a Swiss tour, while the young Henry Owen "who you left a good little boy is now aiming at being a Dandyfied young man, wearing a worked velvet waistcoat, white gloves & a cane!" In every letter, with its many items of small, personal news, there was the implication that it was in England, after all, and not among the marvels of South America that real life was continuing. Caroline might write that "one day passes so like another that nothing I have to tell you", but for Darwin it must have seemed that the changes at home were happening far too swiftly. His sense of exile and the consequent homesicknesses it produced were from now on to mark much of what he wrote to Shrewsbury, and as the months dragged by his impatience to be finished with the voyage became intense. Yet he seems hardly to have wavered, or to have considered his always open option of setting out alone for England.

The temptation must at times have been strong, especially when he received letters from his friends summoning up his nostalgia as well as displaying their desire to see him again. In November, Fox wrote of a visit to

Wensleydale, where Robert Pulleine had a living, "It was just at the commencement of grouse shooting . . . I should so much have enjoyed walking over this beautiful country with my much valued & old friend Darwin, and unless you are much changed, & have learned to despise such small game since you took to Ostriches, you would I think have enjoyed it too." And then there was marriage, now enveloping Fox in its comforts: "I need not set forth to you the manifold advantages of matrimony as you were always a Philogomist and purposed entering that state as soon as you could, I will only say that from my present experience, I warmly recommend it to you & all I wish well to." It must have seemed to Darwin that, for all the activity in it, his own life was the one that had reached a kind of immobility.

What remained positive was the continuing advance in his reputation. The constant supply of specimens and letters which he sent to Henslow were not being jealously kept from the scientific establishment, as they might have been by a less generous man. It was clear from the slightly astonished pride with which the sisters referred to the delight of the experts at what Darwin was sending them that he and his work were being quite widely praised. While his modesty over his achievements and the intensity with which he followed his vocation left little room for him to attempt some grander evaluation of himself, it is probably the case that these reactions not only confirmed him in his intention to devote his life to the natural sciences, they prepared and partly reconciled his family to accept it. Certainly all mention of "the little parsonage" dropped away as the years passed.

It was in some awareness of this, perhaps, that in July Darwin, writing to his old Cambridge friend, Charles Whitley, had asked if he was not "a married man, and may be nursing, as Miss Austen says, little olive branches, little pledges of mutual affection", and had added at once, "Eheu! Eheu! this puts me in mind of former visions of glimpses into futurity, where I fancied I saw retirement, green cottages, and white petticoats. What will become of me hereafter I know not; I feel like a ruined man, who does not see or care how to extricate himself. That this voyage must come to a conclusion my reason tells me, but otherwise I see no end to it." There is an element of duplicity in this, since Darwin had, as we know, the right to end his own voyage when he chose. The reason why he did not he made instantly plain – of course, he bitterly regretted his old friends and pursuits, but in their place "there is much solid enjoyment, some present, but more in anticipation, when the ideas gained during the voyage can be compared to fresh ones. I find in Geology a never-failing interest, as it has been remarked, it creates the same ideas respecting this world which Astronomy does for the universe."

Darwin knew very well that he was in the midst of an intellectual turmoil, an expansion that would alter his ideas, and thus himself, for ever. A farewell to settled notions had meant a farewell to a settled future; but that was the price which, although he understood its heaviness, he was prepared to pay. The choices he took, like the opinions he came to, were the result of deep pondering and were not arrived at without pain. He remained on the *Beagle*, choosing the knowledge that the voyage brought him, although with every month his personal future must have looked more unpredictable.

With the passion of a religious aspirant, he turned to the cosmic truths locked up in geology rather than the domestic pleasures that awaited him in marriage. His tepid involvement with Christianity was burned away by his intense devotion to science; religion became more than ever a question of social order rather than spiritual transcendence. The uneasy promise of intellectual revelation took the place of a steady happiness marked only by the tranquil progression of the rural year. The modest, retiring Darwin, so sparing of information about his inner self, cannot be understood except through his unappeasable hunger to realize the nature and structure of the physical world. It was the attempt to assuage that hunger which governed the choices he made – but that is not to say that such choices were easy. At this precise moment, laid upon his sickbed in Valparaiso, he had no means of knowing what deprivations he was to suffer or even what sacrifices he might already have made as a result of his decision to remain, come what may, upon the *Beagle* expedition.

6

Towards the end of November, 1834, the *Beagle,* unescorted now and once more overcrowded, arrived at San Carlos, on the island of Chiloe. For over two months Darwin crossed its volcanic mountain slopes or watched the sailors trading with the local Indians in remote and rocky hamlets. The start of 1835 seemed more warning than promise, flinging wild rainstorms at their heads. "Thank God", wrote Darwin, "we shall not here see the end of it; but rather in the Pacific, where a blue sky does tell one, there is a heaven . . ." By the time the *Beagle* sailed, on 4 February, he could claim, "I have now well seen Chiloe, having both gone round it & crossed it in two directions."

It took them a day to reach Valdivia, "completely hidden in a wood of Apple trees", one of the oldest Spanish settlements on the western coast. As a result, Darwin was on hand when, on 20 February, the town was shaken by "the most severe earthquake which the oldest inhabitants remember . . . I was on shore & lying down in the wood to rest myself. It came on suddenly & lasted two minutes (but appeared much longer) . . . There was no difficulty in standing upright; but the motion made me giddy. I can compare it to skating on very thin ice or to the motion of a ship in a little cross ripple." Out in the open woods Darwin seems to have thought this interesting, but hardly alarming; hearing that some people had compared it with a very severe earthquake that had partly destroyed Valparaiso a dozen years before, he commented "that in Earthquakes as in gales of wind, the last is always the worst".

Aboard the *Beagle* men had the sensation that the ship had touched bottom, while in the little town many buildings had been wrenched out of shape, though none were destroyed or even badly damaged. This was one of a series of shocks which, they heard, had rippled through the area over the previous two weeks, and as they were sailing on to Concepcion they felt yet another. The mild unease with which they seem to have faced this gave way to something closer to horror when on 4 March they entered Concepcion harbour. Not a house in the town, or the neighbouring one of Talcuhano, remained standing. Seventy villages had been destroyed, and the shore lay strewn with the flotsam of disaster "as if a thousand great ships had been wrecked". Enormous rocks had been torn from the sea-bed and flung high on the beach; vast cracks ran north and south along the ground, some of these splits measuring a yard across. "For the future", Darwin wrote, "when I see a geological section traversed by any number of fissures, I shall well understand the reason. I believe this earthquake has done more in degrading or lessening the island, than 100 ordinary years of wear & tear." To Henslow, Darwin commented, "I wish some of the Geologists who think the Earthquakes of their times are trifling could see the way the solid rock has shivered".

He had now seen at first hand the power of Nature's ordinary forces; it seemed less necessary than ever to explain the facts of geology through any special catastrophes. Nevertheless, his experience of earthquake and observation of its aftermath left him in some confusion. What had caused it? From where exactly had it come? Was it created by some action of the local volcano, Antuco, and, if so, why had the waves apparently come from the south, almost the opposite direction? He circled round and round problems most of which nowadays would hardly disturb a schoolboy, versed in the details of fault lines and the pressures that bear on them, of the movements of continental plates, and the fragility of much of the seabed. One realizes once again how much of their science Darwin and his contemporaries had to create out of almost nothing, how insignificant was the mound of accumulated knowledge upon which they could stand in order to examine the surrounding world.

On 11 March, the *Beagle* was again in Valparaiso – and by the 15th, Darwin had begun to climb into the Cordilleras on his way to Mendoza, on the far side of the mountains. Braving the *puna*, the panting brought on by breathing the rarefied air of high altitude, he worked at his geology at well over ten thousand feet. Clearly at this time his constitution can have had few weaknesses. As, on 23 March, he began his descent towards Mendoza, he noted how different were the plants and creatures to be found on this side of the mountains, as compared with the other. In his *Journal* he explained that these differences were due to the intervening barrier of the Andes, which had existed "since the present races of animals have appeared". Later, he could not prevent himself from adding a footnote that hints at what had become his main scientific preoccupation. "This is merely an illustration of the admirable laws, first laid down by Mr. Lyell, on the geographical distribution of animals, as influenced by geological changes. The whole reasoning, of course, is founded on the assumption of the immutability of species; otherwise the difference in the species in the two regions, might be considered as superinduced during a length of time".

Mendoza, while attractive in its setting of gardens and orchards, "had a forlorn & stupid air . . . the happy doom of the Mendozinos is to eat, sleep & be idle". A day of such inactivity was enough; soon Darwin was clambering delightedly through the mountains again. Crossing the Uspallata range, at well over ten thousand feet, he was amazed to see the fossilized remains of a conifer forest leaning into the thin mountain air. He realized that the trees had once stood by the shores of the Atlantic, until the land itself had sunk to the most profound depths of the ocean. Later, it had risen, shaken off the seas and folded itself into these vast mountain ranges. Wind and weather had, as delicately as archeologists, eventually exposed these petrified remains; now they served the amazed Darwin as instant indicators of terrestrial time. "Vast, and scarcely comprehensible as such changes must ever appear, yet they have all occured within a period, recent when compared with the history of the Cordillera; and the Cordillera itself is absolutely modern as compared with many of the fossiliferous strata of Europe and America".

A few days later, he saw, high in a deserted, waterless valley, the ruins of some Indian houses, similar to those still being built, but, in proof of their antiquity, made of mud instead of stone. Amid such sterility no little village could have sustained itself. "If however a few showers were to fall annually, in the place of one in several years . . . such spots would be highly fertile". He concluded that the climate had radically altered since the huts had been built, and that this may have been the consequence of a quite recent elevation of the land, of which he had "certain proof" in the evidence of the sea-shells he had found. At a lower level, the climate might well have been as balmy and productive as that of the South Seas; "If the mountains rose slowly, the change of climate would also deteriorate slowly; I know of no reason for denying that a large part of this may have taken place since S. America was peopled". Darwin was now a fully-fledged follower of Lyell, seeing the world around him as in a state of constant, low-level flux. There had been change through the millennia, casting forests to the bottom of the sea, hurling them to the tops of mountains, turning them to stone: there was change in the present, lifting whole valleys, altering regional climates and affecting the distribution even of the human race. In such a world, what other alterations might not prove possible? In such a world, what could be taken as fixed?

From Valparaiso, Darwin wrote home, "Since leaving England I have never made so successful a journey: it has, however, been very expensive." Thus he raised "the black & dismal part of the Prospect – that horrid phantom Money . . . In September we leave the coast of America; & my Father will believe that I *will* not draw money in crossing the Pacific, because I *can* not. I verily believe I could spend money in the very moon." The trouble was that when a passing muleteer offered to take him to some wonder a hundred miles away, "I cannot, or rather never have, resisted the Temptation".

Darwin's frequently expressed distress over the money he was spending is curious since, as we have seen, Dr. Robert was both wealthy by the standards of the time and relatively unconcerned about the matter. If anything, he went out of his way, in the messages his daughters passed on, to reassure his son. One cannot help feeling that Darwin's attitude includes an element of play-acting, of providing for his father a somewhat contrived display of contrition. Perhaps, as when he took the lead in criticizing himself, this relieved him of anxiety and left him free to continue behaving as he really pleased. Certainly he seems to have spent more or less what he wished and, though always careful and never, then or later, a spendthrift, travelled as far and as widely as he desired.

After a few days at Valparaiso, Darwin was off on his travels once more, now matching on land the *Beagle*'s pace off shore. In mid-June, he struck inland again, clambering high into the Cordillera where llamas, foxes, vicuña, and the distresses of the *puna* awaited him. By 6 July, he was back on board as the *Beagle* set sail for Iquique.

Had he heeded the advice he was getting from Shrewsbury, he would by then have been halfway home to England. Caroline, responding – four months earlier – to his accounts of his illness, had written:

> Papa . . . wishes to urge you to think of leaving the Beagle and returning home, & to take warning by this one serious illness: Papa says that if once your health begins to fail, you will doubly feel the effect of any unhealthy climate . . . Papa is *very much in earnest*, and desires me to beg you to recollect that it will soon be four years since you left us, which surely is a long portion of your life to give to Natural History. If you will wait till the Beagle returns home, it will be as many years again . . . we are quite in despair about it.

Gossip alters the mood: a Wedgwood cousin, Robert, in his late twenties and a curate, had "fallen vehemently and desperately in love with Miss Crewe, who is *50* years old and blind of one eye . . . She is a clever woman, and must have entrapped him by her artifices . . . It is a regular case of Gobble Boy, I think . . ." But in a postscript Caroline returns to her theme, pointing out, "You have been longer than you originally intended & are not the slightest degree bound in honour to remain as long as the Beagle does . . ." A long letter from Whitley, giving news of all their old Cambridge friends – Heaviside, a tutor; Watkins and Tom Butler, clergymen; Herbert, about to be called to the Bar; Whitley himself, soon to be a professor – may well have increased Darwin's own anxieties, not about his health, but about his future: all those men now so settled and he still on the high seas, his voyage perhaps only half over. Yet nowhere is there the slightest hint that he ever came even close to a decision to go home early.

Nevertheless, his attitude to the places in which he now found himself seems little short of jaundiced. Iquique, of which the aspect "was most gloomy", he described as a "small group of wretched houses"; for relief from this depressing scene he could arrange nothing more enlivening than a visit to a saltpetre works. Callao was "a most miserable filthy, ill built, small sea-port", while the Peruvians, their country in anarchy, seemed "a depraved, drunken set". Although he admitted spending "five very pleasant days" in Lima, the capital, he thought it "in a wretched state of decay". What did draw his appreciative attention, however, were the women of the place.

At intervals, Darwin in his Diary mentions the prettiness of young ladies, but in Lima his appreciation grew very warm. The women there wore a garment called the *tapada* which he especially liked. "The close elastic gown fits the figure closely & obliges the ladies to walk with small steps, which they do very elegantly & display very white silk stockings & very pretty feet. They wear a black silk veil . . . allowing only one eye to remain uncovered. But then, that one eye is so black & brilliant & has such powers of motion & expression that its effect is very powerful." Is the erotic warmth of these observations a clue to deeper turmoils long repressed? Locked away for five years with a bunch of seamen, none of them yet forty years old, himself like most of his companions in his early or middle twenties, high-spirited, healthy and obviously aware of the attractions of women, calling from time to time at some of the wildest of South American cities, Darwin must surely have been at least tempted when his fellows set off – as some of them undoubtedly will have – on their dubious shoreward excursions. Yet he allows us hardly a toehold for speculation. No mention of women but the gentlest ever appears in anything he wrote. It is as if chastity produced no pain or indulgence no remorse; neither is ever reported. Darwin was not, then or later, a man given to bouts of Boswellian candour.

On land, insurrection created its indiscriminate dangers; Darwin spent August quietly on the *Beagle*. At Arauco the survey ship, HMS *Challenger*, was wrecked and Fitzroy sailed in a warship, HMS *Blonde*, to help rescue the survivors. He returned with his spirits uplifted, not only because he had brought aid to a number of old friends, but also as a result of a series of exhilarating quarrels with the *Blonde*'s commander. The *Beagle* prepared for departure. Darwin wrote to Caroline, "I am very anxious for the Galapagos Islands, I think both the geology and the Zoology cannot fail to be interesting."

On 7 September, 1835, the *Beagle* sailed for that significant archipelago. She dropped anchor eight days later in St. Stephen's Harbour, Chatham Island.

7

When we reach the Galapagos the sun will be vertically over our heads, & I suspect my wishes will be fulfilled to the uttermost . . . I trust & believe that this month next year, we shall be very close to, if not in England. It is too delightful to think that I shall see the leaves fall & hear the Robin sing next Autumn in Shrewsbury. My feelings are those of a Schoolboy to the smallest point . . .

Thus Darwin to Susan, in a letter from Peru; but however childlike his feelings, his faculties remained keenly those of a naturalist. On the Galapagos Islands, the geology that had for so long fascinated him gave way a little to zoology and ornithology; there was, perhaps, a slight shift of his attention from the context – earth and time – to what it contained, life and its history.

Yet the belief that here, among these rocks and lizards, Darwin shouted an inward "Eureka!" as the truth about species became clear to him has no evidence to sustain it. Throughout the voyage of the *Beagle* he wrote much more about geology than about the animal world, and his Galapagos notebooks show that while he wrote less about strata and lava flow than he had for a long time, he still wrote three times as much as he did on zoology. It is only the fact that throughout 1835 as a whole he wrote over *eleven* times as much about geology as he did about zoology that makes the Galapagos ratio so interesting. At the time, the principal significance of the Galapagos, as far as Darwin was concerned, lay in their volcanic formation. The real meaning of his work there would not become apparent to him for several years.

Of his first landing Fitzroy wrote that it was "upon black, dismal-looking heaps of broken lava, forming a shore fit for Pandemonium. Innumerable crabs and hideous iguanas started in every direction . . . This first excursion had no tendency to raise our ideas of the Galapagos Islands." Darwin, too, found the archipelago uninviting – "every where covered by sunburnt, stunted brushwood . . . dry and parched surface . . . the bushes smelt unpleasantly . . . wretched-looking little weeds . . ." All about were the cones, craters and fissures, the black rocks and threatening shapes of a volcanic landscape, inhabited by crouching, wattled iguanas, scuttling crabs and the enormous, deliberate turtles from which the islands derived their name. A Darwin, however, judges matters differently from a Fitzroy: "The scene was to me novel & full of interest; it is always delightful to behold anything which has been long familiar, but only by description."

On Charles Island there was a small settlement presided over by an acting Governor, named Lawson. It was his boast, that he could always tell where in the archipelago a tortoise came from, that first alerted Darwin to the differences existing between the creatures, and the plants, of the various islands. This was an idea that was to work deep into his mind; in the meantime he collected with avidity, but in a carelessly wholesale manner, such specimens as the Galapagos as a whole afforded.

Darwin watched the turtles and, in the clear tropical night, observed their painful struggles as they laid their eggs; when they marched in stately procession to the springs to drink, he calculated their speed – it was 360 yards an hour. He examined the various forms of lizards and iguana, those living on the shore which had been labelled "imps of darkness", and their cousins further inland, "hideous animals; but . . . considered good food". He was endlessly struck by the fearlessness of the birds, and how again and again, day after day, this led to their deaths; they could not discover a proper terror of mankind and their avian incapacity to learn drew his wonder. He collected ferns and lichens, mosses, herbs, weeds, examples of cacti, the bark and leaves of the low brushwood, rock specimens and soil samples – only the scarcity of insects baffled him. He noticed that sea-going lizards in a state of terror would not go into the water, so threw them in over and over again, and watched them each time turn in the waves and scramble ashore "urged", he thought, "by a fixed and hereditary instinct that the shore is their place of safety, whatever the emergency . . ." He cut open the land-loving iguanas and discovered their diet: they were vegetarians. He found one digging its burrow and, on impulse, pulled its tail. It turned, he tells us, "and then stared me in the face, as much as to say, 'What made you pull my tail?' " He gathered and sifted and tested and noted for a month, settling first on one island, then on another, like a bee on a bank of flowers. Here were craters, there lava flows, elsewhere black sand; here stony hills, there hovels, somewhere else the thoroughfares of turtles. Everywhere the earth was bare, arid, barren; yet it carried a harvest for him. Finally, on 17 October his Diary entry reads, "In the afternoon the Beagle sent in her boats to take us on board". Two days later, "the Ship's head was put towards Otaheite & we commenced our long passage of 3,200 miles". In a month, like some intellectual Viking, he had plundered the archipelago of its information; it would be more than twenty years before he dared to display his booty to the world.

When, in his cabin on the *Beagle,* and in Cambridge, and later in London and Downe, he had sifted and mulled over the facts of the Galapagos, what were the conclusions that he came to? Why, when his ideas finally began to coalesce and take their shape, was it to this time and to these islands that he

Giant tortoise of the Galapagos.

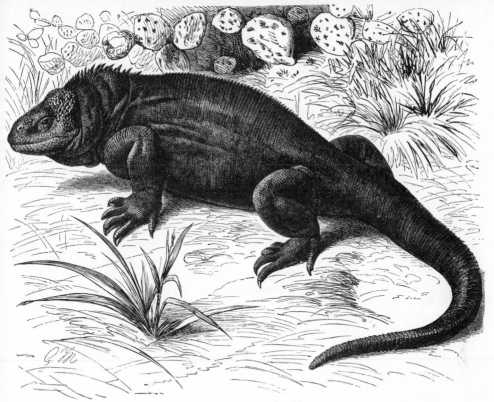

Galapagos Islands land iguana.

felt indebted? One has to remember that at this time he had certainly not progressed past Lyell's position, had not perhaps even reached as far. When he described the Galapagos turtles as "antediluvian", was the adjective being carelessly or precisely used? In any case, he seems still to have believed, with Lyell, that species were and always had been appearing at a constant rate, and that for each there had been a single centre of creation. Enthused by the isolation and comparative newness of the Galapagos, he was to write in his *Journal* that "both in space and time, we seem to be brought somewhat near to that great fact – that mystery of mysteries – the first appearance of new beings on earth". He had already noted, however, that although there was "even a difference between the inhabitants of the different islands; yet all show a marked relationship with those of America . . ."

In a sense, that last sentence again poses, at least by implication, the questions that were nagging him. For *why* was there a difference between the inhabitants of different islands? And why should the organisms of the Galapagos show a marked relationship with those of America? He had seen the Cape Verde Islands, where in a very similar environment the flora and fauna had been very different. There, they had been like the flora and fauna of Africa. In the Galapagos, though separated from the mainland by some

Marine version of the Galapagos iguana.

six hundred miles of ocean, they were like those of America. He had already observed, had indeed collected and become well known for it, the bones of the prehistoric armadillo, the Megatherium. Armadillos still roamed South America. In one region of the earth, therefore, a particular set of plants and animals could be found, ranged both through time and space; in another region, the same was true of a different set. Species, in that case, had not been created once for all to fill a particular environment in nature, wherever that environment existed. Different species fulfilled similar roles in similar environments when those environments were sufficiently divided, by distance or natural barriers. Such a conclusion made the idea of a special creation much less likely. Why should a Creator bother to set upon the earth species different from each other yet performing almost identical functions, just because they had to perform those functions in widely separated locations? Would he not have created one species to perform a certain task wherever that was necessary? But if one removed the Creator, one had to fall back on a different mechanism of creation. When one did that, the original question loomed even larger: why *were* similar creatures in a particular region – in South America, say – apparently related to each other, but not to similar creatures in other regions?

But this raised another, subtly different question: why, even in one particular region, were similar and related organisms, living in comparable environments, not the same as each other? Why, in other words, were creatures of a given kind living on the different islands only fundamentally the same, and not identical in detail? Why, come to that, if the natural life of the Galapagos belonged to the South American region, was it only similar to, not identical with, that of the mainland? What were the differences – and what had caused them? Of course, all these questions were only aspects of a single puzzle, and perhaps Darwin already suspected this. But he was a man who preferred to work first at a detailed, factual level, and so these were the problems that now began to fascinate him.

There was, for example, the matter of the finches. These, he tells us in the *Journal*, were "a most singular group" – all clearly related to each other, yet divided into thirteen distinct species. What differentiated one from another was the shape of the beak, and there was a direct correlation between beak shape and diet. There was the heavy beak of *Geospiza Magnirostris*, which fed on large seeds; there was the longer, curved beak of *Camarhynchus pallidus*, reminiscent of the woodpecker's and signifying its insectiverous, tree-climbing habits (it also shared with its cousin, *C. heliobates*, the habit of using a twig or cactus spine to poke hidden insects out into the open); there was the narrow pointed beak, like a warbler's, of *Certhidea olivacae*, which happily pecked up and ate the tiniest insects.

Apart from the tree climbers, wrote Darwin, "all the other species of this group of finches, mingled together in flocks, feed on the dry and sterile ground of the lower districts". Here, then, one saw a unique cluster of species, clearly related to a familiar genus, the ground finch, where each of the species appeared to have taken up a vacant role in the general order. One kind of hawk, which had some of the habits and characteristics of an American vulture, even to its cry, had undergone a comparable metamorphosis. "Seeing this gradation and diversity of structure in one small, intimately related group of birds," wrote Darwin, "one might really fancy that from an original paucity of birds in this archipelago, one species had been taken and modified for different ends. In a like manner it might be fancied that a bird originally a buzzard, had been induced here to undertake the office of the carrion-feeding Polybori of the American continent".

"One might really fancy" – by the time he came to publish the first version of the *Journal*, he had gone far beyond fancy and had, for well over a year, been hacking away in his notebooks at his central thesis. In 1839, when the *Journal* came out, such passages must have been for him like toes gently dipped into water that might prove too hot for comfort. Meanwhile, he had also been looking over the botanical specimens he had collected from the islands. Although not yet with a basis for any scientific order, for controlling what might become significant factors, he had kept many of these in collections separate for each island. Of course, much of his gathering had been indiscriminate: as late as 1844 he was complaining to Henslow, "I need not say that I collected blindly and . . . just took everything in flower blindly". With neither great botanical experience nor the prescience to know what would be useful to guide him, he always felt that the work he did during these weeks was inadequate to the opportunity he had been given. Yet the work served; it provided in the end much of the evidence he needed. For the moment, however, what he had collected was still to become evidence. The mysteries that were later to obsess him had not yet begun their plaguing; as he began his classifying and labelling in that small poop cabin, he had not even reached the stage of formulating the problem, for all that its constituent parts lay under his hand. While he worked, the *Beagle* rose and fell on the unrestricted waves of the Pacific, bound for her South Seas landfall in Tahiti.

8

Ahead of him, letters were once more accumulating. "I do hope you are careful not to over tire yourself very much," Catherine had written at the end of October, "for fear of giving yourself a dangerous fever in these hot countries." Every change in his circumstances renewed his sisters' anxieties. But now they were beginning to think of his return as an actual and approaching event, "and one not really very far off now". Susan, in November, had commented on his *Journal*, in which the dangers he recounted had made his father shudder. Reporting this paternal reaction did not prevent her from pointing out Charles's further spelling mistakes, however. She had been deeply shocked by his description of the Indian wars: "One can hardly believe anything so wicked at the present day as the conduct of General Rosas". Good people in every generation are always horrified to learn that mankind has not somehow outgrown evil. Susan, however, seems to have found a solution to her dilemma. "Is he a Spaniard?" she asked, acidly. In London, meanwhile, a collection of extracts from Darwin's letters to Henslow had been read to the Geological Society and caused something of a stir. Sedgwick had as a result written to Dr. Robert a letter from which Susan now quoted.

"He is doing admirably in S. America, & has already sent home a Collection above all praise. – It was the best thing in the world for him that he went out on the Voyage of Discovery – there was some risk of his turning out an idle man: but his character will now be fixed, & if God spare his life, he will have a good name among the Naturalists of Europe . . ." And Susan was moved to exclaim, "My dear Charley, I am so happy you have this reward for all your excessive labour & exertions . . ." Erasmus, astonishingly, had begun work as a clerk to Robert Mackintosh, a Commissioner of Public Charities. The fact that Mackintosh was Hensleigh Wedgwood's brother-in-law makes this departure a little more comprehensible. With the affectionate contempt of long familiarity, Susan remarked, "I don't expect that Eras will keep his place long, at least if it requires much work . . ."

On 15 November, the *Beagle* reached Tahiti. Here, it was the people who most fascinated Darwin, since the island's natural history was already well known. "There is a mildness in the expression of their faces, which at once banishes the idea of the savage," he wrote in his Diary, "– & an intelligence which shows they are advancing in civilization." He filled page after page with details of their customs and fashions and of their reactions to their recent conversion to Christianity. Before sleeping on the open mountain-side, during his inland excursions, he noted with approval and respect the prayers of his Tàhitian companions. The missionaries, he felt, had done as much good as could be be expected – human sacrifice, idolatry, war and licentiousness had all been greatly reduced, yet without inducing, as rumour had suggested, a condition of puritan gloom. If he had lost his respect for Christianity as the explicator of the natural world, he seems nevertheless to have seen it still as the arbiter and underwriter of the most important moral values. In his pocket notebook he jotted, "– good Missionaries; never can believe what is heard".

New Zealand, reached in mid-December, proved less attractive. With Fitzroy Darwin visited Kororaki, which would, he wrote, "one day no doubt increase into the chief town". Today it is, indeed, Aukland, the country's largest city; then it was "the very stronghold of vice". The Maoris he found proud and warlike, but noticed with delight "the ceremony of rubbing, or . . . pressing noses". The New Zealand missionaries, he felt, were not offering enough religious instruction, concentrating instead on "the arts of civiliza-tion". But, again, for Darwin religion seems hardly to have been a spiritual matter, but rather a regulatory mechanism, not at all coercive, yet with a social rather than a transcendental function. As for the existing culture of the Maoris, he took the attitude of a man of his times: that it had the slightest intrinsic value, or any purpose other than to display the essential savagery of those who had created it, could never have occurred to him. After the *Beagle* had sailed on, at the end of December, Darwin wrote, "I believe we were all glad to leave New Zealand; it is not a pleasant place; among the natives there is absent that charming simplicity which is found in Tahiti; & of the English the greater part are the very refuse of society".

His landing at Sydney, on 12 January, 1836, occasioned rather different sentiments: "My first feeling was to congratulate myself that I was born an Englishman". With over twenty thousand inhabitants, Sydney seemed very wealthy to him. The town's revenues had increased by £60,000 in a year and a plot of building land of less than an acre had recently been sold for £8,000. The streets were crowded with "gigs, phaetons & carriages" and there were so many people of property that no one knew who they all were.

He made a 120-mile excursion to Bathurst, taking notes on the way of the vegetation and happily meeting a party of aboriginals: "their countenances were good-humoured & pleasant & they appeared far from such utterly degraded beings as usually represented". He added, "In their own arts they are admirable", but implicit in this was the low value of their arts. "They will

SMYTH.

Sydney Harbour a decade after Darwin's visit.

not . . . cultivate the ground, or even take the trouble of keeping flocks of sheep that have been offered them; or build houses & remain stationary." In discussing them, Darwin was pressing closely upon matters which, at further examination, were soon to prove so illuminating. Alcohol, European diseases and the disappearance of the game they hunted were factors already combining to destroy these people. Their children often died from the hardships of a wandering life. "When the difficulty in procuring food is increased," Darwin commented, "of course the population must be repressed in a manner almost instantaneous as compared to what takes place in civilized life . . ." He was seeing at first hand the action of suddenly changed environmental pressures; adapted to the old ones, the aboriginals could not respond to the new. The constant hunting was depleting another native population, that of the kangaroo; the emu, too, was becoming scarce: "It may be long before these animals are altogether exterminated, but their doom is fixed". These seem to have been possibilities that did not particularly disturb Darwin; nor did they lead him on to any general conclusions.

What did cause him some profound and unsettling thought was "the strange character of the animals of this country as compared to the rest of the World". This reflection follows a passage in which he had described the duck-billed platypus, a creature that might excite philosophy in any naturalist. Darwin places in the mouth of "an unbeliever" the suggestion that "two distinct Creators must have been at work", then refutes it. "It cannot be thought so. The one hand has surely worked throughout the universe. A Geologist perhaps would suggest that the periods of Creation have been distinct & remote one from the other; that the Creator rested in his labor." It was the thought of two different species, at opposite ends of the earth, fulfilling the same role in their respective environments that had occasioned these speculations. It is perhaps evidence that his Galapagos collection, examined during that long Pacific passage, was beginning to work upon his imagination. As yet, he was still publicly operating within a religious framework – but the arguments of an unbeliever had at least been postulated. It was a passage, in any case, that he did not think it necessary to transcribe from his Diary to his *Journal*.

Australia, in the end, disappointed him. The country was "rancorously divided" on almost every subject, the convicts and ex-convicts gave society a complexion he did not care for and all that seemed to concern the people was growing rich. In short, "nothing but rather sharp necessity should compel me to emigrate". He cannot have been unhappy when the *Beagle* at the end of January sailed for Hobart – in what was then Van Diemen's Land and is now Tasmania – before journeying on to King George's Sound, not far from where Albany stands today, in Western Australia. Although not caring much for the countryside, which he called "uninviting", Darwin liked the indigenous people – "it is not easy to imagine a more truly good natured & good humoured expression than their faces show". The handful of local settlers feeling it necessary to propitiate a recently arrived tribe, it was decided to organize a great *korroberi* or dance for which, Fitzroy tells us, "Mr Darwin ensured the compliance of all the savages by providing an immense mess of boiled rice, with sugar, for their entertainment."

The reaction of both Fitzroy and Darwin to the actual dancing was rather less than appreciative. The Captain saw "a hundred prancing demon-like figures . . . brandishing their weapons, stamping together in exact accordance, and making hoarse gutteral sounds at each exertion. It was a fiendish sight . . ." Darwin, too, thought it "a most rude barbarous scene", but observing that "the women & children watched the whole proceeding with the greatest pleasure", he began to wonder what significance lay in these intricate gyrations. He noted a dance "called the Emu dance in which each man extended his arms in a bent manner to imitate the movement of the neck of one of those birds. In another dance, one man took off all the motions of a Kangaroo . . . whilst a second crawled up & pretended to spear him." Fitzroy actually used the phrase "hunting dance" in his description, yet neither man seemed able to understand the significance of this ceremonial to a hunting people, nor how central to their lives such evocations of success might be. However, Darwin concluded his account on a pleasantly parish-magazine level, telling us that "the whole party formed a great circle on the ground & the boiled rice & sugar was distributed to the delight of all".

At last Darwin could write, "Farewell, Australia . . . too great & ambitious for affection, yet not great enough for respect; I leave your shores without sorrow or regret." It was 14 March and the *Beagle* was heading out on the two-week journey to Keeling Island (now part of the Cocos group administered by Australia). From Hobart Darwin had written to Catherine, "I confess I never see a Merchant vessel start for England, without a most dangerous inclination to bolt. It is a most true & grievous fact, that the last four months appear to me long as the two previous years . . . There never was a ship so full of home-sick heroes as the Beagle." Two months earlier, writing to Caroline, he had confessed, "For the last year I have been wishing to return, & have uttered my wishes in no gentle murmers; but now feel inclined to keep up one steady deep growl from morning to night . . . There is no more Geology but plenty of seasickness . . . the pleasures have all moved forwards & have reached Shrewsbury some eight months before I shall."

In England, however, his reputation was still increasing, helped now by the extracts from his letters to Henslow, which his gentle patron had had printed and was busily circulating. Dr. Robert had been sent a copy and,

Caroline wrote, with it had come a letter from Henslow* prophesying that Charles would "reap the rewards of your perseverance and take your position among the first Naturalists of the day . . . My Father did not move from his seat till he had read every word of *your* book & he was very much gratified . . ." Erasmus, alas, had given up his post after three weeks. His comment upon his departure had been that "whatever people may please to say, literary leisure is better than work".

Darwin felt himself now to be on the last stages of his journey. But, even as late as this, his application did not waver. Keeling Island was destined to play a part in the establishment of his reputation, for it provided the evidence to support his theories about the formation of coral reefs. Lyell had proposed that coral – which cannot survive below thirty fathoms – built its complex reefs upon the rims of submerged craters. Darwin, who knew that many reefs were far from crater-shaped, thought this theory unlikely. Even more unlikely was it that only those islands where the water was warm enough to sustain coral should have submarine structures of the right height to encourage their growth. Could there not, then, have been a steady elevation of the land, with the slow erosion of wind and wave matching the slow rise of the reef platform? Darwin pointed out that, if that had been the case, all coral islands would be flat, barren and sandy. He summarized his conclusion: "If then the foundations, whence atoll-building corals sprang, were not formed of sediment, and if they were not lifted to the required level, they must of necessity have subsided into it; and this at once solves the difficulty." The land sank downward, the coral built upward. As the subsidence continued, so the polyps built further upon their own drowned cities. The platforms upon which reefs and atolls stood were their own submerged predecessors.

Darwin had largely arrived at this solution to the problem by the time the *Beagle* reached Keeling Island. What he saw there convinced him that it was correct and the subject became the basis for one of his earliest and most successful books, *Structure and Distribution of Coral Reefs*. In his *Journal,* too, he included what amounts to a long essay on the subject; in both he was not content merely to present his theoretical proposals, but also to explore where his ideas might lead. For, given his solution, it is clear that the type and location of a coral reef can be pointers to geological conditions over long periods. Every reef and atoll provides evidence of subsidence or elevation; the absence of coral, as in the West Indies, suggests geological stability. If, as

---

* At the end of December, 1835, Dr. Robert had replied to Henslow, thanking him for the letters and acknowledging how much Charles owed to him. "I thought the voyage hazardous for his happiness but it seems to prove otherwise and it is highly gratifying to me to think he gains credit by his observation and exertion. There is a natural good humored energy in his letters just like himself."

Darwin did in his book, the location of volcanoes is also marked, one can see at a glance how they relate to general earth movements. "We may thus," wrote Darwin "like unto a geologist who had lived his ten thousand years and kept a record of the passing changes, gain some insight into the great system by which the surface of this globe has been broken up, and land and water interchanged."

What his work on coral may also have provided is an indirect insight into the logic of transmutation. It was the interaction of building polyps and subsidence that decided the structure of atoll and reef. As the environment altered during the play of vast terrestrial forces, so the reef changed its character. Lifted by an elevation of the surface, it crept close to the shore; carried down thereafter by subsidence, the same reef might become first a circular barrier reef and then an atoll. If subsidence continued too swiftly, the coral was unable to keep up and the atoll, too, drowned like the land. By 1842 Darwin could write of certain reefs having "an intermediate character", suggesting that he could see clearly how one type might change into another. By then, however, he had already put together the main elements of his theory on evolution. Had he already glimpsed a connection, one is forced to wonder, as he struggled in his cabin with the facts of coral formation and linked them with what he had learned of geology? He was always a great synthesizer, a thinker like a circus acrobat, meticulous about detail, yet given to great leaps. It is not a connection that was beyond him.

On the morning of 12 April, the *Beagle* sailed out of Keeling lagoon. Looking back, Darwin wrote in his Diary that coral islands like Keeling were "amongst the wonderful objects of this world", and added, as he well might, "It is not a wonder which at first strikes the eye of the body, but rather after reflection, the eye of reason." He goes on to give the first outline of his ideas on reef formation. "Under this view," he concludes, "we must look at a Lagoon Isd as a monument raised by myriads of tiny architects, to mark the spot where a former land lies buried in the depths of the ocean." One may also regard them, perhaps, as one of the clues that tantalized Darwin on the way to defining, and solving, some of the riddles surrounding the true nature of species.

9

In a serious sense, the voyage was now over for Darwin. The *Beagle* called at Mauritius, where he took a gentle walk or two and conversed politely with local dignitaries. He wrote from there to Caroline, expressing his pleasure at having visited Keeling, "our only opportunity of seeing one of those wonderful productions of the Coral polypi." But more than anything else he wanted his travels to be over. No country "has now any attractions for us, without it is seen right astern, & the more distant & indistinct the better. We are all utterly home-sick."

In January, Catherine had written, "Papa was settling the other evening what Bedroom you would have, when you come; and I shall much enjoy *turning out* of your room, to give it up to its dear old owner." Caroline, two months later, thought that "it will be as if you were awakened from a dream when you find every thing & every body just as you left them except all of us being pretty considerably aged . . ." Somehow they imagined that life would leap that five year gap, that Shrewsbury, having lent Darwin to the world, would simply take him back again, a little worn, perhaps, but essentially the same. They had, of course, as people do, stayed at the centre of their universe; they had forgotten that Charles had remained at the centre of his, too. In the long interim these cosmic systems had floated irrevocably apart. Shrewsbury was what it always had been, and the sisters going about their small-town lives – chafed and scratched a little by the passing years, no doubt, but essentially unaltered – had remained in their old relation to it. Charles, on the other hand, had changed – and precisely in his essence. In a way, it was a change occasioned less by his new experience of the world, as by what he had made of that experience. His effort to understand what he had seen had turned him into a scientist. What he wrote he addressed now to his peers, to the scientific establishment. Shrewsbury would not prove too small for him because of where he had been, but because of where he was going. His arena had become metropolitan, his audience was in the capital; it was not the jungles of Brazil or the reefs of Keeling Island that would diminish the gardens at The Mount: it was their distance from the Geological Society, from the houses of the men who were about to become his rivals, admirers and friends, from the conversation, the facilities, the music and museums, the endless vitality of London.

He felt that he had time to make up. From Hobart he had written to Fox, "This is to me, so much existence obliterated from the page of life. – I hate every wave of the ocean . . . I look forward with a comical mixture of dread and satisfaction to the amount of work which remains for me in England." That there would be much work still to do on the specimens he had brought or sent from South America and the South Seas was a fact that appeared hardly at all in his letters to his family. But he knew what had to be done, and what it meant in time given up; even if he had not wanted to continue in his science, he had left himself with little choice. Of course, he did want to continue and so was perhaps grateful for the lack of choice. Of all this, however, he wrote very little to the sisters.

Before him there now loomed one or two enormous projects. All the years of geologizing and botanizing, all that probing and examining, speculating and collecting, had finally to be rendered down, given shape and structure: meanings and significance would have to be assigned before his results could be published. Can it have been the effort of trying to extract some general meaning from the welter of information he had gathered that stimulated his scientific imagination and brought him so soon after his return to consider the mystery of species? He had, in a sense, been fortunate in the timing of the voyage. It had come at exactly the right moment in his life, and in the development of natural history. A year or two later he might have been ordained, married, tied down like Fox or Whitley, unable or unwilling to travel. A year earlier, and he would still have been a student.

On the wider time-scale, there was something more than appropriate in the *Beagle*'s excursion coinciding with the publication of Lyell's great book. That had offered to botanists and geologists, with a plausibility they could not ignore, the one indispensable gift geology could bestow: time. It made accessible the aeons of prehistory and stretched existence back into infinity. With this as freshly in his mind as that morning's news, Darwin had moved into the almost unbearable stimulation that was afforded him by the plant life of the tropics, the geology of the Andes, the zoology of the Galapagos, the fauna of Australia, the coral reefs of Keeling Island. At the precise moment when he was at his most ready, his senses and his intellect had been flooded by an endless parade of astounding phenomena, an apparently endless cascade of new information.

He might have been overwhelmed, but he had a record of enthusiasm and an irresistible zeal as a collector and recorder of nature. He was not over-whelmed. He worked almost without ceasing. There were islands on which he collected almost every creature that flew, ran or crawled. He filled well over a thousand pages, each nine inches by eleven, with his geological notes alone; his manuscript diary runs to nearly eight hundred. Then there was botany, and zoology – nearly four hundred pages on that. He filled twenty-four notebooks that he carried with him for his immediate impressions, used as workbooks, or filled with records of what he had sent to Henslow; probably he filled more, for his granddaughter, Nora Barlow, who edited them, believed that three or four must have been lost. He wrote up his Diary from them; and then wrote up his *Journal* from that, and sent it home in installments. All the time he was also writing letters, to his sisters, to Henslow, to his friends. Constantly in the background was his sea-sickness, his hemmed-in, overcrowded discomfort and his increasingly passionate longing to be on his way home. He sent box after box of specimens – skins, stones, butterflies, beetles, plants, seeds – across the seas to the waiting Henslow. He clambered up every accessible mountain, dug out every access-ible bone, rode every accessible mile. His eyes saw and tried to understand everything in his path – the strata of the earth, the customs of the people that lived on it, the plants and animals that shared their world, the politics that ran it. Nomads in Tierra del Fuego, Indians in Brazil, Maoris in New Zealand, convicts and aborigines in Australia. He missed, one fancies, hardly anything, and everything he noticed he described and, where neces-sary, explained.

And his beliefs had altered during the voyage, the way he saw himself, the way he saw the world. He had become a serious person, a man with a future, with a direction. He had found his life task. Not that he had lost his modesty, or his diffidence. When he learned that his letters to Henslow were circulat-ing publicly, he was worried and dismayed rather than gratified. How had they been edited – they had been written to a friend, in a "careless manner" and to print them was "playing with edge tools". Yet he knew that in London and the universities people he respected were learning to respect him. Even those dangerous letters had drawn approval – above all, perhaps, from his father. He had found ground to stand on, a position of his own. It left him free, one feels, to look outwards with confidence; able to regard himself as a scientist, he could act and think like one. He had nothing to prove, either to London or to his father. He had been accepted, and in that acceptance there must have been liberation. He had come to the end of criticism and had no longer to glance back over his shoulder as some disapproving voice remon-strated with him: he could go forward untrammelled. He had left "dear Charley"; he had come back as Charles Darwin.

In his mind there must already have been a great deal of fruitful confusion. He had written of the lice in Chiloe, who lived on Indians but died on white men, that this, if true, was of great interest: "Man springing from one stock according to his *varieties* having different species of parasites. – It leads me into many reflections." The possibilities were complex; if mankind was one species, why could the Chiloe lice live on one race and not another? How was it that a parasite had adapted so well to its usual host, that it could not survive on a different one? How was it that European lice survived on Europeans and Chiloe lice did not? And why Chiloe, an island – was that significant? One can imagine what reflections presented themselves to him. But it was 1834 and he was not yet ready for them. Timidly, he crossed the last sentence out and reneged on the reflections. But in a notebook which most probably he filled in during the long voyage home in 1836, a period during which he ordered much of his work, he wrote of the different varieties of birds inhabiting the Galapagos Islands that "such facts would undermine the stability of species".

By the end of the voyage, therefore, he was ready to face his previously unthinkable reflections. In his geological beliefs, he had moved from a muted catastrophism to an acceptance of Lyell's uniformitarian views. He had learned to think in terms of slow, vast movements of the earth's surface. He had ceased to see, among the strata, the "diluvium" of the clerical geologists. He had accepted a view of time and the cosmos that could at least shelve the problem of a creation, a "steady-state" world in which the scientist could concern himself with mechanisms and processes, not with origins and first causes. He had not yet, in any real sense, faced the problems that surrounded the mutation of species; but he was ready, albeit unconsciously, to face them. He had the status, the self-confidence, the flexibility of mind and the information; he had learned, too, not to be afraid of size, to argue from something relatively minor – say, a coral reef – to the great risings and splittings of the terrestrial surface. He had seen the pressures of environment bear upon species, and the changes that could apparently be worked by isolation, the divergence of closely related groups separated by insuperable natural barriers. Without being aware of it, he had accumulated a great store of the tools and materials he would need. There was very little more he had to do now – except to find the key that would unlock the place where he had hidden them.

In early June, Darwin was in Cape Town. As usual, he went for a jaunt into the local countryside, his guide "a young Hottentot" who "wore a long coat, beaver hat, & white gloves!" He wrote in his Diary, "I saw so very little worth seeing, that I have scarcely anything to say". The important moment for him of his visit was the evening on which he dined with Sir John Herschel: "He never talked much", Darwin wrote of him in his *Autobiography*, "but every word that he uttered was worth listening to".

They sailed to St. Helena, where Darwin "obtained lodgings . . . within a stone's throw of Napoleon's tomb", with which he was very little impressed. He found the plants of the island interesting, since some of them appeared to be unique to "this little world, within itself", as he called it. He sailed from it in reasonable spirits, only to find himself on the way back to South America. On 4 August, he wrote to Susan from Bahia, "I loathe, I abhor the sea, & all ships which sail on it". Complexities of navigation and mapping had made it necessary for Fitzroy to sail back to England by the same route as he had left it. It had given Darwin the chance to wander over Ascension Island and examine its volcanic geology. He hoped, however, to be in England late in October. Now the ports and islands unreeled as the *Beagle* reversed her earliest stages.

Darwin, the voyage at last ending, considered as best he could what its value had been to him. The only thing that made the loss of friends, the lack of space and luxuries, the absence of civilized comfort, domestic society and the arts worth while was the traveller's "decided taste for some branch of knowledge which could by such means be acquired". The sea as such had few attractions, nor were these in any way reinforced if one suffered from sea-sickness. There were, of course, wonderful scenes and wonderful scenery to behold, but the real compensating factor was that "nothing can be more improving in a young naturalist, than a journey in distant countries". But he should beware, since the necessary speed at which one was forced to travel made detailed exploration impossible: "Hence arises, as I have found to my cost, a constant tendency to fill up the wide gaps of knowledge by inaccurate & superficial hypotheses."

What did he most vividly remember? Above all, "the primeval forests . . . whether those of Brazil, where the powers of life are predominant, or those of Tierra del Fuego, where death & decay prevail". Surprisingly, the plains of Patagonia, too, "most frequently cross before my eyes." He hardly understood why; perhaps because of the scope they gave imagination. "They are boundless, for they are scarcely practicable, & hence unknown: they bear the stamp of having thus lasted for ages, & there appears no limit to their duration through future time." No individual object, however, "is surer to create astonishment, than the first sight in his native haunt, of a real barbarian . . . One's mind hurries back over past centuries, & then asks, could our progenitors be such as these?"

He wrote down his list of marvels: "the stars of the Southern hemisphere – the water-spout – the glacier leading its blue stream of ice in a bold precipice overhanging the sea – a lagoon island, raised by the coral forming animalcule – an active volcano – the overwhelming effects of a violent earthquake". With the easy rectitude of his class and time, he looked forward, on the world's behalf, with confidence. "The march of improvement, consequent on the introduction of Christianity, through the South Sea, probably stands by itself on the records of the world." Captain Cook, only sixty years before, "could foresee no prospect of such a change. Yet these changes have now been affected by the philanthropic spirit of the English nation." Perhaps nothing is sadder than the confident optimism of generations vanished long enough ago for us to distinguish the full frailty of their hopes.

But it was time to stop. Through grey seas, the *Beagle* was passing south of the Scillies; surely, in the distance, there was the Lizard? "After a tolerably short passage, but with some very heavy weather, we came to an anchor at Falmouth. To my surprise & shame I confess the first sight of the shores of England inspired me with no warmer feelings, than if it had been a miserable Portuguese settlement. The same night (& a dreadfully stormy one it was) I started by the Mail for Shrewsbury."

It was 4 October, 1836. After fifty-five months, Charles Darwin had come home. He would never be sea-sick again.

The main sources for Part Two were:

On the details of the *Beagle* expedition, *Diary of the voyage of HMS* Beagle, *Darwin and the voyage of the* Beagle, *Darwin's Ornithological Notes, Darwin and Henslow: the Growth of an Idea,* all compiled or edited and introduced by Nora Barlow; Darwin's *Journal of researches*; Volume One of Darwin's *Life and Letters,* edited by Francis Darwin; Fitzroy's *Narrative; Fitzroy of the* Beagle, by H.E.L. Mellersh; *The* Beagle *Record,* edited by R.D. Keynes; Admiral Sulivan's *Life and Letters,* edited by H.N. Sullivan; and various reminiscences, notably King's, among the Darwin manuscripts at Cambridge University Library.

Most of the letters written by Darwin during the *Beagle* years have been published; the originals of almost all these are in the University Library at Cambridge. Previously unpublished material in this section includes Fanny Owen's letters and the many letters from his family and friends sent to Darwin from England; these are also in the University Library. Letters to W.D. Fox not published before can be found in the library of Christ's College, Cambridge.

Material on geology came mainly from Lyell's *Principles of Geology*, from his *Life and Letters*, edited by his sister-in-law, and from an illuminating article by M.J.S. Rudwick, *The Strategy of Lyell's Principles of Geology*. De Beer's *Charles Darwin: Evolution by Natural Selection* and Lack's *Darwin's Finches* shed light on the development of Darwin's ideas.

PART THREE

Marry – marry – marry

1

Only picture to yourself a nice soft wife on a sofa with a good fire and books and music perhaps – compare this vision with the dingy reality of Grt Marlboro' St. Marry – marry – marry.

Darwin, note to himself

The browns, deep purples, faded greens, and yellows of a West Country autumn; the spread of oaks; the asymetric reach of elms, the dark anarchy of yew trees; in blue-grey skies, clerical convocations of rooks, companionably raucous; ranks of round hills, as gentle as cushions; over all, the damp winds of a gathering winter, and one night passing, a second threatening. Hour after hour, the creak and groan of the coach, movement as deep in its frame as in the timbers of the *Beagle* herself, the grinding rattle of the wheels, the pounding of the horses' hooves as they reached again and again for speed and distance, the chime of brass and the soft complaint of leather as the harness took the strain. Then, late on Tuesday night, Shrewsbury, Darwin alighting, stretching cramped legs, perhaps, and breathing deeply air of which he must have remembered every current. As he was to tell Fitzroy in a letter a day or two later, "all England appears changed except the good old town of Shrewsbury and its inhabitants, which, for all I can see to the contrary, may go on as they now are to Doomsday".

That night, it was so late he could not bring himself to disturb his family: not everyone would have been so thoughtful, or so self-effacing. He slept at an inn; early the next morning, on Wednesday, 5 October, 1836, he stepped once more through the plain front door of The Mount. And then? It cannot have been otherwise than obvious and delightful – the cries, the embraces, the kisses, the tears, the lookings at arms' length followed by tighter hugs; then the running of the servants and the barrel broached; the whirlpools and rapids of excited conversation, the attempted questions, the half-answers. Imagination supplies this hubbub, the whirligig of welcome that must after those five onerous years have surrounded Charles on his return. (Only of alcohol is there definite proof: "Two or three of our labourers . . . immediately set to work, and got most excessively drunk in honour of the arrival of Master Charles". Thus Darwin to Fitzroy.)

Charles is come home, [wrote Caroline in a note to her cousin Elizabeth Wedgwood, that very Wednesday] – so little altered in looks from what he was five years ago and not a bit changed his own dear self . . . We have had the very happiest morning – poor Charles so full of affection and delight at seeing my Father looking so well and being with us all again – his hatred of the sea is as intense as even I can wish . . . Now we have him really again at home I intend to begin to be glad he went [on] this expedition, and now I can allow he has gained happiness and interest for the rest of his life.

Charles, however, was determined to renew his old connections himself. Even on that first day, seeing Caroline so busily spreading the news, he was able to sit down amid the excitement and write a short note to his Uncle Jos. "My head is quite confused with so much delight, but I cannot allow my sisters to tell you first how happy I am to see all my dear friends again . . . I am most anxious once again to see Maer, and all its inhabitants, so that in the course of two or three weeks, I hope in person to thank you, as being my first Lord of the Admiralty. I am so very happy I hardly know what I am writing."

Aunt Bessy, Josiah Wedgwood's wife, and Charlotte – once the "incomparable", now Mrs. Langton – sent notes welcoming Charles back to the normality of Shropshire. Meanwhile, as Charles reported to Fitzroy, his sisters continued to assure him "that I do not look in the least different". This seems to have been a somewhat wishful conclusion on their part, since the amenable youth who had departed on the *Beagle* had vanished for ever, replaced by a firm-faced young man with watchful, deep-set eyes, whose thinning hair and wide, slightly compressed lips gave him an air of good-humoured maturity. Inwardly, too, however glad to be home and however loving to his family, he was acquiring an entirely new characteristic: a sense of purpose. It did not cramp the established largeness of his nature nor alter the sweetness of his temperament, but it was to lead him further and further away from the tranquillities of Shrewsbury: his own peace would be different in kind from that of Shropshire's well-to-do.

For in Shropshire, life had not altered. The news of Charles's return spread with country swiftness; it was on that same 5 October that William Owen wrote to express pleasure at his safe return and to say that, were it not for appointments already arranged, "I should certainly be with you at breakfast". The letter invited Darwin to Woodhouse on the following Saturday – "but pray bring your Gun with you, for I have not forgot the amusement we used to have together, and I am anxious to see whether you are *improved by your travels* or whether I am again to be your Instructor". It is probable that many people – and William Owen may have been amongst them – imagined that Charles, after some initial "restlessness", would re-establish the expected pattern of a serene existence. He himself, however, who was not only already altered by his voyage, but would continue in the very process of alteration for months and even years afterwards, had no such placid anticipation.

"I want your advice on many points", he wrote to Henslow on 6 October, "indeed I am in the clouds & neither know what to do, or where to go". In a few days he would have to travel to London, "to get my goods & chattels out of the *Beagle*", and might call at Cambridge on the way: "My dear Henslow, I do long to see you; and [you] have been the kindest friend to me, that ever Man possessed. – I can write no more for I am giddy with joy & confusion." Yet he was already looking forward to the scientific work that awaited him – his "chief puzzle", he wrote, was over who might help him describe the "minerological nature" of his geological specimens. It was not in Shrewsbury that he was likely to find anyone with the requisite skills.

He had time enough to establish himself once again in his family. His father, as he wrote to Fitzroy, "appears more cheerful and very little older than when I left". His own star was, for the moment, in the ascendent. "I do assure you I am a very great man at home; the five years' voyage has certainly raised me a hundred per cent. I fear such greatness must experience a fall."

There was hardly time for a collapse in his reputation. When Fitzroy's first letter, dated 20 October, arrived in Shrewsbury, Darwin was already installed in his brother's rooms at 43 Great Marlborough Street. He had expected the *Beagle* to sail to London for the crew to be paid off; Fitzroy's news was that this would now occur at Portsmouth and that the ship had moved to that port, up the coast from Plymouth.

> I am delighted by your letter [added the Captain] the account of your family – & the joytipsy style of the whole letter were very pleasing. Indeed, Charles Darwin, I have *also* been *very* happy – even at the horrid place Plymouth – for that horrid place contains a *treasure* to *me* which even *you* were ignorant of!! Now guess – and think & guess again. Believe it or not, – the news is *true* – I am going to be *married*!!!!!!! Now you may know that I have decided on this step, long *very* long ago . . .

Even in an age that demanded reserve in a gentleman, Fitzroy's reticence seems superhuman. It lights up a little the recesses of his character to consider what it meant to have travelled for five years in a small ship, on friendly terms with one's companions, and never mentioned once that at home there waited a girl one intended to marry. There seem, however, to have been complications, a small boy whom Fitzroy had promised to make his heir – the reasons are unclear – and whose grandfather had to release him from his promise before he felt himself free to marry. Everyone behaved most properly, however, and that December Fitzroy married his Mary

O'Brien: "My WIFE and I are *snowed up* at Bromham", he wrote exultantly on the last-but-one day of the year.

In that hectic November, Darwin found time to make his promised visit to Maer. "We are getting impatient for Charles's arrival", Emma Wedgwood had written in October. Busily preparing for it, she had read *Rapid Journeys across the Pampas* by Sir Francis Head, published eight years earlier. She dismissed it as "Capt. Head's gallop" and added. "I am afraid it won't instruct me much". Writing to her sister-in-law (who, as Hensleigh Wedgwood's wife, was always known as Fanny Hensleigh) she passed on the information that Charles had been "much struck with the sight of Hensleigh walking up the street with a bandbox in one hand and a child in the other".

This slightly sardonic comment of Emma's suggests that Darwin, as might have been expected, underwent for many weeks small shocks of adjustment to the reality of how much his friends' and relations' lives had altered. Men he had last seen as students had become established in professions and fathers of sizeable families, so that each meeting with an old friend seemed to demand an instant leap over the events of five years of development. What must have made it even more difficult was that it was not a development he had shared. It was a paradox of his situation that, although he had spent these five years in almost constant motion, in a very real sense his life had stood still; that, although he had undergone an intellectual revolution which had not even yet reached its height, his progress towards a full emotional and sexual adulthood had received no assistance. He had learned self-reliance, patience, self-control, application – the virtues imbued by a solitary life. The ordinary social skills and qualities acquired through maturing in a varied and demanding community, expressed in complex relationships, must largely have passed him by. It may be that this is one reason why he retained all his life the childlike quality, the fundamental innocence, to which so many people were to respond. For the moment, however, it is more likely to have meant that his renewing of old connections brought him almost as much bruising as it did pleasure. The fact is, his world had continued without him: for this reason the saying "To go away is to die a little" has for its corollary, "To return is to know what it is to be a ghost".

It must have been with some relief, therefore, that Charles settled for a short while into the remembered ease of Maer. As for the Wedgwoods, "We enjoyed Charles's visit uncommonly", reported Emma to Fanny Hensleigh. Charles had "talked away most pleasantly all the time; we plied him with questions without any mercy". The scene was clearly exactly what it should have been, with Charles the lion and the rest bent towards him in the rapt homage of the stay-at-home for the wayfarer. Emma's sister Charlotte had had her portrait painted not long before, with results Charles found less than satisfactory: "I hope to fate she is not like that picture", he murmured every time he studied it. Is there a touch of acid in Emma's comment? "I suppose he has rather a poetical idea of her, for the picture is certainly very like."

On his return, Darwin had set about re-establishing old friendships; in mid-November his Cambridge crony, Herbert, now studying law at Lincoln's Inn, responded to one of these approaches. "Welcome, right welcome, was the sight of that good, round, unmistakable hand of yours . . . We must have a meeting of the Club to welcome you on yr. return, when you must bring up yr. reports of Transatlantic cookery." By then, however, the new friendships Darwin was forging, in a metropolis made more dazzling by the years of travel and shipboard confinement, must have threatened to overwhelm these more established relationships.

It was becoming clear that in his absence he had created for himself a small but noticeable reputation and that, as a result, some of the most exalted natural scientists of the day were happy to receive him. His first impact on scientific England had been through the extracts from his letters circulated in 1835 by Henslow. Read at a meeting and then printed for the members of the Cambridge Philosophical Society, they had been issued with Henslow's proviso that they should be regarded "as the first thoughts which occur to a traveller respecting what he sees". Sedgwick, however, was sufficiently impressed with them to use them as the basis for a short paper which he read in November, 1835, to the Geological Society of London; eventually, it was published in the *Proceedings* of the Society. These results, coming on top of the small sensation made by the Megatherium and other fossil remains, trophies of the *Beagle* years, and vindication of Peacock's hopes before the expedition set out, ensured that Darwin, even while still under tropical skies, had been taken into the community of the learned. Thus, early in November, 1836, he was able to tell Fox that his first visit to London had been passed "in most exciting dissipation amongst the Dons in science". To be so well known, yet so unprepared for fame, had its disadvantages, however. "You have made me known amongst the botanists," he wrote to Henslow at about the same time; "but I felt very foolish, when Mr. Don* remarked on the beautiful appearance of some plant with an astoundingly long name, & asked me about its habitation . . . I was at last forced to plead most intire innocence, – that I knew no more about the plants which I had collected, than the Man in the Moon."

The first decision that had to be taken concerned the specimens which he had brought or sent back. Where were they to be housed? He wanted them

---

* At the time, the newly appointed Professor of Botany at King's College, London, and Librarian to the Linnean Society.

collated, mounted and described as soon as possible, and by men more expert than he. The situation as it existed in London brought him small comfort. The Museum of the Zoological Society had some one thousand items not yet mounted, and even without these was nearly full. At the British Museum, the botanists had not yet completed their work on the collection King had brought back from the *Adventure* expedition: "I cannot feel . . . any great respect even for the present state of that establishment," Darwin commented dismissively in a letter to Henslow. The latter had suggested that he sort through his material and then cooperate with those experts in the various fields who needed specimens to work with. It would mean living in "this dirty, odious London", in order to be available when "the great men", as he called them, might want to take up his offer.

The great men had been, as a matter of fact, something of a disappointment to him. Lyell and the anatomist Richard Owen (who, knighted, was after the publication of *The Origin* to be a bitter opponent) had proved friendly, "& besides these two I have scarcely met anyone who seems to wish to possess any of my specimens". The rivalry of the men of science worried him, too; he had watched in horror an evening at the Zoological Society "where the speakers were snarling at each other, in a manner anything but like that of gentlemen"; he wondered how, in London, he would be able to avoid such "contemptible quarrels". It was not surprising that, on the whole, he would have preferred his collection to reside in the cultivated order of the Musée d'Histoire Naturelle in Paris, where the labours of Buffon and Cuvier had resulted in an organization mirroring what was assumed to be Nature's own. He had, however, sailed under the aegis of the Royal Navy and this, morally if not legally, bound him to British assignments for his collection.

For a few weeks he established himself at Cambridge, at first staying with the Henslows. He discovered that their "comfortable ways of life however do not suit hard work, and, in consequence, tomorrow I migrate into solitary lodgings in Fitz William St.", as he wrote to Fox on 15 December. Every morning he pored over his specimens and geological fragments – "a most tedious task" – and every evening he wrote. There was no one at the University whom he remembered. He wandered through the Chinese boxes of the Christ's College courts and quadrangles looking up at windows now closed to him by an entire generation of strangers. The student years flicker by so swiftly, one need not be very old to feel like a ghost returned to haunt the suddenly unfamiliar corners of a school or college. Luckily, there were the "gyps", the college servants, for Darwin to greet, fixtures of retentive memory, their constancy kept sharp by the modestly acquisitive expectations of any old retainer.

The fact that Richard Owen was Hunterian Professor at the Royal College of Surgeons helped persuade Darwin to give the College the major part of his fossil collection. Soon casts of the ancient bones were being passed among these expert anatomists. Darwin himself, meanwhile, read papers at the Zoological and the Geological Societies. At the former, he gave a description of the South American ostrich, the Rhea, with something rather more, perhaps, than the normal abstract interest in his subject. "Do you recollect telling me the new ostrich should be called *darwinii*. By an odd chance Mr. Gould has actually so named it . . ." Thus he had written to Fox the day before he gave his talk; it may have been with a certain amount of proprietary passion that he described the hatching behaviour of the male, the numbers of eggs found in a nest, the birds' habits when pursued. In his other paper he gave his reasons for assuming, largely through the evidence of shells, that the mountains of Chile had only comparatively recently been elevated to their present precipitous grandeur.

The ornithological John Gould, who had determined that Darwin's specimen of the Rhea was a new species, was by then working on another of Darwin's projects. This was to publish, with the financial support of the government, a complete *Zoology of the Voyage of the Beagle*, with experts in various fields working under Darwin's general editorship. Richard Owen, even more distinguished than Gould, took charge of the section on fossils; Thomas Bell*, a secretary to the Royal Society and at one time the Professor of Zoology at King's College, London, described the reptiles; the entomologist George Waterhouse worked, perhaps a little unexpectedly, on extant mammals; and Leonard Jenyns, who had so nearly voyaged in Darwin's place on the *Beagle*, undertook to describe the fish.

Darwin by then had been reluctantly drawn back to London – "this odious dirty smoky town", as he described it to Fox, "where one can never get a glimpse at all that is best worth seeing in nature". For, however "dirty" or "odious" the metropolis was, it offered him the scope he now needed, the meetings, the conversations, the debates, lectures, discussions and dinners, the museums, exhibitions and displays which were for the moment so vigorously extending his world. He may have been disgusted by the "mean, quarrelsome spirit" displayed by some of his fellow scientists, but their presence had become necessary to him. They provided an audience, an echo, a source of information and, above all, a constant validation of his own achievements, activities and ambitions. He had found his own supportive tribe and if, a few years later, he would be glad to leave them behind him, to deal with them only through the print and paper of their books and journals,

---

* He became President of the Linnean Society in 1853 and was holding that office when Darwin's and Wallace's momentous papers on the mutability of species were read in 1858. He lived just long enough to see *The Origin* published, dying in 1860.

for the moment they answered the needs of his development.

His letters to Henslow are full of the names of those members of the tribe with whom he was now establishing connections. There were naturalists like the bookseller, and zoologist, William Yarrell, academics like the entomologist and palaeontologist J.O. Westwood, the botanist David Don or the Cambridge mineralogist W.H. Miller; there were museum curators and officials of learned societies, like William Lonsdale, of the Geological Society or Robert Brown, of the British Museum, there were the solidly established men, like Buckland or Whewell, and there were old friends like the geologist Sedgwick, the entomologist Hope and Dr. Grant, once Darwin's Edinburgh mentor, now installed at London University.

There was always in Darwin, however, a fundamental caution, a reluctance to move far from his roots. London, though exciting, provided no more than an environment to which his circumstances forced him to adapt. It offered him so much that was new that it made the familiar more enticing. When he finally established himself in rooms of his own, it was in a house only a few doors away from where his brother lived. Just as his brother's fascination for science may have been central in Charles's early development, so now his presence in London eased an essential, but difficult, stage in his later progress. Without some such familiar connection, Darwin's nostalgia for Cambridge and liking for Henslow might have kept him those crucial sixty miles away in the familiar comforts of that university town. Instead, he had, in his brother's apartment, a permanent metropolitan base, a forward position in which he could pause before continuing his own advance, a dependable fortress within the shelter of which he could set up his own necessary colony.

Erasmus, gentle, ironic, generous, mildly eccentric, witty, dependable, has been thrust paradoxically both into and out of the light by his younger brother's fame. Hovering at what seem the edges of the story, he has hardly been noticed; yet, if there had been no story, he would not have been noticed at all. Carlyle has described him as "a most diverse kind of mortal . . . a quiet house-friend, honestly attached . . . He has something of original and sarcastically ingenious in him; one of the sincerest, naturally truest and most modest of men." Compared with Charles, Carlyle wrote, "I rather prefer him for intellect, had not his health quite doomed him to silence and patient idleness". For Erasmus was another member of the distinguished regiment of Victorian invalids. He had been weak since his schooldays, his general debility persuading even his father that he had neither the strength nor the stamina to pursue a medical career.

Charles, like the rest of his family, imagined for quite a long time that Erasmus was on the point of marrying Harriet Martineau, whom he frequently escorted about London. But Erasmus, tall, thin, distinguished like his brother, lofty-browed as his hair receded, sharp-tongued yet infinitely obliging, remained unmarried as though by vocation. The central relationship of his life was probably that with Hensleigh Wedgwood and his wife, Fanny. "Missis", he called her in the letters he wrote to her, and Dr. Robert, as we know, thought the connection sufficiently close to fear a scandal, even if only in jest. By the late 1830s, however, it was so established that it almost ceased to be mentioned. The three of them went everywhere together; Erasmus and Hensleigh sat on a number of the same committees and had a closely overlapping circle of friends. Fanny, Jane Carlyle, Harriet Martineau, his sisters, the Wedgwood circle – these were the people who provided Erasmus with his emotional security, the continuity of relationship which made sense of life.

It is possible, of course, that he was homosexual, expressing passion only in the secrecy enforced by a censorious age. If that was so, the secrecy was absolute. Aspects of his aestheticism, edged wit and thoughtful generosity might suggest it, but in truth the possibility is only raised by the apparent absence of heterosexual activity. Erasmus may indeed have avoided deep heterosexual entanglements, certainly those demanding some physical participation, but the likelihood is that he was equally repelled or alarmed by all sexual activity. He was agreeable, benevolent, helpful and considerate, one might conclude, not in self-protection, as Charles was, but precisely because he was not a passionate, sexually active man. One may assume that the same attenuations of temperament had caused his lack of true ambition and were the basis of his unperturbed and lifelong indolence. His emotions never blazed; they were warm, but diffused, so that, while he had a number of favourites and one or two women friends, like Fanny Hensleigh and Jane Carlyle, to whom he was quite deeply attached, he seems never to have felt that precise polarization of one's feelings brought about by adult sexual desire.

For Charles, his brother provided a means of entry into social circles that might otherwise have remained impenetrable. They were not circles, however, that he had any deep desire to penetrate. Their literary and political concerns were not his. Perhaps the fact that he was welcomed by them reinforced his gathering confidence, but what he needed now was a man who understood his language, who could follow the logic of his ideas back to their genesis in observation, who was established in his science, but was not afraid of secular speculation, who had grounded his own reputation so solidly he was envious of no newcomer, who was able and willing to inform Darwin without forcing him into the trammels of unexaminable convictions.

That such a paragon existed stands to the credit of the scientific establishment. He was, in fact, someone from whose writings Darwin had already learned many of his most crucial lessons, a man whose own theories had created the very possibility of Darwin's own: Charles Lyell. Throughout his life, Darwin was to depend upon a small group of close friends. His story could be told by tracing the sequence of these relationships. Henslow, Lyell, Hooker, Huxley, Romanes – they follow each other, though naturally overlapping. Every one was a man of great qualities and independent achievement; all were happy in Darwin's friendship and glad to collaborate with him, sometimes over several decades.

In a sense, Darwin used and even leaned on them, hammering out his ideas in conversation with them, drawing from them all the information they could supply, even prepared to see them embroiled at times on what were in fact the battlefields of his own wars. When he eventually withdrew into the comparative isolation of Downe, it was they who over the years supplied the intellectual stimulation another man might have drawn from the easy social intercourse of metropolitan life or the controversies and loaded chit-chat of academic gatherings. They became, so to speak, his panel of advisers, his cabinet, his family-in-science: each became as close as a brother, thus perhaps recreating the relationship Charles had had with Erasmus in that garden laboratory in Shrewsbury so many years before. Yet if Darwin desired their approval as well as their collaboration, he did not depend on this – it took many years for Hooker, Huxley, and, in particular, Lyell, to be persuaded of the validity of his theories, a caution in them which seems never to have diminished his own conviction that he had read and rightly understood the very process of Nature.

Charles Lyell was a Scot, nearly twelve years older than Darwin, who had also taken to natural history early. Despite his father's profound interest in botany, young Lyell's entomologizing was met by "ridicule, or hints that the pursuits of other boys were more manly". In 1815 he went up to Oxford, but managed to combine his studies not only with the collection of beetles, but also with an increasing fascination for geology. After taking his classics degree, he came to London to study law, and promptly joined both the Linnean and Geological Societies. Geology was now his major interest and it was on this that he began to publish. His articles soon made it plain that in the debate dividing that science he stood firmly under Hutton's uniformitarian banner. In 1832 he married the eldest daughter of that Leonard Horner who, only five or six years earlier, had taken the young Darwin to see Sir Walter Scott presiding over the Royal Society of Edinburgh.

Meanwhile, of course, the first volume of his *Principles of Geology* had come out, establishing his reputation among his scientific contemporaries and ensuring his place in the history of ideas. He was therefore one of that community of naturalists who regarded Darwin as their representative in South America and waited with impatience for the *Beagle*'s homecoming. As he wrote to Sedgwick in December, 1835, "How I long for the return of Darwin!"

It was very soon after that return that Lyell and Darwin met; by the end of October, 1836, Darwin could write to Henslow, "Mr. Lyell has entered in the *most* goodnatured manner, & almost without being asked, into all my plans." In those early years, the geologist was an ideal companion for Darwin. Ambitious despite his scepticism, cautious even when iconoclastic, Lyell knew his way through the runs and chambers of the metropolitan warren in a way that Darwin never would. At the same time, he never rejected speculation in favour of dogma, however much he might avoid its public expression in favour of an expedient silence.

By the end of 1836, Lyell was inviting Darwin to "Come up on Monday, January 2, and come and dine with us at half-past five o'clock . . . No one dines with us but Mr. and Mrs. Horner and one daughter, and Mr. Horner will be glad to renew his acquaintance with you . . . one or two are to be here, to whom I should like to introduce you, besides a few whom you know already". He wanted to discuss a paper Darwin had written and "to point out several passages which require explanation, and must have a word or two altered . . ." thus demonstrating in a single paragraph his twin value to Darwin as a mentor both social and scientific.

Lyell's own work had led him naturally to a consideration of the creation and inter-connection of species, the very problems which Darwin's observations had begun to persuade him, too, to re-examine. Darwin was as yet, of course, a long way short of the revolutionary unorthodoxies with which he would shock the conventional a quarter of a century later; when he began to formulate these, he kept them to himself for several years. For the moment, however – and perhaps it was the precise moment when he most needed one – Darwin had found an ally, someone combining knowledge and imagination, rather as he himself did; a man whose good opinion he did not risk by setting out his own ideas and whose judgement, at least on matters of science, he could rely on.

Naturally enough, Lyell had his own theories about species: he believed in "a succession of extinction of species, and creation of new ones, going on perpetually now, and through an indefinite period of the past, and to continue for ages to come, all in accommodation to the changes which must continue in the inanimate and habitable earth . . .", a notion he considered "the grandest which I had ever conceived, so far as regards the attributes of the Presiding Mind". These ideas were very different from those towards which Darwin was to struggle, and it was to be a very long time before Lyell would alter them, but, deistic and arbitrary though they were, they provided a better basis than Genesis for a meeting of scientific minds. Over the years, Darwin learned to have reservations about Lyell, especially about the social Lyell, who was so careful to avoid antagonisms, solicitous of those in power, watchful for his own advancement; but in those first post-*Beagle* years, it was Lyell's friendship perhaps more than any other single factor that supported Darwin as he created his new life: it certified – for him as well as others – that his was an increasingly substantial presence upon the intellectual stage.

2

By the beginning of 1837, Darwin was busily writing his *Journal of Researches*, in which he described all that he was willing or able to reveal of the discoveries he had made during the *Beagle* years. It was a book that would bring him more recognition than anything he was to publish except *On the Origin of Species*. It meant his reorganizing the journal that he had sent home to Shrewsbury in long, thought-provoking instalments, adding dissertations on various creatures that seemed to him significant, on geology and the formation of coral reefs, on the lives of the peoples he had been able to observe, refining material brought over from his Diary, and generally shaping his experiences. In March he wrote to Fox that he was getting ready "*the* book", adding that he was "now hard at work and give up everything else for it". In April, while recruiting Jenyns for the *Zoology,* he said of the *Journal*, "it gets on slowly, though I am not idle". In May he was able to tell Henslow, "I have been working very steadily, but have only got two-thirds through the Journal part alone. I find, though I remain daily many hours at work, the progress is very slow: it is an awful thing to say to oneself, every fool and every clever man in England, if he chooses, may make as many ill-natured remarks as he likes on this unfortunate sentence."

There is, as there was always to be, a great discrepancy between Darwin's seemingly low opinion of his energies and abilities and his actual achievements. The fact is that he wrote the *Journal* in seven months, while at the same time organizing the preparation of the *Zoology* and compiling at least some of the six papers he gave that year. It was in 1837, too, that he began those notebooks in which, through dozens upon dozens of cryptic, energetic, endlessly observant remarks and queries, he worked his way towards the true structure of his ideas on evolution. As always, therefore, one wonders why he was so ready to duck when no one wanted to strike him. Why so swift in defence when there was so small a likelihood of an attack? Why, in other words, disarm criticism when no criticism was logically to be expected?

On some matters at least, and at certain levels, Darwin appears all his life to have stood as though outside himself. From that quasi-external stance, he looked back at himself with a surly, critical gleam in his eye. Was he at those times his father? Was he the elder brother, the Erasmus of the 1820s, pouring out a fraternal scorn? It is hard now to be certain – there had also been at times, after all, a certain stridency in the voices of the sisterhood. Whatever the reason, he seems always to have been ready to play this other person, and to take his part – that of the accuser, the unanswerable critic – against the suspect "I", the working, active self whose efforts were never, despite all the successes through the years, enough to placate that watchful, interior hostility.

While Darwin was creating his new life in London, news of the old was carried to him in a flow of letters from Shrewsbury. William Owen wrote, asking for help in finding a tutor for his son, Charles, "who if nothing better offers I intend for the Church . . ." Wistfully, Owen regretted that there was to be no chance "this Winter of renewing my instructions to you in the *Science* of Shooting – & I am getting so old & so bad on my legs that I fear I shall not be able much longer to attend to or *instruct you*, & you really were so promising a Pupil that I was rather proud of you." But Darwin, busy with his specimens and journals, his eyes on acceptance by the capital, was never to go shooting at Woodhouse again.

Catherine wrote at about the same time, addressing him affectionately as "My dear Charley" and reporting that at Shrewsbury they had been "living as quiet as mice lately, and I hope that you also have at last begun to be really quiet, which I know is what you most wish for". Maer had passed on to them the news that "Hensleigh had been to see your Bones at the College of Surgeons and that the unique head was lying in a room with workmen; which certainly ought not to be – can you do anything about it?"* There is a marvellously proprietary air about these comments; the women of The Mount were not prepared to let their young man slip from their grasp without a struggle.

In letters from Shrewsbury there were often dying echoes of the past. Catherine had visited Woodhouse and met Fanny Biddulph; she reported that Fanny had been "better than when you saw her", an indication that Charles had met his erstwhile "Housemaid" during his earlier visit to Shrewsbury. He had done more, apparently sending her flowers; Fanny, despite her pleasure at this, had complained that Darwin had addressed her too formally in the accompanying note, writing "My dear Mrs Biddulph" as though to a comparative stranger. Clearly he had hedged himself off from any chance of embarrassment by a slightly exaggerated propriety.

In London, meanwhile, the specimens Darwin had brought back from his travels were creating something of a stir, having been recently displayed by the Zoological Society – the *Morning Herald* had written of eighty speci-

---

* Hensleigh's report, if true, runs counter to the College's official gratitude as set out in a letter to Darwin expressing "intire approval of the terms and conditions annexed to your highly liberal offer of your valuable specimens of South American fossil remains".

mens of mammalia and 450 birds. "We were exceedingly pleased to hear of your success in London; especially Papa; and pray *write out* about all your laurels; we enjoy hearing them so much it is hard we should lose any . . . Mr Gould also described the 11 species from the Gallapagos, & all new. – Sarah Williams cut me out this passage, and gave it to me to take to read to Papa."

In February, 1837, there came news of Emma Wedgwood, enjoying an Edinburgh season at the house of her cousin, Lady Gifford. Catherine reported to Charles that Emma "writes word that your Feather Flowers are very much admired, and she finds them exceedingly useful at all her parties. We hear that Emma says she would have preferred the *learned* Season at Edinburgh to the *gay* one . . . I am very much surprised at it, and do not think she can know what she is talking about." As far as the Darwins were concerned, Emma was clearly not among the world's intellectuals – nor, judging from Catherine's acid tone, was she on any short list of those whom Charles, now turning twenty-eight, might be expected to marry.

A few days later, Caroline wrote, enclosing a note from Fanny Biddulph, that message now long vanished. It may be that Fanny was beginning to wonder, as she watched Charles's metropolitan progress from the provincial recesses of Chirk Castle, whether she might have been better advised to wait out the *Beagle*'s five tormenting years; certainly she made efforts to keep alive the old friendship. For Darwin, however, time had closed over the possibility of that passion: he kept her letters and maintained her memory, rather as a widower might trim his dead wife's grave – with one eye open for her successor. Indeed, between the Darwins and the Owens the old association was coming to an end; Charles from time to time during those early London years continued to see Sarah, but from now on Woodhouse figures less and less largely in his story, and that of his sisters.

Lyell was now of greater significance. "My Father is extremely pleased," wrote Caroline, "by Mr Lyell's friendship for you, he thinks it invaluable as a happiness & assistance – and is most flattering as a proof of your information & the value of it – I quite envy Eras being able to hear Lyell's speech" – he had in an address made flattering references to Darwin – "for I suppose men are admitted to hear . . ." There is resignation in her tone. The position of women was so far beyond her powers to redress that even complaint seems to have been unthinkable: acceptance was the only possible response. Meanwhile, Emma had not yet come back from Edinburgh – "Lady Gifford seems to have a very large as well as a very gay set of acquaintances – they take very kindly to Emma . . ." But soon Caroline returned to Charles's new friends and reputation.

Be sure you keep & *shew me* Lyells complimentary letter asking you to go to

London. Can you (if a few words will do) tell me on what points it is that Lyell "fully agrees with your views" on subjects you say you talk over together in London. The Coral islands I know was one subject, but *if* I can understand & *if* you can with out much trouble give me an idea of the other subjects I should be very glad.

There is something touching in her attempts to maintain their relationship even at the intellectual levels on which Charles now seemed most at ease. He, for his part, tried his patient best to explain his new preoccupations and answer her questions about them. The classroom order of his early childhood had been reversed; now it was he who was Caroline's teacher. At the end of February, 1837, for example, he wrote to her:

> You tell me you do not see what is new in Sir J. Herschell's ideas about the chronology of the Old Testament being wrong . . . it is not to the days of Creation which he refers, but to the lapse of ages since the first man made his wonderful appearance on this world. – As far as I know, everyone has just thought that the six thousand odd years has been the right period but Sir J. thinks that a far greater number must have passed since the . . . languages separated from one stock.

If until this moment Darwin had really believed "the six thousand odd years" adequate to explain human history, it argues a late flowering of his transmutational ideas; he was never a man, however, to burden others with disturbing speculations he might more prudently keep to himself. In that Spring of 1837, he was bustling across the plains and peaks of his life with the same energy with which he had penetrated the pampas and the Cordilleras. In mid-March he wrote to Fox, "My good dear old brother lives the same life of tranquillity as usual . . . He seems well contented and happy, but for my own part I would not care for a hundred years of life without a little more excitement." It is probable, however, that his London life, hemmed in though it was by tall facades, coal-smoke and the endless clatter of the horse-drawn traffic, was proving sufficiently exciting – certainly it was ceaselessly active. In May he had to admit to Henslow that he was unable to leave London even when he wanted to. He had planned "to pay my good dear people at Shrewsbury a visit for a few days, but found I could not manage it". That month, however, he took a few hours off to make a nostalgic visit to the *Beagle*, preparing to sail for Australia at the beginning of June. "It appeared marvellously odd to see the little vessel," he told Henslow, "and to think that I should not be one of the party. – If it was not for the sea sickness, I should have no objection to start again."

Yet Darwin worked on despite all distractions. In that May of 1837 he revealed an outline of his ideas on coral formation in a paper delivered to the Geological Society. He had already discussed his ideas with Lyell, who a week earlier had written to Herschell about them: "I must give up my volcanic crater theory for ever, though it costs me a pang at first, for it accounted for so much." Despite his disappointment, it was Lyell who urged Whewell, the president of the society, to arrange Darwin's reading. Quite apart from his conclusions, Darwin's incidental speculations throw some light on the progress of his evolutionary ideas. He pointed out, for example, that since coral formations act "as monuments over subsided land, the geographical distribution of organic beings (as consequent on geological changes as laid down by Mr. Lyell) is elucidated, by the discovery of former centres whence the germs could be disseminated"; as a result, he wrote, "some degree of light might thus be thrown on the question, whether certain groups of living beings peculiar to small spots are the remnant of a former large population, or a new one springing into existence".

Such questions seem at first sight the orthodox opinions of one who has made Lyell's ideas his own; they agree with the phrase Darwin used, at about the same time, of the Galapagos as a possible "centre of creation". They also demonstrate, however, how seriously Darwin was considering the problem of isolated populations and the significance of the often unique characteristics that they displayed. But did they display these, he wondered, because they were the last remnants of what had once been vast armies, the survivors of a once great species, herded into tiny reserves as subsidence steadily raised the level of the sea and submerged their grazing lands? Or were they the forerunners, recently created, of vast armies yet to come? These issues, which Lyell had on the whole avoided, were beginning to tease Darwin. Implied in his questions is a gathering doubt; it is as though even as he attempted to refine Lyell's ideas, to render them more precise, he was in the process of diverging from them.

The activities of the coral polyps may have alerted Darwin to the action elsewhere of organic life upon inorganic matter. Certainly that is the basis of his explanation for the "formation of the superficial layer of the earth, commonly called vegetable mould"; his suggestion that it was the action of earthworms that was responsible began an interest which lasted for the rest of his life – his last published work, in 1881, was *Formation of Vegetable Mould through the Action of Worms*. He set up the simplest of experiments, that ran sometimes for decades, by doing no more than laying lime or marked stones upon the earth and measuring the rate at which they vanished from sight; by its very nature, work of this kind had to continue for a lifetime. Rather in the way that great artists carry for decade after decade concepts arrived at in an early moment of inspiration, to seize on and complete them in old age, so Darwin too worked his ideas over and over through the years, to set them out in public only when he was ready – and the public prepared.

In July, 1837, there occured one of those alliances between cousins which were such a feature of this circle's marital history. Caroline Darwin and the third Josiah Wedgwood decided to get married. There were eight children born at Maer; six of them married – but only two took spouses from outside the family. Of the four Darwin marriages, two were with Wedgwood cousins and a third with the widower of a Wedgwood. Even in the previous generation, Susannah Darwin's brothers, John Wedgwood and Josiah II, had connected their marital choices by becoming the husbands of two of the Allen sisters. It was this Josiah Wedgwood, of course, who was the father of the man Caroline was now to marry. His son was usually referred to as Joe, to distinguish him in his own generation from the two Josiahs who had preceded him. He was a quiet, retiring man, in whom the thrusting energy of the first Josiah appeared to have petered out.

Darwin, writing about the marriage to Fox, described Josiah III as "a very quiet grave man, with very much to respect & like in him, but I wish he would put himself forward more. He has a most wonderful deal of information & is a very superior person, but he has not made the most of himself." For Darwin to consider someone's self-effacement remarkable, it must indeed have been extreme; it is a remark which demonstrates that Darwin's lifelong modesty was always leavened by a measure of shrewdness and an awareness of how the world actually worked, and judged. As for Caroline, he thought she would be very happy, "especially if she has children, for I never saw a human being so fond of little crying wretches as she is". (Caroline, despite the lateness of her marriage, in fact had four daughters and, though the oldest died in babyhood, the others all married and produced "little crying wretches" of their own – one the composer Vaughan Williams.) "But I am an ungrateful dog," Darwin added hastily, "to speak this way, for she was a mother to me during the early part of my life." And, remembering that Fox was now a father, added further, "I must not talk to *you* of crying little wretches – you will not guess that I mean such little angels as all children doubtless are."

The swift activity of his life continued. He was still working on his *Journal* as well as laying the groundwork for the various sections of the *Zoology*. At the same time, he was from time to time giving papers at the Geological Society, of which he was now a member. These had been, he told Fox, "favourably received by the great guns, and this gives me much confidence, & I hope not a very great deal of vanity, though I confess I feel too often like a peacock admiring his tail."

Given all this effort, it comes as no real surprise to find Darwin writing to Henslow in mid-September, "I have not been very well of late with an uncomfortable palpitation of the heart, and my doctors urge me *strongly* to knock off all work & go and live in the country for a few weeks. – I believe I must do this . . ." He asked Henslow, both good-natured and well-qualified, to help him with the proofs of his *Journal*: "I find it most disagreeable work", he warned; "if I attend to sense, I forget the spelling, & vice versa." But, he added, "I feel I must have a little rest, else I shall break down." For the first time, ominously, one detects the note of a genuine concern over his health in Darwin's remarks; like the first hint of twilight, it cools and dampens the brightness of his life before anyone can notice its importance. Implacably, the darkness will steal down, until eventually it will threaten to envelop all, to render his whole world null. "I would not be giving trouble by changing my plans," he wrote, "if I did not feel it was necessary."

On 25 September, Darwin travelled to Maer and Shrewsbury, staying away from London for almost a month. He was now uncertain of his fitness to undertake the amount of work that faced him. In this state of unwonted hesitation, he found himself being asked – on this occasion by Henslow; but not for the first time – to become the secretary of the Geological Society. "The subject has haunted me all summer," he remarked to Henslow. "I am unwilling to undertake the office . . ." Only the previous December Lyell had advised him, "Don't accept any official scientific place, if you can avoid it . . . At least, work as I did, exclusively for yourself and for science for many years, and do not prematurely incur the honour or penalty of official dig- nities. There are people who may be profitably employed in such duties, because they would not work if not so engaged." It was not a very sociable point of view, as Lyell knew very well – "tell no one that I gave you this advice", he requested, "as they would all cry out against me as the preacher of anti-patriotic principles." It was a point of view, nevertheless, that must have chimed with Darwin's own inclinations.

To Henslow he pointed out that he knew nothing of English geology and less of the French language, "so perpetually quoted. It would be disgraceful to the Society to have a Secretary who could not read French." There was the amount of time it would demand, and the little time he had to spare: "All my geological notes are in a very rough state, none of my fossil shells worked up, & I have much to read". He would have to attend the Society's meetings and make abstracts of all papers read there, "but I appeal to you, whether, with my slow manner of writing, – with two works in hand, – & with the certainty if I cannot complete the geological part within a fixed period, that its publication must be retarded for a very long time, whether any Society whatever has any claim on me for three days' disagreeable work every fortnight . . . Moreover so EARLY in my scientific life, with so very much as I have to learn, the office, though no doubt a great honour etc for me, would be the more burdensome." And then there was his health; he doubted if it would "stand the confinement of what I have to do without any additional work. I merely repeat, that you may know I am not speaking idly, that when I consulted Dr. Clark in town, he at first urged me to give up entirely all writing, and even correcting press for some weeks." The agitation that prompted this refusal is clear – so clear, indeed, that it displays how strong was the temptation to accept. "My dear Henslow, I appeal to you in loco parentis, – pray tell me what you think." Four months later, in February, 1838, he accepted the appointment. Thereafter, until 1841, he struggled through his official work as Secretary as well as his own private work as a naturalist, and as the scientific chronicler of the *Beagle* voyage.

The effect of this appointment was to thrust him as an official into one of the most important debating chambers to be found in the world of the natural sciences. Geology had been restructuring, as we have seen, the entire early history of the planet. Because it had pushed far back, into unimaginably distant epochs, the beginnings of those processes which had moulded the earth's surface, it had led its practitioners directly to the questions posed by the origins and development of living species. Geology, after all, provided the ultimate environment, upon which time and weather worked and within which plants and animals flourished or died. Men like Lyell, Sedgwick and Buckland – as well as those from different disciplines, like Herschel or, later, the multi-faceted Spencer – spent their time and energy with enthusiastic prodigality in discussing the "species question".

It was of some importance, therefore, that during the three years that Darwin was Secretary of the Society, its president was William Whewell, one of the sturdiest pillars of the scientific establishment. His father had been a carpenter, but a chance conversation with a local headmaster who was instantly and deeply impressed by the boy had led to his being given a place at a nearby grammar school. A scholarship to Cambridge in 1812, academic prizes and a fellowship saw Whewell established in a university career. He wrote poetry and published on subjects as diverse as ecclesiastical architecture and crystallography. After long dispute, he became in 1828 professor of mineralogy at Cambridge, succeeding Henslow; he resigned in 1832. In 1837, he published his *History of the inductive sciences*, which was to be followed three years later by his *Philosophy of the inductive sciences*. By these works he is still remembered. Eventually, he was to become Master of his old college, Trinity, and Vice Chancellor of Cambridge University. He was a clergyman, having been ordained in 1825, and a friend of the Lakeland poets, especially Wordsworth. Whewell, who had in 1830 written the Bridgewater Treatise on astronomy and natural theology, was a powerful voice on the side of scientific and religious orthodoxy. He believed firmly in a Baconian science, concerning itself with an elucidation of the facts making

up God's created world and eschewing fruitless and unauthorized speculation. His repeated involvement in vehement debates, through print and in
the flesh, over the mutability or fixity of species must have reinforced
Darwin's awareness of the problem's importance.

This focussing of Darwin's attention on the arguments seems more than
likely, despite all Whewell's strictures, to have stimulated his own bent for
speculation to a pitch even higher than had the many suggestive *Beagle*
observations. He heard marshalled the main arguments advanced by the
many shades of opinion, which ranged from Biblical certainty through
various modifications of Genesis and Lyell's notion of a continuous creation
to the acceptance of more or less Lamarckian views. As the person responsible for abstracting papers and recording discussions, there was no way in
which Darwin could escape an understanding of these hypotheses. But the
fact that Whewell and the majority of geologists took what was, on the
whole, a conservative view provided the ideological framework within which
Darwin had to pursue his own ideas. It was against that background that he
felt his way slowly and painfully throughout these years towards his
revolutionary theories – or, more accurately, towards the logical justification of the revolutionary theories that, as the time passed, he held with an
increasing firmness.

Amid these stresses and excitements, he maintained his close connections
with his sisters, a loyalty to his family always strong and natural in him. It
may be, too, that the easy gossip, simple jokes, and trivial news with which
he filled his letters to Shrewsbury offered him some relief from the new
pressures of his life. His sisters would neither judge nor misunderstand him,
so that he could show them feelings and opinions over which he needed to
keep no guard. He had no passionate secrets to reveal, yet it must have been
a comfort to relax on paper in this way.

In April, 1838, he wrote to Susan about a visit to Fitzroy: "The Captain is
going on very well – that is for a man who has the most consummate skill in
looking at every thing & every body in a perverted manner". Darwin himself
had taken up riding again and consequently had not felt "so thoroughly well
since eating two dinners a day at Shrewsbury and increasing in weight in due
proportion". He recounted details of a visit to Cambridge – "In evening
attended Trinity Chapel . . . the last Chorus seemed to shake the very walls"
– he added another *Nota Bene*, this one harking back to his schooldays and
ancient discontents. "I recommend you Mrs. Granny to spell headachs not
head*aches* – there is for you madam – I return you some of your spelling
corrections which you have so often thrown in my teeth." A third "*N.B.*",
however, expressed a certain unease: "I feel some doubts, whether my
severe & very witty criticisms on your spelling is right – I know to my cost

headache in the singular is wrong for I have so written it in my Journal." The pedantries of orthography were never among the skills Darwin learned to master.

Towards the end of June, 1838, Darwin travelled north to Edinburgh by steamship. The trip, he told Lyell, "was absolutely pleasant, and I enjoyed the spectacle, wretch that I am, of two ladies, & some small children quite sea-sick, I being well. Moreover, on my return from Glasgow to Liverpool, I triumphed in a similar manner over some full-grown men." His main purpose in going north was to travel to Glen Roy, near Lochaber, an area around which considerable geological controversy had developed. There, he examined the evidence in "the most beautiful weather with gorgeous sunsets, and all nature looking as happy as I felt . . . I think, without any exceptions, not even the first volcanic island, the first elevated beach, or the passage of the Cordillera, was so interesting to me as this week."

The outcome was a long paper, read in February, 1839, to the Royal Society. During the years of debate that followed, that quality in Darwin which, when he was right, we hail as tenacity was placed at the disposal of a mistaken view and so dwindled into stubbornness. The Parallel Roads of Glen Roy, great horizontal lines running along the sides of this valley system, had clearly not been formed by any divisions between the strata. They were thus a continuing source of frustration to geologists who had become used to solving the problem of terrestrial structures. Everyone agreed that the lines were the remains of ancient beaches – but the action of what water, brought from where, contained how, had etched them there, between 850 and 1150 feet?

The current theory proposed that fresh water had been naturally dammed in the valleys, at various heights and over varying periods, by recurrent obstructions of rocks or alluvial soil. Darwin, proving from the evidence the unlikelihood of this, asserted that the only alternative could be that the Roads had been formed by an arm of the sea. The slow elevation of the land had caused the water level to drop on various occasions, thus creating the beaches; finally, it had cut the valley off entirely from the sea. This was the theory that he defended for over twenty years; one has the feeling that his was the sort of mind which, having sensed that a conclusion is right, cannot easily abandon its allegiance to its own logic. The same powerful imagination which had made it possible for him to consider the vast unfolding of evolution and see it in its entirety could, once misled, seize with the same completeness, the same voracity, upon a mistaken view. Darwin assumed there could be only two solutions to the Glen Roy enigma, the one already proposed and the one he was offering. This assumption was false. Yet up to the 1860s he would struggle to maintain his ideas against those of the farmer-geologist, T.F. Jamieson.

Reverting to the notion of dams, Jamieson proposed that these had been, not of rock or soil, but of ice. As the great glaciers had withdrawn, so these dams had diminished, allowing the level of the water to fall. Periods between the recessions of the ice had allowed the dammed lake to settle into stability again and remain at its new level for hundreds and perhaps thousands of years. Thus at each such level, a beach had formed, creating one of the parallel markings on the slopes of the glen. This solution to the problem appeared both elegant and plausible to many geologists. Yet Darwin clung stubbornly to his own idea: in September, 1838, he wrote to Lyell, hoping to "prove to others' satisfaction what I have convinced myself is the case"; twenty-three years later he was still to admit, "I cannot help a sneaking hope that the sea might have formed the horizontal shelves".

In the end, however, as one might expect from someone of his character, it was with a disarming good grace that he admitted his defeat. "Your arguments seem to me conclusive," he wrote to Jamieson. "I give up the ghost. My paper is one long gigantic blunder . . ." What he learned through this defeat was not to trust in an over-simplified logic: "How rash it is in science to argue because any case is not one thing, it must be some second thing which happens to be known to the writer". It is in fact a wonder that Darwin, galloping as he so often did towards conclusions, fell at so few fences. He had spent eight days in Glen Roy, and on that basis had produced a theory which he was to defend for a quarter of a century; yet in 1861 he could assert, in a letter to Lyell, that the valley should be thoroughly searched for alternative outlets at various levels – "A man might spend his life there". It is an example of how narrow a scientific base he sometimes needed in order to erect the plausible structures of his theories.

This was not the only mistaken hypothesis that Darwin proposed to his fellow geologists. In 1840 he suggested that it was icebergs which had transported what are known as erratic boulders – anomalous blocks of stone found sometimes hundreds of miles from their originating strata. This opposed the view of the French geologist, Jean de Charpentier, who, wandering through the lonely valleys of the Jura, had reinforced with his observations the conviction of Hutton and his exegesist, Playfair, that glaciers had been responsible.

Darwin, basing his ideas on his own observations in South America, was following uniformitarian precept by accepting what he could see in the present as evidence for what was most likely to have happened in the past. Since the carrying of boulders by icebergs was, he wrote, "now in action on the South American shores, we are naturally led to conclude that this was the chief agent in the enormous amount of transportal formerly effected over a

more extended area". Natural though this conclusion seemed to him, it is
Charpentier's view that now prevails. However, Darwin had not this time
offered his solution in any dogmatic spirit; closer scrutiny of the rocks
themselves, he suggested, would "aid us in discovering whether they had
been imbedded in sheet-ice, or carried on the surface of deeply-floating
icebergs".

Meanwhile, in 1838, the leaves darkened, the year turned to high
summer. Darwin paid one of his periodic visits to Shrewsbury, returning to
London early in August. In the metropolis, he had contrived to make his life
even more agreeable than before. Through Lyell, he had widened his
bridgehead in the world of the great men: he had become a member of that
famous club, the Athenaeum, where the established and the mighty walked
ponderously up their wide sweep of staircase to the wood-and-leather gloom
of their hushed Library. He wrote to Lyell,

> I am coming into your way of only working about two hours at a spell; I then go
> out & do my business in the streets, return & set to work again, and thus make
> two separate days out of one. The new plan answers capitally; after the second
> half day is finished I go and dine at the Athenaeum like a gentleman, or rather
> like a lord, for I am sure the first evening I sat in that great drawing-room, all on
> a sofa by myself, I felt just like a duke. I am full of admiration at the
> Athenaeum, one meets so many people there that one likes to see . . . Your
> helping me into the Athenaeum has not been thrown away, & I enjoy it the
> more because I fully expected to detest it.

Lyell, replying, gave Darwin a warning. He used to go to the Athenaeum "by
way of a lounge, and instead of that, worked my head very hard, being
excited by meeting clever people, who would often talk to me, very much to
my profit, on the very subject on which I was writing . . . Now this was all
very well, but I used to forget that this ought to count for work although
nothing had been written . . ." Eventually he had been forced, in order to
preserve his energies, to have himself "driven for a walk into Gray's Inn
Gardens".

Over these nineteenth century decades there lies a paradox – that so much
work, and of such variety, was done by writers, artists and scientists who, to
judge from their diaries and correspondence, were constantly at the point of
physical or mental breakdown. Wordsworth, Coleridge, Carlyle, Lyell,
Darwin himself – all complained about an endless succession of ailments and
disabilities, however complex the projects they attempted, however
resounding the success with which they brought them to conclusion, however widely their fame spread, however enviable the stir they caused around
the dinner tables of the fashionable. It was as if stamina and debility revolved
within them in a state of constant combat; they tottered from desk to sickbed

and back again, apparently as determined to suffer as to achieve. It made them preternaturally aware of the dangerous drain any activity might be on their energies; hence Lyell's hypochondriacal reaction to his over-stimulation by what, for others, must seem the inviolable placidity of the Athenaeum.

In accordance with their widespread yet paradoxical acceptance of over-work, Darwin throughout 1838 had been busy, not only with his geological papers and with taking up his official duties at the Geological Society, but also with the labour of completing his *Journal* of the *Beagle* voyage and preparing it for the presses. With his manuscript written and corrected, he had had to wait for Fitzroy's two companion volumes. Early in the year, he had let Fitzroy read what he had written, in case the *Journal* included anything that might offend the ill-balanced Captain. "I am happy to say", Fitzroy wrote, "that there is nothing whatever in your *excellent* and *well-filled* volume, to which I have any kind of objection to offer . . ." By November, Darwin was seeing the appendix through the presses and the following year the *Journal* was published.

Richard Owen wrote to him that it was "the most delightful book in my collection. It is as full of good original wholesome food as an egg . . . I leave it reluctantly – tired eyes compelling – at night, and greet it as a new luxury at the breakfast table." He was not always to be so gracefully complimentary about Darwin's work. W.H. Fitton, the president of the Geological Society, had derived "the greatest pleasure & satisfaction" from the book, mostly because of "the spirit in which the whole is written, & the absolute want of pretension – & pretence – that goes through it . . . one sees that it is the work of a plain English gentleman – travelling for information, and not for effect – & viewing all things *kindly* . . ." Darwin may well have derived the greatest satisfaction from Fitton's judgement that "your Geology seems to me to be excellent". Buckland thanked him for his copy of the *Journal*, "which I shall always highly value for the Author's sake not less than for its high scientific merit", the sort of politeness that leads to the suspicion that he had not yet read it. Fitzroy's first response made no bones about his not yet having read it – "I have dipped into it here and there" – but anticipated two weeks of attentive work, since "much of it requires *close thinking* I apprehend". He still seemed just a little nervous of what Darwin may have written about him: "I cannot think that there is an expression in it – referring to me personally – which I could wish were not in it – at all events neither I nor my wife have yet lighted upon anything that induces one to doubt in the smallest degree that I shall not be thoroughly at ease in that respect". The convoluted style, so uncharacteristically cramped, suggests an uncomfortable awareness of what Darwin might have written had he had a mind to.

From Brunswick there came a letter from a gentleman named Hartmann, who had translated Lyell's recent *Elements of Geology* and various of Darwin's own published papers and now offered to translate "your very interressant *Journal* . . . one of the best scientific travelworks of this time . . ." Much more to Darwin's delight, however, there arrived from Potsdam a letter of praise from the man who had been throughout most of his adult life his primary hero, Humboldt. The German savant called the *Journal* "your excellent and admirable work" and, noting Darwin's confession that Humboldt's own books had earlier inspired him with the desire to make great voyages, expressed his pleasure at the fact that his "feeble works" had found their real value in contributing to the birth of a better. One can imagine how Darwin, who had travelled the length and breadth of South America carrying Humboldt's account as though it were a Bible, received these conventionalized praises, and how avidly he will have scanned the botanical and zoological details with which, in tiny, compressed hand-writing, Humboldt followed them. If he had had any doubts before, this reaction will have reassured him that he was actually present in the world, a man making his identifiable mark.

Five years later, Humboldt was to write to a friend in Britain, "Alas! you have got some one in England whom you do not read – young Darwin . . . He had succeeded far better than myself with the subject I took up. There are admirable descriptions of tropical nature in his journal, which you do not read because the author is a zoologist, which you imagine to be synonymous with bore. Mr. Darwin has another merit, a very rare one in your country – he has praised me." By then, Darwin had actually met this hero, at the house of the geologist Murchison; in his *Autobiography* he admits that he was disappointed and remembers little about the interview, "except that Humboldt was very cheerful and talked much". For his part, Humboldt was being less than fair to Darwin and the reading public of England: a second and more popular edition of the *Journal* was published a year after he had written that comment, and a third fifteen years later; the book also came out in German and French, and it remains in print, a richly-stuffed classic of travel literature.

But, during the autumn and winter of 1838, despite his preparation of the *Journal*, despite the demands of his new post at the Geological Society, despite the unremitting intensity with which he continued to pursue his own theories and the facts upon which they depended, Darwin had another, more personal absorption. Through September and October his sketchy personal journal records only his scientific interests – papers finished, others begun, ideas contemplated, books read. Then comes the entry, "November 9th Started for Maer", followed by another, two days later, "Sunday. The day of days!" This was followed by the note, "Went to Shrewsbury the next day returned to Maer on the 17th & to London on the 20th". In this laconic, even cryptic fashion, Darwin recorded that he had visited the Wedgwoods, asked Emma to be his wife, been accepted, travelled to The Mount to give his father and sisters the news, returned to spend three days with Emma as her fiancé, and then travelled, altered and exultant, back to his now-redundant rooms in Great Marlborough Street.

3

It is obvious from his letters to Fox that Darwin had always been sexually aware, keenly conscious of the beauty and attractiveness of women. The conventions of his time, imposing on everyone a reticence that it took the flamboyance of a Byron to transcend, makes it impossible to retrace the details of his actual experience with them. Fanny Owen's frivolous and superficial letters, arch, flirtatious, catty, gossiping, give us very few clues; his letters to her have vanished. But from the notes and letters that survive from the 1830s one can see that Darwin's industrious bachelor solitude was becoming less and less comfortable as the decades passed.

In February, 1836, while in Tasmania with the *Beagle*, he had written to Fox, looking forward to the ship's calling at Mauritius, "It will clearly be necessary to produce a small stock of sentiment on the occasion; imagine what a fine opportunity for writing love letters – oh that I had a sweet Virginia to send an inspired Epistle to. A person not in love will have no right to wander amongst the glowing, bewitching scenes. – I am writing most glorious nonsense . . ." Darwin, too, it seems, had been susceptible to the effects of *Paul et Virginie*, the love story by Bernardin de St. Pierre that had for fifty years held the literary public by its sentimental throat and squeezed from it its last tear. When he wrote this letter he was in the throes of that homesickness which ravaged the members of the *Beagle* expedition during its final months; most of the time he had expressed this in the desire to see Shrewsbury and his sisters, but from time to time his thoughts obviously strayed to other possibilities.

Did he take these up when he returned? In May, 1837, Emma, writing to Fanny Hensleigh, mentioned Erasmus's attachment to Harriet Martineau, though in a somewhat oblique manner: "I shall be very curious to know whether Susan and Catherine really like Miss Martineau – I expect they will." Then she added a curious remark – "They seem to take very kindly to their other sister." If Harriet Martineau was to be one sister, brought into the family by Erasmus, who was the other, and how could she become such a relation except through Charles? Tantalizingly, Henrietta Litchfield, Darwin's daughter, who edited her mother's letters, although mentioning a rumour that Darwin was about to become engaged, in the 1915 edition left blank the name of his intended bride. At the end of 1836, there had been that invitation from Lyell to Darwin: "No one dines with us but Mr. and Mrs. Horner and one daughter", he had written. Lyell himself had married one of Leonard Horner's daughters; it would not have been entirely surprising if Darwin, in the euphoria of his return, his setting up in London, his growing reputation and his new friendship with the great geologist, had fallen into some version of love with Mrs. Lyell's sister. When nearly ten years later Catherine Horner actually married Lyell's brother, Erasmus Darwin wrote to Fanny Hensleigh that Charles had "brought back the good news which I dare say you have heard, of Cath. Horner's marriage which more particularly eases his conscience". Why should Catherine Horner have lain on Charles's conscience, and, more to the point, why should this have been in a manner which her marriage eased, if he had not encouraged her to think that he intended to marry her himself and then, for some reason, decided not to?

There is another piece of evidence, tenuous certainly, that links the Horners with Darwin's thoughts on wedlock. Preoccupied by these, he made an attempt to summarize them, and to reach some definite conclusion. Picking up a piece of paper, he set his arguments in two columns. Both were headed "Work finished", looking forward to the time when the tidying up of the *Beagle* findings should have come to an end. The left-hand column began, "If *not* marry" and then had the word "TRAVEL" as a sub-heading. Below this, in a pencilled circle, came, "Europe. Yes?", and underneath, "America????" Then, ringed again, there came a whole paragraph: "If I travel it must be exclusively geological – United States – Mexico. Depend upon health and vigour and how far I become Zoological." Another pencil line ringed the next paragraph: "If I dont travel – Work at transmission of Species – microscope simplest forms of life – Geology –? Oldest formations?? Some experiments – physiological observations on lower animals."

The letter "B" ushered in another set of speculations. "Live in London – for where else possible – in small house near Regents Park – keep horse – take Summer tours collect specimens some line of Zoolog: speculations of Geograph. range & Geological general works – systemize – Study affinities."

The righthand column began "If marry", made the point that his means were limited, and went on, "Feel duty to work for money. London life, nothing but Society, no country, no tours, no large Zoolog: collect., no books. – Cambridge Professorship, either Geolog: or Zoolog: – comply with all above requisites – I couldn't systematize zoologically so well." As though taking a deep breath, Darwin moved down to a new line. "But better than hibernating in the country – and where? Better even than near London country house – I could not indolently take country house and do nothing – Could I live in London like a prisoner? If I were moderately rich I would live in London, with pretty big house and do as (B) – but could I act thus with children and poor –? No – Then where live in country near London; better; but great obstacles to science and poverty."

Like everyone contemplating marriage, except the very rich or the very much in love, thoughts of career and finance hemmed Darwin in. How could he live and work as he wished if he took on unknown responsibilities? He scribbled on. "Then Cambridge better, but fish out of water, not being Professor and poverty. Then Cambridge Professorship, – and make best of it – do duty as such and work at spare times – My destiny will be Camb. Prof. or poor man; outskirts of London – some small square etc. – and work as well as I can." Again he paused; one can see him, regarding himself, regarding his future, trying to understand both, to imagine and so comprehend them. "I have so much more pleasure in direct observation, that I could not go on as Lyell does, correcting and adding up new information to old train, and I do not see what line can be followed by man tied down to London. – In country – experiment and observations on lower animals, – more space –"

The argument seems to peter out, inconclusively. Work, it appears, came first with him. Again and again he returns to the difficulties of making himself space – temporally as well as physically – to pursue the observations and experiments with which he was happiest. What links this inner discussion to the Horners, however, is the fact that it was jotted down on the back of a note from Leonard Horner himself. Is it possible that, receiving it, Darwin fell to musing on Miss Horner, and on the advantages and disadvantages of marriage? In any case, what the note does is to allow us, perhaps, to work out roughly when Darwin was speculating in this manner. Mrs. Litchfield thought it must have been in the course of 1837; Lady Barlow, who transcribed the jottings and was the first to publish them in full, committed herself only to either 1837 or 1838, the two years during which Darwin lived at 36 Great Marlborough Street: the note is addressed to him there.

Brought by hand, however, it has no date stamp and Horner had scribbled only "April 7", omitting the year. It reads, "I learned yesterday that the Factory Act is to be brought into the House of Commons by the Govt. on Monday, and it is material that I should be in the house". Hansard reveals that, in 1837, there was no reference to the Factory Act in Parliament; on that April weekend in 1838, however, two petitions to amend the Act were laid before the House of Commons, one on the day Horner's note was written, which was a Saturday, and one on the following Monday, when Horner felt he should be present. It seems more than likely, therefore, that it was during the second or third weeks of April, 1838, that Darwin mused in this detailed manner on the subject of marriage.

What is not quite clear is whether these were Darwin's first or second thoughts on the matter. For, at what must have been more or less the same time, he wrote another, very similar note, his arguments again organized into two columns. This time the points are more basic, the tone less neutrally judicious. One senses that the decision towards which he seems to be working has in fact been made already, and that this is therefore a later meditation than the other. The two columns are this time headed "MARRY" and "Not MARRY". The first begins at once with a word that made hardly any appearance in that other paper, and when it did was not listed among the advantages:

> Children – (if it please God) – constant companion, (friend in old age) who will feel interested in one, object to be beloved and played with – better than a dog anyhow – Home, and someone to take care of house – Charms of music and female chit-chat. These things good for one's health. Forced to visit and receive relations *but terrible loss of time*.

It would be hard to conceive of a more self-indulgent, almost contemptuous, view of the subservience of women to men; in this, as in so much else, Darwin was a true and conventional son of his times and class. With the underlined remembrance of the time he would lose, he seems to have wavered from the main thrust of his evidence, which had tended to show marriage as in every way agreeable – at the very least, "better than a dog" and "good for one's health". Having allowed himself this momentary petulance, however, Darwin burst out with much more passionate arguments for the other side.

"My God, it is intolerable to think of spending one's whole life, like a neuter bee, working, working and nothing after all. – No, no it won't do. –" Then he set out the terms of what must have been the material reverie: "Imagine living all one's day solitary in smoky dirty London House. – Only picture to yourself a nice soft wife on a sofa with a good fire and books and music perhaps – compare this vision with the dingy reality of Grt Marlboro' St." The comparison overcame him. "Marry – Marry – Marry", he scrawled down.

In the second column, he considered alternatives. "No children," he wrote, "(no second life) no one to care for one in old age. – What is the use of working without sympathy from near and dear friends – who are near and dear friends to the old except relatives." There would be freedom to go wherever one pleased and one could keep social involvement to whatever level one found agreeable. And there would be another advantage – "Conversation of clever men at clubs." His experiences at the Athenaeum had clearly impressed him deeply. "Not forced to visit relatives," he went on, "and to bend in every trifle – to have the expense and anxiety of children –

perhaps quarreling. *Loss of time* – cannot read in the evenings – fatness and idleness – anxiety and responsibility – less money for books etc – if many children forced to gain one's bread. – (But then it is very bad for one's health to work too much)." As he considered the arguments against marrying, he became gloomier, almost vituperative. "Perhaps my wife won't like London; then the sentence is banishment and degradation with indolent idle fool –"

But in fact he had already decided. For below that enthusiastic "Marry – Marry – Marry" in the lefthand column he had written, as though under a proven theorem, "Q.E.D." Turning the paper over, therefore, he could begin to consider new questions. "It being proved necessary to marry – When? Soon or Late." His father advised a swift marriage – it was better to have children young, "and if one does not marry soon, one misses so much good pure happiness." On the other hand, if he leaped into marriage, he would face "an infinity of trouble and expense", with all the problems he had outlined, involving loss of precious working time – "(without one's wife was an angel and made one keep industrious)", he scribbled in optimistic paren- thesis. But if he were obliged to set forth for a daily promenade with his wife, "Eheu!! I never should know French, – or see the Continent, – or go to America, or go up in a Balloon, or take solitary trip in Wales – poor slave, you will be worse than a negro – And then horrid poverty (without one's wife was better than an angel and had money)."

But now he was done with seeking out the difficulties. He rallied himself, became positive. "Never mind my boy – Cheer up – One cannot live this solitary life, with groggy old age, friendless and cold and childless staring one in one's face, already beginning to wrinkle. Never mind, trust to chance – keep a sharp look out. – There is many a happy slave –". Whenever he wrote this – and it sounds from its more personal tone as though it might well be later than the other – he apparently had no bride in mind. To bid himself to "keep a sharp look out" hardly suggests that he already had his eye on Emma Wedgwood or anyone else.

There is another point that strikes one. Everyone who knew him spoke of Darwin's sweetness of temperament, his modesty, his selflessness. Yet nowhere in either of these lists of pros and cons is there the slightest hint that marriage should be anything other than an arrangement ensuring his own comfort. There is no sign that it might demand some emotional contribution from him, nor that he might discover new purpose in a concern for others, a responsibility for a wife and children. On the face of it, these seem curiously self-centred speculations, strangely limited and essentially cold. In reality, of course, he was to be an affectionate and thoughtful husband, and a father both loving and tolerant. The male dominance of his time clearly helped to

Plate 8

The microscope that
Darwin was given as an
anonymous gift by a fellow-
student at Cambridge, later
identified as his friend
Herbert.

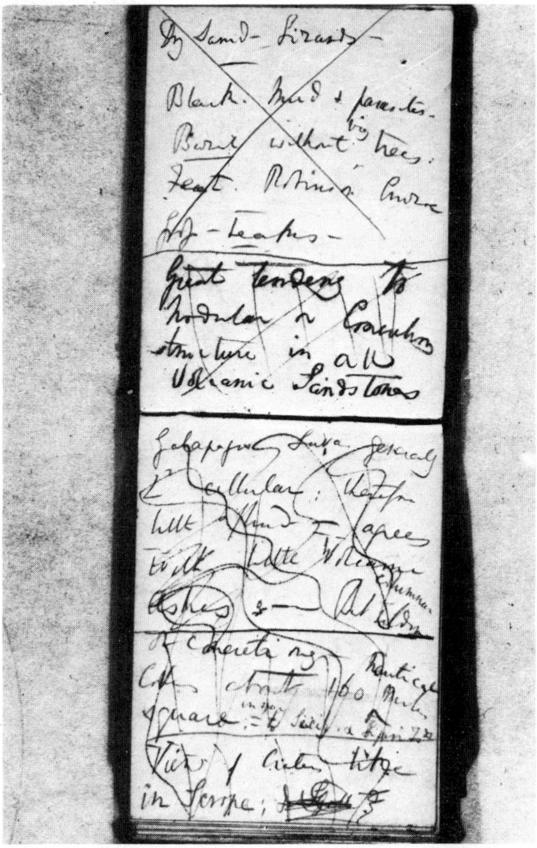

Plate 9

A page from one of the
notebooks Darwin filled
during the *Beagle* voyage, this
one describing some of the
creatures and geology of the
Galapagos crucial to the
development of his ideas.

Plate 10 These caricatures, drawn by Darwin's fellow student, Albert Way, show how important entomology was to the young naturalist during his Cambridge days.

create his attitudes, as did an increasing emotional and sexual reticence that looked forward to Victoria's era. Yet, even given these fashions of the period, there is an emotional emptiness about his ponderings on marriage, a sense that the possibility of deeper feelings has not even occurred to him, which is surprising and at odds with what one might term his public character.

If he jotted these notes during the first half of 1838, then it is also the case that he acted upon them with an almost suspicious swiftness. In just over six months he was engaged, and to one of the most immediately available young women in his life. One cannot help feeling that, once he had come to his decision, almost any reasonable lady, of the right age and class, would have served. It is not that he was without affection and respect for Emma; rather that these were perhaps an affection and respect not originally intended specifically for her. They were to be bestowed upon the woman who would be his wife – whoever was fit for the role became the automatic recipient of those feelings. He was marrying, in short, to make his life easier, more tranquil and comfortable. He needed peace and quiet in which to work; a housekeeper would provide these – and there was the added advantage that she had the duty to soothe all sexual distress: not even desire would long disturb his scientific labours.

Of course, all this appears more monstrous to us than it would have to Darwin's contemporaries. Men and women then went searching for a spouse, not expecting to fall in love, but hoping to find someone with whom they could live, make a home, be comfortable. Love, depending upon when and with whom it occurred, was either a diversion, in both senses of the word, or a bonus. To marry was rather like joining a club, even if it was a club – initially at least – for only two. Darwin was a very "clubbable" man with a gift for friendship, affection and an easy, childlike warmth. If, as is possible, the early loss of his mother had rendered his deepest emotions inaccessible to him, then he had the good fortune to live in a world where this mattered less than perhaps it might have in ours, or in that of a century before. Under Victoria, most people of the middle classes lived emotionally prudent lives, with their passions and desires under close control.

In any case, Darwin himself is not likely to have had the slightest inkling of any subterranean processes of the psyche. It seemed to him self-evident that he should now seek out an agreeable wife. At Maer that summer, he seems to have got on exceptionally well with Emma. They went to the village bazaar together and she sent him a spoof list of the items she had bought. Towards the end of August, he sent her a high-spirited letter from London. "This Marborough St. is a forlorn place – We have no ducks here, much less geese, & as for that sentimental fat goose we ate over the Library fire, – the like of it seldom turns up. – I feel . . . spiteful joy at hearing you have had no other geese . . ." The "goose" here was obviously a long and memorable conversation he had had with Emma, and perhaps it was during it that their feelings for each other altered from an unexamined familial relationship to something more precise, more personal and rather stronger. In any case, Darwin felt impelled to assure Emma that he had been so frequently at Maer "that I have a kind of vested right, so see me you will, & we will have another goose." He ended the letter with a new warmth, "Believe me dear Emma, yours most sincerely Chas. Darwin" – and then, terrified of having over-stepped propriety, crossed out "dear".

Just over two months later came the "day of days" and the announcement of their engagement. At once the mail coaches and the new railways seemed to be taken up with Darwin and Wedgwood correspondence. By 11 November, only two days later, Caroline, now of course a Wedgwood herself, was writing from Newcastle under Lyne that in Emma Charles had found "the very sweetest, most sympathetic of wives – you will be as happy as happy can be & I do most heartily rejoice it is all settled – I was quite taken by surprise not thinking the event was so near taking place." By early November, therefore, it was a possibility of which the family had become quite conscious: "We were talking last night of the chances & probabilities," added Caroline, a trifle shamelessly.

Charles's father wrote to Emma's father, Dr. Robert allowing himself a little humour that he knew Jos would understand. "Emma having accepted Charles gives me as great happiness as Jos having married Caroline, and I cannot say more. On that marriage Bessy said she would not have had more pleasure if it had been Victoria, and you may assure her I feel as grateful to her for Emma, as if it had been Martineau herself that Charles had obtained." Uncle Jos, replying, said that "if I could have given such a wife to Charles without parting with a daughter there would be no drawback from my entire satisfaction in bestowing Emma upon him . . . I could have parted with Emma to no one for whom I would so soon and so entirely feel as a father . . ." He cemented these fine and certainly sincere sentiments in the manner of the time – with money. "I propose to do for Emma what I did for Charlotte and for three of my sons, give a bond for £5000, and to allow her £400 a year, as long as my income will supply it, which I have no reason for thinking will not be as long as I live." It was among Emma's many advant-ages that in Darwin's words, she was "better than an angel and had money". Cynics might think that for Darwin things were not only working out very satisfactorily, they were going according to plan. In a sense, they would be right; the question is, at what levels of consciousness had the plan been set out?

Thus Darwin could write to Lyell that he had "the very good, and shortly since very unexpected fortune, of going to be married . . . I determined when last at Maer to try my chance, but I hardly expected such good fortune would turn up for me." It is as if the whole event was at least as surprising to him as it might have been for any of his friends. No suggestion here that only a few months earlier he had been plotting the outlines and advantages of marriage and determining to end his bachelor solitude.

Emma herself, having accepted Charles, had a momentary hesitation, a feeling that matters were moving faster than she could comfortably bear. "Since Charles went," she wrote to Catherine Darwin on 13 November, "I have been rather afraid of his being in too great a hurry so I hope you will all hold him in a little especially the Dr. I find Elizabeth would be very sorry if it was to happen very soon & that makes me wish more that things may not move too fast. She forgets herself so much that I should like her to have her wish" – and honesty then compelled Emma to add above the line, "besides which I should wish it myself". She could not lay the responsibility for her wish on her elder sister, a popular, busy woman, tirelessly energetic despite a congenital curvature of the spine, who would not have thanked her for being named as an impediment to immediate marriage. In any case, Emma went on, it was not that Charles would disregard her preferences, but simply that, if everyone expected matters to move with excessive speed, "it would make me appear cross & disagreeable on Saturday, when I mean to be particularly happy . . ." That was the day, of course, on which a party from The Mount would descend joyfully on Maer. On the back flap, Emma added, "Tell Charles to be a good boy & do his lessons & take things leisurely, indeed they can't be very fast. How I do wish he would wait till Spring & fine weather! J.A. says it is the happiest time of Emma's life & it is a thousand pities it should be a very short one. Do dear Catty clog the wheels a little slow." The precepts of Jane Austen, who had been so much too young for her death ten years before, still had a direct relevance to the lives of these middle-class young ladies. It is no wonder that Emma called upon her fictitious namesake to bolster her own pleas. Darwin had decided to marry, he had discovered his bride, and the world now had to bear the weight of his cheerfully relentless enthusiasm, delightful yet implacable, rooted in the same strata of stubbornness that enabled him to maintain, and struggle to prove, his unorthodox scientific theories. It is no wonder that Emma felt she was in danger of being swept along at a pace far swifter than her own.

But for Emma, now thirty years old, tall of brow, wide of jaw, with a well-shaped, witty mouth, intelligent eyes set far apart, and the short, strong Wedgwood nose, there were few likely suitors. She had spent a party-going season in Edinburgh and come back no nearer being married than when she had left. Fanny, the sister in every way closest to her, had died six years before. Elizabeth was unlikely ever to marry; Charlotte had married years earlier. During the intervening years her four brothers had followed suit. Emma must have seen before her the lifetime of a middle-class spinster, comfortably off, busy in a brittle way with charities, everyone's aunt and nobody's mother. As the eldest daughter, it was Elizabeth who in the main took responsibility even for the running of the household – for Emma there was no prescribed, self-evident function.

Meanwhile Charles had apparently moved entirely out of her immediate orbit and learned instead to swim in that convivial tide which swirled about the salons and dining tables of intellectual, even fashionable, London. Thus when she broke the news of her engagement to her aunt Jessie, ensconced as Madame Sismondi in Geneva, she confided:

> . . . though I knew how much I liked him, I was not the least sure of his feelings, as he is so affectionate, and so fond of Maer and all of us, and demonstrative in his manners, that I did not think it meant anything . . . He came to see us in the month of August, was in very high spirits and I was very happy in his company, and had the feeling that if he saw more of me, he would really like me. He came down again . . . and on Sunday he spoke to me, which was quite a surprise, as I thought we might go on in the sort of friendship we were in for years, and very likely nothing come of it after all . . . It is a match that every soul has been making for us, so we could not have helped it if we had not liked it ourselves.

Perhaps Charles had simply taken the path of least resistance. He had desired *a* marriage – it was the family that had wished for this particular marriage and he could have had nothing against it. Given his strong liking for Emma, it cannot have been difficult to persuade himself into some slightly more disturbing emotion. With her, too, and their shared memories of Maer, he would be safe: the familiar wrapped him around in the security he seemed to need. That he should have chosen as his wife someone he had known since childhood, a cousin, rather than some comparative stranger met in London, typified the development of his character: he was settling into a new, defensive posture, far removed from that of the congenial hard-riding naturalist of the *Beagle*. It is as if he had decided to guard with a miser's cunning what had become the most important treasure of his life – his burgeoning, unfolding theories about species. It was this that justified, whether consciously or not, the timidity, the emotional conservatism of his choice. Yet this, allied to the element of self-deception and even of calculation that one senses, makes this bridegroom Darwin, for all his pleasantness and warmth, less than entirely appealing. Emma, naturally, saw him somewhat differently. To Jessie Sismondi she wrote:

He is the most open, transparent man I ever saw, and every word expresses his real thoughts. He is particularly affectionate and very nice to his father and sisters, and perfectly sweet tempered, and possesses some minor qualities that add particularly to one's happiness, such as not being fastiduous, and being humane to animals. We shall live in London, where he is fully occupied with being Secretary to the Geological Society and conducting a publication upon the animals of Australia.

This last was, of course, the *Zoology of the Beagle*, still in the long process of preparation. "I am so glad he is a busy man," added Emma. He had, however, his frivolous side, although "he has a great dislike to going to the play, so I am afraid we shall have some domestic dissensions on that head. On the other hand, he stands concerts very well."Charles had wanted to ask her to marry him in August (perhaps during that "fat, sentimental goose"), but had not dared to ask – "and I was pleased to find that he was not very sure of his answer this time." Emma had, it seems, absorbed early the lesson that in a husband's insecurity lies the security of his wife.

Darwin himself made the effort to project himself as a romantic suitor. As soon as he was back in Shrewsbury from his momentous visit to Maer, with his proposal safely over and Emma's acceptance the news he brought his family, he wrote to her, assuring her of "the joy and happiness" of his sisters and adding that "the one conclusion, I exult in, is that there never was anybody so lucky as I have been, or so good as you. – Indeed I can assure you, many times, since leaving Maer, I have thought how little I expressed how much I owe to you, and as often as I think this, I vow to try to make myself good enough somewhat to deserve you." At once, however, he veers from these somewhat conventionalized protestations towards more practical matters – and in these his honesty, his fairness, his genuine affection for Emma make more comfortable reading.

I hope you have taken deep thought about the sundry knotty points you will have to decide on. – We must have a great deal of talk together, when I come back on Saturday. – Do have a fire in the Library – it is such a good place to have some quiet talks together. – The question of houses – suburbs versus central London – rages violently around each fire place in this house. – Suburbs have rather the advantage at present; & this, of course, rather inclines one to seek out the arguments on the other side. – The Governor gives much good advice to live, wherever it may be, the first year prudently & quietly. My chief fear is, that you will find after living all your life with such large & agreeable parties, as Maer can boast of, our quiet evenings dull. – You must bear in mind, as some young lady said, "all men are brutes", and that I take the line of being a solitary brute, so you must listen with much suspicion to all arguments in favour of retired places. I am so selfish, that I feel to have you to myself, is having you so much more completely that I am not to be trusted. Like a child that has something it loves beyond measure, I long to dwell on the words *my own* dear Emma. – as I am writing, just as things come uppermost in my mind, I beg of you not to read my letters to anyone, for then I can fancy I am sitting by the side of my own dear future wife, & to her own self, I do not care what nonsense I talk: – so let me have my way, & scribble without caring whether it be sense or nonsense.

Thus, by talking about houses, Darwin had brought himself back to his own tone of voice. His pleasure in what was happening is apparent, as is his fondness for Emma; but did he himself really believe that his desire for comparative solitude, a desire that was growing stronger year by year, had at its root a passion to keep her jealously to himself? It sounds rather like an attempt to flatter her into acquiescence with plans he was already envisaging, though not yet, perhaps, with absolute clarity.

Now, however, Darwin returned to his family's pleasure in the engagement.

My father echos & reechos Uncle Jos' words "you have drawn a prize!" Certainly no man could by possibility receive a more cordial welcome, than I did from everyone at Maer on Monday morning. – My life has been very happy & very fortunate and many of my pleasantest rememberances are mingled up with the scenes at Maer, & now it is crowned. – My own dear Emma, I kiss the hands with all humbleness and gratitude, which have so filled up for me the cup of happiness – it is my most earnest wish, I may make myself worthy of you. Good bye.

He signed himself, "Most affectionately yours, Chas Darwin", and then scribbled the endearing postscript, "I would tear this letter up & write it again, for it is a very silly one, but I can't write a better one." He was once more at his usual business of envisaging and being the first to utter any criticism to which he might be liable.

Erasmus wrote to Charles as soon as he heard the news. "Not less than to you do I give my congrats to Emma though in writing to you I ought I suppose to word it somehow differently. It is a marriage that will give almost as much pleasure to the rest of the world as it does to yourselves – the best auspices I should think for any marriage." The Sismondis wrote from Geneva, Emma's friends, the Tollet sisters, from nearer at hand. "I hope you will have a chimney that smokes" commented Ellen Tollet, "or something of that sort to prevent your being quite intoxicated." But the letters that Charles and Emma sent each other, full though they were of affection and hope for the future, fell somewhat short of expressing love's imperious intoxication.

William Owen sent his congratulations, affirming that "there is no Man living ... whose happiness & welfare, & I can hardly except my own children, I take a greater interest; & I pray to God to bless & prosper you as you deserve, & to make the Lady on whom you have placed your affections as worthy as I wish & trust she will be of you." He added a characteristic invitation for Charles to come to Woodhouse, "with or without your fair Lady . . . & I promise you I will not scold let your Dog be ever so wild or if you shoot all the Hen Pheasants you see . . ." For Fanny Owen's father, time in its essentials had long ceased to move.

Darwin, meanwhile, had travelled back by rail to London. At Birmingham, as he described to Emma, he had missed the connection by seconds, to the unanimous fury of the passengers. "I can laugh now, though I could not then, at the expression on all faces, as each group turned out of its carriage like bees out of a hive – nothing could be heard, but 'infamous scandalous conduct – directors, parliament, rascals' – one high-minded passenger changed himself, there being nobody to abuse excepting porters, by going to London in a night horse coach, much to his inconvenience." He had eventually travelled to London with "three Manchester hogs", who played whist, drank & sang "half-blasphemous songs" through the night. The next day, he had visited Fitzroy and his wife to give them the news; "he says we shall not know what real happiness there is in man & woman living together, till we have tried it for at least six months". Was this a word of warning about Darwin's sexual expectations? Was Emma to understand "happiness" in a general or a specific sense? Whichever it was, Charles himself had fewer doubts: "I dare say there may be some truth in this, though I suspect the term of probation will be a good deal shorter with us."

In his previous letter, having learned that Emma preferred a longer engagement than he, he had urged her to reconsider. "You must be absolute arbitress, but do dear Emma remember life is short, & two months is the sixth part of the year, & that year, the first from which for my part things shall hereafter date." Now he returned to his arguments, writing of their "term of probation" that he wished it would begin rather earlier, "though I humbly beg pardon for saying so, – will not again – But when I think of those few hours, when we sat together in the Library, hope deferred does make my heart quite sick to call you in truth my wife."

Emma wrote to him on that same 22 November, her tone a little reminiscent of Fanny Owen's coynesses ten years before. "I am afraid the Dr would not think it according to the strictest ettiquette my writing to you before I have received your letter . . ." But Emma had no games to play; her relationship to Charles was real, not make-believe, and she had matters of a fundamental seriousness to discuss.

> When I am with you I think all melancholy thoughts keep out of my head but since you are gone some sad ones have forced themselves in, of fear that our

opinions on the most important subjects should differ widely. My reason tells
me that honest & conscientious doubts cannot be a sin, but I feel it would be a
painful void between us. I thank you from the bottom of my heart for your
openess with me & I should dread the feeling that you were concealing your
opinion from the fear of giving me pain. It is perhaps foolish of me to say this
much but my own dear Charley we now do belong to each other & I cannot
help being open with you. Will you do me a favour? Yes I am sure you will, it is
to read our Saviour's farewell discourse to his disciples which begins at the end
of the 13th Chap of John. It is so full of love to them & devotion & every
beautiful feeling. It is the part of the New Testament I love best. This is a whim
of mine it would give me great pleasure though I can hardly tell why. I don't
wish you to give me your opinion about it.

And on the same line, dismissing religion, Emma went on, "The plaid gown
arrived safely . . ." A little later she reported how her cousin, John Allen, a
twenty-one-year-old student at Oxford, had comically misunderstood the
news travelling down the family grapevine: he had written to his aunt,
"What do you think of this marriage between E.W. & Dr. Darwin. I should
think there must be some disparity of age, though I have never seen either of
these parties". She ended with a lightly-worded postscript that perhaps
disguised some genuine concern. "You will kindly mention any fault of
spelling or style that you perceive as in the wife of a literary man it wd not do
you credit, any how I can spell your name right, I wish you cd say the same
for mine." At times, Darwin must have felt that he had never left The Mount
– and perhaps that as much as anything explains his selection of Emma.

Emma seems to have given some thought to the life she would be entering
as "the wife of a literary man", a member of the country's intellectual elite.
Perhaps the idea overawed her a little: at Maer the writers and scientists of
the world had always been paid due respect. At one moment, for example,
she seemed somewhat overwhelmed at the thought of having been invited by
Sedgwick – "the great Sedgwick", as she called him: "*Me* only think of it!"
But, as one might expect, most of their letters were taken up with almost
dismayingly practical concerns. Kettles and saucepans had been, she wrote,
"weighing a little upon my soul"; their real worry, however, was where such
household goods were finally to be deployed. Even the major question had
not been settled – should they seek a house in central London or in the
suburbs? The centre, said Erasmus predictably; Fitzroy argued powerfully
for the suburbs; on 26 November, Emma reported that "Elizabeth &
Caroline are grown suburban again & it is very puzzling". She herself was
undecided and, oddly, almost unconcerned. In time, she supposed she would
be able to involve herself in "these sublunary matters". She offered a few
suggestions, then threw up her hands: "You have a great deal on your hands
poor old gentleman, but you should have thought of that before."

Over-excited and unable to work, Darwin, often with Erasmus at his side, began criss-crossing London on foot, searching all the possible areas for the most agreeable house they could afford. But in the back of his mind there lurked the thought that, once two or three metropolitan years had established him, he would be able to move out into the country. Weeks before the marriage – and years before the actual move – he was preparing Emma for that possibility. They would eventually have to decide, he wrote, "whether the pleasures of retirement & country, (gardens, walks, &c) are preferable to society &c &c".

This was for the future, however – in the present, houses were few, rents high. He marched up and down the streets near Regent's Park, but was forced to withdraw. He began to quarter Bloomsbury, where prospects seemed brighter. Perhaps it would be cheaper to rent unfurnished and buy what they needed as they could afford it: "Will you rough it a little at first?" he asked Emma. It must have been a relief to him when he learned that Susan had undertaken to buy all their household linen – even though he had still no house in which to put it. He wondered whether living in Bedford Place would suit them; there is a touch of ice in Emma's tone as she scotched the idea – "it would be quite insulting to take the house . . . just opposite the Horneritas". Whom would such a location have insulted? Catherine Horner? Emma herself? Perhaps she had both possibilities in mind – her moment of restrained asperity reinforces suspicions that between Darwin and Miss Horner relations had at one time reached a warmth somewhat beyond simple friendship.

But Darwin, caught up in his personal maelstrom, seems hardly to have registered Emma's comment. Instead, he was abruptly seized by a new fear, though not one his recent experiences can have encouraged: what if he were to find a place far sooner than they needed it? For "would it not be intolerable to discover a good house & then not take it for a month, but to be waiting in agony lest someone else should!" Emma calmed him; there was, she wrote, "no help for it but taking a house that suits when we can catch it". In her tone there is something of the weariness inspired in those close to them by the energetic silliness of great men. Darwin, however, was almost beyond aid. He depicted himself in his distraction – a man "who works all morning in describing hawks & owls; then rushes out & walks in a bewildered manner up one street & down another, looking out for the word 'To let." No wonder that Emma, teasingly, thought it "quite evident that you are on the verge of insanity & we should have to advertize you 'Lost in the vicinity of Bloomsbury a tall thin gentleman &c &c quite harmless whoever will bring him back shall be handsomely rewarded' ". It was, on the whole, just as well that she had decided to come to London for a few days and help him in the search.

In mid-December, therefore, the two of them, sometimes with Fanny Hensleigh or the tall Erasmus in attendance (during the *Beagle* years, had the sisterhood not briefly thought him suggestively attentive to Emma?), wandered past the porches, little parks and elegant terraces of Bloomsbury, intent on finding something in which they might house themselves, at a rent of around £120 a year. Almost everywhere they looked, they discovered that prices were £20 and £30 higher than this; on such a differential, they could have increased their staff by two or three servants. They found a house, at £110 a year, in Woburn Place, but thought it unattractive: "I think it would do quite well only it is not fascinating," was Emma's opinion.

In Gower Street, they discovered a house they preferred. It had bright yellow curtains and azure walls in the drawing room, and Fanny Hensleigh, who came with them, was scathing about the furniture, but it was roomy and central and close to the pretty Tavistock Square, and Emma liked it. The rent, however, was rather more than Darwin wanted to pay or could comfortably afford; everything depended on whether he could argue the landlady, Mrs. Irvine, down to a more reasonable level. Emma, dispirited at the difficulties, wrote from Maer, "I feel rather sorry for your future fate this morning. If a letter should come today to say that the wicked old Jezabel (who I dare say is a charming person) had given in to your terms it would be very well bestowed upon me."

Two days later, on 29 December, Darwin in jubilation was actually "writing to tell you Gower St is ours, yellow curtains & all. – I have today paid some advance money, signed an agreement & had the Key given over to me & the old woman informed I was her master henceforth . . . I long for the day when we shall enter the house together; how glorious it will be to see you seated by the fire of our own house – Oh that it was the *14*th instead of the *24*th . . ." Emma had set 24 January as the earliest date possible for the wedding; Darwin was pawing at it like a dog locked outside a door. Ignoring this, however, Emma expressed her delight that Mrs Irving "had come to her senses . . . I think of Macaw Cottage with the greatest satisfaction." The curtains must really have been virulent to have justified her nickname.

Darwin, whom we usually picture as sober and cautious, was in fact often impatient, wilful, over-eager. He sent off his letter of good news to Emma, then began to think of the new life they were on the point of building together. The winter afternoon dragged on into darkness – cab wheels and hoofbeats in the street outside, then silence. One o'clock sounded, two: Darwin, wide-eyed and restless, lay struggling for sleep. One can assume that the images of a somewhat conventional domesticity passed across his mind – Emma pliant and comforting as he turned from his desk, Emma whisking about the business of a household that had his contentment as its only object, Emma companionable beside the evening fire, Emma sexually available in the muffling darkness of that waiting, Gower Street bedroom. Fitfully, he slept for a while, then woke again, hot-eyed, dry-mouthed. He glanced at his watch: just after five o'clock. An hour or two more of this pre-nuptial discomfort, and he clambered out of bed – work would be the anodyne to dull the sharpness of his expectations. The quiet Sunday morning sat leadenly upon the city. A married Emma leaped *en fête* about his study, the bright ghost of time not yet come. He scratched feebly at the paper in front of him. Near-by, church bells collected the religious, the conformists, those prepared to be polite to God. It was eleven o'clock. Did he sigh, throw down his pen, walk about the room distracted? Perhaps; before in the end summoning Covington.

"I'm very sorry to spoil your Sunday, Covington – but begin packing up I must. I cannot rest."

Covington gaped at him. "Pack up, sir? What for?"

They began, Darwin sorting out papers, Covington, who had once stowed his finds so carefully on the *Beagle*, arranging and packing the first of the specimens. They worked that day and on through Monday; by half past three in the afternoon, the cases and packages were already being placed in the waiting vans. Only some few drawers full of shells still remained, and these would have to be carried by hand. Darwin stared at the amount of his accumulated goods; neither he nor the languid Erasmus could quite account for such a quantity. As the afternoon solidified into night, porters were staggering up the Gower Street stairs, gasping under the weight of boxes filled with geological specimens. The hall, the dining room, the intended study – all were filled with Darwin's cases. By six o'clock, everything was safe. Mr. Darwin – alas, as yet without his bride – had taken up his new abode.

Excitedly, he gathered up pen, ink and paper: "Monday January 1st, 1839," he wrote, then added, "and the first of Our Marriage", and below, in letters large and fat and assertive, set out the address, "!! 12 Upper Gower St^t!" Swiftly he thanked Emma "for your two most kind, dear, & affectionate letters," but then rushed to his real matter. "I will finish this letter tomorrow. I sit down just to date & begin it, that I may enjoy the infinite satisfaction of writing to my own dear wife, that is to be, the very first evening of my entering our house." He scribbled down his tale of unexpected action; outside, everything was quiet. A clock struck nine. "How I wish my own dear lady had been here", he wrote, then left his letter on the table to finish in the morning and went wearily to bed. Did he sleep more easily than on the night before he had decided to move?

The house was roomy and comfortable – Darwin complained that "the only difficulty is that I have not things *enough*!! to put in all the drawers & corners" of his study. Emma could imagine him, proud "in your big house, ordering breakfast in the front drawing room, dinner in the dining room, tea in the back drawing room & luncheon in the study, & occasionally looking through your window on your estate & plantations." Nevertheless, was there a touch of pique in the way she greeted the news that he had taken possession? "I was surprized indeed to find how soon you had moved into your house & I don't wonder you feel triumphant . . . You must have found it very interesting putting all your things away & arranging your sanctum to the greatest advantage, & I should have liked very much to have helped you . . ." Darwin leaped upon the possessive adjective. He desired, he wrote, to give her "a scolding, for writing to me about 'your' house: is it not **our** house; what is there from me, the geologist, to the black sparrows in the garden, which is not your own property".

Meanwhile another, ancillary problem had been agitating them both, that of finding and hiring servants. Emma, searching for a housemaid, had whittled the possibilities down to two. "I think it would be a very good thing if Fanny would take a look at both . . . & if she likes their looks engage them both . . . I don't suppose the housemaid wd come for 109s but that we might settle after Fanny has seen them." Emma was in those early days, both before and after her wedding, to rely quite heavily on Fanny Hensleigh's domestic expertise – an expertise developed in what sometimes seemed a marriage to both her brother and Charles's. (In a postscript to Emma's letter of 27 December that appears to refer to that relationship, she tells Charles, "I have saved F's credit in not mentioning to a soul her bit of folly in going into E's room that day & I hope you will do the same at Shrewsbury". Was "F" Fanny Hensleigh and "E" Erasmus, and if so was the offence only against convention, or were matters between them more robust than has been thought?)

Thus aided, Emma and Charles worked slowly towards the engagement of at least one housemaid – but "I don't know", Emma wrote despairingly, "how we shall settle between the two cooks". This was a dilemma that to some extent resolved itself: in a postscript to his letter of 29 December Charles wrote, "The Cook from Shrewsbury is a failure as she cannot cook & has a drunken husband." Emma, in the peace of Maer, seems now to have abdicated from her responsibilities – it may be for the first and last time. Even if a cook should be chosen, she did not know the wages to be decided. Charles and Fanny "must lay your heads together & settle what you like. I should think 14 guineas & tea & sugar plenty." In the end it was Fanny who took the decision: the cook would be one recommended by Erasmus's maid and the pay would be precisely that suggested by Emma. One by one, crises were being surmounted and problems solved; day by day, the sustaining structures of the approaching marriage were being established and reinforced. Nevertheless, despite Darwin's evident eagerness to be married, the mood of most of the letters that passed between him and Emma owed more to their long-established friendship than to any more recently discovered passion. Neither of them ever actually used the word "love"; Emma came nearest to doing so in a moment of irony after reporting that because of the London visit she had lost her chance of going to a local ball. It had been, she was told, "a very brilliant one, but I feel superior to these vanities & can reflect on having missed it without a pang. Such is the power of true &c &c." She was perhaps the more courageous, and so the more honest, of the two. The marriage suited both of them, though neither for a moment suggested that this was the case; Darwin, however, had worked himself into a noticeably sentimental condition and used language somewhat more lover-like than she. But he too, on the whole, avoided the more ardent extremes, though never achieving the affectionate coolness through which one senses Emma's implicit understanding of their situation.

Of course, she too looked forward to the wedding, and expected happiness from it. When Caroline had written of the sympathy and affection she received from Jos Wedgwood, Emma had commented, "That is a wonderful marriage, I say for the hundredth time, but I think I know one that will turn out quite as happy . . ." At the beginning of January, just over three weeks before the wedding, she wrote, "I begin to feel as if something real was going to happen & it makes me dream and ponder a great deal." But she never wrote with the disconcerted immediacy of Charles: "I wish the awful day was over, I am not very tranquil when I think of the procession, it is very awesome. – By the bye, I am glad to say *the 24th* is on a Thursday, so we shall not be married on an unlucky day . . ." Emma had, perforce, to calm him. "You will have a few more days more time on your hands than you expect my dear Charley as the marriage must be fixed for the 29th instead of the 24th (I always said *about* the 24th) I am afraid you will be rather vexed at this but I hope you will have the Drs maxim that I *must always* be in the right properly impressed on your mind." But feminine contrition at once overcame her – "I do dislike very much doing what you don't like my dear old Charley & I do hope this is the last time I ever shall . . ."

Both could, however, joke about the life that awaited them. A fortnight before the wedding, Darwin reported that Lyell and his wife had visited him. "I was quite ashamed of myself to day, for we talked for half an hour, unsophisticated geology, with poor Mrs Lyell sitting by, a monument of patience. – I want *practice* in illtreating the female sex. – I did not observe

Lyell had any compunction: I hope to harden my conscience in time; few husbands seem to find it difficult to effect this." At the end of the letter, however, he scrawled down more genuine sentiments. Soon he would be on his way to Maer and the ceremony – "I won't forget the way, & do not you forget to keep a bed for me, or lose the Licence."

For her part, Emma had her moment of humour at the scientific cast of his intelligence: "I believe from your account of your own mind that you will only consider me as a specimen of the genus (I don't know what, simia I believe). You will be forming theories about me & if I am cross or out of temper you will only consider 'What does that prove'. Which will be a very grand & philosophical way of considering it." It is clear from this that Darwin was well aware of the narrowing and intensifying of his intellectual effort, of that flowing inward of his energy which led him increasingly to withdraw from all unecessary distractions.

> I was thinking this morning [he wrote to Emma on 20 January] how on earth it came, that I who am fond of talking & am scarcely ever out of spirits, should so entirely rest my notions of happiness on quietness & a good deal of a solitude; but I believe the explanation is very simple. – I mention it because it will give you hopes, that I shall gradually grow less like a *brute*, – it is that during the five years of my voyage (& indeed I may add these two last) which from the active manner in which they have been passed, may be said to be the commencement of my real life, the whole of my pleasure was derived, from what passed in my mind, whilst admiring views by myself, travelling across the wild deserts & glorious forests, or pacing the deck of the poor little *Beagle* at night. – Excuse this much egotism, – I give it you because I think you will humanize me, & soon teach me there is greater happiness, than holding theories, & accumulating facts in silence & solitude.

The attractions of quietness and solitude must have been strong indeed to draw Darwin into so much introspection.

If marriage was, as one may suspect, the way through which Darwin organized the externals of his existence in order to free the inner, intellectual self, intent upon the conundrums of species, then this should become apparent in the attitudes he took to, and the expectations he had of, Emma. At the beginning of December, 1838, he reported to Emma that Lyell's sister had said, "So Mr. Darwin is going to be married; I suppose he will be buried in the country & lost to geology". Darwin's own vision was rather different: "She little knows, what a good strict wife I am going to be married to, who will send me to my lessons, & make me better, I trust, in every respect . . ." Once or twice, quite overtly, he likens his condition to a child's; "I hope my poor old Charley", wrote Emma after they had found their house, "that now your bothers are over you are pretty comfortable & not so done up & can mind your books". It is as if she was ready to accept the quasi-maternal role which would ensure Darwin's comfort and essential peace of mind. "Write soon like a good boy . . ." – such phrases are common between those intending to marry each other, but it is noticeable in this unconscious role-playing that Emma is always the mother, never the child, Darwin always the child, never the father. After he had been shopping with Erasmus, he described his purchases to Emma, then went on, "But I vow I won't go in any more shops, till you come up & take final charge of me."

At times, this thread that runs, faintly yet discernibly, through their correspondence takes on, in the light of the future, an almost sinister aspect. At the turn of the year, a month before the marriage, Emma wrote to Charles, "I want to persuade you dear Charley to leave town at once & get some rest. You have looked so unwell for some time that I am afraid you will be laid up if you fight against it any longer . . . If you knew how I long to be with you when you are not well! You must not think that I expect a holiday husband always making himself agreeable to me & if that is all the 'worse' that I shall have it will not be much for me to bear whatever it may be for you. So don't be ill any more my dear Charley till I can be with you to nurse you & save you from bothers." It is as if during this early period a sort of complicity came into being between them, as if they then took up these parts – mother and child, nurse and invalid – through which for the rest of their lives together they would most easily be able to reach each other. "I do not like your looking so unwell & being so overtired," wrote Emma; "when *I* come & look after you I shall scold you into health like Lady Cath. de Burgh used to do to the poor people." So she offered another aspect of the same archetype, Lady of the Manor and Peasant.

It would be easy to exaggerate this strand in their relationship – perhaps it gives it a false importance even to select it for comment. Yet it demands some sort of notice as one reads the letters, nudging at one's attention with hints, inferences, choice of vocabulary, and so setting one of the prevailing moods of the entire relationship. Nevertheless, Darwin and his Emma discussed many other matters, most of them relatively trivial: they exchanged notes on the books they were reading, for example, she finding *Mansfield Park* "very suitable", he impressed with the foolhardy courage of Mungo Park. Darwin described to her his mornings – "I jump up (following Sir W. Scott's rule, for as he says, once turn over on your side, & all is over) at 8, & breakfast at ten, so that I get rather more than an hour, – & begin again at eleven quite fresh." He wrote of dinners at the Athenaeum and gossiped about the people he had met. Emma wrote comments on his news, gave what there was of her own, from time to time flexed her muscles. "I am *very* glad you resisted the blue coat, you would have looked very unnatural in it," she wrote, thus briskly disposing of his sartorial ambitions.

The time of letter-writing, staple chore of separation, was now nearly over. And perhaps, at the very last, some kind of anxiety gripped Darwin. Safely arrived in Shrewsbury, he wrote to Emma, on the Saturday before the wedding, that he now had the ring, "which is the most important piece of news I have to tell". He then went on, "My last two days in London were rendered very uncomfortable by a bad headache, which continued two days & two nights, so that I doubted whether it ever meant to go & allow me to be married. – The Railroad yesterday, however, quite cured me." With this as a clue, one might wonder whether, as long as he remained in London, he retained the illusion of freedom, of choice: the illusion, that is, that he could after all refuse to make the journey to Maer and the waiting Emma. Perhaps it was the underlying indecisions and consequent tensions that this theoretical possibility caused him which led to his forty-eight-hour headache. Then, however, he caught his train and began his dutiful progress westward. The action committed him, the tensions eased. The headache released its hold and vanished.

When the moment finally came, it passed off quietly: a perfectly conventional little marriage, in Maer Church. Emma's mother – Charles's Aunt Bessy – was ill and bed-bound; when they returned from the ceremony, she was asleep and so they slipped away, without punctilious or over-sentimental farewells. Jos Wedgwood, too, stricken with old age and palsy, could play no prominent part in these nuptials, happy though he was to see them. By the end of the month, with the snow flying down Gower Street, Emma was imposing herself upon her new domain. "I have been facing the Cook in her own region to-day", she wrote to her mother, "and found fault with the boiling of the potatoes, which I thought would make a good beginning and set me up a little". Charles Darwin had, without question, become a married man.

The main sources for Part Three were:

The correspondence between Darwin and Emma Wedgwood, and between Darwin and his family, to be found among the archives of Cambridge University Library; the W.D. Fox letters, kept at Christ's College, Cambridge; *A Century of Family Letters,* edited by Henrietta Litchfield; the *Autobiography* of Charles Darwin, edited by Nora Barlow; Darwin's *Life and Letters,* edited by Francis Darwin, and *More Letters,* edited by Francis Darwin and A.C. Seward.

Also illuminating were the *Life, Letters and Journals of Sir Charles Lyell,* edited by Mrs. Lyell; Jane Carlyle's *Letters to her Family,* edited by L. Huxley and her *Letters and Memorials,* edited by J.A. Froude; Thomas Carlyle's *Reminiscences,* edited by C.E. Norton; Harriet Martineau's *Autobiography* with a memorial by Marie Weston Chapman; *Darwin and Henslow,* edited by Nora Barlow; and Darwin's *Collected Papers,* edited by P.H. Barrett.

PART FOUR

Origin of all my views

1

Had been greatly struck from about month of previous March on character of S. American fossils – & species on Galapagos Archipelago. These facts origin (especially latter) of all my views.

Darwin, Personal Journal

What gives the years between 1837 and 1840 their especial intensity, and their profound importance in the story of Darwin's life, is not that these were the years of his courtship and marriage, nor even that during them he first established his scientific reputation. They owe their true significance to work of which no one at the time had the slightest inkling, to ideas which he pursued with a consuming yet secretive passion, and to the scribbled, almost indecipherable notebooks in which he trapped and caged them. For these are the pages in which one can follow the actual genesis and development of his theory of natural selection, the long search which led to his establishing its principles, and the first excited scramble after the evidence that would support and perhaps confirm it. In a sense, the work laid out in these books provides the underpinning for the scientific endeavour of his entire life.

Reading them today, one sometimes feels goose pimples on one's skin – it is the excitement of observing so closely the snap and dart of that voracious intelligence. Yet, unless we make an effort, the words simply lie on the page, rendered lifeless by a century of exegesis and commentary. It takes an effort of the imagination to thrust back the years, to see those scribbled phrases as though freshly written. We have to realize how much we know, how high our mountains of fact are piled – and how insignificant were the foothills up which Darwin scrambled.

One can see his thoughts beat against the very limits of expression: there was no appropriate vocabulary for him to use, since the disciplines that were to coin it had not yet been devised. Before he could even begin his researches, he had to discern their direction and devise their nature; he conjured questions out of his curiosity. As a result, subjects for potential doctorates flowed from him as though he were some unquenchable academic spring. Yet his attempts to answer his own questions were hampered, more often than not, by his having no means of precise definition. His words were the general ones of everyday use, blurring at times what should have been an edged factuality. He was like a time traveller, trying with an eighteenth-century intelligence to hack his way through the intricate special-izations of twentieth-century science. The solutions he sought were in the end to become the foundations for an intellectual edifice which we still inhabit; the means by which he sought them, however, his sources and authorities, often derived from decades earlier. Unless we realize this, we cannot understand the extraordinary nature of the effort he made.

Not that he was without predecessors – the species question had been for a long time under discussion, as we know. For nearly two centuries, people had been trying in rational terms to explain fossils; for nearly a century, evolutionary ideas had, at intervals, been proposed. Nor was he in any sense a solitary genius in a social landscape made featureless by mediocrity: most of his scientific contemporaries thought themselves competent to consider almost every aspect of Nature. In his notes, however, Darwin seemed to set himself no limits; he ranged far wider than the subject of evolution as most people understood it, or understand it now. He knew that if he was right, then he could exclude nothing, not even the highest human faculties, from the world picture he was creating. The distinction made by both artists and scientists between the natural order on the one side and the human on the other, or between mankind's animal nature and its irreducible spirit, would, if once admitted, falsify his entire scheme. The gradual unfolding of species upon species was, he realized, either totally true or totally false. If some miraculous power had the ability to limit it, then its inner logic was des-troyed. It ceased to be necessary, to answer the evidence; instead it diminished into another arbitrary hypothesis, a plaything to be bandied about between biologists and theologians (where those two functions were not united in a single clergyman).

From the beginning, therefore, his speculations included notes about philosophy, ethics, metaphysics and the more insubstantial aspects of psychology – though, as it turned out, it would be more than three decades before he made some of these ideas public in *Descent of Man*. Nothing, meanwhile, was beyond his questioning, although much proved beyond his capacity to answer. During these three years, 1837–39, he charged at the multifarious phenomena of the earth, ranged before him like some heterogeneous army, as though he had become the young Prince Rupert of biology. It seems a bizarre analogy to use for this tall, bearded man, bald and sickly, benign, undramatic, restrained. His notebooks, however, show where, inwardly, at his centre, his energy and his courage blazed. It was in those pages that he revealed his essential self, brought into existence by the very withdrawal that made him so mild a person in the exterior world. When people wonder what happened to all the vigour he had shown during his

Beagle days, and before, at Shrewsbury and Cambridge, they imagine that somehow, at some point, it had left him. It had not left him. It had merely been directed down a different and much less apparent channel.

2

────────⟨∞∞∞⟩────────

That species were mutable was an idea that stretched back to the beginnings of humanity's intellectual history. The evolutionary unfolding of *prakriti*, the natural cosmos, had been proposed by the Samkhya philosophers of India in the sixth century B.C. Not very much later, the Greek thinker, Empedocles, had devised his own, somewhat cruder, developmental theory. In his *De rerum naturae*, written in the first century B.C., the Roman Epicurian, Lucretius, had suggested something very like natural selection.

With the rise of Christianity, however, and the adoption by the converted West of the Aristotelian version of the universe, all became rigid, immutable. The doctrine of *eidos* – of entities defined by type – and the reverberating descriptions of Genesis managed between them to freeze the cosmos. Existence conformed to the fixed patterns decreed by Providence, and only Providence itself could momentarily suspend these: as Sir Thomas Browne wrote in the seventeenth century, "Nature is the art of God". It was at about that period that the concept of the Great Chain of Being began to be developed, linking the whole of life in what was effectively a single entity. In this vast interconnection of forms, an admirable economy of means was matched by an awe-inspiring profusion of ends. The species were cemented in their places by the all-embracing, complex and inimitable craft of the Designer, mutation was unthinkable, no new forms could ever develop and no old ever become extinct. The kinship between the species had been imposed from the beginning, its basis the fact that all had a common Maker.

If from time to time a more flexible scheme was proposed, such proposals were tentative, heretical or circumlocutory. Yet in this ideological strait-jacket imaginative naturalists like Buffon would, as we have seen, eventually writhe and struggle. Throughout his enormous *Natural History* Buffon scattered indications of his thought, the spoor of an incipient evolutionist hiding his secret – even, it may be, from himself. Sometimes he no more than nudged his readers: "At what distance from man shall we place the large apes? . . ." he asked in Volume IV. Sometimes he presented them with more direct and pregnant questions: "Have not the feeble species been destroyed by the stronger? . . ." He recognized elements of natural selection: in Volume V he pointed out, "Nature turns upon two steady pivots, unlimited fecundity which she has given to all species; and those innumerable causes of destruction which reduce the product of this fecundity . . ." In the same volume, he seized upon the fact of natural variation: "There is a strange variety in the appearance of individuals, and at the same time a constant resemblance in the whole species". He did not, however, bring these two observations together to make, as Darwin was to do, the outlines of a new theory.

A similarly restricted awareness hemmed in many of those who might be considered Darwin's predecessors. Several had pieces of what he was eventually to assemble; none seemed able, or sufficiently interested, to construct the hypothesis that beckoned. The surveyor and engineer, William Smith, for example, crept diffidently into fame by suggesting that rock strata might be dated from the fossils found within them. Yet he did not go on to speculate why at various epochs the life forms had been so different from each other, and from those that still existed. Catastrophism and new creations might have answered him, as it did others – though then it might have been the similarities that needed explaining: why should the fundamentals of each creation remain so much the same? It was the enigmatic Cuvier who smashed for ever the belief in a unified Chain of Being. The four great zoological branchings, Vertebrates, Mollusca, Articulata, Radiata, were devised by him and eventually made credible the postulated divergencies of evolution – yet it was not Cuvier who was to arrive at such a conclusion.

Charles Darwin's own grandfather, Erasmus, put forward evolutionary views in his *Zoönomia*. Indeed, Charles read them while a student in Edinburgh and at the time, as he tells us in the *Autobiography*, admired the book; "but on reading it a second time after an interval of ten or fifteen years, I was much disappointed; the proportion of speculation being so large to the facts given". Between the first reading and the second, Cambridge and the *Beagle* had intervened; Darwin had become a scientist. The fact that he turned to the book a second time, however, suggests that the first must have impressed him greatly – enough, in any case, to lead him back to it when he in his turn was beginning to consider theories of developmental unity.

In *The Temple of Nature*, Erasmus Darwin had shown how:

> . . . smiling Flora drives her armèd car
> Through the thick ranks of vegetable war

and then gone on to demonstrate how far-ranging that war actually was, that it was a struggle involving everything that lived and that it had the entire world for its arena.

> Air, earth, and ocean, to astonish'd day
> One scene of blood, one mighty tomb display!
> From Hunger's arm the shafts of Death are hurl'd,
> And one great Slaughter-house the warring world!

It is difficult to believe that these powerful images had no effect on the young Charles Darwin. The poem's pre-Malthusian vision of relentless struggle is in many ways identical with Charles's later bleak observation about the "dreadful but quiet war of organic beings" constantly being waged in "the peaceful woods & smiling fields". He wrote that in March, 1839, by which time he, too, had come to realize the part played by "the shafts of death" which flew from "Hunger's arm". It is tempting, though quite beyond proof, to see the influence of such verses in the emphasis Charles Darwin was to place on struggle and the ease with which he came to accept that concept.

Was it in his father's library at The Mount, then, that the first stirrings of his most important ideas were felt? Or in Edinburgh, poring over *Zoönomia*? Or at Cambridge, in the midst of some lively discussion in Henslow's dedicated circle? If it was any of these, he did not record them, left no comment, remembered nothing. Certainly neither Lamarck nor Erasmus Darwin can have had more than a general effect upon his ideas during the early years, perhaps helping to create an intellectual climate in which evolutionary theories were at least not unthinkable. Direct influences, however, came later. At Cambridge, as we know, Darwin read one book, for example, that became notable for its delayed effect on him. This was Archdeacon Paley's *Natural Theology*, with its significant subtitle, *Evidences of the existence and attributes of the Deity collected from the appearances of nature.* "I did not at the time trouble myself about Paley's premises", Darwin wrote in the *Autobiography;* when he did become aware of and discard them, Paley's painstakingly collected examples of natural adaptation were left high and dry without explanation or context. He had written, "Design must have a designer. That designer must have been a person. That person is God". Published first in 1802, this was an opinion that prevailed during the early decades of the nineteenth century. It illuminated the eight Bridgewater Treatises, published during the 1830s in order to reassure the general reader that scientists continued to believe in the Creation. Yet had this view not begun to be more and more vehemently challenged, the Royal Society would hardly have thought it necessary to publish them.

Not that those with private doubts were always anxious to make their opinions clear. In December, 1827, Lyell, in deploring another writer's running "unnecessarily counter to the feelings and prejudices of the age", added, "It is an unfeeling disregard for the weakness of human nature, for as it is our nature (for what reason Heaven knows), but as *it is* constitutional in our minds, to feel a morbid sensitivity on matters of religious faith, I conceive that the same right feeling which guards us from outraging too violently the sentiments of our neighbours in the ordinary concerns of the world and its customs should direct us still more so in this." The implication of such an attitude is that there might be a public and a private view of the truth, that prevailing susceptibilities were to be respected even when it meant falsifying or suppressing one's own opinions and that what one said to one's friends in the drawing room should not be repeated to strangers in the lecture hall.

If one says that change was in the air, however, that does not mean that everyone – or even anyone – was waiting expectantly for fundamental alterations in the way the world was perceived. It means rather that positions that had once been held without discussion were now having to be defended; that what men publicly stated was no longer necessarily what they privately believed and that this discrepancy was causing a collective unease; that an academic world which until only a few years before had placed all its weight on the backward-looking study of the classics was beginning to counter this by a new emphasis on the forward-looking sciences; and that even the vast majority who remained unmoved by any premonitions that their beliefs were about to be challenged were falling into a frame of mind which would, when the time came, lead them to regard such a challenge as expected and inevitable.

Men like J.C. Pritchard, whose earlier *De humanis generis varietate* was translated, much expanded and republished in 1813 as *Researches into the Physical History of Man*; the South Carolina doctor, William Wells, a happy expatriate in England, who in the same year brought out his paper, *An Account of a White Female, Part of whose Skin resembles that of a Negro*; and the irritable Scottish botanist, Patrick Matthew, in sections of his otherwise unmemorable *Naval Timber and Arboriculture,* published in 1831, all touched upon some at least of the concepts with which Darwin was to struggle so painfully in the years ahead. In faraway Calcutta the botanist Edward Blyth wrote papers for the *Magazine of Natural History* which Loren Eisely, for one, claims unlocked the gates of speculation for Darwin. Yet not one of these observers ever arrived at the point from which Darwin set out. To reach it, they had to make a step which proved beyond them. They had to accept, to realize, that the uncountable species of living things were mutable. It was this which was for Darwin the paramount fact, understood during some panoramic glimpse of the world and all its history. Once grasped and cloven to, this was the understanding which made Darwin's scientific approach to natural phenomena so fruitfully unique. In any case, when in 1831 Darwin embarked on the *Beagle*, he seems to have had no knowledge of anything that Wells, Matthews and the rest might have written on species development. There simply existed in the scientific world a general subdued volatility of mood, of which these darts of theory were an expression; it was even stronger by the time he returned and would increase through the two decades in which he devised and then fleshed out his theories. There is no evidence, however, that Darwin was overtly aware of the possibilities for biology that were inherent in this widespread, if low-level, ferment. With his support for the Reform Bill, he probably recognized it more easily in politics than in science.

During the voyage, however, as we have seen, what he observed provoked some fundamental questions; so, too, did his reading of Lyell. The lawyer-geologist had long been familiar with the ideas of Lamarck. "His theories delighted me more than any novel I ever read", he wrote to a friend in March, 1827; on the other hand, "I confess I read him rather as I hear an advocate on the wrong side, to know what can be made of the case in good hands. I am glad he has been courageous enough and logical enough to admit that his argument, if pushed as far as it must go, if worth anything, would prove that men may have come from the Orang-Outang. But after all, what changes species may really undergo! How impossible will it be to distinguish and lay down a line, beyond which some of the so-called extinct species have never passed into recent ones."

From the very beginning, then, there was a certain ambiguity in Lyell's response to Lamarck. He thought him wrong – yet fascinating; felt he must be refuted – yet allowed these imaginative notions to stimulate his own thinking. In his *Principles of Geology* he wrote, "It is evident that, if some well-authenticated fact could have been adduced to establish one complete step in the process of transformation . . . time alone might then be supposed sufficient to bring about any amount of metamorphosis". The context was, of course, the accusation that no such fact had been brought forward; yet the statement implies a scientific challenge. In making the case against Lamarck, Lyell proffers to anyone with enough ingenuity the opportunity to nullify his own objections. There is in the detail in which he sets out Lamarck's theories, a hint of the ambivalence found in a tabloid newspaper's condemnation of vice. It is not entirely surprising, therefore, that it was precisely this refutation that first persuaded Herbert Spencer of the truth of the evolutionary hypothesis. It is not unlikely that for Darwin, too, this passage, as well as its uniformitarian views and its pregnant but unanswered questions, gave the book its place in the formation of his theories.

He will have noted, certainly, the special pleading by which Lyell – who was not alone in this – attempted to claim for humanity a unique position. Mankind had put in a late appearance, if the fossil record could be relied on, but there was nothing to show that any continuity of development existed between the animal and human worlds. Man, after all, as Lyell wrote, depended "not on those faculties and attributes which he shares in common with the inferior animals, but on his reason, by which he is distinguished

from them". This assertion may also have seemed to Darwin, once he had
begun seriously to consider it, an implied challenge, and one that he would
have to meet if his ideas on the mutation of species were to pass the criteria
of established science. If he could not devise a scheme that included the
development of human reason, he would be unable to surmount even those
objections which had already been stated.

Lyell also examined an idea to which Darwin was to give much attention,
that of hybridization, the breeding of new individuals by parents of different
species, as the originating agency in the creation of new forms. Lyell dismissed it, because hybrids had not the stamina to stay the course: "In the
universal struggle for existence, the right of the strong eventually prevails
. . ." Lyell, unknowingly, was stating the principle of natural selection, six
years before Darwin found it lurking among the propositions of Malthus.
Unlike Darwin, however, he was in search of an argument for conservation
and stability, not an explanation for Nature's underlying dynamism, and so
he wrote, firmly, that every species had been "endowed, at the time of its
creation, with the attributes and organisation by which it is now distinguished".

Yet Lyell's central proposition, that of an earth subject to constant alteration, seemed to imply that species, in order to survive, had to adapt to these
changes. He considered this, then dismissed it: when the surface went
through one of its constant small convulsions and the environment changed,
the response of living beings was to be found in their reshuffled distribution.
They themselves continued in their new locations exactly the same – except,
that is, for the ultimate alteration : extinction. This occurred when a species,
caught out by a newly-modified environment, found itself challenged in its
own habitat by some group better adapted to survive. Over enormous
periods of time, and by totally mysterious processes, the place of these
vanished creatures was taken by new species, created at intervals by, presumably, a watchful Providence.

The competition implied in this theory had none of the positive results
later to be found in Darwin's. On the contrary, it had only the entirely
negative consequence of keeping the numbers of organisms in phase with
the environment. In this way, Lyell set out some of the terms – adaptation,
distribution, struggle for survival – that Darwin was several years later to
combine into his very different hypothesis. It seems certain that each of
these concepts, so negligently waved away by the geologist, so carefully
scrutinised by Darwin on the *Beagle*, prepared Darwin's mind for precisely
those conclusions which Lyell was attempting to refute. It is not surprising,
therefore, to find Darwin writing to his cousin, Fox, from Lima in 1835, "I
am become a zealous disciple of Mr. Lyell's views, as known in his admirable

book . . . I am tempted to carry parts to a greater extent even than he does."

Where and with whom does an idea begin? The general mood of an entire society, the insights of particular, prescient individuals, the discrepancies that pile up between the accepted truth and the observed facts, perhaps even the centuries-long history of human speculation – all bear upon a certain moment. Of those inhabiting that moment, who will become aware of the pressure? Who will be fit to understand it and to take up the questions it poses? The fund of information is more or less the same for all; the ingredients from which a new truth may be concocted are there for anyone to mix. Who mixes it? Darwin in his moment was young enough to find the correct questions irresistible. He was fortunate enough to have been given the opportunity for gathering his own observations. He was stubborn enough to trust these, rather than the collected observations of other men. He had the inward daring to attempt his own answers and the power of synthesis to combine what he had seen and read until answers had been forged.

Yet at first, this was a process he must have resisted. Indeed, long before it had risen to a level of consciousness at which he had to recognize it as his own, he must have endeavoured to suppress the idea of mutable species. Such suppression would have been automatic: at some stage in the chain of inference, he would have turned away as from an absurdity, an impossibility. There must have been many such approaches and reversals, each one a hammering on a closed door. Just so fourteenth-century men will have turned away from the possibility of a globular earth. The idea was, however, already in being. It had been stated, in various partial forms, and it had been refuted, directly or by implication, on dozens of occasions. Here was Lyell himself immersed in its intricacies. It was not, after all, impossible; it was a concept that one might accept. When Darwin finally realized he believed it, it must have seemed like awakening to a truth of which he had long been already aware, in his sleep, in his dreams, in the unacknowledged darkness of the mind where waits – silent, foetal, patient – all that we do not know we know.

3

"In July opened first notebook on 'Transmutation of Species' – Had been greatly struck from about month of previous March on character of S. American fossils – & species on Galapagos Archipelago. These facts origin (especially latter) of all my views."

So Darwin wrote in his personal journal when recording the events of 1837. By that summer, therefore, he was sufficiently certain that the species were not eternally fixed to begin a book of speculative jottings on the subject. And he looked back to the previous March, to a time when the *Beagle* was hissing and booming down the long winds that carried her from Australia to Keeling Island. For two weeks the ocean had locked the ship into a solitude in which he had been free to consider his work and the meanings that might be derived from it. Perhaps it was then – bundled into the hammock that was his inadequate refuge from sea-sickness, notebook in hand, the beams about him noisy and the wind calling in the rigging – that what had always seemed unthinkable had suddenly revealed itself as truth. This was the divide which was to determine the shape and purpose of his life: on one side of it he had been a collector, a classifier, albeit with a clutch of interesting ideas; on the other, he would become the synthesizing pioneer, the innovator, the scientist able to effect a fundamental alteration in the way human beings thought about themselves and their world.

His earliest jottings lie haphazard on the pages of almost the last of those small notebooks he had carried with him on all his *Beagle* excursions. It is therefore just possible that he wrote them during that long run home in the late summer and autumn of 1836. There are his first impressions of St. Helena in that notebook, his earliest reconsiderations of the geology of the Cape Verde Islands – but there are also fleeting memoranda scribbled down in 1838 as he searched London for a house to which he could bring Emma. Most probably, therefore, they were hurriedly written down as he went about his other London business. Whenever he wrote them, the notes show the very beginnings of the intellectual effort that six years later would result in the first coherent formulation of his proposals and almost all of them, usually developed to a further stage, make an appearance in the *Transmutation Notebooks*.

Although, even when writing these stray thoughts in 1837 or 1838,

Darwin was still only devising questions and defining areas of research, his journal entry makes it obvious that when he looked back to this entire period it seemed to him that it had been in that March of 1836 that he had begun to shape his evolutionary theories. But perhaps all that really happened then was that his troubled speculations about species, gathering over the previous two years or more, coalesced into doubts that were to prove irresistible.

By the time, more than a year later, that he found it essential to write down the snatches of thought, the glimpses of truth, the gropings and speculations that fill his *Notebooks*, he had come much closer to the views that were to form the basis of his life's work. Thus the importance of these jottings, largely inaccessible to the general reader, cannot be stressed enough. If the years of the *Beagle* voyage provided Darwin with a fund of information that was to last him, in one fom or another, for the rest of his working life, then the mental voyage charted in the *Transmutation Notebooks* created a reservoir of ideas that he called on and developed, decade after decade, in an exactly similar way. It has to be remembered that not only *On the Origin of Species,* but almost everything he did throughout his productive years – and they spread over five decades – sprang from his overriding interest in the formation of species. It was this interest that created, and then drew on, the contents of these *Notebooks*.

In the story of Charles Darwin, *The Origin* glitters with the fascination of a hypnotist's lure. The eyes of commentators and biographers are filled with its brilliance; for the millions of non-specialists who have some knowledge of Darwin, its glow renders everything around it pale, almost invisible. Even when they wake from their trance, they cannot prevent its taking the central place in all the tales they tell. In one way, this is as it should be; the book both brought Darwin fame and summarized the work through which he had earned it. But just as the excitement it provoked makes us liable to forget how well known Darwin was before its appearance, so its obvious import-ance tends to make us overlook the books he brought out afterwards. We look at his life and work almost entirely in the light of this one production, disregarding the distortion it must cause. For *On the Origin of Species* was not, by any means, the book that Darwin planned to write.

In other words, to see Darwin's earlier work as leading up to that momentous publication in 1859, and all his later work as its constantly diminishing aftermath, is tempting and even plausible; it is not, however, true to the events of Darwin's life. The *Transmutation Notebooks* formed the basis of a first outline of his ideas that he wrote in 1842. This in turn was much expanded in the lengthy sketch he produced two years later. But these, and the work of detailed investigation, of gathering information, of refining his concepts that continued painfully through the 1840s and the mid-1850s,

Plate 11

Capt. Fitzroy, the irascible
commander of the *Beagle*
expedition, who, despite his
friendship for Darwin, was a
fundamentalist who came to
regret that he had ever invited
the naturalist to join his ship.

Plate 12 At the mouth of the Santa Cruz River, the *Beagle* was hauled ashore and
swiftly careened; with her bottom cleared of barnacles and newly caulked, she was
ready to proceed the following day.

Plate 13 Botofago Bay, near Rio de Janeiro, on the shores of which Darwin established himself while the *Beagle* continued with her survey of the coast.

Plate 14 Valparaiso Bay, where Darwin found hospitality under the roof of an old schoolfellow – whose household expenses, he noted, were half what they would have been in England.

were not intended to lay the foundations for a book as brisk and accessible as *The Origin*. Darwin saw that as no more than an abstract of his real book, and only the insistence of his publisher, John Murray, was to prevent his saying so on the title page.

The work he actually intended – his big "species book" – was begun as planned. When its progress was interrupted in 1858, Darwin had written over a quarter of a million words of it – though this covered only half its intended scope. That was the book for which he was to raid the *Transmutation Notebooks*, clipping out pages containing references and conjectures that promised to be useful. In that book, too, he deployed the full scholarly apparatus which haste would make him reduce in *The Origin* itself. Professor R.C. Stauffer, who has published what remains of this enormous manuscript in his *Charles Darwin's Natural Selection,* estimates that the final length of the book would have come to some 375,000 words; as he points out, "the scale does not seem inordinate considering the standards of the days of double-decker and triple-decker novels" – and considering too, perhaps, the breadth, complexity and importance of the subject. Nevertheless, if he is right, it would still have been shorter than, say, Lyell's *Principles of Geology*. Whatever its eventual size would have been, it was this work towards which all Darwin's efforts were to be bent, for more than a decade; if his approach to it was slow, it was almost inhumanly thorough. When at last he was forced to abandon the book, to quicken his pace, to prepare for the swiftest possible publication, it seemed to him a catastrophic alteration in his plans (see p. 412 *et seq.*).

He hoped for a long time that he would be able to return to this enormous, unified and comprehensive exposition of his theories. As he hurried to write a shorter version of the book, however, it was as if what had been the central labour of his ambition burst asunder. Once *On the Origin of Species* was published, the purpose of the work that he had first intended seemed to have been served. The gravity of logic which had held its elements together weakened, and it fell apart. Each of the resultant fragments, however, retained elements of their original unity. For that reason, his books form an indivisible *oeuvre*, in exactly the same way as the fictions of some eminent novelist. They continue to express the coherence of theme which was to underly the enormous book he had planned. *The Variation of Animals and Plants under Domestication, The Descent of Man, The Expression of the Emotions in Man and Animals,* even *The Effects of Cross and Self Fertilisation in the Vegetable Kingdom* and *The Power of Movement in Plants* – these and the rest are, in essence, sections of a single work, of which *The Origin* admittedly remains the core. Concerned with one all-embracing subject, they draw on the material intended for the original project. And the entries in the *Transmutation Notebooks* – and the "M" and "N" Notebooks on metaphysics and psychology – are markers on the route towards the book that Darwin envisaged even if at the time he wrote them he had not yet imagined it with any clarity. He knew that some day he would present "my theory" to the world and, looking ahead, he must have seen some fore-shadowing of how he was to do it. In such moments, it was not *The Origin* that he saw, but rather some comprehensive summary, the shape of "the big species book" which would encompass all his ideas within a single structure.

The *Notebooks*, therefore, bear upon *all* his work. They are the store-house into which he poured the harvest of an astonishing period of intellect-ual activity, to draw on as and when he needed to. To make it necessary to open them, his mind must have been in a constant turmoil of questions, observations, faintly glimpsed possibilities, tenuous connections and hoped-for conclusions. Pressed by that excitement, however, that as yet indefinable expectation, open them he did, writing firmly at the top of the first page: "ZOONOMIA". Probably it was shortly before this that, driven by similar imperatives, he had reread his grandfather's book and been so disappointed. Almost at once, in considering the essential differences bet-ween asexual and sexual reproduction, he found himself struggling with the most fundamental issues: *eros* and *thanatos* confronted him. It was Erasmus Darwin who had pointed to the invariable replicas produced by grafts or replanted root slivers, "whereas the seminal offspring of plants, being supp-lied with nutriment by the mother, is liable to perpetual variation" (a typically eighteenth-century mixture of true observation linked to false causation).

Darwin wrote down, "Why is life short, why high object – generation". "Generation" was the word he generally used for sexual reproduction; he realized from the beginning that death, propagation and the volatility of life's order were intimately linked.

> We *know* world subject to cycle of change, temperature & all circumstances, which influence living beings. We see the young of living beings become permanently changed or subject to variety . . . Again we know, in course of generation even mind & instinct becomes influenced. Child of savage not civilized man . . . There may be unknown difficulty with *full grown* individual with fixed organisation thus being modified, – therefore generation to adapt & alter the race to *changing* world. – On other hand, generation destroys the effect of accidental injuries, which if animals lived for ever would be endless (that is with our present system of body & universe. – therefore final cause of life.)

Darwin had leaped straight for the central issue. He needed to establish why flux was necessary in the organic world; in the inorganic, Lyell had long established the principle of constant change. Death was the key – in the immutable system, what need was there for individuals to die? Yet the environment was changing the whole time; death and new life allowed the world of living beings a responsive flexibility.

From this profundity, Darwin was drawn by a somewhat more practical question: "With this tendency to vary by generation, why are species constant over whole country". Because he knew of no mechanism for passing on characteristics unaltered from one generation to the next, he believed that some form of blending occurred, mingling the traits of an individual's parents. This ensured that in any species the characteristics of the majority would prevail, thus maintaining its overall unity: "Beautiful law of inter-marriages partaking of both parents & then infinite in number", he wrote. But how, in that case, were useful variations preserved? How did divergence from the main body of a species occur? The mathematics showed that, in ten generations at most, any such modifications were bred out. Darwin worked out a solution based on his *Beagle* observations – if you placed a breeding pair "on a fresh island, it is very doubtful whether they would remain constant . . . Let a pair be introduced & increase slowly, from many enemies, so as often to intermarry – who will dare say with what result. According to this view animals, on separate islands, ought to become different if kept long enough apart, with slightly differ circumstances. – Now Galapagos Tortoises, Mocking birds, Falkland Fox, Chiloe fox . . ." Isolation avoided the contaminating normality which fashioned, and was fashioned by, the majority, so that any variations produced would be retained by the interbreeding of a small number of individuals.

A little later in the *Notebook*, Darwin linked these ideas with those of "centres of creation" and the continuous appearance of new forms which he had earlier taken over from Lyell. "If species made by isolation, then their distribution (after physical changes) would be on rays – from certain spots." And he pointed out that such a conclusion agreed with Lyell's "to a certain extent". He had, in fact, made a crucial alteration to Lyell's theory, substituting for centres of creation what might be termed centres of transmutation (though he was from time to time to return to a concept of creation that he seemed at this period unable to abandon).

In his view, however, such centres were clearly points of arrival as well as departure. In isolated areas, such as islands, newcomers vied with long-established species, the more recent arrivals being still very similar to those found on the nearby mainland, while "others old ones (of which none of the same kind had in interval arrived) might have grown altered. Hence the type would be of the continent, though species all different." He had answered the question by which he had first been struck when considering the

"Americanness" of the Rhea. Nor was this similarity true only in space, but in time as well – the plants and creatures of a certain locality were likely to be very similar to those that had existed there millions of years before: "Propagation explains why modern animals – the same type as extinct, which is law almost proved". Because the similarities ran through such unimaginably long periods, an adaptation crucial to the effectiveness of a remote ancestor might no longer seem of obvious value. Inheritance, however, had maintained it in existence, either as it was or in some vestigial shape. "Hence antelopes at C. of Good Hope & Marsupials at Australia."

At this point, Darwin reconsidered life's beginnings: "Will this apply to whole organic Kingdom when our planet first cooled." He peered back towards the earliest times. "This presupposes time when no mammalia existed," he wrote, leaping over geological aeons like an athlete. "This view supposes that in course of ages, & therefore changes, every animal has tendency to change." Though unorthodox, it was a suggestion already made by Lamarck; the causes of change, however, were unknown. Darwin wrote, "Volcanic island – Electricity," as though these were clues then added, "Each species changes. Does it progress." Already, it is clear, he was looking along the whole uncoiling chain of organic development, from its incomprehensible beginnings right down to its most recent manifestation – the human race. "Man gains ideas," he commented, then answered his own question. "The simplest cannot help becoming more complicated; & if we look to first origin, there must be progress."

Briefly, he now took up a concept his recourse to which most commentators have ignored, but to which Professor Howard Gruber in *Darwin on Man* has drawn attention – that of monads. A hundred and fifty years earlier Leibniz, in his *Monadology,* had postulated a universe composed of an infinite number of sealed entities, each separately set in motion by a Creator to act in "pre-established harmony". These "windowless monads", every one of which was self-sufficient, mirroring the entire universe with greater or lesser efficiency, were like clocks, acting in unison because separately wound up and regulated. Darwin seized on a similar idea when considering the rise and extinction of species. "If we suppose monads are constantly formed," he wrote – reviving in a new form the idea of a continuing creation – "would they not be pretty similar over whole world under similar climates and as far as world has been uniform at former epoch."

He appears to have believed in these ultimate units as regulators of form in a species, as well as controllers of its time on earth. Coming spontaneously into existence, they determined the nature of the different species, developing greater complexity the longer they continued to exist. The number of forms present in nature, however, appeared to be constant, hence some species had to disappear, making room for this increase in complexity. Some of the oldest species therefore had vanished, as the fossil record showed; by corollary, some of the most complex species were the most recent: "We may look at Megatherium, armadillos & sloths as all offspring of some still older types, some of the branches dying out . . . If we suppose monad definite existence, as we may suppose in this case, their creation being dependent on definite laws; then those which have changed most, owing to the accident of positions must in each state of existence have shortest life. Hence shortness of life of Mammalia. –"

The monads were Darwin's first solution to a problem which had vexed the orthodox, and thus had been widely discussed, ever since the nature of fossils had been correctly defined. For what was one to think of a God, supposedly benevolent, supposedly paternal, who created entire species, allowed them to flourish for a while, then wiped them out? The scheme that Darwin proposed removed God from the picture, substituting as the primal cause of species these spontaneously generated monads with the inherent power of development and with a specific life span. When that life span had been completed, the species concerned became extinct. His thoughts had evidently returned to the horses of South America, flourishing since their Spanish re-introduction and relishing an environment in which the earlier, indigenous species of horse had died out. He wrote, "The absolute end of certain forms from considering S. America (*independent of external causes*) does appear very probable: – Mem.: Horse, Llama, etc etc –"

This seems to be as far as Darwin took his idea. His next note reads, "If we grant similarity of animals in one country owing to springing from one branch, and the monucle has definite life, then all die at one period, which is not .·. MONUCULE NOT DEFINITE LIFE". Given that "monucle" or "monucule" is a synonym for monad, it appears that Darwin here abandoned the notion that the inherent time scheme of these fundamental biological particles determined that of their dependent species. Yet he was still faced with the problem of species extinction. "I think . . ." he wrote, and then drew his thought in a diagram: his Tree of Life, the branches and twigs of which were the divisions and subdivisions that define the great collectives of the earth's living beings.

This vision of life's many branching forms had been with him since his first conception of the role of the monads. He had written:

> Every successive animal is branching upwards different types of organisation improving . . . simplest coming in and most perfect and others occasionally dying out . . . Organized beings represent a tree, *irregularly branched*- some branches far more branched, – hence genera . . . Would there not be a triple branching in the tree of life owing to three elements – air, land & water . . . If

each main stem of the tree is adapted for these three elements, there will be
certainly points of affinity in each branch.

A little later, realizing that what seemed discontinuities in the record of
species development were perhaps no more than vanished records, he
wrote, "The tree of life should perhaps be called the coral of life, base of
branches dead, so that passages cannot be seen".

Now he came to realize that this model was of itself sufficient to explain
what happened to the species. He had already arrived at a common-sense
acceptance of large-scale extinction: "There is nothing stranger in death of
species, than individuals". Death was death – it made little difference
whether it took organisms singly or in great armies of the doomed. However,
if monads did not limit specific kinds of life to specific periods of time and
species did not die out abruptly, with that suddenness which had shocked the
pious, then they must vanish gradually. If that was so, there was ample time
for them to pass through periods of transition and modification. In other
words, species did not become extinct before, just like individuals, they had
been immortalized in their offspring. In their case, of course, such offspring
were new species, new twigs and branches on the tree of life – and, just as in
the case of individuals, they did not always occur. Indeed, that seemed to
him essential, "so as to keep the number of species constant". From the rush
of notes that followed, all dependent upon this basic concept, it is clear that it
was a vitalizing one for him.

Darwin's first attempt at a coherent theory, then, was founded upon a
mistake, the introduction of his monads to explain what seemed an inherent
tendency in species to die out. This he associated with the model of a tree, or
of a coral growth, the branchings of which eventually seemed to him sufficient explanation of the facts as he came to see them. The monads fell into
limbo, while the tree of life flourished, to remain a constant in his work, even
if it was one which he lost sight of from time to time. Here, in his first
Transmutation Notebook, it appeared, labelled with letters that mark the
geography of divergence; in *The Origin* the same diagram, albeit much
developed, helped to explain the same phenomenon.

At this point, of course, no principle animated his tree; it had grown and
now existed, but why it thrust forth certain branches while others withered
remained unclear. Certainly interaction with the environment was a key
factor, recognized by Lyell and others before him – but how did it actually
work? What was the energy that actively worked upon the species, sculpting
life into tenable shapes? How did variations occur, and how were they
maintained? By what energy was natural development fuelled? Darwin
returned to the idea of divine creation, from which the monads had dis-

tanced him. "The Creator has made tribes of animals, adapted preeminently for each element, but it seems law that such tribes, as far as compatible with such structure, are in minor degree adapted for other elements."

This notion of organisms connected by certain basic affinities now led Darwin up another blind alley, one constructed by a certain William Sharp Macleay. This was the Quinarian System, which divided the entire animal kingdom into five groups, each of which was in turn divided into five, each of which again comprised five parts, and so on to the least significant individuals. Each of these groups and sub-groups was arranged in a notional circle, so that every member of a group had a neighbour on either side. With both of these that member had affinities, a relationship that must have made the entire system more plausible in Darwin's eyes. Eventually, its very regularity – based on a mystical, rather than scientific, view of the world – came to discredit it for him, especially once he had gained a much more intimate understanding, through the work he was to do on the cirripedes, of the unpredictable complexity in which Nature was actually clothed. For the moment, however, the branchings and interconnections of the system seemed sufficiently like his own vision of the world to attract him; he even tried to modify it, proposing four and then three as the number of units in each group.

The idea of an endlessly interconnecting system opened up new lines of speculation. One was the possibility that a common ancestor might be found in the prehistory of genera. For "the father of Mammalia" Darwin proposed the Ornithorhynchus – the duck-billed platypus:

> If this last animal bred – might not new classes be brought into play. – The father being climatized – climatizes the child? – Whether every animal produces in the course of ages ten thousand varieties (influenced itself perhaps by circumstances) & those alone preserved which are well adapted? this would account for each tribe acting as in vaccuum to each other. [After a few pages, he returned to his original point, taking the platypus this time to demonstrate that] we have not the slightest right to say, there never was common progenitor to mammalia & fish . . .

The geology that underlay his reasoning on distribution led him to a concept we have only recently adopted. "Speculate", he wrote, "on land being grouped towards centre near Equator at former periods and then splitting off." A little later, considering the unexpected anomalies of distribution, he proposed "world divided into Zoological provinces, united – and now divided again." It seems clear that he was considering some version of what we now call Continental Drift. On the other hand, he was even more intrigued by the possibility, then almost universally accepted, that habits and characteristics found useful during an individual's lifetime were passed on to its progeny. "Can the wishing of the Parent produce any character in offspring?" he asked. "Does the mind produce any change in offspring?" He had already noted, "The condition of every animal is partly due to direct adaptation & partly to hereditary taint . . ."

This in turn brought ecological questions to his attention, since adaptation involved a consideration of the relationship between species, and between each species and the general environment. Darwin's conclusion was to see these interconnections as significant: "There must be progressive development; for instance none? of the vertebrata could exist without plants & insects had been created; but on the other hand creations of small animals must have gone on since from parasitical nature of insects & worms. – In abstract we may say that vegetables & most of insects could live without animals, but not vice versa . . ." Thus he was again able to lift himself above the vast jungle of detail and see for a moment that forest in its entirety, glimpsing an interdependent system stretching through both space and time, always the same in essence although undergoing constant development and influencing through the complex relationships of its constituent parts, its own slowly unfolding history.

In all this, Darwin had two problems with which he constantly wrestled. The first was the scientific one of how inheritance actually worked; the other was the metaphysical question of the Creation. He struggled all his life with the mathematics of inheritance, without ever formulating the matter in mathematical terms. The material for a Mendelian experiment existed in his experience and his reading; he quoted various observations of the offspring of parents with very different characteristics. It is clear, however, that he never knew what exactly to make of these, or how to bring these facts together in a theory in which he had any real confidence. The discussion becomes mixed with that on hybridization – with which of course it is closely linked – and is again and again turned away from its main path. The uniformity of species, too, becomes an aspect of this series of speculations. Throughout his entire scientific life, Darwin was to feel uncomfortably aware that he had not discovered a principle upon which he could base his convictions about heritable characteristics, and that without such a principle his theory, bolstered though it was by a mountain range of supportive facts and, eventually, the agreement of almost the entire scientific community, remained dangerously vulnerable.

The problem of the Creation, on the other hand, he eventually solved by largely ignoring it. For his purposes, it was sufficient that life existed; given that it did, his task was restricted to explaining how it had assumed its thousands upon thousands of forms. In his own notes, however, he returned to the subject several times and he continued elsewhere to use at least the phraseology of orthodox belief. Indeed, the fact that he used the words "creation" and "creative" to mean both a divine and a natural process sometimes blurs the clarity of his ideas on these matters. He was also using the phrase "my theory" with increasing frequency and aplomb, an indication of the importance it had assumed, even though he had as yet been unable to establish anything like a complete hypothesis. Nevertheless, he had enough of its elements to be able to make out something of its distinctive shape. It was for this reason that he could concentrate, not on quasi-theological argument, but rather on the outlines of his main proposition, which already postulated the mutation of species effected through variation, the results of which were spread or maintained by sexual propagation within a restricted population, a group isolated either through geological action or the inherent limitations of a structured ecological system.

Such a process operated throughout the whole of Nature, in Darwin's view – and it was a view that he seems to have held from the beginning. Life was a single event and all its manifestations were connected. But there were nevertheless glaring discontinuities that would, he felt, have to be accounted for: "The difference intellect of man & animals not so great as between living things without thought (plants) & living things with thought (animal)". Until biochemistry allowed us to learn something about the basic building-blocks of all life – the amino acids and the protein chains they formed – it was a gap that could be bridged only by the mystic and the sentimentalist: science was unable to find a verifiable way across it.

The unity of Nature implicit in Darwin's scheme had the consequence, too, of removing the distance which others had been at such pains to establish between human beings and the rest of the earth's creatures. Even in these very early days of his serious work on species transmutation, Darwin never considered excluding mankind from its effects. It is in this first *Notebook* that Darwin wrote a strange sentence which has snagged the attention of many commentators. "If all men were dead", he wrote, "then monkeys make men. – Men make angels." This derived from his assumption that Nature provided a place for each of its creatures – but a place that, like a vacuum, had to be filled. If men vanished, then monkeys – or their successors – would fill their ecological niche. The world was not static, but dynamic. Apes might change – and so might human beings. Dying, the latter became angels in the popular view; regarded from the scientist's, they became through their own development creatures so advanced that "angels" might be chosen as a useful metaphor to describe them. (Or perhaps, since there were no angels, humans simply took on that status in the unfolding hierarchy.) Whatever Darwin meant, however, it is clear that he saw a continuity of creatures which led up to and included humanity – a continuity not static, as in the Great Chain of Being postulated by earlier thinkers, but one that flowed and changed without cease in a plasticity as old as life itself. He returned to this idea when developing the theme that separate, but similar, species may have a common progenitor, although their development would always continue on divergent lines. He thought it unlikely, for example, that monkeys would ever produce a human type, "but both monkeys and men may produce other species". As a result of a new blending, "other species or angels produced". Mankind was part of a process that was not yet concluded, a view contrasting sharply with the opinion that *homo sapiens* is unique and under the particular care of Providence. Those who maintained the truth of the latter view found the idea of the human race as simply one more member of the animal kingdom, distinguished from the rest only by degree, offensive both to humanity's dignity and to the mercy of God. This was a view with which Darwin would have no truck. "Animals whom we have made our slaves," he wrote, "we do not like to consider our equals. – Do not slave-holders wish to make the black have other mind? – Animals with affection, imitation, fear of death, pain, sorrow for the dead – respect." That catalogue of qualities was the consequence of his effort to find correlations elsewhere in Nature for the human emotions and the human intellect. It was the reason he saw so profound a discontinuity, threatening to his theory, between plant life, in which no such qualities could be discerned, and animal life, in which they could. His later analysis of, for example, the power of movement in plants, was part of his effort to reduce this discontinuity as much as he was able.

In any case, mankind had greatly developed since its progenitor's earliest days – that precursor's "arts would not then have taken him over the whole world". Even those who believed in a soul accepted that it had been introduced into human beings already physically existent; "animals not got it", wrote Darwin, presumably pointing out that this was the accepted factor differentiating them from mankind. But suppose accepted opinion was wrong? "If we choose to let conjecture run wild, then animals – our fellow brethren in pain, disease, death, suffering & famine, our slaves in the most laborious works, our companions in our amusements – they may partake from our origin in one common ancestor, we may be all netted together." The creatures of the earth were one, no soul marked out a human difference; and in the dark beginnings of time our joint progenitor thrust its unicellular way among the weeds and sandbanks of unimaginable oceans. Lofty minds, which had no need to mark the human out by extraneous arguments, would accept their unity with the other orders of nature: "Those will not object to my theory, those philosophers who soar above the pride of the savage, they perceive the superiority of man over animals, without such resorts". In his imagination, he had already presented his hypothesis to the world and heard the arguments that it aroused; in fantasy, "philosophers who soar" had already given it their approval.

So the thoughts of Darwin – these and a hundred associated others – swirled and swooped throughout the second half of 1837, and into the early weeks of the following year. It was as if, having been cooped up for the five years of the *Beagle* voyage in that tiny ship, to emerge at intervals as no more than the observer, the gatherer of specimen and fact, Darwin now felt himself freed to consider for the first time everything that he had seen and noted. He had perhaps been constrained by his role as the expedition's naturalist. He was hemmed in by the very fact of the expedition, sponsored by the Admiralty and commanded by a naval officer. On his shoulders there had lain his responsibilities as the representative of British science. At times, he had been uncertain whether he was doing the right things, selecting the right specimens, making the right observations. He had been in an environment in which very few people were able or sufficiently interested to understand his work; at best, he was supported by the superficial, fashionable fascination of gentleman-officers who followed natural history as an agreeable hobby. He had lived in close, sometimes uncomfortable, proximity with men whom he liked well enough, but with whom he could share very few of his most important preoccupations. The only one who might have understood him, Fitzroy himself, had settled into views diametrically opposed to his own and held them with an increasingly intractable passion. From that situation Darwin had been catapulted into the respectful plaudits of Cambridge and scientific London, the friendship of men like Lyell and Richard Owen, the attention of the Geological, the Entomological, and even the Royal Society. It is no wonder that he should have felt during these years so hectic a surge of energy, nor that for month after month, as he worked at his books, his secretaryship, and his papers; as he was married, hunted houses, became a father, and felt the first insidious intimations of illness; his ideas should have come tumbling out like the endless coloured ribbons of some conjurer, to lie sprawling and intermingled at last across the tight-packed pages of his *Notebooks*.

And when he had finished the first *Notebook*, he turned at once to the second. The flow was not now to be interrupted. Ideas must have seized him at the most awkward moments, to be scrawled down – as had been his thoughts on marriage – on any convenient piece of paper. Later, one fancies, he will have transferred them to one of the *Notebooks*, with additions and adumbrations, sometimes with excisions and corrections. At other times, he obviously worked directly in the books, the thoughts, whether disconnected or not, following each other in a sequence. Sometimes, one imagines, ideas he had discovered in the course of conversation – debating with a Lyell, an Owen or a Murchison – were dashed down at the earliest opportunity, the late candle flickering, the pen making its swift, acerbic little noise, Emma elsewhere, already asleep, the maid long retired, Darwin at his solitary desk with the light softly reflected in that straight brow left bare by the receding hairline, the eyes in shadow, and on the wide mouth, perhaps, the faint, absorbed smile of a man shaping solutions for problems that have long plagued him.

There lies between the lines of the second *Notebook* – Notebook "C" – a new sense of purposefulness. It is as if Darwin were at last beginning to take himself seriously. More and more he looked forward to the time when his ideas had been made public and must be defended. As a result, he was prepared to equate his position with that of scientific martyrs in the past. "Mention persecution of early Astronomers – then add chief good of individual scientific men is to push their science a few years in advance only of their age . . . must remember that if they *believe* & do not openly avow their belief they do as much to retard as those whose opinion they believe had endeavoured to advance cause of truth." It was a firm affirmation of a noble truth – but it was followed by two decades of silence. Perhaps the clue to that lies in the phrase "a few years in advance only" – innovatory theories had to be publicized with a nice sense of timing if they were to be ahead of general opinion, but not too far ahead.

Darwin, too, was becoming very conscious of the objections that might be raised by critics. The inability to trace the stages of development in such delicate organs as the eyes, adapted so precisely to their function, was "perhaps greatest difficulty to whole theory". A little later he was writing, "Insects shamming death most difficult case to imagine how art acquired." Such apparently learned behaviour as the hoarding by squirrels of stores for the winter posed problems, too, since in order to show how intellect had developed he needed to differentiate between it and instinct. "My theory must encounter all these difficulties," he wrote, firmly. Certain squirrels had apparently learned to take ears of corn instead of nuts, an alteration in their behaviour that "surely is not worthy interposition of deity". Nevertheless, the question teased him, especially when he considered the human mind. He seems to have decided, however, to treat it like any organ especially developed by particular species: "The greater individuality of mind in man is analogous to greater individuality of bodies of some animals over those of others."

In this there are indications of a tougher attitude than before to the question of humanity's place in nature. "Let man visit Ourang-outang in domestication", he wrote, "hear its expressive whine, see its intelligence when spoken, as if it understood every word said – see its affection to those it knows – see its passion & rage, sulkiness & very extreme of despair; let him look at savage, roasting his parent, naked, artless, not improving, yet improvable and then let him dare boast of his proud preeminence." He remembered his Patagonian experience: "Not understanding language of Fuegian puts on par with monkeys". There is something much harder edged about this, almost a hint of anger, of misanthropy, as if Darwin, hemmed in now by his London life, half exulted in the blow that his ideas might strike at mankind's self-esteem. "Let him dare boast" is a phrase from something stronger than mere scientific analysis. A little later, in discussing the relationship between "thought (or desires more properly)" and brain structure, he wrote, "Love of the deity effect of organization", then broke off to admonish himself, "oh you materialist!" A line or two later, he returned to his earlier scorn. "Why is thought being a secretion of the brain, more wonderful than gravity a property of matter? It is our arrogance, it our admiration of ourselves." The pen has flown across the page, the word "is" has been omitted in his haste; he has, one senses, achieved a state of mind unfamiliar to us and far removed from the gentle, obliging Darwin to which we have become used. One supposes this to have been a private anger, a mood he concealed, or contained. His metropolitan life, his decision to marry, the construction, demolition and reconstruction of his theories combined, perhaps, to crack for a time the gentle façade by which the world knew him, by which he knew himself. Briefly, something darker and fiercer seems to have appeared.

How demanding the intellectual effort required to fashion his ideas actually was it is hard now to understand. One has to recreate for oneself the dead weight of a long-vanished orthodoxy, a situation in which much of what we now take for granted had painfully to be brought into existence. Darwin rarely mentioned the difficulty of his task, but on page 74 of this *Notebook* he did: "The believing that monkey would breed (if mankind destroyed) some intellectual being though not MAN, – is as difficult to understand as Lyells doctrine of slow movements &c. &c. The multiplication of little means & bringing the mind to grapple with great effect produced is a most laborious & painful effort of the mind . . . Once grant that species and genus may pass into each other . . . & whole fabric totters & falls. – Look abroad, study gradation, study unity of type, study geographical distribution, study relation of fossil with recent. The fabric falls!" Darwin had passed from complaint through argument to affirmation.

He turned again to the situation of Man, who "is not a deity, his end under present form will come, (or how dreadfully we are deceived) then he is no exception." – How powerful, yet how enigmatic, seems that sudden parenthesis: "or how dreadfully we are deceived". The mind recoils from it, for we cannot tell whether Darwin is looking forward to a Christian millenium, regarding with an ironic biologist's eye the bleak extinction of his race, or proposing humanity's apotheosis, perhaps as those heavenless "angels" of his earlier metaphor. One thing remained clear: "Man in his arrogance thinks himself a great work worthy the interposition of a diety. More humble & I believe truer to consider him created from animals." And Darwin called in testimony a faction whose opinions he detested: "Has not the white man, who has debased his nature by making slave of his fellow Black, often wished to consider him as other animal". Perhaps he realized at this point that his new materialism offered him only a thin logic to support his anti-slavery convictions; in any case, he turned back. He wrote, one suspects hastily, that he believed those "who soar above such prejudices yet have justly exalted the nature of man," and, with that single adverb, "justly", he set a limit to his misanthropy.

Meanwhile, he was already beginning to work towards a selection theory; at least there was a burgeoning recognition of the creative role played by death. "The death of some forms & succession of others . . . is absolutely necessary to explain genera & classes", he wrote; meaning, however, that the gaps left by the vanished forms marked the divergence of the surviving species: "if extinct forms were all fathers of present, then there would be perfect series or gradation." A little later he commented, "It is very remark-able, with so much death, as has gone on, no greater gaps". At the same time, he overturned that favourite postulate of Natural Theology, the Chain of Being, writing, "It is capable of demonstration that all animals have never at any one time formed chain", since creatures were perishing even before the carboniferous age, proving that "there always have been gaps, & there now must be, ∴ extinction of species bears relation to existence of genera &c. &c." As so often, however, having made a statement, his mind continued examining it until he was forced into modification: "Discussion useless, until it were fixed what a species means". Yet the question continued to nag. "Is the *extinction & change of species* two very different considerations", he wondered. He hovered about mortality like an undertaker, having realized from the beginning that the disappearance of species was among the facts that he had to explain, yet not quite being able to fit it into the picture. He had yet to realize, perhaps, that species were made up of individuals and that it was what happened to them that was of the first importance.

He struggled still with the problems of heredity and the significance of mutants – "monsters", he called them, and "monstrosities". At the same time, he was beginning to doubt that acquired characteristics could be passed on. He realized that "changes after birth do not affect progeny", citing the practice of lopping the tails of both dogs and sheep for generation after generation, "yet there is no record of any effect. – New Hollanders have gone on boring their noses &c. &c.", yet their children were still born with noses as ordinary as those who had never drilled holes in them. Again, it seems as if he was moving towards a concept of crucial adaptations, those adaptations that lead to survival; he wrote of "hare becoming white in winter of Arctic countries few will say it is direct effect . . . but adaptation. – Albino however is monster, yet albino may so far be considered as adaptation, as best attempt of nature colouring matter being absent." He was like someone playing blind man's buff, stumbling to and fro, arms outstretched, knowing his quarry was there, almost close enough to touch, yet never quite able to seize it. Apart from anything else, the crucial difference between boring a hole in one's nose for cosmetic purposes and turning white in an Arctic winter is that the latter marks an interaction with the natural environment and the former does not. Within two pages Darwin had considered both, yet a comparison between the uselessness of a bone through the nose and the usefulness of a white coat on snow did not occur to him. A line or two later, however, he was discussing the possible value of the undeployable wings on certain beetles. One has the feeling that, at least subliminally, he had already made the necessary connections. What was needed now was some catalyst, some agent that would lift knowledge into the light of consciousness.

In a letter to Fox in the summer of 1838 Darwin made one of his few early references to the ideas that actually were preoccupying his mind. He had obviously asked his cousin for information on the cross-breeding of domestic stocks and Fox, always fascinated by the natural sciences, had undertaken to supply the facts he needed. "I am delighted," wrote Darwin, "you are such a good man, as not to have forgotten my question about the crossing of animals. This is my prime hobby & I really think some day I shall be able to do something on that most intricate subject, species & varieties . . ." Three months later, however, in September, his tone is his Journal was less enthusiastic: "Frittered these foregoing days away on working on Transmutation theories . . ." By then, perhaps, other considerations had temporarily occluded the bright constancy of his intellectual passion, for he was beginning to move towards his proposal to Emma. Nevertheless, when that moment came, he was deep in his work on the mutability of species. His ideas had, he himself claimed, begun to join together in a new coherence; he had found his catalyst in the ideas of Malthus.

In his *Autobiography*, Darwin tells us, "In October, 1838, that is, fifteen months after I had begun my systematic enquiry, I happened to read for amusement Malthus on *Population*, and being well prepared to appreciate the struggle for existence which everywhere goes on from long-continued observation of the habits of animals and plants, it at once struck me that under these circumstances favourable variations would tend to be preserved and unfavourable ones destroyed. The result of this would be the formation of new species. Here, then, I had at last got a theory by which to work . . ." Time, and the undemanding nature of memoirs written for family consumption, have allowed Darwin to telescope a process that took rather longer than he makes it sound. There was, too, nothing "at last" about his having "a theory by which to work" – he had always had some hypothesis, however partial, and had formulated it sufficiently clearly to use almost from the beginning the phrase, "my theory". What he had now, however, was a theory which explained enough of the facts to make it plausible; he had always envisaged defending his ideas in public, but now he had the foundations for a coherent system. Although from the second *Transmutation Notebook* on there had been an air of optimism and conviction about Darwin's theorizing, the fact that in looking back he saw October 1838 as the moment when possibility turned to likelihood suggests that his earlier work had filled him with unacknowledged doubts. Nevertheless, the actual tone of his notes at the time, both before and after, hardly demonstrates any violent change in mood or certainty.

Malthus's basic proposition, of course, compared the growth of populations with that of resources and demonstrated by formulae how the first was bound to outstrip the second. Writing at the end of the eighteenth century, he seems as a clergyman to have been unduly pessimistic about the intentions of the deity as worked out in his creation. As a mathematician, he tended to a certain rigidity. As a prophet, therefore, he had definite limitations. Nevertheless, the general picture that he painted of a constant pressure on resources by expanding populations is one that has become terrifyingly familiar two centuries after its first appearance. Darwin, however, perhaps of a different cast of mind from Malthus, saw in these ideas evidence of a positive rather than a negative force. He was in need of a context that could provide variation with an obvious function, and population pressure seemed to offer one. It established the criteria which would make certain variations more significant and useful than others. It created the mechanism through which less successful adaptations were eliminated. He had found a solution to his central problem.

He came across the idea he needed on 28 September. On page 134 of his third *Transmutation Notebook* he wrote, rather defensively at first,

> We ought to be far from wondering of changes in numbers of species, from small changes in nature of locality. Even the energetic language of Decandolle* does not convey the warring of the species as inference from Malthus. –

increase of brutes must be prevented solely by positive checks, excepting that famine may stop desire. – in nature, production does not increase, whilst no check prevail, but the positive check of famine & consequently death . . . Population is increase at geometrical ratio in FAR SHORTER time than 25 years – yet until the one sentence† of Malthus no one clearly perceived the great check among men . . . The final cause of all this wedging, must be to sort out proper structure, & adapt it to changes . . . One may say there is a force like a hundred thousand wedges trying force every kind of adapted structure into the gaps on the economy of nature, or rather forming gaps by thrusting out weaker ones.

Darwin had discovered the force, the energy, which drove that vast unfolding he envisaged, that process, wide as nature, directing life into its multifarious forms. For several months, however, he apparently continued to think of "the warring of species" as the point at which that process might be perceived. He had understood that his theme was struggle, but he had not yet clarified exactly which struggle it was. When he finally did select the significant confrontation, it was seen to be not between species at all, but between individuals of the same species. Here was the rivalry that threatened the least well-adapted, here the turmoil out of which the changed species one by one emerged.

Not that Darwin had been instantly enthused. He had, one imagines, simply set down some sentences that interested him, two filled pages among the hundreds he would write, and then gone on to finish Malthus's book. He must have done so some time early in October. He did not return to the subject until he opened his new – fourth and last – *Transmutation Notebook* later that month. This, however, he began with notes on Malthus's theory, apparently going over the book again in order to jot down comments on what seemed to him important. It was then, one assumes, that he began incorporating Malthus's ideas in his own, finally cobbling together what amounted to the final version of his theory. For the moment, however, Malthus had only provided him with one notion among a hundred others, an intellectual titbit which he seized, as he had so many more, before turning to new and different matters.

For example, he was still wrestling with the problems of genetic inherit-

---

* The botanist Augustin Pyrame de Candolle who, though Swiss, did his best work in France in the two decades before 1816. He was the leading systematist of his day, setting out the structure of the botanical world. The last ten of his seventeen great volumes became the responsibility of his son, Adolphe, who continued the work after his father's death in 1841.

† "It may safely be pronounced, therefore," wrote Malthus (Vol. 1, p. 6), "that the population when unchecked goes on doubling itself every twenty-five years, or increases in a geometrical ratio."

ance. "An animal in either parent cannot transmit to its offspring any change from the form which it inherits from its parents stock without it be small & slowly attained. N.B. The longer a thing is in the blood the more persistent any amount of change . . ." From such a view as this, close to the truth, yet inadequate, and in its fundamentals quite mistaken, Darwin could veer to what we might think no more than a peasant rumour: he began a long entry under the heading, "Proved facts relating to Generation", with the statement, "One copulation may impregnate one or many offspring, it affects the subsequent offspring, though other male may have copulated". It is this superstitious version of genetics that continues to induce hysteria in dog-owners when a mongrel mounts a pedigree bitch.

Distribution still fascinated Darwin, as did the function and capacity of hybrids, the models provided by the breeding of domestic animals, and Macleay's Quinarian System; in an aside he even mentioned the Deluge and the fact that among the fossil shells of Europe and the Americas "there is no appearance of sudden termination of existence". The sexual instinct, its manifestations and attendant organs interested him more than they had before, and it need not be a prurient point to see in this a sublimated reflection of his own sharpened sexuality. He was, after all, beginning seriously to contemplate marriage, and such a correspondence between areas of emotional and intellectual intensity is not to be wondered at. His actual approach to the subject in the *Notebook* was, of course, admirably dispassionate, although at times one wonders if one is reading the worksheets of a scientist or a poet. "The passion of the doe to the victorious stag, who rubs the skin off horns to fight, is analogous to the love of women . . . to brave men." At once, however, he was off at a tangent, considering the consequences of castration.

Sexual desire between individuals of different species bore directly upon his theories. He noted, therefore, instances of monkeys who, according to an informant, "big & little that ever he saw knew women. – he has repeatedly seen them try to pull up petticoats, & if women not afraid, clasp them round the waist & look into their faces & make the st. st. noise . . . These monkeys had no curiosity to pull up trousers of men . . . These facts may be turned to ridicule, or may be thought disgusting, but to philosophic naturalist pregnant with interest."

Hermaphroditism caught his interest, since it demonstrated the fact that organs might develop in a number of possible ways. He realized that to think men and women completely different, with two different sets of organs, did not match the facts, and that the existence of hermaphrodite forms made this apparent. He pointed out that "those organs which perform nearly the same function in both sexes, are never double, only modified, those which perform very different, are both present in every shade of perfection. – How comes it nipples though abortive, are so plain in man, yet no trace of abortive womb, or ovarium, – or testicles in female. – the presence of both testes & ovaries in Hermaphrodite – but not of penis & clitoris, shows to my mind that both are present in every animal, but unequally developed." There was an underlying unity in nature's diversity, and Darwin sought it wherever he could, whether between the species or between the sexes. More specifically, the development of the sexes from the animal world's asexual progenitor posed problems for anyone attempting to establish the truth of evolution. Underlying similarities, offering clues to how that development might have taken place, were therefore of great importance. "In my theory I must allude to separation of sexes as very great difficulty, then give speculation to show that it is not overwhelming."

Read now, nearly a century and a half after they were dashed down, his thoughts intrigue us not only as history, but also from time to time as prescience.

> Why does Gecko produce always different tail? The whole grown to that part – in the separated part every element of the living body is present . . . If it possible to *support* the arm of man, when cut off, it would produce another man. – That the embryo the *thousandth* of an inch should produce a Newton is often thought wonderful, it is part of same class of facts, that the skin grows over a wound . . . A mans arm would produce arm if *supported*, & in making true bud some such process is effected, – a *child* might be so born, but it would be very different from true generation . . .

Tissue culture, cloning, test-tube babies – the outlines are here, over a century before the techniques. Genetic engineering was always, it seems, waiting in the wings until the brightening illumination on the stage allowed it to appear – abruptly, perhaps, like the Demon King. A little later Darwin returned to the same theme: "The *sympathy* of parts is possibly part of same general law, which makes two animals out of one & heals piece of skin, – if the tail knows how to make a head, & Head a tail, & the half both head & tail – no wonder there should be *sympathy* in human frame." He was considering the meaning of regeneration in snails and worms – but his generalized "sympathy" is our particular DNA. Darwin would not have been astonished by our skills in organ transplantation.

He tried to curb his more imaginative flights, distrusting unstable structures in which one theory rests upon another. "*Pure hypothesis* be careful," he warned himself, considering some potential law of nature. And, a little later, "The only advantage of discovering laws is to foretell what will happen & to see bearing of scattered facts." What was true explained the world; what did not explain the world was not true – that was his basic scientific creed. "In comparing my theory with any other, it should be observed not what comparative difficulties (as long as not overwhelming) [but] what comparative solutions & linkings of facts." This was a demand he amplified later in the *Notebook*: "The line of argument often pursued throughout my theory is to establish a point as a probability by induction, & to apply it as hypotheses to other points, & see whether it will solve them." It is perhaps his failures that mark the exactitude of his methods; he proposed no implausibilities nor conjured any law of progressive development out of the air. As with the problem of genetics, when he had not resolved a difficulty he knew it.

When in 1856 Darwin began to work in earnest on "the big species book", he simply tore out of the *Notebooks* whatever pages he needed for reference. Many have since been recovered, but the first two pages of the fourth *Notebook* have not. It was on these, almost certainly, that he wrote his first considered responses to *An Essay on the Principles of Population*. Only a few days earlier he had scribbled down those sentences from the book which had struck him immediately, but now he seems to have given Malthus's ideas rather more thought. The first surviving entry in the *Notebook,* on page 3, reads, "Epidemics seem intimately related to famine, yet very inexplicable" – a reference to the kind of natural disaster through which, Malthus had reassured his readers, the Lord placed a necessary curb on population growth.

But Darwin soon turned from considering Malthus to defending the theory he himself was outlining with increasing firmness. The very slowness of the development he was proposing put it, he felt, in line with the geological picture of the earth. "If the change could be seen to be more rapid I should say then some link in our train of geological reasoning extremely faulty." He considered the continuing problem of variations being swept away by the fixed characteristics of the majority. "No structure", he wrote, "will last without its adaptation to *whole* life of animal . . . it will decrease & be driven outwards in the grand crush of population." As swiftly as this – the note is on page 9 of the *Notebook* – he was applying the lessons he had derived from Malthus. Fifty pages later he had moved beyond "the grand crush of population" to consider the consequences: "When two races of men meet, they act precisely like two species of animals. – they fight, eat each other, bring diseases to each other &c., but then comes the most deadly struggle, namely which have the best fitted organization, or instincts (i.e. intellect in man) to gain the day . . . Man acts & is acted on by the organic and inorganic agents of this earth like every other animal." Nothing humanity did was, or by definition could be, outside the normality of nature. Its range and distribution were what might have been expected, and its geological history was "as perfect as the Elephant if some genus holding same relation as Mastodon to man were to be discovered." It is a condition that *homo erectus* seems to have fulfilled.

Another thirty pages on, and his basic idea is clearly enunciated. He was discussing the acclimatization of plants and wondering whether, in the course of time, warm-climate plants grew hardier in colder regions. "Now my principle" stated Darwin, thus promoting what had only been a theory, "does not apply to any plant reared artificially . . . my principle being the destruction of all the less hardy ones & the preservation of *accidental* hardy seedlings . . . to sift out the weaker ones: there ought to be no weeding or encouragement, but a vigorous battle between strong & weak." He had moved to the crux of his matter, which is not the struggle between species, but the intra-specific struggle of individuals with the same, competing needs. Having reached such a conclusion, no wonder that a few pages later he made his comment on the underlying horror of that conflict: "It is difficult to believe in the dreadful but quiet war of organic beings going on [in] the peaceful woods & smiling fields."

Soon he was capable of mentioning "my Malthusian views" in a manner so matter-of-fact it suggests that by the spring of 1839 he had melded these opinions totally with his own. He wrote then, "Seeing the beautiful seed of a Bull Rush, I thought, surely no 'fortuitous' growth could have produced these innumerable seeds, yet if a seed were produced with infinitesimal advantage it would have better chance of being propagated & so &c." There at last, after months of discussing the various propositions he had from time to time called "my theory", Darwin was able to put with simple clarity the hypothesis which the world was to accept and with which we have become so familiar.

Meanwhile he struggled with the concepts he had inherited – Lamarck's conviction that a principle of development underlay the whole of Nature, Lyell's contrary certainty that there never had been any development at all – and with the observable realities of the world around him. He saw that "as the forms became complicated, they opened *fresh* means of adding to their complexity. – but yet there is no *necessary* tendency in the simple animals to become complicated . . . if we begin with the simplest forms & suppose them to have changed, their very changes tend to give rise to others." There might indeed be a reverse process – what he called "dis-development" – partly because ecological niches, once existing, would be filled. "I doubt not if the simplest animals could be destroyed, the more highly organized would soon be disorganized to fill their places." Darwin always realized how important, and how delicately balanced, was that interlocking totality we call the ecology.

The way he was to deal with the human race when it came to setting out his ideas continued to stimulate comments. "The dog being so much more intellectual than fox, wolf &c &c – is precisely analogous case to man exceeding monkeys. – Having proved mens & brutes bodies one type: almost superfluous to consider minds. – as difference between mind of a dog & a porpoise was not thought overwhelming – yet I will not shirk difficulty . . ." Later he is moved to make a sudden aside: "What a chance it has been, (with what attendant organization, Hand & throat) that has made man". Monkeys might have been made "intellectual", he thought, given similar circumstances, "but almost certainly not made into man." It was a nicety of definition which his less subtle critics were later to find it difficult to match.

With a more settled structure for his ideas, he was able to think more about their ramifications, what they explained, what their significance might be, and how they might best be defined. "Three principles", he wrote grandly, "will account for all", and then set them out in a small table:

1) Grandchildren like grandfathers
2) Tendency to small change especially with physical change
3) Great fertility in proportion to support of parents

Continuity of general form, variations, and the increase in fertility that resulted from good – i.e., supportive – conditions were of primary importance in the scheme as he now proposed it. He used the word "law" a great deal as he strove to isolate specific factors in the welter of activity that made up the general process of nature. "The effect of one part being greatly developed, on another, must not be overlooked. – It makes fourth cause or law of change." And, "The existence of a 'law of organization' had better be shown . . . and all varieties must be presumed to be result of such laws."

He nagged at the problems posed by asexual reproduction, since he now based his hypothesis on the changes that might be produced in a mingling of parental characteristics. By what other method, he wondered, could new forms come into existence? "My theory only requires that organic beings propagated by gemmation* do not now undergo metamorphosis, but to arrive at their present structure they must have been propagated by sexual commerce". The mingling of parental characteristics, however, by doubling the effects of the species' predominant traits, also maintained its stability – how therefore could asexual reproduction have the same result? It was a fact, he wrote, that "throws a very great difficulty on my theory"; his solution lay in the simplicity of those forms which had continued with asexual reproduction – "This simple forms perhaps oldest in world & hence

---

* A botanical term for a form of asexual reproduction in which a small cell-group – known as a gemma – develops into a new individual. If is found most often in mosses and similar plants.

most persistent – if forms exceedingly difficult to vary, the run of chances, would prevent it varying . . ."

The opposition he might run into stimulated him to an unwonted fierceness. "I utterly deny the right to argue against my theory because it makes the world far *older* than what geologists think"; it would be no more than a repetition of what geologists themselves had had to face fifty years before. In any case, what did "older" mean in such a context – "what relation in duration of planet to our lives"? Again the note of firmness and self-confidence sounds: "Being myself a geologist, I have thus argued to myself, till I can honestly reject such false reasoning."

The *Notebook* dribbles away in a spatter of scribbled notes on the inside back cover. "Grandfathers handwriting to compare with my own", runs the last. All have been cancelled by a light scoring out. He had, it seems, filled his reservoir, his storehouse; the basic formulations of his theory, as far at least as he had been able to take them, were clear to him. Time was the ground upon which his theory stood, providing both foundation and limits. The pressure of population, constantly threatening resources, supplied the energy. Variation produced the wide spectrum of individuals which that energy selected – for survival or for death. Sexual reproduction both slowed and spread the effects of that selection, ensuring that by and large the general type was maintained. Change was therefore gradual, taking its cue from the time-scale of geology – millions and hundreds of millions of years were involved. Isolation, accelerating change, led to divergence. Thus, as circumstances slowly altered, living things were enabled to make their response of survival. That there were gaps and vulnerable silences in his theory – notably over the problem of inheritance – Darwin knew very well. If he felt that he could ignore them – though not without some nervous glances over his shoulder – it was because his hypothesis described as nothing else did the point at which living things interacted with each other and with the infinitely slow capriciousness of their surroundings.

To arrive at these conclusions Darwin had struggled for over three years with the intractable ignorance of the world. He was in advance of most other thinkers because not enough was known to make clear the ideas towards which he was struggling. What was known had not been systematized or brought under the kind of academic control which made it accessible. He read without ceasing: books, journals and pamphlets cascaded into his house. He went to hear lectures and papers read, he talked endlessly with the learned men who had become his friends. But there was no branch of science called "Evolutionary Studies", no accumulation of knowledge labelled "Genetics"; no one had gathered or predigested the material he needed, or could even be certain what that material was. The men who had written directly about the mutability of species – men like his grandfather and Lamarck – had disappointed him by the inadequacy of their facts. Others worked only in contiguous fields, at a tangent, often upon what were from his point of view irrelevancies, yet now and then producing some morsel of information he could seize on – provided he became aware of it. It was paradoxically the opponents of species change who had inadvertently done some of his work for him.

Among Darwin's most important gifts was his sharp independence of mind. It enabled him to read deeply without being influenced, to evaluate other men's conclusions by setting them beside the facts they sought to explain, and to filch from them information they had taken to be evidence for their views and use it to support his own. For Lyell he felt both friendship and profound admiration, indebted to him as he was for facts, ideas and methods; yet all this did not prevent his rejecting totally Lyell's principled objections to all mutation theories. Uniformitarianism meant for Lyell small-scale change in large-scale stasis; upon his postulated earth, nothing ever altered in any fundamental way. Darwin refused to accept this picture of a world without any development, when to have done so under the influence of Lyell's book and personality would have been more than understandable.

He read Paley with the greatest interest, and very early. Again, it would have been reasonable to suppose Paley's *Natural Theology* a primary influence so powerful that it was hardly to be surmounted. Darwin, with the judo-flick of an intellectual black belt, used the book's strength against itself. Adaptation turned out not to be the result of some limitlessly benevolent design, but the very mechanism through which natural selection was expressed. When the time came, he took from Malthus the crucial observations about how populations related to food supply, but not his depressed view of species immutably bound into their situations. For Malthus, human beings were kept from general disaster by particular tragedies – the constant culling of individuals was all that maintained some balance between people and supplies. Nothing followed from this, nor was the situation open to any fundamental alteration. By introducing the concept of variation between individuals, Darwin reshaped Malthusian pessimism into the dynamic hypothesis of natural selection.

How difficult in the prevailing convictions of the time it was to assert such independence one can hardly assess today. In *The Origin of Species* Darwin tells us "that nearly all the breeders of the various domestic animals and the cultivators of plants, with whom I have conversed, or whose treatises I have read, are firmly convinced that the several breeds to which each has attended are descended from so many aboriginally distinct species". De Candolle among others was of the same opinion. Men whose work Darwin used in the *Transmutation Notebooks* to fire his own ideas, looked back to a prehistoric diversity just as great as that to which they were accustomed. In their breeding techniques they applied principles which, as theorists, they were unable to discern, let alone proclaim. It was in the context of this general blindness that Darwin pursued his vision, unique not so much in what he saw, as in having the will to see at all.

At the same time, even when he had taken his concept so far as to justify his titling it "my theory", he was never tempted to plug the gaps in it by calling upon some vague general formula like Lamarck's developmental impulse, the innate tendency to improve. Darwin was clear about the primacy of the fact. As long as Lamarck remained attached to the factual world, as in his classificatory system, Darwin gratefully accepted the value of his work; when he departed into the insubstantial vapour of theories that described but did not explain, Darwin admired the sweep of the imagination displayed, but found himself unable to follow. For him, the only way was the painstaking route of the scientist, testing what he supposed to be the case against the reality of the natural world. It is true that sometimes the intended rigours of this method became a little blurred in practice. The line between testing the theory against the facts and finding facts to support the theory was hard to define and, even where defined, proved permeable. Yet Darwin, as his *Notebooks* prove, knew very well which details of biology offered immediate evidence for his views, and which presented difficulties of varying degrees. He had read widely enough to discover that the observations of some scientists supported him, while others appeared to refute him. In such circumstances, he did not cheat. Opposition had to be faced and defeated, difficulties had to be overcome, possible objections met. He did not ignore the awkward fact or the contradictory opinion. Certainly he tried to meet them on the basis of his theory, but no one, faced with the varied complexity of the world, can attempt to explain it without a working hypothesis. There is no other way to decide what is relevant and what can be discarded. The scientist, however, modifies that hypothesis as the evidence he gathers begins to operate upon it. Darwin, as the *Notebooks* show, changed his ideas several times, despite an underlying constancy.

From now on, it was the search for facts to illustrate species change that was to occupy his time. The *Notebooks* show how farflung his enquiries already were. Quotations from books and papers fill them, small insights gained in private conversations, information sent by correspondents, material culled from his own observations. In the years to come, these would continue to be drawn in, to lie in that gargantuan storehouse of the mind beside the harvest of the *Beagle* years and the ideas, casked and pleasantly fermenting, that he had worked out in the *Transmutation Notebooks*. Beside them, too, waiting to add their dimension to the totality Darwin was constructing, were the perceptions and intuitions about mankind with which, in the previous eighteen months, he had filled the "M" and "N" Notebooks.

4

For many, Lyell, as we have seen, among them, there was a splendour about the human mind that lifted the entire species out of the ordinary systems of nature. Whatever might be true of other living organisms was not necessarily true of humans – they were different. Gods and angels were of the general order they belonged to, not squid or antelopes, or even the humanoid orang-utan. It was mind that made the essential difference, even for those who would have no truck with soul. Mind led to fantasy, to the imagination; it led to intellect and the lofty speculations of philosophy; it led, above all, to self-awareness, to the individual's sense of himself and the anguish of solitude and expectation of mortality that resulted.

These are, of course, the concepts of the Romantics. Darwin compiled his *Notebooks* in the 1830s, at a time when England, like the rest of Europe, saw a whole generation posture and declaim in the fashionable aftermath of the mighty dead: Keats, Shelley, Coleridge very shortly, but Byron above all. Scientists of the period were not immune from the prevailing modes of thought and feeling. Certain of them, indeed, attempted to create a synthesis between these ideas and those of science and Christianity; as Professor W.F. Cannon has pointed out, Sedgwick and Whewell were among the foremost in this group.

Darwin knew very well the arguments that supported the conviction such men had that humanity was special within the general scheme of the Creation. Human beings had not not only reasoning power, they also had profound feelings unique in being elicited by abstractions – love of beauty, for example, or a passion for right conduct, a knowledge of and admiration for the good. No purely materialist scheme, simply following the physical clues that linked mankind to other animal forms, was likely to satisfy critics basing themselves on such opinions. They took their stand on the innate qualities, on the emotions and the moral sense with which the human race was imbued, or which, even where it shared them with other mammals, existed in men and women at a unique pitch. No universal outline of species development could be called that if it excluded human beings; but no theory dealing with human beings could exclude these rarified attributes. Indeed, they were precisely – even when vague in themselves – what made human beings human.

Darwin, therefore, was faced with the task of trying to understand qualities of which the point was, in the Romantics' litany, that they were beyond understanding. It was that transcendent element which lifted mankind to a different and higher plane. If they proved to be understandable after all, elements in a comprehensible scheme, then the sublime part of the human being would be whisked away. It was this that forced Darwin into a position of irreducible materialism, quite as much as his doubts about a creator-god. He had to find a place in his hypothesis for the emotions, the instincts, the faculty of reason, the ability to love, for all the abstract apparatus through which our existence is both complicated and elevated. He spent some time on this effort, as we have seen, in the *Transmutation Notebooks*. But it was in the "M" and "N" Notebooks that he took up the challenge with all the energy and intellectual intensity of which he was capable.

By their nature, such books are not sequential. Thoughts, impressions, questions, speculations and reactions to other people's writings tug and pull the thread in all directions. Yet there is such a thread, for what Darwin was investigating here was the development, the continuity, of consciousness across the whole spectrum of life. How habit was linked to instinct and instinct to reason, the inter-specific similarities in the emotions and how they were expressed, the merging of memory into daydream and daydream into dream – he tried to cover the whole range of human conjecture from psychology to metaphysics.

He did not exclude even the vegetable world from his enquiries. He wondered, for example, whether plants understood cause and effect – "they have habitual action which depends on such confidence when does such notion commence?" – and how their memories, if any, operated – "must be association, – a certain round of actions take place every day, & closing of the leaves, comes on from want of stimulus, after certain other actions, & hence become associated with them." To establish this linkage "will help my theory of sensitive Plants", he added. If the natural world was one, and man was a part of the natural world, then his faculties were not unique to him, but might be found in rudimentary form in any living organism. Decades later, he was to publish his work on insectivorous, climbing and twining plants, setting his suppositions upon a more scientific basis.

To chart the underlying continuity of animals and humans, on the psychological as well as the physical plane, Darwin relied on similarities in their involuntary reactions and expressions. Yawning, smiling, pouting, the grimaces of fury and fear, all seemed to him evidence that supported his unifying vision. In fact, his catalogue of similarities goes only a little further than the anthropomorphic exclamations of a crowd in a menagerie, yet he could see what he could not wholly explain, and what he saw made him certain of the connections between the species. He summed up his conclusion: "The whole argument of expression more than any other point of structure takes its value from connexion with mind, (to show hiatus in mind not saltus between man & Brutes) no one can doubt this connexion . . . Nearly all will exclaim, your arguments are good but look at the immense difference between man, forget the use of language & judge only by what you see. Compare the Fuegian & Ourang-Outang, & dare to say difference so great . . ." Unity, continuance, merging, development – the common attributes of living creatures blurred the textbook rigidities of species and showed him the links he sought.

The slow rise of animal intelligence led him to consider its means of expression, language. "Probably, language commenced in some necessary connexion between things & voice, as roaring for lion, etc etc . . . crying yawning laughing being necessary sounds . . . not produced by will but by corporeal structure". How far along the developmental trail, he wondered, could one trace the beginnings of communication? In the human species, "the possibility of poets describing gentle things in gentle language, & vice versa, – almost proves that at earliest times there must have been intimate connection between *sound* & language". (Darwin may have been influenced in these views by the theories of Hensleigh Wedgwood, who, attempting in his etymological works to establish the origins of language, suggested that it may have derived from inarticulate sounds. Regarded as extremely plausible today, this idea was met with derision by the experts of Hensleigh's era.)

Darwin, however, resisted the over-simple conviction that development must of its nature always take an upward direction, despite the fact that so many of the most significant human attributes seemed to have come into being only after millennia of slow improvement: "Man's intellect is not become superior to that of the Greeks (which seems opposed to progressive development) . . . Man's intellect might well deteriorate." And he added a parenthesis that showed once more how clear he was about the difference between change and advancement. "In my theory there is no absolute tendency to progression, excepting from favourable circumstances!"

Yet mankind's characteristic qualities – its moral sense, for example, and its awareness of beauty – were of necessity fitted into the general developmental context provided by Darwin's ideas. The Dark Ages, which he cites as evidence for his doubts about progress, were after all no more than a minor stumble in humanity's long climb. Awareness of good and evil was an essential element in Man's cultural inheritance, and it had grown in acuteness and significance as the centuries had passed. Nevertheless, he felt that "one can remonstrate with a dog, & make him ashamed of himself, in manner quite different from *fear*", a fact which may be linked with an earlier observation on the origins of wickedness. "Men having some instincts as revenge and anger, which experience shows it must for his happiness to check ... with lesser intellect they might be necessary & no doubt were preservative, & are now, like all other structures slowly vanishing ... Our descent, then, is the origin of our evil passions!! – The Devil under form of Baboon is our grandfather!" But if the moral sense was accounted for, then religion necessarily followed – everything had to be accommodated within Darwin's final theory. He therefore followed up these conjectures, a little later, by wondering whether moral systems arose "from our enlarged capacity" being guided in ways as yet obscure by "strong instinctive sexual, parental & social instincts", and then went on: "? May not idea of God arise from our confused idea of 'ought', joined with necessary notion of 'causation', in reference to this 'ought', as well as the works of the whole world." Not for the first time, Darwin was prepared to turn accepted opinion upside down: if our feeling for right conduct had instinctive roots, he argued, it would precede any Voice we might invent to proclaim what that feeling enjoined. If the need to invent such a voice were coupled with our need to discover causes for the phenomena surrounding us, we would have created a god responsible both for the external world and the inner self-commandment. It was a sizeable speculation to fill one short sentence.

In a similar way he tried to search out the beginnings of our aesthetic sense. He scribbled into a consideration of how our idea of beauty came into existence, the note that "male glow worm doubtless admires female, showing no connection with male figure". This led him to the conclusion that our feeling for the beautiful was not, as a sense, under our control and that thus it must fall into the realm of ordinary natural development. Academic notions of aesthetics, like those advanced by Sir Joshua Reynolds, might explain why one culture disagreed in its standards of beauty from another, "but it does not explain the *feeling* in any one man." Darwin made his own opinion plain: "Beauty is instinctive feeling, & thus cuts the Knot."

It is clear from his note about the glow-worm that Darwin saw the aesthetic sense as closely linked to sexual selection. As in the third *Transmutation Notebook*, written at about the same time, there seems a slightly increased emphasis placed on sexual matters, seriously though these are always treated, and this perhaps reflects an inner preoccupation as the time of his marriage drew closer. But he saw that sexual feelings and the ways in which these were expressed cut across species lines, and expressed this recognition with un-Victorian directness:

> A dog *whines*, & so does man. – dogs laugh for joy ... Many of actions, as
> hiccough & yawn are probably merely coorganic as connexion of mammae &

womb. – We need not feel so much surprise at male animals smelling vagina of females. – when it is recollected that smell of one's own pud* not disagree. – Ourang outang at Zoology Gardens touched pud of young males & smells its fingers. Seeing a dog & horse & man yawn, makes me feel how all animals built on one structure.

Sexual desire, and the means of its expression, just like – mysteriously – yawning, linked all mammals and were thus, perhaps, an indication of some far distant, common progenitor.

If one of the characteristic attributes of human beings was the faculty of reason, Darwin's attempts to understand it were crucial to his establishing a comprehensive theory of human development. As a result, he found himself interested in the examples of unreason, of insanity, with which his father's practice had made him partially familiar. He realized that there were several varieties of mental illness, although he had no labels to attach to the clusters of symptoms he could discern. He examined what it meant for "the brain having whole train of thoughts, feeling & perception separate from the ordinary state of mind", linked this with the unconsciousness of habitial behaviour and with the case of a certain Dr. Ash, who had "struggled as it were with a second & unreasonable man". It was as though Darwin were stretching towards concepts of the unconscious that were not seriously proposed until the end of the century.

There are moments, too, when he seems to anticipate the idea of a race memory, one of Jung's favourite concepts. He noted various examples of people remembering in senility the songs of their childhood and then commented, "Now if memory of a tune & words can thus lie dormant, during a whole life time, quite unconsciously of it, surely memory from one generation to another also without consciousness, as instincts are, is not so very wonderful". It is clear that he is attempting to understand instincts and is using memory as an analogy to help him – an example of how limited the vocabulary at his disposal was – but his conclusion is not vastly different from that of Dr. Jung. He returned to the same concept weeks later when, early in the "N" Notebook, he wrote, "The existence of taste in human mind is to me clear evidence, of the general ideas of our ancestors being impressed on us."

These ideas led him on inevitably to consider the age-old problem of free will, and to arrive at a solidly materialist conclusion: "I verily believe will & chance are synonymous. – Shake ten thousand grains of sand together & one will be uppermost, – so in thoughts, one will rise according to law". So rigorously mechanistic a view made nothing whatsoever of the supposed uniqueness of the human situation, and it is therefore not surprising to find

---

* *Pud* – his contraction of the word "pudenda".

him drawing conclusions that eliminated all difference between the psychological plane and the physical: "To study Metaphysics, as they have always been studied appears to me like puzzling at astronomy without mechanics – experience shows the problem of the mind cannot be solved by attacking the citadel itself. – the mind is function of body. – we must bring some *stable* foundation to argue from." There is a slightly condescending air about the last sentence as he dismisses with a wave of the hand legions of head-in-air metaphysicians.

In a sort of triumphant aside, however, written in August, 1838, Darwin had already proclaimed his mastery over metaphysics. Locke, too, he implied, had been or was about to be outstripped. He wrote, "Origin of man now proved, – Metaphysics must flourish. – He who understand baboon would do more toward metaphysics than Locke". While this seems hard on the seventeenth-century philosopher, a pragmatic, commonsensical sort of thinker, it is clear that sudden excitement had whirled Darwin off into a mood of irresistible optimism. Diffidence dropped from him: he – "who understand baboon" – would make the underlying unity of all life plain for everyone to realize and so would make the real truth about that enigmatic creature, the human being, finally accessible. In the identity of all animals lay the ultimate secrets – the true roots of the passions, the well-springs of behaviour, the nature of free will and the origins of mind. Whoever unravelled the connection between the species would reap the harvest – a new knowledge, wider and deeper than any that man had possessed before.

It is as if, for a moment, there glittered before Darwin the ancient, inexhaustible temptation of Faust. But ambition for Darwin was circumscribed, precisely delineated: he wanted to be a discoverer, and for his discoveries he wanted the respect and admiration of his peers. Not flesh nor place nor gold could move him. He was Faustian only in one thing – his constant passion, patiently obeyed, to know what was true about the world.

5

While his intellectual life was continuing at this intense and demanding level, Darwin was establishing with Emma the undramatic but fulfilling happiness of their marriage. Certainly Charles, sentimental in an uncomplicated way, seems never to have questioned the serenity of their relations. There is perhaps something too swift and easy in his adjustment: it is as though he had willed into being something he badly needed. But Emma knew very well what shape he wanted his life to take. She seems very quickly to have blossomed into one of those architects of Victorian domesticity who built around their husbands great bastions of kindness, concern and respect, thus tending their pride, providing their comforts and ensuring their security.

Her letters present Emma Darwin as sensible, humorous, affectionate, intelligent without being in the least intellectual, firm of character and of a fundamental, self-aware honesty. In editing her letters after her death, her daughter Henrietta painted a fuller portrait. Naturally, she remembered her mother, who lived into her late eighties, only in middle and old age, but one imagines that by the time of her marriage Emma's essential characteristics were already fixed. Only the increasing gravity of her later years seems to have made a profound alteration, obscuring the quirky, slightly sardonic humour and light-heartedness of her youth. Indeed, during the last three or four decades of her life, people who first met her were often overawed, and even rendered nervous, by her controlled reserve. Perhaps the maternal role into which Darwin's needs had thrust her, his frequent ill health and the long struggle to validate theories which she neither fully understood nor wholly approved of, exerted a combined pressure which did to some extent remould her.

However, the issue of religion had weighed heavily with her from the beginning. It was the only one in which she and Darwin were so clearly ranged on different sides. In his *Autobiography*, Darwin tells us that he too, during the 1830s and 1840s, "was led to think much about religion" – to him the Old Testament had by then become unreliable as history and misleading as the basis of Christianity. It related to an older, more barbaric view of divinity than that offered by the New Testament – but the Gospels, too, with their reliance on miracle and the increasing likelihood that they had been written long after the events they described, could not easily be accepted as stemming from divine revelation. The morality of the New Testament was certainly beautiful, but literal belief in the events it related posed problems for him. "Thus disbelief crept over me at a slow rate, but was at last complete . . ."

Soon after their marriage, Emma had written Darwin a long statement on the subject, a letter which he kept all his life and, as he made clear, read many times. The paper is old; the folds in which it has lain for a century and a half are stained and brittle, but the words are as clear as Emma's round hand can make them. She wanted, she said, "to feel that while you are acting conscientiously and sincerely wish and trying to find out the truth, you cannot be wrong", but this was a comfort she could not always find. He was so single-minded in pursuing his scientific goals, other ideas tended to be discarded as mere interruptions, and he was thus unable to give his attention to both sides of the question. Then there was the fact that Erasmus had led the way towards scepticism – "is it not likely to have made it easier to you and to have taken off some of that dread fear which the feeling of doubting first gives . . . May not the habit in scientific pursuits of believing nothing till it is proved, influence your mind too much in other things which cannot be proved in the same way, and which if true are likely to be above our comprehension." The matter was of the profoundest importance to her, for in giving up revelation there was a danger that one might cast off "what has been done for your benefit as well as for that of all the world and which ought to make you still more careful, perhaps even fearful lest you should not have taken all the pains you could to judge truly."

She summoned up that fair-mindedness which seems to have marked all debate among Wedgwoods and Darwins. "I do not know whether this is arguing as if one side were true and the other false, which I meant to avoid, but I think not." They had obviously talked about the relation of belief to morality, because she went on, "I do not quite agree with you in what you once said that luckily there were no doubts as to how one ought to act. I think prayer is an instance to the contrary, in one case it is a positive duty and perhaps not in the other." That "perhaps" suggests that Darwin's scepticism had not after all gone very far – or, possibly, that he had not yet confessed how far it had actually gone. Emma went on, "But I daresay you meant in actions which concern others and then I agree with you almost if not quite."

She wanted, she said, no reply – her satisfaction came from writing what she felt; when she spoke to him on these subjects, "I cannot say exactly what I wish to say, and I know you will have patience with your own dear wife. Don't think that it is not my affair and that it does not much signify to me. Everything that concerns you concerns me and I should be most unhappy if I thought we did not belong to each other for ever. I am rather afraid my own dear Nigger will think I have forgotten my promise not to bother him, but I am sure he loves me, and I cannot tell him how happy he makes me and how dearly I love him and thank him for all his affection which makes the happiness of my life more and more every day."

Darwin, it seems, had briefly extended his earlier conceit about becoming a "happy slave" in marriage into the nickname "Nigger"; this humble apellation had however, concealed a reality in which Emma found it necessary to promise "not to bother him" – by which she meant, presumably, not unleashing her certainties to harass his doubts. He had written, in the margin of her letter, "When I am dead, know that many times, I have kissed and cryed over this", and signed it with his initials. Without doubt the fact that his work might distress Emma caused him some anguish and confusion; on the other hand, her convictions did not for a moment halt his progress towards the quiet, undemonstrative atheism at which he eventually arrived. Science had its own imperatives and, however regretfully, he was never able to deny them. He had all his life a deep affection and deeper need for Emma, but when it came to what he thought true, he searched for understanding, clarity and proof. The obfuscations, as he thought them, of religion, even when reinforced by the convictions of his wife, and even at the cost of her profound unhappiness, he could not bring himself to accept as truth. He did, however, read as she had requested in that early letter, the selected verses from St. John's Gospel, so earning Emma's gratitude: "To see you in earnest on the subject will be my greatest comfort & that I am sure you are".

What seems never to have altered was her naturalness, her unaffected response to the life around her. She was always an immediate, spontaneous person, with an unselfishness founded on a childhood spent in a large, happy, and endlessly reasonable family. It was this, too, that gave her a continuing ability to sympathize with others, and especially the young – she must have been in many ways an ideal mother. Small things delighted her – flowers, birds, some tiny domestic incident, a view, a flash of sunlight. Like her husband, she had no gift for introspection; with those inner depths unexamined, she was free – again like Charles – to leap to waiting conclusions. Unlike him, however, she had no scientific ideal to give her ballast, and was easily bored. The meticulous work with which he attempted to prove his insights held no attractions for her; she was hardly prepared to hear even two sides of a question.

Unaffected herself, she responded to simplicity in others; she probably found elaboration tedious. Much of life seemed to her self-evident; one can imagine that her religious disagreements with Darwin baffled as much as distressed her. But she needed his easy warmth, shallow in some ways though that might have been, to counterbalance her rather self-contained nature. The Darwins were, on the whole, more exuberant and eccentric than the Wedgwoods, and certainly more demonstrative, so that, although she was always pleased by his expressions of affection for her, she found it difficult to offer him her own. What she provided, more importantly, was calmness and strength. She was what she was, without pretence or that maternal coquetry which puts the love of children on constant trial. She could be trusted, always and without question, for level-headed, unstinting support, untarnished by sentimentalism or meaningless gush. Her very reserve reinforced the impression of reliability she gave, that certain distance which she preserved between herself and the world allowing no one, not even her sons, to consider her for one moment negligible. (Her daughter remembered her saying, "I do not feel my sons are my sons, only young men with whom I happen to be intimate" – not the remark of a woman destined to become the object of filial contempt.) Her lack of pretence made her almost invulnerable – however sacred a cow might be to others, if she disliked it she either said so or ignored it. She tried to enter in some measure into Darwin's work, found she could not and ceased the attempt. "I am afraid this is very wearisome to you", he said during a lecture. "No more than all the rest," she replied, placidly crushing.

Over the years, she clearly became the emotional base upon which Darwin rested his entire life. He gave his external, physical self over to her. There is no suggestion that other women ever caught his interest, or that he for a single moment felt constrained by his marriage. On the contrary, he retreated into it as into a citadel. With its walls around him, he was free to turn inward into his own mind, there to pursue to their conclusion the ideas and theories which, in the years just before and after his wedding, whirled and danced their compelling patterns in his brain. The happy paradox of his condition was that, the more securely he was anchored by Emma's selfless strength, the freer he became. Long before the question of their being man and wife had even been thought of, they had developed the habit of friendship. Their ties to each other were linked to childhood and the very beginnings of memory. They had a common history, a joint tradition. It is hard to think their relationship a passionate one, but it was happy, and the happiness had deep roots.

Darwin himself remains in many ways a mysterious figure. The paragraph in which he explained to Emma his increasing love of solitude is almost the only passage of genuine introspection in his writings. He offered to the world a self that turned away all controversy and pre-empted all criticism. He concealed the firmness of his purpose behind the pliability of his manner. He was always ready with a nostalgic protestation, but it was the friends who were useful to him whom he saw: Henslow, Lyell, Hooker a little later. He was warm and generous, yet careful enough to keep account books in which he noted the spending of every halfpenny. He was always disarmingly friendly and affectionate, but, as with his marriage, one detects elements of calculation in his behaviour that hint at inner steel.

In the two notebooks concerned with psychology that Darwin began in 1838 – the "M" and "N" Notebooks – he sometimes, as we have seen, used himself as specimen and experimental subject. He was, after all, the one creature whose inner processes he was uniquely qualified to chart. It may not be entirely fanciful, therefore, to see in such entries a clue to the kind of man Darwin actually was at this time.

One perhaps inconsequential aspect of his mind that strikes one is how important vision was to him. He was, of course, first and foremost, an observer; what he thought was based upon what he saw. But it is interesting to realize that he was among those people who respond to music by creating images in the mind; perhaps this explains the pleasure it brought to him, almost tone-deaf though he was. Singing affected him more directly, making "his blood run cold". But he was affected by the symmetry of forms – "this gives beauty to a single tree", he wrote – and by the natural elegance of perspective.

As a result, a panorama would rouse his imagination rather like a piece of music. Memories, snatches of poetry, recollections of other views would crowd into his mind, while his intellect would attempt a geologist's analysis of structure. He would look up at the trees and see them as great colonies of creatures, "great compound animals united by wonderful & mysterious manner". Even the geology would be transmuted, rendered marvellous by the imagination – "land covered with ocean, former animals, slow force cracking surface etc truly poetical".

It is no wonder that he noted in himself a tendency to reverie and daydream. He thought this useful, leading as it sometimes did to harder, more sequential thought. Such imaginative constructions were by their nature insubstantial, and so were distinguishable from the true thought they sometimes led to, based as that was upon recoverable premises buttressed by notes, papers and references. Yet Darwin knew that "such castles in the air are highly advantageous", and it is clear that in his own inventiveness he shuttled between the two states of mind. One can almost see him, at times dreamy and abstracted, walking perhaps in Regent's Park or slumped in a comfortable chair, at others intent, filled with purpose, notebooks and papers about him, reference books open, pen busy, working his way towards some wished-for, half-anticipated conclusion.

This habit of daydreaming seems to have been one way in which he controlled an inner anger of which he was surprisingly conscious. He depicted himself, "thinking over somebody who has, perhaps, slightly injured me, plotting speeches . . . From habit the feeling of anger must be directed against somebody." He had irrational furies – he recalled one that overcame him when, very tired one evening, he was listening to the piano – and at other times felt anger so overwhelming that it drove him to involuntary movement: "When a man is in a passion he put himself stiff, & walks hard . . . I noticed this by perceiving myself skipping when wanting not to feel angry." A little later he referred to his "wish to improve my temper . . .", as though this were a very familiar ambition.

Within a few years of his return from the *Beagle* voyage, Darwin began to experience the symptoms of the chronic ill health that was to constrain all the rest of his life. As yet, these bouts of illness – headaches, nausea, vomiting, eczema – were infrequent. Yet during these attacks he was seized with profound anxieties, although reason told him these were groundless. He would awaken terror-stricken in the night, then try to reason himself back to serenity. At times, too, he had periods of depression – though he noted, somewhat inexplicably, that this, like involuntary feelings of anger, gave "strength & comfort to the body". Intense mental effort brought on instant headaches, though lighter reading or conversation would relieve these: he noted that tales by Dickens or "allowing my mind to skip from subject to subject as quick as it chose" had a therapeutic effect. By the time of his marriage, however, such headaches were clearly playing a depressingly noticeable part in his life.

Marriage, of course, was Darwin's induction to a life of overt and sanctioned sexuality. So reticent was he on this subject, in the circumspect manner of the times, that it is hard to consider this aspect of his character at all. He was uxorious, had a full complement of children and remained faithful: perhaps little more needs to be said. Yet it is apparent from his entries at and just after the time of his marriage, he felt impelled to consider various aspects of sexuality with an intensity he showed nowhere else. In the late Spring of 1839 he noted, "I often have (as a boy) wondered why *all abnormal* sexual actions or even impulses (where sensations of individuals are same as in normal cases) are held in abhorrence. It is because instincts to women not followed . . ." This is his only reference to any childhood interest in sexual behaviour and if he was indeed a boy when he wondered this, then it seems most likely to refer to conventional attitudes to masturbation. That there was some homosexuality at Shrewsbury School is also more than probable – it is hard to believe that the boys of the 1820s were so different from those of a century later. For a boy, given to daydreams and a delight in solitude, masturbation would be a natural pleasure, while as a boarder he would have known, through rumour and testament, if not direct experience, of the sexual activities of his schoolmates.

In August, 1838, while trying to discover significant similarities between human and animal behaviour, he wrote, "Stallion licking udders of mare strictly analogous to men's affect for women's breasts" – proof not only that men were pleasantly aware of the female bosom long before Hollywood and advertising agencies exploited the fact, but also that Darwin understood this very well. In September of the same year, less than two months before he proposed and a month after he had wanted to do so but refrained, he dreamed "that a person was hung & came to life, & then made many jokes about not having run away & having faced death like a hero, & then I had some confused idea showing scar behind (instead of front) (having changed hanging into his head cut off) as kind of wit showing he had honourable wounds." It is foolhardy to take such images and try and hammer them into immediate sense, yet to interpret this in sexual terms is tempting. Professor Gruber thinks the dream refers to Darwin's work, approaching success being heralded by the idea of resurrection. In a man contemplating marriage, limbering up to ask his "overwhelming question", a dream like this – experienced as witty, shot through with laughter, dealing with a coming to life, demonstrating a scar mysteriously moved from in front to behind and concerned with some not very serious encounter with death (a frequent synonym in myth and language for orgasm) – almost forces one to consider it as referring to his sexual hopes and anxieties. Perhaps it is to the point that Darwin's next entry reads, "What is the Philosophy of Shame & Blushing?".

Two weeks after Emma had accepted him, he was noting, "Sexual desire makes saliva flow", then adding on the next line, "yes, *certainly*", a moment of unscientific enthusiasm he attempted to rescue with "curious association", written immediately below. A few lines later, however, he was back upon his preferred track, suggesting that such salivating pointed to "our distant ancestors having been like *dogs* to bitches", and ending the passage with a boast: "How comes such an association in man – it is a bare fact, on my theory intelligible".

A few days later, Darwin jotted down some thoughts on the effects of the mind on the body. He considered blushing, then dropped in a quite different observation – that "like erection shyness is certainly very much connected with thinking of oneself". He saw, too, the connection between blushing and sexuality, even if he did not go to the Freudian lengths of "displacement from below upwards" in order to make that connection even closer. A few lines further on, however, he returned to his previous illustration, certainly an apposite one: "If you fear you shall not have e—n, or wish extraordinarily to have, you wont". This sounds as though based on his own experience, yet there is nothing in the known details of his life that allows one to presume an occasion in which he wished to have an erection, feared he would not, and in fact failed to have one. Was he following hearsay? The sentence sounds so personal, so directly knowledgeable, one suspects he was not. And it is succeeded at once by, "No surer way to blush, than particularly to wish not to do so". It is almost like an outline for one of those small tragedies of virility and masculine pride that most men have in their secret histories.

The year turned. In four weeks, Darwin was to be married. He wrote, "A man shivers from fear, sublimity, sexual ardour." It was the beginning of January. On the 6th, he added, "What passes in a man's mind, when he says he loves a person – do not the features pass before him, marked with the habitual expression of those emotions, which make us love him, or her. – it is blind feeling, something like sexual feelings." Then the marriage took place. It was the end of sexual references in the Notebooks.

One can make of these entries what one pleases. Darwin's main purpose in scribbling then down was scientific; it is his books that are the true progeny of the emotions that drove him to fill those pages. Unspoken in the humility and gratitude with which he received her accepting him as husband, implied in the recurring description of himself as "brute", one senses the sexual "demand", that physical transaction in which the wife gives in, as graciously as she can and the husband, almost despite himself, struggles briefly for his own satisfaction. Convulsed by guilt, he afterwards thanks her for permitting such violation, and lives out his sexual life in a mixture of resentment and contrition. It is unlikely that the marriage of Charles and Emma was very different from that of any other middle-class, early Victorian couple. What is apparent is that they worked out a *modus vivendi*, whatever its terms, and on the whole managed their lives happily enough.

Thus, through the Notebooks, we have at least a glimpse of the actual Darwin. He was a man of active senses, delighting in symmetry, rhythm, landscape, in smells and sounds and colours. Despite the intensity of his thought, there was nothing arid in his attitude to life. He had, too, a clear, untormented approach to sexuality: it was one fact among others determining or modifying the behaviour of advanced organisms. He had a vivid and easily aroused imagination, and turned this to his intellectual advantage, allowing his thoughts their first form in the easy shapelessness of reverie, his "castles in the air". He was, for all his impetuosity and warmth of feeling, capable of an almost frightening objectivity, regarding his most intense emotions with a laboratory detachment. He was, at least during these years, almost preternaturally aware: no detail, no passing question or hint of an answer, was too small or fleeting for him to seize on.

His introspection was entirely in the service of his work. Not for a moment does he seem to have been interested in elucidating who and what he was for its own sake – and that, too, in its negative way, adds to our definition of him. Another absence was any reference to the characters of literature or drama; a different man might have found exemplars of the ideas he sought in the classics or Shakespeare, the Bible or Jane Austen. That other nineteenth century sage, Sigmund Freud, plundered mythology for analogies: not so Darwin. He was happy to confine himself to his chosen reality. Even the politics which had so interested him in his youth hardly ever figured in his letters or, one must assume, his conversation – although this was a time when the vociferous protesters of Chartism were at their most active, when Peel became Prime Minister, when inflation, bad harvests and thoughtless management led to the collapse of jerry-built railway companies and insecurely founded banks, when Mehemet Ali was again challenging the Ottoman Empire abroad while at home Daniel O'Connell's misleadingly ferocious oratory was simplifying the complexities of the Irish Question. Not one of these various great issues and events was even fleetingly reflected in anything that Darwin wrote.

His timescale had been adjusted to the aeons of geology. It was the history of the entire planet, and of the life it bore, that now fascinated him; contemporary events appear to have diminished into little more than the inconsequential chatter of gossips. His social life revolved about his scientific interests, his private life about his marriage, his intellectual life about the theories that, still in careful secrecy, he was excitedly developing. He had begun his withdrawal into the encapsulated life, guarded, self-contained and dedicated, within which he was to do the work that would startle the world and alter forever its most fundamental concepts.

6

---ᘛᘛᘛ---

In the distance, tragedy darkened other lives: Caroline's first baby died. It was a reminder of the constant chances of mortality that in those days lurked about the nursery. We think that such close and continuous attendance by death must have hardened people, but Emma's sister Elizabeth reported Jos, overcome with grief, frequently having to leave the room, weeping, and Caroline made ill by misery. The news shocked Emma, but she, after all, had an entire new life to live. Shopping, she bought a satin morning dress in a dark claret, one of the muddy colours then in vogue. A piano arrived, a wedding present from her father, splendid and mellow in its mahogany case. In return, the ailing Jos wished for a portrait of her; the merits of various artists were discussed and in the end George Richmond was chosen. From his deft drawing she looks out at us, ringleted, open-faced, with something just a touch mocking and sardonic in the faint smile with which she favours us. The face is attractive and intelligent, too broad in the jaw-line for beauty, but marked with strength and honesty.

Charles sat for the same artist. He gazes down the decades with a hint of suspicion. His shadowed eyes keep secrets. Under the receding hairline, the brow dominates the face. The mouth is guarded, serious; prepared to smile, but for the moment held firm, almost pinched. His hands clutch each other, noticeably unrelaxed. His left leg, crossed over the right, is drawn across his body as though to protect him from our regard. He looks clever, but uneasy, and his warmth and charm are for the moment in abeyance. Emma, however, was happy. Living with Charles, she reported to Elizabeth, "I am cockered up and spoilt as much as heart can wish and I *do* think . . . that there is not so affectionate an individual as the one in question to be found anywhere else. After this candid and impartial opinion I say no more."

Prints and drawings relieved the awful azure of the drawing room walls. Every evening, Emma played the piano for Charles's pleasure (was it on one of these occasions that fury so inexplicably seized him?). The servant, Edward, decked in new livery, served at their first dinner party, its foundation a turkey. Erasmus teased him – their meal was only an imitation of his own "and certainly the likeness was very striking", admitted Emma. "But when the plum-pudding appeared he knocked under, and confessed himself conquered very humbly."

Henslow and his wife came on a visit. At Darwin's table he renewed his friendship with Lyell and met for the first time Robert Brown; the two botanists chattered science merrily across the dinner table. A noted geologist, Dr. Fitton, could match Lyell, stratum for stratum, and Darwin must have presided happily. Below the masculine hammer-and-tongs of the naturalists, however, one hears the light feminine interventions of Mrs. Lyell and her sister Leonora, of the witty, acerbic Mrs. Henslow, who in the past had frightened Darwin, and Emma herself: did they draw the men from the parochial gravity of their own subjects, talk of babies, introduce the general topics that animated intelligent London? Was Emma able to draw on her Wedgwood experience and organize a discussion like those that had brightened the drawing room at Maer? We hear the rise and rattle of the voices, but can make out no words. Emma later described Lyell as "enough to flatten a party, as he never speaks above his breath, so that everybody keeps lowering their tone to his . . . Mrs. Henslow has a good loud, sharp voice which was a great comfort, and Mrs. Lyell has a very constant supply of talk". But of what exactly that talk consisted she gives us no hint.

Darwin fell ill again; even in that first married year of 1839, he continued ominously unwell. He and Emma abandoned giving or going to dinner parties and other gatherings – "they agree with neither of us", wrote Darwin to Fox in October. He was probably deceived in this, since in her early letters from Gower Street Emma had given no sign of not enjoying visitors and visiting. But they both liked walking up and down their thirty yards of garden and breathing fresh air, increasingly clouded though it was by the coal-smoke of a million fires. Charles wrote to his sister Caroline of "the extreme quietude in which we are living . . . we see nothing, do nothing & hear nothing, & this to my mind is the perfection of life. – I find I cannot stand going out in the Evening – I can just last through the 24 hours if I am quite quiet after dinner. – I can barely stand the Hensleigh's & Erasmus." He described his usual day for her:

> Get up punctually at seven leaving Emma dreadful sleepy & comfortable, set to work after the first torpid feeling is over, and write . . . till ten; go up stairs about half an hour, eat our breakfast, sit in our armchairs, – and I watch the clock as the hand travels sadly too fast to half past eleven – Then to my study & work till 2 o clock luncheon time: Emma generally comes & does a little work in my room & sits as quiet as a mouse. – After luncheon I generally have some job in some part of the town & Emma walks with me part of the way – dinner at six – & very good dinners we have – Sit in apoplectic state, with slight snatches of reading, till half past seven – tea, lesson of German, occasionally a little music & a little reading & then bed-time makes a charming close to the day. – I fear poor Emma must find her life rather monotonous . . .

At the end of the year, the Darwins' first child was born. Delighted, Emma's mother, still with six difficult years of life ahead of her, wrote to offer congratulations: "It cost me a good cry, but such tears are precious and I was very happy while shedding them". She guessed that the boy's name would be Robert; Emma and Charles instead chose William Erasmus. Elizabeth was with Emma when the child was born – "He is a sort of grandchild of hers," wrote Emma to her Aunt Jessie, and it is true that Elizabeth, the elder by fifteen years, had become more mother than sister to her. Even after her marriage Elizabeth had congratulated her with the curious remark, "what mother ever was not rejoiced at a daughter's making a happy marriage", as though this was in fact their relationship.

Now Emma had to divide her attention between her new baby and her sick husband. She described the former to her aunt: "He has very dark blue eyes and a pretty, small mouth, his nose I will not boast of, but it is very harmless as long as he is a baby." Like Charles, she seems to have been capable of clarity over even the most emotion-charged facts. As for Darwin, he improved slowly; Emma responded to his need for her with an almost suspect delight. He was "not like the rest of the Darwins, who will not say how they really are; but he always tells me how he feels & never wants to be alone, but continues just as warmly affectionate as ever, so that I feel I am a comfort to him".

That Darwin, despite his illnesses, was happy becomes evident when one sees the lightness of his mood in his early letters to Emma. In April, 1840, he visited Shrewsbury again; the account of his rail journey to the West is almost worthy of Dickens.

> In my carriage there was rather an elegant female, like a thin Lady Alderson, but so virtuous that I did not venture to open my mouth to her. She came with some female friend, also a lady, & talked at the door of the carriage in so loud a voice that we all listened with silent admiration. It was chiefly about family prayers, and how she always had them at half-past 10 not to keep the servants up. She then charged her friend to write to her either on Saturday night or Monday morning, Sunday being omitted in the most marked manner . . . As soon as we started our virtuous female pulled out of her pocket a religious tract & a very thick pencil. She then took off her gloves & began reading with great earnestness, & marking the best passages . . . Her next neighbour was an old gentleman with a portentuously purple nose, who was studying a number of the *Christian Herald*, and his next neighbour was the primmest she-Quaker I have ever seen. Was not I in good company?

Emma, for all her deeply held beliefs, was evidently quite capable, in Darwin's view, of seeing how absurd such ostentatious religiosity was. Despite the laughter, however, that dark, censorious mood was spreading and, like a paralysis of the imagination, busily destroying for ever the old, robust spirit of a vanishing England.

In Shrewsbury, Darwin picked his father's medical brains for information about Emma's health, and the baby's, Dr. Robert as usual suggesting the most sensible, least alarmist courses. Alone in the big double bed at The Mount, Darwin slept badly – "in which respect," he chidingly remarked to Emma, "I have shown much more sentimentality than, it appears, you did." Throughout the year, he gathered strength and some version of his former health – in January, 1841, he wrote to Fox, "I was at one time in despair & expected to pass my whole life as a miserable, useless valetudinarian, but I have now better hopes of myself . . ." Nevertheless, he lived, even in London, like a recluse, seeing very few people outside his immediate family and even with them keeping his conversations short and undemanding.

In March, Emma's second child, a girl named Annie, was born. That summer they went to Maer, while Darwin with his son, William, visited Shrewsbury; soon, as he was quick to write to Emma, Charles "became bad & shivery, wh. ended in sharp headache & disordered stomach (but was not sick) & was very uncomfortable in bed till ten. – I was very very desolate & forlorn without my own Titty's sympathy & missed you cruelly." (In the early days of their marriage, "Titty" was the nickname he gave Emma.) The next day, however, he was "pretty brisk & enjoying myself". Once again, Darwin, with hypochondriacal diligence, mined his father's expertise for information about his family's health, and Dr. Robert gave it willingly enough, despite having discovered a serious flaw in Charles's household: Bessy, the new maid, had not been given a cap to wear, and from the Doctor and the sisterhood there came a constant barrage of reproaches – "It looks dirty" and "She's like a grocer's maid-servant" and finally, from Dr. Robert himself, "The men will take liberties with her, if she's dressed differently from every other lady's maid". Darwin warned Emma, "If they open on you, pray do not defend yourself, for they are very hot on the subject". One feels for the moment the weighty rigidities of a society obsessed with maintaining its conventions.

During Darwin's stay, the family went through its annual accounts. Expenditure for the year had been £1,380, which was £10 less than it had been in the previous year. "Is not this marvellous, considering my father's personal expences & presents, & everything except his children's allow-ances, are included in this?" What makes such an expenditure even more marvellous is that Dr. Robert's account book shows his investment income for that year at £7,178, a figure one would have to multiply by at least ten in order to calculate today's equivalent. Anyone spending ten thousand with an income of seventy thousand would think himself well on the clever side of prudence, especially as until 1843 tax made very few inroads on these profits.

Small events like these were the milestones of Darwin's domestic life. He had settled into an existence from which such dramas as were under his control had been eliminated; his own ill health, the traumas afflicting child-birth, and the various disabilities of babyhood were more than sufficiently distressing. If it had been his intention to exclude everything that might have distracted him from his work, his constant sufferings undermined that pur-pose. "I have scarcely put pen to paper for the last half year," he told Fox in July, "& everything in the publishing line is going backwards . . . At present I only want vigour – in wanting which, however, one wants almost all that makes life endurable." The quiet of his life in London was no longer enough for him; he sought a deeper seclusion. "I think we shall never be able to stick all our lives in London, & our present castle in the air is to live near a station in Surrey about 20 miles from Town."

It was his intention to leave London in the Spring of 1842; it would take him that long, presumably, to disentangle himself from his domestic and professional obligations. He and Emma were already actively in search of a house – they went out to the west of Windsor in order to look one over, and a little later were tempted by another near Bagshot, but found it too expen-sive. They came close to making an offer for a third, a place named West-croft, but finally nothing came of it. Constant now was Darwin's detestation of the city: "I long to be settled in pure air, out of all the dirt, noise, vice & misery of this great wen, as old Cobbett called it". What marriage had brought out in him, meanwhile, was a profound, if unselfconsciously senti-mental, love of children. He thought his son William "a prodigy of beauty & intellect", and defied "anybody to flatter us on our baby, for I defy anyone to say anything in its praise, of which we are not fully conscious . . . I had not the smallest conception there was so much in a five month baby." Then – and one can almost see a wry, self-deprecating smile on his face as he wrote – he added, "You will perceive from this, that I have a fine degree of paternal fervour." Fox, to whom these boasts and confessions were made, must have smiled himself, remembering the student days when Darwin would proclaim his horror of small children.

Although they were now determined to leave the city, London life con-tinued to provide them with its small adventures. Emma took Hensleigh's children to the pantomime. Charles witnessed Erasmus's election to the Athenaeum. Emma travelled to Maer, Charles to Shrewsbury. Rail travel had altered all perspectives – Emma reported that her journey back to London on her own had worried her "no more than a drive to Newcastle", the country town near Maer were her brother Jos lived with Caroline. The children, meanwhile, were picking up the accents of the London streets, especially that substitution of a "v" for a "w" that we know from Dickens; their eldest son now announced himself as "Villy Darwin".

From Shrewsbury, Darwin wrote to Emma, proclaiming that his stock had fallen for letting "Doddy" – William's pet name – fight his Wedgwood cousin Johnny. "Katty declares she shall always say I was once a good father. They think I probably misuse you very much, otherwise you could never be quiet while I teach my son such pranks, – poor dear old Titty is a misused old soul, poor old Titty so very sick & squashy this very minute . . ." Emma, in that indomitably fruitful Victorian way, was pregnant once more. For Charles, aware of his own constant ill health and so of the sickroom realities, this must always have produced some anxiety; perhaps he reassured himself by his own improvement. He went for a long walk and reported it to his wife: "The day was very boisterous, with great black clouds & gleams of light, & I felt a sensation of delight which I hardly expected to experience again." He had a new zest for conversation, enjoyed his games of whist and was even able to complain at Sir Robert Peel's reintroduction, for the first time since the Napoleonic Wars, of an income tax – though one might smile ruefully at Darwin's indignation over having to give up seven pennies in every pound, a fraction over three per cent.

In March, 1841, however, he received news that must have brought home to him the true fragility of his happiness. His cousin and old friend, William Darwin Fox, wrote to tell him that his wife had died. Mrs. Fox had long been ill, but Charles and his cousin were still comparatively young men and hardly prepared for such bereavement. Darwin wrote instantly to Fox:

> I truly sympathise with you, though never in my life having lost one near relation. I daresay I cannot imagine how severe grief like yours must be, & how little the longest expectation can resign one to the blow when it falls . . . Your children must be now an infinite comfort to you; I trust they are well & again cheerful. for it is their peculiar blessing to love sweetly & yet not to mourn long . . .

Did he look forward to the hazards of childbirth through which Emma would soon have to pass? In a second letter, he returned again to the hope that from one's offspring one might derive strength in such a crisis. "What a comfort it must be to you – that is, I think I should find it the greatest – the having children – it must make the separation seem less entire – the unspeakable tenderness of young children must soothe the heart & recall the tenderest, however mournful, rememberances . . ." It is almost as though he were musing on mortality and noting his thoughts for his own benefit. Yet in a paragraph or two he works himself back into a more mundane frame of mind: his "two dear little children are very well and very fat" while Emma "is uncomfortable enough all day long & seldom leaves the house, this being her usual state before her babies come into the world". With such slightly insensitive self-satisfaction he thrust away the reality of death.

Back in Gower Street, the Darwins settled again to a metropolitan Spring. Emma assured her Aunt Jessie in Geneva that, though they had no plans to move immediately, "my inclination for the country does not diminish". As for Charles, almost all intellectual exertion now produced its reaction, so that his work took wearisome weeks longer than he planned, or wished. In mid-May, 1842, Emma set off for Maer again; Darwin was lonely without her and the children, while his work for the Geological Society increased the demands on his energies. He wrote to Emma, "Yesterday I went at 2 o clock & (had) an hour's hard talk with Horner on affairs of the Geolog Soc & it quite knocked me up . . ." But his children – "the chickens", he called them – gave him continued delight and, one must believe, sustenance for his spirit. Censorship has here given a touch of raffishness to his expression of this affection; he ended his letter, "I long to kiss Annie's . . .", but a heavy scrawling-out obscures what it was he wished to kiss. Long and scholarly scrutiny restores to us the innocent expression, "botty-bott".

Although they had deferred their intention to move, Emma and Charles had continued their search for a country house within reach of London. By the second half of summer, they were approaching choice. Placed among the woods and flower-studded fields of the Kentish chalklands, Down House – named after the adjoining village – was wrapped as closely as they could desire in rural peace and a brisk cleanliness of air. Less than ten miles away stood Beckenham Station; London was less than twenty miles away. Standing in eighteen acres of ground, the house was set in a wide lawn shadowed by a file of lime trees. It had no profound social or architectural pretension, but was a square, honest, open-fronted structure, somewhat bare, with straightforward windows and an intimidating front door, built of worn, though serviceable, brick.

At the end of July, Charles and Emma stayed in the village inn in order to take a leisurely look at the house. On his return to London, he described what they had found in a letter to Catherine.

> I calculate we were two hours' journey from London Bridge. Westcroft was one-and-threequarter from Vauxhall Bridge. Village about 40 houses with old walnut tree in middle where stands an old flint church and three lanes meet. Inhabitants very respectable; infant school; grown up people great musicians; all touch their hats as in Wales, & sit at their open doors in evening; no high road leads through village. The little pot-house where we slept is a grocer's shop and the landlord is the carpenter. So you may guess the style of the village. There is one butcher and baker and post-office. A carrier goes weekly to London & calls anywhere for anything in London & takes anything any-

where . . . The country is extraordinary rural & quiet with narrow lanes & high hedges & hardly any ruts. It is really surprising to think London is only 16 miles off.

He noted the absence of a view from the drawing room, the abundance of the surrounding trees, some of them pleasantly productive of fruit, the kitchen garden, chalky of soil but, despite appearances, suitable for its purpose, and the profits to be gained from the adjoining hayfield: in 1842, a bad year, the hay had fetched £30, the year before £45. "Does not this sound well, ASK MY FATHER?" The house itself was "ugly, looks neither old nor new; walls two feet thick; windows rather small; lower story rather low; capital study 18 × 18. . . . Three stories plenty of bed-rooms. We could hold the Hensleighs & you & Susan & Erasmus all together . . . I have no doubt, if we complete purchase I shall at least save 1,000£ over Westcroft or any other house."

Emma had not liked the surrounding countryside at first, not having the flat boredom of Cambridgeshire with which to compare it, as Darwin did. By the evening of the inspection, she had a bad headache, and a toothache to compound it, but the next day the richer scenery they passed through altered her mood. The house itself and its immediate grounds she had, if anything, taken to rather more enthusiastically than her husband. Soon Darwin saw that she was "rapidly coming round". And he noted what must have been something of an attraction for him – that nearby, on three thousand ancestral acres, there lived Sir John Lubbock, a well-known astronomer and natural scientist. However, it was likely, he thought, that Lubbock, said to be "very reserved . . . will never know us".

Through late summer they hesitated and negotiated. Darwin's account books note four journeys to Downe between mid-July and mid-August. Did they like Down House enough to take it? It had advantages, other than its situation and price. Unlike many of the houses they had seen, it was likely to need very few alterations – at most, they would have to build a new drawing room; it seemed, as Darwin pointed out to his family, "very solid throughout, though oldish & ugly", suggesting that they were not to be faced with constant repairs; and the agent, Mr. Cressy, was nudging them towards commitment with his promise to buy it back for at least £2,000 if after a year or so they found themselves displeased with it. By now, Emma was weary of searching the Home Counties for anywhere better; with her pregnancy advancing, she was finding the journeys more and more demanding. If they turned away this opportunity, it would be six months at least before they were able to begin their hunt again.

"Mr Cressy is a sensible man & very friendly – if I am deceived in him I am done for: but I don't think it . . ." So wrote Darwin, nervously, edging

Down House seen from the garden.

towards decision. The house was on the market at £2,500 and most of those they had looked at had been priced at over £3,000; his father having agreed to advance him the money, he gingerly offered £2,020. At once the wheels of commerce whirled, catching him up in their glittering cogs – all was suddenly signatures, packing, bustle. By 14 September, perhaps a little out of breath, they were moving into their new home. Darwin had found his retreat, rural, undemanding, conveniently close to London. It was to give him the seclusion and shelter he had dreamed of. For forty years it was to be his refuge, his citadel; only death would prove strong enough to evict him.

The main sources for Part Four were:

Darwin's manuscript notebooks in the archives of Cambridge University Library, and their transcripts in *Notebooks on the Transmutation of Species* and a further selection, *Pages excised by Darwin*, both edited by De Beer; the Darwin correspondence in Cambridge University Library; the W.D. Fox letters at Christ's College, Cambridge; Darwin's *Life and Letters*, edited by Francis Darwin; *A Century of Family Letters*, edited by Henrietta Litchfield; *Darwin on man*, by H.E. Gruber and P.H. Barrett; Erasmus Darwin's *Essential Writings*, edited by D. King-Hele; *Darwin's Century*, by Loren Eisely; *Natural Selection before the "Origin of Species"*, by C. Zirkle; and *Charles Darwin: Evolution by Natural Selection*, by De Beer.

PART FIVE

The Speculatist

1

*. . . this confounded variation, which, however, is pleasant to
me as a speculatist, though odious to me as a systemist.*
Darwin, letter to Hooker

From the time of his grateful retreat to Downe, the physical Darwin, active in
the world, ceased in some sense to exist. Of course, he put in an appearance
from time to time in London, and on occasion made the journey to Shrewsbury and Maer; he took very seriously his responsibilities within the village
community; he fathered children and played his part in rearing them; he
kept an eye on the household accounts; and, either with his family or alone,
he travelled at intervals to a seaside resort, a hydro or a spa. All these,
however, even his marriage, had to fit in with what now became central in his
life, the link and the struggle between his illness and his work.

Darwin had become an intellectual. He was a new phenomenon, a man
without a prescribed social role who carved out a place for himself simply by
applying himself to those problems which he found intriguing. He made his
name through his work, not through his position. He was not a dilettante
aristocrat, trifling away the leisure hours with experiments of varying usefulness. He was not an academic, established by title upon the intellectual
scene. He was as self-created as any artist, a man who would have been of
small consequence had he not possessed exceptional abilities and the determination to use them to impose himself upon the world. In a few decades,
when science had become more institutionalized, it had become impossible
for men like him to succeed. His opportunity was the very confusion which
his gifts would order.

If one simply concluded that, during the years that followed the *Beagle*'s
return, ill health reinforced inclination to motivate Darwin's slow withdrawal from the world, one would be giving a false emphasis to the passive,
the negative elements in his character – though, to be sure, such elements
existed. The fact is, however, that a person is a collective of frequently
opposing characteristics, and if one can detect in Darwin a flinching away
from the swift to and fro of London life, one may also discern a new pride in
his withdrawal upon his own resources. The story of these years is, among
other strands, that of his burgeoning self-belief. He always had a particular

kind of intellectual self-confidence, born as much from enthusiasm as arrogance, which allowed him to leap upon disciplines – and to conclusions – with only the slightest preparation. The history of his development as a geologist is a case in point: a handful of conversations and rambles with Sedgwick, occasional debates, lively though they doubtless were, while in Henslow's circle, a little reading, and he felt himself ready to propound new theories and to propose new solutions to old problems.

That such theories were often of great perspicacity, and so proved in time of value, was as much a consequence of the general flux obtaining in the sciences during the early decades of the nineteenth century as it was of his personal abilities. His was a peculiar mixture of qualities. On the one hand, there was the jackdaw catholicity that marked his search for facts and near-facts, his collection of observations both professional and amateur, his grab-bag of correspondence in which proof, memory and rumour jostled side by side. On the other hand, there was his leaping gift for synthesis, for seeing the meaning beyond the detail, for making unsuspected connections and so giving a retrospective significance to what his voracity had earlier collected – on the basis of which he then collected even wider and farther. It was a mixture that made him the ideal person to operate in the confused and confusing conditions of his time.

Fortunately, despite his eyes for the overriding process, for the meaning in a landscape or in the quiddities of variety and inheritance, he took no overt, limiting stand on matters philosophic or metaphysical. He allowed expression to no cosmic theories, made public no notions about the true nature of man, God or the universe: as far as anyone can tell, speculations of this kind never interposed themselves between his seeing and what he saw, or between what he saw and what he subsequently thought about what he had seen. Yet it seems on the face of it misleading simply to assume from this that he had no beliefs: surely his assertion of these lies implicit in his work. Thus, at the foundation of his faith there lay, not a presiding Intelligence, but the central operations of Nature; the elucidation of those operations was probably as far as he wanted to go in making that faith clear. His Christianity remained to him as a social factor, a means of acting in the world – a question of manners, then, of the dues one paid in effort, cash and attitudes to the community.

He was from the beginning, therefore, free to concentrate on what most drew and interested him. He was free in another way, too – he had enough money to live without labouring for an income. Not for him the parading and politicking that precedes a university appointment, nor the drudgery of lecturing that follows it. The problems that faced a Huxley or a Wallace were spared him, as was the corrosive hypocrisy of an ecclesiastical career in the major premises of which he now had no true belief. The work that lay before him as he and Emma began to settle into their new home in Kent made what must have seemed a self-evident demand; his private money, though no fortune, ensured that he could allow himself to answer it, at his own pace and constrained only by its logic and the availability of proofs. What made this even easier was the scientific reputation he had already built during his metropolitan years: in a sense, he was able to leave London with such equanimity precisely because he had established himself there so securely.

It was earlier in that year of the great removal, 1842, that Darwin had published *Structure and Distribution of Coral Reefs*. In a letter to Emma, he calculated the time that he had spent on the book. "I commenced it 3 years & 7 months ago, & have done scarcely anything besides – I have actually spent 20 months out of this period on it! & nearly all the remainder sickness & visiting!!!" He probably wrote those words just after he had finished correcting the proofs of the book, since he recorded in his Journal, using almost the same phrase, that he had completed that task on 6 May. In March he had visited Shrewsbury, to discover his father for much of the time too large and gouty to move. In mid-May, he travelled to Maer, but found that too a melancholy experience, the house utterly changed, the brightness of its talk and games, the ebb and sparkling flow of its many visitors all ended, and Jos Wedgwood and his wife feeble invalids tied to their beds.

Despite such depressing signs of time and mortality, however, despite the many months of labour on his coral theories, despite the illnesses and the social duties, Darwin managed to gather his thoughts, revive his speculations and turn once more to the species question. It was that July, during later visits to The Mount and to Maer, that he pencilled down one of the most significant manuscripts of his intellectual career – the first extended outline of his views. His theory can hardly ever have been far from his mind, and one imagines him toying with and tugging at its details during whatever spare hours he was permitted. He scrawled down his thoughts, the soft pencil slashing and curtseying across the limp paper, syntax, punctuation and superfluous words torn aside by the speed of his advance, erasures and additions mottling the already complicated pages. It is clear that his first formal statement of his theories was intended for no one's eyes but his own.

The manuscript is divided in ways that later, longer versions were to make significant, indications of the single-mindedness which unified Darwin's entire working life. In every detailed statement of his thesis, for example, he began at the same point, the study of variation and selection as it is seen in the domestic breeds developed for humanity's support. This is followed by an examination of how the same process can be observed more slowly at work in the wild. The selection of suitable varieties, either by human choice or the impartial exigencies of nature, was of course the core of his theory, but the absence of a truly comprehensive hypothesis to explain inheritance and its imperfections meant that he could never understand the full significance of sexual reproduction in the evolutionary scheme: the causes of variation therefore continued to baffle him, as did the mystery of why some survived while others swiftly vanished. What he did do was to emphasize the critical role of variation in providing a great number of possibilities within a species, possibilities that were then rigorously selected by the preferences of breed-ers or the much slower but equally obdurate workings of the environment. In time, he suggested, this process would lead to the formation of new species – "a thousand wedges are being forced into the economy of nature", he wrote, carrying forward a reflection found in the *Transmutation Notebooks*.

He devoted an entire section to the instincts "and other mental attri-butes": the spectrum of reactions that he proffered in evidence supported his contention that these too had come about by infinite gradations, just as physical structures had been modified over many thousands of years. This concluded the first part of his sketch; Part Two (which by mistake Darwin once or twice called "Part III") provided his supportive evidence. There was the fossil record; the way in which plants and creatures were distributed about the earth and how this related to long-term geological change; the affinities between classes of living organisms, which we could recognize despite functional similarities and differences which might have misled us (he suggested as an example "an otter-like animal amongst mammalia and an otter amongst marsupials" where we could see that "external resemb-lance and habit of life and *the final end of whole organization* very strong, yet no relation"); the similarities to be found in creatures of the same general class, "this wonderful fact of hand, hoof, wing, paddle and claw being the same"; and the continuance, sometimes in rudimentary or atrophied form, of anatomical features which were of no practical use in the present, but could be assumed to have had a true function in the life-style of some far distant progenitor.

It was with this first sketch, of thirty-five or thirty-seven pages (Darwin claimed the latter, but only the former number survive), in his luggage, that in September, 1842, he made his migration to Down House. It was the conclusion of the first phase of what he had now recognized was the centre of his scientific life. For five years he had been pursuing the fugitive elements of a constantly developing theory. Now, at last, he had been able to fix it in a single comprehensive statement. It was, however, more a beginning than it was an end. He had established the foundations for what he must have known was to be years of effort. If he was shown to be categorically wrong on a single point, his proposals would be damaged in a crucial way: his critics needed to demolish only one assertion, but he had to prove all of them. There now began, therefore, the long middle phase of his life when, guarding his hypothesis like a citadel, he buttressed it with the constant slow piling up of fact, creating the high walls, the towers and battlements that would keep it safe once its inevitable siege began. Around it spread the clutter of his life, but it was the nucleus that give purpose to all the rest.

The movement of his entire existence, therefore, was inward now, towards that centre. Darwin, who had been all activity, who had expressed himself when young in the physical world, imposing himself upon it as hunter and collector, withdrew gradually towards stillness. The intensity with which he had formerly looked outwards was refocussed. It turned towards what he was learning and gathering, leaving what was sometimes no more than a token energy for the duties and obligations that pressed upon the social self. If the shape of his life and his identity, considered as a single, unified phenomenon, could have been laid out in diagrammatic form during the years that led to *The Origin of Species*, it would have looked like a series of concentric rings.

On the periphery there lay that part of his life which interacted with the great world beyond. It was the least important part of his new existence, and more and more he came to resent the time and effort it took up. His response was to withdraw, to abandon that outermost circle almost entirely. That was, indeed, one of his principal reasons for moving from the metropolis. Because he withdrew so completely from this part of his life, it all but died, turning into an almost impenetrable integument. As the years went by, he travelled with increasing rarity on any but personal business – only the desire to see his family in Shrewsbury or to seek out a cure for his continuing illnesses drew him from home. Close by though London was, he visited it only at lengthening intervals and, until the last decade of his life, very few people were encouraged to make the journey to Downe. For the most part, only letters crossed the barriers that increasingly separated Darwin from the ordinary activities of the scientific and academic communities – though that paper tide seemed constantly in spate. But meetings, dinners, lectures, exhibitions, the functions of societies and clubs, scientific conferences and debates, as well as the individuals who took part in them – all were kept at bay to expressions of unconvincing regret from a Darwin publicly available only through the written word.

Within this circle lay that of his immediate neighbourhood. Unthreatening and almost entirely unconcerned with his scientific status, this nourished rather than drained him. It allowed him to potter to and fro, intermittently busy with village affairs, with charities, church and school, in a manner that continued the benign traditions of both Darwins and Wedgwoods. It allowed him, one feels, to locate himself in his preferred context of place and class, and so to affirm that nothing essential had altered in his situation. He remained a man of the country, of quasi-squirearchical status, and he was happy to accept the obligations that followed from such a definition of his role. In fulfilling the expectations of his neighbours, both rich and poor, he confirmed the legitimacy of his own; no matter where his ideas might lead him, his identity within the village community was clear, uncontroversial and accepted by all.

Within this again lay the circle of his closest friendships. Here existed his peers, his mentors, the men upon whose expertise he sometimes relied and whose approval he desired. It was these men whom he still saw, whom he allowed through the outer defences of his life: Henslow had been the first, then there had been Lyell, soon there was to be Hooker, later perhaps the most important of them all, Huxley, and in his final years there would be the young Romanes – these formed about him a sort of lifelong scientific cabal. He was to have correspondents among the scientific community all over the world and some, like Buckland and Sedgwick, Wallace and Asa Gray, were to become important and eventually even close, yet it was this handful of men who through the years remained a continuing panel of advisers, a kitchen cabinet freely discussing ideas long before they were prepared to share them with the public at large, passing on information in their various specialities, often defending Darwin from his rivals and opponents, testing, modifying and eventually often adopting his theories. And, once his ideas had finally crystallized, it probably seemed more important to Darwin to convince this little group of their truth and value than it was to convince all the rest of the world that he was right.

Next stood his family, the Darwins and Wedgwoods: some important, though remote; others, like Fox or Hensleigh, friends rather than cousins. These, with his sisters, his brother Erasmus, his father until his death – and even, perhaps, after it – circled like planets, close enough to comfort with their brightness. And just beyond them, dim and silent, yet never forgotten, swung in orbit his older friends, the heroes of his Cambridge days, companions of his Shrewsbury youth: nostalgia was always more powerful than force in piercing his defences and men like Herbert, Eyton or Albert Way would be instantly and gladly accepted even after decades of estrangement. Friends scientific, friends personal, aunts and cousins, then the immediate Darwins of The Mount – so the rings closed about the central serenity of his life.

And at Down House itself there stood the inner circle, his nearest satellites, attached to each other and to him by the action of a single gravitational field: Emma, protective, affectionate, watchful, firm, the mother of the place, and around her the children – among whom, one senses, Darwin often counted himself. Here, science became a game as well as a serious pursuit, a cooperative process involving everyone who had a mind to join in. The group faced inwards, their backs collectively towards the outside world, their faces towards each other. Protected by their father's isolation from all dramatic interventions, stilled by his repeated illnesses, yet wrapped in his unfailing gentleness, his generosity and fair-mindedness, the Darwin children expanded in a rare security. Emma, guarding all, allowed them to feel protected. The serenity this generated provided for Darwin the atmosphere in which he could best become himself. His challenges were all internal; he did not thrive on instant and abrasive competition.

But the circles continue, tighter and tighter as the centre approaches. Next comes the ring of his scientific activities, his experiments with plants, with the cirripedes, with his breeding pigeons, with the stones that marked the slow working of the earthworms. Darwin, withdrawing from the world, did not stop the detailed labours of the scientist. He no longer ranged the countryside; instead, he had its products brought to him, so that in his defended citadel he might dissect, observe and understand them.

Within this there lies what might be termed the circle of his general speculations. Here he worked out his thoughts on the elevation of mountain ranges, the action of ice, the strength of climbing plants, the formation of mould. At this level he asked the thousand questions that from time to time caught his imagination. He hammered out ideas that dealt with the particular issues such questions raised, and fed them into the scientific community by means of the papers that he wrote throughout his life. These ideas, however, were not separate from the theories he had developed about the evolution of species. Even though only peripheral, they usually had some connection with his innermost concerns, feeding and fed from those constant convictions.

So one arrives at the centre. Here is the intense focus of all his intellectual energy, the energy that had once carried him day after day across the pampas or thousands of feet up among the peaks of the Andes. It is a fire, unsuspected from his gentle exterior, sustained by the fixity of his purpose and fuelled by a boundless stamina. His will bends his attention to the problems that he desires to resolve. Day after day, week after week, month after month, he aligns his thoughts with the precision others might bring to the laying of a gun – or to the meditations of a religious order. He had written in the "M" Notebook, "I suspect . . . that whole effort consists in keeping one idea before your mind steadily, & not merely thinking intently . . . Then if one endeavour to keep any simple idea – as scarlet steady before mind for period, if this scarlet were before one effortless (but) one is obliged to repeat the word, & think of qualities . . . Is the effort greater if the idea is abstract as love . . . than if simple idea as scarlet?"

There is a Sanskrit term, *manaskara*, which translates as "mind-work". It describes the meditative practice of Hindu mystics, whose world lies in dimensions other than Darwin's, yet whose mental processes seem so similar. They too attempt to keep "one idea before your mind steadily" – achieving what they term "one-pointedness" – and they too repeat a single word over and over in order to focus and maintain their concentration. Just as Darwin used the "simple idea" of scarlet as an example, so it is occasionally their practice to "flood" their minds with a single colour and use it as the medium, so to speak, of their meditation. Thus they induce in themselves that condition of absorption which is, as Darwin wrote, "not merely thinking intently", but something much deeper. In mystics that would be the meditative trance; in Darwin, the profound state of concentration in which he pursued his theories. The comparison indicates the intensity that Darwin could generate during those seminal years, the all-demanding inner effort that he called, in the same note, the "excessive labour of inventive thought".

For such levels of mental endeavour one must have a consuming motivation. In the case of Darwin, it is clear that he was being driven by a passion very akin to religious faith. Everything else must for a while have become marginal to him, existing only to feed or protect this inner quest. The rest of his life became his armour, within which he could search in safety for the Grail. For, as we have seen, the intensity of questioning and speculation that he displayed in the Notebooks, and in the species work that followed, testified to a depth of feeling which he could rarely articulate nor, it seems, match by any other passion. It was his paramount desire and it raged within him as vice or ambition rage in other men – *the desire to know*. He hardly ever mentioned it, partly because he was not given to self-examination, but partly, one suspects, because it must have appeared to him as totally self-evident.

2

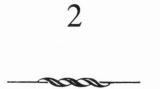

The long years spent by the Darwins at Down House, in retrospect so tranquil, began with tragedy. Ten days after they had moved in, Emma gave birth to a daughter, Mary Eleanor. She lived three weeks; on 16 October, she died. "Our sorrow is nothing to what it would have been if she had lived longer and suffered more", wrote Emma reassuringly to Fanny Hensleigh. It was Charles she worried over, for he had faced the funeral with forebodings and intimations of weakness, but in the end survived that ordeal without damage to his health. Emma, who had seen in the baby some fetching resemblances to her mother, turned for consolation to the other children. "With our two other dear little things you need not fear that our sorrow will last long, though it will be long indeed before we either of us forget that poor little face." In the balance of grief and hope, in her care for Fanny Hensleigh's feelings and her concern for Charles, all Emma's strength, level-headedness, selflessness and generously distributed affection are made clear.

Darwin settled into his new life, while keeping many connections with his old one. For example, he remained on the Council of the Geological Society and, for purposes such as this, he planned to spend a night in London every two or three weeks, "& so not to turn into a complete Kentish Hog". He was not yet so unworldly that the contacts and politics of the scientific world had lost their fascination. Nevertheless, the focus of all his immediate activities now became his new house. Inwardly, geology, the species question and the metaphysics of mind may have retained his most intense attention, but, when he was not actually working, his existence revolved around the renovation, improvement and buttressing of his fortress. The problems that obsessed him concerned the rebuilding of old rooms and the addition of new ones. He sought ways to beautify the grounds, or render them more functional. For the first time in his life, after all, he had become the lord of an estate, the monarch of a demarcated kingdom. The walls which he had painted or papered, the walks he had laid down, the extensions he had built belonged to him; his orders decked out or created them, his money made sure that his orders were followed. The work delighted as much as it tired him and, like the main labours of his life, had the merit of never coming to an end.

"We are now exceedingly busy", he informed Fox in a letter written in March, 1843, "with the first brick laid down yesterday to an addition to our house; with this, with almost making a new kitchen garden & sundry other projected schemes, my days are very full." The work destroyed his usual, more leisurely schedules; in April he was writing half complainingly to Susan, "I was called off yesterday to speak to workmen at 9 oclock & excepting an hours rest on the sofa at luncheon time I was on my legs till 5 oclock: this is the way I pass my days & am so much knocked up in the evenings". Eventually, the house would be a substantial one, but "as one of the bricklayers often says to me with a gloomy shake of his head, 'a most deceptious property to buy Sir' ". It was not to be "deceptious" in the future; a new bedroom for Emma was being constructed, as well as the new drawing room; outside, a flint-stone wall was put up beside the lane, to increase privacy, and a new path laid in the kitchen garden. Extra work on the road itself cost, as Darwin scribbled in graphic horror, "38£!!"

"Thank my Father for his offer of lending me money," he wrote gratefully to Susan; "I shall indeed be run short before July & I think the least sum which will carry me through will be a cool 300£, which will make, I think, 2,500£ altogether borrowed: on reflection I am pretty sure 300£ will not be enough altogether though perhaps it will be for the present half year. – I will write in time when I want to borrow. – I have got 429£ in Bank & 84£ in my great iron-chest." The somewhat hectic tone of the paragraph suggests that Darwin was more than a little disturbed at the cost of alterations he yet could not bring himself to postpone.

By September he was able to tell Fox that the work was nearly finished and "almost all the workmen gone & the gravel laying down on the walks – Ave Maria how the money does go – there are twice as many temptations to extravagance in the country compared with London". In his account book he wrote "Man making Walk (I think 6s per 100 yds good pay)" and noted a payment of seven shillings; but at Christmas he gave the two men then working on the paths beer to the value of 4s. 6d. And once the initial renovatory assault was over, Darwin began to luxuriate in the peace of Down House – "its thorough rurality is invaluable", he reported to Fox, around the beginning of 1845. And to Emma, visiting Maer and Leith Hill at about that time, he wrote, in anticipation of her return, "Try & remember just before you drive in at our gate, to rise from your seat & look over the wall & see how nice the place looks".

More inside alterations, too, were being contemplated. The servants had put forward their own proposals: "It seemed so selfish", commented Darwin, "making the house so luxurious for ourselves & not comfortable for our servants, that I was determined if possible to effect their wishes". Parslow,

Plate 15

Darwin in 1849, already
settled at Down House,
struggling against ill health
and with his theories
firmly established.

Plate 16

Emma Darwin's kindly strength,
which sustained her husband for
over forty years, was clearly to be
read on her features in old age.

Plate 17 For cartoonists, Darwin and his ideas seemed heaven-sent
and in the decades after *The Origin* came out their drawings, like this one
published in 1874, made their own contribution to the debate.

the butler, was too confined for efficiency in his small pantry; and, for the moment, everything the servants carried had to be brought through a frequently busy kitchen. A new pantry and a new corridor would remedy these inconveniences. A schoolroom would be needed, since the small children and later the girls were not to be sent away to school; it was decided that at the same time, two small extra bedrooms would be built. "So I hope", begged Darwin "the Shrewsbury conclave will not condemn me for extreme extravagance, though now that we are reading aloud Sir Walter Scott's life, I sometimes think that we are following his road to ruin at a snail-like pace . . ." But Darwin's sober, comfortable retreat was a far cry from the neo-Gothic, pseudo-chivalric folly that had bankrupted Sir Walter, nor, for all his forebodings, were his expenses ever beyond his control or his father's powers of rescue.

Perhaps the most directly useful of all the work that was put in hand during those early days was the creation of the Sandwalk. This Darwin came to call "my thinking path", and for decade after decade hardly a day passed when he would neglect to stroll up and down that pale, looped route, shadowed as the years passed with the trees – alder, birch, hazel, dogwood, hornbeam – that he had planted himself. A high hedge hid the kitchen garden and the house; the little wood cut off the outside world. Here and there larger and older trees lifted above the saplings of the Darwin era – a great hollow ash, blackened within, and a vast beech named, by the Darwin children then or later, The Elephant Tree. Birds nested on the springy, spreading branches, and squirrels leaped and chirruped among the leaves. Darwin, careful and soft-footed, would stalk these creatures with solitary patience – once so successfully that a brood of young squirrels ran up his legs and whisked across his back, thinking him something slower and friendlier than a man. For over thirty years Darwin rented the growing wood by and through which his favourite path wound; in 1874 he exchanged it, with the landlord, Sir John Lubbock, for a field of the same size, and so at last became its owner.

In the course of the years the house grew almost like a living thing. The drawing room became the dining room, and a new drawing room was built. In the old dining room Darwin placed a billiard table, a game he delighted in and one that, so many years before, he had urged Fanny Owen to learn. In the 1870s, a special billiard room was built, with a reception and a bedroom above it. The front door was moved and a portico added. A verandah, glass-roofed and facing grass, trees and flowers, became the summer centre of family life. The kitchen garden was moved to a new location. A hothouse was constructed under the supervision of Horwood, Sir John Lubbock's gardener: "Without his aid," wrote Darwin modestly to Sir John, "I should never have had the spirit to undertake it; and if I had I should probably have made a mess of it". At the very end of Darwin's life, a hard court for tennis was laid down, sign of the infectious enthusiasm for sport that overtook the late-Victorian young. With such zeal and energy did Darwin tend his refuge and turn the gaunt, unappealing house he had bought into a home which his children and grandchildren always looked back to with nostalgia.

Gwen Raverat, Darwin's granddaughter, knew the house at the end of the century, but it is clear that what she felt was an emotion the whole family shared: though her charming American mother found the country dull, creating only a boredom that had to be borne with good-humoured patience.

> But to us, everything at Down was perfect. That was an axiom. And by us I mean, not only the children, but all the uncles and aunts who belonged there ... Everything there was different. And better. [She remembered the stones that surfaced the path beside the verandah] ... large round water-worn pebbles, from some sea beach ... stuck down tight in moss and sand, and ... black and shiny as if they had been polished. I adored those pebbles. I mean literally, *adored*; worshipped ... And it was adoration that I felt for the foxgloves at Down, and for the stiff red clay out of the Sandwalk clay-pit; and for the beautiful white paint on the nursery floor.

This was the house, the home, the atmosphere, that Charles and Emma had created around them and rooted strongly enough to survive his death and her partial withdrawal from the place. In it, he must have felt secure, untroubled; it turned away the world's threats. Thus anchored physically, he could brave the tempests of his own speculations. He could recreate the world of his childhood, but one in which he was master. Nature, which his ill health made so often inaccessible to him, he brought cunningly to his own doorstep. No tiring journeys intervened between him and its rhythms, scents and sounds, its winds and clouds and the scurrying multiplicity of its creatures. Not certain whether he could outface his challengers, he created a universe where they could be kept at bay, and he could reign unchallenged. With Emma as Regent, the chosen viceroy of his empire, he could relax, both master and mastered.

3

Once Darwin had settled into Downe, he established a routine that hardly varied until the feebleness of his age began to curtail it slightly. He would stroll on the Sandwalk before breakfast and after it, from about eight o'clock, work in his study for an hour and a half. Then, for an hour or so, he would rest on a sofa and be read to – the morning's letters or a section of a novel. The Darwins usually had two or three books that were being publicly read at the same time, the lighter offering some relief from the more substantial. They read most of the novelists of high reputation: Dickens, Thackeray, George Eliot and Trollope, about all of whom they had some reservations, and Walter Scott, Mrs. Gaskell, and Jane Austen, whom they admired without stint. Biographies and autobiographies pleased them, and they sometimes read works of popular theology or philosophy. Novels, Darwin thought, should have a happy ending and contain "some person whom one can love, and if a pretty woman so much the better". They were, on the whole, "a wonderful relief and pleasure to me, and I often bless all novelists".

After these readings, he would work hard for another hour and a half; this was the most important working period for him and what he managed to do then determined whether or not he had had a satisfactory day. He gave up around noon and, whatever the weather, went out for some exercise. Although there was a period during his later years when this consisted of riding – a venture which a fall or two persuaded him was too dangerous even for a one-time sporting man – he usually went for a walk, either round the Sandwalk or out into the world beyond. Neither cold, rain nor heat ever stopped him, but he would be back by the time that lunch was served at one o'clock. For this the family would gather, giving it always a small sense of occasion and a special happiness. Darwin would perhaps drink a glass of light wine and – despite repeated resolutions to give them up – eat a few postprandial sweets. With one of these in his mouth, he would take one more to the sofa for his daily reading of *The Times*. Even the support that paper gave to the South in the American Civil War, offensive though that was to the slavery-hating Darwin, could not persuade him to stop reading it. "*The Times* is getting more detestable than ever", he wrote to his American friend and ally, Asa Gray. "My good wife wishes to give it up, but I tell her that is a pitch of heroism to which only a woman is equal. To give up the 'Bloody Old *Times*' as Cobbet used to call it, would be to give up meat, drink and air."

The afternoon was the time when he wrote to his many correspondents all over the world, many of them the informants upon whom he relied for the curious testimony with which he supported his theories. Emma would read to him then, too, while he lay listening and smoking and, occasionally, falling asleep. When this happened, she would often continue so that he might rest easily against the background of her voice. Towards the end of the afternoon he sometimes managed a little more work, before looking in on whoever was in the drawing room and then going off for another period of rest in his bedroom. A very simple supper was almost always followed by backgamm-on with Emma: they played two games in a session and one can have some idea of how often they took out their board from a letter Darwin wrote Asa Gray in January, 1876. "Now the tally with my wife in backgammon stands thus: she, poor creature, has won only 2,490 games, whilst I have won, hurrah, hurrah" – here his triumph demanded a line to itself – "2,795 games!" Sometimes, as his daughter Henrietta remembered, he would himself read aloud in the evenings, but by half past ten he was almost always in bed, ready for the early morning walk that would recommence the routine's new round.

This was the order which Darwin built around himself like a fortress of which Emma was the chatelaine. It left him free to settle to his work; its walls would withstand the assaults and sieges of the world outside. The vagaries, both tragic and triumphant, of a familiar mortality proved rather harder to resist. Death had been the first experience they had had to face after their move to Downe; he and Emma sorrowed a long time for their lost child, that Mary Eleanor who had died after so short a time. Over the years to come, the deaths of those close to them, more frequent in the days when families were large, repeatedly punctuated the serenity of their secluded lives.

Even before the move, in the summer of 1842, Emma's uncle by marriage, the historian Sismondi, had died in Geneva. It must have hurt Emma, not only because she knew him quite well, having visited the Sismondis in Switzerland, but also because of her affection for her now-widowed Aunt Jessie. "He so filled every instant of my life", wrote Jessie in answer to Emma's letter of condolence, "that now my feeling of desolation passes all description . . . If I can but keep off the monster despair, which at times approaches so near it makes me tremble, I shall learn to bear my own deprivation . . ." What thoughts did such grief arouse in a young wife whose own husband was declining into a chronic invalidism?

Almost exactly a year later, Emma's father, Charles's Uncle Jos, also died; Emma, once more pregnant, travelled to Maer in order to be with him during that final illness. Early in 1846, when Emma was back at Maer, the dedicated Elizabeth was still nursing Bessy Wedgwood, Jos's widow, bed-ridden and declining towards death. In March, not very long after Emma had returned to Downe, Bessy died. The long dissolution of that house had come to its conclusion: the conversations, the urbane debates, the gossip and flirtations, the readings in the library and the walks across the grounds, the shooting parties and the coachloads of guests sent laughing off to some local ball or dinner – all had ended forever. Hensleigh, Emma, Charles, Erasmus and the others of their generation doubtless reminisced over them from time to time, reviving some tattered scandal or dusty joke, but the house itself was now dark, empty, forlorn: "I think . . . there is little use in lingering", wrote Elizabeth to Emma, "and that we shall probably not stay more than a month. I don't feel that leaving the place (though I shall never see another I shall like anything like it) will be much of a grief."

In 1847, like a refugee from that final assault of mortality, Bessy's sister, Sarah Wedgwood, moved into a house in Downe village, a place named Petleys, the trees of which shadowed the village pond. There, caped and shawled and bonnetted and gloved, she lived a frugal life of determined seclusion, attended by her three servants, devoted to her charities and finding her true pleasure in her books. In 1856, she too died. Three years earlier it had been the turn of her sister, Jessie Sismondi; Aunt Jessie's last letter to Emma, dated a month before her death, had remained full of life and an excited curiosity about the state of the world. The Wedgwood training lasted for life.

By then, Darwin had had to sustain far bitterer and much more directly personal blows. "My father is perfectly collected, and placid in his mind in every way," wrote Catherine to Charles Darwin on 11 November, 1848, "and one of the most beautiful and pathetic sights that can be imagined, so sweet, so uncomplaining . . . He attempted to speak about you this morning, but was so excessively overcome he was utterly unable; we begged him not to speak as we knew what he would have said . . ." Two days later, Dr. Robert died: "God comfort you, my dearest Charles," wrote Catherine, "you were so beloved by him."

Darwin, telling his friend, the botanist Hooker, of this months later, wrote that "no one who did not know him would believe that a man above eighty-three years old could have retained so tender and affectionate a disposition, with all his sagacity unclouded to the last." At once he turned to his own illnesses and their symptoms, which suggests that his loss had reinforced old anxieties, long-buried guilts perhaps associated with the death of his mother, as well as placing him, as the passing of one's parents always does, in the frontline of life's resistance and among the most vulnerable of the survivors. He could not find the strength to attend the funeral, felt he could not act as his father's executor; all winter his illness seemed to him extreme – "I thought I was rapidly going the way of all flesh", he told Hooker. It was the following March that, desperate, he made a pilgrimage, the first of many, to Malvern and the renowned water-cures of Dr. Gully. Slowly he recovered – but worse was to come.

In 1850, his daughter, Annie, then nine years old, became ill. She was a girl filled with a joyous life, cheerful, affectionate, energetic, her behaviour intelligently touched by a certain mischievous shrewdness. It was this that rescued her from a sugary conformity with the more sentimental Victorian ideals of childhood. Darwin was distracted – the thought had begun to haunt him that he carried some hereditary weakness which had been passed on to his children. He took Annie to a South Coast resort in the autumn of that year and, in March, 1851, to Malvern.

Although attended by Dr. Gully, the girl became feverish. The doctor seems not to have had any great idea of what to do, being reported as thinking "that in some respects Annie was better and in some worse, but there is yet a chance". Emma, once more pregnant, was quietly desperate, not only on the child's behalf, but also because she was, as her aunt, Fanny Allen, wrote, "so afraid that this anxiety may injure Charles's health, which is always affected by his mind . . ." Darwin, however, seems to have stood the strain with undeviating staunchness, writing constantly and in detail to his wife as Annie's condition fluctuated.

On 17 April, Dr. Gully was confident, but by the next day, "Sometimes Dr. G. exclaims she will get through the struggle, then, I see, he doubts. Oh my own, it is very bitter indeed." On Saturday, 19 April, he sent Emma a telegram, giving her the reassuring news that Annie was better. But in a letter he wrote the same morning, he added a warning: "You must not suppose her out of danger . . . You would not in the least recognize her with her poor hard, sharp pinched features; I could only bear to look at her by forgetting our former dear Annie . . ."

Emma reacted with a premature relief to Darwin's telegram: "What happiness! How I do thank God! but I will not be too hopeful." It was as well that she was not. Annie's pulse became tremulous; the outlook remained sinister. "She asked for orange this morning, the first time she has asked for anything except water", reported Darwin, clutching at straws. "Our poor child has been fearfully ill, as ill as a human being could be . . ."

Included in Darwin's letters, though not in the published version, nor in those bedroom scenes which so cleverly sweetened death and disease for the Victorians, were details of the bladder and bowel movements, debilitating, uncomfortable and alarming, which were a part of the corrosive reality.

"Poor Annie is in a fearful mess, but we keep her sweet with Chloride of Lime; the Dr. said we might change the under sheet if we could, but I dare not attempt it yet." In the evening, Annie took a spoonful of tea, and Dr. Gully saw her again. "She has slept tranquilly almost all the afternoon", scribbled Darwin, and added, with controlled anguish, "perhaps too tranquilly." He had reason for his foreboding – Annie's sleep was now more and more the induction to her death. Two days later, at noon on 23 April, she made that transition.

"Our poor dear dear child has had a very short life," wrote Darwin, "but I trust happy, and God only knows what miseries might have been in store for her. She expired without a sigh. How desolate it makes one to think of her frank, cordial manners. I am so thankful for the daguerrotype. I cannot remember ever seeing the dear child naughty. God bless her. We must be more & more to each other, my dear wife . . ." Emma answered him:

> My feeling of longing after our lost treasure makes me feel painfully indifferent to the other children, but I shall get right in my feelings to them before long. You must remember that you are my prime treasure (and always have been). My only hope of consolation is to have you safe home and weep together. I feel so full of fears about you. They are not reasonable fears: but my power of hoping seems gone.

In her diary, Emma wrote simply the time of Annie's death: "12 o'clock". After that she rarely spoke of her loss; Darwin himself, never. A week after she died, as though in some private memorial service for a congregation of one, he wrote a eulogy for her. He remembered her "boyant joyousness . . . her sensitiveness . . . her strong affection". He tried to maintain her reality, to fix for ever the quality of her character and, even more, the physical fact of her, to hold on to her existence with cables of words.

> All her movements were vigorous, active, and usually graceful. When going round the Sand-walk with me, although I walked fast, yet she often used to go before, pirouetting in the most elegant way, her dear face bright all the time with the sweetest smiles . . . She often used exaggerated language, and when I quizzed her by exaggerating what she had said, how clearly can I now see the little toss of the head, and exclamation of "Oh papa, what a shame of you!" . . . We have lost the joy of the household, and the solace of our old age.

Emma, for her part, kept all her life a little store of mementoes – the child's notebooks, a clutch of written texts, a piece of wool she had been working – as a testimonial to the continuing pain of that death. Nor was it only the parents who sorrowed – the Scottish nurse, Brodie, was so altered by grief that she left Down House for good, retiring to Scotland in desolation; she recovered sufficiently in time to make long visits to the children she had helped nurture, but she never worked for the Darwins again.

But there were many births to balance the family account. William had already been born when the Darwins moved to Down; Henrietta came in 1843, George two years later, and two years on again, Elizabeth. In 1848, Francis was born, Leonard and Horace in 1850 and 1851; four years later came the last child, the tenth that Emma bore, Charles Waring. Sickly and retarded, the joy he brought them was tempered by doubt, then by anxiety. But, "My dear Emma," wrote Jessie Sismondi to her niece in 1852, "how I do love you when you talk of your children! You never speak so prettily as then. You are poetic without knowing it, which is the prettiest poetry of all."

When the children were babies, Darwin, as his letters have shown, doted on them. Later, however, concern over their future clouded a little his happiness. In March of 1852 he wrote to Fox, "I congratulate and condole with you on your *tenth* child; but please to observe when I have a tenth, send only condolences to me. We have now seven children, all well, thank God, as well as their mother; of these seven, five are boys; & my father used to say that it was certain that a boy gave as much trouble as three girls; so that *bona fide* we have seventeen children." He worried over what professions they should take up – it made him sick, he said, perhaps with unconscious precision – and then added a parenthesis, only half humourous, about his "three bugbears", which were "Californian & Australian gold, beggaring me by making my money on mortgage worth nothing; the French coming by the Westerham & Sevenoaks road, & therefore enclosing Down; &, thirdly, professions for my boys". Considering that he had an income of over £4,000 a year, that Britain was not to fight a European war for another sixty years and that his sons grew to wealth, honour and a brace of knighthoods, he seems once more to have been exercising his capacity to worry profoundly about very little. At the same time, of course, he was able to stand far enough away from himself to laugh with Fox at these mild eccentricities.

He returned to them, nevertheless, in another letter six months later – "oh! the professions; oh! the gold; and oh! the French – these three oh's all rank as dreadful bugbears" – in which, not for the first time, he considered the problems of education. William, at Rugby, seemed settled and contented, but Darwin had strong reservations about boarding schools: he said categorically that he hated them "and the whole system of breaking through the affections of the family by separating the boys so early in life; but I see no help, & dare not run the risk of a youth being exposed to the temptations of the world without having undergone the milder ordeal of a great school." He was, obviously, a concerned and active father, in a period when men of his class often shut themselves away from any too pressing connection with their families. But Darwin's warmth, and the need he felt to have warmth around him, his loving disposition and his need for love, worked together to make him an effective, if at times over-anxious, parent.

Darwin's altruistic concern was not, however, confined to his family: he had an abiding hatred of injustice, and slavery remained a subject which could always excite his anger. Writing to Lyell about the geologist's book, *Travels in North America*, published in 1845, he said, "Your slave discussion disturbed me much; but as you would care no more for my opinion on this head than for the ashes of this letter, I will say nothing except that it gave me some sleepless, most uncomfortable hours." Later, he gave his approval to Susan's work for the abolition of that monstrous institution, the use of child sweeps – small boys who clambered up the tortuous flues of the houses of the wealthy dragging their brushes behind them: "We have set up a little Society in Shrewsbury to prosecute those who break the law. It is all Susan's doing . . . but the brutal Shropshire squires are as hard as stone to move . . . It makes one shudder to fancy one of one's own children at seven years old being forced up a chimney – to say nothing of the consequent loathsome disease and ulcerated limbs, & utter moral degradation." He urged Fox to play his own part in the campaign – "add to your many good works, this other one, & try to stir up the magistrates."

4

In the causes he supported, in the size and routine of his household, in the provisions he made for his children, Darwin maintained the decencies, obligations and comforts of his class. To do so was clearly self-evident – the social effort would have come from any attempt to deviate from these standards. Brought up as a member of the prosperous provincial bourgeoisie, his friends drawn mainly from the ranks of the rural gentry, his metropolitan years had been as much a diversion from the natural course of his life as had his period on the *Beagle*. As the owner of a large house in a well-to-do village, Darwin found life very congenial – especially as that village lay within such easy reach of London.

The account books that Darwin kept meticulously all his life help to anatomize his pleasantly squirearchical existence. One constant, necessary expense was the upkeep of a horse and carriage to connect Down House with the railway. There were harness oil, carriage repair, the mending and replacement of harness, feed for the horse, its periodical shoeing, the cost of keeping the animal in readiness for the return journey from the station. The family's phaeton, together with a small carriage for the children, had been bought just after the move from London, at a cost of nearly £70. Once installed in the country, Darwin faced various agricultural expenses: in 1842, he bought a cow at an auction, for just over £11; he paid thirty shillings for two pigs, and bought two or three more at the beginning of every year, presumably to have them butchered a year later. He bought a pig trough, too, and "14 iron Hurdles", to make a fence, or temporary pens when needed. Despite the helpful presence of the cow, manure was bought at intervals, at around £1 a load. Feed for the livestock took occasional sums, the meadow had to be rolled and, later, mown, seeds had to be bought for the garden and stakes for beans and sweet peas. Now and then there appears the delicate item, "Cow to Bull", each such visit costing two or three shillings.

Then there were the charity payments expected of a man in Darwin's position. Money was given annually to Rev. Brodie Innes's Sunday School, for example, and to the "Cruelty Soc." – otherwise the Society, not yet royal, for the Prevention of Cruelty to Animals. One suspects Emma's hand in another sum paid out at intervals, to the Society for the Protection of Young Females. Money was given for the upkeep of the church and for the Coal

Club, which ensured the warmth of the poor in winter. Then there were the smaller, more personal sums, dispensed to "Beggar" or "Poor man" – presumably people who came to the door to ask for alms. These were usually amounts of sixpence or a shilling, but on 15 October, 1844, "Poor woman" was given five shillings and at moments of extreme generosity the sums might be as high as ten or twelve shillings – one quarter of a servant's annual wage.

There were payments for specialized services – the mole catcher, for example, earned 3s. 6d. for a visit. Chimney sweeps, plumbers, bricklayers, labourers at haymaking time – all took their little sums, and most had them augmented with beer bought at Darwin's expense. Trips to London were quite frequent during these early years, and there hansom cabs and omnibuses had to be taken; what all this cost was carefully set down. The luxuries were not forgotten, either: "3 doz sherry. 1 doz Mad. 2 doz Port", wrote Darwin on 11 April, 1845, noting additions to his cellar costing over £15. In July, he bought snuff for 13s. 6d. – snuff was a recurring item of expenditure. Books were bought, though these were probably more utilitarian than recreational, and Mudie's Circulating Library – of which the reverse was true – was steadily supported. In 1852 a piano, a Broadwood, was bought for £12 5s., and tuned a few weeks later, at a cost of thirty shillings; thereafter the piano tuner paid periodic visits. The Athenaeum subscription was kept up – at six guineas in the 1850s, a guinea more thirty years later – as were those of the various learned societies to which Darwin belonged. There were subscriptions, too, for such publications as the *Times*, the *Westminster Review*, the *Geological Journal* and the *Daily News* Sixteen shillings bought Darwin a hat in August, 1851, and he made regular payments to his tailors, Stuart & Huntsman.

As they grew up, the children made their appearance in these ruled, dog-eared notebooks which so faithfully reflected all Darwin's interests and priorities. "Mechanical toys & Recreation £2.4.6", he wrote as Christmas approached in 1854. The older boys had by then acquired their own tailor, a man named Cooper who also made clothes for the servants. When it was time for William to go to school, down went a note about his pocket money and fare to Rugby, and, a little later, his fees for the school there (around £60 a half). The girls remained at Downe with the younger children; in the account books one finds that their governess was paid fifteen, and later twenty, pounds a quarter.

The faint spoor of what remained of Darwin's political interests can also be found in these pages. He was a member of the Corn Law League, dedicated to the repeal of the infamous tariff on wheat which was enriching the landlords while starving the poor. Over the years, his main political contribution was to the West Kent Liberal Association – the Liberal Party was, of course, the direct successor of the Whigs, to whom Wedgwoods and Darwins had given their allegiance for at least three generations.

The state of Darwin's health had a continual impact on the accounts. The cost of his first visit to the hydro at Malvern, in 1849, when he took his entire family and rented a house, came to £120, including £50 for medical fees. After his return, these fees continued at almost a guinea a month for several years, while at intervals other medical men, including Sir Henry Holland (second cousin to the Darwins and Wedgwoods, a fashionable doctor in London and physician to Queen Victoria), had their share of the money Darwin paid out in order to alleviate his anxieties. Holland, however, also attended the children and was the family's principal physician, despite the doubts expressed at intervals about his competence and intelligence – he became, at times, almost a figure of fun in the general correspondence. Nevertheless entries like that for 4 November, 1854, "Sir H Holland for Georgy/ with Physic 5s/ £1.6.0.", were not infrequent. Small items of medical equipment and bills paid to chemists also figured in these lists, even down to such entries as "Sticking Plaister 1/6".

Darwin's life-style, unostentatious but comfortable, was made possible by the fact that, although not rich during the early years of his marriage, he was never, even remotely, in want and, after his father's death, could be thought of as distinctly well-off. He had his share of his father's marriage settlement, as well as the money settled on him at his own wedding; Emma had been given £5,000 at the same time, her allowance until her father's death, and her inheritance after it. All these monies had been well administered for many profitable years by Jos Wedgwood and Dr. Robert. From the early 1840s on, Darwin took on more and more of the administration of his own money, and his ledger shows how he switched and altered his investments over the years, at the same time taking charge of Emma's income. Early on, he followed his father, who, like all active, if not alway prudent, mid-nineteenth century investors, was busily transferring his money from canals to railways. Darwin kept an eye on the various properties he owned, paying out for tithes and repairs. At times, he sold stocks at a loss, setbacks which he recorded with his usual meticulousness. By 1851, Darwin's income from the interest on his investments totalled £3,671, more than enough to maintain Down House even without the direct profits from the sale of stocks and shares or the royalties earned by his writings. The latter were not negligible, for the *Journal* of the *Beagle* voyage was by then selling its second English edition as well as coming out in various translations. Ten years later, in 1861, his investment income had risen to just under £5,000; by the time he died, it was running at around £8,000 a year. That he became rich in his later years was partly the result of his inheriting substantial sums from his father, but it was also the result of good management. Certainly he received from his father's estate some £40,000, but at the same time he managed to create year after year a surplus of income over expenditure of anything between £1,500 and £2,500; in the last decade of his life it was frequently much more than this. These sums were then available for reinvestment, a course the prudence of which must have recommended it to a man who remained all his life oddly anxious about money.

The good nature of the Darwins, as well as the standards of comfort such an income permitted them, created the conditions in which servants could over the years reign and flourish. Emma's Geneva aunt, Jessie Sismondi, who had stayed in the Gower Street house in 1840, wrote in her letter of thanks that "everything went to our heart's content; be it observed that Parslow is the most amiable, obliging, active, serviceable servant that ever breathed. I hope you will never part with him." The Darwins followed this advice as nearly as mortality made possible. Parslow (for whom as we have seen Darwin had enlarged the pantry) governed the domestic staff at Down House, to which he had moved with the rest of the household in 1842, for a total of thirty-three years. In 1875 he retired, returned now and then to potter about the grounds and shoot at the birds that threatened the garden; in this enviable condition, he survived his erstwhile master, being among the spectators when in 1885 a statue of Darwin was unveiled at the Natural History Museum in Kensington. Emma continued to visit him, though after 1891 she ceased to employ him even on the most irregular basis, despite his requests. He died in 1896, at the age of eighty-six.

A butler named Jackson took Parslow's place, and one can imagine that, holding the place until the early 1880s, he found it somewhat uncomfortable to be constantly under his predecessor's eye. The fact that he had earlier been a groom was unlikely to have inspired confidence in an orthodox indoor servant. The energetic Mrs. Evans ruled in the kitchen through the 1860s and 1870s, and into the next decade; there were the maids, Bessy, Anne and Emily Jane, supplemented later by an Esther; Comfort had had a boy to help in the garden, and so later did Lettington, each such lad now known to us only by his first name, carefully preserved in the account books. Indoors, meanwhile, there was Moffat, provided by the Darwins with livery at various intervals in the twenty years after he was first taken on in 1858, and therefore probably a footman.

There were always, of course, those members of the Down staff concerned only with the children and their upbringing. Early on there was Brodie, the Scottish nurse who seems to have arrived at Down with the family. She was surprisingly sensitive, going into a sort of decline when Bessy, the maid, treated her less respectfully than she thought she deserved. "We sent the maids to a concert at Bromley on Monday", wrote Emma to Fanny Hensleigh in the autumn of 1843, "and it has done Brodie such a wonderful deal of good . . . I have told Brodie that I shall not keep Bessy if she is pert to her, and matters have gone very smooth since." Brodie had the orange-red hair and pale blue eyes of an East Coast Scot, and though her face was scarred from the effects of smallpox, she had a most genuine and winning smile. Darwin's daughter Henrietta remembered her "sitting in the little summerhouse at the end of the Sand-walk", accompanied by "the constant click-click of her knitting-needles".

Later, there were the governesses – Miss Thorley, who travelled with the family on that first therapeutic trip to Malvern; Miss Pugh, who arrived in 1856 and swiftly went insane; Miss Grant, who arrived in 1858 and, even more swiftly than Miss Pugh, departed for unspecified reasons; Mrs. Latter, who after a year or so became a teacher at a nearby school, taught Henrietta and Elizabeth there and perhaps returned from time to time to give them special tuition; Fräulein Ludwig, who was German, taught that language to the girls and trailed the borrowed glamour of an officer brother who sailed in the liner *Teutonic*; and a handful of other specialists, including a Mlle Barellien, who supplemented Fräulein Ludwig's German with her own French.

Emma, of course, had her own maid – for a long time, the dignified, Scottish Mathison, who always addressed her in the third person: "Will Mrs. Darwin be getting up now?", she would ask, as though face to face with royalty. And there were others as time went on, men and women now anonymous, their very shades dispersed, the unheralded conscripts of this small domestic army. When Gwen Raverat was a girl and Bernard Darwin a boy, during the 1880s and 1890s, there seem to have been as many as six maids, a number that may or may not have included the beautiful head maid, Harriet; the footman; the coachman and the gardener – with, persumably, the usual boy to help him; Mrs. Brummidge, the cook; and Emma's personal maid. One may wonder, as the sunlight fades from that distant, late-Victorian summer which glows so ceaselessly in our imaginings – the very essence of our collective nostalgia – what on earth so many servants could have found to do all day. Mrs. Raverat provides the clue:

> There was no bathroom at Down, nor any hot water, except in the kitchen, but there were plenty of housemaids to run about with the big brown-painted bath-cans. Just as there were plenty of hands to lay and light the fires, scrub the floors, black the grates, polish the silver and the brass, dust the mantelpieces, wash the clothes and mend them, clear the windows, range the china on its shelves, wax the woodwork, carry the dishes filled or empty . . .

Just out of sight, in the shadows of the back stairs and the kitchen passage, hardly to be heard, almost unnoticed, almost unnoticeable, there is the scurrying of feet, the faint clash of metal and the flick and slop of water. Somewhere a little bell rings, brightly, once and then again – even in this most friendly of houses, this most liberal of families. Someone calls, in tones given just the slightest edge by a gathering impatience; and, up the dark stairs, echoing in the stone-floored passage, a high, clear voice replies breathlessly, "Coming, madam – quick as I can!"

5

Within these living ramparts Darwin sought his solitude. It was with a mole-like intensity that he followed the dark tunnels of his speculations: little disturbed the even surface of his life to reveal the activity below. Perhaps this was necessary to protect the dangerous nonconformity of his ideas. Constant ill health meant that he needed to conserve his energies and expend them only on what he thought essential. He had from the beginning detested the hurly-burly of scientific debate. His withdrawal had logic and convenience to recommend it.

In his comparative isolation, however, he faced the debilitating likelihood of losing contact with his intellectual peers. It was a danger he avoided by maintaining, like bridges to the mainland, a handful of close relationships: we have seen how crucial in his life had been the parts played by Henslow and Lyell. As important as these to him was a man whose name has begun to appear regularly in his story: the botanist Joseph Hooker. Over the fifteen years that culminated in the publication of *The Origin*, he became the confidant, critic, informant and mentor without whom Darwin's ideas might never have reached their full maturity.

So profoundly was botany a part of Hooker's family heritage, that he was able towards the end of his life to describe himself, in an after-dinner pleasantry, as "the puppet of Natural Selection". His father, Sir William Hooker, was for many years the Professor of Botany at Glasgow University, and created there the botanic gardens and herbarium which became centres of reference and admiration for the natural scientists of Scotland. He in turn had inherited his interest from *his* father, who was widely known for his success in growing rare and exotic plants, and been supported in it by his banker father-in-law, Dawson Turner; like Erasmus Darwin, Turner was one of those versatile eighteenth-century men whose successes in his own profession did not prevent his acquiring fame both as an antiquary and as a botanist specializing in ferns, mosses and similar spore-bearing plants.

Like Darwin, Hooker studied medicine at Edinburgh and varied it with unremitting attention to natural history. Again like Darwin, he was put forward for the post of naturalist on an Admiralty expedition – that in which Captain Ross took the *Erebus* and *Terror* deep into Antarctica – somewhat before he was entirely prepared for the opportunity. Unlike Darwin, he saw

Joseph Hooker, Darwin's staunch ally, in 1868.

the post given to someone older and more experienced, and sailed instead under the less satisfactory title of Assistant Surgeon and Botanist.

Darwin, who had returned from his own expedition only two years before, was during that time much in Hooker's thoughts. At his own interview, Ross had pointed out that the man who took the position of Naturalist to the expedition "must be perfectly well acquainted with every branch of Nat. Hist., and must be well known in the world beforehand, *such a person as Mr. Darwin*; here I interrupted him with 'what was Mr. D. before he went out? he, I daresay, knew his subject better than I now do, but did the world know him? the voyage with Fitzroy was the making of him (as I had hoped this exped. would me).' " So the young Joseph described to his father his frustrations and desperate arguments, in the Spring of 1839.

Later that summer, while Hooker was still waiting for his appointment to be confirmed, he and Darwin actually met, briefly. He was walking in Trafalgar Square "with an officer who had been his shipmate for a short time in the *Beagle*" when they met Darwin and for a moment chatted to him. From this first introduction, Hooker wrote later, "the memory that I carried away and still retain was that of a rather tall and rather broad-shouldered man, with a slight stoop, an agreeable and animated expression when talking, beetle brows, and a hollow but mellow voice . . ." For the young Hooker, used though he was to eminent men, this must have been an encounter of some moment – Charles Lyell's father had given his father the proofs of Darwin's *Journal*, and these Sir William had passed on to his son. Pressed for time, struggling to finish his medical studies before the Ross expedition left, Hooker slept with the uncorrected book under his pillow, in order to read it in the moments between waking and getting up. When he sailed, it was with a copy of the book with him; not only he but all the other officers under Ross read it with apparent avidity during the long years of their voyage.

During the four years that he was away, Hooker, like Darwin, collected and analysed with an assiduity that built him a developing reputation at home. The official naturalist, McCormick, "takes no interest but in bird shooting and rock collecting . . . I am, *nolens volens*, the Naturalist", he wrote in his journal in March, 1840; on the naval surgeon's unconcern, he built the foundations of his own career. As he gathered, collected and drew his specimens, bent over a table under one of *Erebus*'s stern windows, working often until two or three in the morning, he was also gathering new experience, and information that he sent in a series of letters to Charles Lyell, his mentor hardly less than he had been Darwin's. These, Lyell passed on to Darwin, who read them with fascination – impossible that they did not revive his own memories of travel, discomfort, discovery and triumph. When

Hooker returned therefore, late in 1843, Darwin wrote to him.

"I suppose you are very busy now and full of enjoyment: how well I remember the happiness of my first few months of England – it was worth all the discomforts of many a gale!" Henslow had sent Hooker the botanical collection Darwin had made in Patagonia and Tierra del Fuego, areas where Hooker had also worked; now Darwin hoped that Henslow would add the plants of the Galapagos as well. And he pointed Hooker towards answers he himself would have liked to have:

> Do make comparative remarks on the species allied to the European species, for the advantage of botanical ignoramuses like myself. It has often struck me as a curious point to find out, whether there are many European genera in T. del Fuego which are not found along the ridge of the Cordillera . . . Do point out in any sketch you draw up, what genera are American and what European, and how great the differences of the species are, when the general are European, for the sake of the ignoramuses.

For Darwin, of course, wrestling with the details of his evolutionary theories, the questions of distribution, and of how genera diverged from each other when widely separated by geography, were crucial.

Hooker sent Darwin an outline of his conclusions about the distribution of plants in those far southerly regions, and from that moment the two men drew closer and closer together, what had begun as a coincidence of scientific interests warming into the ease of genuine friendship. Darwin was soon using Hooker as one of the most important of the many sources of the information he was avidly gathering in order to make his own theory watertight. Letters filled with questions and speculations were year after year hurled at the knowledgeable Hooker.

They next met in Erasmus Darwin's house in Park Street, not long after he had moved in, during the autumn of 1844. Soon, Hooker was making the short journey to Down quite often; he recalled meeting there the botanist, Hugh Falconer; Edward Forbes, the marine biologist; and a man named Waterhouse, probably the architect Alfred Waterhouse, designer of the Natural History Museum in Kensington. With these, Hooker remembered, "there were long walks, romps with the children on hands and knees, music that haunts me still. Darwin's own hearty manner, hollow laugh and thorough enjoyment of home life and friends, strolls with him all together, and interviews with us one by one in the study to discuss questions in any branch of biological or physical knowledge that we had followed and which I at any rate always left with the feeling that I had imparted nothing and carried away more than I could stagger under."

Slowly, Darwin's health began to collapse. The other visitors were one by one denied a hospitality that now drained him. Only Hooker continued to make that journey with any frequency. After breakfast, the two men would settle for half an hour in the study, Darwin with a bundle of little paper slips in his hand, from which he would read out questions he had written down as they occured to him. This intensive seminar in natural history over, Darwin would talk for a while about the progress he was making, the ideas he was considering, the evidence upon which he was preparing to base himself; on these and similar matters he wanted, or perhaps needed, Hooker's opinions. For seven years, perhaps for eight, Darwin had struggled alone with his heterodox ideas; now, having confided in Hooker, he must have enjoyed the sensation of speaking openly about his theory to a man who, whatever his own conclusions on the matter, was able to understand it in all its ramifications. It provided him with an intellectual sounding board – and, perhaps, a partner, however passive, who could take from him some of the burden of apprehension, excitement and guilt.

These discussions rarely lasted much more than half an hour. Darwin had no stamina for such intense and disturbing sessions. They enriched him, but they also threatened him. He responded with headaches, weakness and a swift fatigue; Hooker remembered him, after such meetings, "taking a complete rest, for they always exhausted him, often producing a buzzing noise in the head, and sometimes what he called 'stars in the eyes', the latter too often the prelude of an attack of violent eczema in the head during which he was hardly recognizable." These migraine-like symptoms were Darwin's frequent reaction, as we have seen, to intense mental effort; they may also, as Dr. Colp has suggested, be a sign of the anxiety, the anguish of shame, which it caused Darwin to reveal the continuing inadequacies of his ideas. Given his sensitivity to potential, rather than actual, criticism, perhaps just raising so controversial a subject was enough to set off the eczema which would make it clear – as always, long before anyone else had been able to point it out – what a grotesque he had become. The claim, "I am a fool", not only diverts censure, it pre-empts it – just as the claim, "I am an invalid", softens it. From Darwin's unconscious reactions one may guess how dangerous this ground was, even to him, and how much it cost him, day after day, to venture upon it. It is a mark of how close he and Hooker had now become that it was only in the botanist's company that he dared to make such forays.

At noon, a recovered Darwin would go outside and call Hooker down, and together they would stroll in the shaded seclusion of the Sandwalk and talk of "foreign lands and seas, old friends, old books and things far off to both mind and eye." They might take another such walk in the afternoon, and then they would meet again at dinner, when the whole household assembled. Even if Darwin was not well enough to take his place at table "he generally managed to appear in the drawing-room, where seated in his high chair, with his feet in enormous carpet shoes, supported on a high stool – he enjoyed the music or conversation of his family."

It is no wonder that when, in 1845, it seemed as if Hooker would be appointed to the Chair of Botany at Edinburgh, Darwin thought that it would be "a heavy disappointment" to him – "in a mere selfish point of view, as aiding me in my work, your loss is indeed irreparable". Politics blocked the offer, and Hooker travelled on a botanical expedition to India instead; the loss, while it lasted, was almost total, but he was lost for a shorter while. He left in the *Sidon* on 11 November, 1847: in October, Darwin was already bemoaning his departure. "It will be a noble voyage and journey, but I wish it was over, I shall miss you selfishly and all ways to a dreadful extent . . ." He tried to say his farewells in person, but, "I am very unwell", he wrote apolgetically, "and incapable of doing anything . . . I shall not now see you. Farewell, and God bless you." He signed himself, "Your affectionate friend".

Hooker came back to England in 1850 and, after a few years of uncertainty, became officially assistant to his father, by now installed as the Director of the Royal Botanic Gardens at Kew. It was already obvious that he would follow his father in that influential post. His *Flora Antarctica*, two volumes of description and illustration, had appeared in 1847; the *Flora of New Zealand* was published in 1853 and that of *Tasmania* in 1859, shortly before Darwin's *Origin* startled the world into a new view of itself.

It is hard to imagine that Darwin could have come so successfully through the years when he struggled to realize, formulate and prove his theories without the friendship of Lyell and Hooker. Their acceptance of his ideas was for a long time partial and equivocal; their acceptance of him, of his seriousness and the importance of the work he had begun, never faltered. Often it was they who urged him on. Distracted by ill health, isolated from the intellectual hurly-burly of London, Darwin might have sunk into the self-indulgent torpor of a provincial dilettante, collecting his facts for ever, their collection his hobby and their publication his myth, had it not been for the encouraging attentions of these friends and scientific equals. To suggest this might seem to diminish Darwin, but the truth is that one cannot distinguish the moral contribution of Lyell and Hooker from the force of his own inner resolution. His courage and patient stubborness at times drew upon their spirits as much as his own. The quality of their attention confirmed for him the reality, the significance, of what he was about. Without them, he would have been alone, in an intellectual darkness through which he would have had nothing to guide him but his own sense of direction; there was no one else he would have trusted to show him whether or not he was on course.

Of his two friends, it was Hooker who became the more intimate. It was he who was the first to learn how serious Darwin was in his work on species, and it was he who was the first to be persuaded by its logic. It was he, and not Lyell, who publicly supported Darwin during the storms that followed the publication of *The Origin*. It was he, above all, who repeatedly made the journey to Down, breaching the isolation within which Darwin had settled; it was he alone who was consistently permitted through the ramparts of sickness. Nothing can lessen Darwin's achievement; but from that achievement, Hooker's contribution can hardly be separated.

6

Almost as soon as he had arrived at Down House in 1842, Darwin began his book on volcanic islands. It was to follow his work on coral islands as the second geological report of the *Beagle* expedition. By the following June, the manuscript was complete enough to be sent to Hooker for comment. Even before it was published in 1844, Darwin had begun the third, filling this with more general observations and conclusions. This was to take him another eighteen months to finish; part of it was given as a paper to the Geological Society in 1846.

At the same time he was preparing what would become the revised, 1845 edition of his *Journal* of the voyage, while writing as always a varied succession of letters, essays, articles and proposals. In 1844, for example, his mind seemed to flicker across the complex disciplines of the natural sciences like the fingers of a pianist over a keyboard. As a zoologist he described in great detail the seaborne, invertebrate arrow-worm and the slug-like planaria. As a geologist he discussed analogies between the structure of rocks and icebergs, and debated the significance of the dust that sometimes falls on ships as they pass the Atlantic coasts of Africa (perhaps alerted to this by his interest in the way seeds or minute organisms may be distributed). Here and there, the subterranean stream of his evolutionary speculations rises as though through a tiny spring, clue to the hidden flow below. In September, 1844, for example, *Gardener's Chronicle*, a favourite medium with him, published a letter he had written on variegated leaves: young box trees which he had planted had nearly all produced leaves with white tips. "Those growing in deep shade are not tipped, nor are some older trees. These facts may appear trivial; but I think the first appearance, even if not permanent, of any peculiarity which tends to become hereditary . . . deserves being recorded." Thus Darwin, thinking now as a botanist, and with one eye upon theories of transmutation.

It was at the beginning of 1844 that he ventured for the first time to reveal something of his vision to Hooker, with whom he had only recently struck up his friendship. He wrote to the botanist that he had been:

> ever since my return engaged in a very presumptuous work, and I know no one
> individual who would not say a foolish one. I was so struck with the distribution
> of the Galapagos organisms, &c. &c., and with the character of the American

fossil mammifers, &c. &c., that I determined to collect blindly every sort of fact, which could bear any way on what are species . . . At last gleams of light have come, and I am almost convinced (quite contrary to the opinion I started with) that species are not (it is like confessing a murder) immutable. Heaven forfend me from Lamarck nonsense of a "tendency to progression", "adapt-ations from the slow willing of animals", &c.! But the conclusions I am led to are not widely different from his; though the means of change are wholly so. I think I have found out (here's presumption!) the simple way by which species become exquisitely adapted to various ends. You will now groan, and think to yourself, "on what a man have I been wasting my time and writing to". I should, five years ago, have thought so . . .

The effort involved in this confession is reflected in the contortions of the style. Behind the bold mask of the innovative scientist, can there be glimpsed again the uncertain, almost cringing, figure of the motherless child? Yet, even as his arm rises to ward off the expected blow, he continues to assert his opinions with undeviating fluency. The courage of his obstinacy outfaces not only the exterior threat, but also the inner betrayal. He has seen a truth, and he will bear witness to it – today to a friend, but in time before the world. It has been suggested that such testimony was not as difficult to proclaim as we like to believe; the truth had been more than half-glimpsed already. The tone that Darwin adopted in his letter suggests that this was not a conviction he shared. For him, with Whewell, Sedgwick, Buckland, Murchison and the rest all giants in a landscape to which he was still by comparison a newcomer, the certainties to which he was opposing his own hypothesis were real, constant and, collectively considered, menacing.

Nevertheless, Darwin believed with absolute conviction that he had had a glimpse of the true workings of nature, and he wanted to work out the details of what he had seen. He had, as it were, been liberated into reality – a strange enough place for a man so cautious, and in many respects so conventional, to find himself. Whig he may have been, but he was neither revolutionary nor radical; he read his *Times* and minded his own business. Yet, even if only for a moment, he had been free enough in his perceptions to recognize how falsely human preconceptions lay across the actuality of nature.

How and why was it Darwin who achieved the insight that led to his theory? Is it the case, as Dr. Rankine Good has claimed, that "Darwin *did* revolt against his father"? Dr. Good says that "in a typical obsessional way" he transposed "the unconscious emotional conflict to a conscious intellec-tual one – concerning evolution. Thus, if Darwin did not slay his father in the flesh, then . . . he certainly slew the Heavenly Father in the realm of natural history." But it is hard to see where this fruitful animosity can have come from; so little ruffles the apparent serenity of the relations between Dr. Robert and his son that to assume suppressed patricidal impulses on Darwin's part seems less than entirely plausible. And did he really kill the Heavenly Father? Was he ever a devout and passionate Christian, suffused with the reality of a creator-god? There is no evidence to show that he was, or played more than the sober, decent, restrained and unembarrassing role in the congregation that was expected from a man of his background. His father was not a believer, while his brother Erasmus was almost, if not entirely, an atheist. The Heavenly Father, never very apparent in Darwin's personal firmament, seems rather to have faded away than been dramatically killed.

It may even be that the nebulous character of such a god, the largely conventional nature of Darwin's Christian beliefs, provided the conditions in which his natural ability to observe and synthesize his observations could come into play untrammelled. The intellect of a genius need not, like a computer, be switched on by some definable mechanism. It is precisely because it comes to unexpected or unprecedented conclusions, because it can work its way towards previously unsuspected connections, that we understand it to be that of a genius.

More to the point, perhaps, might be to ask how Darwin, essentially an unconfident and in some ways even a timid man, found the resolution to struggle his way for year after year towards a public statement of views so dangerously controversial. Neither the crushing weight of the task, nor the enmity of established scientific authority that it risked, halted or diverted him. Whatever his overt motives might have been for this or that personal decision, taken together they resulted in a paring down of his life that provided the precise conditions he needed in order to continue his work. His speculations brought him again and again to the brink of physical breakdown – either, as he believed, because of the intensity with which he pursued them or from some other, darker reason – yet he never wavered.

What was the source of his energy, which allowed him to continue in this way for so long? From the evidence of the *Notebooks* one is tempted to think that there lay within him a pool of unsuspected anger that he could draw on, so letting him attempt his lifelong answer to his father and, more especially, his sisters – the sisters of his childhood, not the staid, respectable and properly deferential ladies they became – for the doubts and exhortations with which they had once burdened him. He would show them – that they were wrong, that after all he was worthy of their respect and admiration. His capacity to see the thing in front of him as it was and not as some other thing he had been taught to expect, together with his ability to draw from such observations the richest inferences, combined to provide him with his scientific opportunities; the deep structures of his character, neurotic or not, ensured that he could seize them. Perhaps in some such configuration lies one part of the solution to the enigma that Darwin still presents. As we shall see, it is not the only explanation for his tenacity, the uncharacteristic self-assertion of his lonely, stubborn speculations.

In that summer of 1844, Darwin wrote the long essay which, copied in the clear hand of the village schoolmaster, Fletcher, set out the theories he had only been able to scrawl down briefly in pencil two years before. Its pages interleaved with blanks to permit further Darwinian comment, the book was again divided into two parts, the first three chapters following the pattern set in the early sketch. He entitled Part II "On the Evidence Favourable and Opposed to the View that Species are Naturally Formed Races, Descended from Common Stock". Here, as in the 1842 version, he faced the problems raised by the fossil record – problems which remained just as great when he published *The Origin* and which continue to create perplexity today*.

The fact is that the incompleteness of the fossil record (the earliest specimens deposited in rock were metamorphosed by the movements and pressures of millennia and so rendered unrecognizable) means that there is little evidence of early, transitional species ever having existed. It is therefore often difficult to support by direct proof the branching model of species development proposed by Darwin. One has to recognize, however, how partial the fossil record by its nature must be. To be created and preserved, a fossil must almost always derive from a creature with some hard parts, whether shell, bone, teeth, claws or tusks; it must have been preserved from destruction after death; and it must have been cocooned in a preservative material, such as the ooze of the ocean bed, deposits of tar, volcanic ash or the mud and quicksands of a bog. That there are gaps in the record should be the cause of no surprise.

Darwin himself, in this 1844 essay and later, thought that if no fossils older than those of the Palaeozoic Era were discovered, it must, as he put it, lead to the abandonment of his theory, "as it limits *from shortness of time* the total number of forms which can have existed on this world . . ." Today, the period before the Palaeozoic began, some six hundred million years ago, is divided into the two sections of the Pre-Cambrian Era. The first, over two thousand million years long, has been name the Archeozoic. From its mangled rock formations, pulverized by earthquakes and volcanoes, spread into vast ocean beds only to be heaped and rumpled into jagged mountain ranges, eroded into dust again and carried by gale and torrent back into the sea, no direct evidence of life has survived. Only certain deposits containing

---

* They gained wide publicity when presented in November, 1978, by Dr. Niles Eldredge, of the American Museum of Natural History. In the correspondence that followed in the London *Guardian*, they were seized on by Sir Fred Catherwood and others in terms reminiscent of those used by Archdeacon Paley 170 years before – proof of the durability of the Creationist arguments for design.

high percentages of carbon suggest the existence of anything organic. The Proterozoic Era, also a period of violent events, some volcanic, some glacial and some marine, began over two thousand million years ago; from it some testimony does survive to indicate the presence of living entities. These consisted of algae, worms, sponges and radiolaria, a kind of protozoic plankton; they seem all to have been entirely seaborne, but widely distributed. By the beginning of the Palaeozoic Era, marked by the Cambrian Period of six hundred million years ago, life existed in abundance. Trilobites, looking rather like marine woodlice, proliferated and would continue to do so for the millions of years that remained before their extinction; those fixed shellfish, the brachiopods, clung to their narrow lives in numbers they cannot match today; and the precursors of the world's vertebrates flickered busily below the waves. The earlier sponges, snails, worms and similar creatures had meanwhile maintained or consolidated their hold on life. Hordes of creatures existed in fruitful diversity, with hundreds of millions of years before them for their further development.

Thus, even if those overwhelming progenitors known to contemporary myth as "missing links" have not been discovered, both existing and fossil forms offer examples of points where branching seems to have occured. That unchanging genus of oyster, *Ostrea*, has had split from it lines of variant descendants which have subsequently evolved with some rapidity. The fossil forms known as calcichordates, found in marine strata laid down as much as six hundred million years ago, combine a skeleton much like that of starfish with features that look forward to the vertebrates. The opinion is strongly held that they were the forerunners of both fish and mammals. They had heads that were mostly mouth and gills and a tail that propelled the creatures through the water by swinging rapidly from side to side. What brain they had was centrally placed, behind the head, before the tail; while not a particularly appealing ancestor to look back to, the calcichordate was probably itself a variant of the even more primitive organism which was the original starfish*. A similar, but surviving creature is the tropical *Amphioxus*, a delicacy for Chinese fishermen, who share with it an ignorance of the role it plays in biology as another possible precursor of all vertebrates. The fossilized form of a small, upright ape, *Ramapithecus*, lurks beyond both *Australopithecus*, failed and deceased, and *Homo erectus*, shambling ancestor of us all. It is as if we saw the Tree of Life through a swirling mist – here a glimpse of the trunk, there the tracery of the outermost branches. Slowly, it may be, the mist will float away on the world's breezes; if it does, the shape

---

* Darwin had a not dissimilar vision in 1860. Writing to Lyell he said, "*Our* ancestor was an animal which breathed water, had a swim bladder, a great swimming tail, an imperfect skull, and undoubtedly was an hermaphrodite! Here is a pleasant genealogy for mankind."

we will see may not be quite what we expect – but unless our eyes totally deceive us now, it will certainly be a tree.

For Darwin, the mist was thicker. It was on that, indeed, that he based his arguments. He conceded that, should certain evidence be found, his theory collapsed. If different evidence were discovered, however, his theory would be confirmed. Neither, he felt, was likely; he made his stand, in other words, on the unavoidable inadequacies of the record. It was the medium itself that was imperfect – the earth, settling into its unpredictable shapes, restlessly undulating through the aeons, had rendered the discovery of any record complete enough for certainty very unlikely. But in the margin of one page Darwin had scribbled, "There can be no doubt, if we banish all fossils, existing groups stand more separate". He may have meant only the pachyderms and ruminants he was referring to at the time, but the remark has general relevance. The significance of the fossil record can most clearly be seen in the biological isolation of existing species that would result from its obliteration. The additional information provided by the fossils helps to create our sense of unity in nature, a unity which can sometimes be felt like an instinctive confirmation of transmutational ideas.

The rest of the Essay continued to follow the lines laid down in the original Sketch. Darwin faced another long-established difficulty that loomed in the contemporary consciousness, that of the extinction of species. Again he carried over his response from the *Transmutation Notebooks*: "To marvel at the extermination of a species appears to me to be the same thing as to know that illness is the road to death . . ." He then considered the question of species distribution, harking back to that similarity of forms in a given continental context which had so struck him during the *Beagle* voyage, and especially at the Galapagos. He pointed out that the development of a new form was unlikely to occur in more than one location. It would spread from there to the limits of possible migration. The rise and fall of great land masses would spread and split populations; these, during such turbulent epochs, would evolve into many different species, each of which would, nevertheless, show some rudimentary likeness to all the rest, so that "the inhabitants of the most *dissimilar* stations on the same continent would be more closely allied than the inhabitants of two very *similar* stations on two of the main diversions of the world". It was a proposition for which, as in *The Origin*, he could call his Rhea as witness.

He ended this long essay with a persuasive statement of his beliefs, at times reminiscent of the closing speech of an advocate determined to sway a suspicious jury.

It is derogatory that the Creator of countless Universes should have made by individual acts of his Will the myriads of creeping parasites and worms, that since the earliest dawn of life have swarmed over the land and in the depths of the ocean . . . From death, famine, and the struggle for existence, we see that the most exalted end which we are capable of conceiving, namely, the creation of the higher animals, has directly proceeded . . . There is a grandeur in this view of life with its several powers of growth, reproduction and of sensation, having been originally breathed into matter under a few forms ["perhaps into only one", added Darwin in pencil at this point], and that whilst this planet has gone cycling onwards according to the fixed laws of gravity and whilst land and water have gone on replacing each other – that from so simple an origin, through the selection of infinitesimal varieties, endless forms most beautiful and most wonderful have been evolved.

The final sentence is a modification of the one that ends the 1842 sketch; modified again, it also ends *On The Origin of Species*. Such correspondences are the fibres in the long thread of Darwin's thought that runs from 1837 through 1859 and onward to the end of his life.

In a late addition to the essay, Darwin tackled the problem of divergence – if varieties were species at the beginning of their formation, why and how in the course of their development did they increase the differences between them? For a solution he seized upon the principle that life will fill an ecological niche where one exists. There were "many and widely diversified places in the polity of nature", the diversity within a species matched these, enabled its members to take advantage of them and so favoured different adaptations in each group: such favoured adaptations became the particular characteristics of the new species.

When, early in July, 1844, the essay was finally written, Darwin understood very clearly what he had achieved. In seven years he had hammered out a theory that, as it were, ran by its own intrinsic logic. It needed no extraneous principles to activate it, as Lamarck's had, but, like the railway engines then beginning to criss-cross England, generated its own power. He was the first – and he knew he was the first – who by rejecting the received orthodoxies had freed himself to gather all the available evidence and so had been able to postulate, not the idea of evolution – there was little novelty in that – but an integrated model of how evolution worked.

Why did he not publish? The answer must be the simple one that he was not ready. Before he dared to launch his vessel on the seas of scientific controversy, he had to make sure that its every seam was caulked and watertight. The fact that its design was novel meant it would have to survive both close inspection and hard knocks. Eight of the next ten years were to be lost to the all-demanding cirripedes; much of the remainder to publishing what was left of the *Beagle* results – and to illness. How important he considered the work he had done is made plain by the letter he wrote to

Emma on 5 July; equally clear, however, from the request it contains, is his awareness of how much still had to be done before his Essay became the closely argued book, made respectable by the full foot-noted panoply of academic rectitude, that he knew it had to be to convince the neutral and silence the bigoted. To prepare such a book would take every minute, and more, of the years that remained to him between the dissection of his last barnacle and the intervention of the faraway Wallace. To his wife, therefore, he wrote:

> I have just finished my sketch of my species theory. If, as I believe, my theory in time be accepted by even one competent judge, it will be a considerable step in science.
>
> I therefore write this in case of my sudden death, as my most solemn and last request, which I am sure you will consider the same as if legally entered in my will, that you will devote £400 to its publication, and further, will yourself, or through Hensleigh, take trouble in promoting it. I wish that my sketch be given to some competent person, with this sum to induce him to take trouble in its improvement and enlargement. [Both Darwin's heavily annotated books and his "scraps", papers bearing references and quotations, should be made available.] . . . As the looking over the references and scraps will be a long labour, and as the *correcting* and enlarging and altering my sketch will also take considerable time, I leave this sum of £400 as some remuneration, and any profits from the work. I consider that for this the editor is bound to get the sketch published either at a publisher's or his own risk. Many of the scraps in the portfolio contain mere rude suggestions and early views, now useless, and many of the facts will probably turn out as having no bearing on my theory.

The best editor would be Lyell, who would "find the work pleasant, and he would learn some facts new to him." Because "a geologist as well as a naturalist" was ideal, Darwin's next choice was "Professor Forbes of London"*. Although he was giving the names in order of preference, he found it difficult not to be polite to his nominees even *in absentia*: "The next best (and quite best in many respects) would be Professor Henslow. Dr. Hooker would be *very* good." Then came H.E. Strickland, another all-round naturalist and traveller; finally there appears the crossed-out sentence, "Professor Owen would be very good; but I presume he would not undertake such a work." If money proved the reason for a good editor's refusing the post, and another £100 might make the necessary difference – "I request earnestly that you will raise £500."

---

* Edward Forbes, who died in 1854 when not quite forty. He was a geologist, botanist and palaeontologist, a traveller, witty and gregarious, a man who, like Darwin himself, had been a naturalist on an expedition overseas. In 1844, he gave up the chair of botany at King's College, London, to become official paleontologist to the Geological Survey. In 1853 he became one of the youngest Presidents of the Geological Society there has ever been and, in the year of his death, was appointed Professor of Natural History at Edinburgh University.

Then or later, Darwin added, "Lyell, especially with the aid of Hooker (and if any good zoological aid), would be best of all. Without an editor will pledge himself to give up time to it, it would be of no use paying such a sum . . . If there should be any difficulty in getting an editor who would go thoroughly into the subject, and think of the bearing of the passages marked in the books and copied out of scraps of paper, then let my sketch be published as it is, stating that it was done" (here the words "several years ago and" have been added) "from memory without consulting any works and with no intention of publication in its present form."

Although the new sketch, when copied, ran to 231 pages, it is clear from this letter that Darwin considered it no more than a rudimentary outline for the work he intended to write. Having, so to speak, appointed his reserves, he now turned to the task of editing, revising, annotating and supporting this lengthy summary. At the same time, he began what no editor would have been competent to do, a series of experiments in botany and zoology meant to clarify some of the points he was describing. Many of his results would appear years later, in the dependent books that followed *The Origin*. But his theory would stand or fall by the validity of its supporting evidence – and he was leaving nothing but the workings of evolution itself to chance.

While his species work, as always, seized his deepest and most central interest, its ramifications now led him away from theory, towards the tedious practicalities that confronted the systemizing naturalist. In 1846, he noted in his journal, "Oct. 1. Paper on new Balanus Arthrobalanus . . ." He had begun his long wearisome labours on the whole genus of barnacles. (Ironically, this first paper seems never to have been published.) While in Chile he had found a form "which differed so much from all other Cirripede that I had to form a new sub-order for its sole reception". In order to understand its structure, he had to understand that of barnacles as a whole, to see in what ways it was peculiar within the genus, "and this gradually led me on to take up the whole group". For eight years he laboured over these small and unresponsive molluscs, dissecting, examining, classifying and describing; in the process, he became a practical biologist, a worker with scalpel and microscope, a compiler and collator of minute results, in a way that he had never been before. That is not to claim, as Huxley later would, that it was his intention when he began to use these investigations as a training prog-ramme. He was slowly drawn into them by his own intellectual compulsions, a sort of fastidiousness which did not permit him to leave what had not been thoroughly explored. Had he simply wanted to train himself in previously neglected methods and techniques, a few months' hard work with a single species and an exhaustive monograph at the end of it would have been enough. Instead, having set out for himself his task, he pursued it despite his increasing boredom and despite, above all, the speculations on species which more and more clearly he saw as his real, his central interest.

That he was bored is clear. In 1848 he was writing to John Gray, the Keeper in the Zoological Department of the British Museum, "In truth never will a mountain in labour have brought forth such a mouse as my book on Cirripedia: it is ridiculous the time each species takes me". To Hugh Cuming, a naturalist and collector, he wrote a few months later, "I quite dread the genus Balanus". He was, fortunately, always able to summon up some interest in what he was doing, even at times a little amusement. Early in 1853 he dissected what he calls "a curious cirripede" and found on the female specimen twelve males attached. "These males I suspect are the most negative creatures in the world; they have no mouth, no stomach, no thorax, no limbs, no abdomen, they consist wholly of the male reproductive organs in an envelope," he wrote to Lyell. Barnacles came and went through the house at Downe as though on their own mysterious tides. The British Museum lent him its collection, Hugh Cuming allowed him to work on his, individuals like the geologist J.S. Bowerbank, who sent him fossil specimens, or the Irish botanist G.C. Hyndman, who sent him larvae of *Balanus*, or the French naturalist, Henri Milne-Edwards, who had himself published work on the crustacea, gave him help, encouragement and advice. No wonder one of the young Darwin boys, visiting the Lubbocks, asked solemnly about Sir John, "And where does he do his barnacles?"

What kept Darwin at his dogged labours? His character, with internalized authority constantly ready with its criticisms, supplied its own imperatives. Yet even for him these would not have proved sufficiently commanding to divert him from what had quite consciously become his life task. Before beginning his monographs, he had written to Hooker, "I hope this next summer to finish my South American geology, then to get out a little zoology, and hurrah for my species work". That had been in the Spring of 1845; why had he continued to toil so long and painfully at "a little zoology" which he himself obviously thought peripheral? In the autumn of the same year he had written, also to Hooker, "All of what you kindly say about my species work does not alter one iota my long self-acknowledged presumption in accumulating facts and speculating on the subject of variation, without having worked out my due share of species". Seven or eight years later, still to Hooker, he was writing, "How painfully (to me) true is your remark, that no one has hardly a right to examine the question of species who has not minutely described many". He was discussing the credibility of foreign authors, but clearly was disturbed about his own.

Perhaps this is the clue – Darwin was not training himself with the Cirripede, he was *qualifying* himself. He was establishing his right to deal

Plate 18

The anatomist Richard Owen, a disciple of Cuvier, who became the bitterest of Darwin's scientific opponents.

Plate 19

Huxley who, in 1857, when this photograph was taken, had still to be convinced by Darwin's ideas, but who later became their most zealous defender.

Plate 20

A.R. Wallace, who in the aftermath of fever dreamed up a theory of natural selection so close to Darwin's own that for a while Darwin believed he would have to cede priority to the other man.

Plate 21

Charles Lyell's great book, *Principles of Geology,* opened for Darwin the vast aeons without which natural selection became impossible, though ironically Lyell himself was never entirely persuaded by Darwin's ideas.

with the problems that obsessed him. He would be challenging men who had worked all their lives in the classification of organisms on the lines first laid down by Linnaeus. "My only comfort is (as I mean to attempt the subject), that I have dabbled in several branches of Natural History . . ." But that would have been small comfort had he abandoned his tedious sea creatures. Worse than never having attempted the analysis of such a group would have been to begin the task and fail to complete it. Once he had set his hand to it, he could not falter or turn back. To leave it half done, whether he could afford eight years or not, would have made him vulnerable to the counter-attacks of the intellectual establishment. It would have opened to them the possibility of disregarding his ideas while attacking his right to hold them. The four volumes that resulted, the first two on the stalked, the second two on the directly attached species, covering both fossil and contemporary specimens, were not merely significant contributions to the classification of the natural world, which remained the standard works for many years after their publication in 1851 and 1854. They were also among the most important of his credentials when the time came to reveal his wilder, farther-reaching and far more controversial speculations on the mutability of species.

Not that his detailed work now did not have its repercussions on his opinions. The slow alteration of one species into another during its long interchange with its environment depended upon the existence of significant differences between one individual and another. Only then would times of crisis offer to the first advantages from which the second was less likely to benefit. Darwin realized from his dissection of cirripede how widespread such variations were, how different from all the others, even if only in minute ways, each individual actually was. "Systematic work would be easy", he wrote to Hooker in the summer of 1849, "were it not for this confounded variation, which, however, is pleasant to me as a speculatist, though odious to me as a systemist". Difference was grist to his mill, though it was uniformity that provided the logic of his labours.

One particular variation that he found, however, seemed to verify important elements in his theories. Safe under the protective mantle of these normally hermaphrodite creatures he found what appeared to be tiny parasites. It was his thinking on the mutability of species which allowed him to identify them as those rudimentary males which, five years later, he was cheerfully to describe to Lyell as "the most negative creatures in the world". It had already appeared to him probable that species bearing the organs of both sexes were likely in the course of time to throw up individuals in which the characteristics of one sex were beginning to predominate over those of the other. The logic of survival would then lead to the appearance of individuals whose sexual development was opposite and complementary to that of the first group – "and here we have it", he wrote to Hooker, "for the male organs in the hermaphrodite are beginning to fail, and independent males ready formed".

What Darwin in his precise and very comprehensible descriptions managed to do was not only to demonstrate how gross was the variation between the typical cirripede with its seventeen segments and its cluster of organs, and the attenuated males with their three segments, single eye and sexual organ – a variation which itself helped forward his mutation argument – but also to show the link between the various types, leading the reader, by way of a chain of similarities and correspondencies, to a conclusion of diversity which he could clearly understand. It needed only another step or two to arrive at the threshold of the unorthodoxy hidden under the meticulous restraint of his descriptions. In a sense, this was true of the species work of other men, too, since there had been discussion for a hundred years on the exact nature and limits of species. Perhaps it was the weight of the definitions themselves, the very solemnity of the heavy Latin nomenclature, that anchored the species immovably in their places. The words lay across nature like a judgement, reinforcing the great creative act of Adam, the giver of names; the organisms of the living world stood trapped in the vast grid of identity which mankind had laid over them.

It is interesting to see how little the outside world by now impinged on that which Darwin had created, and in which he laboured with such intensity. The Chartists and reform at home; abroad, the slow collapse of Turkey and the revolutions of 1848; the rumbustious hide-and-seek of Parliament, where Russell, Palmerston, Peel, Gladstone and Disraeli were making their various assaults on history – none of these had the slightest effect on life at Down House or received more than passing mention in the letters Darwin so tirelessly wrote or received in his worldwide correspondence. Many of these letters, of course, referred to the cirripedes – to the loan of specimens, the progress of the work and the quirks and oddities of the creatures themselves. With Lyell, Darwin continued to discuss the minutiae of geological theory – but "it makes me groan to think that probably I shall never again have the exquisite pleasure of making out some new district, of evolving geological light out of some troubled dark region." Resignedly, he added, "So I must make the best of my Cirripedia", but, as he had already written to Hooker, ". . . do not flatter yourself that I shall not yet live to finish the Barnacles, and then make a fool of myself on the subject of species . . ."

By 1854, the monographs on the cirripedes, detailed, exhaustive and rigorous, had finally appeared. During these years of the barnacles, Darwin's general output of papers had naturally dwindled: between 1846 and 1855 there were only seven articles published, most of them minor. The only lengthy piece was his advice to peripatetic geologists in a contribution to the *Manual of Scientific Enquiry*, brought out by the Navy, under Herschel's editorship, in 1849. Darwin, certainly remembering his own beginnings, comforted the neophyte with the thought that "perhaps no science requires so little preparatory study as geology" – a pair of hammers, a chisel, a compass, a small pickaxe and a clinometer were the only essential tools. Armed with these, a magnifying glass and Lyell's works, almost anyone, apparently, could act as a geologist. Let the apprentice label every item he collected, draw accurate diagrams, examine numerous specimens, "and by acquiring the habit of patiently seeking the cause of everything that meets his eye, and by comparing it with all that he has himself seen or read of, he will, even if without any previous knowledge, in a short time infallibly become a good geologist . . ." Clearly Darwin in his modesty felt that what he had done, anyone might do.

In his personal journal, Darwin wrote on 9 September, 1854, "Finished packing up all my Cirripedes . . . Began Oct 1 1846. On Oct 1 it will be 8 years since I began! but then I have lost 2 or 3 years by illness." So he marked the moment when he arrived at the point for which he had been aiming ever since his return from the *Beagle* expedition. That voyage had supplied him with his raw material; the publication of its results had founded his reputation. Because of the latter, he had been able to develop a network of scientific connections, the closer of whom supplied him with the controversy upon which he could sharpen his ideas, and the more distant, with the information he needed to feed and develop them. The work he had done, the papers, articles and books he had published, his secretaryship at the Geological Society, and his membership of other learned bodies, had both established and protected his position. As the time had passed in this profitable manner, so his still unpublished theories had become clearer, more extensive and increasingly supported by his researches. Now he felt himself ready to begin the final phase of his work – that which would at last lay his speculations before the world.

7

Darwin must have wondered, however, as he began to gather and collate the notes he had written and the evidence he had collected on the mutability of species, whether his physical strength would allow him to finish the task he had set himself. The ill health which had already robbed him of so many years of work and circumscribed his relations with his friends, constrained him in every department of his life. It governed the reading and writing he did, the people he saw, his leisure, exercise and diet, ordained his happiness or depression, brought calm or disorder to his days and nights. His migrations were planned, undertaken and terminated according to his physical condition. And how much of his energy was spent in wondering about the nature of his ailments, worrying over their effects and considering how they might best be treated? How much more was spent in undergoing the actual treatments – long treks to hydros, hours taken up with water therapies at home, douches, enemas – and in the precautions that he and his family took to keep the Down world equable, unobtrusive, obliging, undemanding and amenable?

Nor was it, of course, only Darwin himself whose life was dominated by the fluctuations in his health. It became over the years the unseen presence that ruled his entire household. One is therefore brought to ask how much his indefinable maladies set the seal upon the dependence through which he controlled Emma and the children. That Emma, able by mothering to manage him, connived at this does not divert the question. Was ill health both his method of governing and his way to an inner contentment? Was it physical feebleness that he brought to the inner transactions of his marriage, receiving in return a close, maternal care – the kind of care which early deprivation had taught him to construe as love?

To speculate on the origins of Darwin's constant ill health, and even to wonder in what way it was of use to him, is not to deny the genuineness of his sufferings. These were real and he detested them – that this should be so was, indeed, the very condition of their value to him. He was not, after all, either a confidence trickster or a hypocrite. It is obvious from his constant laments – to his family, his friends, his scientific colleagues, even comparative strangers – how much he overtly regretted his condition. As early as June, 1841, he was forecasting in a letter to Lyell that he would ail for years to come, so that – since "the 'race is for the strong' " he would have to "be content to admire the strides others make in Science."

Two years later he was complaining to his father, though without receiving much satisfaction, "of my dreadful numbness in my finger ends"; as he wrote to Emma, "all the sympathy I could get was 'yes, yes exactly – tut-tut, neuralgic, exactly, yes yes' . . ." By 1845, Darwin was not only safely installed at Down House, he was also solidly established in the role of invalid. That Spring he wrote to Fox, "It really is one of my heaviest grievances from my stomach, the incapability & dread I have of going anywhere. I literally have not slept, I believe, out of inns, my own, Erasmus', Shrewsbury & Maer houses, since I married".

The fact is, Darwin always had the ability to present perfectly normal circumstances as evidence of debility. In the six years since his marriage he had made frequent visits to his parents and parents-in-law, had attended scientific meetings, had covered the Home Counties in his search for a country house, and had set up two successive establishments, the second one large, landed and in considerable need of alteration. Another man might have taken the same record as evidence of considerable energy – even without bringing into account the secretaryship of a learned society, the preparation of a number of scientific papers, the publication of two books, the collation of the zoological results of the *Beagle* voyage and the drafting of an evolutionary theory which was to alter the intellectual climate of the world.

What was the precise shape of Darwin's misery; how did his debilities manifest themselves? Most commonly, he suffered from flatulence. Some flaw in his digestion produced, apparently, great excesses of intestinal gases which, creating inner pressures followed by the turmoils of relief, caused him very frequent pain. Dr. Lane, who attended Darwin in the 1850s, wrote later, "In the course of a long professional experience I have seen many cases of violent indigestion, in its many forms, and with the multiform tortures it entails, but I cannot recall any where the pain was so truly poignant as in his. When the worst attacks were on he seemed almost crushed with agony . . . it was then that I first perceived the wonderful sweetness and gentleness of his nature, his patience, and the gratitude with which he received the most ordinary services and tokens of sympathy."

Such periods of acute pain were, fortunately, never very long-lasting; sometimes he vomited as a result of them. Headaches, too, plagued him, often occuring at the same time and probably as a consequence of his flatulence. Often he suffered from boils, less frequently from rashes or other skin conditions. He was subject to colds, though these seem rarely to have led to any complications. His fits of flatulence would leave him weak and trembling, which is hardly surprising if they caused him the agony described by Dr. Lane. At the same time, he would experience feelings of fear and anxiety, or the heavy torpor of depression. On occasion he seemed to suffer a noticeable diminution of his energies, feeling languid and weak and finding it necessary to take to his couch, or his bed.

Yet all this time he maintained a steady output of work, and played his part as a husband and father. Children were cherished as they grew and, from time to time, their numbers were added to. His weaknesses, however, constantly distressed Darwin and, when conventional medicine offered him no relief, he began to seek less orthodox alternatives. He was no more to be limited by the received convictions of the world in this than in his scientific ideas, but, perhaps significantly, it was only after his father's death in 1848 that he began seriously to consider alternative therapies. He wrote to Fox early in 1849 to ask him about treatments at the increasingly fashionable hydros. The previous autumn his old comrade from the *Beagle* expedition, Sulivan – now clambering swiftly through the ranks of naval hierarchy – had recommended these for people with poor digestive systems and, a little nervously, Darwin now wanted to know more about them. Fox passed on the little he knew; "Thank you much for your information about the water-cure: I cannot make up my mind: I dislike the thought of it much – I know I shall be very uncomfortable then – & such a job moving with 6 children," wailed Darwin in reply.

Nevertheless, anxiety about his condition forced him into action. On 10 March, 1849, with his horde about him – wife, children, governess, servants and all the baggage they demanded; the journey alone cost him over £22 – he set himself up in a house at Malvern, very close to the hydropathic estab-lishment of Drs. Gully and Wilson. It was his knowledge of the successful spas and hydros of Europe that had led James Wilson to help found this therapeutic centre, but the guiding and enthusiastic spirit of the place was James Manby Gully. The son of wealthy Jamaican settlers, he had been educated at Edinburgh and Paris; a year younger than Darwin, he must have reached the Edinburgh medical school only a little while after Darwin had left it. Setting himself up in London, he soon laid the foundations of a reputation as a medical iconoclast – his *The Simple Treatment of Disease* offered alternatives, often enlightened, to the conventionalized responses of his colleagues. In 1842, he opened his Malvern hydropathic clinic, giving that old spa an infusion of new energy, and four years later published his explanation of what he was doing, *The Water Cure in Chronic Disease*. It is a tribute to his lucidity and the widespread hypochondria of the Victorian era that his book went through nine editions. His clinic, meanwhile, attracted an impressive stream of the rich, the fashionable and the famous – including

Erasmus's friend, Carlyle, and Darwin's later enemy, Bishop Wilberforce of Oxford. For later generations, alas, Dr. Gully's fame was to be more luridly established through his involvement in the Bravo murder case: when in 1876 Charles Bravo died, his wife was suspected of having poisoned him, and Gully, as her lover and a medical man, of having supplied the necessary drugs. He was never directly accused and in the trial that followed Mrs. Bravo was acquitted, but his reputation did not survive the lurid publicity. All this, however, still lay almost thirty years in the future and, in the meantime, belief in Gully and his methods remained fervent and wide-spread.

It was Dr. Gully's objective to create by artificial means a "nervous irritation" in some part of the patient's body, analogous to that naturally, and distressingly, occuring in the stomach, but distant from that organ. Thus the patient was wrapped in or rubbed with soaking sheets, or persuaded into a sitz bath, in order to draw the blood away from the chronically inflamed stomach to some other part. Periods of sweating, followed by cold baths, were supposed to "rouse" the system – a theory which continues to enrich the owners of saunas – while a regimen of bland foods would offer the delicate stomach the minimum of stimulation. Regulated exercise helped the process along, while calculated discomfort helped the patient to forget the primary distresses which had originally persuaded him through Dr. Gully's doors. What Gully forcefully rejected, however, was the value of medication. It was permanent organic regeneration that he was after, and not some temporary muffling of the system in a drug.

Nine days after his arrival, Darwin sent Susan his "hydropathical diary":

> A ¼ before 7 get up, & am scrubbed with rough towel in cold water for 2 or 3 minutes, which after the few first days, made & makes me very like a lobster – I have a Washerman, a very nice person, & he scrubs behind, while I scrub in front – drink a tumbler of water & get my clothes on as quick as possible & walk for 20 minutes – I cd. walk further, but I find it tires me afterwards – I like all this very much. – At same time I put on a compress which is a broad wet folded linen covered by mackintosh & which is "refreshed" – i.e. dipt in cold water every 2 hours & I wear it all day except for about 2 hours after midday dinner; I don't perceive much effect from this of any kind.

Sugar, butter, spices, tea, bacon "or anything good" were excluded from his diet, though "plain pudding" had finally been admitted. "At 12 o clock I put my feet for 10 minutes in cold water with a little mustard & they are violently rubbed by my man . . . After dinner lie down & try to go to sleep for one hour – At 5 oclock feet in cold water – drink cold water & walk as before." Supper ended the day, a regimen which left Darwin with "much sickness", but stronger and less depressed. "Tomorrow," he added, "I am to be packed at 6 oclock" – here, half boastfully, half plaintively, one feels, Darwin inserted "a.m." – for 1½ hours in Blanket, with hot bottle to my feet & then rubbed with cold dripping sheet; but I do not know anything about this."

Four months of the therapy produced, for whatever reasons, the hoped-for result. "I consider the sickness as absolutely cured", proclaimed Darwin to Fox. "The Water Cure is assuredly a grand discovery & how sorry I am that I did not hear of it, or rather that I was not somehow compelled to try it some five or six years ago." After sixteen weeks – he was never again to be so long away from Downe – Darwin, relaxed and rested, led his entourage home once more. He began to take early morning walks; he had a bath-house built near the well in the grounds and there had Parslow give him daily water treatments; and he began to keep a meticulous record of both these uncomfortable therapies and his resultant health.

He was even earlier keeping notes on at least the changes in his weight. In October, 1843, he wrote to Emma from Shrewsbury, "I weighed *yesterday* before luncheon 11st 2½lbs: please enter it in your book . . ." Even at that stage, therefore, some sort of record was being maintained on certain aspects of his health; that this was so seems consistent with his habits of close observation and his passion, dating from the *Beagle* days, for writing copious notes. Now he began to list most meticulously the waxing and waning of his disabilities. His comments were based on a scale that determined his state of health as well very, well, poorly or poorly very, these categories being refined by occasional underlinings. He remarked on "fits", too, these being presumably bouts of painful flatulence and indigestion.

Later, he was able to code his repetitions – "Sw" for sweat, for instance, or "Sh" for his shallow bath, "D" for his douche and "Dr" for treatment with a dripping sheet. He recorded his weight on Monday, 23 July; he was, "without Hat or compress, in grey trousers & shoes", exactly eleven stone, or 154lbs. A little later, he began to note that he was "Well, VERY", and from 1850 he began to count up these "double dashes", as he called them, in order to keep some statistical account of his condition. In 1850, too, there appear occasional little ticks in the record, four or five a month, and it is possible that these marked the occasions of sexual intercourse. It seems unlikely that he would have neglected this factor, yet impossible that he would have mentioned it directly. There is no indication, however, that such a conclusion is correct, rather than based on the wishful prurience of a biographer.

On Tuesday, 16 January, 1855, he wrote "Well *very*" and noted that the night had been "good", then abruptly brought his records to an end. If one glances at other evidence – his letters, for instance, or account books – there seems no reason for his having done so. The piano tuner called at Down,

£1.7s.6d was paid to charity; nothing of special significance occurred. On 18 January, however, feeling that a change of air was needed, Darwin transported his entire family into the bustle of London, taking a house in York Place, off Baker Street. The whole of Europe was clutched in a vicious winter. In the Crimea, inadequately clothed soldiers froze in the encampments of a trumped-up war; betrayed by a tight-fisted Parliament, they shivered under the bulging walls of Sebastopol or died by the thousand in disgusting hospitals. At Down, two of Darwin's sons had already caught bronchitis. Now, in London, he and Emma both fell ill; when any of them did venture out, the unrelenting frosts depressed them further. (This was a stay which was to cost Darwin £13 in "Dilapidations".) It seems likely that if the Diary of Health was not forgotten in the departure from Downe, it was neglected in the general misery. Faced eventually with a gap of several weeks to fill, Darwin may simply have abandoned his now incomplete record.

By this time, although still convinced by the claims of hydropathy, those of Dr. Gully seemed to him exaggerated. Clairvoyance and mesmerism had joined homeopathy in Gully's medical armoury, and these were all matters on which he had inherited his father's scepticism. A visit to a clairvoyante, at Gully's urging, did nothing to change his mind, nor did Harriet Martineau's strident advocacy of mesmerism persuade him of it or endear her to him. "I do not think I shall have courage for Water Cure again", he admitted to Fox in February, 1857. He was dosing himself with "mineral acids", he said; the Victorians, with their "chronic dyspepsia" a widespread malady, believed the cause might be the inadequate production of acids by the stomach. Darwin was clearly attempting to right this supposed deficiency – "with, I think, good effect", he reported.

By the end of April, however, working with steady intensity at the enormous book, *Natural Selection*, which it was then his intention to write, he felt so exhausted that the old water therapies regained their attractions. This time he travelled to Moor Park, where Dr. Lane was the resident physician to the hydro. Lane, too, had studied his medicine at Edinburgh, but, thirteen years younger than Darwin, had been there more than twenty years later. Like Gully, he had published a book on hydropathy, subtitling it *The Natural System of Medical Treatment*. He was a less flamboyant and extrovert character than Gully, perhaps more thoughtful, more concerned with the philosophy, the ethics and the theory of medicine. "I like Dr. Lane & his wife & her mother, who are the proprietors of this establishment very much", Darwin confided to Fox. "Dr. L. is too young, but that is his only fault – but he is a gentleman & very well read man. And in one respect I like him better than Dr. Gully, viz that he does not believe in all the rubbish which Dr. G.

does . . ." What Dr. Lane did believe in, as his book announced, was nature's own inherent powers of healing, the *vis medicatrix naturae* of medieval medicine, coupling this with the realization that its "cardinal medicines are the apparently simple medicaments of air, exercise, water, and diet . . ." He was sufficiently of his time and place to consider that these had to be supplemented by "healthy moral influences".

Lane became as much a friend as a doctor to Darwin. Together they would walk through the open woodlands that surrounded the house. After Darwin's death, Lane remembered these rambles, during which, as he wrote, "No object in nature, whether Flower, or Bird, or Insect of any kind, could avoid his loving recognition". What he saw brought back to Darwin memories of his *Beagle* days a quarter of a century before, and the stream of anecdote, memory, scientific fact and speculation were delivered, Lane said, "in a manner so full of point and pith and living interest, and so full of charm, that you could not but be supremely delighted . . ."; such a conversation was "a vast intellectual treat to be never forgotten", such promenades "red-letter days in your calender".

The possible causes for Darwin's persistent ill health have provided the one course of speculation and even controversy that centres on his private life. It has stimulated psychotherapists to outface, or outflank, experts in tropical medicine, and pathologists to comb Darwin's diaries and letters for clues. Most of the theories that have been advanced are considered in some detail by Dr. Ralph Colp in his book, *To Be an Invalid**, which chronicles Darwin's ailments; none of the physical explanations, based on common-sense internal medicine, are in any way definitive, while those which look to anxiety, guilt and neurosis for the cause cannot be definitive by their nature. We are faced by that delight of academics, the insoluble problem.

For a long time, it was thought that Chagas' disease provided an answer. Proposed by an Israeli parasitologist, Professor Saul Adler, this was a theory based on a diary entry made by Darwin during the *Beagle* years. On 25 March, 1835, he had, he reported, been bitten by "the great black bug of the Pampas". This had occured in Mendoza Province, in Argentina, where, it was claimed, over half the population suffered from or carried Chagas' disease, and nearly three-quarters of a certain group of insects, *Triatoma infestans*, carried the microorganism which caused it. Named *Trypanosoma cruzi*, this organism damaged heart muscle and intestinal nerve tissue. The disease, therefore, between periods of remission, made itself apparent through cardiac deficiencies and intestinal disorders. Discovered in 1909, it was not an ailment Darwin could have known. If *T. cruzi* was also to be

---

* Published in 1977, it must place all subsequent biographers in its debt.

recognized under the prizefighter alias of "great black bug of the Pampas", therefore, the likelihood was strong that the source of Darwin's maladies had been identified.

After a while, however, doubts began to be heard. Darwin, after his encounter with the bug, continued voyaging for another eighteen months, suffering only from the debilities of sea- and homesickness. That seems a long time for Chagas' disease to sit within the body, unnanounced, inactive. Even after his return, over a year went by before his complaints began. And where were the signs of cardiac weakness? Even when under therapy at Moor Park, in 1858, he was able to walk over four miles without any reported chest pain. True, in his old age he developed angina, but one did not need to call in the fangs of *T. infestans*, or those of *T. cruzi*, to explain that. Rather, it was perhaps up to the proponents of the theory to describe how the heart flutters he had felt before his departure on the *Beagle* fitted into the picture. And the exzema that had afflicted him at Cambridge. And the swellings and the boils that attacked him at intervals throughout his middle years.

The more Chagas' disease was looked at, the less likely a candidate it seemed. Corrected statistics more than halved the reported incidence of the disease in Mendoza; those who caught it had usually lived in the area over several years. One bite, it seemed, was not enough to cause it – it was secondary contamination, not the direct consequences of the bite, that created the conditions for the disease to take hold. Various other proposals were made over the years, but to all similar objections apply – they explain some, but not all, of Darwin's reported symptoms. Arsenic poisoning, brought on by the medicines which he took at various times during his life, was suggested, and some of the symptoms would support this. Others, however, as Dr. Colp has pointed out, would not: the fluctuations of Darwin's weight, for example, the state of his hair and teeth, the incidence of rheumatoid pains. Thus these and other possibilities – was he, for instance, allergic to some of the creatures with which he worked? – were one by one dismissed. (The pattern of stimulus and response throughout his life seems to make allergies unlikely; they would have had to wax and wane in extraordinary ways.)

If we are forced to eliminate any one physical cause for Darwin's long-standing debility, however, we cannot avoid serious consideration of its possibly psychogensis. Such theories, less constrained by evidence, have proliferated to make a tangled riot of speculation. Forbidding fathers are invented, for Darwin to react against. Emma stalks his imagined dreams, grim guardian of Christian orthodoxy. God leans threateningly from his heaven, pointing a vast finger of accusation at Darwin's heretical assumptions. None of these visions leads to an entirely satisfactory hypothesis, yet the uncomforable feeling persists that somewhere in that tangle the answer lies.

Some conviction of his own unworthiness burrowed all his life into Darwin's confidence. Only retreat guaranteed his safety, and his peace. Ill health served him in the preservation of this peace. That its symptoms were unconsciously recognized as useful can only have reinforced their palpable violence. But it had another effect – it set Emma in the role of mother. Susannah Darwin had died, as we know, when he was eight – it is hard to believe that this had no effect. A bed-wetting child plays out, in its bereavement or deprivation, the role of baby, through which it may recreate a coercive dependance. Darwin's illnesses may have been his personal equivalent. As he matured, he needed such a regression less; in his later years, Darwin was usually in better health than he had been between the ages of thirty and fifty-five.

As we have seen, an early nickname that Darwin gave Emma was "Titty". One can make too much of such hints, and the name was not unusual in Victorian days, but it remains a fact that Webster's New International Dictionary, for example, defines "titty" as "Childish diminutive of tit, teat – used familiarly; also milk from the breast". Later, Darwin changed "Titty" to outright "Mammy": "My dearest old Mammy" is how he addressed Emma in a letter from Shrewsbury in 1848. After giving her a bulletin on his health, he went on, "Susan was very kind to me, but I did grieve for you. Without you, when sick I feel most desolate . . . Oh Mammy I do long to be with you & under your protection for then I feel safe." Could one really tell from the tone whether that was a husband writing to his wife or a child to its mother? If one stretches fancy a little further, one may even begin to wonder at the constancy of that dyspeptic symptom, flatulence – is it anything more than the "wind" that mothers pleasantly pat out of their babies? Such a question, to be sure, adds a highly speculative dimension to the widespread digestive problems of the Victorian age: perhaps not only the excessive meals, but also the strict containment of emotion, and the lurid sentimentality that took its place, had a part to play in the intestinal discomforts of the nineteenth century.

Even if in Darwin's case such a hypothesis were true, it would not follow that Emma was always or only a mother-equivalent. But the main pattern of their relationship may be seen as one in which Darwin turned to her for comfort and protection, and she provided it. The tendency to psychogenic illness, which, for example, might have made him miss the *Beagle*'s departure, had he not so rigorously ignored it, could now have free and secure rein. It would no longer prevent his doing what he wished; on the contrary, it would now provide the conditions in which he could do it best. It enabled him, in however childish a way, to organize his environment, without creating antagonisms which he could not face. On the contrary, instead of anxiety-creating hostility, it ensured that he was surrounded with sympathy. Thus protectively encircled, he could pursue, unchallenged and unharassed, his most absorbing, frighteningly comprehensive theories. It meant that for some of the time he was incapacitated – his physical symptoms were real, after all; as they had to be to convince *him* – but one remembers Sir Peter Medawar's comment, that "three or four hours' work a day is not at all a bad stint for someone engaged in difficult writing". Despite his own complaints, accepted by nearly everyone at their face value, his losses were small compared with his gains: the scope and extent of his output makes this obvious. It is hard to see what, or how much, more he could have achieved.

Overlaying these profound, if relatively straightforward, processes, there would have been the effects upon his hesitant nature of the ideas he was pursuing. For years he worked in stubborn solitude, hammering out the essentials of his theory, the framework, the structure of its expression. He set himself to his task like an amateur – no professional, in other words, understanding the impossibility of what was to be attempted, would have allowed himself to begin. In the immensities of geological time, observing the endless, microscopic alterations of the universal flux, understanding with an oppressive clarity that almost everything accepted as true by the people around him was in fact false, he was totally, and vulnerably, alone. The nearer he came to concluding his work, the closer must have seemed confrontations of the kind he had always found it necessary to avoid. Yet he had a clear intellectual duty to conclude it, as well as being impelled by the justifiable tug of ambition. He wanted to offer the world his theories – but perhaps he also wanted not to be the person who had done so. He knew very well what controversy, what vilification, awaited him. Reactions of anger, however, such as those that inevitably lay ahead, provoked him, not to an answering anger – perhaps because he so rigorously controlled his temper – but to states of anxiety. In the years to come, Darwin's response to the unavoidable crises of his career was usually to be recorded in a flaring-up of his old symptoms. With vomiting and flatulence, boils and eczema, Darwin fought to keep his immediate universe in subjugation, demanded its sympathy and, it just may be, punished himself for presuming to challenge both earthly and heavenly authority.

On the other hand, it must not be forgotten that his sufferings were real. For days and nights he would be in wretched misery, punctuated by moments of extreme pain. He felt himself imprisoned by his disabilities, unable to travel or visit his friends. At times, as hints in his letters show, he must have compared his condition in the present with the vigour of his *Beagle* days, or of the sporting years before. The actual symptoms that he presented were not only disagreeable, but humiliating. For him, there were no advantages in them, nothing to be gained; indeed, whatever unknown anxieties caused his illness can only have been increased by this evidence of his continuing invalidism. The fact that, looking back, primed with the psychiatric theories of the last hundred years, we may see causes and reasons for his condition, means that we can explain it, but cannot explain it away. For Darwin, pain, weakness, depression and humiliation were one dark element in the background against which he had to continue his work, just as the affectionate support of his wife, children and friends made a countervailing brightness.

He was in deadly earnest when he wrote to Hooker at the beginning of that stressful year, 1858, "Oh health, health, you are my daily & nightly bugbear & stop all enjoyment in life". It was utterly typical of him that he should at once see how this might look in another's eyes – and instead of deleting, apologize for it: "But I really beg pardon, it is very foolish & weak to howl in this way. Everyone has got his heavy burthen in this world." As usual, he had been able to get in both the howl and his disclaimer of it. What gives this emotional double-dealing its dignity is the genuine anguish of the howl, and the true honesty of the disclaimer.

8

Such were the circumstances of Darwin's life in the two decades that preceded the publication of *The Origin*. Constantly battered by his illnesses, yet maintaining the intensity and the momentum of his work, he cocooned himself in the routines of his household, allowing the affectionate concern of his family, his friends and his servants to protect him. Despite the waxing and waning of his disabilities and the long development of his ideas, he seems to have remained almost entirely unchanged. As he described it to Herbert in 1844 or 1845, "we live like clock-work, & in what most people would consider the dullest possible manner." Musing on his circumstances in 1846, however, he came to more positive conclusions; he put them in a letter to Emma, then in Tenby. The day had been intermittently stormy, and he himself sick, as so often before; the printers were demanding manuscript copy that was far from ready, "and I am tired & overdone. I am an ungracious old dog to howl, for I have been sitting in the summer-house, whilst watching the thunderstorms, & thinking what a fortunate man I am, so well off in worldly circumstances, with such dear little children . . . & far more than all with such a wife. Often have I thought over Elizabeth's words, when I married you, that she had never heard a word pass your lips which she had rather not have been uttered, and sure I am that I can now say so & shall say so on my death-bed, bless you, my dear wife."

He maintained his main connections with the intellectual world at large. In 1846 he travelled to Southampton for that annual scientific jamboree, the meeting of the British Association for the Advancement of Sciences. "I enjoyed my week extremely, and it did me good," he commented. Three years later he was rather more jaundiced about the BAAS meeting for which he had travelled to Birmingham: it had been "very flat" and "the place was dismal," while his final remark was irritably disenchanted. "One gets weary of all the spouting," he wrote to Hooker after it was over.

He was rather attracted by the thought of being elected to the Philosophical Club, founded to promote discussion between those members of the Royal Society "who are actively engaged in cultivating the various branches of Natural Science", as the first article in its rules proclaimed. It met early, at 6 p.m., so that those dining there together might be encouraged to go on to the evening meetings of the Royal Society. The fact that their numbers were strictly limited to forty-seven made membership something of an honour, and when Hooker suggested that he might be chosen, Darwin responded with some enthusiasm. "With respect to the Club, I am deeply interested; only two or three days ago, I was regretting to my wife, how I was letting drop and being dropped by nearly all my acquaintances, and that I would endeavour to go oftener to London; I was not then thinking of the Club, which, as far as any one thing goes, would answer my exact object in keeping up old & making some new acquaintances." He thought that his health would allow him to attend at least every other meeting: "But it is grievous how often any change knocks me up". If he found he could not appear as often as this, he promised to resign after a year's trial; "If you can get me elected, I certainly shall be very much pleased". On 24 April, 1854, Darwin was indeed elected and remained a member for ten years; presumably he dined there often enough to make good his pledge.

There were occasionally other excursions to London, though no more of the migrations which had added so considerably to the miseries of the "Crimean winter". Within the strict defences erected by his illness – paradoxical ramparts, his weakness like granite – the work he was engaged in obsessed him. In 1846 he had written to Hooker, "I am going to begin some papers on the lower marine animals, which will last me some months, perhaps a year, and then I shall begin looking over my ten-year-long accumulation of notes on species & varieties, which, with writing, I dare say will take me five years, & then, when published, I dare say I shall stand infinitely low in the opinion of all sound Naturalists – so this is my prospect for the future." While this outline of his programme was right in general, it proved wrong in almost all its detail. His "papers on the lower marine animals", as we have seen, turned into his four enormous volumes on barnacles and took him eight years to produce; it took him nearly seven years to prepare his work on species, and even then it was only a short version of a projected book that would have taken as long again; when it came out, "sound Naturalists" on the whole ensured that his reputation should soar infinitely high. But these were the projects upon which his life centered during the 1840s and 1850s.

Except to Hooker, however, he was always a little cautious about confessing what his exact intentions were in his "species work". "I am hard at work," he informed Fox in 1855, "at my notes collecting & comparing them, in order in some two or three years to write a book with all the facts & arguments, which I can collect, *for and versus* the immutability of species". This was true enough, as far as it went, but implied a stance of scientific neutrality which it was never his intention to take up. Darwin needed Fox, as he did so many others, to feed him the detailed information through which his theory would be seen at work; as a clergyman, he might have been less ready to supply it had he known the full extent of Darwin's iconoclastic intentions. In Darwin's very caution, however, one may find a hint of the tension under which he lived, his complicated and perhaps even fearful expectations, his nervous stubborness and one of the major causes of his recurring ill health.

But there were along the route incidental excitements and satisfactions. He decided, in 1855, to collect every plant growing in a field which had by then been left fallow for fifteen years. His problem was his lack of experience as a classifying botanist: "How dreadfully difficult it is to name plants", he complained to Hooker. However, he and the helpful governess, Miss Thorley, gathered and labelled and examined, and at the end of that same letter, Darwin could write, "I have just made out my first grass, hurrah! hurrah! . . . I never expected to make out a grass in all my life, so hurrah! It has done my stomach surprising good . . ."

There was, too, the detective's satisfaction of seeing one's logical predictions come true. From descriptions of the plant life of the Azores, Darwin inferred that icebergs had once been stranded there. His own theory – later disproved – that those vast transported stones known as "erratic boulders" had been deposited by icebergs made him suggest that such rocks should be looked for. Lyell wrote on the subject to the German geologist and traveller, George Hartung; pleasantly boastful, Darwin reported to Hooker that "now H. says my question explains what had astounded him, viz large boulders (and some polished) . . . some 40 & 50 feet above the level of the sea . . ." No wonder he added, "Is this not beautiful!", and prefaced the little story of his triumph with, "I have just had the innermost cockles of my heart rejoiced . . ." Such feelings sustained him; it was the beauty of seeing his ideas proved and the joy that this created in him that offered him his rewards. What he had thought about the world, what he had imagined and recreated in his mind, had been matched by the physical reality; such revelations must have led to a strange and overwhelming exultation, blurring the distinction between the analyst and the creator. Darwin, picturing a possible world, watched it come into actual, verifiable being as clearly as though he had built it himself. This was the emotional reward that must, over the years, have reinforced that secret, undeviating determination.

It was not, however, the only reward he looked for. He very much desired the reassurance fame would bring, though he had before him a sterner ideal, that of the scientist disinterestedly pursuing truth and seeing fame as at best a distraction from the real business of his life. In 1857 he confessed to Fox, after mentioning how deeply he was involved in his writings on species, that "I wish I could set less value on the bauble fame, either present or posthumous, than I do, but not, I think, to any extreme degree: yet, if I know myself, I would work just as hard, though with less gusto, if I knew that my book would be published for ever anonymously". In his usual fashion, he both advances and retreats; the subject is a difficult one and leads him into contortions. That fame was desirable in *any* degree was unpleasant to him; yet, after all, others desired it more. He would work just as hard if no one ever knew of his efforts, and yet the fact that they would know added energy to his labours. As always, one sees him standing outside himself, making judgments based on an impossible notion of perfection. Falling short, he becomes contemptuous of himself – in a world of pure motives, the ethical man would not even be aware of fame as a possibility, a reward. The value of the work he did would be his only necessary validation. Yet Darwin could not achieve this lofty unconcern; ambition nagged him. That others were worse became his only justification. Sometimes one has the feeling that he set up such ideals in order to fall short of them, so providing himself with an occasion for that self-castigation through which he managed and contained, at least in some measure, his lifelong anxieties.

These were, despite their secluded calm, years of desperation. The constant struggle was to overcome himself, to defy the inner sense of his own unworthiness, to remain true to the energy-sapping task he had taken up. His solitude exposed him to every doubt; his illnesses and periods of health were indications of the to and fro battle. Every hour at his desk marked a tactical advance, every chapter a new step in his grand strategy. That the battles created by his inner divisions, the war his strategy demanded, raged at levels of the self of which he was hardly at all aware does not alter their fierceness, nor diminish in the slightest his ultimate victory.

9

Throughout the first half of the nineteenth century, there was a speculative, indeterminate restlessness that agitated opinion on the mutability of species. A belief in the possibility of constant change was considered fanciful, yet not incredible, rather as the conviction that life exists elsewhere in the universe is regarded today. As the 1830s came to an end, and the next decade began, as Darwin settled into Down House and wrote his own extended essay on the subject, this sussuration on the wilder edges of science continued.

The very fact that there was a constant surreptitious flirtation with evolutionary ideas by a handful of recalcitrant scientists and laymen worked to harden the orthodoxies of the majority. All over Europe and in the United States a flow of more or less agitated argument maintained that the stability of species was not only correct in science, but necessary in morality and absolute in religion. Lamarck, in Britain known to most of those interested only through Lyell's refutation, remained unique as a figure of consequence in the natural sciences who had proposed and held to a developmental theory. In this climate of opinion, in 1844, Darwin could write to Hooker, that "in my most sanguine moments, all I expect, is that I shall be able to show even to sound Naturalists, that there are two sides to the question of the immutability of species; – that facts can be viewed and grouped under the notion of allied species having descended from common stocks. With respect to books on this subject, I do not know of any systematical ones, except Lamarck's, which is veritable rubbish; but there are plenty . . . on the view of the immutability."

Darwin himself at about this time was reading – in "stiff German" – *Geschichte der Natur* by H.G. Bronn, one of the leading zoologists and palaeontologists in Europe, a professor at Heidelberg, who six years later was to win a competition, set by the Paris Academy of Sciences, for the best paper on the species question. Bronn then came down without equivocation against any developmental process, stating his belief "that all species of plants and animals were originally created by an unknown natural force and did not develop through the transformation of a few natural forms". Nevertheless, Darwin found his work "a wonderful book for facts on variation . . . it forestalls me, sometimes I think delightfully, and sometimes cruelly."

Into this atmosphere of slightly nervous calm there now dropped like a small avalanche a book which must for a moment have looked to Darwin as though it would forestall him much more comprehensively. The concerted scream of fury and dismay that arose from the scientific community was proof of the tensions that underlay what had appeared to be unshakeable certainties. The book was called *Vestiges of the Natural History of Creation*, it was published in that same year, 1844, and the boldness of its views was only emphasized by the anonymity of its author. Its great harvest of indiscriminate and not always accurate information was intended to support a single tendentious proposition: "The inorganic has one final comprehensive law, GRAVITATION. The organic, the other great department of mundane things, rests in like manner on one law, and that is, – DEVELOPMENT." It was, as the writer claimed, "the first attempt to connect the natural sciences into a history of creation".

It suffered from a number of defects, the first of which was that its author, with no scientific training to call on, had no criteria by which to select his evidence nor a body of knowledge against which he might test its validity. Thus the findings of astronomers, paleaontologists, botanists, geologists and the rest jostled in his grab-bag beside the assertions of phrenologists, lay experimenters with "the electrical fluid" and farmers relying more on superstition than observation. The book was written by Robert Chambers, an energetic but low-level polymath who was one of the great popularizers of the Victorian age, a man directed by both duty and profit to bring to the newly self-aware middle and working classes the varied knowledge of the period.

For over two years, Chambers, cloistered in the isolated little university town of St. Andrews, had steeped himself in the findings of contemporary science. He began his book, therefore, with the developmental theories arrived at by the astronomers, from which arose the pregnant conclusion "that the formation of bodies in space is *still and at present in progress*". His italics proclaim the importance of the finding – everything was still in the process of being formed.

Settling finally upon the earth, Chambers turned to geology, flirting with catastrophist notions of the Flood – or a flood – and relying for evidence on the prevalence of "diluvium" and Darwin's own hypothesis that it was icebergs which had transported erratic rocks. Having set the stage, he considered the question of the introduction of life upon it, valiantly attacking head-on the idea of special creation. The Creator had devised laws, and then stepped back to allow them to operate. The picture of a divine artificer stooping to mould every piffling life form seemed, to Chambers, a demeaning one, especially when one saw the earth in perspective, "third of a series which is but one of hundreds of thousands of series, the whole of which again form but one portion of an apparently infinite globe-peopled space . . . Is it conceivable, as a fitting mode of exercise for creative intelligence, that it should be constantly moving from one sphere to another, to form and plant the various species which may be required? . . ."*

How then had life been formed? The contortions and suppositions of the chapter in which Chambers attempts to face this problem underline the good sense of Darwin's refusal to make a similar effort. Fact slides into fantasy, hypothesis into superstition, analogies are stretched beyond breaking point. Chambers thought significant the tree-like markings left when electricity strikes, believed spread lime induces the creation of white clover, suggested the spontaneous generation of the intestinal worm. He accepted the experiments of Andrew Crosse, who, using "a powerful voltaic battery" upon various chemical compounds, claimed to have produced "insects" – though these, it subsequently turned out, were common mites, parasitic on humans, that he had brushed off during his preparations.

Having now dealt with the appearance of Life, Chambers was free to demonstrate what his next chapter heading proclaims: "Hypothese of the Development of the Vegetable and Animal Kingdoms". He expressed himself with an almost self-destructive clarity:

> The idea, then, which I form of the progress of organic life upon the globe . . . is, *that the simplest and most primitive type, under a law to which that of like-production is surbordinate, gave birth to the type next above it, that this again produced the next higher, and so on to the very highest,* the stages of advance being in all cases very small – namely, from one species to another . . . Whether the whole of any species was at once translated forward, or only a few parents were employed to give birth to the new type, must remain undetermined . . ."

So at the centre of Chambers's argument there lies a vagueness reminiscent of a bar-room debate: imprecisions like "a law" are not made more convincing by an outburst of italics. He supported his views by an endless parade of analogies and possible progressions, those linking groups of the world's languages somewhat more plausible than others which, for instance, suggested that the physiology of the non-European races mirrored the stages of foetal and infant development among Caucasians (he even went so far as to write a footnote on "the beard, that peculiar attribute of maturity", which

---

* In the London Library copy of the *Vestiges* – which, though of course annonymous, was donated "With the Author's Compliments" – some theologically alert reader, aware of the Deity's supposed omnipresence, has underlined the word "moving" and written in the margin the deflating question, "Why?"

was, he felt, significantly "scanty in the Mongolian, and scarcely exists in the Americans and Negroes").

Darwin read the *Vestiges* closely, made notes on what he read and here and there must have found echoes of his own ideas. Chambers, for instance, seized on the evidence of mutations, though like any other pre-Mendelian he had little idea of how they occured: "We are ignorant of the laws of variety-production", he wrote, a statement Darwin might well have echoed. Like Darwin, Chambers was interested in communication between animals and saw this as the precursor of language. Chambers, indeed, had his greatest impact, and perhaps his greatest importance, in his blithe leaping of the supposed gap between the animal world and the human. "There is," he wrote, "in reality, nothing to prevent our regarding man as specially endowed with an immortal spirit, at the same time that his ordinary mental manifestations are looked upon as simple phenomena resulting from organization, those of the lower animals being phenomena absolutely the same in character, though developed within much narrower limits."

The fact is that, for all his indiscriminate harvesting of fact, fantasy and wishful thinking, Chambers did at least set out, and expansively, an evolutionary plan. It was the blueprint for a machine that still wanted a power source to run it, but it showed the necessary connections and the possible capacity of such a construction. The result was, at last, the public debate which had for so long been threatened by the private smoulderings of scholars. It was, on the whole, conducted in tones of horror and terms of vilification. "If our glorious maidens and matrons may not soil their fingers with the dirty knife of the anatomist," wrote Sedgwick, his style furiously ponderous, "neither may they poison the springs of joyous thought and modest feeling, by listening to the seductions of this author . . ." The *Vestiges* offered them "the serpent coils of a false philosophy, and asks them again to stretch out their hands and pluck forbidden fruit", it taught them "that they are the children of apes and the breeders of monsters" and – in Sedgwick's splenetic italics – *"annulled all distinction between physical and moral . . ."*

Public denunciation in the *Edinburgh Review* was matched by private expressions of abhorrence, as in a letter Sedgwick wrote Lyell in April, 1845: "The sober facts of geology shuffled, so as to play a rogue's game; phrenology (that sink-hole of human folly and prating coxcombry); spontaneous generation; transmutation of species; and I know not what; all to be swallowed without tasting or trying, like so much horse-physic!! Gross credulity and rank infidelity joined in unlawful marriage, and breeding a deformed progeny of unnatural conclusions!" Everywhere, the book was being discussed, reviewed, supported, refuted – and, above all, read. Between October, 1844, and the time, six months later, that Sedgwick wrote to

Lyell, it had gone through four editions; before the *Origin* had begun to make its impact in 1859, another seven had come out. The reviews, those bastions of Victorian opinion, fired their various salvoes – the *Westminster* felt the fault lay with the scientists, who had turned from their task of making what they had discovered comprehensible to the layman; the *Quarterly* hoisted the battle flag of Biblical fundamentalism; while the *Edinburgh,* having set off Sedgwick as the prime piece in its battery, fell back upon an alarmed obscurantism which seemed to suggest that all knowledge, once disseminated, was bound to become dangerous. At a less exalted level, the discussion centred on the absorbing question of who had actually written the book. Sedgwick believed it must have been a woman, so charmingly was it written, and so blithe were "its ready boundings over the fences of the tree of knowledge, and its utter neglect of the narrow and thorny entrance by which we may lawfully approach it". Others believed that Lyell had written it, or Thackerey or even the Prince Consort, Albert himself.

There was another theory: in February, 1845, Darwin wrote to Fox, "Have you read the strange, unphilosophical, but capitally written book, the *Vestiges*, it has made more talk than any work of late & has been by some attributed to me – at which I ought to be much flattered & unflattered." Hooker seems to have thought the book of no great consequence, and to have treated it with humour, for Darwin wrote to him, at about the time it was published, that he had been "somewhat less amused at it than you appear to have been: the writing and arrangement are certainly admirable, but his geology strikes me as bad, and his zoology far worse." The secret of the book's authorship was kept for another forty years, but some people clearly had an early suspicion of the truth. In 1847, Darwin remarked, in a postscript to a letter largely concerned with variation, that he had "only made one new acquaintance of late, that is, R. Chambers; and I have just, received a presentation copy of the sixth edition of the *Vestiges*. Somehow I now feel perfectly convinced he is the author." The following year, Darwin became involved with Chambers in one of his intermittent disputations on the Parallel Roads of Glen Roy and confessed in a letter to Lyell that "Chambers has piqued me a little"; referring to *Ancient Sea Margins,* a new work by the industrious man of letters, he added, somewhat waspishly, "If he be, as I believe, the Author of the Vestiges this book for poverty of intellect is a literary curiosity". Some time later, however, discussing the species question with Hooker, Darwin wrote, "Lamarck is the only exception, that I can think of, of an accurate describer of species . . . who has disbelieved in permanent species, but he in his absurd though clever work has done the subject harm, as has Mr. Vestiges, and, as (some future loose naturalist attempting the same speculations will perhaps say) has Mr. D. . . ."

The effect of the *Vestiges,* then, lingered on in Darwin's mind. That last reference was made in the early 1850s, by which time almost a decade had passed since the first furore. It seems probable, especially in view of this final linking between them, that Darwin's painstaking collection of truly scientific evidence, and perhaps even his tacit refusal to deal with the origins of life, owed something to the ramshackle nature of Chambers's book – and more perhaps to the rumbustious nature of its reception. Yet the *Vestiges* had turned a subject barely thinkable into one that was widely discussed. It forced the conservative thinkers, anxious to preserve the fragile synthesis of the scientific with the Biblical, into the construction of alternative schemes. By raising the entire question, these in turn opened the way to further debate, both on the true relations between natural science and religion and on the origins of existing life forms.

A general intellectual ground was being prepared upon which the simple, yet awe-inspiring structures of evolutionary theory would in time be placed. In the minds of ordinary people, this created a basis for discussing such concepts as the continuity, across the whole spectrum of nature, of living things – a continuity which might well include the human race itself. Such a foundation, laid down in the public understanding long before Darwin unveiled his own hypothesis, was in a large measure his legacy from Robert Chambers and the controversy aroused by the *Vestiges.*

In working towards the elucidation of his own ideas, Darwin had to some extent altered his practice as a naturalist. Hitherto, he had been largely an observer, one who garnered facts and argued from them towards the conclusions they supported. Now he had become an experimenter, working upon what existed and seeing how the results matched his expectations. It was a long stride from the classificatory operations to which naturalists had been restricted only a few years before and even from the dissections of the anatomists or the assemblages of the palaeontologists. Perhaps the long hours spent at physical grips with his cirripedes made the difference. In any case, he now began to devote considerable time to breeding, observing and dissecting pigeons and rabbits*, to fertilizing, crossing and placing under the microscope a number of different plants.

He wanted to solve the problem of how varieties were formed, how new characteristics were passed on and maintained down the generations. In a sense, he discovered through his experimental cross-breeding the clue that he was seeking. He did not recognize it. Varieties of pigeons when cross-bred soon revert to the original, the *ur*-pigeon. This blue-grey bird seemed

---

* In view of Darwin's dislike of such inhumanities as vivisection, it is pleasing to note that he took advantage of the recent discovery of chloroform to kill his laboratory animals as painlessly as possible.

enigmatic to Darwin, appearing like the ghost of some early progenitor after a hundred generations had apparently obliterated it. Modern biology tells us that its genes lie latent in each variety; crossing doubles their potency and the ancient bird is recreated. Ignorant of genetics, Darwin could not realize that a characteristic once created, in other words, continues to exist down the generations, one heritable entity among thousands. Careful breeding – even by those ignorant of the actual mechanism – ensures that it remains latent. Thus isolation, whether arranged by man for his own purposes or by the environment in neutrality, creates varieties and, in time, species. Darwin, in wondering how the original rock-pigeon could so quickly be bred back into existence, was asking one question too many. That it could was, in essence, his answer – it was always present, had never disappeared, had lurked within the basket of pigeon inheritance waiting for the right conditions to reappear. Emerging from its egg, it testified to the impregnability of its survival. That impregnability was the mark of particulate inheritance, of the indefinite conservation of characteristics – but it was a mark Darwin was never to be able to read.

In his botanical experiments, he often had Hooker as mentor, aide or friendly rival. He planted sixteen kinds of seed in his meadow; out of these, he reported to Hooker, "fifteen have germinated, but now they are perishing at such a rate that I doubt whether more than one will flower". He marked out six square feet of ground and took note each day of "each seedling weed as it has appeared . . . and 357 have come up, and of these 277 have *already* been killed . . ." He had tiny plots of earth dug up and cleared, and watched with some surprise the flourishing of charlock seedlings, though none was growing wild in the vicinity. He pointed out in the *Gardeners' Chronicle* "that the power in seeds of retaining their vitality when buried in damp soil may well be an element in preserving the species . . ."

The power of seeds to survive, not only in stable conditions, but also while covering great distances, was crucial to Darwin's theories. Widespread distribution of species allowed him to propose a single location for the appearance of each species, instead of an unlikely multiplicity of similar mutations; it also led to the unified character of living organisms over great areas and it allowed organisms to achieve those conditions of isolation in which new varieties would be best produced. Darwin was anxious to know, therefore, whether seeds were able to survive for long periods in the cold salt water of the oceans. He kept the seeds for his experiments – initially chosen at random, but later selected on principles devised by Hooker – in a tank in the Down House cellars and for many weeks maintained the water at near freezing temperatures by having his children replenish it with the snows of a hard winter. Others he placed in bottles and left outside the house. One of the incidental hazards he faced was the increasingly offensive odour as the stagnating water turned putrid. Emptying them at the end of the desired period must have entailed its own kind of heroism.

He kept most seeds immersed for forty-two days, calculating that, since the average speed of Atlantic currents was thirty-three nautical miles per hour, a seed might in that time be carried over 1,300 miles. Lettuce, carrot, celery and, not unexpectedly, cress were among those plants which germinated and grew strongly even after the full period of immersion. A snag, however, was that seeds seemed to float very badly; indeed, as he wrote in *Gardeners' Chronicle*, "all the 40–50 seeds which I have have as yet tried sink in sea-water; this seems at first a fatal obstacle . . ." Darwin's ingenuity was swift with its counter: plants fell into the oceans whole and so floated, "being carried down rivers during floods, by water-spouts, whirlwinds, slips of rivercliffs, &c . . ." to new locations hundreds and even thousands of miles away. His final sentence, in a piece published in 1855, flicked a cautious straw or two into the wind of public opinion. "But when the seed is sown in its new home then, as I believe, comes the ordeal; will the old occupants in the great struggle for life allow the new and solitary immigrant room and sustenance?" Through such hints and nudges, Darwin in the 1850s attempted both to test and prepare his potential readership.

At the same time, Darwin began to fluster correspondents all over the world with a bombardment of questions none the less demanding for being wrapped in a smokescreen of apologies. He was no hero in direct confrontations – frequently, after some acrimonious meeting of a learned society, he accused himself in a letter to Lyell or Hooker of having been "chicken-hearted" – but once in pursuit of a fact he had a sort of deferential persistance that very few were able to resist. If they proved laggardly, he was not above sending a reminder, still wrapping tenacity in politeness – but with redoubled zeal.

The botanist and entomologist G.H.K. Thwaites, in Ceylon, was given a long list of queries, most concerning the changes that might have occured in introduced species, and asked to send the skins of various fowl, including leg and wing bones. Was there much variation in plants "*recently naturalized*" as Darwin vehemently put it, underlining hard. "The course of my work", he explained, "makes me more and more sceptical on the eternal immutability of species; yet the difficulties on the other theory of common descent seems to me frightfully great". Writing in March, 1856, he did not envisage publishing "for 2 or 3 or more perhaps years". Meanwhile, he would like more pigeon skins – "I have now all English breeds of Pigeons alive, & am carefully observing them, making skeletons & crossing them". Ducks would be acceptable as specimens, too, as would rabbits and poultry of all sorts. Ruefully, Darwin apologized for asking so much – but "when a beggar once begins to beg he never knows when to stop!"

The Indian civil servant, Walter Elliot, like Thwaites later to be a Fellow of the Royal Society, was another Darwin sought out for assistance, having met him at the 1855 British Association meeting in Glasgow. A Dr. Oldfield was approached over a comparison he had made between dogs in Assyrian art and similar types he had seen in Tibet and Nepal. The paleontologist T.W. St. C. Davidson, an expert among other things on the shellfish genus Brachipoda, was asked whether the little creatures might provide facts to clarify whether "a variable species is or is not equally variable at all times & places". Eyton, who was much harried on the subject of pigs, the ornithologist and conchologist E.C. Layard, Darwin's cousin Fox, Hooker above all – everyone was drawn into Darwin's network. Having read S.P. Woodward's book on shells both contemporary and fossilized, he wrote at once to congratulate his naturalist friend – and to warn him that he had compiled a list of questions for him to answer when next they met. When he came across an article in the *Gardeners' Chronicle* written by a J. Egan from Hungary, he leaped in with a question about stripes on Hungarian horses. Three weeks later, he was thanking Egan for the reply – an example of how efficient the network could be.

The facts that Darwin wanted his correspondents to search out were almost always small and very precise. As a result, they often involved specialist knowledge, and Darwin, at home in the scientific community, was never reticent in calling upon this. One feels his disciplined curiosity straining at distance as he tried to manipulate his helpers with sharp questions and soft politeness, at times following up with the persistence of the obsessed some point which had caught his attention. He had, indeed, become a sort of monomaniac – he ended a letter to Fox with the words, "Do sometime, I beg you, let me hear how you get on in health; and *if so inclined*, let me have some words on call-ducks".

It is as well that his friends shared his passions and intellectual priorities, otherwise such single-mindedness might have proved boring and even offensive. Indeed, coupled with his frequent complaints about his health, this over-determined pursuit of his aims produces what should be rather an unattractive picture. Yet it is not unattractive, partly because Darwin remained aware of what an imposition his interests and, above all, requests could be, partly because his own character, that essentially anxious character of the over-supervised child, still maintained its pleasing aura. The absence of any harshness, of force or power directed out at us, renders his letters mysteriously readable even when the style is arid and the subject matter abstruse, and even now, over a century after they were written.

"May 14th Began by Lyell's advice writing Species Sketch" – so wrote Darwin in his Journal in 1856, marking the beginning of what he must have thought would be the final stage of his long effort. There was a certain admirable disinterestedness in Lyell's urging, since he was not as yet convinced that Darwin was right in his theories. He foresaw, however, as he wrote to Hooker in July, 1856, that "whether Darwin persuades you and me to renounce our faith in species (when geological epochs are considered) or not . . . many will go over to the indefinite modifiability doctrine." There is a hint that Lyell saw in this the possibility of intellectual anarchy, since once – with Hooker's own ideas on the definition of species to help them – people began to think that a species was not "a separate and independent creation . . . every man becomes his own infallible Pope." However, it made no immediate difference to the work Hooker and Lyell were doing, in the same way that constellations might shift their positions in the course of aeons, "but it is certain that we may ignore the movement *now*, and yet astronomy remains still a mathematically exact science for many a thousand year".

Nevertheless, Lyell urged Darwin to put his ideas in publishable form and make them available, largely because he did not want his friend to lose the chance of claiming priority for his idea. The *Vestiges* was still selling and still appearing in new editions. The ubiquitous Herbert Spencer (who was to the world of the intellect rather what Selfridge would become to that of commerce) was beginning to publish the results of his conversion, inadvertently caused by Lyell himself, to a belief in species mutability; his first essay on species creation and development came out, in a periodical called *The Leader*, as early as 1852.

In 1855, the Savilian Professor of Geometry at Oxford, a clergyman with the illustrious name of Baden Powell, published a book of three essays, the last of which, entitled *The Philosophy of Creation,* categorically accepted a developmental thesis: Baden Powell stated in the course of it that "the general fact would be simply that *species (within certain limits of deviation) are permanent during very long periods, but beyond these periods a change, in some sense, occurs*; and this bears some relation to changes of external conditions . . ." The cause of such a change would be, he thought, "slight changes of forms accompanying corresponding changes of condition, acting through periods of incalculable length" and, summarizing his speculations, he proposed "the existence of a stage in the early evolution of every class and order, during which a community of form belongs to them all. At this stage, there exists no difference between them, and out of this primitive common germ or rudiment any one of the more distinct specific forms might, as far as we know, be equally produced, provided the *determining causes* for that particular modification were present."

Variation interacting with environment to produce species descended from a single common progenitor – Powell had left Darwin only one area of self-confessed ignorance in which to plant the flag of scientific conquest. To the problem of "the determining cause", Darwin could propose his theory of natural selection; it was, of course, the very heart of his theory. Darwin, too, had his great storehouse of observations from which to draw the evidence that would lend scientific weight to his ideas. Yet Baden Powell had come down with threatening firmness on the side of evolution, his view of it uncomfortably close to that bull's eye at which Darwin had for so long been aiming. The book enjoyed a certain vogue: later, reviews of *The Origin* were to cite it. Darwin or his friends will certainly have known of it and may even have read it; Darwin's own testimony on the point is a little ambivalent. "If I have taken anything from you, I assure you it has been unconsciously", he wrote to Powell after *The Origin* came out, but later he remembered that he had actually acknowledged Powell's work in the preface he had written for his never-published larger book. This passage he included in the historical sketch which he added to later editions of *The Origin*, lauding there the "masterly manner" in which Powell had handled his theme. It seems, therefore, that Powell's ideas represented both rivalry and reinforcement for Darwin's own; in either event, they were a further proof that the intellectual tide was catching him up with a disconcerting swiftness.

More certainly influential in awakening Lyell at least to the dangers besetting Darwin's chances of priority was a paper that appeared in September of that same year, 1855, in the *Annals and Magazine of Natural History*. Entitled *On the Law that has Regulated the Introduction of New Species*, it was by a naturalist named Wallace, who had sent it in from his base in Ternate, an island in the Moluccas, tucked away beyond the western extremity of New Guinea. Based on his experiences and observations in Borneo, the article enlarged upon a point already made by Baden Powell – that the similarities between past and present species suggested development rather than constant new creation. If Wallace was still some way from an evolutionary theory, it was clear that he had found its spoor.

Wallace was one of the many men who had clambered out of obscurity by way of the natural sciences, having left school in his middle teens and worked as an assistant teacher in a Leicester school of little consequence. The passionate desire to collect and understand the products and processes of nature had turned him into an excellent practical naturalist and a swift, original intelligence made him very soon considerably more than that. He spent years collecting in the Amazon Basin before travelling in 1854 to the Far East. Born in 1823, he had been able to read Darwin's *Journal* as part of his programme of self-education; Humboldt, Malthus and Lyell were others whose books had made their contribution.

Wallace had long believed in the transmutation of species. There is a myth that the entire notion seized him between fits of malarial fever in 1858, but the fact is that he was thinking about the subject as early as 1845, three years before he made his first journey to South America. In December of that year he wrote to H.W. Bates, who was to become his partner on the Amazon expedition; the subject was the catalytic *Vestiges of Creation*. Wallace had a better opinion of the book than Bates. "I do not consider it as a hasty generalization, but rather as an ingenious hypothesis strongly supported by some striking facts and analogies but which remains to be proved by more facts & the additional light which future researches may throw upon the subject. It at all events furnishes a subject for every observer of nature to turn his attention to; every fact he observes must make either for or against it . . . I would observe that many eminent writers give great support to the theory of the progressive development of species in animals & plants." Wallace then went on to expound his theory that the various races of mankind were true species; his open-mindedness at this stage makes a contrast with the moralizing hysteria of a self-righteous intellectual establishment. (The fact that Wallace was, like Chambers, among those who took phrenology seriously may also have made his reaction to the *Vestiges* more positive than was, say, Sedgwick's.)

Lyell, therefore, disturbed at these signs of innovative activity on the subject of species, tried to persuade Darwin to organize his views once and for all. Darwin was uncertain; he knew that he would have to overwhelm potential critics with the wealth and relevance of his evidence – "every proposition," he wrote to Lyell early in May, 1856, "requires such an array of facts. If I were to do anything, it could only refer to the main agency of change – selection – and perhaps point out a very few of the leading features, which countenance such a view, and some few of the main difficulties. But I do not know what to think; I rather hate the idea of writing for priority, yet I certainly should be vexed if any one were to publish my doctrines before me." Pride, modesty, ambition, diffidence – not for the first time, these qualities fought for primacy within him. Six days later, he wrote on the subject to Hooker.

> If I publish anything it must be a *very thin* and little volume, giving a sketch of my views and difficulties; but it is really dreadfully unphilosophical to give a *resumé*, without exact references, of an unpublished work. But Lyell seemed to think I might do this . . . I thought of giving up a couple of months and writing such a sketch, and trying to keep my judgement open whether or no to publish it when completed . . . Eheu, eheu, I believe I should sneer at any one else

doing this, and my only comfort is, that I *truly* never dreamed of it, till Lyell suggested it . . .

Two days later, he wrote again, having had an approving reply from Hooker: "I am extremely glad you think well of a separate 'Preliminary Essay' . . . I certainly think my future work in full would profit by hearing what my friends or critics (if reviewed) thought of the outline." The rest of his letter is a confused and somewhat desperate winding to and fro about the matter, tiptoeing towards a conclusion only to leap away in a sort of terror; and then what is one to think about that half-touching, half-irritating, Uriah Heep-like parenthesis, "if reviewed"? The end of the letter reflects Darwin's perplexity and irritation: "I begin *most heartily* to wish that Lyell had never put this idea of an Essay into my head".

Lyell, however, was not without allies. A correspondent identified by Professor Stauffer as Sir Charles Bunbury, Lyell's brother-in-law and a friend to whom Darwin had spoken of natural selection as early as 1845, wrote to Darwin in April, 1856, "I am exceedingly interested by all you tell me about your researches & speculations on species . . . & am delighted that you are going on working at the subject. I trust that you will not on any account give up the idea of publishing your views upon it . . ." Bunbury was himself a botanist, an expert on early plant life and a Fellow of the Royal Society, so that his advice had a value beyond that of one of Lyell's relations. The fact that he disagreed with Darwin's conclusions gave his wish to see them published an added potency.

Darwin's brother, Erasmus, had also taken to pointing out that "you will find that someone will have been before you," and Darwin consequently settled to his work; he had, after all, the essay of 1844 to provide a basis, though he began by subjecting it to new and stringent analysis. By October, however, he realized that there was no possibility of setting out his views for the world to examine in any but the fullest form. If he had wanted no more than priority, a staked claim in the goldfields of history, he could after all have published that earlier sketch twelve years before. He wrote to Fox that he had "found it such unsatisfactory work that I have desisted, and am now drawing up my work as perfect as my materials of nineteen years' collecting suffice, but do not intend to stop to perfect any line of investigation beyond current work. Thus far and no farther I shall follow Lyell's urgent advice . . . I find to my sorrow it will run to quite a big book."

Fox had not wanted Darwin to write a mere sketch of his ideas – "Your remarks weighed with me considerably", commented Darwin – but it is doubtful if he would have begun writing at all had it not been for the pressure of his friends. In the more than twelve decades of evolutionary studies since 1856, research has not arrived at its goals nor has controversy been stilled by scientific certainty. What generations of workers have been unable to achieve was hardly in Darwin's lifetime compass. At what point would he have been able to settle to his desk, secure in the knowledge that he had gathered all the facts he needed? Left to himself, he could not have reached such a point. Yet, without reaching it, could he ever have made himself begin the book he had planned?

He had criticized his grandfather and attacked Lamarck for the airiness of their views, their lack of factual ballast; he had seen the *Vestiges*, only ten years before, clawed by reviewers and professors for the indiscriminate nature of its evidence as well as the immorality of its opinions. When would he – could he – have felt himself safe from a similar savaging? His friends, on the whole, did not accept his views. Lyell, as we have seen even thought commitment to them irrelevant. Hooker, while tending towards them, was not yet a convert.

Thus Darwin was essentially isolated, even within his own circle; beyond it, so far as he could tell, there waited only the great killer sharks of orthodoxy, the sharp-toothed guardians of authority for whom the idea of a dynamism within nature, expressed in constant fundamental change, was not a scientific theory, but a major immorality: a heresy. Perhaps they might tolerate such opinions in private; their public expression, leading to the disorientation, even the corruption, of the believing masses and the righteous bourgeoisie, could not be permitted. For the sanctity of women and the innocence of children were inextricably linked with the conviction that human beings were unique because modelled upon the divine and endowed with a soul. Beyond the pride which insisted upon the separation of the human from the animal, there lurked a fear of the consequences if that separation were not maintained.

Just out of sight, in the encircling darkness, the nauseating beast bounced and gibbered, that beast kept at bay by the steel bars of convention and the dazzling brightness of religious assertion. If the bars gave way and the brightness died, the beast would be amongst us. Worse, it would be seen to *be* us. In that moment, the terror of such thinkers implied, we would be forced into an acceptance of our primeval violence, our primeval sexuality. With such an acceptance there would come a collapse of the certainties – especially the certainty of human goodness, human nobility – which supported nineteenth century morality. Optimism would be undermined, relations between the sexes would be utterly transformed, all transcendental inducements to right behaviour would be swept away. The opponents of evolutionary theories, having lost the debate, have been displayed ever since as misguided conservatives, feebly maintaining outdated concepts for no better reason than that these were the concepts they had been brought up to.

None of them, however, looking down the decades at us, is likely to think himself, in any essential respect, wrong in the stand he took.

Yet, with every stroke and dot of Darwin's pen, their Nemesis was coming closer. He left the first chapter of his book, on domestic breeding, incomplete, but by the end of the year had written his second chapter, the more factual part of his thesis on variation under domestication; his third, on the effects of crossing and its prevalence in nature – proof of the underlying unity of species – and was setting about the fourth, which concerned the crucial matter of variations occurring in the wild. "Jan 26th Finished Ch. 4 Var: Nature", is his first Journal entry for 1857. Chapter Five dealt with the struggle for existence and was done by the beginning of March; by the end of that month, Chapter Six was also complete, although clearly Darwin felt he had not done its crucial subject justice and, in April the following year, while at Moor Park, he went over it again. Its heading was "On Natural Selection". By the end of 1857, however, another three chapters had been written: those on the laws of variation, on transitions between species and on hybrids.

In the Spring of 1857, Darwin replied to a letter Wallace had sent him from the East Indies the previous autumn. He referred to the article that had startled Lyell into his galvanizing advice and went on:

> I can plainly see that we have thought much alike and to a certain extent have come to similar conclusions . . . This summer will make the 20th year (!) since I opened my first note-book, on the question how and in what way do species & varieties differ from each other. I am now preparing my work for publication, but I find the subject so very large, that though I have written many chapters, I do not suppose I shall go to press for two years . . . It is really *impossible* to explain my views (in the compass of a letter), on the causes & means of variation in a state of nature; but I have slowly adopted a distinct & tangible idea, – whether true or false others must judge . . .

The tone is one of cautious cordiality, the easy generalities of a poker player prepared to give nothing essential away.

At the end of the year, Darwin was able to write again to Wallace, this time in response to a second letter in which the distant naturalist had wondered why his article had provoked so little response. Darwin reassured him, first praising Wallace's current work on distribution, planned "in accordance with theoretical ideas."

> I am a firm believer that without speculation there is no good & original observation . . . You say that you have been somewhat surprised at no notice having been taken of your paper in the *Annals*. I cannot say that I am, for so very few naturalists care for anything beyond the mere description of species. But you must not suppose that your paper has not been attended to: two very good men, Sir C. Lyell, and Mr. E. Blyth at Calcutta, specially called my attention to it. Though agreeing with you on your conclusions in that paper, I

believe I go much further than you; but it is too long a subject to enter on my
speculative notions . . . You ask whether I shall discuss 'man'. I think I shall
avoid the whole subject, as so surrounded with prejudices; though I fully admit
that it is the highest & most interesting problem for the naturalist. My work, on
which I have now been at work more or less for twenty years, will not fix or
settle anything; but I hope it will aid by giving a large collection of facts, with
one definite end.

Darwin had, in his *Notebooks*, and thus in his own thoughts, faced and dealt
with the problem of how and where the human race fitted into the general
scheme of nature. But in none of his extended descriptions of his theories,
from the very first sketch of 1842, had mankind figured among his examples.
Wallace was interested in the provenance of human varieties, and later
Darwin was to show himself equally interested in the subject. For the
moment, however, he allowed caution to dictate the contents of his book –
what he had to say was controversial enough, without his meeting its central
difficulty head-on. Everything he was writing implied the coherence of
nature, from the most miniscule organisms to mankind; he had no intention
of opening out that implication into a bald statement. Another twenty years
would pass before he felt himself ready to take such a step.

There is something about the tone of these letters, however, which
suggests that Darwin had a wary eye on Wallace from the beginning. In both,
he went out of his way to mention to the younger man the length of time he
had already spent on the species problem. It was clearly something he
wanted to establish very firmly in Wallace's mind. It was the other's paper
that had made Lyell acutely aware that Darwin stood in danger of being
overtaken. Now he was sending letters halfway round the world to raise with
Darwin such subjects as variation, distribution and selection, and to raise
them from a standpoint similar, and sympathetic, to Darwin's own. It would
not have been surprising if Darwin, used to standing alone in this matter –
and perhaps taking a certain grim pleasure in his solitary and beleaguered
statues – had begun to be a little alarmed at Wallace's interventions. There is
about that reiterated "twenty years" something of a bull's hoarse bellowing
as he stamps out his territorial rights.

Throughout these years of intense and debilitating labour, Darwin was
distracted by a long-drawn-out domestic crisis. In 1857, Etty – his daughter
Henrietta – had fallen seriously ill. Whatever it was that afflicted her
lingered on intermittently for years, to be diagnosed at the end of the decade
as some form of persistent fever, perhaps typhoid. "Poor Etty will long be an
invalid," wrote Darwin to his oldest son, "but we are now too happy even at
that poor prospect." In the end she recovered, to live out her life with at least
her share of the Darwin hypochondria. Gwen Raverat described her in old

age, when "her business in life, her profession, was taking care of healths, her own and other people's . . ."

Despite his constant concern over his daughter, and his own repeated bouts of illness, Darwin worked steadily at the enormous manuscript of his book. At times, it seemed as if the task might overwhelm him. "The work has been turning out badly for me this morning," he wrote to Hooker in 1858, "and I am sick at heart; and, oh! how I do hate species & varieties." In the same year, writing to Emma from the hydro at Moor Park, he described a walk he had taken amid "the fresh yet dark-green of the grand Scotch firs, the brown of the catkins of the old birches, with their white stems, and a fringe of distant green from the larches . . . At last I fell fast asleep on the grass, and awoke with a chorus of birds singing around me, and squirrels running up the trees, and some woodpeckers laughing, and it was as pleasant and rural a scene as ever I saw, and I did not care one penny how any of the beasts or birds had been formed." Yet, at other times, he felt all the fascination that had first drawn him to his work, and responded to that with a sense of happy resolution. He told Fox in a letter in 1858 that he was possibly working too hard at his book: "It will be very big, and I am become most deeply interested in the way facts fall into groups. I am like Croesus overwhelmed with my riches in facts, and I mean to make my book as perfect as ever I can."

Throughout the first half of 1858, Darwin worked on, bent over his vast production. Its scrawled pages, clogged with corrections, were in danger of becoming illegible. The pile they made mounted, a monument to mid-Victorian industry. He travelled to Moor Park for his cures, but nothing interrupted or, one would have thought, could have interrupted, his dedicated labours. For three months he hammered out his chapter on "Mental Powers and Instincts of Animals" – it was, as he wrote to Asa Gray, the botanist from Harvard who was to be one of his greatest supporters, "a despairing length of time". He travelled once again to Moor Park, there preparing his ideas "on large genera & small", as his Journal tells us, "& on Divergence & correcting Ch. 6." He "finished June 12th & Bees cells", an entry that suggests that he returned to the chapter on instincts, in which the complex behaviour of bees plays a prominent part. The next entry reads, "June 14th Pigeons (interrupted)."

10

June, 1858, was perhaps the worst month of Darwin's life. While Etty struggled with her fever, his youngest child, Charles Waring, was very plainly ailing. The months had passed, but he had neither walked nor spoken. Emma had been forty-eight when he was born; he suffered the consequences that sometimes follow on a late conception. On 28 June a fever, perhaps mercifully, whisked away his life. For a short while, Darwin suffered the repetition of an earlier anguish. Wounds not long healed were threatened once more. And death seemed to have prepared a double blow, striking not only at fatherhood, but also at his chance of fame. For it was at this moment, with that sad little boy first ill, then dying, finally a continuing memory in his house, that Darwin had to face the appearance of a rival in the field where he had for so long been alone.

From the far side of the world there arrived the message which he had, perhaps, half expected, about the likelihood of which Lyell, Hooker and Erasmus had warned him and which, in a thin flutter of pages, seemed to him for the moment to have overturned his life. For, in three weeks of convalescence, Wallace had worked his way to the same theory that had obsessed Darwin for two decades. His notion of natural selection paralleled that of Darwin; even some of the phrases he used were identical. Now, succinctly, in a paper that was in fact no more than a letter, he had outlined these ideas for Darwin's examination.

Restricted by the weakness that follows fever, Wallace had been resting in his quarters at Ternate when, musing on species, he had remembered reading Malthus a dozen or so years before. He considered how many had to die in order to contain the numbers that unchecked breeding would produce – and abruptly made the connection, Darwin's connection, turning the same lock with the same key. He realized – "it suddenly flashed upon me" – that "in every generation the inferior would inevitably be killed off and the superior would remain – that is, *the fittest would survive*." When the environment changed, therefore, as it was known it did from time to time, then, "considering the amount of individual variation" that he knew from experience existed, Wallace could see "that all the changes necessary for the adaptation of the species . . . would be brought about; and as great changes in the environment are always slow, there would be ample time for the change to be effected by the survival of the best fitted in every generation." He realized that "in the very process of this modification the unmodified would die out, and thus the *definite* characters and the clear *isolation* of each new species would be explained." For an hour, Wallace tells us in his autobiography, he pondered on Lamarck and the *Vestiges*, considered their deficiencies, and "saw that my new theory supplemented these views and obviated every important difficulty". Two days later, he had set down the outline of his ideas in the four thousand-word paper which, in that appalling June, landed upon Darwin's life with the impact of a military bombardment. In less than a week, Wallace had clawed his way, helped perhaps by fever and the accompanying imposed immobility, to the centre of the mystery which Darwin had been cautiously approaching for years.

Wallace's paper began exactly where Darwin's great book did: he had written his first paragraph on variation in domestic breeds. He had gone on to argue that species in the wild were not "in all respects analogous to or even identical with those of domestic animals . . . The life of wild animals is a struggle for existence". The very phrase was the one Darwin had chosen to head his Chapter Five. Wallace summarized the Malthusian calculations and their theoretical consequences, then drew the logical conclusion: "The numbers that die annually must be immense; and as the individual existence of each animal depends upon itself, those that die must be the weakest . . . Now, it is clear that what takes place among the individuals of a species must also occur among the several allied species of a group . . ." In such a situation, variation then became crucial, as Darwin had already realized. If a variety had "slightly increased powers of preserving existence, that variety must inevitably in time acquire a superiority in numbers." If conditions became critically stringent, the weaker, parent stock and all other varieties would vanish: "The superior variety would then alone remain . . . The *variety* would now have replaced the *species* . . . Such a variety *could not* return to the original form; for that form is an inferior one, and could never compete with it for existence . . . But this new, improved, and populous race might itself, in course of time, give rise to new varieties . . . Here, then, we have *progression and continued divergence* deduced from the general laws which regulate the existence of animals in a state of nature . . ." Throughout the essay, Wallace drew on examples similar to, and sometimes the same as, those chosen by Darwin. He hit on a similar structure and, at times, on the same phrases. And when he had finished, it was to Darwin he sent it.

Rueful acceptance, the desire to do the honourable thing, sorrow, a hollow reassurance – all mix together in Darwin's letter to Lyell with which he enclosed, as Wallace had asked him to, this disconcerting paper. He sent it on the same day as he received it, recommending it as "well worth reading.

Your words have come true with a vengeance – that I should be forestalled ... I never saw a more striking coincidence; if Wallace had my MS. sketch written out in 1842, he could not have made a better short abstract! Please return me the MS., which he does not say he wishes me to publish, but I shall, of course, at once write and offer to send it to any journal. So all my originality, whatever it may amount to, will be smashed, though my book, if it will ever have any value, will not be deteriorated; as all the labour consists in the application of the theory."

When he wrote to Hooker, however, Darwin showed how shattering that June's double shock had been. "I am quite prostrated, & can do nothing ... I dare say it is all too late. I hardly care about it." The reputation he had so reluctantly hoped for, the vindication of his years of labour – perhaps even, if one's guesses are true, the reversal of the family verdict passed on him thirty-five years before (a verdict actually irreversible, the sentence as long as life) – all were suddenly endangered. And to lose all that would be to slide into a darkness equivalent to death. It is no wonder that for a short while Darwin was in despair.

It was a moment of mental and emotional turmoil that Darwin eventually withstood. He had, after all, long faced the possibility that someone else might reach the same conclusions he had. On the other hand, he could say with certainty that no one on earth had thought about these subjects as deeply as he, or investigated them with more persistence. He had been, as it were, secure in his insecurity, perched on the end of the branch he had chosen. His situation was lonely – but it had its grandeur. Now, at the last moment, someone had climbed out to join him. He had thought that this would not concern him, that he might even be pleased to have company. To his own horror and self-disgust, he hated it. Despite all the promptings of honour, he wanted to be known as the man who had first sat on that dangerous branch, and had sat on it alone.

A week later, he wrote to Lyell again. There was nothing in Wallace's ideas, he pointed out, that could not be found in his 1844 essay. He had sent a short sketch of his own hypothesis to Asa Gray the year before, "so that I could most truly say and prove that I take nothing from Wallace. I should be extremely glad now to publish a sketch of my general views in about a dozen pages or so; but I cannot persuade myself that I can do so honourably ... I would far rather burn my whole book, than that he or any other man should think that I have behaved in a paltry spirit." He had thought about the matter for days, while having to endure the terrifying illnesses of his children. What was happening was almost more than he could bear, stirring as it did the very wellsprings of his life's effort.

He wanted to be acknowledged as the originator of the theory he had worked on for so long; at the same time, he could not bear to run counter to his inner model of behaviour. Through modesty, diffidence, the assertion of unworthiness, he manipulated his existence. That he was genuinely modest and frequently benevolent does not alter the fact that these were the weapons with which he organized his relationships and influenced his friends. It was, one may suppose, the method he had learned in childhood and it had stood him in good stead. He could not bear to be seen flying these other, more aggressive colours. The appearance he proffered of himself as a person was, for the first time, in conflict with that of the scientist; the resultant inner struggle was fierce and, in a sense, irreconcilable. In despair, he abdicated, passing the decision over to his closest friends. The responsibility was beyond him.

"My good dear friend, forgive me," he ended his letter to Lyell. "This is a trumpery letter, influenced by trumpery feelings." In a postscript he added, "I will never trouble you or Hooker on the subject again." And he did not write – until the following day. He had felt it necessary to strengthen the case against himself, putting in Wallace's mouth the accusing sentence, "You did not intend publishing an abstract of your views till you received my communication". Darwin, if he published, would be taking advantage "from privately knowing that Wallace is in the field. It seems hard on me that I should thus be compelled to lose my priority of many years' standing, but I cannot feel at all sure that this alters the justice of the case."

Lyell and Hooker considered the matter; while at Down House, scarlet fever struck down Darwin's sad little two-year-old and threatened the other children. "I cannot think now on the subject," he wrote to Hooker the day after his son had died, "but soon will." Hooker and Lyell, meanwhile, arrived at a conclusion that combined fairness to the scientists with the enterprise due to science. Wallace's paper should be published, but jointly with extracts from Darwin's 1844 essay and the letter written in 1857 in which he had outlined his theories for the benefit of Asa Gray. Wallace, who became one of Darwin's foremost supporters and even published a book on evolution entitled *Darwinism*, never from the moment this solution was suggested to him gave the slightest appearance of resentment or disagreement. One wonders, all the same, whether he ever thought of what would have happened had he sent his paper to one of the learned journals, as a contribution, instead of to Darwin, as a communication between naturalists.

The chances are that very little would have happened. Lyell and Hooker presented the papers, under the joint title *On the Tendency of Species to Form Varieties; and on the Perpetuation of Varieties and Species by Natural Means of Selection*, as by Charles Darwin and Alfred Wallace, and they were read at the Linnean Society on 1 July, 1858. Brought in at short notice, they took the place of one by George Bentham* on, of all the possible vagaries of coincidence, the fixity of species. If Darwin had expected outcry and furore, he was disappointed – or, more probably, reassured. There was hardly any reaction from the assembled members, although Hooker felt that there was an intense interest among the audience. He thought that Lyell's presence as a sort of sponsor, and Hooker's own at Lyell's side, "rather overawed the Fellows, who would otherwise have flown against the doctrine". Nevertheless, when the President, Thomas Bell, a firm believer in the immutability of species, gave his account a few months later of the year's activities, it is clear that he had heard nothing that impressed him. The period, he declared, had not "been marked by any of those striking discoveries which at once revolutionize, so to speak, the department of science on which they bear".

Wallace's reaction to this reading was relaxed and matter-of-fact. Writing to a friend, still from the East Indies, in October, 1858, he devoted one paragraph to it in a letter of four pages. "An essay on *varieties* which I sent to Mr. Darwin has been read to the Linnean Soc. by Dr. Hooker & Sir C. Lyell on account of an extraordinary coincidence with some views of Mr. Darwin, long written but not yet published, & which were also read at the same meeting". After that, he simply asked his correspondent to obtain copies of the paper if it was published and distribute them to those of his friends who were unable to hear it read. Wallace, in fact, could hardly have found a cooler tone in which to refer to the matter.

Darwin's mood, as we have seen, was very different. He had left the organization of the reading, and the publication which followed it, almost entirely to Lyell and Hooker. Even with this out of the way, he remained confused, anxious not to lose priority, equally anxious not to be seen to care whether he did or not. Consciously or not, he must have sensed that there was a danger that he might lose his protective appearance of unworldliness. Only his withdrawal from competition had left him free to compete; the thrust, scrimmage and bustle of London scientific, or even Cambridge academic, life had been a distraction and a threat. Now, with this quandary, it had surrounded him once more; at the same time, sickness and death had struck at the serenity with which he had endeavoured to surround himself. He felt bewildered, exposed, totally uncertain.

Hooker was, he had written, again on 29 June, "too generous to sacrifice so much time & kindness. It is most generous, most kind . . . It is miserable in

---

* George Bentham was the nephew of Jeremy Bentham, the expert on law and the constitution. He was a linguist who could read fourteen modern languages, and made a name in philosophy and legal studies before turning to botany in 1831, in which he had previously been only an amateur. He became one of the great systemists, as from his law studies one might have expected, and President of the Linnean Society, 1861–74.

me to care at all about priority . . . I will do anything. God bless you, my dear kind friend. I can write no more." Hooker agreed to write to Wallace about what had been done, and Darwin wrote to him on 13 July to say that his letter "seems to me perfect, quite clear and most courteous . . . I always thought it very possible that I might be forestalled, but I fancied that I had a grand enough soul not to care; but I found myself mistaken and punished; I had, however, quite resigned myself, and had written half a letter to Wallace to give up all priority to him, & should certainly not have changed had it not been for Lyell's & your quite extraordinary kindness."

To Lyell, five days later, he wrote in similar terms, while he and his family were beginning their recuperation on the Isle of Wight. "I certainly was", he repeated, "a little annoyed to lose all priority, but had resigned myself to my fate. I am going to prepare a longer abstract; but it is really impossible to do justice to the subject, except by giving the facts on which every conclusion is grounded, – that will, of course, be absolutely impossible". Whether it would "do justice to the subject" or not, the abstract that Lyell had suggested years before – albeit now in a much longer form – would this time be written: Darwin and his friends had had a fright. It was clear that he could not afford to take the time needed to finish *Natural Selection*.

There was perhaps another factor, one that resulted precisely from the closeness of the intellectual relationship between Darwin and those whom he admitted to the secrets of his work. He longed to convert them to his ideas, yet in doing so set in motion a sort of seepage of theory that again put at risk his priority. Hooker, in particular, was beginning to write from a standpoint increasingly Darwinian. The long introduction he was preparing for his almost completed *Flora of Tasmania* clearly demonstrated the influence of Darwin's ideas, now held the more firmly for having been confirmed by his own observations. For this essay makes it plain that the more precisely he attempted to classify what he had collected, to systematize, to fix definitions upon the natural world, the more aware he became of the lack of true divisions between one plant species and another. The overall fluidity of nature, to which Darwin's endlessly repeated views had alerted him, had become too obvious to ignore.

"You cannot imagine", wrote Darwin to Hooker in July, 1858, "how pleased I am that the notion of Natural Selection has acted as a purgative on your bowels of immutability". Yet perhaps, consciously or not, he may not have viewed with quite such enthusiasm as he expressed the possibility of even his closest scientific friend making so clear a statement of his new mutational beliefs. In any case, it was during that month that he began his projected summary. In his Journal there is the entry, "July 20th to August 12th at Sandown began Abstract of Species book". At last the long progress of his destiny had brought him to the crucial moment: he had begun to write *On the Origin of Species*.

He worked swiftly, but under an increasing burden of ill health. On 23 October he was able to record in his diary that he had been working on Part IV of the book: "Difficulties finished", he wrote, and one can almost hear his sigh of relief and satisfaction. Yet he must have felt weakened by the effort: two days later, he went to Moor Park. On 13 November he wrote to Fox, "I have lately spent a very pleasant week at Moor Park, & Hydropathy & idleness did me wonderful good & I walked one day $4\frac{1}{2}$ miles, – quite a Herculean feat for me!" He spent most of the following February at Moor Park, but complained to Fox while there, "I have been extra bad of late, with the old severe vomiting rather often & much distressing swimming of the head: I have been here a week . . .& it has already done me good . . . My abstract is the cause, I believe of the main part of the ills to which my flesh is heir to . . ." Perhaps he saw more truly than he realized: it is possible that the tensions underlying his relapse had been created not so much by the effort of writing the book as by the knowledge that soon the scientific and academic communities were to be confronted with his unorthodox ideas.

Through most of the Spring of 1859, Darwin struggled to finish the book which would encapsulate his views. In April, there arrived the anxious moment when the prospective publisher, John Murray, read the first chapters of the manuscript: in relief, Darwin wrote to Hooker that "he abides by his offer". A month later he was thanking Hooker for his high opinion of the book – but "Good Lord, how I do long to have done with it!" A few days later he was claiming, "My health has quite failed", and rushing off to Moor Park. Yet another month over, and he was deep in his corrections: "I get on very slowly with proofs", he admitted to Murray. He had thought that little would have to be altered; the meticulous reality was otherwise. "I find the style incredibly bad, & most difficult to make clear & smooth . . . How I could have written so badly is quite inconceivable, but I suppose it was owing to my whole attention being fixed on the general line of argument . . ." To Lyell, at almost the same time, he wrote, "I long to finish, for I am nearly worn out" – he still had over 350 pages to correct. By September he was complaining to Hooker that his "health has been very bad, & I am becoming as weak as a child, & incapable of doing anything whatever, except my three hours daily work at proof-sheets . . . I had a terribly long fit of sickness yesterday, which makes the world rather extra gloomy today, & I have an insanely strong wish to finish my book . . ." And on 11 September, he reported to Lyell, "I corrected the last proof yesterday . . . So that the neck of my work, thank God, is broken . . . As soon as ever I have fairly finished I shall be off to Ilkley, or some other Hydropathic establishment . . . Murray proposes to publish the first week in November. Oh, good heavens, the relief to my head & body to banish the whole subject from my mind!"

Ilkley House, in Yorkshire, had opened for hydropathic business some three years earlier. Its physician, Edmund Smith, was a man of fifty-five for whom Darwin had small respect – "he constantly gives me the impression as if he cared very much for the Fee & very little for the Patient". In November, Darwin had trouble in finding a house near by for his family, and for a while thought he would be isolated in his northern water cure. Then he learned that a Miss Butler, whom he had befriended at Moor Park, was touring in Scotland and, a little desperately, wrote to her "to know whether there is any chance of your being at Ilkley in beginning of October. It would be rather terrible to go into the great place & not know a soul. But if you were there I should feel safe & home-like." Two days after he arrived at Ilkley on 3 October, he was tetchily admitting to Fox that he detested "the whole place & everything except one kind lady here, whom I knew at Moor Park". Miss Butler had evidently arrived.

The publication of *The Origin* was now only weeks away. Advance volumes were shuttling through the posts, to friends and enemies, admirers, rivals, sceptics, converts – above all, those whose pronouncements would shape the opinion of the world. If nervousness and uncertainty were building up in Darwin, no one can be surprised. He had been working towards this moment for more than two decades. The subject had long been a field on which the orthodox were prepared to give furious battle. His book, carved out of one much fuller and longer, had been hastily prepared, almost cobbled together; the scholarly scaffolding that would have supported the original work had been flung aside: speed of construction rather than safety had been the criterion. If it failed, however, all failed – his life would have been turned to ridicule. No reasons, no plea of imposed conditions, would be able to excuse or exorcise that.

So, bewildered in Yorkshire, miserable in unfamiliar surroundings, with Emma distant, the tensions and anxieties mounting, Darwin now underwent a whole catalogue of sufferings. He sprained his ankle. His leg swelled until it appeared like a case of elephantiasis. His face became covered in a rash; then it too swelled, almost sufficiently to close his eyes. Finally, he was overwhelmed by "a frightful succession of boils." No wonder he felt as if "living in Hell."

But of course he was not to be denied the fame he so much desired – and so much despised himself for desiring. There must have been one unexpected consequence of publishing his theory however: his life became integrated in a way that it had not been until then. His inner and his external selves were welded into one. Few people had known of his ideas; now, the entire world discussed them. He had worked almost alone, almost in secrecy; now he, and those who believed him to be right, were forced by public outcry to become public men. Darwin continued to maintain the physical seclusion which had for so long protected him, but despite this he was henceforth to be a presence in the world.

The effect was to bring together the life he lived and the ideas he held. He became the progenitor and vessel of those ideas, in the eyes of all beholders: he became the Charles Darwin of history, of our own legend, a century on. There had been a disunity in his life: on the one hand, there had been the husband, the father, the owner of one of the locality's big houses, a man who like his neighbours was what the material reality proclaimed; on the other, the person who in the privacy of his study or his garden, worked out his heterodox ideas. There had been a kindly, gentle, endlessly agreeable semi-invalid, who had been the Darwin everyone knew and liked, and there had been an obsessed, demonic, endlessly energetic scientist, the Darwin few knew and many would have thought – and now did think – monstrous and dangerous. His silence about the inner Darwin had left the external to potter about his village world almost like a husk; there is a sense in which his entire life outside science had until that moment been little more than a mask, almost a sham.

Now the dramatic revelation of his true, complete identity through the publication of his ideas linked the inner and outer areas of his life. Each could be seen in something like its true proportions. All these years his true centre had lain not, as it had appeared to do, in his drawing room and his children's nursery, but rather in the solitude of his study, where he had scribbled down his endless observations and the page after page of his intended book. From 1836, when he returned from the *Beagle* voyage, until the moment in November, 1859, when *The Origin* came out, the most significant outflow of his energies had, unknown to almost everyone, been directed towards the creation of a self-consistent model of the natural world which allowed for the endless flux he had discerned, and explained its slow, millennial mutability. It was a model which, half triumphantly, half despite himself, he was about to reveal – a process in which he would also, but much more inadvertently, reveal himself.

The main sources for Part Five were:
  Letters, manuscripts, account books and the Diary of Health from the Darwin papers in Cambridge University Library; letters from the Darwin archives in the Library of the American Philosophical Association, Philadelphia; the W.D. Fox

letters from Christ's College, Cambridge; Darwin's *Autobiography*, edited by Nora Barlow; Darwin's *Life and Letters*, edited by Francis Darwin and *More Letters*, edited by Francis Darwin and A.C. Seward; *Emma Darwin: a Century of Family Letters*, edited by Henrietta Litchfield; *Down, the Home of the Darwins,* by Sir. H. Atkins; *Period Piece*, by Gwen Raverat; *To Be an Invalid* by R. Colp.

Evolution by Natural Selection, edited by Sir G. de Beer: Darwin's *Collected papers*, edited by P.H. Barrett; Darwin's *Natural selection*, edited by R.C. Stauffer; *Vestiges of Creation* by R. Chambers; *Darwin's Century*, by Loren Eisley; Hooker's *Life and Letters*, edited by L. Huxley; *Creative Malady*, by Sir G. Pickering; Sedgwick's *Life and Letters*, edited by Clark and Hughes; *Darwin's Victorian Malady*, by J.H. Winslow; *My Life* by A.R. Wallace.

PART SIX

My Abominable Volume

1

"You will think me presumptuous", Darwin had written to Hooker in April, 1859, "but I think my book will be popular to a certain extent . . . amongst scientific and semi-scientific men; why I think so is, because I have found in conversation so great and surprising an interest amongst such men . . ." Even so mild an anticipation of success had quickly disturbed him; a few days later he had written, "Please do not say to anyone that I thought my book on Species would be fairly popular, & have a fairly remunerative sale (which was the height of my ambition), for if it prove a dead failure, it would make me the more ridiculous".

In May, Murray himself had expressed uncertainty about the book – he had found it entirely unbelievable, "as absurd as though one should contemplate a fruitful union between a poker and a rabbit", and passed on to Darwin the suggestion, made by the editor of the *Quarterly Review*, Whitwell Elwin, that the bulk of the book should deal with the experiments on pigeons: "everybody is interested in pigeons". By June, there had been a gathering and strengthening of Darwin's fears. He had written to Hooker. "You say that you dreamt my book was *entertaining*; that dream is pretty well over with me, & I begin to fear that the public will find it intolerably dry & perplexing". At the end of September, he had informed Fox that the book was almost ready for its final printing: "So much for my abominable volume, which has cost me so much labour that I almost hate it."

On 24 November, with Darwin struggling against his physical disabilities at Ilkley, the book finally appeared: 1250 green volumes, nearly five hundred pages of small type in each, every one a package of ideas, evidence and speculation which, like a letter bomb, was primed to detonate when opened. The potential victims, however, rushed to meet their fate; the first edition, at fifteen shillings a copy, was sold out before publication. Murray, who had originally intended to print an edition of no more than five hundred, wrote urgently to Darwin for the revisions that should go into a second printing. Darwin, to his astonishment and delight, received the letter on the very morning of publication. Murray, he wrote at once to Lyell, "wants a new edition instantly, and this utterly confounds me".

He set about making minor changes. For example, he attempted to placate the religious feelings that he had outraged by here and there adding

ON

THE ORIGIN OF SPECIES

BY MEANS OF NATURAL SELECTION,

OR THE

PRESERVATION OF FAVOURED RACES IN THE STRUGGLE FOR LIFE.

By CHARLES DARWIN, M.A.,

FELLOW OF THE ROYAL, GEOLOGICAL, LINNÆAN, ETC., SOCIETIES;
AUTHOR OF 'JOURNAL OF RESEARCHES DURING H. M. S. BEAGLE'S VOYAGE
ROUND THE WORLD.'

LONDON:

JOHN MURRAY, ALBEMARLE STREET.

1859.

Title page of *The Origin's* first edition.

the phrase, "by the Creator", so suggesting the belief that matter had first achieved life through the intervention of some divine agency. Meanwhile, he had the reactions of his earliest readers to sustain him, those whose standing had allowed them the priviledge of an advance copy. "I have just finished your volume", wrote Lyell in October, 1859, "and right glad I am that I did my best with Hooker to persuade you to publish it . . . It is a splendid case of close reasoning and long substantial argument throughout so many pages . . ." Charles Kingsley, a clergyman and natural scientist as well as a novelist, wrote in mid-November to thank him "for the unexpected honour of your book . . . All I have seen of it *awes* me; both with the heap of facts and the prestige of your name, and also with the clear intuition, that if you be right, I must give up much that I have believed and written". Kingsley had not taken long to get to the crux of the matter.

A few days later the botanist, H.C. Watson, wrote to Darwin, "Your leading idea will assuredly become recognized as an established truth in science, i.e. 'Natural Selection'. It has the characteristics of all great natural truths . . . You are the greatest revolutionist in natural history of this century, if not of all centuries." Hooker, setting down the terms of his enthusiasm amid the gravities of the Athenaeum, thanked Darwin "for your glorious book – what a mass of close reasoning on curious facts and fresh phenomena – it is capitally written, and will be very successful." And, a few days later, from the School of Mines in Jermyn Street, there came a letter of mixed praise and prophecy, sent by the most recent of that chain of friends by whom Darwin was guided and supported throughout his life.

The letter stated firmly that, in the nine years since reading the essays of von Bär – an embryologist from the shores of the Baltic who was among the most eminent of Darwin's predecessors – "no work on Natural History Science I have met with has made so great an impression on me. Nothing, I think, can better the tone of your book . . . I trust you will not allow yourself to be in any way disgusted or annoyed by the considerable abuse and misrepresentation which, unless I greatly mistake, is in store for you. Depend upon it, you have earned the lasting gratitude of all thoughtful men. And as to the curs which will bark and yelp, you must recollect that some of your friends, at any rate, are endowed with an amount of combativeness which (though you have often and justly rebuked it) may stand you in good stead." One can almost hear the tone of anticipatory glee as the writer adds, "I am sharpening up my claws and beak in readiness".

Thus T.H. Huxley announced his readiness for the coming battle. Huxley was the son of an Ealing schoolmaster who, after a period scattering brilliance and gathering prizes as a student at Charing Cross Hospital, began his career, as had both Darwin and Hooker, by joining the scientific staff of a naval expedition. After four years in the southern waters of the Australasian continents, he had returned in 1850 to England and comparative poverty. Yet the work he had done had caused the better established to take notice of him: a few months after his return, he was elected a Fellow of the Royal Society. His new standing excited him, as years before it must have excited Darwin – though Huxley, less reticent than Darwin, was not afraid to express what he felt. To his future wife he wrote, in November, 1851, "I have at last tasted what it is to mingle with my fellows – to take my place in that society for which nature has fitted me, and whether the draught has been a poison which has heated my veins or a true nectar from the gods, life-giving, I know not, but I can no longer rest where I once could have rested."

Huxley was one of the first scientists to be directly converted by *The Origin* itself. Unlike Hooker, he had not accepted Darwin's ideas before reading the book; unlike Lyell, he had little reason to hold out against the Darwinian hypothesis once he had read it. Darwin, in a letter to Wallace, acknowledged Hooker as an adherent, then added, "If I can convert Huxley I shall be content." Not that such a conversion demanded any profound rearrangement of Huxley's thinking: like other scientists, he needed less the reiteration of a belief in transmutation, than an explanation of how transmutation might occur. As he put it himself, "The facts of variability, of the struggle for existence, of adaptation to conditions, were notorious enough; but none of us had suspected that the road to the heart of the species problem lay through them, until Darwin and Wallace dispelled the darkness, and the beacon-fire of the *Origin* guided the benighted."

Huxley, with his strong nose and deep-set eyes, his bony face and brown hair falling over his collar, looked the hawk-like, aggressive contrast to the placid Darwin that he was. He had swooped down and seized the central thesis of Darwin's book the moment he had been able to see it clearly; thereafter, though he might have been discredited as a result, might even have found himself with a smashed career, he defended it with wholehearted energy and all his fierce power.

"We . . . shall have, I am convinced, all young and rising naturalists on our side," wrote Darwin to Hooker, and it is true that the intellectual world was now dividing as though opposing armies were rallying to their banners. Here stood the young, the radical, the empirical, the materialist, the revolutionary, there the conservative, the authoritarian, the idealist, the God-fearing, the defenders of established order. Darwin's adherents were in the minority, but they had the strength of recent converts. Often it was Darwin's logic rather than his evidence which drew them. "In fact", as Erasmus wrote to his brother, "the *a priori* reasoning is so entirely satisfactory to me that if the facts won't fit in, why so much the worse for the facts is my feeling". The cannonading of this verbal war became so fierce, and the issues it centred on were so fundamental, that it forced itself on the attention of everyone. It became a topic of general conversation, at whatever amused or trivial level. "Have you seen 'The Colleen Bawn'*?", Mild Youth asked Horrid Girl in *Punch,* to which – "with extreme velocity" – she replied, "Seen 'The Colleen Bawn'! Dear, dear! Yes, of course. Saw it last October! And I've been to Crystal Palace, and I've read the Gorilla Book!" Thus did Horrid Girls lay claim to social preeminence in the London summer of 1861.

The matter in dispute lay in the first five chapters of *The Origin.* As in every extended exposition of his views, Darwin had begun with a study of how breeders and farmers exploited the vagaries of genetics, seizing on differing variations in order to produce new types of domestic fowl or animal. His second chapter demonstrated that the effects of variation in nature, though undirected by any human agency, might be equally important. In Chapter III, dealing with the universal battle for existence, it was the heading of the final section that made what was perhaps the centrally significant point: "Struggle for Life most severe between Individuals and Varieties of the same Species". In his fourth chapter Darwin drew together all that he had outlined – much of which was not in dispute – and brought to bear upon it his revolutionary but unifying principle, natural selection. The fifth of these crucial chapters seems now much weaker than the other four; the ideas on genetics with which it deals were unavoidably vitiated by the prevailing ignorance of science on the subject.

In the rest of the book, Darwin discussed at some length the objections that might be raised against his theory; he attempted to explain the development of the instincts (those behavioural equivalents of crimson plumes or snow-white fur); demonstrated that sterility was not the necessary outcome of attempts to mate between the species (important in showing that species could have arisen from varieties); dealt with the geological evidence for his version of prehistory; and finally attempted to explain the significance of the geographical distribution of species and, more particularly, of the otherwise anomalous physical similarities between them.

One can see that the structure of his book followed fairly closely the plan he had laid down for his first paper in 1842. It is as though the theory had been in its essentials fully formed from the beginning; he had seen no need to change either his ideas or the sequences of evidence and exposition through which he explained them. Perhaps this consistency stemmed from the isolation in which he worked. That had now been swept away for ever and he had become open to the world's opinion. Over the following decade, the

---

* A highly successful play by the Irish-American dramatist, Dion Boucicault, who brought it to London after an acclaimed run in New York.

alterations he was to make to the text of *The Origin* demonstrate that, even protected by his faithful colour-guard, he was deeply affected by the cannonading of his opponents.

It was in the new year that this barrage began to achieve its full ferocity. During the last weeks of 1859, Darwin could take comfort in reactions that were either neutral or, through the tricks of infiltration, positively friendly. At the beginning of December, writing to a French correspondent, probably the anthropologist Quatrefages, about the possibility of a French translation, Darwin was sounding positively jubilant. "Sir C. Lyell, who has been our chief maintainer of the immutability of species, has become an entire convert; as is Hooker, our best & most philosophical Botanist; as is Carpenter, an excellent physiologist, & as is Huxley, & I could name several other names." The list is a little suspect – neither Lyell nor Carpenter were as yet wholehearted supporters – but then Darwin was trying to exert a shrewdly commercial pressure in order to extend his readership to France.

Meanwhile a highly favourable review had appeared in *The Times*, an unexpected venue for such sympathy. "Mr Darwin abhors mere speculation as nature abhors a vaccuum", wrote this anonymous supporter of natural selection. He saw in the theory an explanation "for many apparent anomalies in the distribution of living beings in time and space" and the pointer "to a region free from the snares of those fascinating but barren virgins, the Final Causes, against whom high authority has so justly warned us". Darwin wrote to Hooker, "I cannot avoid a strong suspicion that it is by Huxley . . ." and to Huxley himself asserted, "Certainly I should have said that there was only one man in England who could have written this essay, and that *you* were the man. But I suppose I am wrong, and that there is some hidden genius of great calibre." Darwin, however, was right: the journalist who had been given the book to review had found it too difficult a task and had asked for Huxley's expert help. Huxley wrote later, "I was . . . anxious to seize upon the opportunity of giving the book a fair chance . . . and being then very full of the subject, I wrote the article faster, I think, than I ever wrote anything in my life . . ."

These columns of praise and understanding had appeared just in time to counter the doubts and criticisms raised by a not unexpected source. On 24 December, Professor Sedgwick had settled down in his rooms at Cambridge to write Darwin a long letter. He had been in the forefront of the battle to damn the *Vestiges,* and he was not prepared to let the same heresy – as he saw it – flourish even when proposed by a friend, colleague, and ex-student. Confronting Darwin directly, however, he wrote in restrained and scholarly vein. He had, he said, read the book "with more pain than pleasure. Parts of it I admired greatly, parts I laughed at till my sides were almost sore; other parts I read with absolute sorrow, because I think them utterly false and grievously mischievous." His main criticism was that Darwin had based his conclusions "upon assumptions which can neither be proved nor disproved", yet had expressed them "in the language and arrangement of philosophical induction". As for natural selection – "your grand principle" – it was no more than "a secondary consequence of supposed, or known, primary facts". It was the will of God that ordered the world, "and I can prove that He acts for the good of His creatures". Everyone admitted there was a battle for life and development was "a fact of history: but how came it about? . . . There is a moral or metaphysical part of nature as well as a physical. A man who denies this is deep in the mire of folly. 'Tis the crown and glory of organic science that it *does* through *final cause*, link material and moral . . . You have ignored this link; and, if I do not mistake your meaning, you have done your best in one or two pregnant cases to break it. Were it possible (which, thank God, it is not) to break it, humanity, in my mind, would suffer a damage that might brutalize it, and sink the human race into a lower grade of degradation than any into which it has fallen since its written records tell us of its history."

Much of this was, from Darwin's point of view, irrelevant and all of it might have been anticipated. Sedgwick had said, "You write of 'natural selection' as if it were done consciously by the selecting agent", but Darwin had done no such thing; if anything, he had erred on the side of making natural selection a positive and active entity, almost as personified a force within nature as an ancient god. Reviews, now appearing thick and fast, tended to repeat both Sedgwick's opinions and his errors. They derided Darwin's ideas as wild speculation; they allotted to Biblical accounts of the Creation the scientific status of observed and tested fact; and they accused Darwin of attempting to destroy the credibility of divine revelation, upon which rested both morality and the religion that authorised its sanction.

Darwin's supporters, whether long-established or newly converted, rallied as vigorously as they could to what had become their cause. The foremost of them, Huxley, in his lectures described the true scientist as "the sworn interpreter of nature in the high court of reason". Yet what use was his honesty, "if ignorance is the assessor of the judge, and prejudice the foreman of the jury?" In the *National Review*, the physiologist, Carpenter, wrote sympathetically and with understanding. He faced the religious issue squarely, and dismissed it as irrelevant, since "any theological objections, even to Mr. Darwin's startling conclusions, much more to his very modest premises, seem simply absurd". After fourteen pages of description and analysis of Darwin's and Wallace's ideas, he came to judgement: "We are disposed to believe, then, that Mr. Darwin and Mr. Wallace have assigned a *vera causa* for that diversification of original types of structure which has brought into existence vast multitudes of species, sub-species and varieties . . ." In grateful jubilation, Darwin wrote to Carpenter, "It is a great thing to have got a great physiologist on our side."

Jenyns, Darwin's old Cambridge companion and Henslow's son-in-law, offered his praise for *The Origin,* but also his reservations. He clearly felt that it had moved too far towards the atheist position. Darwin replied that it would have been "dishonest to quite conceal my opinion" about the question of humanity's genesis. "Of course it is open to every one to believe that man appeared by a separate miracle, though I do not myself see the necessity or probability." In the book itself, however, he had been careful to be much less outspoken, having realized from the beginning that this was the crux of the objections he would meet. If the human race was no more than one species among many, created like the others by the long process of transmutation, what became of divine ordinance and the image of God?

His own silence on so critical an issue did not ensure that of his opponents. They took their stand on humanity's ethical sense, on its freedom to choose its course of action. "Look at the educated Englishman", wrote the *London Review* with invincible smugness, "and the Australian aboriginal; the one gaining more and more mastery over the laws of this world, the other almost as helpless a victim of those laws as the brutes around him. Never in nature's kingdom do we see this immense gulf between individuals of the same species; we see it in man alone, because he alone in creation was free to rise or fall." (The writer refrained from considering the position of his "educated Englishman" if cast adrift in the central wastes of Australia, and what lessons might usefully be drawn from that!)

The *Dublin Review*, securely rooted in its Catholicism, wrote in patronizing mock-sorrow. Mr. Darwin, it told its readers, "has the misfortune not to believe in Adam and Eve, and he has filled up the gap thus left in his mind by substituting in their place some prototype of far more venerable antiquity . . . he looks back through a bewildering number of years to his simple progenitor, a worm, perhaps, or a bit of sponge, or some animated cellule . . . The work itself, in the main, we will say frankly, seems to us so valuable . . . that we cannot say how grieved we are that the book should be marred by the introduction of so gratuitous and so repulsive an idea . . ."

Sedgwick returned to the attack in the *Spectator,* anonymity protecting a certain lack of restraint. He expressed his "detestation of the theory, because of its unflinching materialism; – because it has deserted the inductive track, the only track that leads to physical truth; – because it utterly repudiates final causes, and thereby indicates a demoralised understanding on the part of its advocates . . . Each series of facts is laced together by a series of assumptions, and repetitions of the one false principle. You cannot make a good rope out of a string of air bubbles."

And, also anonymously, freely citing himself as an authority, there was a long essay in the *Edinburgh Review* by Richard Owen. He was the Lucifer in Darwin's cosmos, the fallen angel who might have been among the mighty of heaven had not stubborness and pride made it impossible. Thus Darwin and his friends attacked Owen with a bitterness not matched by the tone they used for anyone else among their opponents. Neither Sedgwick nor the Swiss-born catastrophist Agassiz were ever mentioned with the contempt that shaped their comments when they referred to him. Owen was an anatomist almost as skilled in the assignment and assemblage of bones as had been Cuvier, whose follower he was. Like Cuvier, Owen for a long time rejected all developmental or transmutational ideas. He was, in the philosophical sense, an idealist, believing that every vertebrate species was in fact only a modified version of the perfect model of a vertebrate that existed eternally in the imagination of the Creator. The fact that this was thought a scientific rather than a theological hypothesis indicates the confused intellectual climate in which *The Origin* was published. Because Owen so confidently opposed Darwin, the non-scientific felt emboldened to do the same. If there was a Huxley to speak for Darwinism, there was an Owen to speak against it. "Had they agreed," wrote *John Bull* in 1863, "We should . . . have been compelled to accept Mr. Darwin. As it is, we can adopt one side or the other, with the comfortable assurance that a champion whose blows all must respect is fighting with us."

Darwin, who found it difficult to be angry with his peers and usually discovered something polite to say about them, whatever the disagreements, became uncharacteristically abusive when mentioning Owen. His reaction turns this somewhat pompous anatomist into an adversary of the first importance, and makes vanquishing him appear like a victory of great consequence. In fact, Cuvier's flag at the masthead marked Owen's as a sinking ship, and no one realized this as well as he; as unobtrusively as he could, he struck his colours as he foundered, hoping that he might pass in the end for a ship of the newer fleet that had defeated him. But he had been outmanoeuvred too decisively for that; he sank, leaving behind him, not his inherited theories, but the meticulous and unimpeachable work he had done over the years.

In his vexed fury, the disconsolate energy of the dispossessed, Owen allied himself to the most virulently anti-Darwinian party. He became a kind of *ex officio* scientific adviser to its leader, Samuel Wilberforce, the Bishop of Oxford, a man whose unctuous agility in sermon and debate has been immortalized by his nickname, "Soapy Sam". We know his critical methods best from an article on *The Origin* that appeared in the *Quarterly Review* – "I can plainly see Owen's hand", wrote Darwin to Hooker.

The article misunderstood Darwin's thesis with what seems deliberate obtuseness: it magnanimously accepts "a struggle for life", which it describes as a tendency "continually to lead the strong to exterminate the weak", a view rather different from Darwin's, in which organisms strive to exist in an unconcerned and occasionally inimical environment. It saw natural selection as working through variations that are such "as truly to exalt those individuals above the highest type of perfection to which their least imperfect predecessors attained . . .", so introducing precisely that principle of progression which Darwin was so careful to exclude. It found an opening in the Darwinian armour however, when it attacked the mathematics with which Darwin attempted to demonstrate the geological age of the Kentish Weald, a proof that was to be abandoned in later editions. It quoted with an unsurprising approval from Owen himself, particularly recommending his statement that "the sum of the animal species at each geological period has been distinct and peculiar to that period", a commitment to the catastrophist position that denies any possibility of evolution by whatever means.

The article went on to raise the subject of human descent; mankind's manifest qualities were "utterly irreconcilable with the degrading notion of the brute origin of him who was created in the image of God . . ." Fortunately there was an Owen to redress the philosophical balance by stating firmly, "Man is the sole species of his genus, the sole representative of his order and subclass. Thus I trust has been furnished confutation of the notion of a transformation of the ape into the man." Since this was not a transformation Darwin had proposed, the salvo seems misdirected; but it is what the public thought Darwin had said and therefore may not have fallen so wide of its real mark – Darwin's reputation, his credibility, rather than his ideas. With that end in view, the article attacks the man by insulting his conclusions, likening them to "the frenzied inspiration of the inhaler of mephitic gas. The whole world of nature is laid for such a man under a fantastic law of glamour, and he becomes capable of believing anything . . . able, with a continually growing neglect of all the facts around him, with equal confidence and equal delusion, to look back to any past and to look on to any future".

It is no wonder that the public, fascinated but bewildered, turned in some excitement to that year's annual meeting in Oxford of the British Association for the Advancement of Science. Wilberforce was going to appear there, and though his article had not yet been published, everyone knew what his position was and that he intended to assert it. With Owen to advise him, he was obviously preparing to rest his case on the logic of this world as

The BAAS meeting in 1866.

well as the next. Then, as now, the BAAS was the forum at which disparate disciplines made brief contact with each other, and where Science coyly invited the laity into its mystifying cloisters. The clash of factions would therefore take place under the eyes of spectators both committed and uncertain.

Predictably, perhaps, Darwin's health proved too fragile to permit his own appearance. He was the philosopher who had established the tenets of his cause; he was neither its champion nor its commander in the field. By letter, he rallied, congratulated and, at times, cajoled his supporters, but in person he remained in his fastness at Downe or, as now, retreated even further, to the damp sheets and saline solutions of a water cure. He explained to Hooker that, since his "stomach has utterly failed", he could not be in Oxford; then he shut himself away in Dr. Lane's new hydropathic clinic at Sudbrook Park, in Richmond, just southwest of London.

On the day that he placed himself in Lane's care, 28 June, 1860, there was fought the preliminary skirmish to the main Oxford battle. On that Thursday the University's professor of botany, Dr. Charles Daubeny, read to the Zoological Section a paper "On the Final Causes of the Sexuality of Plants", a potentially calming piece which suggested impending dissent only in its subtitle, "with particular Reference to Mr. Darwin's Work 'On the Origin of Species by Natural Selection' ". Daubeny was prepared to go some way in Darwin's support, pointing out that a union of the sexes in plants allows for variation in the offspring and that, if one accepted the hypothesis of natural selection, that might be considered the purpose of vegetable sexuality. But, as the account of the meeting in the *Athenaeum* hastened to add, "Whilst . . . he gave his assent to the Darwinian hypothesis, as likely to aid us in reducing the number of existing species, he wished not to be considered as advocating it to the extent to which the author seems disposed to carry it". This somewhat grudging approval, with its sweeping caveat, at once opened the possibility of a wider debate.

Henslow, who was the chairman of this section of the BAAS and therefore probably eager to be fair to Darwin, asked Huxley to speak. Huxley, however, was reserving his fire. He felt, he said, "that a general audience, in which sentiment would unduly interfere with intellect, was not the public before which such a discussion should be carried on" – an attitude of high-handed elitism that explains to some extent the antipathy he aroused in the more consciously arrogant Owen.

After some inconclusive debate, much of it centering on whether monkeys could learn to break oysters and, if so, how they did it, Owen himself rose to speak. His attitude was that of a man who, were he willing, could easily destroy any claims made for the truth of the natural selection hypothesis:

speaking "in the spirit of the philosopher" he affirmed the "conviction that there were facts by which the public could come to some conclusion with regard to the probabilities of the truth of Mr. Darwin's theory". Perhaps unfortunately for him, he proposed as the first of these facts the difference between the human brain and that of the gorilla, the latter, in his submission, presenting "more differences, as compared with the brain of man, than it did when compared with the brains of the very lowest and most problematical of the Quadrumana" (the "four-handed" genus to which all apes and monkeys belong).

Huxley had, over the previous two years, made a study of exactly this subject. He had confirmed for himself the profound structural similarities that existed between the brains of human beings and the higher apes, and he had included his findings in his public lectures. He cited as authorities the German anatomist Tiedemann and others, who had themselves dissected and examined various organs with precisely this object in mind. Between humans and the highest Quadrumana, he asserted, there were fewer differences than there were between the highest monkeys and the lowest. He thus met Owen's claims with a "direct and unqualified contradiction" and promised that he would "justify that unusual procedure elsewhere". A year later he was to publish a paper in the *Natural History Review* that would demolish Owen's case – though the argument was to drag on, reanimated at intervals and always with Owen's name cited as authority, long after it had been won and lost.

Huxley, as he had already made clear, felt no desire to debate the Darwinian issue before this unpredictable and largely uninformed audience. His wife was staying with her sister near Reading, not very far away, and on Saturday morning he had intended to join her there. On Friday afternoon, however, he happened to meet Robert Chambers, who, although he had seen his *Vestiges* supplanted by Darwin's book as the anti-Bible of the evolutionists, still adhered to the transmutational cause. He pleaded with Huxley not to desert those fighting for it – "Soapy Sam" Wilberforce, whose claim to speak on scientific matters derived from a First in mathematics, had vowed to "smash" Darwin and the Darwinians once and for all. With such a champion uttering such a challenge, was Huxley to retreat?

Swayed by Chambers's appeal, and perhaps drawn by his own pleasure in battle, Huxley remained in Oxford. On a day when nothing less was to be debated than the origins and status of mankind, it is not surprising that a vast crowd of the partisan, the concerned and the curious began early to push their way into the lecture hall of the New University Museum. Soon it had become obvious that there would not be room for them all and the venue was changed to the much larger West Room. There, Huxley mounted the platform, with beside him another reluctant participant, Hooker. Owen, who was to have taken the chair, perhaps prudently absented himself; with what one may imagine was some reluctance, Henslow agreed to take his place.

The opening of the debate was anticlimactic: with well over seven hundred people craning forward to hear him, the American, Prof. J.W. Draper, began to intone his lecture – which had, after all, been the lure drawing so many spectators to this room. Entitled "On the Intellectual Development of Europe, considered with Reference to the Views of Mr. Darwin and Others, that the Progression of Organisms is determined by Law", it tried to show that a fundamental alteration in their physical circumstances would swiftly modify human societies and institutions. It followed that, as the *Athenaeum* report put it, if "the existing apparent invariability presented by the world of organization . . . should suffer modification, in an instant the fanciful doctrine of the immutability of species would be brought to its proper value". In this roundabout manner the New York chemist declared himself an unenthusiastic adherent of the Darwinian theory. His flat and monotonous delivery, however, the length of his address and the fact that much of it was irrelevant to the confrontation these hundreds had come to witness, all threatened to wreck the occasion before it had fairly begun.

Other speakers rose: a clergyman named Greswell took issue with Draper, but the audience, especially the students among them, were losing patience and after a few minutes began to interrupt and shout him down. Sir Benjamin Brodie, the President of the Royal Society, a clutch of students around him like a Praetorian Guard, then stated his opposition to Darwin: the existence of a "primordial germ" had not been proven, nor was it likely that the power of self-consciousness could have originated in lower animals that did not possess it. A Mr. Dingle, with misplaced assurance, now stepped forward, chalk in hand. He scrawled on the blackboard. "Let this point A", he drawled, "be man, and let that point B be the mawnkey . . ."

Patience burst, turned into derision, threatened soon to become fury. "Mawnkey! Mawnkey!" yelled the students in fierce mockery. Mr. Dingle, overwhelmed, sat down; his head vanishes below the sill of history. Into the spreading silence of expectancy, the Bishop of Oxford rose to his feet. The women sitting in the windows of the west wall waved their handkerchiefs, signals of their allegiance to the Christian cause, their hope that Darwin would once and for all be crushed by the incontrovertible logic of the church; then they too settled down.

Huxley, who had the day before shrugged and said, almost offhandedly, to Chambers and his pleading, "Oh, if you're going to take it that way, I'll come and have my share of what's going on", now sat forward tensely. He was not tense for very long – it was soon clear, to him if not to the Bishop's supporters, that whatever his university standing in mathematics might have been, "Soapy Sam's" grasp of natural science was inadequate for his task. Wilberforce cited the evidence of the mummified animals of Egypt to show that modification did not take place; he pointed out that no experimenter had ever been able to change one kind of animal into another; he claimed that the distinction between humanity and the lower animals was absolute, there being no sign that the latter had the slightest tendency to become rational and self-aware beings. Everything he said showed, to those fully familiar with it, that he had only the weakest understanding of Darwin's proposition.

Wilberforce spoke with an easy assurance. He enjoyed speaking. He enjoyed being listened to, and creating effects. He was moving towards the end of his speech, which was to be grave, a reiteration of Old Testament truths, and he needed a moment of lightness before he began it. He paused, looked out at his audience, then said, "I should like to ask Professor Huxley, who is sitting by me and is about to tear me to pieces when I have sat down, as to his belief in being descended from an ape. Is it on his grandfather's or his grandmother's side that the ape ancestry comes in?" Then his voice dropped, his face took on an episcopal gravity and he moved into his peroration, the sonorous rhetoric appropriate for the defence of a Victorian deity. But Huxley had turned to his neighbour, Sir Benjamin Brodie, and said in whispered triumph, "The Lord hath delivered him into mine hands!" And as Sir Benjamin stared at him in bewilderment, he began to turn over in his mind the terms of his reply.

Applause, the cries of enthusiastic undergraduates, the white flowering of those religious handkerchiefs; then a slow settling as Huxley stood. "I am here", he told his listeners sternly, "only in the interests of Science – and I have heard nothing which can prejudice the case of my august client". He pointed out that Darwin's was an explanation of the phenomena found in the organic world, just as the wave theory of light – proposed by the English scientist Thomas Young nearly sixty years before – explained the phenomena of luminescence. A light wave had never been halted and measured, but no one asserted that this disproved the undulatory theory. He explained that Darwin was not proposing that species could change into each other, but rather how various forms that had become to all intents and purposes permanent had developed their present characteristics from a common ancestor. Mankind might differ from the rest of the world's animals because it alone had consciousness, but who was able to say at what precise moment in an individual's development conscious intelligence came into being? "You say that development drives out the Creator", he said, turning to Wilberforce. "But you assert that God made you: and yet you know that you yourself were originally a little piece of matter, no bigger than the end of this gold pencil-case."

Finally he came to the issue of personal descent, which the Bishop had raised with such easy insolence. Afterwards, various witnesses tried to reconstruct his precise words, but no account struck those who had been there, or Huxley himself, as absolutely accurate. (There were even some who insisted that he had replied to Wilberforce at once, leaping to his feet while the taunt was still fresh, but if this was so it seems strange that anyone could have forgotten it; those who believed it may have been so impressed by the force of Huxley's words that in retrospect they heard them as immediate refutation of the Bishop.) What Huxley seems to have said, as nearly as possible, is, "I asserted – and I repeat – that a man has no reason to be ashamed of having an ape for a grandfather. If there were an ancestor whom I should feel shame in recalling it would rather be a *man*, endowed with great ability and a splendid position, who should use these gifts to . . ."

And here a great crashing of applause, as the audience leaped upon Huxley's meaning, appears to have obscured for ever the words he actually spoke. Every hearer seems to have recalled the rest of the statement in his own personal style. More honestly than most, *Macmillan's Magazine* reported Huxley as a "slight tall figure, stern and pale, very quiet and grave", who "stood before us and spoke those tremendous words – words which no one seems sure of now, nor, I think, could remember just after they were spoken, for their meaning took away our breath, though it left us in no doubt as to what it was. He was not ashamed to have a monkey for his ancestor; but he would be ashamed to be connected with a man who used great gifts to obscure the truth. No one doubted his meaning, and the effect was tremendous. One lady fainted and had to be carried out; I, for one, jumped out of my seat." To be fair, not everyone was swept into approval; as the High Church weekly, *The Guardian*, observed, what would become of the British Association if "Professors lose their tempers and solemnly avow they would rather be descended from apes than Bishops . . ." Huxley himself, however, later recalled "inextinguishable laughter among the people, and they listened to the rest of my argument with great attention".

If this was the fiercest and most dramatic moment of the debate, it was not the last. Like some strange avenger for a long-forgotten crime, Fitzroy of the *Beagle*, his hair grey and receding, his long face pouched and jowled, but his haughty nose as imperious as ever, rose from among the crowd. There was, he cried, no logic in *The Origin*, and Huxley had no right to claim there was. He had read it, but the reading had pained him; he recalled, whether from memory or fancy, his shipboard protests nearly thirty years before against his companion's reservations over divine revelation. He held high a ponder-

Plate 22

Despite the damage caused to it by the workings of time, this photograph of Darwin with his eldest son, William, expresses all the tenderness and delight he felt in fatherhood.

Plate 23

Darwin's older brother, Erasmus, who as a schoolboy helped to create Charles's fascination for science, but who went on to live the agreeable life of a moneyed literary dilettante.

Plate 24

Collier's portrait of Charles Darwin in old age, now in the National Portrait Gallery

ous Bible, displaying it like the Mosaic tablets themselves – there, he cried, was the single, unimpeachable authority from which all truth derived. But so comprehensive a denial of the claims of science appealed to few in that assembly: he was shouted into silence. Defeated, Fitzroy – an Admiral, once the Governor of New Zealand, at another time chief of the Government Meteorological Department, who as he had always wished had been elected long before a Fellow of the Royal Society, but who during all these years of service and reward had become more and more zealous in his Christianity, more and more fundamentalist, until now his faith had curdled into mono-mania and obsession – Fitzroy accepted silence and withdrew, that day from the Oxford meeting and afterwards further and further from the irreverent doings of a blasphemous world, to die by his own hand less than five years later, his suicide the last gesture of his bitter bewilderment.

The debate grew more predictable, with divines and older academics on one side, the most respected practising scientists on the other. Darwin's Kent neighbour, John Lubbock, pointed to the flaws in the arguments of those who supported the permanence of species, to the implications of embryology as evidence for development and thus transmutation, and pro-claimed himself a follower of the Darwinian hypothesis since it provided the best available explanation of the facts. Finally, the erstwhile reluctant Hooker stood up to speak. And Hooker, like Huxley, was quite prepared to take on Wilberforce in the most direct manner.

Wilberforce, he began, had claimed that all reputable scientists were opposed to Darwin's ideas; since Hooker was in favour of them, he ob-viously could not claim to speak with any scientific authority. However, it seemed to him that the Bishop had largely misunderstood Darwin's hypothesis – Darwin had never proposed that one species could change into another. To say that he had was so contrary to Darwin's writings that it seemed inconceivable that anyone who had actually read *The Origin* could make such a mistake. The Bishop had claimed that the characteristics of species were such that no careful, thinking naturalist could possibly accept Darwin's views: Hooker's experience was, however, quite the contrary. At least half the known kinds of plants could be grouped into species connected by varying characteristics. He pointed out that the belief that each separate species was an original creation was also no more than an hypothesis, in itself no more entitled to acceptance than anything proposed by Darwin. He had himself accepted it on that basis; his experience as a botanist who had worked in many different parts of the world had persuaded him that Dar-win's hypothesis was the superior one. He would use it as his best basis for future research, but was quite prepared to change it to another, or back to the old creationist one, should the evidence demand it.

Huxley's response has obscured Hooker's. Historians seem hardly to remember that Hooker spoke at all. Yet the *Athenaeum* report of the meeting gave Hooker by far the greater amount of space, and Hooker himself was in no doubt about the value of his intervention. His was the first report of the meeting to reach Darwin; he wrote it two days later, his breeziness unable to disguise his remembered excitement over what had happened:

> Well, Sam Oxon got up and spouted for half an hour with inimitable spirit, ugliness and emptiness and unfairness. I saw he was coached up by Owen and knew nothing . . . Huxley answered admirably and turned the tables, but he could not throw his voice over so large an assembly, nor command the audience . . . The battle waxed hot. Lady Brewster fainted, the excitement increased as others spoke; my blood boiled, I felt myself a dastard; now I saw my advantage; I swore to myself that I would smite that Amalekite, Sam, hip and thigh . . . I hit him in the wind at the first shot in ten words taken from his own ugly mouth; and then proceeded to demonstrate in as few more: (1) that he could never have read your book, and (2) that he was absolutely ignorant of the rudiments of Bot. Science . . . Sam was shut up – had not one word to say in reply, and the meeting was dissolved forthwith, leaving you master of the field after 4 hours' battle.

Darwin, a little bemused at all this belligerence, replied, "How I should have liked to have wandered about Oxford with you, if I had been well enough; & how still more I should have liked to have heard you triumphing over the Bishop. I am astonished at your success and audacity. It is something unintelligible to me how anyone can argue in public like orators do. I had no idea you had this power." Darwin wrote to Huxley, too, about these "awful battles which have raged about species at Oxford . . . I often think that my friends (& you far beyond others) have good cause to hate me, for having stirred up so much mud, & led them into so much odious trouble. If I had been a friend of myself, I should have hated me. (How to make that sentence good English, I know not.) But remember, if I had not stirred up the mud, some one else certainly soon would. I honour your pluck; I would as soon have died as tried to answer the Bishop in such an assembly . . ."

It would be quite untrue, however, to imagine that by winning this battle the Darwinians had also won their war. They had not; indeed, it is not clear that everyone believed them to have won the battle, whatever they themselves claimed. It gives shape and drama to the story to bring it to its climax of confrontation in that Oxford summer of 1860, but the fact is that the articles and reviews, the debates, the letters, the skirmishing and sniping, continued throughout the decade and beyond; they have not ceased yet. At the annual meetings of the British Association, the debate continued year after year, well into the 1870s, the earlier years marked by Owen's more and

Asa Gray, American botanist and Darwin's early confidant.

more desperate efforts to defend his position.

As late as 1866 the *Contemporary Review*, only founded in that year, could attack *The Origin* as though it had just been freshly published. "Beautiful, ingenious and self consistent as is the Darwinian theory", it stated, "yet it has not been removed from the region of hypothesis into that of demonstrated facts . . ." By then, the struggle between the Darwinians and their opponents had long become a worldwide one. Even in 1860, a sympathetic article in the *Calcutta Review* was pointing out that "religious prejudice only, and not religious convictions will stand between Mr. Darwin's theory and acceptance among religious men". In Britain's lost dominion, too, the forays and trenches of this war had made their appearance. It was at the very end of 1859 that the Fisher Professor of Natural History at Harvard began to read his copy of *The Origin*. He was already more familiar than most other people with the trend of its ideas, for his name was Asa Gray and it was a letter to him, outlining the theory, that had helped Darwin to prove his priority over Wallace eighteen months earlier. With his own perceptions modified by Darwin's conclusions, Gray had discerned that similarities between the flora of eastern North America and Japan were evidence that before the Ice Ages there had been a unified distribution of plants throughout the earth's Arctic regions. This one-time interconnection, and the differences that had evidently developed in the plant life of the various regions once they had separated, gave him an empirical base from which to fight the Darwinian battle.

He fought it on every possible level, in debate, in his writings, and by making sure that *The Origin*, originally brought to the American public in a pirated edition, should be published with Darwin's approval, from Darwin's text and to Darwin's profit. It was fortunate for the cause of natural selection that when *The Origin* was to be reviewed in the *American Journal of Science*, it fell to Gray to write the article; Dana, the senior editor, who would have been against it, had suffered a breakdown and was recuperating in Italy, while the third in line of the editors was Agassiz, perhaps the most obdurate defender, among the world's major scientists, of catastrophism, creation, design and the unalterable fixity of species. Indeed, Gray used the views of Agassiz, which proposed, in Gray's words, "that each species originated simultaneously, generally speaking, over the whole geographical area it now occupies or has occupied", as the extreme in orthodox opinion against which Darwin's theory might be judged.

Gray was much more interested than was Darwin in reconciling science with religion and made it his interest to integrate the idea of natural selection with that of heavenly design, but the former, he insisted, "must be regarded as a legitimate attempt to extend the domain of natural or physical science". It was precisely this, of course, that such disciples of Cuvier as Agassiz could not admit. Gray however, was determined that, as he had written to his fellow botanist, Hooker, in January, Darwin "shall have fair-play here". He and Darwin corresponded about *The Origin*, swinging praise, criticism and explanation to and fro across the Atlantic; in February, having read proofs of Gray's forthcoming article, Darwin wrote, "Your Review seems to me *admirable*; by far the best I have read. I thank you from my heart both for myself, but far more for the subject's sake." Darwinism had found its champion in the United States – albeit one who had his reservations about the doctrine in its purest form.

France, having largely rejected Lamarck, made no very vigorous response to Darwin. Even when evolutionary ideas returned to intellectual respectability, they had for a long time a Lamarckian tinge. In 1870, attempts sponsored by the botanist Quatrefages to have Darwin elected to the French Academy of Sciences foundered on the implacably anti-evolutionist opposition of the Academy's Permanent Secretary, Pierre Flourens. Another eight years were to pass before Darwin became a member of the Botany Section. Quatrefages liked and admired Darwin, while consistently opposing his ideas. Just before his first, abortive effort to bring Darwin into the Academy, he had written in a letter to him, "You are incontrovertibly the leading proponent of mutational theories, the only one who has proposed a theory based on scientific considerations alone . . . It is therefore with you above all that I have battled . . . But I hope I have never misconstrued the greatness of your work." A handful of scientists were working to increase Darwin's evidential base, notably the Marquis Gaston de Saporta, demonstrating the links between the evolution of flowers and the markings of insects, and the zoologist Albert Gaudry. Darwin wrote a little bitterly to Quatrefages, early in the 1870s, that "a week hardly passes without my hearing of some naturalist in Germany who supports my views, & often puts an exaggerated value on my works; whilst in France I have not heard of a single zoologist except M. Gaudry (and he only partially) who supports my views".

In this more responsive Germany, the zoologist and palaeontologist H.G. Bronn, a Freiburg professor, supervised a translation of *The Origin* by a linguist named Schweitzerbart, but it was another zoologist, Ernst Häckel, who most enthusiastically took up Darwin's cause. He read *The Origin* when it first appeared, while studying marine organisms on the Sicilian shore, and was swiftly and totally convinced by it. When he published, in 1860, his monumental study of the tiny radiolaria, whose star-shaped silicate skeletons enrich the oozes of the ocean floor and reinforce the layered strengths of flint, he showed he had absorbed the Darwinian precept by assuming in his classifications that all these tiny organisms derived from one original type. By 1863, he was declaring, at a meeting of German scientists, that Darwin was the "Newton of the organic world"; in this opinion, as in his adherence to the theory of natural selection, he stood almost alone among his compatriots. He became so fierce in his advocacy and so vulnerable in his solitary stand that Darwin himself became alarmed: "All that I think", he wrote in 1867, "is that you will excite anger, and that anger so completely blinds every one, that your arguments would have no chance of influencing those who are already opposed to our views. Moreover, I do not at all like that you, towards whom I feel so much friendship, should unnecessarily make enemies, and there is pain and vexation enough in the world without more being caused. But I repeat that I can feel no doubt that your work will greatly advance our subject . . ." Darwin's horror at direct opposition and the energetic confrontations of scientific dispute was plainly aroused on his adherents' behalf as easily as on his own.

Thus the campaigns of this rarefied war, with its intellectual cannonading, its besieged ramparts of prejudice, its clerical furies and academic spites, its underlying theme of liberalism *versus* despotism, of democrats *versus* authoritarians (Czarist Russia, after an attempt in 1866 to assassinate Alexander II, banned *The Origin* as subversive), boomed through the lecture halls of Europe and America, or erupted in great barrages of books and articles. It was a situation which from time to time changed Darwin's sanctuary at Downe into the inspirational centre of a worldwide cause. The bulletins from his supporters read like reports from a warfront. In return, Darwin sent letters congratulating, cajoling, explaining, clarifying, and exhorting his champions, persuading the timid to speak up, pacifying those who opposed him, reassuring those who agreed with him only partially, and restraining those who wanted nothing more than to take on the ecclesiastical cavalry singlehanded. At the same time he kept a careful watch on what his critics said; and, in the successive editions of *The Origin* that appeared during the 1860s and into the next decade, he modified his exposition to accommodate their doubts, reinforce his case, and shore up his own uncertainties.

Popular recollection has simplified these campaigns, with the combatants divided neatly into two armies: the religious on one side; the scientific on the other. In fact, the picture was rather more confused than that and the antagonisms more complicated. Certainly there stood on one side a phalanx of orthodox clerics resolved to defend Genesis to their last breath. But there were others, just as committed to Christianity, who felt that their religion could accommodate an intelligent theism, and that an intelligent theism could accommodate Darwin's ideas. There were scientists who felt the same. Charles Kingsley was an example of the first, Asa Gray of the second. There were scientists, like Agassiz, more obdurate than almost all the clerics, and others, like Sedgwick, who actually were clerics and apparently saw this as their first role. There were scientists who found Darwin's theory plausibly applicable to most of nature, but who refused to accept that it could explain human development. There were others who wanted to believe Darwin, but found one or another aspect of his reasoning suspect. There were Darwin's own adherents who nevertheless disagreed with him upon some point, and so wished to modify his hypothesis. Even Huxley belonged in this category, though Darwin's opponents will never have thought so. Finally, there was a small regiment of devoted Darwinians, who had seen the cosmos through their prophet's eyes and found it both marvellous and convincing. Darwin, tinkering with his text and conscious of his critics, does not seem himself to have belonged in this group.

The grounds for debate were therefore various. Nevertheless, whatever might have been the motives of those raising them, the arguments themselves did finally divide into either the scientific or the religious. Scientists and theologians brought these up indiscriminately, clerics damning Darwin as a poor scientist, scientists accusing him of atheism. The fact that they could do so illustrates the intellectual priorities, and perhaps confusions, of the time, the paramount role played by religion, and the widespread belief in the truth, objective and absolute, of the Scriptures. The Bible was considered by many Christians – as are, for example, the Vedas by orthodox Hindus – a witness to reality as sure as any sensory experience. It was this that led to the circular nature of so many anti-Darwinian arguments, the Bible often becoming the only source of evidence to prove that the Bible was the only proper source of evidence.

The keystone to Darwin's proposition was his belief in the infinity of variation. It was the ability of organisms to produce offspring marginally different from themselves that enabled natural selection to find its leverage, picking out those slightly better adapted to survive. It was this, in turn, of course, that leavened the dour forecasts of Malthus and snatched a reality of development out of that clergyman's prophecies of destruction. The subject of variation, therefore, became one of the most warmly contested centres of the battle.

"The many slight differences which appear in the offspring from the same parents . . . afford materials for natural selection to act on and accumulate", wrote Darwin in *The Origin*. But Agassiz was categorical in opposition: "Whatever views are correct concerning the origin of species, one thing is certain, that as long as they exist, they continue to produce, generation after generation, individuals which differ from each other only in such peculiarities as are related to their individuality." The point was not only that one could see no sign of variations blossoming into species; it was also the fact, known to all breeders, that there seemed to be an actual limit to the amount of variation possible. After reaching this, new generations of no matter what organism became attenuated, infertile, distorted and valueless. As Lyell himself had written, in the influential second volume of his *Principles of Geology*, "The entire variation from the original type, which any given kind of change can produce, may usually be effected in a brief period of time, after which no farther deviation can be obtained . . . the least possible excess beyond the defined limits being fatal to the existence of the individual".

In the third edition of *The Origin*, Darwin, assaulted by such critics both in Britain and America, some of them his own adherents and champions, conceded that his theory "that the process of variation should be thus indefinitely prolonged is an assumption, the truth of which must be judged of by how far the hypothesis accords with and explains the general phenomena of nature". But, riding the blows of his opponents, he counter-punched at once: "On the other hand, the ordinary belief that the amount of possible variation is a strictly limited quantity is likewise a simple assumption".

In fact, the solution to these antagonisms lay hidden, as some of Darwin's friends suspected, in a phenomenon called "saltation" – the larger leap than simple variation which nature sometimes makes between generations. As far as Darwin was concerned, this could result only in "monstrosities", unfortunate specimens of genetic distortion which, deservedly sterile and shortlived, were certain to be rejected by the remorseless workings of natural selection. But even so close a supporter as Huxley found himself unable to agree with this: "We believe", he wrote in the *Westminster Review*, ". . . that Nature does make jumps now and then, and a recognition of the fact is of no small importance in disposing of many minor objections to the doctrine of transmutation".

What bedevilled debate on all such subjects was the patchiness of the scientific knowledge that could be brought to bear on them. Without any real understanding of even the rudiments of genetics, naturalists, whichever view they took in the Darwinian discussion, had hidden from them the secret process which ensured that, on the whole, like produced like, but which also from time to time created the small significant changes upon which natural selection could work. This lack of knowledge led to yet another debate, one not concerned in whether new characteristics appeared by Darwin's "continuous variation" or Huxley's "saltation". It centred rather on what happened to such new characteristics once they had appeared. The prevailing view of inheritance in the middle of the nineteenth century was that it fused the elements from both parents into a new physical and psychological compound and that it did so, on the whole, on a fifty-fifty basis. The features resulting from this were an exact and equal compromise: each offspring, ideally, bore the balanced and balancing trends of both its father and mother.

It is obvious that if one accepted this view of inheritance as a blending, a new variant could survive and flourish only in very exceptional circumstances. Whatever the effects of natural selection – and particularly if, as Darwin claimed, these only made themselves apparent over enormous periods of time – an otherwise favourable variation would soon vanish under the steady flow of normality assured by repeated matings with the unmodified. In ordinary natural conditions, breeding had the effect only of conserving the species, since any abnormal characteristic would in a very few generations be swamped by the one already established in all the other members of the group. The only solution was for Darwin to point out those exceptional circumstances that would enable a new characteristic to survive in a breeding population. The most plausible, and the one that put variation under least pressure, was isolation. The new endowment, if it was truly advantageous, might spread through a small, cut-off population in quite a short time and only a few generations.

There was another approach. Darwin's conviction that variations of evolutionary significance were almost imperceptible allowed him to believe that they were not necessarily rare. A number of more or less similar variations might occur within a group, maximizing the advantage they offered and bypassing the swamping effect. The majority without the new characteristic would be, by definition, less able to deal with the environment than the minority with it and would tend to be eliminated more swiftly; meanwhile there would be a sufficient number of individuals with the characterstic for it to continue in being. Eventually, those sporting the modification would become the majority and novelty would have become normality.

For Darwin's critics, however, the swamping effect seemed an essential element in maintaining species. Without it, how would groups of organisms remain self-consistent at all? The Darwinian counter was to propose levels of the inheriting power, using a concept scientists called prepotency – as close an approximation to the idea of genetic dominance as mid-Victorian biologists could achieve. Thus Huxley, in his *Westminster Review* article, was able to suggest that there was "a prepotent influence about a newly-arisen variety which gives it what one might call an unfair advantage over the normal descendants . . ."

This aspect of the anti-Darwinian view was most forcibly expressed in 1867, in the *North British Review*, by the Professor of Engineering at Glasgow University, Fleeming Jenkins: "Darwin's theory requires that there shall be no limit to the possible difference between descendants and their progenitors . . . But if man's selection cannot double, treble, quadruple, centuple any special divergence from a parent stock, why should we imagine that natural selection should have that power?" Jenkins proposed the idea of "a sphere of variation" which contained the type of the species with all its possible modifications. He did not believe, as Darwin did, that the limits of this sphere could be transcended by the mere operation of time. Even if, through saltation, what might be thought the nucleus of a new species could come into existence, the swamping effects of inheritance by blending would ensure that it could not survive: "the advantage, whatever it may be, is utterly outbalanced by numerical inferiority". Thus Jenkins's attack was two-pronged, pointing out the limits to variation on the one hand, and the vulnerability of saltations on the other. "Fleeming Jenkins has given me much trouble", wrote Darwin to Hooker, "but has been of more real use to me than any other essay or review".

If anything, Jenkins's remarks confirmed Darwin in his convictions. "I always thought individual differences more important", he wrote to Wallace, discussing the article; "but I was blind & thought that single variations might be preserved much oftener than I now see is possible or probable". In other words, he had not been persuaded to reconsider his belief in the paramount importance of small variations, continued over many thousands of years, while his scepticism about the value of saltation had been deepened further by Jenkins's expressed doubts.

Beyond these and other criticisms of the details of Darwin's proposals, however, there ran a deeper debate, concerned in the main with the role of science – how it should be conducted and what its value was, compared with that of religion. The two questions were linked, since the respect a scientist might accord natural phenomena would alter with his view of what they were. On one side of this debate there stood the religious idealists, whose most prominent spokesman within science was Whewell. For them, the world was imbued with forces and imperatives that derived from an active but unanalysable First Cause. Nature could best be regarded as a series of effects, which it was the scientist's duty to examine and describe, but which finally represented nothing more or less than the workings of a transcendental power.

All this seemed obfuscating nonsense to the opposing empiricists. It did not seem to them necessary to postulate an Unknowable to cover the area of the unknown. What happened in nature was no more than what was observed to happen. Such happenings might be codified into laws, upon the basis of which predictions might be made. New observations might falsify those predictions and, out of these disappointed expectations, new laws could be formulated. To assign to these workings some transcendental cause explained nothing, but simply altered the phraseology of ignorance. As Huxley put it in the *Contemporary Review* in 1871, "In ultimate analysis everything is incomprehensible, and the whole object of science is simply to reduce the fundamental incomprehensibilities to the smallest possible number". To rename what was incomprehensible "God" or "the Creator" did not allow one to understand it any better; the fact that the religious hugged precisely that incomprehensibility to them in the name of faith did not endear them to their opponents.

For Christians, there were also some doctrinal points which made the defence of Genesis more than a matter of conventional piety or stubborn conservatism. What meaning could there be in the idea of redemption, crucial though this was to the purpose of Christ, if humanity had never fallen? Yet the concept of the Fall was inextricably a part of the story of Eden. In its turn, Eden was a part of the story of the Creation. Thus the significance of the Crucifixion could not easily be separated from the factual truth of the Mosaic account of the world's, and humanity's, beginning. It is for this reason that many theologians considered it a matter of the highest importance that ideas such as Darwin's should be discredited. The Victoria

Institute, founded in 1865, took it as its function to examine "the most important questions of Philosophy and Science" that bore upon "the great truths revealed in Holy Scripture, with the view of defending these truths against the opposition of Science, falsely so called".

Even twenty years after the publication of *The Origin*, a religious period-ical, *The Record*, Low Church, conservative, could begin a hectoring series entitled "Devices of the Enemy" with a long article on the evils and short-comings of Darwinism. "We learn that man originally came and still comes from a hairy, tailed quadruped, the inhabitant of woods . . . So soon as a living man, capable of reason and of speech, shall introduce us to a she-ape incapable of both, and shall offer us incontrovertible proof that the creature was his mother, we shall grant that a real problem not easy of solution has been offered to us."

Such crude misrepresentations came typically from those who most ve-hemently resisted Darwin's views. At the other extreme were the thinkers who endeavoured to intertwine the principle of natural selection with those of their religion. "I aver", said the Rev. W.H. Spencer from his Mas-sachusetts pulpit in that same year of 1877, "that not only is Darwinism in general harmony with the ethics of Christianity, but that Christianity, as a great historic religion, is a beautiful illustration of the principle of Darwin-ism itself . . . Christianity, as a religion, has had to struggle for its life . . . Why did it conquer? For the simple reason that its dogmas and ethics were a little better adapted to the religious demands of the age."

Darwin, throughout all this, avoided any sort of public commitment, any sort of stand, whether on atheism, anarchy or convention. One has the feeling that he wanted people to accept his theories, yet to do so without becoming upset, without upsetting the tenets by which they had hitherto lived. He wrote letters of encouragement, gratitude and exhortation to those who had taken up the cause of his theory, but found himself unable to venture onto the barricades. The acerbic style of a Huxley disturbed him and the consequences of direct argument and harsh debate made him nervous. He wrote to Hooker, "I am not sure whether it would not be wisest for scientific men quite to ignore the whole subject of religion". There is a feeling of impatience about his attitude, a sort of weariness, as if he wished the subject could have been dropped, leaving him free to continue his work untramelled by irrelevant discussions. He had had a vision of nature as process, a view perhaps founded upon old-fashionedly mechanistic and materialistic beliefs, but one that had struck him not only with its plausa-bility, but also with its grandeur. It was precisely because it showed nature running without the necessity of guidance or intervention that it excited him; it was the fact that it seemed, so to speak, a miracle *within* nature, organized by logic and proceeding by its own energies, that had led to his years of devotion to his theory, and to his stubbornly reiterated defence of its principles. He resented it when great scientists like Herschel wrote that "an intelligence, guided by purpose, must be continually in action to bias the direction of the steps of change", since it was precisely the elimination of that hypothetical intelligence that seemed to him his greatest triumph.

Yet in his *Autobiography* he acknowledged "the extreme difficulty or rather impossibility of conceiving this immense and wonderful universe, including man with his capacity for looking far backwards and far into futurity, as the result of blind chance or necessity. When thus reflecting I feel compelled to look to a First Cause having an intelligent mind in some degree analogous to that of man; and I deserve to be called a Theist." This somewhat grudging affirmation was swiftly modified by the confession "that it has gradually with many fluctuations become weaker". His more orthodox faith he had lost earlier, having apparently relinquished it by 1840, the rate at which disbelief encroached having been "so slow that I felt no distress, and have never since doubted even for a single second that my conclusion was correct". It may be that the expressed scepticism of both his father and grandfather eased his way towards a profitable doubt.

Darwin's scientific rationality and the implications of his own work provided the intellectual context within which he was able comfortably to change his mind: "The old argument of design in nature, as given by Paley, which formerly seemed to me so conclusive, fails, now that the law of natural selection has been discovered." One has the feeling that, as he said, he never felt very strongly "the religious sentiment"; it came to be important to him only because his ideas had stirred up such profound theological and clerical opposition. Had he ever had a profound sense of a world circumscribed by Biblical ordinances and Christian definitions, it would have been impossible for him to see time in vast geological spans or species as mutable. Having been given his answers, he would have felt no need to seek others; had they presented themselves to him, he would have had to shun them. Had he been unable to prevent himself from realizing their truth, the consequence would have been profound spiritual turmoil. Darwin, however, had no capacity for such turmoil, nor for the passionate beliefs which might have caused it. It was the concrete that swept him off his feet with its magnificence, the proofs of science that elicited his dogged devotion. It was the best explanation of the facts that he proposed, and then stubbornly defended, his personal theology overturned only by a new and better explanation. As for religious faith, "I cannot pretend to throw the least light on such abstruse problems. The mystery of the beginning of all things is insoluble by us; and I for one must be content to remain an Agnostic."

It was not long after the publication of *The Origin* that Emma wrote Darwin a letter which was in part, and perhaps obliquely, about religion, but which seems in the main a note of reassurance to him, a reaffirmation of a deeply established love that by then he can hardly have doubted. She writes of her compassion for his sufferings, and it is clear that he has been undergoing one of his bouts of illness – perhaps the one which, by its severity, kept him from Oxford at the time of the British Association meeting. She thanks him for "the cheerful and affectionate looks" his discomforts have not prevented his giving her.

> I am sure you know I love you well enough to believe that I mind your suffering nearly as much as I should my own and I find the only relief to my mind is to take as from God's hand, and to try and believe that all suffering and illness is meant to help us to exalt our minds and to look forward with hope to a future state. When I see your patience, deep compassion for others, self command and above all gratitude for the smallest thing done to help you I cannot help longing that these precious feelings should be offered to Heaven for the sake of your daily happiness. But I find it difficult enough in my own case. I often think of the words "Thou shalt keep him in perfect peace whose mind is stayed on thee." It is feeling and not reasoning that drives one to prayer.
>
> I feel presumptuous in writing this to you. I feel in my inmost heart your admirable qualities and feelings and all I would hope is that you could direct them upwards, as well as to one who values them above everything in the world.

It was the pressure of her emotions that had made her write; the words once on paper brought her relief. Some time in 1861, when she was feeling "cheerful and comfortable again about you", Emma gave the letter to her husband. "God Bless you", he wrote fervently at its foot. Perhaps he remembered the letter when, writing his *Autobiography* nearly twenty years later, he set down Dr. Robert's view: "Before I was engaged to be married, my father advised me to conceal carefully my doubts, for he said that he had known extreme misery thus caused with married persons. Things went on pretty well until the wife or husband became out of health, and then some women suffered miserably by doubting about the salvation of their husbands, thus making them likewise to suffer."

In 1873, Darwin's son George wrote a sceptical essay on religion and gave it to his father for comment. Darwin asked him to "remember that I am not a good critic as I have not read much on such subjects" – then, catching himself claiming by implication to be a good critic on other matters, added above the line "(nor indeed any subject)". Neither age nor paternity, it seems, could erode his deep-seated modesty. After a few general remarks on the piece, he told George:

> . . . for several reasons I wd. urge you not to publish it for some months, *at the*

soonest, & then to consider whether you think it new & important enough to counterbalance the evils; remembering the cart-loads which have been published on the subject. – The evils are giving pain to others, & injuring your own power and usefulness. Last night — and Litchfield* were talking about J. Stuart Mill never expressing his religious convictions, as he was urged never to do by his Father. Both agreed strongly that if he had done so, he wd. never have influenced the present age in the manner in which he has done. His books wd. not have been textbooks at Oxford. To take a weaker instance, Lyell is most firmly convinced that he has shaken the faith in the Deluge &c. far more efficiently by never having said a word against the Bible, than if he had acted otherwise. –

The rest of the letter veered away from religious questions, though indirectly illuminating Darwin's own approach to scholarship. He urged George, as a young author, to publish "only what is very good & new" and described himself as "rather alarmed at your getting into the habit of . . . writing short essays (& therefore temporary) on important subjects . . . I wish that you were tied to some study on which you could not hope to publish anything for some years". He warned George that "an enemy might ask who is this man, & what is his age & what have been his special studies, that he shd. give to the world his opinions on the deepest subjects?" Perhaps these suggestions and enquiries help to explain the long years that lay between Darwin's conceiving his theory of natural selection and the publication of his conclusions.

In a postscript, Darwin returned to the main subject: he had been reading Morley's biography of Voltaire, "& he insists strongly that direct attacks on Christianity (even when written with the wonderful force & vigour of Voltaire) produce little permanent effect, real good seems only to follow from slow & silent side effects. – I have been talking on this head to Litchfield, & he strongly concurs, & insists how easily a man may for ever destroy his own influence." Later in the same month, having presumably heard more from George, Darwin wrote, "It is a fearfully difficult moral problem about the speaking out on religion, & I have never been able to make up my mind."

He expressed the same uncertainties to others. He wrote on the subject to F.E. Abbot, editor of the American rationalist periodical, *The Index* (which stated truculently on its masthead that it "accepts every result of science and sound learning, without seeking to harmonize it with the Bible"). In a passage that Francis Darwin omitted from a note he published in the *Life and Letters of Charles Darwin*, his father had told Abbot, "Many years ago I was strongly advised by a friend never to introduce anything about religion in my works, if I wished to advance science in England . . . Had I foreseen

---

* Henrietta's husband, Richard Litchfield, whom she had married in August, 1871.

how much more liberal the world would become, I might have acted differently." Yet what exactly was his personal feeling when he wrote to Abbot in 1871, "I can never make up my mind how far an inward conviction that there must be some Creator or First Cause is really trustworthy evidence"? And was it his version of a religious conviction when a few months later he predicted, "A firm belief in the laws of nature will some day reign supreme"?

For the committed freethinkers, the attempt by clergymen to incorporate Darwin's doctrines in their own was something to be combatted. It was with this end in view that Edward Aveling, an energetic spokesman for atheism who became Karl Marx's son-in-law, published the account of a visit he had paid Darwin towards the end of his life. In 1881 he brought to Down House Dr. Ludwig Büchner, president of the International Federation of Freethinkers. Büchner had helped to publicize Darwin's ideas in Germany and had no intention, Aveling claimed, of discussing religion. It was Darwin himself who raised the issue:

> When once we were within the walls of his study, and he was sitting in most unconventional fashion in the large, well-worn easy chair, almost the first thing he said was, "Why do you call yourselves Atheists?" . . . Very respectfully the explanation was given, that we were Atheists because there was no evidence of deity, because the invention of a name was not an explanation of phaenomena, because the whole of man's knowledge was of a natural order, and only when ignorance closed in his onward path was the supernatural invoked. It was pointed out . . . that whilst we did not commit the folly of god-denial, we avoided with equal care the folly of god-assertion.

Darwin, claimed Aveling, agreed "with point after point of our argument", commenting at last, "I am with you in thought, but I should prefer the word Agnostic to the word Atheist". His visitors' counter to this was that " 'Agnotic' was but 'Atheist' writ respectable, and 'Atheist' was only 'Agnostic' writ aggressive."

Darwin smiled at this. "Why should you be so aggressive?" he asked. "Is anything to be gained by trying to force these new ideas upon the mass of mankind? It is all very well for educated, cultured, thoughtful people; but are the masses yet ripe for it?" A little later, speaking of Christianity more specifically, Darwin said that he had not given it up until he was forty years of age. "Asked why he had abandoned it, the reply, simple and all-sufficient, was: 'It is not supported by the evidence'." Aveling, of course, had a case to prove, and Darwin was always influenced in what he said, on questions that did not involve his scientific convictions, by the expectations of his hearers; nevertheless, the picture of the reticent agnostic, the secretive rationalist, that emerges from Aveling's account is not unlike the one created by Darwin on other occasions.

Hensleigh Wedgwood's daughter, Julia, wrote a long letter on the subject to Francis Darwin, in October, 1884. Darwin himself had been dead by then for over two years, and she was trying to summerize her impressions of this aspect of his beliefs:

> Every one, I suppose, who feels Religion infinitely the most important subject of human attention, wd be aware of a certain hostility towards it in his attitude, so far as it was revealed in private life. And what is to me very remarkable I should say that it was a growing hostility while all the apparent reasons for it were vanishing quantities . . . He was far more sympathetic with religion when his books were considered wicked by the religious world . . .

She had not forgotten hearing, before *The Origin* came out, some of Darwin's ideas on evolution and natural selection. "And I recall my own expression of extreme repugnance to this idea & the sense of loss in giving up the belief in Creation." Darwin's response was cool: "I cannot conceive any *wish* about the matter one way or another", she remembered his saying, adding, "at least both the meaning & the tone of voice & the look comes back to me now though perhaps the words may not be exactly literal. He felt that he was confronting some influence that *adulterated the evidence of fact*."

She recalled words he had spoken during one of the last conversations she had ever had with him: "The reason that I can never give in to the belief we are all naturally inclined to of a First Cause is that I look upon all human feelings as traceable to some germ in the animals". She herself could not understand why these origins for feelings so widespread should automatically make them suspect, but for Darwin the argument was obviously sufficient. She felt, however, that "he had no hostility towards Religion, as a view of the ultimate origin of things . . . yet when Religion appeared as concerning itself with forces now at work in the world . . . then I think it always seemed to him a belief that brought disorder, & was hostile to all true Science. And so of course he was hostile to it."

One comes to the conclusion that Darwin, by the last two decades of his life, had long discarded the entire ideology of Christianity, that his own theories had many years before filled up the inner space that this might once have taken up, and that the belief he maintained in a First Cause was weak, rudimentary and not of a kind to give him either spiritual or intellectual discomfort. He was clearly very conscious of the politics of scepticism, of the effects on his career of too robust a stand against religion. Yet in his advice to his son George, he equated "attacks on Christianity" with doing "real good", suggestive of an attitude much harder than the one he defined a little later in the *Autobiography*.

Darwin was a reluctant polemicist, even in his own field – even, perhaps, within his own mind. Abstractions disturbed him; he preferred his view of the cosmos to be firmly based on perceptible facts. Love of family, which he constantly experienced, was real to him; he saw it as humanity's prime cause of happiness, even when all else brought suffering. It seemed to him one of the great universals. The Christian God, however, and the creation legends that were part of his story, lay beyond his capacity to believe. There is no evidence that his lack gave him pain, except to the extent that it pained Emma. Instead, it freed him, enabling him to explore his theories to the limits of their capacity, and his own. For the sake of peace, both in his home and in the wide, censorious world, it may be that he minimized the extent of his freedom, and dressed his vestigial religious feelings in the solemnity of an earnest agnosticism. The fact is that, except when he was forced to, he seems to have given religion very little real thought, reserving the passionate drive of his mind for those matters that concerned the palpable world. For Darwin, reality had to come dressed in proofs before he was prepared to take it seriously.

2

In 1881, Emma wrote to her son George about the visit of a distant Darwin cousin. "We quite like the young Capt. tho' a regular Philistine. He liked his visit too I think. He told Leo he wanted to see F, he had been so chaffed about him & called *Origin & Theory*. He expected to find a regular philosopher but found he knew about all sorts of things & was quite good company." The "F" she wrote about stood for "Father", and the letter suggests how widespread Darwin's fame had become, twenty years after *The Origin* was published, yet how little it had changed him. Some version of what he had proposed lay among almost everyone's intellectual equipment, sufficiently familiar to be the raw material for jokes in the officers' mess; yet at the centre of his reputation he could remain "good company" for a young man of limited cultivation.

Darwin kept his fame at a distance. He wanted continuity above all, the regularity of a dependable daily round. Every day he could be relied on to be in bed until 6.30, to be up before 6.45. Every day he bathed his face in cold water, keeping the jug on his window sill to cool on summer nights. Every day, by the time he sat down to breakfast at 7.30, he would have taken two turns around the Sandwalk, and at breakfast every day he drank from the same cup, its blue worn into blotches and its gold tarnished. Every day when he arrived to read the mail in the drawing room at about 9.30, he would have done some two hours work in his study, and every day, as he read his letters, he would murmur an accompanying commentary: "Oh, dear, here's this bothersome fellow again", or, "Here's a note from Hooker".

In this way he maintained the architecture of his private life. There was something obsessive about the way he regulated his daily comings and goings. It was as if he felt some superstition about it, as if an indefinable unpleasantness might overtake him the moment he broke the smooth round of habit. It seems likely that the strict repititions of his timetable, intended to minimize the strain of work or visitors on his physical health, helped also to maintain his psychological equilibrium. In the outside world, his name had become part of the common coinage of conversation. People unknown to him revered or reviled him, explained, extended, adapted or misconstrued his ideas; safe in his enclave of countryside on the edge of London, he created for himself not only the stone walls of his domain, but also these fencelike constraints of activity so rigidly defined and programmed that outsiders had little chance of breaking in.

Every day there was the reading aloud of a novel, usually Emma's task, the book often negligible, its chief requisites, in his son George's words, "a pretty girl and a good ending". Every day before lunch there were two hours or so of work and a walk in the garden, with the meal always at one o'clock. By two-thirty the newspaper was read and Darwin free to begin dictating replies to his many correspondents; half an hour later, he was ready to rest and smoke and be read to. So the day would pass, in work and reading, rest and strolls in the grounds, with backgammon keenly contested after dinner, music often after nine o'clock, bedtime at ten-thirty. One has the feeling that the need to placate authority which Darwin had carried from childhood had found expression in the tidiness of this daily programme. The day's plan became the impersonal power to which he now had to conform; had he broken into its regularity with some spontaneous adventure, he would probably have felt overwhelmingly guilty. "A very strong characteristic", his son William recalled after his death, "was his deep respect for authority of all kinds . . . He could not endure the feeling of breaking any law of the most trivial kind, even the most harmless form of trespassing made him uncomfortable and he avoided it." At Down House, it was Emma who spoke for the necessary coercive power: she would break into his conversations with a brusque, "You've talked enough", and he would go with her instantly, for his assigned period of rest.

It was through letters that the attention and curiosity of the outside world was most frequently expressed. Towards the end of 1874, Darwin wrote to his son Leonard that "my bothering correspondents seem steadily to increase in number, & I think in folly, for I have just answered two precious fools". Sometimes such correspondents even broke into lamentable verse:

> The learned Darwin states that Moses taught confusion
> For Man, he boldly says, descends from Ape or Monkey –
> I, having read his book, am come to this conclusion,
> Darwin (at least himself) descends from Ass or Donkey.

Such was the opinion of one critic, perhaps a little blunted by its anonymity, which arrived in Darwin's mail in 1875. Bad poetry was not the exclusive prerogative of his opponents, however. From the depths of Pennsylvania, a Dr. J.W. Abernethy sent his pastiche of Burns:

> Ha! Darwin, what a root you are;
> Your logic taut doth shoot so far,
> Old Fogy's prigs a brute or waur
>   Maintain ye must be,
> Your book, they can't refute or mar;
>   Belike they'll bust ye.

It is as well that, as Darwin confessed in the *Autobiography* he had long lost his youthful taste for poetry: Dr. Abernethy, as his leaden-footed verses trample down the page, does not improve.

In humourous periodicals like *Figaro*, *Fun* and *Punch*, the cartoons, skits and passing witticisms continued throughout the 1860s and 1870s. In France, *La petite lune* put Darwin on its cover, portrayed as a monkey swinging from the branches of "*l'arbre de la science*". Darwin knew of them all; he or his family collected them, they still lie like fairground tinsel among the sober pamphlets, manuscripts and correspondence of his thousands of surviving papers. He knew very well what his name meant to millions of people throughout Europe and the United States and there must have been moments when that knowledge became oppressive. He responded, as he had ever since the days when he was first married and safely esconced in Gower Street, by turning his back on those distant crowds, limiting his life so that it fitted neatly into that of his house and his village, and placing at its centre the absorbing continuity of his work.

During these years, one of his closest friends was Rev. Brodie Innes, who had been the Vicar of Downe since 1846. They stood together when dissension threatened: "He held the view," Innes wrote later, "that where there was no really important objection, his assistance should be given to the clergyman, who ought to know the circumstances best and was chiefly responsible." And there were village feuds and scandals – fences were threatened, paths closed, trees overhung. There was, too, the passing drama of Mr. Robinson, to whom Darwin wished, in September, 1868, to hand the responsibility, hitherto his own, of keeping the National School* accounts. Within a few months, the odour of scandal was hanging about Mr. Robinson; a slightly breathless postscript in a letter from Darwin to Innes suggests the nature of the man's shortcomings: "Mr. Allen knows nothing from his own observations, but rumours certainly are rife against Mr. R. The name of the girl is Esther West. Mr. Allen's cook saw Mr. R. talking to her in the road near the house. He had heard from Mrs. Allen that the mother of the girl (who has left Mrs. Allen) had written to Mr. R. forbidding him to call at her cottage; also that Mr. R. had been seen to go into some house in the village where some girl supposed to have a bad character lives . . ." The incident offers us a vision of Darwin in a different context, active like any other member of the rural middle class in maintaining the restrictive mesh of moral preconceptions that bound Victorian England.

---

* The National Society for Promoting the Education of the Poor in the Principles of the Established Church organized schools in the Anglican interest throughout the country, sharing the task of education with the British and Foreign School Society until the state took up some of the burden in 1870.

MONKEYANA.

Punch cartoon, 1861, linking the abolitionist Wedgwoods with Darwin's theory.

Because of the effect his scientific work had, there is a temptation to regard Darwin as in some general and fundamental way a rebel. In fact, he was so profoundly a conformist that the puzzle is rather how he could have brought himself to devise theories so dazzlingly revolutionary as those he proposed in *The Origin*. In his politics he was always, certainly, a Liberal, but the party of Mr. Gladstone fell a long way short of being a radical Left. He remained all his life vigorously against slavery, writing frequently to Asa Gray of his approval for the northern cause during the war between the states in North America. With the exception of Gladstone, he despised politicians, talking contemptuously of their "jawing" in Parliament; at the same time, there were reforms he desired: notably a truly national system of education that would give proper value to science; and, to ensure a similar respect in the national life as a whole, a Minister for Science in the Cabinet (a reform that it took nearly a century to achieve). None of these positions, however, involved the searching re-examination of reality that marked his work in natural history.

Part of the reason is that Darwin consistently refused to bother himself with any but scientific issues. Problems in general philosophy, in theology, in political science doubtless had their interest, but it was an interest that Darwin preferred to ignore. He had, he insisted, only so much energy available, and this he wished to direct into those activities that really concerned him. He was simply not prepared to give up the time necessary to consider with the intensity they deserved these other and, to him, peripheral questions.

This response, however, which he often made to correspondents, somewhat begs the question. Other men, as beset as he by weakness and ill health, found time and energy enough to consider the meaning of human life. The truth is that Darwin never was a rebel, even within the sciences that were his central interest. The fact that he came to revolutionary conclusions was the result rather of his profound respect for authority. What made him different from others was the authority to which he chose to defer. As his son William testified, he kept his deepest respect, not for the laws of man or of God, but for those of nature. "No man", wrote William Darwin, "could feel more intensely the vastness and the inviolability of the laws of nature, and especially the helplessness of mankind, except so far as the laws were obeyed".

What was it about these laws that placed them, for him, far above those of the jurists or the theologians? Almost certainly, it was the fact that they could be clarified by experiment, and that, once clear, they proceeded with a logic that could not be denied or overthrown. To that logic, Darwin gave an absolute respect, one that effortlessly overrode every other form of allegiance. Probably it was during the *Beagle* voyage that he had made this almost Faustian surrender, but whenever it was, once he had made it he had set himself on the route to paradox. The more sedulously he complied with the imperatives that the laws of nature set him as a scientist, the more completely would he be forced to deny the orthodoxies preached by every other authority. It was the priority of his devotion that decided his course of action and that made him seem, in the context of those other orthodoxies, the revolutionary that he never actually was. The contrast, therefore, between the turmoil caused by his theories and the quiet life of Down in which he immersed himself, was more apparent than real; the certainty with which he pursued his vision of what was true in nature was of precisely the same order as the conviction, placidly conventional though it was, that he brought to his quotidian village life. And perhaps it was the consequent certainty that all his beliefs had the support of a relevant authority – respectable middle-class opinion in the one case, Nature itself in the other – that allowed him to ride with such apparent ease the storms of ridicule and insult howling about his name for the better part of two decades.

The placid tenor of the life he actually lived will also have helped him to bear that distant turmoil. Its continuity must have reassured him; he detested change and had to be cajoled and bullied, especially by Emma, before he would even go on holiday. From time to time, nevertheless, he could be persuaded to take that ultimate luxury of the Railway Age, the personal saloon carriage, a travelling drawing room which maintained the comfortable separation of the gentry from the grubby commonality. Yet he was never at ease in doing so; Francis Darwin recalled that "he considered it a piece of presumption and extravagance for one in his station in life".

What he liked best was to work, and to work at Downe, with his family within reach and familiar sights and sounds around him. It was there that, towards the end of 1860 and into the early weeks of the new years, he prepared the first real revision he had undertaken of *The Origin*. Intending at first to take up his critics' points one by one, elucidating this, refuting that, demonstrating how one had misunderstood him and another misread the evidence, aiming his own cuts at those who had all these months slashed at him, he finally accepted Lyell's pacifist advice. He altered and revised; he did not counter-attack. It was now that he added the Historical Sketch which appeared in every edition from then on, giving a short account of his forerunners and their attempts to formulate a viable evolutionary theory. Wells was given his due, and the combative Patrick Matthew, whose letter to the *Gardener's Chronicle* had already drawn Darwin's apology; Geoffroy Saint-Hilaire, who had recognized as early as 1850 a relationship between variability and a changing environment; and other naturalists and geologists of varying degrees of fame, including at the last his faithful supporters,

Huxley and Hooker. In April, 1861, the two thousand copies of the third edition were issued to the world.

On 16 May, Henslow died. During all the years since Darwin's student days, Henslow had been constant in his scientific firmament. The two men had corresponded throughout that time, usually brisk and practical in the things they wrote. Darwin, as he did of everyone, had asked the questions that for the moment had possessed him and Henslow had tried to answer them. Beneath and around this utilitarian directness their old affection had continued quietly to flourish. "I fully believe a better man never walked this earth", Darwin wrote now to Hooker. He had never forgotten, not only what Henslow had done to found and further his career, but the warmth and gentleness which had made his apprentice days in Henslow's circle at Cambridge so delightful. Yet it is also true that he had grown past and away from Henslow; he had new and younger colleagues now, who agreed with his theories as Henslow could not, and other informants and advisors, like Asa Gray, more in tune with the science he himself practised. He sorrowed for Henslow, he remembered him with gratitude and affection, but the progress of his life did not falter. "He wrote me by dictation a most kind note from his death-bed", he told Fox, reporting the event, but then moved on at once to wonder whether his cousin intended visiting the British Association meeting in Manchester later in the year.

In the same May that Henslow died, Darwin sent to John Murray a paper he had originally written for publication in the Linnean Society *Journal*. Looking at it again, he wondered if it might not provide the basis for a book. Entitled *On the Various Contrivances by which British and Foreign Orchids are Fertilised by Insects*, it dealt with the special adaptations by which orchids ensure that they are cross-pollinated. For example, the pollen sacs in such flowers are attached to curious organs which come away with the proboscis of a nectar-seeking insect as it withdraws. Some thirty seconds later, Darwin discovered, these detached organs bend forward so that, when the insect visits another flower, the pollen can be rubbed off. The pollen itself, too, is not like the pale dust of the wind-fertilized, but is heavy with a sticky secretion that ensures its remaining in place until the insect rubs it off against the stigma of a receptor flower.

How imbued Darwin was with the prevailing morality can be seen from his comment in the covering letter he sent Murray: "The subject of propagation is interesting to most people, and is treated in my paper so that any woman could read it". His usual detestation of putting himself forward, his total inability to do so, was soon apparent. "It could be a very little book", he wrote, "and I believe you think very little books objectionable. I have myself *great* doubts on the subject. I am very apt to think that my geese are swans . . ." No one ever had to look far to find arguments for denying or refuting anything that Darwin proposed.

However, Murray felt that, with Darwin's reputation so widely established, it was worth publishing his new book, despite its specialist nature. It was Darwin himself who had the doubts. In September he wrote to Hooker, wondering "whether I am not going to do, in publishing my paper, a most ridiculous thing"; in October, it was Lyell's turn for these diffident confidences: "The subject is, I fear, too complex for the Public & I fear I have made a great mistake in not keeping to my first intention of sending it to the Linnean Socy's [*Journal*] but it is now too late, & I must make the best of a bad job." But five weeks after it was published, he was able to write, "Well, my Orchid-book is a success . . ."

Sickness struck the Darwins, while elsewhere death drew away Charlotte Langton, Emma's sister, the "incomparable Charlotte" over whom Erasmus and Charles had once sighed in unison. Leonard lay critically ill with scarlet fever; there were signs of typhoid, doctors grew uncertain in prognosis. With his recovery, there came again one of those great family migrations: William's house in Southampton became a staging post on the way to Bournemouth. (Well set up now, that eldest son, a partner in a bank; Darwin had subsidized him, confiding to Fox, "I had so good an offer it seemed a pity to reject it".) In Bournemouth, Emma, perhaps exhausted by sickbed demands, fell ill herself with scarlet fever. Darwin took a second cottage to make sure that the contagion did not spread.

Every year, as the summer advanced, Darwin wondered if he might not make the journey to the British Association's annual gathering. He longed to go, yet dreaded it. In 1862, it was to be held in Cambridge and that held a double attraction for him. But by mid-September he was writing to Fox, still from Bournemouth, "I have begun to turn tail & have resolved to go home". It was to be the same that year as it had on others. He set down one of the most common formulae of his nostalgia. "I should like to see the old place once again, where I have spent so many happy hours; but I am not sure whether it will not be more melancholy then pleasant, for I know I shall feel knocked up & unable to ramble about & see the old haunts. What pleasant hours we have spent together at our alternate breakfasts & teas. There were no fears & anxious looking forward in those days. And poor dear Henslow is gone . . ." Darwin's nostalgia was always swift, though it is hard to know how deep it was. In his daily life he was either occupied or ill; he had little time to spare for looking back. Yet it is clear that his years at university lay glowing in his memory, a period recalled as one of the happiness and hope. "About two years ago," he told Fox, "I stumbled at Downe on a *Panagaeus crux major*: how it brought back to my mind Cambridge days! You did me a great service in making me an entomologist: I really hardly know anything in this life that I have more enjoyed than our beetle-hunting expeditions . . ."

The following summer, ill once more, Darwin withdrew to Malvern; it was his first visit there since the death of his daughter Anne, and at first the journey had to be postponed, so bad did his eczema become as the day of departure drew nearer. He put himself, not under Dr. Gully, but a medical man named Ayrehurst, and installed himself in the Villa Nuova. Early in September, Emma went to visit their daughter's grave, and to her horror found the gravestone gone. Darwin wrote at once to Fox, who had a few years earlier seen the grave: what year had he gone to Malvern? What kind of stone had it been? Where exactly had it stood? The cemetery had been altered recently – could the stone have been moved? Fox replied, with his usual precision: "I am glad", Emma wrote to him at the end of the month, "that by the help of your directions, & the lady at whose house our poor Annie lodged, we have found the tombstone". Despite these tragic absurdities, Darwin, having suffered appallingly all that winter, returned to Malvern early the following Spring. He wanted desperately to be well: as when he had first begun to write down in detail his ideas on evolution, the work that he was now engaged on had begun to expand, proliferate, to grow almost unmanageably complex.

This proliferation was, in part, the result of Darwin's desire to be absolutely clear. Faced with a total lack of understanding of his theories on genetics, he complained to Hooker that "I took such pains, I must think that I expressed myself clearly". At about this time he was giving help and advice to John Scott, then working in the Royal Botanical Gardens at Edinburgh, later – largely through Darwin's and Hooker's influence – appointed Curator of the Botanical Gardens in Calcutta*. Scott, largely self-educated, had been writing papers on botanical subjects that interested Darwin as a scientist, but slightly distressed him as a reader. He became Scott's self-appointed, though respected, tutor and set down for his protégé his thoughts on writing.

> I really think you cannot go on better for educational purposes than you are now doing; observing, thinking & some reading beat, in my opinion, all systematic education. Do not despair about your style: your letters are excellently written; your scientific style is a little too ambitious. I never study style; all that I do is to try and get the subject clear as I can in my own head, & express it in the *commonest* language which occurs to me. But I generally have to think a good deal before the simplest arrangement & words occur to me . . .

---

* Darwin gave him the money for his fare to India; when in 1871 Scott offered to pay him back, Darwin assured him that "there is nothing discreditible to you . . . in receiving a gift from a rich man, as I am . . . Pray do not rob me of my small share in the credit of aiding to put the right man in the right place."

He added a sentence or two that perhaps throws a little light on his long delay before publishing his ideas on species: "I would suggest to you the advantage at present of your being very sparing in introducing theory in your papers (I formerly erred *much* in geology in that way): *let theory guide your observations*, but till your reputation is well established be sparing in publishing theory. It makes persons doubt your observations." This little passage answers in part the questions that are asked about Darwin's approach to his work: "let theory guide your observations". It is a precept some way from the ideals of a Baconian science, or from the classificatory devotion of his teachers' generation.

In other letters to Scott, Darwin returned to the analysis of style, happily taking his own practice as a model. "I find it a good rule to *imagine* that I want to explain the case in as few & simple words as possible to one who knows nothing of the subject", he wrote on one occasion. On another he declared, "It is a golden rule always to use, *if possible*, a short old Saxon word. Such a sentence as 'So purely dependent is the incipient plant on the specific morphological tendency' – does not sound to my ears like good mother English – it wants translating . . . I go on plan of thinking every *single* word which can be omitted without actual loss of sense is a *decided* gain. Now perhaps you will think me a meddling intruder: anyhow it is the advice of an old hackneyed writer who sincerely wishes you well."

Such were the rules that guided Darwin as he struggled with his new work. When *The Origin* had first been published, he had taken it as no more than a signal to return to the larger book he had for all these years been contemplating. He began to write again the early chapters, only to discover that the problems of variation were so central that they demanded extended treatment. As he attempted to codify his thought on the matter, he began to be distracted by a new fascination. A few years earlier it had been orchids; now it was insectivorous plants. Perhaps the vision that he had of the unity of nature led him to view plant life as a whole in a manner peculiar to himself. Emma wrote to Lady Lyell, in the summer of 1860, when his new interest was in its earliest stages, "At present he is treating Drosera just like a living creature and I suppose he hopes to end by proving it to be an animal". *Drosera rotundifolia* is the sundew, the round leaves of which are traps to which insects stick; the leaf, slowly curling over, then absorbs and digests its prey. It is clear that Darwin saw in this carnivorous behaviour a mechanism linking, in some way perhaps more metaphorical than actual, the vegetable and animal worlds.

Thus work on *Variation of Plants and Animals under Domestication* progressed slowly. The reason was not only to be found in his other interests, in his growing reputation and the demands it made, nor in the constant illnesses that left him so depressingly enfeebled; it lay also in the fact that it was in this volume that he decided to present a genetic theory explaining the developmental processes he had described in *The Origin*. The lack of such a theory had left the most important of the gaps still to be found in his hypothesis.

He called his theory "Pangenesis", a name he was not really happy about: he asked his son George whether he knew "any good Classic who cd suggest any Greek word expressing cell, & which cd be united with genesis? . . ." The word, he wrote, "implies that the whole organization, in the sense of every separate atom or unit, reproduces itself". He envisaged tiny particles, which he named gemmules, being gathered into sperm, ovum or pollen-grain by the interior circulation of the organism – in animals, by the blood-stream. In the offspring, these would disperse again, travelling to the appropriate area of the embryo. There, they would determine how it developed and what it eventually looked like. Thus a continuity of appearance and function was ensured as between one generation and the next.

It was a theory that solved a number of puzzling problems. Variation, of which he had been challenged again and again to described the cause, could finally be explained: a few gemmules more or less from one or the other parent would be enough to cause alterations in the particular limb, organ or characteristic for which they were responsible. Reversion to an earlier type could be the result of retained gemmules from several generations back having an effect. Deformations were caused by gemmules not reaching the area of their intended operations. The inheritance of acquired characteristics, belief in which Darwin had never relinquished, and which he held to with increasing firmness as his convictions over the evolutionary effects of small variations were criticized more and more fiercely, could also be explained by pangenesis. Darwin visualized the gemmules as being produced throughout the lifetime of an organism; an organ that had become in some way modified would reflect that modification in the gemmules it produced. These would sometimes pass this modification on to the next generation, thus establishing a situation in which natural selection could do its work.

Genetics in Darwin's day was a mixture of superstition, inadequate observation and frank bewilderment. Biochemistry, of course, had no existence. Knowledge of cell structure was rudimentary. Darwin was, almost of necessity, brought to rely upon some mechanistic explanation that looked back to the ideas of the eighteenth century rather than forward to those of our own. Given all these constraints, his was a brave and comprehensive attempt to understand and explain the phenomena of inheritance. It included the idea of a precise and particular coding, which we now know to be the function, chemically exercised, of the nucleic acids; and the resultant transmission of inviolable characteristics, which we have now determined to be the function of the chromosomes and their uncounted numbers of genes. It would be misleading, however, to give the impression that Darwin had come close to solving the genetic mystery. He had not. He thought the gemmules carried quite large fragments of information, concerning whole organs and limbs. He believed that if an organ or limb were altered in the course of an organism's life, the gemmules sometimes incorporated information about that alteration and so passed it on to the next generation. He believed the gemmules from each parent mingled with those from the other, thus perpetuating the theory of a blending inheritance. On the whole, Darwin was cripplingly far from the truth on this crucial matter.

It is one of the better known ironies of scientific history that almost at the same time that Darwin was working out the final details of pangenesis – though he had in his usual fashion been pondering the theory for some twenty years – a stout, bespectacled monk of benign appearance was conducting experiments into the mathematics of inheritance in a monastery garden in Moravia. Scrutinizing his results, this monk, whose name was Gregor Mendel, realized what only the rigidities of received opinion had prevented others from seeing – that whatever the units were that passed characteristics from one generation to the next, they did not affect each other. There could be, in other words, no such thing as the famous "swamping effect" that had been so useful to Darwin's critics. Characteristics, once established, could survive and would appear, often in predictable percentages, in later generations. Some were dominant and others, therefore, recessive, but all continued to exist.

Even had Darwin known of Mendel's work (and it has seemed a mystery to many that Mendel never wrote the letter which would have given him that information), and grafted its results to his own genetic hypothesis, it would not have saved his theories. The fact is that he had done something which, when he came across it in the work of others, he despised: he had invented, without having the slightest real evidence to support his idea, a process which had in the end no other function than to answer the questions and solve the problems with which he was faced. Huxley tried to persuade Darwin not to publish his chapter on pangenesis, but the same stubborness which had rightly made him cling to his evolutionary theory, and wrongly to his ideas about Glen Roy, now led him to bring out and hotly defend his genetic hypothesis. Mendel, on the other hand, who had worked backwards from the evidence of his generations of carefully tended peas to the notion of particulate inheritance, found that he had not the slightest need to defend his conclusions. Despite his meticulous statistical work (recently under somewhat severe and disapproving scrutiny), which had precisely that rigour missing in this instance from Darwin's approach, nobody took any notice of his results at all.

Darwin broke off his work on variation and pangenesis in the Spring of 1864, to pursue once more the chimera of the vegetable as animal. He had become fascinated by the apparent volition of climbing plants, just as he had earlier by the voracity of the sundew. He began to write a paper on the subject for the Linnean Society *Journal*, working on it intermittently for the rest of that year. Meanwhile, around his head, there buzzed and spluttered a new controversy, a more personal version of the one that he had unleashed with the publication of *The Origin*. It had been proposed that he should be given the Copley Medal of the Royal Society, awarded to "the living author of such philosophical research, either published or communicated to the society, as may appear to the council to be deserving of that honour". The question was, did Darwin's work so appear to the council, and if it did, which aspect of his work was it to which they were giving their approval?

A considerable faction with strong doubts about Darwin had successfully prevented his winning the award the previous year. When, in 1864, they looked likely to lose the day, a group, powerfully led by the president of the society, attempted at least to have *The Origin* excluded from whatever honour was finally done its author. Huxley was furious, and wrote to Darwin of "the more ferocious sort" who had "begun to whet their beaks and sharpen their claws in preparation for . . . any failure of justice this time". But the medal was after all graciously bestowed, and Darwin was able in his milder way to write to Fox, "The Copley being open to all the sciences & all the world is reckoned a great honour, but . . . such things make little difference to me. It shows, however, that Natural Selection is making some progress in this country & that pleases me." This was precisely the impression, of course, that the president of the Royal Society was afraid would be given.

These were strange years for a man living an apparently placid life deep in the serenity of the Home Counties. They were years of honour and insult, achievement and controversy, the loss of old associations, the establishment of a new generation. As Darwin prepared himself to work on a new edition, the fourth, of *The Origin*, news came from Shrewsbury that his sister Catherine had died. Three years earlier, aged fifty-three, she had taken Charlotte Wedgwood's place as Charles Langton's wife. Now Susan had fallen ill; Catherine had returned to The Mount to nurse her, and had unexpectedly perished herself. It was Catherine who, younger than Darwin, had been his confidante and playmate, his schoolroom companion, his natural ally in a world of older people. "Sad, sad Shrewsbury! which used to look so bright and sunny . . ." Thus Fanny Allen to Elizabeth Wedgwood – Emma's aunt to Emma's sister.

Three months later, Darwin found himself well enough to attend the Royal Society's annual Soirée, "where assemble all the scientific men in London", as Emma reported to her aunt. It was so long since his colleagues had seen him that Darwin, disguised by a flourishing beard, had to introduce himself to many of them. The president – was it with some secret reluctance? – presented him to the guest of honour, the Prince of Wales, "a nice good-natured youth, and very gentlemanlike", as Emma's verdict ran. The Prince, perhaps as confounded by genius as genius might be by royalty, murmured something incomprehensible. Bearded Darwin, unable to reply, bowed as deeply as his physical resources permitted and withdrew. Bence Jones, his doctor, a fellow-guest that evening, was jubilant, seeing in Darwin's appearance the triumphant vindication of his treatment.

Achievement, recognition, loss: six months more, and Susan too was dead; once the most beautiful of the sisters, vivacious at parties and balls; Sarah Owen's friend, often censorious at home; the "Granny" whose sharp eye had raked through Darwin's youthful orthography and picked out its frequent weeds; the one Darwin daughter to have remained lifelong at The Mount, guardian of the family's tradition, bringing there her elder sister Marianne's four children when their mother died – Susan vanished and with her the Darwins passed from Shrewsbury. In November, all the contents of The Mount were sold, the familiar books, the overstuffed furniture, the glassware and cutlery dispersed; a little later, the house itself had passed to other hands and Darwin's last direct link with his own youth had fallen from the lengthening chain of his life.

In his middle fifties, however, Darwin was still living most actively in the present. By the end of the year, the bulk of his book was at last ready. The size of it dismayed both publisher and author – it was more than double the length of *The Origin* – but Darwin needed it to be an exhaustive study of how variation had been manipulated by mankind for its own benefit. He had been working on it, intermittently, for six years, drawn to and fro by the different lines of investigation that became apparent as he worked. He had done his own experiments, had followed with avidity those of others, had collected the lore and practice of the breeders, had drawn on the literature of ancient civilizations and the findings of modern archeology. Old friends reappeared between its covers – a study of the sundew fills out Chapter 11 – and the investigation into the development of and the variety within a species was detailed and as complete as his immense industry could make it.

He marked the enormous differences to be found in the types of the domestic dog, and argued from this not only the extreme adaptability of the species *Canidae*, but also the likelihood that it had had a variety of ancestors in the wolves and jackals of the Paleolithic world. He noted how horses, too, had been bred for many uses and thus had been made to produce a number of varieties. Cats, on the other hand, though differing somewhat from place to place, were of homogeneous type in any given place: intractable, secretive, often absent and thus mating as they pleased, they had resisted the human race's general tendency to breed particular traits into its domestic companions. Darwin understood, too, how social factors might have a bearing on the matter – European owners of donkeys had almost always been poor, since the rich possessed horses; each such owner, therefore, would rarely have had more than one or two animals; without a large herd from which to select, directed breeding became impossible; thus among domestic donkeys there was found very little variation. He spread his net to cover every form of living organism that had historically been pressed into human use – he dealt even with goldfish, even with trees. And in five chapters on the laws governing variation, he returned once more to his fundamental conviction, the belief upon which *The Origin* had rested, that the forms of life were infinitely malleable, subject not only to human intervention but to that, both more powerful and more haphazard, of the environment, and that the changes which resulted had been enough, given the length of the earth's existence, to produce the near-infinity of species which now flew or ran, slithered or burrowed upon it.

The first edition sold out and a second was put in hand. "This has done me a world of good", wrote Darwin to Hooker, "for I had got into a dogged hatred of my book". A review in the *Pall Mall Gazette* had delighted him, "more perhaps than is reasonable", and he wished to discover who had written it. It was in fact G.H. Lewes, George Eliot's companion, an occasional correspondent of Darwin's and a keen amateur scientist. A snarling and contemptuous review in the *Athenaeum* pleased Darwin less; on the development of species, the article stated loftily, "Mr. Darwin has nothing, and is never likely to have anything, to say", although his new book could be considered "a valuable store-house of facts for curious students and practical breeders". The *Gardener's Chronicle*, however, was approving and, as Darwin said, with that and the *Pall Mall* on his side, "I do not care a damn".

Pangenesis, on the other hand, had been met by incomprehension, doubt and downright antipathy: it was, as Darwin said, "stillborn". He clung to his theory, nevertheless, and confided to Hooker, "You will think me very self-sufficient, when I declare that I feel *sure* if Pangenesis is now stillborn it will, thank God, at some future time reappear, begotten by some other father, and christened by some other name". In this he was over-optimistic.

It had been his intention, after expanding the opening chapter of *The*

Plate 25 Down House, with its wide lawns and guardian trees, was Darwin's home and refuge for nearly forty years, enabling him to survive the fiercest controversy of the century from behind its bastions.

Plate 26

This famous photograph of Darwin is by Julia Margaret Cameron and was taken when he was staying in her house during the summer of 1869.

Plate 27 The work table at Down House, where Darwin would analyse and ponder over his specimens. The microscope is the one presented to him during his time as a student at Cambridge.

Plate 28

This statue of Darwin, sculpted after his death and unveiled in 1888, still stands as tribute to him in the natural History Museum.

Origin into one volume on domestic variation, to deal in a second with the subject of the next chapter, the development of varieties in nature. Instead, thoroughly tired of such complexities, he decided to come to grips at last with a much more crucial subject: the origins of mankind. He had planned to include a section on this most domesticated of species in his first volume, but in the end had not done so. In *The Origin*, he had dismissed the matter in a single sentence – "Much light will be thrown on the origin of man and his history". This evasion of his scientific and philosophic responsibilities had not, as he had perhaps hoped, helped him to escape the jeers of his critics. Readers and reviewers had understood very clearly the latent message of his book. Now, ten years later, he decided to make his viewpoint more directly apparent and to throw that light on humanity and its history which he had predicted.

In 1863, Lyell had published his *Antiquity of Man*. Darwin, at first nervous that the wily geologist might steal his thunder – priority remained an issue – became indignant instead at Lyell's cautious refusal to provoke a storm of any kind. He was, he informed Hooker, "deeply disappointed . . . to find his timidity prevents him giving any judgement". What most annoyed him was Lyell's refusal to be as firmly committed in public to an evolutionary conclusion as he seemed to be in private – though "the best of the joke is that he thinks he has acted with the courage of a martyr of old." Now, six years later, Darwin was going to set out on the campaign from which Lyell had hung back. It must be admitted, however, that the potential dangers of such a foray had greatly diminished over the intervening years, while he himself had become a formidably authoritative figure in the public eye. However, Darwin was no crusading polemicist and could hardly have braved the subject earlier; on the other hand, almost face to face with his sixtieth birthday, he may have felt that he could hardly keep away from it much longer.

He was pushed further in this direction by his growing interest in what he called sexual selection – the effect on a species, over many generations, of the particular choices made by individuals in the selection of their breeding partners. He had begun to realize that there might be more than the simple ability to survive the Malthusian shortages of nature that determined which organisms should flourish and produce offspring like themselves; it was the aesthetic preferences of their prospective mates that decided which of these survivors actually moved on to parenthood. Humanity, with its freedom of choice, seemed to Darwin the richest field for his new principle. When, in 1864, Wallace published a paper in the *Anthropological Review* entitled "Human Races and Natural Selection", Darwin wrote to him, praising his ideas, but offering his own opinion "that a sort of sexual selection has been the most powerful means for changing the races of man . . . Among savages the most powerful men will have the pick of the women, & they will generally leave the most descendants".

This was actually the first exchange in a long disagreement between the two men. Wallace was beginning to consider human beings as different in kind from the rest of the living world; the nobility and apparently infinite power of their minds seemed to him evidence of some prior divine intervention, an indication of the one special creation in the history of the earth. "I rather differ on the rank . . . which you assign to man", responded the sceptical Darwin; "I do not think any character simply in excess ought ever to be used for the higher diversions. Ants would not be separated from other hymenopterous insects, however high the instincts of one, however low the instincts of the other". For his part, Wallace came to feel, as he considered the evidence, that Darwin had hugely exaggerated the effects of sexual selection.

It seems strange that Darwin, with such disagreements looming, should have written, "I have collected a few notes on man, but I do not suppose I shall ever use them", and should then have offered them to Wallace. Certainly he was still at that time deep in *Variation under Domestication*, yet he must have known that it was from him that the world wanted some definitive word on the history of mankind. Huxley had already written on the subject, and Lyell; but the gap remained. Was he trying to make amends for having ten years before headed Wallace off from immortality? Whatever the reason, Wallace declined; significantly, he began the paragraph in which he did so by reiterating firmly that natural selection had been, always and only, Darwin's idea. "You had worked it out in details I had never thought of, years before I had a ray of light on the subject, and my paper would never have convinced anybody or been noticed as more than an ingenious speculation, whereas your book has revolutionised the study of Natural History, and carried away captive the best men of the age." Only after having cleared the air in this way did he return to the subject of human descent and Darwin's suggestion: "I may possibly some day go a little more into this subject, and if I do will accept the kind offer of your notes." For Wallace, obviously, Darwin's had been an attempt at reparation.

Three years later, matters were rather different. "I have lately hit upon a generalisation connected with sexual characters which pleases me very much", wrote Wallace to Darwin, "and I make no doubt will interest you". It was in fact his own thesis that he was proposing, suggesting "that the primary action of sexual selection [in birds] is to produce colour pretty well equally in *both sexes*, but that it is checked in the female by the immense importance of *protection* . . ." Darwin, this time far from offering notes, was swift in defence, pointing out almost brusquely that:

. . . your view is not new to me. If you will look at p.240 of the fourth edition of the *Origin* you will find it very briefly given . . . I have long entertained this view, though I have never had space to develop it . . . In your paper perhaps you will just allude to my scanty remark in the fourth edition, because in my Essay on Man I intend to discuss the whole subject of sexual selection, explaining as I believe it does much with respect to man. I have collected all my old notes, and partly written my discussion, and it would be flat work for me to give the leading idea as exclusively from you. But, as I am sure from your greater knowledge of Ornithology and Entomology that you will write a much better discussion than I could, your paper will be of great use to me. Nevertheless I must discuss the subject fully in my Essay on Man . . . It is curious how we hit on the same idea.

One cannot help thinking that it was the memory of traumas suffered ten years earlier that had triggered Darwin's anxieties. For the moment it must have seemed to him that every time he had a new theory to propound, there was Wallace ahead of him, already propounding it. In fact, Wallace was concerned with the way natural selection had created well protected but drab females out of distant, dangerously resplendent earlier generations. He had little confidence in the workings of sexual selection; he preferred the impersonal processes of nature to the suggestion that an element of individual choice had helped to create the species in their present forms. The emotionalism of his attitude to human development contrasted strangely with the harsh objectivity with which he regarded the rest of the natural world.

Perhaps taken aback by Darwin's vehemence, Wallace in his turn now offered up his notes for the other's use. There is not in Wallace's behaviour that strain of hypocrisy, the suspicion that he is trying to make a good impression, to placate a critic or divert the dangerous judgements of other people, that one senses from time to time in Darwin's. He thought and did those things that seemed to him right and gentlemanly, largely for their own sake, partly because he had begun as an outsider and owed himself the duty of honourable behaviour. Thus he not only offered Darwin the notes – the kind of offer that in the nature of things must always invite refusal – he actually sent them.

Darwin had been outmatched in generosity, a drubbing that must have stung him. He sent the papers back, writing in his covering letter that "it would vex me to take so much from you, as it is certain that you could work up the subject very much better than I could . . . I confess on receiving your note that I felt rather flat at my recent work being almost thrown away, but I did not intend to show this feeling . . . Your paper on the sexual colouring of birds will, I have no doubt, be very striking. Forgive me, if you can, for a touch of illiberality about your paper."

Darwin worked on sexual selection and the foundations of what he was calling, rather grandly, his "Essay on Man" during the early summer of 1868; by the end of July, he and his family had moved to Freshwater, on the Isle of Wight. The house they took belonged to Mrs. Julia Cameron, a lady deemed by Henrietta "sociable and most amusing". It helped to make her amusing that she had made herself expert in the new art of photography; no one realized then, not even she herself, that her portraits were to make her posthumously famous and would, a century later, help to form the nucleus of the photographic archives in the National Portrait Gallery. Her place in society assured her a steady supply of the famous and the mighty; while the Darwins were her guests, Tennyson called several times, as did his fellow poet, Longfellow. Mrs. Cameron's photographs of Tennyson are among the best known ever taken of him, and the picture she took of Darwin during that summer, which Henrietta rightly called "excellent", places him before us in an almost unexpected humanity.

This was the summer, too, when it became clear that the young Darwins were growing up. Earlier in the year, the family had learned that George had stood second among those receiving a first class honours degree in mathematics from Cambridge University – or, in the esoteric language of that place, had taken his tripos and come out second wrangler. Darwin wrote to him, "I always said from your early days that such energy, perseverance and talent as yours would be sure to succeed . . . Again and again I congratulate you. But you have made my hand tremble so I can hardly write." Now Leonard had come second among that year's entrants to the Royal Military Academy, Woolwich, the Sandhurst of the engineers, and Darwin warned his youngest son, Horace, "I shall burst with pleasure at Leonard's success". Only Horace himself, a year younger than Leonard, was still at school, and he too would soon be moving to Cambridge. The children decided, therefore, to stop calling their parents Papa and Mama: Darwin would be "Father" from now on. "I would as soon be called Dog", he growled morosely when he learned of this, but in her letters to the young Darwins Emma had soon contracted him to "F".

The following summer his melancholy was tightened a notch by what he must have known would be the last visit he was to pay to Shrewsbury and The Mount. It had a new owner, a man both hospitable and over-conscious of the eminence of his guest; he fluttered through the rooms, escorting, guidelike, this nostalgic party. He walked with them even through the garden. Darwin, though stubbornly polite, was saddened: "If I could have been left alone in that greenhouse for five minutes," he murmured, "I know I should have been able to see my father in his wheel-chair as vividly as if he had been there before me".

Then they all moved on to their summer holidays, at the Barmouth where Darwin, forty years before, had worked in desultory fashion at mathematics and marched across the hills on day-long entomological adventures. He felt his present, contrasting weakness, his mood one of a gentle bitterness; in April, his horse, Tommy, had stumbled and fallen, throwing him, then rolling on him. He had given up riding; now he could see, in these surroundings both so old and so new, how restricted his physical universe had become.

By contrast, that which his mind commanded stretched as widely as ever. It had its walls, its fenced-off areas, estates where other landlords ruled: when the imperious Frances Power Cobbe, a lady of Amazonian proportions notable for her part in the early struggles for women's rights, spoke to him of Kant and Mill, his response was polite patience rather than interest. He swiftly returned the copy of Kant's *Critique of Pure Reason* that Julia Wedgwood had lent him, reporting that it had "said nothing to him". But in his own domains, his industry, interest and command of detail remained as keen as ever. Through all the first half of 1870 he worked on *Descent of Man* and, by August, Murray had the manuscript, freshened and sharpened by the contributions of Henrietta, who worked on the early chapters while wintering in Cannes. Darwin told her that "your corrections and suggestions are *excellent* . . . You have done me real service; but, by Jove, how hard you must have worked . . ."

The manuscript was again longer than *The Origin*; John Murray found in it only a single sentence that he wished to change, one carrying the unthinkable implication that females might feel sexual desire. Later, he sent proofs to Whitwell Elwin, who had earlier distinguished himself by wishing to trim *The Origin* into a description of pigeon-breeding. Ten years had increased Elwin's scope no more than they had diminished Darwin's: he found the book almost incomprehensible, not worth taking seriously, "little better than drivel". Darwinism, in any case, a fad of the times, would be demolished as soon as there arrived on the scene "a really eminent naturalist". Fortunately, Murray was a publisher – he wanted to be rich, not right. By now it was clear that there existed a public fascinated by Darwin's ideas and prepared to buy his books; this made their intrinsic value irrelevant. In February, 1871, *Descent of Man* appeared.

The book made the anatomical case for mankind's animal origins – a concept which it admitted had originated with Lamarck – and showed, in detail after detail, how humans and the higher apes were more nearly the same than those apes and the lower primates. They carried the same parasites; they had the same reactions to drugs; they responded in the same way to chemicals. Only "our natural prejudice", Darwin wrote, "and that arrogance which made our forefathers declare that they were descended from demi-gods" had hidden from us the obvious fact that "man and all other vertebrate animals have been constructed on the same general model". Opinions, however, were changing, and "the time will before long come when it will be thought wonderful, that naturalists, who were well acquainted with the comparative structure and development of man and other mammals, should have believed that each was the work of a separate act of creation."

The constant argument of his opponents, however, was that human beings were much more than the sum of their physical parts. They had minds, were imbued with a moral sense, had an instinct for worship, an awareness and expectation of the numinous. These were matters Darwin now faced, as he had known he would one day have to when, thirty-five years earlier, he had first dashed down his ideas in those seminal *Notebooks*. His observation of animal behaviour had shown him, what everybody else had seen but not always noted, that all the higher creatures shared a range of emotional responses: such feelings as pleasure, rage, fear, pain and jealousy were not confined to human beings. It was Darwin's overriding vision of an inter-connected natural order that made him regard this not merely as a psychological curiosity or the result of the Creator's economy of effort, but as evidence of true relationship.

Animals, he pointed out, had a greater or lesser capacity to reason; many used tools; all used a communications system of some subtlety and complexity. He drew on his memories of the Fuegians to begin bridging the abyss between man and animal from the other side. They had had, he said, no religious sense, no pantheon of gods, no rituals of worship, proving that these were not innate human needs or characteristics. As for the moral sense, that was a concomitant of collective living – many animals had learned to work for other members of their family or group. Given the development of mental powers to a human level, a true morality, based upon abstract concepts of right behaviour, was only to be expected.

Despite Wallace's defection to a more mystical camp, Darwin was still firmly of the opinion that natural selection was enough to explain the development even of such a species as the human. However, the book was flawed by Darwin's pursuit of evidence for the sexual selection by which he set such store. Wallace suggested that it was really two books rolled into one, and he was right: only about a third of it deals directly with the subject its title proclaims. The rest is taken up with the usual Darwin apparatus of detailed information supporting a proferred hypothesis. The reaction to the book was, by comparison with that to *The Origin*, muted and undramatic. Many readers were disappointed – the book had little of the verve that had

given the arguments of *The Origin* their energy. This does not seem particularly surprising, since the debate that had followed that first statement of
Darwin's view had never died down, and had from the beginning dealt with
the issues covered in *Descent of Man*. Opponents were confirmed in their
opposition by this further evidence of Darwin's godlessness; supporters
were happy to have openly stated what they had always known Darwin
believed. As for the devout but neutral, Emma had already spoken for them
when she had first read parts of the manuscript: "I think it will be very
interesting, but that I shall dislike it very much as again putting God further
off".

Darwin, perhaps because he had given so much space to sexual selection,
realized, even as the book was appearing in the shops, that he had far from
exhausted the subject. It was the demonstrable unity of all behaviour that
continued to fascinate him; he had for years been observing or asking others
to observe the way in which animals, babies and every sort of adult expressed
their feelings. He had, from the time of his own first child's birth, observed
how young humans managed even before the age of speech to make their
feelings plain; now he systematically extended these enquiries, involving as
always correspondents all over the world in the attempt to discover whether
gesture and facial expression differed according to race. As a result, he was
able to formulate certain principles governing expression: for example, that
some reactions, like snarling in humans, reflected an inheritance from
remote ancestors which had long lost its direct practicality – the snarl had
been of real use only when mankind's precursors had had dangerous canines
with which to threaten their enemies. Another such principle was that of the
antithetical movement, when a direct and practical response to a situation is
reversed as perception of the situation is reversed – he cited the signals of
aggression as contrasted with those of fear or friendship in dogs. The third of
his main principles defined a quite different class of reaction, those that were
extensions of the normal, automatic responses of the nervous system, such as
trembling or shivering.

The Expression of the Emotions in Man and Animals was the last of the
books in which Darwin directly tackled the central theme of his intellectual
life, the last in which he mined that great pile of material which was to have
been the one all-encompassing book he had once planned. It was the lightest
of them, too, with its examination of actors' techniques, its use of photographs and drawings, its references to art and its examples drawn from
lunatic asylums. On the day that it appeared, in November, 1872, it sold over
five thousand copies. Almost as he finished the manuscript, however, Darwin began yet another revision of *The Origin*, this the sixth and last.

In January, 1871, there had been published a bitterly anti-Darwinian book entitled *The Genesis of Species*. Its author was an Anglo-French biologist, a Catholic and one-time lawyer named St. George Jackson Mivart. He had originally been persuaded by Darwin's arguments, but had noted and agreed with many of the criticisms that had been levelled against them. He had noted, too, and found wanting Darwin's various attempts to find an answer to them. It is not clear why his antagonism to Darwin and Darwin's ideas developed the vituperative edge that they did. There was something personal, almost malevolent, in the contemptuous gusto with which he mounted his attacks. Aggrieved, Darwin complained to Hooker that Mivart "shows the greatest scorn and animosity towards me . . . I suppose that accursed religious bigotry is at the root of it." Whatever the root, the branches flourished: in his book, Mivart deployed his biologist's learning with a lawyer's skill. He may have abused the supporters of natural selection as "a great crowd of half-educated men and shallow thinkers", but he laboured long and hard to refute their beliefs. Darwin, therefore, reworking certain parts of *The Origin*, hardening and sharpening its style by eliminating qualification wherever he could, was forced to add a section directly refuting Mivart's attack.

The result of his accumulated revisions, this tinkering with the text under the pressure of criticism, was to make *The Origin* in its final shape somewhat contradictory. By eliminating some of the hesitations and uncertainties, he made it a more positive statement of his beliefs. But, in trying to answer or incorporate so many of the objections, culminating in his effort to combat the comprehensive assault mounted by Mivart, Darwin blurred and even compromised those beliefs. He had had a vision of life on earth slowly changing and unfolding under a single agency of selection, an agency which worked upon the organisms of the planet uninfluenced by anything but its own simple logic. Survival was a constant struggle; those creatures which were, by some chance, better adapted to that struggle than others would survive it. The rest would perish. The process was without end, working throughout countless aeons upon the plasticity of living nature.

With sexual selection, with the new emphasis he placed upon the effects of use and disuse, Darwin introduced a quite different factor: that of individual choice. In selecting a male, a female exercised volition; in using or adapting a limb, a creature might well do the same. However slight this factor was – and it became more important as one considered the ranks of the higher vertebrates – it muddled the simplicity of the original vision. It was an element which conflicted with the impersonal logic of a selection process that derived only from the interaction of organism and environment.

Nevertheless, Darwin had said his last direct word on the subject. The new edition of *The Origin* was published early in 1872. The *Expression of*

Emotions came out in November of that year. He was beginning to clamber through his middle sixties and there were other fascinating matters that were drawing his attention, matters not unconnected with the ideas he had been pursuing all his life, but more peripheral than those to which he had devoted most of his life since he had begun to work on his projected book in 1859. Perhaps he was tired of being in the centre of the storm; perhaps he felt that he could never placate his critics and thus that uneasy part of himself which to some extent agreed with them. He knew that his explanations of natural selection were not watertight; that was why he had had to shuffle the pieces on the biological board to and fro, searching for the perfect, inviolable defence. In the absence of a true science of genetics, it could not be found.

For all the work he had done on variation, for all the efforts he had made to render pangenesis plausible, he knew that no such science had yet been created. A thousand miles away, unknown to him, Mendel had discovered its foundations; but no one had discovered Mendel. So Darwin, always happier when working painstakingly at the details of his science, removed himself even further from the battles he had started. All his working life he had been asking questions; now he had an endless supply of them, each one demanding answer. For example, why did flowers so often have both male and female organs? Was it really, as botanists believed, in order to be self-fertilizing? And if it was, why did each plant, unmodified by the genetic inheritance from another of identical type, not produce one generation after another of progeny so varied that soon the entire species would dissolve into chaos? There was still a vast amount to be learned about the sundew. And how exactly did climbing plants weave themselves about their supports? And then what about the soil? He had been wondering about that since the *Beagle* days. What about the soil, and the formation of loam, and the part played in all that by the earthworms? . . .

Thoughtfully, caped and bearded, Darwin strolls out into his garden, his head whirling with possible answers, with experiments that might test those answers, with questions that the answers have suggested. He pauses in his hothouse, gazes benignly around: there is still a great deal to be done. He walks thoughtfully on towards the Sandwalk, and into the last decade of his life.

3

In these years, some inner tension seems at last to have relaxed in Darwin. Was it that, with the acceptance of his theories and the worldwide admiration that this had created, he had at last hoarded self-esteem sufficient to sustain him, to keep him secure for the rest of his life? For years he had had love enough, and money, yet had never changed his placatory attitude to the world. Had he, for all that time, feared at some secret level of his being the harsh word that would invalidate all he had done? If so, he no longer seemed to believe that it would come. Finally, he had achieved enough; finally, he had become able to believe that he was what the world thought him.

His health improved. Down House, for decades his shelter, almost his hospital, behind the walls of which he had guarded his therapeutic isolation, began to welcome guests. Old friends, long greeted only on paper, at last appeared again in the flesh: de Candolle came to see him, their first meeting for forty years. Häckel came several times from Germany, to be revitalized by every contact with his master. Strangers arrived from all over the world – once an Australian who rushed in, wordlessly shook hands with him and would have left at once had he not been stopped; mysteriously, he was heard of later, tramping in poverty across California, his only possessions a pipe and a faded letter from Darwin. Most of those who came, however, were scientists, savants, occasionally pursuers of the famous, often pompous, at times incomprehensible. Fortunately, older friends came too – Hooker, of course, and Huxley: as a neighbour, Lubbock would at times stroll over, perhaps with one or two congenial friends.

For the visitors, Down House offered an unpretentious welcome. Life would not be disrupted by their arrival, nor disturbed at their departure. Darwin's routine, supervised by the watchful Emma, survived no matter who came calling. There were books in profusion, the piano, the garden and grounds to amuse the guests who stayed over the weekend, those cavernous, Victorian, Thursday-to-Monday weekends that punctuated the industrious productivity of nineteenth century intellectuals. Emma would continue her daily rounds, her overseeing of the household, her wideflung charities, her readings to Darwin, her sewing in the drawing room. As for Darwin, he brightened to the arrivals, exuding unsuspected energies, reviving, it may be, memories of endless conversations held over the beer and through the pipe-smoke of his Cambridge days.

His son George, remembering a few years later that weekend talk, recalled how Darwin "threw himself into it heart and soul, and was never languid or torpid". He would talk easily and fluently, yet remained always a patient listener, drawing talk from others; unlike his father, he never attempted to dominate or monopolize a conversation. George's older brother, Francis, indeed thought him a reluctant, even an inadequate conversationalist, though he enjoyed laughter and, having once decided that a man was humorous, would be ready to laugh at almost anything he said. When he himself spoke, he still had at times the flat vowels of the Midlands and used a handful of dialect words that he had carried with him since childhood ("boss", for example, a Staffordshire word for a grass-tussock, he used for footstool). With women he used a curious mixture of teasing and deference, which he himself would describe as flirting; with men, he enjoyed using slang and what George called "vigorous expletives" – "Devil take it!" he would exclaim when thwarted. "Confound the thing!" The consequence of these displays of energetic bonhomie was a predictable exhaustion: Darwin, however much he had enjoyed himself, almost always heaved a sigh of relief as his guests departed on Monday morning for the nearby station.

In August, 1871, Henrietta was married to R.B. Litchfield, an active social reformer perhaps best known for his part in the founding of the Working Men's College in 1854. In his love of music and his reverence for science, he proved a suitable son-in-law for Darwin. Ten years before he had written, in an article for the College's *Magazine*, "It is the scientific mind which is habitually one of reverence; meaning by reverence not a trembling horror of the unknown, but a deep feeling of the awfulness and mystery of the great world". Clearly a kindred spirit had joined this rational, science-orientated family. But the years were whirling on: only a little while before, it must have seemed, Henrietta had been a sickly child, an adolescent invalid threatened week by week with relapse and even death. And within a few years, first Francis, then William, were also to be married – indeed, Darwin would be a grandfather and Francis a widower before the decade ended.

Darwin was looking an old man now, older than a man in his sixties might be expected to look. In his new manifestation, he steps out of his present into ours – he has become the Darwin with whose appearance we have remained so familiar. Shadowed by the jutting cliff of his brow, there gleam his watchful, blue eyes; under the shaggy beard, white and oddly pugnacious, his mouth, both generously wide and firmly thin-lipped, can be seen. The expression is a little withdrawn, observing us across a silent century: he is as interested in us as we in him. The wide-brimmed hat, the dark cloak (often replaced inside the house by a shawl), the broad frame – we seem to know him as well as did the village children who ran to open gates for him when they saw him on his regular walks. He stares out at us from the pages of a book, or down from a wall, framed, fixed, caught for ever during those last peaceful years of authority and honour: the Sage at home. The uncertainties, the hesitations, the self-doubts seem to have vanished, as well as whatever there was of vanity and self-importance (especially those subtle versions that stem from not being vain, not being self-important). Baffled, we turn away, to leave him standing for ever looking quizzically back at us as he leans against a tree or, as in Leonard's splendid photograph of him, pensively regards something in his own life which continues eternally just beyond the frame, tantalizing us, but perhaps comforting him as he relaxes on the wicker chair on his verandah.

In 1873, Darwin, perhaps conscious of his own lifelong comfort and the serenity of his old age, became active in helping a close friend who had never had similar good fortune. Over the previous few years, Huxley had become dispirited, unhealthy, overworked. He felt keenly the financial insecurity which, for all his lofty intellectual stances, was constantly threatening to lay him low. With one or two friends, notably the physicist John Tyndall, Superintendent of the Royal Institution and a noted writer and lecturer on science, Darwin decided to collect a sum of money for Huxley's use. The amount they agreed on was £2,000; it was a contribution, appropriately enough, from the president of the Royal Society that brought them to their intended total.

Darwin wrote to Huxley about the fund and why "some of your friends (eighteen in number)" had decided to raise it.

> We have done this to enable you to get such complete rest as you may require for the re-establishment of your health; & in doing this we are convinced that we are acting for the public interest, as well as in accordance with our most anxious desires. Let me assure you that we are all your warm personal friends, & that there is not a stranger or mere acquaintance among us. If you could have heard what was said, or could have read what was, I believe, our most innermost thoughts, you would know that we all feel towards you as we should to an honoured & much-loved brother . . .

Huxley was overwhelmed. He had felt himself, he wrote, for the first time in his life "fairly beaten – I mean morally beaten . . . I have for months been without energy & without hope . . ." Now he would be able to take a holiday "without feeling that I am potentially guilty of fraud – and when my peculiar little blue-devil dances about me (as dance he will for some time yet) I shall fling the cheque for £2,100 at his head as Luther did the inkstand." He ended with a paragraph of gratitude for Darwin: "Have I said a word of

Darwin in the last year of his life.

appreciation for your own letter? I shall keep it for my children that their children may know what manner of man their father's friend was & why he loved him."

Such generosities apart, Darwin had a cautious, watchful attitude to money. Until the end of his life he remembered the financial precepts and investment advice of his father. During his last months, suggesting to Caroline that she should buy "ordinary Government 3 per cent Stock", he reinforced his advice by adding, "My Father used to say that everyone ought to hold some of this Stock." Yet at the same time, as in the case of John Scott, of Huxley and others, where he saw a need he could respond swiftly. When his correspondent, friend and near-protégé, Fritz Müller, a German naturalist living and teaching in Brazil, was said – in a somewhat exaggerated report – to have had his house destroyed by floods, Darwin offered instant aid. "From you, dear Sir", Müller replied, "I should have accepted assistance without hesitation . . ." Darwin was not only ready to help his friends, he had the knack of making that help acceptable, of lightening the load of obligation it implied. Yet, at Down House, he would hurry to snuff out a candle that seemed to be burning uselessly, he used scrap paper rather than new whenever he could, cannibalizing even his old manuscripts to do so, and at the end of every year summoned the family to what they nicknamed "the workhouse season", an annual accounting loud with his lamentations and his forecasts, made at least half seriously, of poverty to come.

Towards the end of his life, Darwin began a small but effective agitation to have the Government give Wallace a pension. With his more straitened background, Wallace had always had to struggle much harder than many of his middle class colleagues. He had, perhaps, had to work too hard and at too varied a set of projects – though his versatile intelligence and speculative cast of mind would always have sent him in directions Darwin preferred to avoid. By writing to Hooker in 1879, Darwin set in motion the ponderous mechanisms of governmental gratitude: Hooker, as Director of the Royal Botanic Gardens, had easy access to the bureaucracy. Darwin continued to press, Hooker to argue; in January, 1881, Gladstone himself wrote to Darwin to announce that the battle had been won, the pension granted. "How extraordinarily kind of Mr. Gladstone", commented Darwin, "to find time to write under the present circumstances. Good heavens! how pleased I am!"

Darwin had both a gift and an abiding need for friendship. Now, in his mid-sixties, when all the major relationships of his life might have been thought long forged, he found himself establishing the last of those close scientific associations that had sustained him since the days of Henslow at Cambridge, of Grant at Edinburgh. George Romanes, with his strong, square face, his wide brow and powerful nose, his open, enquiring expression, was forty years younger than Darwin; at Cambridge, he had intended like Darwin to become an Anglican clergyman. Unlike Darwin, he had done so out of a serious commitment to religion; again unlike Darwin, who had not had the opportunity, he had read for the natural history tripos, taking his degree at the same time, though at a less exalted level, as Francis Darwin. (The examination paper had included a question on natural selection – Romanes had been unable to answer it.) As science seized his interest, religion faded; like Francis, again, he began to study medicine. His first publication, however – written when he was convalescing after one of those long, mysterious illnesses which were of such assistance in sharpening Victorian minds – was entitled *Christian Prayer and General Laws*: in 1873 it gained him a typical example of the esoteric rewards that decorate British academic life: the Burney Prize.

In 1874, after reading a letter from him in *Nature*, Darwin invited Romanes to visit him. Romanes had already decided to spend his life as a serious research scientist, and had sharpened his general medical training into the expertise of a physiologist. He had, by now, read Darwin's books and the summons both awed and delighted him. He made the pilgrimage to Down House and, as his widow was to record in the biography she wrote of him, "From that time began an unbroken friendship, marked on one side by absolute worship, reverence, and affection, on the other by an almost fatherly kindness . . ."

Thus Romanes took his place as a junior member in the resplendent circle that gathered around Darwin: Lyell, Hooker, Huxley, Lubbock, as well as many others of equal ability and prestige, but – in that context – of less significance. One had the impression that, at least for a while, Darwin intended Romanes to bear onward the torch of pangenesis – as he put it in a letter written in 1876, Romanes would "some day, I hope, convert an 'airy nothing' into a substantial theory . . ." As late as 1881, the two men were still debating the subject in their correspondence. But their letters cover a great variety of other scientific matters, as well as touching upon two issues that interested both of them, in varying degrees: spiritualism and the controversy surrounding vivisection.

Darwin took part in two or three seances, held at his brother's house in Queen Anne Street, in London. One was in January, 1874, which he called "grand fun" and at which Charles Williams, the medium, made various objects leap about the drawing room, while George Darwin, who had arranged the meeting, and Hensleigh Wedgwood held his hands and feet. Darwin's report, alas, was only hearsay, for "I found it so hot & tiring that I went away before all these astounding miracles, or jugglery, took place.

How the man could possibly do what was done passes my understanding." A few days later, his wonderment had somewhat abated and he declared to Huxley that "the more I thought of all that I had heard happened at Queen Anne St., the more convinced I was that it was all imposture".

Huxley, too, attended one of these gatherings and reported to Darwin; and a year later, on April Fool's Day, 1875, Darwin himself went to another one, at Hensleigh's house. He reported to his son George that:

> . . . one girl was put in dark room with hands tied & sealed – & tied & sealed to floor. The other girl was in the partly lighted room in a trance on the sofa & not tied, with all the spectators. – All that happened was that the spirits talked & chatted much, & Hope* thinks that she saw lips of girl on sofa moving. – There was only one appearance & even Hensleigh admitted that it presented no distinct appearance: Hope (who believes in spirits) says it might have been merely a white handkerchief . . . One of the spirits first asked who & how many were present, & made each one give his honour that he w_d not try to seize hold of any spirit!

Next morning, Darwin suggested to Fanny, Hensleigh's wife, that the tied medium must have wriggled out of her bonds – "& then it came out that the seal by which she was fastened to the floor was broken!! . . . Good Heavens, what rubbish the whole does seem to be."

Vivisection had become an issue for debate by 1870, as scientists began increasingly to take ordinary human curiosity as a quasi-divine imperative. In 1875, a Royal Commission was appointed to consider it and the following year a Bill was presented in the House of Lords which, as is the way with controversial issues, was thought by some too harsh and by others too permissive. Darwin detested vivisection, but it seemed to him an evil that serious research made necessary – "but not", as he said in 1871, "for mere damnable and detestable curiosity". To his daughter, four years later, he wrote that the only sure counter to cruelty in the laboratories was "the improvement of humanitarian feelings". He was not happy about the coercive alternative: "If stringent laws are passed, and this is likely, seeing how unscientific the House of Commons is, and that the gentlemen of England are humane, so long as their sports are not considered, which entail a hundred or thousand-fold more suffering than the experiments of physiologists – if such laws are passed, the result will assuredly be that physiology, which has been until within the last few years at a standstill in England, will languish or quite cease."

As a result of his views, he found himself unable to sign a petition being presented by the formidable Miss Cobbe, who was with typical absolutism

---

* Hensleigh's youngest child – yet another Wedgwood later to marry a cousin.

entirely against vivisection. Instead, with Huxley and a handful of other scientists, and aided by Litchfield, he drafted a Bill of his own, an initiative that led in the end to no practical result. Meanwhile Huxley had had to defend himself in the *Times* against accusations that he was teaching vivisection to schoolchildren; it is not surprising that Darwin a little later was writing to Romanes, "It seems to me the Physiologists are now in the position of a persecuted religious sect . . ."

The conflict continued during the remaining years of Darwin's life (and has never completely died down since, a sign of its intractable nature). In 1881 he wrote a letter to Professor Holmgren, who taught physiology at the University of Upsala, in Sweden; as an expression of his views, it was published in the *Times*, and in the course of it he asserted that "physiology cannot possibly progress except by means of experiments on living animals, and I have the deepest conviction that he who retards the progress of physiology commits a crime against mankind." Thus Darwin in his old age had been drawn, as he never had been by the battles over his own ideas, into open polemics in the newspapers. Miss Cobbe, still active in the struggle against vivisection, wrote a spiritedly argumentative letter in an attempt to refute Darwin's contention, Darwin tried to prove her mistaken, she riposted – although, Darwin claimed, she had in the meantime changed her ground. Later the same year, Romanes asked him to write on the subject, one article in a symposium that the Physiological Society was organizing. "I have been thinking at intervals all morning what I could say, and it is the simple truth that I have nothing worth saying," Darwin replied, offering instead the use of quotations from his *Times* letters – "I still abide most strongly in my expressed conviction".

Throughout all these years he continued to work at a rate that seems almost undiminished. In 1875, his studies of climbing and of insectivorous plants were published, and towards the end of the year, a second edition of *Variation under Domestication*. The following year he brought out *Effects of Cross and Self Fertilisation in the Vegetable Kingdom*, in which he began by demonstrating the frequency with which plants had developed structures and processes favouring cross-pollination. Even in hermaphrodite flowers, self-fertilization was prevented by the organs of one sex ripening at a time different from those of the other. By experiment, Darwin found that plants which had been cross-fertilized almost always grew taller and stronger than those which had pollinated themselves, even when they were commonly self-fertilizing: he had work on more than fifty species, done over twelve years, to provide the evidence. This was clearly a strong, if circumstantial, proof of his central thesis, natural selection: the adaptations to ease cross-fertilization were connected with a general increase in vigour; vigorous

SUGGESTED ILLUSTRATION

FOR "DR. DARWIN'S MOVEMENTS AND HABITS OF CLIMBING PLANTS."

(See Murray's List of Forthcoming Works.)

*** We had no notion the Doctor would have been so ready to avow his connection with his quadrumanous ancestors—the tree-climbing Anthropoids —as the title of his work seems to imply.

Caricature draw in 1875 by Sambourne.

plants were more likely to survive in competitive circumstances; thus over the vast periods of evolutionary development, plants making cross-fertilization easier, by however slender a margin, will always have had an advantage over those that did not; in the course of time, therefore, the self-fertilizers will have perished, while the others, going from strength to strength, took over the species.

The following year, 1877, *Different Forms of Flowers on Plants of the same Species* was published, a book that pushed Darwin's investigation of vegetable sexuality into more specialized areas. Certain plants have two or three forms of flower, with varying stamen lengths and varying depths of style (the tube that carries pollen to the ovary). Closer examination shows that pollen sizes vary also. Each individual plant produces flowers of only one type, invariably passing this singular faculty on to its progeny. Darwin also discovered that a flower dusted with pollen of its own type rarely proved fertile – the fertility of short-styled flowers, for example, was only guaranteed by pollen from those with a long style. He had again demonstrated the advantage of the genetic spread produced when two different organisms were involved in the creation of a new generation, an advantage expressed here in greatly increased fertility.

In 1880, Darwin published *Power of Movement in Plants*. He had already analysed the manner in which plants used supports to carry their leaves nearer the sun, his precise observations clarifying an area in which almost everything had hitherto been taken for granted. Now he wanted to find out what vegetable mechanism it was that enabled them to move in so purposive a manner. Obviously the means of movement stemmed from one side of a stalk or tendril growing more swiftly than the other; that was a long-established observation. But what triggered this crucial differential? The answer, Darwin discovered, was light, playing upon the sensitive tip of the shoot: lower on its stem, the plant would respond to these signals, the greater growth always taking place on the dark side.

But Darwin was unable to determine the way in which these signals are transmitted. Only the tip of the shoot has this sensitivity, and the stem lower down will respond even if itself protected from the light. Now Darwin discovered that the twisting of climbing plants was only an extreme development of a general ability; delicate experiments with cabbage shoots showed that all plants thrusting towards the light twirled in constant circles, while the thrusting tips of their roots behaved similarly in the soil. Theirs was no passive response to forces and structures outside themselves, but a constant, if blind, searching for advantage. Young shoots arched themselves like tiny springs in order to burst out of the earth, protecting at the same time the first fragile growth of leaves. To straighten itself, the plant used the same technique of differential growth as the climbing plants. Mature plants, too, he discovered, maintained the same questing circling, multiplying their opportunities for growth and establishing a basis of general behaviour from which evolution had been able to select the particular development of the climbing plants. The runners of such plants as strawberries showed themselves to be not only energetic, but also what in an animal one would call resourceful. Darwin laid obstacles in their path, then watched them wind around or over them. He made them pass between pins driven into the ground. One, too thick to push between them, stopped, seemed to gather itself, then simply "leaped" over the top. They too appeared to "perceive" their environment by means of the slow circling of their sensitive shoot tips.

Darwin turned next to another phenomenon that seemed to unite the vegetable and animal orders: the fact that so many plants dropped into a sort of sleep at night. To de Candolle he had commented, "It always pleases me to exalt plants in the organic scale", but he was not besotted by his vision of unity. "Hardly anyone", he wrote now, "supposes that there is really any anology between the sleep of animals and that of plants". In fact, Darwin discovered, the drooping of the leaves that occurred at night not only protected plants from the cold, as Linnaeus had suggested, but by setting them at right angles to the zenith, kept them away from dangerous radiation.

What Darwin was always unable to determine is how signals are transmitted within the plant, what serves it in place of the nervous system. Only the tips of shoots and roots have the sensitivity he observed; from their perceptions stem a complex variety of reactions elsewhere in the plant. How are they connected? Because of his demonstrations, these questions have vexed generations of botanists, micro-biologists, biochemists. Today we know at least that it is hormones in the plants that carry the necessary messages, and that plant cells can move the hormones, or prevent their moving, along the stem. How and under what circumstances they do so is not yet understood.

Once more, Darwin had initiated an entire line of enquiry, setting in motion a century of effort. He had the capacity, arising perhaps from a certain bluntness, of asking directly relevant questions couched in the simplest of terms. Modest himself, he was not afraid of enquiring into humble matters – the entire living world, after all, mankind included, had been developed from the simplest of organisms. Because he was laying the foundations of a science, he was fortunate in having the opportunity to ask so many original questions, and to do so much original work while attempting to answer them. On the other hand, he was forced to leave many such questions unanswered, and out of these the twentieth century has fashioned whole colleges of specialists. Some of today's scientists may envy Darwin the straightforwardness of the problems that faced him, however subtle and complex their solutions. It is possible, of course, that such problems continue to exist, lacking only the eye of genius that can discern them.

For example, ever since his return from the *Beagle* expedition, and perhaps even before, he had been intrigued by a problem hardly anyone else had regarded as such at all. In 1827, a field near Maer had been spread with lime; ten years later, a series of holes revealed half an inch of turf, two and a half inches of fine mould beneath that, and beneath the mould what remained of the lime. In the year that he had settled into Down House, 1842, chalk had been spread on a field not far away; a trench dug in 1871 showed seven inches of mould above the chalk remains. Whatever was strewn on fields, it appeared, sank at an average rate of a quarter of an inch a year; put another way, a quarter of an inch of valuable mould was annually deposited for the farmers to use. Where did it come from? What agency deposited it?

Darwin had been dealing with these questions as early as 1838, when he had published a paper on the subject in the Geological Society's *Proceedings*. He had presented there a solution first suggested to him by his Uncle Jos, that it was earthworms which, by bringing up their castings, were continuously, if imperceptibly, burying the surface. Now, over forty years later, he began to take a more considered look at the evidence. He gathered in the assistance of his sons: Francis, living at Down House with his small son, Bernard*, already acted as his principal assistant, while the others, not for the first time, were conscripted by letter. In his garden, William had an acacia; worms were said to draw the stalks of its leaves to their burrow. "I want much to know whether they draw them in by blunt base or by apex – & whichever end is drawn in, whether this is uniformly done". To George, in Cambridge, he wrote, "Please find out when Cloisters in Neville's Court are swept & examine just before the time so as to see whether any connection between sagging of pavements & castings," adding rather glumly, "I suppose not."

Darwin, tending earthworms, calculated the work rate of these unconsidered creatures. They eat decaying vegetable matter and, as they pass through the soil, grind it down to a powder which, melded into pellets or castings, they deposit on the surface. Patiently, Darwin and his son Francis weighed the castings brought to the surface on a square yard of pasture, did their arithmetic with care and came to the conclusion that over a year the earthworms in an acre of land carried up into the daylight some eighteen tons of earth. The worms sank their tiny shafts to a depth of about twenty inches; to that depth, therefore, they were responsible for turning, reducing

---

* Bernard Darwin became, in due course, one of the most distinguished writers on golf that there have ever been.

and aerating the soil – responsible, in other words, for the rich mould in which plants set and grow so well. It is also worms, he discovered, that are the prime agency active in burying ruins: abbey, castle, or peasant's hut, all when once abandoned have to bow to the ceaseless energy, the grinding gizzards and constant, mindless hunger of these ubiquitous, disregarded annelids.

Darwin took the manuscript to Murray. "Here is a work", he said, "which has occupied me for many years. I fear the subject will not interest the public, but will you publish if for me?" In October, 1881, the book appeared. Two thousand copies were sold at once; it went into six editions in a year, and in three years sold over 8,500 copies. "It has been a complete surprise to me how many persons have cared for the subject", commented Darwin to a friend. The very ordinariness of the earthworm, its familiarity, contrasted with the enormous geological work Darwin attributed to it, seemed to attract readers. They knew the earthworm well; as a result, perhaps, they felt they could understand what Darwin had written about it. It was, in commercial terms, a greater success than *The Origin* had been.

During these years, Darwin wrote two short biographies – that of his grandfather and his own. His *Autobiography* was not, ostensibly at least, intended for publication, though perhaps one can see in his disclaimers something of his habitual diffidence, his shy creeping into our attention. Another man of similar fame might have thought himself sufficiently secure to admit that the world would probably like to know more about him; Darwin declared that he would tell his life story only to his immediate family. Such an intention might have become an inhibiting factor during his writing of it – had he needed one. But he did not.

The fact is that Darwin was a man incapable of the exuberant self-revelation that good autobiography demands. As in his letters, there is something curiously impenetrable and elusive in everything he writes about himself; his view is lucid and objective, yet guarded. He lived in an era of greater circumspection than ours, but not everyone wrote as though what went on inside their own minds was as inaccessible to them as to any outsider. The portrait he paints is, for all the limited distribution he intended – or claims he intended – a public one, although it may be the case that a man is at his most careful when presenting himself for his family's judgement.

That is not to say that he was in any sense deliberately misleading. He had the habit of writing very clearly about things which he had closely observed and, to the extent that it was possible for him, he did the same here. His views on religion were firmly enough put for Emma to have them edited before the *Autobiography* was finally published, a few years after Darwin's death, as part of Francis's *Life and Letters* of his father. It is accurate, modest and

Sambourne caricature in 1881 *Punch*.

likeable, as Darwin himself seems to have been, and claims nothing to which it has no right; indeed, it claims rather less. But – again as in his letters – it displays no idiosyncracy, no profound self-questioning, no apparent interest in the true deeps and darks of the mind, no raging animosities or overwhelming allegiances: in short, it gives no hint of anything demonic, uncontrollable, disturbing within the man it attempts to describe. And perhaps in this it told the truth.

Somehow, over the years, the emotions had become shallow in Darwin; the language in which he wrote to his friends of affection or nostalgia was flaccid with much use. For such matters, as for his science, he reached for the nearest practical phrase, almost the nearest available response. Certainly he felt what he wrote, but there was no pressure in the feeling. His emotions had been long ago locked away, to sob or gibber in some closed chamber of the soul, out of the sight and hearing of their master. This left him to do his work; it left him free, too, to like and be liked, to be equable, affectionate, caring, considerate, sentimental – everything, in fact, but passionate.

He had, after all, been born only a little while after the eighteenth century had ended. His intellectual style was much influenced by the standards of the Age of Reason. Perhaps for this reason he was happy to work on the biography of Dr. Erasmus, the gargantuan grandfather whom he never saw. The German writer Hermann Krause had written an essay on Erasmus Darwin's work and evolutionary ideas. To the English translation of this, it was decided that Charles Darwin should write a long biographical introduction. Darwin worked hard over it, writing to almost every cousin he could trace in the various collateral lines of Darwins for information, relics, pictures; many responded, with interest if not with material, happy to have an excuse to make or renew connections with their illustrious relation. "The more I read of Dr. D. the higher he rises in my estimation", wrote Darwin to one of these, adding apologies for untidiness, "but I am very tired to death with writing letters; half the fools throughout Europe write to ask me the stupidest questions."

The book was published in November, 1879. It was greeted with pleasure by the family and politeness by the world, the one notable exception being Samuel Butler, author of *Erewhon* and grandson of Darwin's old headmaster at Shrewsbury. Once an enthusiastic advocate of Darwin's ideas, he had sidled away into a somewhat convoluted admiration for the theories of Lamarck, a preference which he had increasingly translated into direct and personal animosity against Darwin. In May, 1879, his book *Evolution Old and New* had appeared, lauding Lamarck, placing beside him on the podium Buffon and Erasmus Darwin, and consigning Charles, with contumely, to the periphery of the arena. Now Krause, preparing his essay for English publication, made a few late additions critical of Butler's assertions. Characteristically, Butler concluded that to bring out these criticisms had been Darwin's main purpose in publishing the book. He launched a vituperative attack in that ever willing anti-Darwinian periodical, the *Athenaeum*. Darwin, somewhat against his own judgement, was persuaded not to send a reply that might have soothed his opponent, and Butler, a man often drunk on his own furies, continued his ranting attacks on him. These were to break out again from time to time, expressions of a raw and inexhaustible anger that continued long after its object had become only a venerated name in history.

So at last the cascade of Darwin's books ceased. For over forty years he had offered his observations to the world, and the long unrolling scroll of evidence that supported the central thesis of his intellectual life. In this final decade he had published eight new titles, if one includes *Erasmus Darwin*; in the same period, new editions had been brought out of *The Origin*, his early work on coral reefs and *Variation under Domestication*, as well as a second printing of *Descent of Man*: if this was the semi-retirement of a sickly man, it matched what most of the healthy might produce at the height of their vigour.

At the same time, life continued as richly as ever at Down House. The ball flew to and fro across the tennis court as merrily as when the Darwin boys first played the game. Emma wrote of these comings and going in her letters to George: in 1881, the last full year of Darwin's life, the traffic of visitors was as swift and varied as it had ever been. The family were often there, maintaining the contacts and realities of their childhoods. "My dear George", wrote Emma, "we can manage very well if you don't mind the little room . . ."; at another time, "The Litches [i.e., Litchfields] came at lunchtime from Bromley, & we sat in the verandah & dawdled about". On a different occasion they brought a certain Elsie Blunt with them – "a very nice tasteful girl; but very plain". Then "Uncle Harry & Arthur & Rowly are here" – that is, her brother Henry with two of his sons; or, a little later, "Our Sunday guests were Caroline W. [probably Henry Wedgwood's daughter] & Miss Tyler, a nice natural woman, with whom I had topics enough . . ." A Madame Hemholtz was brought on a visit, "a very lively agreeable woman & F. flirted very prettily with her". The great Sanskrit scholar, Max Müller, appeared, a man long interested in the evolution of language, and regaled them with tales of the singlemindedness of Japanese students.

More robustly, the Sunday Walking Party of the Working Men's College was, at long intervals, invited to Down House, and then great tables would be set on trestles on the lawn, seventy or eighty guests would arrive, tea would be served, and strawberries, there was music under the trees and, with a flash of straw hats and a whirling of long skirts, there would be dancing under the trees. In the nearby field, the men would play cricket and other games, while Darwin himself would wander about the garden, grey-bearded and beaming, very different from the hermit he had been during his middle years. "My father's cordiality and warmth delighted everyone", wrote Henrietta, whose husband had organized the feast. "There never was anyone like him for making a sense of exhilaration and glow in the atmosphere . . ."

These were the years when Darwin moved beyond controversy and into adulation. On his sixty-eighth birthday, in 1877, he was sent from Holland an album containing photographs of 217 of his most eminent supporters there, a curious tribute, suggesting that the Dutch had learned something about trophies from the headhunters of their East Indian possessions. Nevertheless, it was a sign of how widespread admiration for his work had become. Towards the end of the year, however, there came an acknowledgement of his new position in the intellectual firmament that must have meant more to him than almost any other. He was granted an honorary degree from the University of Cambridge, a doctorate of law that seemed to admit his role as one of the jurists of the natural order, a man who had helped to establish the terms of its irreversible legislation. "To appoint a special congregation of the senate", remarked the scientific journal, *Nature*, "for no other business but the conferment of a solitary degree, although it be *honoris causâ*, is only resorted to in exceptional and important cases . . . The building was packed, and the inevitable pastime of the undergraduates assumed a form extremely appropriate, however questionable its taste may have been." Readers of *Nature* had to turn to other publications if they wanted to discover that the students had hung across the Senate-house, from gallery to gallery, the effigy of a large monkey dressed in academic robes. Darwin, entering through a side door with the Master of his old college, Christ's, was greeted with genuine applause, but when the Public Orator stood to deliver his Latin eulogy, he was constantly interrupted by yells of "Construe!", "False quantity!" and, with rather less erudition, "Cut it short!"

From York Villa, Lower Avenue, Southampton, a certain Charles Hoare was moved to send Darwin his versified congratulations.

> "Darwin"; the sunset of thy life is cheered,
> By recognition; – Honours never sought,
> Though nobly earned; will make thy name revered!
> Few have so gallantly for Science fought,
> Maligned, abused, with falsehoods too assailed,
> Disdaining answer; – but Truth has prevailed.

Mr. Hoare continued at some length in this vein, but not everyone shared his view. The award had revived something of the earlier controversies. The religious periodical, *The Rock*, said, a little haughtily, "No doubt the affair has its ludicrous side, though a believer will scarcely regard the honour paid to the apostle of Evolution as by any means a laughing matter." The *Manchester Weekly Times* was more urbane: "If the evolution theory upon which the Public Orator at Cambridge threw the splendour of his approving rhetoric is true, Mr. Darwin has made considerable havoc in the groundwork of Christianity . . . I can only wonder how the Cambridge Doctors of Divinity and official guardians of orthodoxy will manage to square accounts with Mr. Darwin. Perhaps it is believed that a niche may be found for him in some sequestered corner of the Christian fabric."

Such isolated cannonades, however, were rarer now. More typical was the scene at the Royal Institution four years later, when Darwin walked in to hear a lecture by the physiologist Burdon Sanderson. At once the entire audience rose to applaud him and he was brought, reverentially but somewhat to his distress, up on the platform, there to be placed beside the chairman. For Darwin, the situation had its own anticlimax – he had come to hear about movement in plants, but, as he wrote to his son George, Sanderson spoke for so long about animals, "he never got to plants . . . & had to shut up without saying a word about them".

Truth to tell, adulation brought with it its share of small burdens and disappointments. Later in 1881, he was a delegate at the International Congress of Medicine, and so was one of the guests – the Prince of Wales was another – at the great luncheon at which the meeting was celebrated. For Darwin, however, as he explained, this time in a letter to his son William, the event "was a failure, as there was an immense crowd of all the greatest scientific swells and much delay and I was half dead before luncheon began. I sat down opposite the Prince and between Virchow and Donders*, who both spoke bad English incessantly and this completed my killing . . . The Prince spoke only a few civil words to me. The Crown Prince of Germany was there, to whom I was presented, and he looks a very nice and sensible and fine man." This, of course, was not a verdict Darwin's countrymen endorsed when, during the First World War over thirty years later, they were to nickname him "Kaiser Bill". At this luncheon, Huxley was also a guest. Seeing Darwin shaking hands with sundry savants, he came over and gravely asked if he too "might be introduced to Mr. Darwin". When the honour was done him, he bowed most profoundly – "like a foreigner", wrote Darwin, "until his back was horizontal". Such are the schoolboy jokes of genius.

---

* Rudolf Virchow, one of the founding theorists of modern medicine, contributed greatly to the understanding of cell function; F.C. Donders was an eminent Dutch physiologist and occasional correspondent of Darwin.

Yet another consequence of the esteem in which people now held him – though one of a very different kind – was the Rich inheritance, a curious tribute from which he himself was never to prosper directly. An Honorary Fellow of Caius College, Cambridge, Anthony Rich belonged, with his sister, to the last remaining generation of a moderately wealthy family, owners of property in the City of London. He had decided that his heir would be someone who had spent his life in work beneficial to mankind; Charles Darwin was the person he had chosen. Rich, aged seventy-four, and his sister, a year younger, would retain the property until both had died, after which it would pass on to Darwin or his heirs. Since the income from the buildings, which stood on Cornhill, amounted to something over £1,000 a year, it would made, as Darwin wrote to Erasmus, "a fine addition for our children". It was to be 1891 before Rich actually died and the Darwin children came into his inheritance (with Huxley receiving Rich's house and its contents, all of which he promptly sold), but that would not have altered Darwin's verdict: "The whole affair has astonished me greatly & has pleased me much".

Throughout these years, however, there runs the dark note of Time's unwinding. Darwin's nostalgia became keener. In 1874 he wrote, almost audibly sighing, to his old companion, Fox, that "as for one's body growing old there is no help for it, & I feel as old as Methusalem [*sic*]; but not much in mind, except that I think one takes everything much more quietly, as not signifying so much. And as you say one looks backwards much more than forwards & can never expect to have nearly such keen enjoyment as in old days, as when we breakfasted together at Cambridge & shot in Derbyshire."

Curious echoes of his youthful days punctuated the calm of these final years. A man named Thomas Burgess wrote to him; he had been a sailor on the *Beagle* – did Darwin remember his "calling you upon Deck one night, when the Beagle lay in Chilnay, to witness the Volcanic Eruption of a Mountain when I was on duty on the Middle Watch, and you exclaimed, O my God, what a Sight, I shall never forget." He had served in the Cheshire Constabulary and had now retired on a pension of £32 a year – a sum that puts Darwin's £7,000 and more into some perspective. In a later letter he asked for one of Darwin's books, none of which he had ever read. "I should like to have the opportunity in my Lifetime, which cannot be so long at the longest. If you should condescend to send me one with your name as a present to one of the Beagle's Crew I should think it a small fortune. I feel honoured by you sending me your Pothograph [*sic*] and I shall prize it while I live . . ."

From Stoke-on-Trent there arrived a letter that evoked memories from an even earlier time. "Some 56 years ago you, as a senior at Shrewsbury, took me a walk along the Severn banks, with your botanical box in hand to collect specimens of wild flowers." The letter had been sent by a man named E.J. Edwards. He had, he said, come across a portrait, presumably of Dr. Robert, since it was "of one who was very kind to me always as a Shrewsbury School boy – as he was to several other hungry schoolfellows whom he admitted to his table on the monthly Holiday Saturday. Yourself or some of the family will I am sure like to have it."

And there arrived one morning a letter that must for the moment have rolled away all the years to the happy, simple time before the *Beagle*, when everything had seemed certain in the present and possible in the future: health and sport and love, and the easy planes of a familiar land, peopled by those who posed no threat, had surrounded him then with a comfort he was only to achieve again through the deliberate circumscriptions of his life at Down.

> Yesterday I read in a leading article of the *Times*, 'Of all our living Men of Science, none have laboured longer, or to more splendid purpose than Mr. Darwin', & it recalled to my mind, your boyish assertion, made many many years ago, that "if ever Eddowes" newspaper alluded to you, as 'our deserving Fellow Townsman', your ambition would be amply gratified' – So you may believe with what sincere gratification, I see your fondest hopes more than gratified & realized – you have hosts of friends, but few older, or more sincere than myself, for you are associated with the happiest memories of my youth . ...

Thus Sarah Haliburton, who had been Owen (and Williams in the meantime, until widowed), leaping the years with a bravery perhaps customary with her. "My dear Charles Darwin", she had begun, and added, with a nervous coquetry, in brackets, "For I really cannot address you in any other way". She imagined old William Owen's delight in Darwin's success – "I can fancy his carrying that newspaper about, & reading it to everybody". Perhaps, she suggested, they might yet meet.

Darwin was even less tentative than she: "Dear Sarah", he wrote, and then congratulated himself with, "You see how audaciously I begin; but I have always loved and shall ever love this name . . . I often think of the old days and of the delight of my visit to Woodhouse, and of the deep debt of gratitude which I owe to your father". He wanted to see her again, but not at Down, "for we feel very old and have no amusement, and lead a solitary life". By 1880, this was no longer as true as it had been in 1860, but it seemed to Darwin sufficient reason to arrange a meeting in Erasmus's house. So they met, in the house in Queen Anne's Street, early in December, 1880, the two old people; he with his wife, his brother, his reputation; she almost certainly alone, twice widowed, repository of whatever memories remained of the young Charles delirious with summer among the strawberry beds, a youth in whom could be discerned no lineament of the sage he would become, a young man besotted with the hunt, with guns, with horses, and perhaps with her beautiful young sister: a young man in whom passion had not yet guttered out. Afterwards she wrote to him, to tell him of her pleasure at seeing him again, "& to feel assured that the old times are still fresh in your memory, & your friendly regard unabated . . ." In a postscript she added, "Our meeting had but one drawback, you called me '*Mrs Haliburton*' twice, this offence must not be repeated –" For a moment, the old Sarah appears, mock-astringent, flirtatious, safely imperious with beauty to protect her, her tone, precisely remembered or never relinquished, authentically that of the Owen sisters of Woodhouse, pursuing their "shootables" in a Shropshire now far off, long vanished, a golden land, innocent and undisturbed, before the railways, before natural selection, before the withering of youth.

By contrast, therefore, the present was dark, and darkening further: Darwin belonged to a generation now beset by death. In 1875, Fanny Allen died, Emma's aunt, the last survivor of her mother's generation. She was ninety-four. She begged her relatives to feel no sorrow: "There is nothing in my death that ought to grieve them, for death at my great age is rest", she wrote in a message left for them. Earlier that year, Darwin had suffered a harder blow – Sir Charles Lyell had died. For all the impatience Darwin came to feel over Lyell's equivocations about natural selection, he could not forget that in Lyell's acceptance of him he had found the first serious confirmation of his own scientific destiny. The man whose book had re-organized his vision had offered him respect and friendship; his mentor had taken him to be his peer. He wrote to Lyell's secretary, Miss Buckley, "I never forget that almost everything which I have done in science I owe to the study of his great works". To Hooker he confessed, "how vividly I can recall my first conversation with him, and how he astonished me by his interest in what I told him". Gloomily he added, "Well, he is gone, and I feel as if we were all soon to go".

Poor, bent Elizabeth Wedgwood, Josiah Wedgwood's oldest child, who all her life had treated Emma more like her daughter than her younger sister, died at her house in Down in 1880. Her twisted spine, her frailty, later her failing eyesight, always drew out the concern of others; when she tapped her way into Down House, calling for Emma, her dog, Tony, beside her, Emma would drop whatever she was doing and answer the summons. Fifteen years older than she, Elizabeth had taken over Maer from their mother when Emma was still a child, and respect as well as affection ordered Emma's attitude.

Ten months later, Erasmus died, in August, 1881. His tall elegance, his charm and wit, had declined at last into melancholia; he had begun to find life wearisome. As a boy, as a young man, he had had a brilliance that must have raised his own expectations of success and fulfilment. He had maintained a small laboratory in his apartment long after he had settled in London. Had he hoped that somehow his dilettante curiosity might be translated into discovery and fame? He had spent his time among the intellectuals and *literati* of the capital – had he hoped perhaps to become one of them, to bring out as they did some series of elegant or perceptive volumes? It is hard not to believe he did, in that dreamer's way that postpones action until all possibility of action has passed. Hard not to believe, too, that sometimes, alone in the tasteful comforts of his little house, he did not contrast the fundamental emptiness of his own life with all the richness that his younger brother had achieved. Both fame and family had evaded him, while Charles, the dullard in the sporting field while he had been the young hopeful at Cambridge, had gathered in both. Not that it would have made him envious – he had neither the temperament nor the energy for a feeling so ungenerous and extreme – but it might at times have saddened him. With the passing of the years, even his small function as the companion of the talented had almost vanished. Harriet Martineau was long gone; Carlyle had died that February. It is no wonder that, tired, he had turned away from life.

He had been ill earlier in the year, but had seemed to recover. Darwin had reported to his son George that "Uncle Ras . . . now sits up in his bedroom for some hours in the afternoon & is very cheerful". But he was not cheerful, and he was not recovering. Writing of him after his death, Darwin said in a letter to Hooker, "He always appeared to me the most pleasant and clearest headed man, whom I have ever known. London will seem a strange place to me without his presence . . ." In a long black cloak, Darwin stood, a cold rain falling, and watched his brother being buried; on his face, his son Francis recalled, there was "a grave look of sad reverie". Bit by bit his own history was being eroded; those among whom he had been young were vanishing. Every such loss loosened his own hold on life. Now Erasmus, who had been there always, ally, guide, observer, friend, had slipped away and left him, in some sense, alone.

The world he had constructed, however, held fast. There was a constant coming and going of his children at Down House, maintaining by their visits the integrity of his citadel. Indeed, when Francis's wife had died in childbirth, in 1875, he had retreated to the safety of those familiar walls; installed at Down House again, he became Darwin's assistant and secretary, the only one of the sons to continue a naturalist's work into another generation, becoming himself a scientist of repute as well as the meticulous biographer of his father.

Darwin had always been affectionate and liberal with his children, careful not only of their welfare, but also of their autonomy. In their childhood, as George was to recall, they had regarded him "with a sort of familiar awe", while his study had seemed "a sort of sacred place not to be invaded in the morning without some really urgent cause, such as a piece of string or a footrule". Only when they had interrupted three or four times would they face the paternal edict, "You really must *not* come again!" It did not prevent them running about the house, shouting at their play, or rolling across the drawing room floor on the castors of the microscope chair, propelling themselves with a walking stick. Never at any point did Darwin attempt to force knowledge on them, or direct them towards the science in which he had spent his life. "When however we freely exhibited any wish to learn, there was no amount of trouble which he would not take . . ."

Now they had grown up, and for Darwin had become a constant source of pride; he had the happiness that stems from success at the ordinary business of living – perhaps even more difficult to achieve than success in one's career. When, a little belatedly, William became engaged in 1877, Darwin wrote to his American fiancée, Sara Sedgwick, "I can say with absolute truth that no act or conduct of William has ever in his whole life caused me one minute's anxiety or disapproval. His temper is beautifully sweet and affectionate and he delights in doing little kindnesses." It is no wonder that, many years later living as a widower in London, William should have reminded some of his uncle, Erasmus, whose treatment of others had been so similar.

Early in 1880, Horace, the youngest son, married Lord Farrer's daughter, Ida – one by one, the children stepped away into their own lives. Yet the affection remained; that same January, they clubbed together to buy their father a vast fur-coat, spending on him a sum that he would never have laid out for his own comfort. Francis crept conspiratorially into the study and left it there, furry side out, for Darwin to discover before setting off on his afternoon walk. "My dear Children", he wrote in thanks, "I have just found on my table your present of the magnificent fur-coat. If I have to travel in the winter it will be a wonderful comfort . . . The coat, however, will never warm my body so much as your dear affection has warmed my heart."

In the summer of 1881, they went away for the last of the leisurely family holidays which had throughout the years sustained them. The house they took was in Patterdale, in the Lake District, not far from Ullswater. "This place is magnificently beautiful", wrote Darwin to the absent George, "but the weather is nothing less than damnably cold, & this precludes much enjoyment. There was snow on the mountains yesterday . . ." But to Hooker he was more despondent, complaining that "idleness is downright misery to me, as I find here, as I cannot forget my discomfort for an hour. I have not the heart or strength at my age to begin any investigation lasting years, which is the only thing which I enjoy . . . So I must look forward to Down graveyard as the sweetest place on earth." He spent his time quietly, nevertheless, watching the others leave to take pleasant little outings by boat; when he climbed a nearby rock, "a fit of his dazzling came on", as Emma described it, and he was forced to come down again.

That October – perhaps already wearing his fur-coat – he went on what was to be his last visit to Cambridge, to spend a week with Horace and his wife, pregnant with their first child – "our happy week at Cambridge", Emma called it. As their "chief dissipation", they had taken the tram to King's College Chapel, to hear the choir singing in that tall, narrow, marvellously sculpted box where Darwin half a century before had shivered at the glories of the music.

In December, visiting Henrietta in London, Darwin found that his pulse had become irregular. Emma went to consult their physician, Dr. Clarke. "I told him about the pulse, and he said that shewed that there was some derangement of the heart, but he did not take a serious view of it." Darwin himself was less insouciant; to his friend, the geologist John Judd, he said that he had had his warning and that he was certain his heart was seriously affected.

At the end of February, 1882, Emma reported to George, "F. is pretty well but sometimes has returns of the pain that stops him walking & makes him afraid of going further than the sandwalk." A week later, on 7 March, Darwin had so sharp an attack that he reached the house with some difficulty. From then on, the Sandwalk, too, became part of the world that was bit by bit being filched from him. Dr. Clarke came to examine him, "& he fully hopes & believes", Emma assured her son, "that with care to avoid every exertion that brings on the pain it will either be quite overcome or kept in abeyance . . ." By 14 March, she could write that "F., each day . . . has been a little stronger & less uncomfortable than the last", though he remained "oddly weak".

Dr. Clarke, however, had been very hurried in his examination; he had arrived late, spent no more than half an hour and, to the distress of the Darwins, refused a fee – "it was most unsatisfactory", commented Emma. They decided to consult a rising young metropolitan physician, Dr. Norman Moore, whose diagnosis was somewhat less severe than Clarke's had been. This reassured Emma and may have lightened Darwin's gathering depression. By now, the entire outside world was barred to Darwin; he came downstairs, sometimes for most of the day, but he no longer went into the garden. A surgeon named Alfrey was consulted, adding his expertise to Dr. Moore's. But through the first half of April Darwin's chest pains persisted, sometimes waxing, sometimes waning, but never really leaving him. In his diary his notes tell of "very slight attack Pain" or "Some pain" or "only trace of pain", but make no mention of any lengthy relief. He was taking amyl nitrite tablets for the *angina pectoris* from which he was suffering, and these sometimes gave him a little ease. On 15 April he noted "no pain & no dose at Dinner – dropped down", an entry recording his giddiness while eating that day, and his fainting as he tried to reach the sofa.

During the night of 18 April, he woke up with the severe pains of heart disease, roused Emma and sent her to fetch the amyl nitrate he needed from his study. By the time she came back, he had become unconscious. Brandy revived him, but he felt that he was probably passing through his final moments. It was just after midnight; he told Emma those things he wanted her to know, and which she never repeated, then added, "and be sure to tell all my children to remember how good they have always been to me." He paused, then murmured, "I am not the least afraid to die". Dr. Allfrey arrived, summoned by one of the household, and stayed with Darwin until eight o'clock.

All that morning, Darwin suffered from nausea, retching and, at times, vomiting. "If I could but die!" he muttered again and again. Francis and Henrietta were at his bedside, from time to time offering sips of the neat whisky Alfrey had prescribed. It was decided to call in Dr. Moxon, of Guy's Hospital, to add his expertise to that of the other medical men, but until he arrived the family could do no more than continue their anxious nursing. The entire house now had for its nucleus and focus the old, bearded man, beset and breathless under the covers of his bed. Emma had through all these hours maintained her usual controlled practicality, but her underlying anguish was clear; she was persuaded to take an opium pill and lie down for a rest. Darwin, bloodless, all his strength gone, slept, woke to his feebleness, within minutes slipped into his uneasy doze again: "It is wonderful how I keep dropping off to sleep every minute", he said. Francis lifted his hand, pale now and covered with a cold mortuary sweat, to try and take his pulse, but it was too weak even to be perceived.

Just before half past three in the afternoon, Darwin murmured, "I feel as if I would faint". Henrietta, calm despite her distress, asked Francis to call their mother. Emma hurried in at once. Three teaspoonfuls of whisky brought Darwin once more back to consciousness. He struggled to sit up; Emma tried to make him lie flat, but he would not and so they propped him against his pillows. After a few moments, his eyes closed again; his breathing became thicker, louder, more desperate. From downstairs there came the ringing of the door bell: Moxon and Allfrey had arrived. Like Emma, however, like Henrietta and Francis, like the silent servants, they could do no more than watch, and wait for that terrible breathing to stop.

Darwin's study, still to be seen at Down House.

4

Late April: the world beginning again. Outside, blackbird and thrush worked their way busily towards an evening of song. Within, Darwin, dying, slipped into the waiting dimension of legend. In that moment, the conventional man of family, living out his domestic, middle-class round, and the intellectual, searching with a demonic intensity for evidence to support his palatial hypotheses, were absorbed by, recreated as, the legendary hero of science. This is the figure whose transforming presence bestrides the century that has passed since then. For some, a little absurdly, he remained the demon he had seemed in 1860. Their myth was at once dark and ridiculous. It was the Darwin of their nightmares with whom, twelve years after this deathbed afternoon, the Lord Himself, they claimed, signalled his discontent. At that time, the people of Darwin's native Shrewsbury were proposing to set up a monument to his memory. An obdurate minority stood out against this decision – they wanted no sign in their town that the godless Darwin had been born and bred there. At the height of this controversy, a gale came slashing across the West Midlands and tore down the spire of St. Mary's, one of Shrewsbury's churches.

For its vicar, Rev. Newdigate Poyntz, the message was clear and indisputable: God had expressed his anger, Shrewsbury, intent on celebrating a heretic, had been given its divine warning. The *Shrewsbury Chronicle,* however, remarked that "the fall would have been much more impressive, and much more likely to have its intended effect, had it happened upon a windless night"; it also pointed out that "a judgement at St. Chad's, where the Vicar is supporting the memorial, would seem more appropriate than a disaster at St. Mary's, where Mr. Poyntz is free from any complicity in the matter".

Thus the swift rationality of the nineteenth century robbed us of the simplest legend: Darwin the God-hater, the Anti-Christ, Faust-Darwin in his pride challenging the Lord. Three centuries earlier, the falling of that church steeple might have become the nucleus for a whole bundle of folk tales. The actual legend that grew up was subtler, less precise, more pervasive – and we are not done with it yet. For many, of course, Darwin has remained little more than a name, an undefined presence behind a doctrine that continues to be controversial, or is at best reluctantly accepted. For others, who may nevertheless be less than clear about how natural selection actually works, he stands in the lists of history as one of the great champions of reason. For those who accept this aspect of his legend, the success of his theory appears as one of the crucial trimphs of truth over belief, of proof over revelation. Refined, this version of the myth develops into that of Darwin as an archetype: the Scientist. Misunderstood, assailed by prejudice, the Scientist stubbornly pursues his self-imposed mission. Eventually – from this side of the grave or the other – he manages to convince the world of the truth and value of his discoveries. In Darwin's case, the tale is made sweeter by the fact that he lived to see his victory. There is, as we have seen, much that is true in this view of him. If that were all, however, it would be no more than might be said of half a hundred similar researchers. What gives Darwin's legend its particular energy is the revolutionary nature, for most people almost undiminished, of what he proposed. His ideas on human descent touched so profound a nerve that the anguish he caused has not yet ceased its reverberations.

Nor is this simply a matter of sentiment, the result of some romantic but popular misconception. In the most factual world of all, his work continues: his presence permeates the sciences in which he worked. A century after his death, his successors continue to flesh out the theories which are their inheritance from him. The most recent and most controversial developments in evolutionary studies, the theories propounded by the sociobiologists, hark most rigorously back to his doctrines. A great array of academic specializations, some old, some new – embryology, biogeography, anthropology, systematics, genetics, ethology, palaeonotology, animal psychology and a dozen others – extend, modify or continue work that Darwin either began or to which he made substantial contribution. Beyond that, the principle of natural selection (derived as it may partly have been from Adam Smith's theories, then all-pervasive, of a fiercely competitive economy) has become a staple of the everyday rhetoric through which we now define ourselves.

All of us, in other words, have been forced to accommodate ourselves to the inescapable transformation worked by his ideas. Finally, it is the superhuman scale of this transformation that underpins the legend: in the space of two decades, Darwin redesigned the natural world. That is to say, he altered the way most of us in the developed world perceive the cosmic order. Himself a man who drew back from metaphysical speculation, he nevertheless gave a new significance to such abstractions as Divinity, Nature, Time and Death. He relocated God and redefined his functions. To mankind he gave a new and perhaps diminished character. Reorganizing the history of life on his planet, he redirected humanity's gaze from the past of Eden to a future opened up by change. Most of these things he did not do knowingly; they flowed inevitably from the comprehensive hypothesis that both ordered and crowned his scientific life. All of them, and more, happened as a direct result of his work. It is this that invests him with the grandeur of his legend.

Yet for several decades after his death it did not appear that this was to be the likely outcome. The absence of a genetic theory able to accommodate what Darwin had said were the evolutionary facts had sapped much of his reputation. The failure of pangenesis under dissection and experiment and the lack of an alternative had left unanswered those major criticisms of Darwin's work which had been so succinctly marshalled by Fleeming Jenkins. Natural scientists were discouraged: most of them believed in what Darwin had taught them, all the evidence of physiology and palaeontology confirmed it, yet they had no explanation for how it worked. As the biologist William Bateson, born some eighteen months after the publication of *The Origin*, was to write early this century, "In the study of evolution progress was well nigh stopped. The more vigorous, perhaps the more prudent, had left this field of science to labour in others where the harvest is less precarious and the yield more immediate".

The search for a solution drew scientists not only into the field, the hothouse, the dissecting room and the laboratory, but also into the library to see what clues had been left in the books and papers of their predecessors. And it was there that they found details of the research that was to validate and so give new life to the Darwinian hypothesis. Tschermak in Germany, Correns in Austria and de Vries in Holland all came independently upon the forgotten papers of that forgotten monk, Gregor Mendel, left disregarded for over thirty years in the *Proceedings* of the Natural History Society of Brünn (now Brno). Thus resurrected, they were at once seen to have a potential ignored before: men now were ready, were looking, for the information they contained. Bateson, who translated these articles, wrote the retrospective sentences quoted above in the preface to his book, *Mendel's Principles of Heredity*. He added, "Each of us who now looks at his own patch of work sees Mendel's clue running through it: whither this clue will lead we dare not yet surmise".

In 1902, when that was written, the picture was still unclear. For, curiously, biologists did not at once bring Darwin and Mendel together in a marriage of scientific convenience. Indeed, basing himself on Mendel's work, the Dutch botanist, de Vries, proposed his own theory of mutational change, apparently superseding with it Darwin's earlier hypothesis. For if organisms could be altered quite dramatically at a single Mendelian stroke, what value lay in Darwin's cumbersome scheme of small variations and natural selection? It was to be another twenty years before the geneticists, J.B.S. Haldane and Sewall Wright, and above all the statistician, Sir Ronald Fisher, began to publish the work that was to create modern genetics and, in the process, rehabilitate Darwin.

It became clear that mutations as such simply occured: in themselves they had no value and were, indeed, more likely to be harmful than beneficial. It was the action of the prevailing circumstances that determined whether they were of use or not. In stable conditions and within an established species, natural selection normally acted precisely as Darwin's critical contemporaries had said it did – it maintained the genetic integrity of the species. But the survival of many mutations as recessive genes meant that there were, locked away in the collective storehouse of the species, an unknown number of possible, as yet unrealized, variant forms. When the patterns of climate or predation, geological activity or food supply began to change, this spread of available variation offered the species new directions for survival.

Once it became clear that natural selection had precisely that importance in biology that Darwin had claimed for it, it became possible to find solutions for many of the problems that had plagued Darwin himself. Mendelian genetics proved to be the key to most of the mysteries which had so long and so often provided his opponents with the grounds for their most damaging criticisms. The calculations of those who believed in "blending" – that in four generations only one-sixteenth of a new characteristic would remain to any one individual – could now be wiped for ever off the scientific blackboard. Where offspring have characteristics which appear to blend those of their parents, it is now known that this results from several genes working as one. It is such gene-clusters that lead to the continuous variation which for Darwin was always the raw material of evolutionary change.

This is not to say, however, that Darwin's ideas have blossomed into a full-blown, unchallengeable law. Some of the old debates continue, albeit in modified form. We are, for example, born with some adaptations which we might instead have expected to develop through use – the lines on our hands are one such instance, and the thickening of the skin on our heels is another. And there are strange anomalies, recently discovered, in the body's reaction to foreign tissue: immunities acquired very early by one generation seem to reappear in the next. Is that dry sound we hear the ghostly chuckling of Lamarck? There is still some discussion over where the burden of evolution lies, with the species or the individual. Like Darwin, most biologists now feel that advantage must accrue first to the individual if a new adaptation is eventually to alter a species. This view, however, has not yet convinced all those who think they can discern some principle giving first place to species survival; they feel that at times this transcends any drive ensuring individual well-being, leading to the sacrifice of single members for the benefit of the group. For them, the question remains open. Such special adaptations as the eye, delicate and complex organs with specific functions, also continue to stimulate the critics. Beyond their doubts lingers a hankering after Design, the word that sums up the cosmic operations of some transcendental artificer, and it remains true that there is no intrinsic reason why a world picture based upon Design, as Paley's was, should be wrong.

In the United States can be found the major bastions of opposition to Darwinism, just as it is there that Darwinian orthodoxy has been pushed to its extremes. It is only just over fifty years since the propounding in schools of natural selection fell foul of the law in Tennessee, and in what became known as the "Scopes Monkey Trial" a young teacher was indicted for spreading these atheistic doctrines. Today, wealthy foundations pursue what is known as "creationism", putting their effort and their money into an energetic attempt to discredit Darwin's conclusion. The passing of the years has not, despite the slow accumulation of evidence supporting natural selection, offered the debate a really decisive fact; and the opposition to the Darwinian position has remained in remarkably good fettle.

There are also difficulties arising from the underlying logic of evolutionary theory, the most fundamental statement of which has been attacked as a tautology. It seems to say no more than that survivors survive. If true, this would be self-evident without being explanatory. Certainly the scale of evolution is so great and its unfolding so slow that it defies human observation. In the laboratories of the geneticists, the generations of the fruitfly demonstrate the mechanisms of inheritance, but the work remains, in essence, that of Darwin's pigeon breeders. It is suggestive, but hardly conclusive. Evolution itself eludes the scientific eye – and, say its critics, since it can therefore never be falsified, it can also never be proven.

Even if evolution could be directly observed, however, any formulation about it would remain, in the critics' terms, tautologous. That is, anything precisely rather than generally true about it must, in the nature of things, be retrospective. Evolution is a responsive process, the result of a continuous interaction between organism and environment. The evolutionary response can never be predicted, because the constantly shifting variables in the environment make it impossible to foresee what particular adaptation will ensure future survival. For example, whether thick fur will do so must depend upon the weather. Are we about to enter a new Ice Age, or will the "greenhouse effect" bring tropical heat to the poles? Even if the temperature drops, will that make thick-furred animals such desirable prey for shivering humans that they will soon face extinction? Or will shivering humans instead conserve and farm them? In circumstances so beset by unknowns – and one could add food supply, altered habits of predation, inter-species rivalry, and a transformed habitat as other factors – no statement about possible survivors can avoid tautology. Since it cannot in the nature of things be accurately predictive, in other words, such a statement must be retrospective. And no retrospective formulation can avoid that suspect structure: the survivors are those that have survived.

There are, however, various incidental facts and verifiable predictions that may be taken to validate the central thesis of evolutionary studies. Evolutionists will state, for example, that in a species not in decline there will always be more offspring than parents and thus, very soon, more offspring than can be sustained in the prevailing conditions. Simple statistics confirm this. They will state further that such offspring will always vary both among themselves and compared with their parents, within the range that specifies the type. They will state that, given the numbers of offspring in the environmental circumstances, not all can expect to survive to maturity. Evolutionists would predict that in a species long suited to its environment, those which most nearly conformed to type would be the likeliest to survive; given an abrupt alteration in conditions, however, the prediction would be either the extinction of the species, or the rapid spread of an adaptation ensuring the survival of those individuals in whom it had developed. Both observation and experiment seem to prove such predictions right.

More generally, perhaps, sexual reproduction itself becomes cumbersome and meaningless the moment one removes the evolutionary theories that provide its relevance. It is, in other words, an unnecessary biological complication if variation is not to be its outcome, and variation has no function if it is not to be the prelude to selection. In a non-evolving world, the asexual reproduction of offspring identical with their parents seems the simplest way to continue a species. Alternatively, there might in those circumstances be a provision even simpler: immortality. Death makes little sense in a world where change has no priority.

The debates surrounding evolution and Darwin's theory of natural selection never entirely dwindle away to nothing. Their continuing intensity, whatever one's own conclusions may be, demonstrates the reality of this legendary Darwin who began to come into his own at the moment of his death. It is as if he were still in his quiet retreat at Downe, watching and listening while the savants of the world fight out the battles his ideas have started. Distant giants – Galileo, Descartes, Newton – take their places quietly in history; even the more recent ones begin to lose their relevance. Darwin's near contemporary, Karl Marx, petrifies into granite within the lowering institutions that now protect his name; year by year, the influence of Freud continues to wane. But around the ideas of Darwin the same arguments rage as did a hundred years ago; their story remains unfinished. Certainly his thesis has become the central orthodoxy of biology – reinforced by the convinced materialism of today's sociobiologists – yet the voices of the heretics and dissidents have not been stilled. In the last analysis, the issue remains undecided. Around it, controversy quickens, curiosity focuses, interest constantly revives, just as they did – often in the same terms – while Darwin was a direct observer. To that extent, he remains a participant, the sense of his presence permeating the biological sciences. Nor is this surprising: his subject, after all, was the shape taken by life itself.

When one looks back to the genesis of his major theory, it is hard not to believe that Darwin's first vision was one that realized even as it defined the unity of all things. In the words of Sylvan S. Schweber, in his article *The origin of the* Origin *revisited*, "by July 1838 Darwin had a unitary evolutionary view of everything around him: the planetary system, our own planet, its geology, its climate, its living organisms and their social organizations". The whole of existence was one continuous and interlocking process, in his eyes. He refused to categorize its multifarious manifestations, nor to fix them forever in their places, as though the cosmos were some comprehensive entomological cabinet. He saw that life *was* – no more and no less. It existed and, being what it was, might be expected to be volatile. He looked across the ages and saw the species in their perpetual flux, itself a response to the perpetual flux of their environment. He saw that some had perished so that others could arise, saw all struggle, watched the victors reach for self-awareness. He understood early that each of them was a part of all, and that finally there existed only one all-embracing phenomenon.

This overwhelming vision had perhaps come to him during the *Beagle*'s voyage home from Australia; certainly after his return to England he had pursued it with an utterly absorbing devotion, through periods of intense mental effort, to a conclusion of convincing clarity. The singleminded penetration of this effort had given him an insight into the minutiae of nature that allowed him to elucidate a great variety of its particular mysteries. This appears to have reinforced the respect he had already learned for its laws, and that respect came in many ways to take the central place of a religion in his life. As a religion, it seems to have extended its ethical sanctions to cover what, from every other point of view, he knew was his iconoclasm. Sustained in this way, he found the courage to carry his investigations forward through the years to their unavoidable end of worldwide controversy.

An illuminating vision, an absorbing mental effort, a pervasive sense of certainty: the combination suggests a man seized and utterly changed by a profound inner experience. Whatever brought this about, the analogies that spring to mind come less from the world of science than from that of deep meditation and religious trance. Those who have travelled to the limits of human spirituality bear witness that their reward is a direct awareness of an underlying cosmic unity. In the late Middle Ages, Meister Eckhardt wrote, "Say, Lord, when is a man in mere understanding? I say to you, 'When a man sees one thing separated from another'. And when is he above mere understanding? That I can tell you: 'When he sees all in all . . .' "

It is not to stake a claim for Darwin as a mystic to suggest that an unprecedented intensity of intellectual effort during the weeks when he was first attempting to grasp all that he had seen on his journey had ended in a moment of profound illumination. His inner absorption may well in such a period of mental excitement have paralleled the ecstacy of the religious visionary (one recalls him as a child, so deeply in his mysterious dreams that he could fall while walking). The outcome may have been a flashing vision of nature as an all-embracing unity, a moment of insight so profound that it brooked no further argument. Certainly by the time he came home, or at the latest shortly afterwards, he had become convinced that species were mutable. What occupied him in the years that followed, the years of the *Notebooks*, was the question of how exactly their transmutations had taken place. The foundations of his theory had been laid, and he never in all the difficult decades that followed doubted their solidity. He could not have been more unshakeable in his conviction if he had indeed seen, directly perceived, the undifferentiated singularity which is the universe of the mystic. The clarity of such a vision, if it ever came to him, will not have seemed more mysterious than any other moment at which one becomes aware of the truth, yet the truth in this case was so fundamental, so pervasive, so transforming, that its effect on his life – the way he thought, the way he lived, his ambitions, his career – could not have been more complete. The entire current of his existence changed; it could have changed no further if the experience had in fact been spiritual rather than intellectual. And perhaps the total concentration of a powerful mind may create such an effect, even in a man untrained in the subjective disciplines of the religious.

In any case, clearly something convinced him, and his conviction did lead him to see the earth and all that appertained to it as one unified process. But not even his years of devotion to this vision could, for all his success, do more than set in motion a new kind of science; it was a process which, once begun, could have no ending unless it was discredited. Not yet disproved, it continues into our own day. Thus, as Darwin gasped away the last fractions of his physical self on that April afternoon a century ago, it is in this sense true to say that his greatest triumphs still lay ahead. Today he is known across the world, in a way that was not yet the case when he was alive: his legend now draws an undoubting respect to his name that was necessarily less common then – no one could be sure what people would be saying of him a hundred years on.

In the days immediately after his death, it was his warm and abiding humanity that drew the attention, and the grief. That he would become in some sense a legend already seemed inevitable to many; that the legend would survive for any length of time was less certain. For those at his bedside, little of this was important: the event was personal. Even for the world that awaited the news and would receive it with some distress, Darwin still retained the ordinariness of a contemporary; gigantic though he was acknowledged to be, he was still a human among humans, a sort of distant cousin, talked about, respected, flesh and blood – a member of the family. It is we, inheriting him, who are free to give him his legendary dimension; remembering rather than experiencing him, we have perhaps no choice. For Emma, on the other hand, the closest to him of all, he could be no more and no less than her husband.

5

"I was not unprepared", Emma wrote to Hensleigh, her brother, and Fanny, his wife.

> I felt 2 months (& before that in the winter – tho' that fear passed away) – that our secure happiness (& oh what happiness – but I have appreciated it all along – it seems now) was all shattered . . . The days have been filled up, with the arrival of all the dear sons on Thursday – Their grief so violent and affecting – it did me good too & made me cry . . . I hardly know how I shall get through my days so empty & desolate; but I do feel life worth having & that my children want me . . . I feel that the memory of his life is so full of sweetness that I shall always like to speak of him.

Her long, deep affection for Darwin shines through her words. Her grief marks them, but also her fundamental composure, her readiness to reach for new resources and create other meanings in her life. She was to live on many years, placidly gathering in love and respect, offering her strength to her children and grandchildren. For Darwin, meanwhile, there were other, grander obituaries, the measured verdict of the world he had left, the varied comments of the self-appointed jury of his peers.

When Darwin died, almost a quarter of a century had passed since the high point of the controversy aroused by *The Origin*. Even his opponents had long allowed him the stature of genius, and the numbers of those opponents had been dwindling year by year. His adherents and supporters could be found across the entire empire of science. His death was therefore the signal for the widespread admiration, and even affection, in which he had been held to be enthusiastically expressed. Nevertheless, even at this moment of valediction, there were some who clung to their doubts, and others to their enmity; the chorus was worldwide, but it was not without its discords.

The *Times* was quick to point out that the old quarrels – in which it had itself taken part, albeit not always on the same side – had long outworn their fury.

> The storm which hurled around *The Origin of Species* at its first appearance has subsided . . . The story of such scenes as those which took place at the celebrated meeting of the British Association at Oxford, in 1860, and of the battle royal between Bishop Wilberforce and Mr. Huxley, reads at the present

day like a scene from ancient history; like an episode in the persecution of Galileo, or a preliminary to the excommunication of Spinoza . . . Great as he was, wide as was the reach of his intelligence, what endeared him to his many friends, what charmed all those who were brought into even momentary contact with him, was the beauty of his character.

The conservative *Standard* phrased the historical argument rather more bluntly. "Time has toned down the irritability that Mr. Darwin's name first evoked". And its attitude to Darwin's future standing was equivocal. "What rank future generations may accord to the illustrious naturalist who has left us it is hard to say . . . Discoveries may be made . . . which may prove that Darwinism was all an unsubstantial dream." With a sigh, however, the newspaper finally accepted the realities: "Everything is possible, but these things, judging from the facts which are every day coming to light, are not probable". The weekly *Saturday Review* annexed Darwin to the transcendental cause. "The work of Mr. Darwin consisted in making it probable to civilized man that the history of animated nature on our globe had been different from that which it had been previously supposed to be . . . That the order of the universe is the order of a supreme mind working silently and closely through the ages, and not spasmodically through centuries, is now as much an accepted idea of civilized man as the theory of gravitation." The uncomfortable syntax suggests some uneasiness at this glib conclusion.

The Liberal *Daily News* was categorical in its praise. "Contemporary science in England boasts one indisputably great man, and we have lost him . . . His place, it is almost impossible to doubt, must be where Newton and where Kepler are, with Aristotle and Copernicus." The Unitarian *Spectator* thought very much the same. "By the death of Charles Darwin England has lost the most original, as well as far the most celebrated, of modern men of science – the one man whom European science would, with one voice, probably agree to consider the most eminent scientific writer and thinker of the present century". The *Morning Post,* as its High Church conservatism would lead one to expect, was less extravagant in its view, calling upon its own hero to set out the terms of its praises. "If, as Lord Beaconsfield said, a great man is one who changes the spirit of his age, then Darwin was a great man, and we who cannot respect all his theories can admire his life."

The *St. James's Magazine* saw Darwin as "not only a discoverer, but a captain and organizer of discovery . . . He not only knew, he was master of all his knowedge: to the power of a man of science he added the genius of a philosopher." *The Pall Mall Gazette*, the Liberal evening newspaper which had long supported him, wrote, "The bustle of daily politics is for the most part but dusty sterility compared with the vast effect of the labours of the thinker who from his tranquil hilltop in his little Kentish village shook the world . . . We have lost a man whose name is a glory to his country – one who belongs to that illustrious band of whom the Greek statesman said that the 'whole world is their tomb'."

In the United States, his death was received in terms no less laudatory. The New York *Herald* compared his life with that of Socrates, the *Tribune* thought him "a giant among his fellows". There had been some plans made to welcome him to America later that year, so that in much of what was written there was a discernible disappointment. In France, every Paris newspaper carried long obituaries. *La Liberté* wrote, "Charles Darwin occupies a place of his own in the scientific world, and the most implacable opponents of the doctrine of descent are unanimous in paying homage to his exceptional qualities. His doctrine has had a calamitous influence on our age, but Science can only feel grateful for the rich store of new ideas which she owes to him". *Le Temps*, though patriotically pointing out Lamarck's priority in proposing an evolutionary theory, added, "Darwin's great claim to originality is his discovery of the natural laws proving that theory. The mass of facts collected, classified and explained by this patient observer is truly marvellous." In *La France* his work was declared an epic – "the great poem of the genesis of the universe, one of the greatest that ever came from a human brain" – while he himself was compared not only with Leibnitz, Bacon and Descartes, but declared "worthy to rank with Homer and Virgil". It was the same in other countries – Germany, Holland, Austria: into the Babel that was Europe, his name, repeated from every corner, brought a momentary linguistic unity.

As this extraordinary paean rose from the journals and periodicals of the world, a universal sussuration of praise, Darwin's body lay amidst the mourning of Down House. But while the family grieved, and friends called in subdued succession to offer condolence and what comfort they could, there began throughout the country a slow swelling of opinion, a gathering demand that Darwin's body should lie among those of his peers, in Westminster Abbey. As the *Standard* said later, "It would have been a national reproach to have denied Charles Darwin a place with the illustrious dead who have made the country famous . . . to refuse national recognition of the labours of one so distinguished would to-day savour of the bigotry of dark and bygone ages." Twenty Members of Parliament, Lubbock amongst them, wrote to the Dean of Westminster: "We hope you will not think we are taking a liberty if we venture to suggest that it would be acceptable to a very large number of our countrymen of all classes and opinions that our illustrious countryman Mr. Darwin should be buried in Westminster Abbey." The Very Rev. G.G. Bradley, away on holiday, replied by telegram and, somewhat whimsically, in French, *"Oui sans aucune hesitation regrette mon absence"*.

Four horses drew the funeral car that carried Darwin's body from the peace of Down to the grandeur of the Abbey. The three younger sons, Francis, Leonard, and Horace, followed it on the sixteen miles of its final journey. In the gathering darkness of an April evening, William and George awaited their arrival. It was eight o'clock before the coffin, of plain, unpolished oak, was ready to be carried into that vast church. It was set in the chapel of St. Faith, between the south wall and the chapter house, a small, gloomy place of ancient stonework, weakly lit by two dim lanterns.

By eleven the next morning, that of 26 April, the mourners were beginning to assemble. The Lord President of the Council was there, The Speaker of the House of Commons, the Lord Mayor of London, the Chancellor of Oxford University; France, Italy, Germany and Spain were represented; the president of the Geographical Society had come, as had the president of the College of Surgeons; the Royal Society, the Linnean, Geographical, and Geological Societies, had sent almost every member of their councils; the Master of Christ's College was there, as was the Headmaster of Shrewsbury School. There were those too who, like Darwin himself, owed their position to nothing but their own achievements: Herbert Spencer, Max Müller, and a host of scientific and artistic notables, including, perhaps a little surprisingly, Thomas Hardy. But the Vice-Chancellor and Council of Cambridge University were absent – they had arranged to select their new Regius Professor of Hebrew on a day that, at such short notice, they had been unable to change. And no one in that distinguished congregation represented those who still survived from the *Beagle* expedition: Stokes lived in retirement far to the west, in Pembrokeshire, and Sulivan, like Stokes an admiral now, had been kept away by scarlet fever.

The procession of mourners formed just before noon. A pall of black velvet edged with white silk covered the coffin, hiding the little plate that carried Darwin's name and the dates of his birth and death. The pall-bearers came forward – the Dukes of Devonshire and Argyll; the Earl of Derby; the United States Minister, J. Russell Lowell; the president of the Royal Society; and Canon Farrar, the rural dean of Westminster, a Fellow of the Royal Society and author of that admonitory children's classic, *Eric or Little by Little*. With them stood a small phalanx of Darwin's closest friends, Huxley, Hooker, Lubbock, and Wallace. A diffused light flowed across the church, picking out the clear white flowers of the many wreaths. As the coffin was lifted and the procession began to move, it was met by a small group – Darwin's children, their husbands and wives, their closest connections. Only Emma had found it impossible to take part; her antidote to sorrow was solitude.

The voices of the choir spread under the Gothic vaulting. The clergy

Darwin's funeral in Westminster Abbey.

formed in surpliced ranks. The coffin stood before the communion rail as Purcell's music stitched the centuries together. An anthem, composed for the occasion, carried words selected from *Proverbs*: "Happy is the man that findeth wisdom, and getteth understanding. She is more precious than rubies, and all the things thou canst desire are not to be compared unto her . . .

The coffin was carried to where its grave awaited it, in the northeast corner of the nave. Now it was the grandeur of Handel that sounded: "His body is buried in peace, but his name liveth evermore". The coffin descended, its eternity congenially peopled – Sir John Herschel lay close by; Sir Isaac Newton's monument overlooked it. So the darkness took Darwin. He had left the world, but before his departure he had changed it utterly. So profound was that change, so extensive its consequences, so continuously present the world's response to it, that his death remains in some sense unreal, a necessary biological fiction disguising a profound intellectual truth. He remains amongst us, since he affects us as he did his contemporaries, through his ideas.

Darwin's loss as a person was felt by those who loved him, but they have died in their turn and their sense of loss has vanished with them. What remains to us is precisely the Darwin whom the great world honoured a hundred years ago; we know him through the same books, the same papers, the same observations and theories. As they did, we express our admiration and pick our quarrels, discovering his greatness at one time, his limitations at another. We continue to struggle with his thesis, trying to understand it, to recognize the world we live in through its terms, to apply its terms to what we discover of that world. His influence persists – even if only to tempt naturalists into flouting, denying or transcending it. The sciences he helped to found continue to animate their specialists, and to reach out for newer truths. There is no discontinuity between his work and that of his successors.

Darwin wanders equally through our century as he did through his own, constant, modest, endlessly perceptive, endlessly enquiring, his blue eyes watchful but friendly, his sage's beard gleaming; behind his tall brow questions spin and, any moment now, he will stop to bend and stare at something you and I have hardly noticed, have all our lives taken for granted. Be careful – what he asks when he straightens up may revolutionize your life.

Sources of Illustrations

The following organizations, to whom grateful acknowledgement is made, have given permission for illustrations to be reproduced in this volume:

The Mary Evans Picture Library, for illustrations on pp. 91, 95, 181, 196, 197, 198, 361, 443, 490, and 495; and for Plates 4 and 17.

The Mansell Collection, for illustrations on pp. 203, 330, 435, 461, and 521; and for Plates 7, 12, 15, 19, and 21.

The Royal College of Surgeons (Medical Illustration Support Service), for illustrations on pp. 131, 182, 426, and 507; and for Plates 2, 3, 8, 9, 11, 16, 20, 22, 23, and 27.

Cambridge University Library, for the illustration on p. 77; and for Plates 10 and 25.

The National Portrait Gallery, London, for Plates 1, 18, 24, and 26.

The British Museum (Natural History), for Plate 28.

Darwin Manuscripts

The main repository of Darwin manuscript material is the library of Cambridge University. The only collection remotely comparable with this is to be found in the library of the American Philosophical Society in Philadelphia. A reciprocal scheme now ensures that each holding is supplemented by microfilm material from the other, so that in one form or another almost the entire range of Darwin manuscripts will be available at both locations.

No other collections of any significance exist elsewhere, although there is material to be found at Down House, the Royal Society, the Royal College of Surgeons and the British Library.

Works by Darwin

Journal of Researches during the Voyage of the Beagle. 1840.
Structure and Distribution of Coral Reefs. 1842.
Geological Observations on Volcanic Islands and Parts of South America. 1846.
Monographs on the Cirripidae. 1851–54.
On the Origin of Species. 1859.
On the Various Contrivances by which British and Foreign Orchids are Fertilised by Insects. 1862.
Variation of Animals and Plants under Domestication. 1868.
Descent of Man. 1871.
Expression of Emotion in Man and Animals. 1872.
Insectivorous plants. 1875. (July).
Movements and Habits of Climbing Plants. 1875 (September).
Effects of Cross and Self fertilisation in the Vegetable Kingdom. 1876.
Different Forms of Flowers and Plants of the Same Species. 1877.
Life of Erasmus Darwin (with E. Krause). 1879.
Power of Movement in Plants. 1880.
Formation of Vegetable Mould Through the Action of Worms. 1881.

Life and Letters (edited by Francis Darwin). London 1887.
More Letters (edited by Francis Darwin and A.C. Seward). 1903.
Diary of the Voyage of HMS Beagle (edited by Nora Barlow), London, 1933.
Autobiography (edited by Nora Barlow). London, 1958.
Ornithological Notes (edited by Nora Barlow). British Museum of Natural History Bulletin, 1969.
Journal (edited by Sir Gavin de Beer). British Museum of Natural History Bulletin, 1969.
Notebooks on the Transmutation of Species (edited by Sir Gavin de Beer). British Museum of Natural History Bulletin, 1969.
Notebooks on the Transmutation of Species: Pages Excised by Darwin (edited by Sir Gavin de Beer). British Museum of Natural History Bulletin, 1971.
Collected Papers (edited by P.H. Barrett). Chicago, 1977.

Bibliography

Allen, D.E. *The Naturalist in Britain*. London. 1976.

Allen, G. *Darwin*. London, 1885.

Allen, M. *Darwin and his Flowers*. London, 1977.

Appleman, P. (editor) *Darwin: Texts, Backgrounds, etc*. New York, 1970.

Atkins, Sir H. *Down: the Home of the Darwins*. London, 1976.

Aveling, E. *The Religious Views of Charles Darwin*. London, 1884.

Barlow, N. (editor). *Charles Darwin and the Voyage of the Beagle*. London, 1945.

—— *Darwin and Henslow: the Growth of an Idea*. London, 1967.

Barnett, S.A. (editor). *A Century of Darwin*. London, 1958.

Bartholomew, M. "Lyell and Evolution". *British Journal for the History of Science*, vol. 6, 1972–73.

Benn, A.W. *A History of English Rationalism in the Nineteenth Century*. London, 1906.

Bettany, G.T. *Life of Darwin*. London, 1887.

Birdsell, J.B. *Human Evolution*. Chicago, 1972.

Bradford, G. *Darwin*. Boston, 1926.

Buckland, W. *On Geology and Mineralogy*. (Bridgewater Treatise). London, 1837.

Buffon, G.L.L. *Natural History*. 10 vols. London, 1807.

Burke, H.F. *Pedigree of the Family of Darwin*. Privately printed, 1888.

Butler, S. (editor). *Life and Letters of Dr. Samuel Butler*. 2 vols. London, 1896.

Cannon, W.F. "The Whewell-Darwin controversy". *Journal of the Geological Society*, London, vol. 132, 1976.

Carlyle, Jane W. *Letters and Memorials*. (edited by J.A. Froude). 3 vols. London, 1883.

—— *Letters to her Family*. (edited by L. Huxley). London, 1924.

Carlyle, T. *Reminiscences* (edited C.E. Norton). London, 1887.

Carroll, P.T. *Annotated Calendar of the Letters of Charles Darwin in the Library of the American Philosophical Association*. Wilmington, 1976.

Chambers, R. *Vestiges of the Natural History of Creation*. London, 1844.

Chancellor, J. *Charles Darwin*. London, 1974.

Colp, R. *To be An Invalid*. Chicago, 1977.

Cuvier, G. *Essay on the Theory of the Earth*. London, 1827.

—— *Recherches sur les ossements fossiles*. 10 vols. Paris, 1834.

Darlington, C.D. *Darwin's Place in History*. London, 1959.

Darwin, E. *The Botanic Garden*. London, 1824.

—— *Essential Writings* (edited D. King-Hele). London, 1968.

—— *The Temple of Nature*. London, 1825.

Dawkins, R. *The Selfish Gene*. Oxford, 1976.

De Beer, Sir G. (editor). *Charles Darwin and Alfred Russell Wallace: Evolution by Natural Selection*. Cambridge, 1958.

—— *Charles Darwin: Evolution by Natural Selection*. London, 1963.

Eisley, L. *Darwin and the Mysterious Mr. X*. London, 1979.

—— *Darwin's Century*. New York, 1958.

Ellegård, A. *Darwin and the General Reader*. London, 1958.

Essays and reviews. London, 1860.

Farrington, B. *What Darwin Really Said*. New York, 1966.

Fitzroy, R. *Narrative of the Surveying Voyages of HMS* Adventure *and* Beagle. London, 1839.

Gage, A.T. *History of the Linnean Society*. London, 1938.

Gillispie, C.C. *Genesis and Geology*. New York, 1959.

Gould, S.J. *Ever Since Darwin*. New York, 1977.

Gray, A. *Darwiniana* (edited H. Dupree). Cambridge, Mass., 1963.

Greenacre, P. *The Quest for the Father* (Freud memorial lecture). New York, 1963.

Greene, J.C. "Darwin and Religion". *Proceedings of the American Philosophical Society*, vol. 103, no. 5, 1959.

Gruber, H.E. and P.H. Barrett. *Darwin on Man*. London, 1974.

—— and V. Gruber. "The Eye of Reason: Darwin's Development During the *Beagle* Voyage". *Isis*, vol. 53, no. 172, 1962.

Hardy, Sir A. *The Living Stream*. London, 1965.

Hays, H.R. *Birds, Beasts and Men*. London, 1973.

Himmelfarb, G. *Darwin and the Darwinian Revolution*. New York, 1959.

Hofstadter, R. *Social Darwinism in American Thought*. Boston, 1955.

Hooker, Sir J.D. *Life and Letters* (edited by L. Huxley). London, 1918.

Huxley, Sir J. and H.B.G. Kettlewell. *Charles Darwin and his World*. London, 1965.

Huxley, T.H. *Darwiniana*. London, 1893.

Irvine, W. *Apes, Angels and Victorians*. London, 1955.

Jefferies, R. "First of the Vertebrates?" *New Scientist*, vol 80, no. 1131, 1978.

Jenyns, L. *Memoir of the Reverend John Stevens Henslow*. London, 1862.

Keith, Sir A. *Darwin Revalued*. London, 1955.

Kelly, M. "Robert Darwin's Splendid Character". *Isis*, vol. 55, no. 179, 1964.

Keynes, R.D. (editor). *The* Beagle *Record*. London, 1979.

King-Hele, D.G. *Doctor of Revolution: the Life and Genius of Erasmus Darwin*. London, 1977.

Kingsley, C. *Letters and Memories of his Life* (edited by Mrs. Kingsley). 2 vols. London, 1877.

Krause, E. *Erasmus Darwin* (with introductory essay by Charles Darwin). London, 1879.

Lack, D. *Darwin's Finches*. London, 1947.

Leakey, R.E. and R. Lewin. *Origins*. London, 1977.

Litchfield, H. (editor). *Emma Darwin: a Century of Family Letters*. 2 vols. London, 1915.

Lyell, Sir C. *The antiquity of man*. London, 1863.

—— *Life, Letters and Journals* (edited by Mrs. Lyell) 2 vols. London, 1881.

—— *Principles of Geology* (10th ed.) 2 vols. London, 1867.

Macbeth, N. *Darwin Retried*. New York, 1971.

Macleod, R.M. "Evolutionism and Richard Owen, 1830–1868." *Isis*, vol. 56, no. 203, 1965.

Malthus, T.R. *An Essay on the Principle of Population*. London,

McKinney, H.L. "Wallace's earliest Observations on Evolution". *Isis*, vol. 60, no. 203, 1969.

Medawar, Sir P. *Darwin's Illness*. New Statesman, 3 April, 1964.

Mellersh, H.E.L. *Fitzroy of the Beagle*. London, 1968.

Mivart, St. G. *On the Genesis of Species*. London, 1871.

Moorehead, A. *Darwin and the Beagle*. London, 1969.

Morrell, J.B. "Science and Scottish university reform: Edinburgh in 1826". *British Journal for the History of Science*, vol. 6, no. 21, 1972.

—— "The University of Edinburgh in the late eighteenth century". *Isis*, vol. 62, no. 212, 1971.

Musgrove, F. "Middle-class education and employment in the nineteenth century". *Economic History Review*, no. 12, 1960.

Owen, R. *Life of Sir Richard Owen*. 2 vols. London, 1894.

Paley, W. *The Works*. 5 vols. London, 1837.

Paston, G. *At John Murray's*. London, 1932.

Pickering, Sir G. *Creative Malady*. London, 1974.

Powell, B. *Essays*. London, 1855.

Raverat, G. *Period Piece*. London, 1952.

Replies to "Essays and Reviews". London, 1862.

Rogers, J.A. "Russian opposition to Darwinism in the Nineteenth Century". *Isis*, vol. 65, no. 229, 1974.

Romanes, G.J. *Darwin, and after Darwin*. 2 vols. London, 1895.

—— *Life and Letters* (edited Mrs. Romanes). London, 1896.

Rudwick, M.J.S. "The strategy of Lyell's Principles of Geology". *Isis*, vol. 61, no. 205, 1970.

Ruse, M. *Sociobiology: Sense or Nonsense?* Dordrecht, 1979.

Russell, C.A. (editor). *Science and Religious Belief*. London, 1973.

Schweber, S.S. "The origin of the *Origin* revisited".*Journal of the History of Biology*, vol. 10, no. 2, 1977.

Sedgwick, A. *Life and Letters* (edited Clark and Hughes). 2 vols, Cambridge, 1890.

Shepherd, P.M. *Natural Selection and Heredity*. London, 1958.

Simpson, G.G. *The Major Features of Evolution*. New York, 1953.

—— *The Meaning of Evolution*. Oxford, 1950.

Smith, J.M. *On Evolution*. Edinburgh, 1972.

—— *The Theory of Evolution*. London, 1975.

Spencer, H. *Essays Scientific, Political and Speculative*. 3 vols, London, 1891.

Stauffer, R.C. (editor). *Darwin's Natural Selection*. Cambridge, 1975.

Sulivan, Sir B.J. *Life and Letters*. (edited H.N. Sulivan). London, 1896.

Thompson, F.M.L. *English Landed Society in the Nineteenth Century*. London, 1963.

Thomson, K.S. "H.M.S. *Beagle*, 1820–1870". *American Scientist*, vol. 63, Nov.–Dec., 1975.

Venn, J.A. *Alumni Cantabrigiensis*. Cambridge, 1951.

Vorzimmer, P.J. *Charles Darwin: the years of controversy*. London, 1972.

—— "Darwin and Mendel: the Historical Connection." *Isis*, vol. 59, no. 196, 1968.

Wallace, A.R. *Darwinism*. London, 1889.

——*Letters and Reminiscences*. (edited J. Marchant). 2 vols. London, 1916.

—— *My Life*. 2 vols. New York. 1905.

Ward, H. *Charles Darwin: the Man and his Warfare*. London, 1927.

West, G. *Charles Darwin, the Fragmentary Man*. London, 1937.

Whewell, W. *History of the Inductive Sciences*. 3 vols. London, 1837.

—— *Philosophy of the Inductive Sciences*. 3 vols. London, 1840.

Wichler, G. *Charles Darwin: Founder of the Theory of Evolution*. London, 1961.

Winslow, J.H. *Darwin's Victorian Malady*. Philadelphia, 1971.

Woodall, E. *Charles Darwin*. Shrewsbury, 1884.

Zirkle, C. "Natural Selection Before the Origin of Species". *Proceedings of the American Philosophical Society*, vol. 84, no. 1, 1941.

Index

Nimrod I.
⟵ = route of *H.M.S. Beagle* 1831-1836

THE WORLD
ON MERCATOR'S PROJECTION.
by William Shawe. F.R.G.S.